MICHAEL BROADBENT'S
POCKET
VINTAGE
WINE
COMPANION

This book is dedicated to Rita Mackintosh, whose unwaveringly sunny disposition and extraordinary and selfless efficiency have been of invaluable help in preparing this Pocket Companion, *as with* Vintage Wine.

MICHAEL BROADBENT'S
POCKET
VINTAGE
WINE
COMPANION

Over Fifty Years of Tasting
over Three Centuries of Wine

Harcourt, Inc.
Orlando   Austin   New York   San Diego   London

www.HarcourtBooks.com

First published in 2007 by Pavilion Books
An imprint of Anova Books Company Ltd
10 Southcombe Street
London W14 0RA
in association with Christie's

Created for Pavilion Books and Harcourt, Inc., by
Websters International Publishers Ltd

Library of Congress Cataloging-in-Publication Data available upon request
ISBN 978-0-15-101261-9

Editor: Fiona Holman
Designer: Nigel O'Gorman
Desktop Publishing: Keith Bambury, Lesley Gilbert, Jayne Clementson

Printed in China
First edition
K J I H G F E D C B A

AUTHOR'S ACKNOWLEDGEMENTS
Apart from Rita, to whom this book is dedicated, I am particularly grateful to
Fiona Holman, the most patient, thorough and supportive of editors.

CONTENTS

Introduction

In *Vintage Wine*, published in 2002, I wrote, 'This is a very personal, somewhat idiosyncratic book, I praise and admonish, I mix unconcealed adulation and quirky dislikes. The reader does not have to agree with me, but perhaps what I have to say might stimulate some original thoughts'. Since then many readers have told me how helpful it would be to have a distillation of the original 560 pages in a handier format and with updated notes.

Pocket Vintage Wine Companion is that distillation. I hope it will be both a companion to the big book as well as an introduction for those who want to go deeper into the world of fine wine. Since 2002 I have tasted and noted thousands more wines, the best of which have been summarised in this Pocket Companion; and I have updated notes on older wines as well as included notes on more recent vintages.

I have to admit that there are several shortcomings. One is fairly obvious: the coverage is extremely uneven, for several reasons: first that it is totally impossible in a pocket book to include every country, district and wine in the now greatly expanded world of wine. Certainly not with tasting notes.

A glance at the contents will expose what looks like prejudice and favouritism, and to a certain extent this is true. But I make no apologies for dwelling on first growth clarets; on Yquem and Climens in Sauternes; the Domaine de La Romanée-Conti and Leflaive in Burgundy; Guigal, Jaboulet and Beaucastel in the Rhône; Zind-Humbrecht in Alsace; Egon Müller in the Mosel and so on, for these are the luminaries who represent the touchstones, the ultimate in typicity and quality.

My other excuse is that for a period during the preparation of this update I have been unable to attend several key tastings, 2005 burgundies and Rhônes, for example, which accounts for some unavoidable gaps. The use of other tasters' notes, would have evened out the coverage, but the very quirky personal element would have been diluted and confusing.

I make no apology for the preponderance of French wines in my books, my tasting notes and my life. I regard France as the cradle of fine wine, for, with the honourable exceptions of Germany and its Rieslings and Italy with Sangiovese and Nebbiolo, virtually every major grape variety and style of wine can be traced back to a region of France. At their best and most typical, French wines set the standards that others seek to emulate.

Happily it is not essential to describe a wine in order to enjoy it. I hope that my tasting notes go some way towards putting the elements of quality and condition of a wine into words. But a glass in the hand will always be better than a guide in the pocket.

Stars and when to drink

Stars are my assessment of a wine at the moment of tasting, intended to be a general indication of quality and, as indicated on page 8, brackets are occasionally used to indicate the full or anticipated maturity; similarly, the 'when to drink' assessment is necessarily rough and ready. In any case I am aware that a lot of people are happy to drink wine in its youth, whilst others have the patience (and means) to wait for full maturity – whenever this might be is certainly not all that easy to predict.

Postscript: I trained as an architect but in 1952, at the ripe age of 25, I took a bold or foolhardy different direction. With no wine background, I became a 'trainee' (cheap labour) under the brilliant but quirky Tommy Layton. Within a week of joining him, he gave me the best advice I ever received, and one that I pass on freely to the reader: when tasting, make a note. It also acts as a useful *aide-mémoire*.

My first tasting note, jotted down in a little red book was made on 13 September 1952. Over 90,000 notes later, and just about to embark on my latest volume, identical in layout, I still dutifully note, briefly, sometimes extensively, depending on the context, every wine that I look at, smell and taste. A fetish, I admit. It also provides evidence of my intake of alcohol – which is only revealed to my medical advisors!

My early career was in the wine trade, involved in every aspect, becoming a Master of Wine in 1960. Resigning as UK Sales Director of Harveys of Bristol, I joined Christie's in 1966 to head up a completely new Wine Department. It was a challenge, but the best move I ever made. The international market for fine and rare wines as we know it today did not exist. I travelled widely, met collectors, conducted auctions and moderated tastings and invariably made handwritten tasting notes (more than 90,000 in small, identical red books – 148 to date). I have loved every minute and consider myself very lucky.

Lastly, though in moderation, I do drink wine every day, with every meal (including fresh orange topped up – and enlivened – with a little champagne at breakfast). I think it is not only good for one's health, but one of life's civilised pleasures.

Michael Broadbent
2007

NOTES FOR READERS

VINTAGE ASSESSMENTS Each vintage or year is given a star rating (see below); where relevant I describe the weather conditions during the growing season. (v) indicates a variable vintage.

WINE NOTES Below each vintage heading, the wines, in red type, are listed in ascending vintage order and then within alphabetical order (in the case of Bordeaux, preceded by the first growths; in Red Burgundy, by the wines of the Domaine de la Romanée-Conti (DRC); and in White Burgundy by Montrachet). Also, whenever appropriate, the name of the wine is followed by that of the producer, estate or domaine in **bold type**. This is followed by my tasting notes (each culled from my tasting books). At the end of the tasting note *the information in italics* states the date of the last time I tasted the wine, followed by my star rating for the wine and when to drink, if appropriate.

PUNCTUATION Semi-colons are used to divide 'appearance' of the wine from its 'nose' (aroma, bouquet) and 'palate' (taste in the mouth). In my tasting books these three elements are noted in vertical columns; in the text these have been translated into semi-colons.

WINE ASSESSMENTS Within each chapter the quality and state of maturity of individual wines are assessed. Throughout the book, I have used the 'broad brush' 5-star rating system I use in my tasting books. Although I occasionally use a 20-point system at blind tastings to supplement my notes they relate only to a particular wine tasted at a particular time. In my opinion, the 100-point rating system is flawed because it is inflexible and does not allow for bottle variation and context.

STAR RATINGS (relating to individual wines ★ and vintages ★)

★★★★★	Outstanding
★★★★	Very good
★★★	Good
★★	Moderately good
★	Not very good, but not bad
No stars	Poor

QUESTIONMARKS WITH THE RATINGS These indicate that I am uncertain about a wine's future or feel I need to retaste it. The same applies to the rating of a particular vintage or year, especially one where the wines are too young to assess properly.

BRACKETS To give the reader an indication of the present drinkability, and a prediction of the ultimate quality of a young wine, I use brackets, for example:

A wine rated ★(★★★) means 1 star for drinking now: (the wine is immature, unready); but the 3 additional stars show that its potential at full maturity is 4 star or 'very good'.

A wine rated ★★★(★★) can be drunk with pleasure now but should be 'outstanding' when fully mature after further bottle ageing.

WHEN TO DRINK For certain wines I offer a rough and ready guide to drinkability based on the quality of the vintage, the 'pedigree' of the producer and my own first-hand notes and experience.

For example: 'Now–2012' means that I consider the wine is ready for drinking but will continue on its plateau of maturity until around 2012. This does not mean, however, that the wine will suddenly drop off its perch. Unless the cork and storage conditions are bad, wines tend to decline relatively slowly.

Vintages at a Glance

VINTAGE ASSESSMENTS Within each chapter each vintage or year is given a star rating (see below). (v) indicates a variable vintage. The top vintages are listed here for easy reference.

STAR RATINGS
★★★★★	Outstanding
★★★★	Very good
★★★	Good
★★	Moderately good
★	Not very good, but not bad
No stars	Poor

Red Bordeaux

VINTAGES AT A GLANCE

Outstanding ★★★★★ 1784, 1811, 1825, 1844, 1846, 1847, 1848, 1858, 1864, 1865, 1870, 1875, 1899, 1900, 1920, 1926, 1928, 1929, 1945, 1947, 1949, 1953, 1959, 1961, 1982, 1985, 1989, 1990, 2000 (v), 2005

Very Good ★★★★ 1791, 1814, 1815, 1821, 1861, 1869, 1871, 1874, 1877, 1878, 1893, 1895, 1896, 1904, 1911, 1921, 1934, 1952 (v), 1955, 1962, 1964, 1966, 1970, 1971, 1986, 1988, 1994 (v), 1995, 1996 (v), 1998 (v), 1999 (v), 2000 (v), 2002 (v), 2003, 2004

Good ★★★ 1787, 1803, 1832, 1863, 1868, 1887, 1888, 1892 (v), 1898 (v), 1905, 1906, 1914, 1918, 1919, 1924, 1933, 1940, 1943, 1946, 1948, 1952 (v), 1975, 1976 (v), 1978, 1981, 1983, 1991 (v), 1993 (v), 1994 (v), 1996 (v), 1997 (v), 1998 (v), 1999 (v), 2000 (v), 2001, 2002 (v)

Dry White Bordeaux

VINTAGES AT A GLANCE

Outstanding ★★★★★ 1928, 1937, 1943, 1945, 1971, 1976, 1978, 1989, 1990, 2005

Very Good ★★★★ 1926, 1929, 1934, 1947, 1949, 1955, 1959, 1961, 1962, 1975, 1983, 1985 (v), 1994, 1995, 2000, 2001, 2002, 2003

Good ★★★ 1927, 1933, 1935, 1940, 1942, 1948, 1952, 1953, 1966, 1970, 1979, 1981 (v), 1982, 1985 (v), 1986, 1996, 1997, 1998, 1999, 2004

SAUTERNES

VINTAGES AT A GLANCE

Outstanding ★★★★★ 1784, 1802, 1811, 1831, 1834, 1847, 1864, 1865, 1869, 1875, 1893, 1906, 1921, 1929, 1937, 1945, 1947, 1949, 1955, 1959, 1967, 1971, 1975, 1983, 1989, 1990, 2001

Very Good ★★★★ 1787, 1814, 1820, 1825, 1828, 1841, 1848, 1858, 1871, 1874, 1896, 1899, 1900, 1904, 1909, 1926, 1928, 1934, 1942, 1943, 1953, 1962, 1976, 1985 (v), 1986, 1988, 1995, 1996, 1997 (v), 1998, 1999, 2003, 2004, 2005

Good ★★★ 1818, 1822, 1851, 1859, 1861, 1868, 1870, 1914, 1918, 1920, 1923, 1924, 1935, 1939, 1944, 1950, 1952, 1961, 1966, 1970, 1978, 1979, 1985 (v), 1997 (v), 2000 (v), 2002

Red Burgundy

VINTAGES AT A GLANCE

Outstanding ★★★★★ 1865, 1875, 1906, 1911, 1915, 1919, 1929, 1937, 1945, 1949, 1959, 1962, 1969, 1978, 1985, 1988, 1990, 1999, 2002, 2005

Very Good ★★★★ 1864, 1869, 1870, 1878, 1887, 1889, 1904, 1920, 1923, 1926, 1928, 1933, 1934, 1943, 1947, 1952, 1953, 1961 (v), 1964, 1966, 1971, 1986, 1989, 1993, 1995, 1996, 1997, 1998, 2003, 2004

Good ★★★ 1858, 1877, 1885, 1886, 1893, 1894, 1898, 1914, 1916, 1918, 1921, 1924, 1935, 1942, 1955, 1957, 1961 (v), 1972, 1976, 1979, 1980 (v), 1983 (v), 1987, 1992, 2000, 2001

White Burgundy

VINTAGES AT A GLANCE

Outstanding ★★★★★ 1864, 1865, 1906, 1928, 1947, 1962, 1966, 1986 (v), 1989 (v), 1996, 2005

Very Good ★★★★ 1899, 1919, 1923, 1929, 1934, 1937, 1945, 1949, 1952, 1953, 1955, 1961, 1967, 1969, 1971, 1973, 1976, 1978, 1979, 1982 (v), 1983, 1985 (v), 1986 (v), 1989 (v), 1990 (v), 1995, 1997, 1998, 1999, 2001 (v), 2002, 2003 (v), 2004

Good ★★★ 1941, 1950, 1957, 1959, 1964, 1970, 1982 (v), 1985 (v), 1986 (v), 1988, 1989 (v), 1991(v), 1992, 1993 (v), 1994 (v), 2000, 2001 (v), 2003 (v)

Rhône

RED VINTAGES AT A GLANCE

NORTHERN RHÔNE (CORNAS, CÔTE-RÔTIE, CROZES-HERMITAGE, HERMITAGE, ST-JOSEPH)

Outstanding ***** 1929, 1945, 1949, 1959, 1961, 1969, 1971, 1978, 1983, 1985, 1990, 1998, 1999, 2005

Very Good **** 1933, 1937, 1943, 1947, 1952, 1953, 1955, 1957, 1962, 1964, 1966, 1967, 1970, 1972 (v) (except Côte-Rôtie), 1979, 1982, 1988, 1989, 1992, 1995, 1996 (v), 2000, 2001, 2004

Good *** 1934, 1942, 1976 (v), 1981 (v), 1991, 1997, 2002 (v), 2003 (v)

SOUTHERN RHÔNE (MAINLY CHÂTEAUNEUF-DU-PAPE)

Outstanding ***** 1929, 1945, 1949, 1952, 1959, 1961, 1970, 1978, 1983, 1985, 1989, 1990, 1995, 1998, 2005

Very Good **** 1934, 1937, 1947, 1955, 1957, 1962, 1964, 1967, 1969, 1971, 1982, 1999, 2000, 2001 (v)

Good *** 1939, 1944, 1953, 1966, 1972 (v), 1979, 1980, 1981 (v), 1986, 1988, 1992, 1996 (v), 1997, 2001 (v), 2002 (v), 2003 (v), 2004

Loire

SWEET VINTAGES AT A GLANCE

Outstanding ***** 1921, 1928, 1937, 1947, 1949, 1959, 1964, 1989, 1990, 1997, 2003, 2005

Very Good **** 1924, 1934, 1945, 1962, 1971, 1976, 1985, 1986, 1988, 1995, 1996, 1998 (v), 2001, 2004

Good *** 1933, 1953, 1955, 1966, 1969, 1975, 1978, 1982, 1993, 1998 (v), 1999, 2000, 2002

Alsace

VINTAGES AT A GLANCE

Outstanding ★★★★★ 1865, 1900, 1937, 1945, 1959, 1961, 1971, 1976, 1983, 1988 (v), 1989, 1990, 1995 (v), 1997, 2002, 2005

Very Good ★★★★ 1921, 1928, 1934, 1964, 1967, 1981, 1985, 1986 (v), 1988 (v), 1992 (v), 1993, 1995 (v), 1996, 1998, 2000 (v), 2001 (v), 2003 (v), 2004 (v)

Good ★★★ 1935, 1953, 1966, 1975, 1986 (v), 1988 (v), 1992 (v), 1994 (v), 1999 (v), 2000 (v), 2001 (v), 2004 (v)

Germany

VINTAGES AT A GLANCE

Outstanding ★★★★★ 1749, 1811, 1822, 1831, 1834, 1846, 1847, 1857, 1858, 1861, 1865, 1869, 1893, 1911, 1921, 1937, 1945, 1949, 1953, 1959, 1967 (v), 1971, 1973 (v), 1990, 1993 (v), 2003 (v), 2005

Very Good ★★★★ 1727, 1738, 1746, 1750, 1779, 1781, 1783, 1794, 1798, 1806, 1807, 1825, 1826, 1827, 1942, 1959, 1862, 1880, 1886, 1904, 1915, 1917, 1920, 1929, 1934,1947, 1964, 1975, 1976, 1983, 1988, 1989 (v), 1992 (v), 1993 (v), 1994 (v), 1995 (v), 1996 (v), 1997, 1998, 1999, 2001, 2002, 2003 (v)

Good ★★★ 21 vintages in the 18th century, including 1748 in the text, 20 vintages in the 19th century, and 1900, 1901, 1905, 1907, 1926, 1942 (v), 1943, 1946, 1952, 1961 (v), 1962 (v), 1963 (v), 1966, 1969 (v), 1970, 1979, 1985, 1986 (v), 1989 (v), 1991 (v), 1992 (v), 1994 (v), 1995 (v), 1996 (v), 2000 (v)

California

VINTAGES AT A GLANCE

Outstanding ★★★★★ 1941, 1946, 1951, 1958, 1965, 1968, 1969 (v), 1974, 1985, 1991, 1994 (v), 1997, 1999, 2001, 2002

Very Good ★★★★ 1942, 1947, 1956, 1959, 1963, 1964, 1966, 1970, 1972 (v), 1973, 1978, 1980, 1982, 1986 (v), 1989 (v), 1990, 1992, 1993 (v), 1994 (v), 1995 (v), 2000, 2003, 2005

Good ★★★ 1944, 1949, 1955, 1960, 1961, 1967, 1971, 1972 (v), 1975, 1976, 1979, 1981 (v), 1984, 1986 (v), 1988, 1989 (v), 1993 (v), 1994 (v), 1995 (v), 1996, 1998 (v), 2004

Vintage Champagne

VINTAGES AT A GLANCE

Outstanding ★★★★★ 1857, 1874, 1892, 1899, 1904, 1911, 1920, 1921, 1928, 1937, 1945, 1952, 1959, 1964, 1971, 1982, 1985, 1988, 1990, 1996, 2005

Very Good ★★★★ 1870, 1914, 1923, 1929, 1934, 1943, 1947, 1949, 1953, 1955, 1961, 1962, 1966, 1970, 1976, 1979, 1981, 1989, 1992 (v), 1995, 1997, 1998, 1999, 2002, 2004

Good ★★★ 1915, 1919, 1926, 1942, 1969, 1973, 1975, 1983, 1986 (v), 1992 (v), 1993, 1999 (v)

Vintage Port

VINTAGES AT A GLANCE

Outstanding ★★★★★ 1811, 1834, 1847, 1863, 1870, 1878, 1884, 1900, 1908, 1912, 1927, 1931, 1935, 1945, 1948, 1955, 1963, 1966, 1970, 2000, 2003, 2005

Very Good ★★★★ 1815, 1851, 1853, 1868, 1875, 1896, 1897, 1904, 1920, 1924, 1934, 1944, 1947, 1960, 1977, 1982 (v), 1983, 1985, 1991, 1992 (v), 1994, 1997, 2004

Good ★★★ 1820, 1837, 1840, 1854, 1858, 1869, 1872, 1873, 1877, 1881, 1887, 1890, 1893, 1895, 1910, 1911, 1917, 1922, 1933, 1942, 1950, 1954, 1958, 1961, 1980, 1982 (v), 1987 (v), 1989, 1990 (v), 1992 (v), 1995, 1996, 1998 (v), 1999, 2001, 2002

Red Bordeaux

Bordeaux still dominates the fine wine market. The names of its top châteaux are the best known, the most revered and, particularly over the past few decades, the most traded wines in the world. A knowledge and understanding of what lies behind the label, the wine name and the vintage, is vital. The way each wine has evolved or is likely to evolve over a period of time is of very much more than purely academic interest.

The greatest influence on the region is its maritime climate. The unpredictable fluctuations of weather during the growing season are mainly responsible for the style and quality of the wine. Add to this the differences of microclimates and geology, not to mention the ministrations of individuals, and one becomes aware of the almost infinite permutations.

The proportions in which the different vine varieties, the *cépages* (for red Bordeaux mainly Cabernet Sauvignon, Merlot and Cabernet Franc), are planted and used in the final blend by each château create the unique complexity of the red Bordeaux. Then there is time. The red wines of Bordeaux not only keep but – and this is the crucial point – are capable of evolving in bottle, being transformed from fruit-dominated young wines to something fragrant, harmonious, mature and infinitely subtle.

My half century in wine has been dominated by Bordeaux because its top wines set the standards. Good claret is not 'old hat'; it remains the best of all beverages. Its colour tells us much about its content and, very accurately, its maturity; its nose – smell, fragrance – gives not only sensual pleasure but awakens the salivary glands; it is rarely too heady, too alcoholic; its acidity refreshes, its tannin, obtrusive when the wine is tasted alone, does several jobs. Tannin leaves the mouth clean and dry between one forkful of food and the next. It is an antioxidant, preserving the wine and, the medical world agrees, helping to keep our arteries clear. Claret aids the digestion, calms the soul, stimulates civilised conversation.

Claret works on many levels, appealing to both intellect and the senses. What more can one want?

Outstanding vintages
1784, 1811, 1825, 1844, 1846, 1847, 1848, 1858, 1864, 1865, 1870, 1875, 1899, 1900, 1920, 1926, 1928, 1929, 1945, 1947, 1949, 1953, 1959, 1961, 1982, 1985, 1989, 1990, 2000, 2005

Late 18th and 19th centuries

For the whole of this period red Bordeaux dominated the fine wine market. Shipped in cask and sold by merchants under their own name, simply as 'claret', it had been a staple drink of the English since the Middle Ages. Bordeaux's first growths were already firmly established by the latter half of the 18th century and the first vineyards to be named in a Christie's catalogue were Lafete (*sic*) and Château Margau (*sic*), both in 1788. The importance of the châteaux and the growth of the Bordeaux wine trade increased throughout the 19th century. However, by the 1870s, the disastrous pest phylloxera was beginning to make itself felt in the vineyards and the last top-class pre-phylloxera vintage was 1878. Due to the ravages of phylloxera and then powdery mildew (oidium) the late 19th-century period was fairly dismal, though the century did end on a high note with the outstanding 1899 vintage.

In this section I have concentrated on the top vintages and selected top wines. I have included a few older tasting notes just to illustrate how wonderful some of these wines were, and, indeed, still can be. A much more complete list of old vintages, châteaux and first-hand tasting notes appear in *Vintage Wine*.

VINTAGES AT A GLANCE

Outstanding ★★★★★ 1784, 1811, 1825, 1844, 1846, 1847, 1848, 1858, 1864, 1865, 1870, 1875, 1899

Very Good ★★★★ 1791, 1814, 1815, 1821, 1861, 1869, 1871, 1874, 1877, 1878, 1893, 1895, 1896

Good ★★★ 1787, 1803, 1832, 1863, 1868, 1887, 1888, 1892 (v), 1898 (v)

1784 ★★★★★
The most renowned vintage of the period.

1789
A notorious year – the French Revolution.
Ch Lafite Recorked by the *maître de chai* in 1984. Palish, open appearance; sweet, delicate and fragrant on nose and palate. A faded old lady but delicious, still with wonderful flavour and length. *June 2004* ★★★★★★ *(6 stars)*

1811 ★★★★★
The famous 'comet' vintage. Fairly abundant crop of very good wines.
Ch Lafite Labelled '*CHÂTEAU LAFITE grand Vin, J J Van der Berghe, Bordeaux, recorked at the château in 1980*'. Pale with hints of red; immediately forthcoming old

bouquet reminding me of spearmint, then Chartreuse; a touch of sweetness on the palate, distinctive, minty flavour, vestiges of sustaining tannin and acidity, good length. *June 2001* ★★★

1815 ★★★★
The renowned 'Waterloo' vintage.
Ch Lafite Two notes. The first slightly corked which tainted the otherwise rich and impressive taste. Coincidentally the following month, a bottle recorked at the château in 1984: similar appearance to the 1789, with pale green rim; rich madeira-like bouquet; medium-sweet, good flavour, excellent tannin and acidity. *Last tasted June 2004. At best* ★★★★★

1821 ★★★★
Ch Lafite Recorked, date unknown, very good level. Medium-deep, richly coloured; spicy bouquet, lovely fruit still; sweet, perfect weight, lean, elegant, delicious flavour. *May 2004* ★★★★

1832 ★★★
Ch Lafite A superb bottle, recorked in 1980, neither pale nor delicate but deep and rich-looking; a faultless, spicy, almost eucalyptus bouquet; full-bodied, excellent flavour, lots of grip and still tannic. *Last tasted June 2001* ★★★★★

1844 ★★★★★
Ch Lafite This was the first wine that made me realise what sensationally good wines were made well before the commonly accepted 'pre-phylloxera' period 1858–1878. Most recently, recorked by the *maître de chai* in 1987: good colour though slightly cloudy (not rested enough before decanting); a whoosh of fragrance, very rich yet, after 20 minutes, a whiff of old straw and sourness. Dry, perfect weight, lovely drink but showing its age, and drying out. *Last tasted Nov 2005. At best* ★★★★★

1847 ★★★★★
A very abundant crop and the wines were contrarily described as 'full-bodied yet exquisite'.

1858 ★★★★★
By 1858 an effective treatment for oidium had been discovered. This year marked the start of an extremely prosperous period, particularly for the Bordeaux merchants.

1864 ★★★★★
Vins complets. One of the greatest vintages of the 19th century. Despite the heat at vintage time, there was an abundant crop of superbly balanced wines.
Ch Lafite I have been privileged to taste, to drink, this wine on seven occasions. The first five notes all superb. Next, labelled '*Lafite Bon (Baron) de Rothschild, R. Galos*' in 1995, almost too sweet. Most recently, perfection, complete, harmonious. *Last tasted June 2001* ★★★★★
Ch Latour Most recently, a bottle with a pictorial label; spicy bouquet,

creaking a bit after 40 minutes; exceedingly flavoury, delicious. Distinguished. Venerable. *Last noted June 2001* ★★★★★

1865 ★★★★★
Another great vintage, sturdier than the 1864 and, in my experience, the most dependable vintage of this period.
Ch Lafite Many notes, the virtually perfect best from the 'pristine' cellars of Lord Rosebery and the Meyrick family, sold between 1967 and 1970 and tasted several times since. Most recently, a bottle recorked at the château in 1980: medium-dry, lovely colour, amber rim; showing its age and slightly malty at first but after an hour had got its 'second wind'. Dry, a hefty style, very tannic. Very impressive. *June 2001. At best* ★★★★★
Ch Latour Outstanding. Five perfect bottles. Still fairly deep, with a good mature rim; whiff of eucalyptus; good flavour, balance, condition, length. Faultless, even allowing for a slight touch of the vintage's tannic astringency. *Last noted June 2001. At best* ★★★★★
Ch Kirwan One of the most remarkable finds of my long career at Christie's. Twenty-five bottles found unlabelled, plain capsules and unidentifiable. The corks were fully branded '1865 Kirwan'. At 105 years of age, perfection. Most recently, a slightly ullaged bottle showing its age, but still deep. *Last tasted March 2001. At best* ★★★★★

1870 ★★★★★
A magnificent classic pre-phylloxera vintage. Spring frosts reduced the potential crop and a bakingly hot summer escalated the sugar content, leading to an early (from 10 September) harvest of superripe, concentrated wines.
Ch Lafite One of the all-time greats and, at its best, a powerhouse. In fact, such a powerful and tannic wine that it was virtually undrinkable for half a century. Nevertheless, bottlings varied and, as always, provenance plays a part. Tasted on 18 occasions. The most magnificent were (and still can be) the Coningham-bottled magnums from Glamis Castle. Most recently, a magnum, deep, brown-rimmed but alive; spicy, eucalyptus yet not very enticing bouquet; excessively tannic and austere but improved in the glass. *Last tasted August 2005. At best* ★★★★★★ *(6 stars)*
Ch Mouton-Rothschild Most recently, rebottled by Whitwham's in 1981: fairly deep, ruddy colour; a faded old lady, fragrant, held well; very sweet, its delicious flavour disguising encroaching acidity. *Last tasted Sept 2005. At best* ★★★★★

1874 ★★★★
Abundant and high quality. The wines are now variable.
Ch Lafite Many notes. Lean but very drinkable. *Last tasted Nov 2000. At best* ★★★★

1875 ★★★★★
An even more abundant crop and reputed to be the biggest from the start of records until 1960. These were wines of great delicacy.
Ch Lafite Many notes. At best soft, silky textured, rich, lovely. *Last tasted Sept 1995. At best* ★★★★★

1888 ★★★

An abundant and good quality vintage.

Ch Montrose From the château. Palish but healthy colour; showing its age, fragile but fragrant bouquet and aftertaste. *Sept 2005. At best* ★★★

1890 ★★

A mediocre crop of full-bodied wines.

Ch Montrose Two bottles from the château, both surprisingly deep, rich core, open rim. Slight bottle variation. The best had an intriguing bouquet of coffee, 'old ivy', violets. Sweet. Delicious. *Sept 2005. At best* ★★★★

1893 ★★★★

An extraordinary year. Bakingly hot summer. Exceptionally early and abundant harvest from 15 August. Some of the grapes must have been like raisins. To my surprise I have over 50 notes but only one recently.

Ch Montrose Medium-deep; amazingly vibrant bouquet, minty, spicy; sweet, glorious flavour, a touch of volatile acidity, prolonged aftertaste. *Sept 2005* ★★★★

1896 ★★★★

An abundant crop; fine and delicate wines.

Ch Latour Amazingly deep, intriguing bouquet, reminiscent of gnarled oak, toffee and fresh mushrooms; sweet, no signs of decay on the palate, good length, dry finish. *June 2004* ★★★★★ *(for its age).*

1898 ★★ to ★★★

Small crop. Tannic wines, some of which have survived.

Ch Montrose From the château. Very fragrant, verging on pungent; sweet, rich though delicate flavour. *Sept 2005. The best of two bottles* ★★★

1899 ★★★★★

The first of the renowned *fin de siècle* twin vintages. A perfect growing season and an abundant harvest. Wines of stature, yet with delicacy and great finesse. I have 45 notes, the most recent being:

Ch Lafite Even in a vintage like this, Lafite sold their wine in bulk to Bordeaux *négociants* for bottling or shipping on to other merchants. Most recently, a spectacular, recorked double magnum: fragrant, gentle, beautifully balanced. *May 1999. At best* ★★★★★

1900–1919

The Edwardian era conjures up flamboyance, opulence and splendour. Importers on both sides of the Atlantic were doing well as, in Bordeaux, were the *négociants*. Then the shortage of both labour and materials in World War One made life difficult for the producers. The weather conditions did not help, 1915 being a complete disaster. Some people profited by the war – wine merchants from northern France and the Low Countries were able to move to Bordeaux and to buy châteaux: for example, Cordier, Ginestet and the Woltners. Post-war recovery was slow, the Volstead Act of 1919 heralding the end of a prosperous era for the US wine trade.

VINTAGES AT A GLANCE

Outstanding ★★★★★ 1900
Very Good ★★★★ 1904, 1911
Good ★★★ 1905, 1906, 1914, 1918, 1919

1900 ★★★★★

Wines of the second of the renowned twin vintages were more structured, well balanced and more obviously impressive. A superabundant crop following perfect weather conditions. The wines were uniformly excellent.

Ch Lafite Some outstanding bottles tasted from the mid-1970s. Most recently, two bottles, both outstanding: each had a good colour; ripe, mulberry-rich bouquet; sweet, soft, lots of life, delicious. *Aug 2005. At best* ★★★★★

Ch Latour One of Latour's greatest vintages. No recent notes.

Ch Margaux The greatest Margaux of the period. Most recently, two bottles, one oxidised, the other palish, with a bright, ruddy glow; whiff of mushrooms yet still fragrant; sweet, *faisandé*, better flavour than nose. *June 2004. At best* ★★★★★

Ch Ausone Two bottles, one in poor condition, the other remarkable with rich, strawberry-like bouquet, very sweet on the palate, crisp, distinctive flavour and good acidity. *June 2004* ★★★★

Ch Montrose Initially showing its age on the nose but quickly cleared to reveal amazing fragrance. Alas, on the palate fading, tart. *Sept 2005* ★★

1904 ★★★★

Abundant crop of very good wines. Many notes, but none recent.

1906 ★★★

Robust wines of good quality. Some remarkable survivors.

Ch Margaux The best wine of the vintage. A dozen notes, varying from oxidised to superb. Most recently: fragrant nose, holding well; sweet and delicious in its dotage. Almost decrepit but a survivor. *Last tasted Nov 2000. At best* ★★★★

Ch Montrose From the château. Lovely, open, healthy colour; very fragrant old bouquet, autumn leaves, privet; sweet, delicious. *Sept 2005. At best* ★★★★

1911 ★★★★

A small but good crop.

Ch Montrose Two bottles from the château: both fully developed; attractive, 'faded old lady' bouquet; sweet, rich. *Sept 2005* ★★★

1916 ★★

Hard, tannic, long-lasting but mainly charmless wines. Several old notes.

Ch Montrose From the château: attractive colour; crisp, *gibier* bouquet, aged but fragrant. Surprisingly sweet and attractive. *Last tasted Sept 2005. At best* ★★★★

1918 ★★★

A good summer with ripe grapes harvested just before the Armistice.

Ch La Mission Haut-Brion Variable. Most recently: surprisingly deep; vanilla, earthy, then meaty, almost caramelly; sweet, remarkably sound, rich yet still tannic. *Dec 2002* ★★★★

Ch Montrose Two bottles from the château. Both surprisingly deep; full, rich, yet delicate, *gibier* bouquet; sweet, full body and flavour. Tannic. *Sept 2005. At best* ★★★

1920–1939

The 1920s and 1930s were periods of great contrast. The 1920s was one of Bordeaux's most successful decades ever, the 1930s one of the most difficult. The prosperous upper classes were well served by Bordeaux in the 1920s, with the plethora of splendid vintages and prices, even for the best, that were well within reach. The decade ended on a high note with the renowned vintages of 1928 and 1929.

The 1930s were difficult, both for grower and merchant. The decade opened with three atrocious vintages, poor wines for which there was no market and the Great Depression: growers were in despair, producers lost money, châteaux changed hands at give-away prices. The end of Prohibition in 1933 coincided with somewhat better growing conditions and trade, but the US market was slow to recover. British merchants and their customers were awash with the '28s, '29s and earlier vintages. In 1935 the French took steps to improve their wine quality and protect names by introducing the *appellation contrôlée* system. There was some recovery by 1937 and that vintage was welcomed, though the reds never threw off their astringency.

VINTAGES AT A GLANCE

Outstanding ★★★★★ 1920, 1926, 1928, 1929
Very Good ★★★★ 1921, 1934
Good ★★★ 1924, 1933

1920 ★★★★★

Small production, high quality. Several older notes.

Ch Montrose Superb nose, delicious flavour, sweet, complete, good tannic grip. *Sept 2005* ★★★★★

1921 ★★★★

The hottest summer and earliest harvest since 1893, with singed grapes and overheated vats. Some magnificent wines, laden with alcohol, extract, tannins.

Ch Mouton-Rothschild Several notes, all good. In 1998 a jeroboam at the château: ripe, sweet, gamey bouquet and taste. Full, rich, soft. Most recently an oxidised bottle. *Nov 2005. At best* ★★★★★

Ch Latour-à-Pomerol Immensely deep; far too sweet, rich, chewy. Impressive but lacking finesse. *March 2001* ★★ *to* ★★★★ *depending on one's taste.*

Ch Montrose Two bottles from the château. Deep, fairly intense; one sweet, good fruit, but the other with whiff of cork. *Sept 2005. At best* ★★★

1924 ★★★

An abundant crop of attractive wines. Over 100 notes, but few recent.

Ch Haut-Brion Top-shoulder level. Fairly deep; sweet, fragrant bouquet; delicious flavour but creaking – a touch of sourness. *Feb 2004* ★★★

Ch Pavie Small, firm, original cork. Pretty colour; gentle, fragrant, arboreal bouquet; sweet, crisp fruit, attractive, still tannic. *June 2004* ★★★★

1926 ★★★★★

Great vintage. Small crop of high-quality wines put on the market at commensurate prices in the buoyant late 1920s.

Ch Latour Many notes, mainly excellent. Most recently, recorked at the château in 1998: high-toned nose, showing its age; still sweet, more than vestiges of tannin and acidity. A great wine in its old age. *Dec 2000. At best* ★★★★★

Ch Haut-Brion The best Haut-Brion until we reach the '45. Noted in different contexts and sizes: bottle, magnum and jeroboam. Its nose and taste very distinctive, totally unlike the *1er cru* Médocs. Most recently, still almost opaque; harmonious, rich nose; fairly sweet, full flavoured, powerful. *Last tasted Sept 2000* ★★★★★

Ch Cheval Blanc One of the most magnificent wines I have ever tasted. Most recently, showing well, a magnum, delicate and fading but with finesse and great length. *Last tasted May 1987* ★★★★★ *It could still be superb.*

Ch Montrose Distinct whiff of mocha, a bit tart. *Sept 2005* ★★

Ch La Tour Haut-Brion Interesting nose, fine rich tea, after 25 minutes reminding me of the smell of an old steam train. Rich, smoky Graves flavour, showing its age, very tannic, raw. *March 2001* ★★

1928 ★★★★★

The first of the famous twin vintages of the 1920s; both great but of contrasting substance and style. Summer heat thickened the skins, from which were extracted deep colouring matter and tannin; exceptionally good ripening conditions were responsible for the richness and body. The longest-lived vintage of the decade. Huge stocks remained unsold throughout the 1930s, much remaining in British wine trade cellars until after World War Two. In the 1950s, they were still on merchants' lists, which is why I have so many notes, almost 200.

Ch Latour This was, and still is, the star of the vintage. Like the 1870 Lafite, so dense, powerful and bitterly tannic that it was a full half century before it was mellow enough to be enjoyed. Most recently, an impressive bottle, fragrant, drinking perfectly. *Last tasted Jan 2000. At best* ★★★★★

Ch Margaux Eight notes. Slight bottle variation but mainly very good: deeply coloured; sweet, singed, cedary, fragrant bouquet; 'sweet, tanned and tannic'. Most recently: rather too sweet and caramelly; rich yet still very tannic. *Last tasted Nov 2000. At best* ★★★★★

Ch Mouton-Rothschild Fragrant, sweet, crisp, attractive, remarkably sweet on the palate, lighter than expected. Delicious. *Last noted June 2000. At best* ★★★★

Ch Cheval Blanc Many critical notes. Some fragrance and charm but faded. Whiff of geraniums (sorbic acid). *Last tasted June 2000. At best* ★★

Ch Cheval Blanc Belgian-bottled by Vandermeulen. Two notes: glorious, reminded me of the '26: rich, meaty, and with none of the château-bottled faults. *Last tasted March 2001* ★★★★

Ch Figeac Bottled by Corney & Barrow. Ruddy mahogany colour; an appealing bouquet of eucalyptus and spearmint; very spicy flavour with touch of spearmint on the finish. A surprisingly delightful drink. *Dec 2004* ★★★★

Ch Montrose Still fairly deep; faultless nose; gloriously mouthfilling flavour, good tannic grip and length. *Last tasted Sept 2005* ★★★★★ *and time in hand.*

1929 ★★★★★

The end of an era. At its best it was the epitome of elegance and finesse.

Ch Margaux Medium-pale, soft cherry; initially showing its age on the nose but settled down, rich, slightly chocolatey; better on palate though with sweetness of decay. Good tannin and acidity. 'Decadent'. *Last tasted June 2004. At best* ★★★★★

Ch Mouton-Rothschild Once the 'star' of the saleroom. Fleshy, often corrupt, yet always exciting. Most recently, a top-shoulder bottle; medium-deep, healthy glow; opened up richly in the glass; sweet, very flavoury, still exotic though showing its age, good length. *Last tasted Feb 2004. Now, at best* ★★★★

Ch Haut-Brion A strange wine that I have never liked, but some do. Still fairly deep, richly coloured; singed Graves nose, rich yet slightly sour; concentrated, almost port-like. A matter of taste. *Last noted Feb 2004. 'The jury is out.'*

Ch Léoville-Poyferré One of the most perfect '29s and the end of a great era for Poyferré. Alas not tasted in its prime. Recently a disastrous bottle. Faded, not even a whiff of its pristine sublimity. *Last tasted Dec 2005.*

Ch La Mission Haut-Brion A magnificent '29, one of the best ever La Missions, certainly the richest. Variable though, the best from the original Woltner cellars. Most recently: lovely colour, warm, touch of orange; singed old oak; dry, tangy, showing its age but characterful. *Last tasted Feb 2004. At best* ★★★★★

Ch Montrose Two bottles from the château: medium-deep, open rim; slightly cheesy, meaty, rich, ripe stables! Very sweet, delicious flavour. Perfect for its age – on the palate. *Sept 2005* ★★★★

1934 ★★★★

The best vintage of the decade. An abundant harvest, very good wines. Now risky, but the best still drinking well.

Ch Lafite Most recently: lovely colour, glowing, rich 'legs'; immediately forthcoming, fragrant bouquet, with sweet, honeyed development; sweet, soft, fleshy, excellent flavour and still quite a bite. *Last tasted Nov 2005. At best* ★★★★★

Ch Margaux Despite some poor bottles, my favourite '34. So very Margaux. Most recently, bouquet very attractive; richly flavoured, but just misses greatness. *Nov 2000. At best* ★★★★

Ch Mouton-Rothschild Most recently, ullaged almost to mid-shoulder: fully mature, open, orange-tinged; overripe bouquet; sweet, deliciously ripe, *faisandé* old flavour, decadent and astringent. *Last tasted June 2004. At best* ★★★★★

Ch Cheval Blanc Arguably the finest and in my experience one of the most reliable of the '34s. Most recently, magnum with upper-mid-shoulder level. A bit hazy; nose disappointingly neutral though much better on the palate; sweet, complete, fading gracefully but still drinking well. *Dec 2000. At best* ★★★★★

Ch Montrose From the château. Surprisingly deep; good, rich, *gibier* nose; sweet, showing its age but with very good, positive flavour. *Last tasted Sept 2005* ★★★★

1937 originally ★★★★, now ★★

Once rated as highly as the '34, now one of my least-liked major red Bordeaux vintages. The wines were tannic from the start but, in time, this turned into astringency. Avoid, unless the wines have high levels and a dependable provenance.

Ch Montrose Fairly deep; woody, yet with fragrance and depth. Surprisingly sweet and rich, with '37 tartness. *Last tasted Sept 2005* ★★

1940–1959

Many traditional markets were badly dislocated and economically weak as a result of World War Two; British post-war restrictions lasted well into the 1950s. However, three of the post-war vintages (the '45s, '47s and '49s) were of almost unsurpassed quality. The 1950s was a period of recovery. In Bordeaux the proprietors struggled to renovate and replant, the merchants to restock. *Négociants* still ruled the roost and, with the cosy relationships resumed, British shippers (importers) and their wine merchant customers had a head start. Competition was limited. The Americans were only starting to appreciate – and drink – good Bordeaux.

Bordeaux still dominated the British wine lists and, for the comfortably off, it was the last period in which they could drink decent claret every day, and First Growths at the weekend. Château proprietors made very little money, yet there were some lovely wines and more than the decade's fair share of really good vintages including my favourite, 1953, and the 1959, not only the most impressive of the decade, but one of the greatest of the century.

Vintages at a Glance

Outstanding ★★★★★ 1945, 1947, 1949, 1953, 1959
Very Good ★★★★ 1952 (v), 1955
Good ★★★ 1940, 1943, 1946, 1948, 1952 (v)

1940 ★★★
Some attractive wines, though uneven.

1943 ★★★
The most successful of the wartime vintages, the best wines still drinking well. I have over 50 notes, but none recent.

1945 ★★★★★
One of the greatest vintages of the 20th century. Magnificent, long-lasting wines of the highest quality. The very small crop was the result of severe frosts in May. The wines' exceptional ripeness, concentration and power were due to a summer of drought and excessive heat. The best, and best kept, are still superb. I entered the wine trade at the right time (in 1952), for I have over 200 notes of this great vintage.

Ch Lafite Nearly 30 notes, yet despite the varying occasions and contexts, what is remarkable is the relatively little bottle variation. Just about every note refers to a glorious fragrance which seems to unravel itself after 15 or 20 minutes in the glass. Most recently: another faultless bottle: lovely soft colour; classic bouquet, sweet, touch of iron, fragrant, developed richly; also sweet on the palate, mouthfilling flavour, life-preserving tannin still evident. A lovely wine. *Last tasted Nov 2005* ★★★★★

Ch Latour A great wine. Surely one of the best ever Latours, drinking beautifully now but with many years more life. Thirty notes made over five decades. Always deep, with an opaque core; spicy bouquet, eucalyptus, cedar, smoky tea (Lapsang); full-bodied, rich, complete, silky tannins, complex, great length. Most recently, sweet yet still very tannic. Very distinctive flavour. Living up to its reputation. *June 2004* ★★★★★

Ch Margaux A magnificent wine. Nothing fragile and feminine about it, at least not in its early years. Its fragrance, the hallmark of Margaux, variously described as ripe mulberry, crystallised violets, cedar cigar box, creamy – and always glorious. Its initial tannins ameliorating, now soft and velvety. Still showing at its magnificent best. *Last tasted Nov 2000* ★★★★★

Ch Mouton-Rothschild One of the greatest clarets of all time, certainly the most distinctive and consistent. Virtually identical recent notes: still impressively deep with a jewel-like ruby sheen; inimitably exotic bouquet, an eruption of spice, eucalyptus, lavender and violets; amazingly sweet, wonderful fruit, concentrated yet vivacious, crisp, endless length. Still tannic. *Last tasted Nov 2005* ★★★★★★ *(6 stars)*

Ch Haut-Brion A superb wine, possibly the best ever Haut-Brion. Consistently deep in colour, 'warm ruby' with a rich, mahogany rim; bouquet variously described as 'vanilla chocolate', tobacco, earthy, always harmonious, honeycomb, touch of liquorice; silky texture, crisp fruit, luscious, perfect weight, great length. A gentle giant. *Last tasted Dec 2000* ★★★★★

Ch Ausone Still richly coloured but tiring; 'autumn leaves', old straw, *gibier* – over-mature; still rich on the palate, distinctive, dry, with slightly sour finish. Idiosyncratic. Over the top but interesting. *Last tasted April 2005. At best* ★★★★

Ch Pétrus A dozen notes over the past 30 years. Unquestionably impressive and, for a big wine, elegant. Most recently, three magnums at a dinner: amazing colour, opaque, velvety, ruby rim; rich, spicy, fruit-packed; sweet, concentrated, still very tannic. *Last tasted Aug 2005* ★★★★★

Ch La Conseillante A superb magnum: fabulous fruit, perfect balance, complete. *Last noted Sept 2000* ★★★★★

Ch Lafleur Excellent level. Opaque core; strange, arboreal, sweaty (tannic) nose; sweet, full-bodied, packed with fruit, good length. *Sept 2004* ★★★★

Ch Léoville-Barton Full maturity noted in colour, bouquet and on palate. Ripe, high quality, still tannic. *Sept 2003* ★★★★

Ch Léoville-Barton Bottled by Berry Bros. Virtually opaque; bouquet arboreal then 'meaty', 'almost carvable', finally ripe and 'stably'; a powerful wine, incredibly concentrated, sweet, rich but still tannic. Superior to, or stored better than, the château-bottled. *Dec 2002* ★★★★★

Ch Lynch-Bages Belgian-bottled: luminous colour; lovely bouquet, glorious, spicy, eucalyptus flavour. Delicious but cracked up within 20 minutes. *Feb 2000* ★★★★

Ch Montrose Two bottles from the château: fairly deep and attractive; rich, fragrant, almost meaty; fairly concentrated, rich, very spicy, tannic. *Sept 2005* ★★★★

Ch Talbot Consistently glowing notes. Most recently, a beautiful double magnum. *Last tasted April 2000* ★★★★★

OTHER EXCEPTIONALLY GOOD '45S LAST TASTED IN THE 1990S
Ch Calon-Ségur deep, velvety, rich mahogany colour; mature nose, touch of vanilla and coffee, fleshy, cedary; rich though drying out a bit. Still tannic; still impressive. *At best* ★★★★; **Ch Cantemerle** low-keyed, typically fragrant, soft, rich and lovely wine ★★★★; **Ch Cheval Blanc** usually noted for its fragrance, deft touch and elegance. Flavoury but acid-edged magnum ★★★★; **Ch Le Gay** variable but some bottles fabulously rich, with great concentration. Tannic though superb aftertaste. *At best* ★★★★★; **Ch Gazin** retaining its lovely colour; sweet, old, cedary bouquet; still rich, perfection but in decline. *At best* ★★★★★; **Ch Gruaud-Larose** at its best in the 1970s. But always tannic. A sensational jeroboam, deep ruby, multi-dimensional, full of fruit but after 30 minutes drying and dying. *At best* ★★★★; **Ch Langoa-Barton** a wonderful wine. Bordeaux-bottled by Barton-Guestier. Fully mature-looking; glorious, rich bouquet; excellent cedary flavour and dry finish ★★★★★; **Ch La Mission Haut-Brion** vying with the '29 as La Mission's greatest vintage. A magnum, displaying its characteristic tobacco-like, gravelly flavour, very sweet, full, rich, spicy ★★★★★; and **Ch Pontet-Canet** Bordeaux-bottled by Cruse. A good '45, severe and tannic well into the early 1970s. Now sweet, rich, more mellow. *At best* ★★★★

1946 ★★★
Quite good but rarely seen.

1947 ★★★★★
The second of the three great post-war vintages. Hot summer with picking in almost tropical conditions causing serious fermentation problems. Quite a few wines suffered from high volatile acidity. On the whole, exceptionally rich almost voluptuous wines, though some living dangerously.

Ch Lafite Two half-bottles from Berry Bros' cellars: attractive bouquet; now lean but very agreeable. *Last tasted April 2005. At best* ★★★★ *Drink up.*

Ch Margaux Variable notes, from a very flavoury but tart mid-shoulder bottle to a well-constituted magnum, sound, harmonious, but lacking inspiration. *Last tasted Nov 2000. At best ★★★★ but not dependable.*

Ch Mouton-Rothschild One of the great '47s. Earlier notes ecstatic. In April 2005: deep, rich; impressive and distinctive, spicy, dramatic, eucalyptus bouquet and flavour. Five months later, despite good level, rich but volatile, overripe. *Last tasted Sept 2005. At best ★★★★★*

Ch Haut-Brion A great '47. Most recently, upper shoulder level, superb; still very deep; distinctive scent of vanilla and mocha. Very fragrant. Superb though beginning to show its age. Still tannic. *Last tasted March 2003. At best ★★★★★*

Ch Cheval Blanc Not only the most famous '47 but, at its best, one of the greatest Bordeauxs of all time. Well over two dozen notes. At its zenith in the 1990s but variable. Most recently, a perfect bottle: beautiful colour, still lively; blissful fragrance, rich, superb; very sweet, perfect weight and balance. *Last tasted June 2004. At best ★★★★★★ (6 stars)*

Ch Cheval Blanc Belgian-bottled by J van der Meurlin-Decannière. These dependable Vandermeurlen bottlings appear on the market frequently enough to warrant comments. Most recently, an excellent bottle, good level: very deep, intense; gentle yet rich, slightly tangy nose; very good flavour, balance and condition. *Last tasted March 2003. At best ★★★★*

Ch Pétrus Variable, depending on provenance. Very deep, very red appearance; gloriously complete and harmonious on nose and palate. Fairly sweet, a wine of great power and concentration. *Last tasted, from a good English cellar, April 2006. At best ★★★★★ but ascertain provenance and condition before paying an astronomic price.*

Clos L'Église-Clinet Curiously, bottled by Jean Terrioux, Pauillac. Intense, taste better than nose. Good length. *March 2001 ★★★*

Ch Cos d'Estournel A superb Justerini & Brooks bottling from a perfect English cellar: fragrant, faultless; very good flavour. *March 2006 ★★★★★*

Ch Lafleur Good notes on several bottlings, including an excellent Danish and two gloriously rich, fragrant and absolutely correct Vandermeurlen bottlings. Most recently, château-bottled: lovely colour; sweet bouquet and flavour, perfect condition. *Last tasted June 2004 ★★★★★*

Ch Lascombes Good level: rich, 'warm', appearance; ripe nose; distinctly sweet, rich, remarkably good despite a touch of '47 tartness on the finish. *Dec 2002 ★★★★*

Ch Latour-à-Pomerol Very deep, opaque core; bouquet like rich tea; sweet, excellent flavour, extract, tannin and acidity. *March 2001 ★★★★*

OTHER GOOD '47S LAST TASTED IN THE 1990S **Ch Batailley** deep and still drinking well ★★★★; **Ch Calon-Ségur** lovely bouquet and flavour. Still surprisingly tannic but otherwise perfect ★★★★★; **Dom de Chevalier** an elegant, crisp and fragrant magnum ★★★★; **Ch L'Église-Clinet** opaque; very sweet, slightly caramelly nose; very full, rich, laden with fruit. Excellent, though acidity lurking ★★★★★; **Ch Figeac** at its opulent best. Most recently, one dried out yet beguiling, the other sweet, positive and attractive. *At best ★★★★*; **Ch Gruaud-Larose** richly evolved, with good Gruaud fruit. *At best ★★★★*; **Ch Haut-Bailly** three Swedish-bottled, pale but delicious, a fourth, Danish-bottled with deeper colour; scented vanilla fragrance; rich, good fruit, excellent acidity. *At best ★★★★*; **Ch La Mission Haut-Brion** a deeply coloured wine with very distinctive nose and taste – 'dried leaves', 'tobacco', 'cedar'. I even noted 'peat' on the palate. An extraordinarily rich, idiosyncratic Graves ★★★★★; **Ch Pichon-Baron** very variable, the best being Danish-bottled, and a richly-coloured Marie-Jeanne with harmonious bouquet and lovely flavour. *At best* ★★★★; **Ch Pontet-Canet** *at best* ★★★★; **Ch Siran** soft, rich, sweet, lovely ★★★★; and **Ch Trottevieille** fine mature colour; very fragrant; sweet, soft, rich, perfect balance and condition. ★★★★★

1948 ★★★

A good enough vintage though largely ignored by the British trade. Some of the wines had an aggressive masculinity and lacked charm, others had a more dextrous fragrance.

Ch Haut-Brion A perfect magnum: rich, mature; sweet, harmonious; lovely flavour and weight, though drying out a bit. *Last tasted March 2001. At best* ★★★★

Ch Montrose From the château: fine, deep mature colour; moderately sweet, full-flavoured, dry finish. Much better than I expected. *Sept 2005* ★★★

THE BEST '48S LAST TASTED IN THE 1990S **Ch Margaux** very fragrant; sweet, rich, lovely flavour, good length. An elegant '48 ★★★★; **Ch Cheval Blanc** a deep, intense, still red magnum; rather peppery but sweet, with crisp fruit. *At best* ★★★★; **Ch Pétrus** not overtly aggressive, sweet, soft, fleshy. *At best* ★★★★; **Ch L'Évangile** magnum: opaque; crisp fruit; lovely texture, silky tannins ★★★★; **Ch Lafleur** rich and attractive magnum. *At best* ★★★★; **Ch Latour-à-Pomerol** magnum: rich, almost molasses on the nose; sweet, full, rich, chewy ★★★★; **Ch Léoville-Barton** exquisite wine. By far the most attractive '48 and, in fragrance and delicacy, on a par with Mouton '49. Still beautiful ★★★★★; **Ch La Mission Haut-Brion** a great '48 though variable. At best opaque, spicy, earthy, sweet, fleshy with silky tannins. Losing some of its colour but rich, velvety; showing its age but very fragrant; very Graves, very dry but with lots of fruit and character. *At best* ★★★★★; **Ch Nenin** rich, gentle, vanilla, tannic, with attractive aftertaste ★★★★; and **Ch Palmer** lively ruby colour; rich, biscuity, then a tangy, almost pungent, smell of thoroughbred stables. Rich, quite a bite. Slightly tart finish but very drinkable ★★★★

1949 ★★★★★

The third of the great trio of post-war vintages. Wines of great style, avoiding some of the constraints and excesses of the concentrated '45s and the ripe and more opulent '47s. An almost unprecedented heatwave, 43°C recorded in the Médoc on 11 July. Finally, a late harvest in fine weather. The best are still superb but living precariously; storage and provenance are vital.

Ch Lafite Capricious and inconsistent, judging by over 20 notes spanning 50 years. Most recently, a double magnum: lovely colour, open rim; rich, strawberry-like fruit, just a whiff of sourness; high extract, chewy, fragrant, teeth-gripping tannins. Risky but very drinkable – needs food. *Last tasted Aug 2005. At best* ★★★★

Ch Latour Fairly deep, richly coloured; classic nose and flavour; slightly sweet, perfect weight and balance. Fully mature yet time in hand. *Last tasted, from an immaculate cellar, May 2007* ★★★★★

Ch Margaux Some variation. Most recently a perfect bottle, perfectly cellared: medium deep, autumnal, relaxed; a truly amazing spicy, high-toned fragrance; very sweet, exquisite flavour. Sheer perfection. *May 2007. At best* ★★★★★ *Good provenance essential.*

Ch Mouton-Rothschild Unquestionably the finest '49. A wine that, at its best, has an inimitable fragrance and deftness of touch. From the start I found it enchanting, rich and ripe yet with an indefinable delicacy, and a complete contrast to the magnificent, lordly, '45. Perhaps its secret lies in the modest alcoholic content: 10.5%. Most recently, a medium-deep autumnal colour; vivacious, fragrant, floral bouquet; rich yet with a lacy delicacy, and exquisite flavour. *Nov 2003* ★★★★★★ *(6 stars) but drink before it starts to fade away.*

Ch Cheval Blanc Another wonderful wine imbued with the most perfect expression of the vintage. Lovely, fragrant, soaring bouquet; sweet, perfect weight, classic, superb. *Last tasted, from an impeccable cellar, May 2007* ★★★★★

Ch Pétrus Hard to fault. Six notes. All the component parts *in excelsis*! Impressively deep; ripe, fleshy, mulberry-like nose; sweet, mouthfilling, velvety and soft despite its life-preserving tannin. *Last tasted, from a good English cellar, April 2006* ★★★★★

Ch Batailley Always dependable 'even unto this day' yet the big surprise of an evening of great '49s: rich, floral, slightly vegetal – not cabbages!, bouquet: medium sweetness and body, delicious flavour, perfect condition. *May 2007* ★★★★

Ch Montrose At its impressive best in 1985: sweet, ripe, spicy, with silky tannins. Alas, most recently, two disappointing bottles from the château. *Last tasted Sept 2003. At best* ★★★★ *still worth looking out for – preferably from a cold English cellar.*

THE BEST '49S LAST TASTED IN THE 1990S **Ch Calon-Ségur** Calon-Ségur made particularly good wine in 1945, '47 and '49. In 1994 it was showing gloriously well; indeed perfection, and a slightly leaner but elegant magnum the following year ★★★★; **Ch Cantemerle** a top vintage for this once elegant wine. The '49 had a particularly beautiful colour. *At best* ★★★★; **Ch Figeac** several excellent notes. Most recently, sheer perfection: surprisingly deep in colour though a fully mature rim; a sweet, rich, totally delicious bouquet and flavour ★★★★★; **Ch La Fleur** a fragrant, opulent magnum. Sweet, full, rich, lovely fruit, balance and finish. And for a wine of such blatant magnitude, great charm ★★★★★; **Ch Haut-Brion** a curious wine. It often is. Still very deep and fairly intense; yet relatively low-keyed nose with touch of honey; a wine of power and length with an end taste of singed heather ★★★★; and **Ch La Mission Haut-Brion** the high peak of the Woltner brothers' long stint at La Mission and said by them to be the best-ever La Mission, on a par with their '29. A dozen notes, all, I am fairly certain, emanating from the original cellars and all outstanding except a double magnum with high volatile acidity. Consistently more masculine and assertive than Haut-Brion, deep in colour, its bouquet distinctive, strong, with whiffs of cedar, liquorice, molasses, spice and mocha. On the palate sweet, rich, earthy with marvellous velvety texture, 'toasted bracken, dry leaves and tobacco'. *With one exception* ★★★★★

1950 ★★

Abundant, but of uneven quality. Best in Pomerol, Margaux and Graves. Some wines surviving well.

Ch Cheval Blanc Little consistency, partly due to different bottlings in the UK and in Bordeaux. Most recently: fairly deep colour, rich 'legs'; mature, classic

Right Bank nose; very sweet, good fruit and flesh. *Last tasted Feb 2003. At best* ★★★
Ch Malartic-Lagravière Remarkably good colour, still ruby; showing some age but very good. Dry, very flavoury and refreshing. *April 2003* ★★★
Ch La Mission Haut-Brion One of the best '50s. Most recently, touch of iodine on nose, vegetal on palate. Much more enjoyable than it sounds: good texture and fruit. *Last tasted June 2000* ★★★★
TWO TOP POMEROLS LAST TASTED IN THE 1990S **Ch Pétrus** powerful, spicy ★★★★; and **Ch Lafleur** three notes, all in the 1990s. All very sweet, immensely powerful, packed with fruit and tannin. Enormously impressive to taste but hardly suitable to accompany a meal. Most recently, a magnum: opaque; singed, black treacle nose; high extract, concentrated and certainly very impressive ★★★★★ *for sheer monumentality,* ★ *for drinking.*
AND FINALLY, an old note but at the time it was my best wine of the vintage:
Ch Margaux Attractive, with Margaux femininity and style. Most recently, a gentle fragrance, fading a little; still with some sweetness and charm. *Last tasted May 1987* ★★★★ *Should still be good, though becoming frail.*

1952 ★★ to ★★★★

Popular with the British wine trade. Most clarets were shipped in cask and bottled by merchants. The growing season was very satisfactory up until September, which was cold and unsettled; the unripeness of some of the crop is responsible for its variability: best in the Graves and on the Right Bank, harder, more unyielding in the Médoc.
Ch Lafite A rather ungracious and unsatisfactory wine though it was agreeable enough in the early to mid-1960s. My best note is of a flavoury magnum in 1980. Most recently, a magnum: fairly deep, slightly drab, with weak rim; showing its age, scent of something like beetroot and living dangerously; medium sweetness and body, mushroomy, drying out and tannic. *Last tasted Dec 2000. At best* ★★
Ch Margaux Initially severe, still astringent, though sweet, crisp with good flavour. *Last noted Nov 2000* ★★
Ch Mouton-Rothschild Seven notes, its fragrance and flavour making up for the hard tannins. Most recently: most attractive, un-Mouton nose; sweet, fleshy, assertive though not a tough '52. *Last tasted Feb 2003* ★★★★
Ch Haut-Brion Definitely one of the best surviving '52s. Distinctive, slightly chocolatey, earthy bouquet which opened up well; citrus-like fruit, good flavour but very tannic. I thought it would go on and on. *Last noted June 2000* ★★★★
Ch Pétrus Six notes. Characteristically deep in colour; finely textured, combining power and flesh; its sweetness and high alcoholic content masking its sustaining tannin. *Last tasted April 2000. At best* ★★★★★
Ch La Mission Haut-Brion Spicy but less aggressively masculine than usual. Crisp, very good fruit. Delicious. *June 2000. At best* ★★★★★
Ch Montrose A good period: a classic wine needing bottle age. Still fairly deep though fully mature; nose dusty at first but opened up; better on the palate: medium-dry, rich, good flavour, tannin and acidity. *Last noted Sept 2005* ★★★★
OTHER GOOD '52S LAST TASTED IN THE 1990S **Ch Latour** the combination of Latour and a tough vintage like 1952 did not augur well. For many years austere and tannic. Most recently, my 21st note, a magnum maturing nicely; bouquet fully evolved; sweet, very rich but still tannic. Will it do a '28? I

doubt it. *At best* ★★★; **Ch Ausone** basically very good though strange, with its curious over-mature colour and idiosyncratic nose. Variable. A very good Vandermeurlen bottle: richly coloured; nice gentle fruit, 'singed', good depth, perfect weight, its tannin and acidity serving to preserve and refresh. *At best* ★★★; **Ch Cheval Blanc** definitely one of the best '52s, almost from start to finish – except that it is nowhere near finished. Most recently: very deep, mature-rimmed; very good classic Cheval Blanc nose and taste, very sweet, good body, nice weight (12.6 % alcohol) and tannic grip. *At best* ★★★★; and **Ch Cantemerle** a good period and a much better than average Médoc. Good colour; very attractive bouquet; a splendid lively wine, fruit holding hands with tannin ★★★★

1953 ★★★★★

One of my all-time favourite vintages, combining fragrance, finesse and charm, epitomising claret at its best, the antithesis of some latter-day blockbusters. The late harvest produced wines which were easy, lovely to taste even in cask and throughout its development.

Ch Lafite A wine of exquisite charm and finesse, Lafite at its beguiling best. Most recently: fully mature, open, rosy-hued; perfect fragrance; touch of sweetness, lovely, soft yet beautifully balanced. Top claret. *July 2006* ★★★★★★ *(6 stars). Now past its peak and unless a perfect bottle from an ideal cellar one can expect some frailty.*

Ch Margaux Now here's a wine. One of the loveliest of all vintages of Margaux. Most recently, magnums: fully mature, open-rimmed (as opposed to intense); very fragrant 'oyster shell', iodine bouquet; very rich, lovely but – it has to be admitted – past its best. *Last noted May 2005. At its best* ★★★★★

Ch Mouton-Rothschild Over 20 notes over 40 years, and not one less than outstanding: always a glittering, dazzling bouquet and flavour, with incomparable spiciness and zest. Most recently: lovely colour; very fragrant, complex, a whiff of spicy eucalyptus, glorious; fairly sweet. Perfect flavour and weight. Indescribably magnificent. *Sept 2005* ★★★★★★ *(6 stars)*

Ch Haut-Brion Rich, autumnal colour; scent of old stables, iron, earthy. Rich, characterful, but a touch of decay. *Last noted Dec 2002. At best* ★★★★★ *Now tiring.*

Ch Pétrus Medium-deep, mature; deep, fleshy, delicious; fairly sweet, rich flavour, perfect balance. *Immaculate cellar, April 2007* ★★★★★

Ch Pétrus Bottled by Averys. Lovely, relaxed, bright ruby sheen; very fragrant, meaty; citrus whiff; rich, yet crisp, excellent body and flavour. Good acidity, dry finish. *April 2004* ★★★★★

Ch La Mission Haut-Brion Many good notes, though its very distinctive flavours recorded, included singed, burnt, peaty, dried bracken, tobacco and a slightly aggressive masculinity. Not a lightweight '53, though plenty of fragrance and some elegance. Still impressive, idiosyncratic. *Last noted June 2000. At best* ★★★★★, *and will continue.*

Ch Pontet-Canet Bottled by Harvey's of Bristol. Healthy appearance; sound nose, whiff of celery; sweet, soft, perfect weight. Lovely wine. *July 2002* ★★★★

Ch Talbot In its youth, a bit raw and lacking charm. But this *is* the fascination of good Bordeaux, and shows why it should be given time to mature. Most recently, a good, rich, ripe magnum from the château, delicious but beginning to dry out. *Last tasted April 2000. At best* ★★★★

Ch Trottevieille In 1995, an almost unrealistically deep appearance; low-keyed but harmonious nose; surprisingly full and rich, vigorous, but with a certain coarse 'un-'53-like' masculinity. Most recently, showing well. *June 2003* ★★★

OTHER GOOD '53S LAST TASTED IN THE 1990S **Ch Latour** not a great '53, the '52 having more character, the '55 better balance. However, having scanned nearly 20 notes, most warrant 4 stars despite its leathery tannic finish. Most recently, an immediately forthcoming, mature, bricky, slightly medicinal Pauillac bouquet; a sweet, ripe entry, a touch of decay yet a rich drink and still tannic. *At best* ★★★★; **Ch Cheval Blanc** exactly two dozen notes charting its progress. A soft, mellow brick red with shades of ruby; the sort of fragrance that can't wait. Mocha, a touch of lime blossom; a most lovely wine with perfectly integrated component parts. Light in style and only 12% alcohol. *At best* ★★★★★; **Ch Pétrus** not one bad note among the 18 made since 1956. An early developer with lively fragrance. Most recently, a perfect magnum. *At best* ★★★★★; **Ch Calon-Ségur** still drinking quite well. *At best* ★★★★★; **Ch Cos d'Estournel** another popular wine at the time, and an early developer. Superb: surprisingly deep for a '53; glorious, fragrant bouquet. Claret at its very best, delectable flavour, weight and balance. *At best* ★★★★★; **Ch Figeac** excellent. Bouquet very original, slightly caramelly, tea and tobacco. A soft, easy, earthy wine with a dry finish. Past its best but delicious. *At best* ★★★★★; **Ch Grand-Puy-Lacoste** consistently excellent and always dependable. Most recently, an *impériale*: rich, mature colour; showing a bit of fungi at first but it opened up brilliantly. On the palate, the sweetness of age and ripeness. Fragrant. Good length and aftertaste. A delicious wine though its seams beginning to show. *At best* ★★★★★; **Ch Gruaud-Larose** yet another fragrant and fruity '53. Most recently, a voluptuous *impériale* ★★★★★; **Ch Lynch-Bages** an enormously popular wine and certainly one of the most attractive and drinkable '53s. My most recent note: a lovely, mellow-looking wine with an immediately fragrant bouquet. Ideal weight, sweetness and balance. Perfection ★★★★★; and **Ch Pichon-Lalande** a lovely '53. Elegant. Stylish. Most recently, a magnum, fully developed with a gentle, fragrant, harmonious, cedary bouquet and lovely flavour. On the light side, drying out, with attenuated finish. *At its best* ★★★★ *Now fading.*

1955 ★★★★

A somewhat underestimated yet useful vintage, now undeservedly neglected. A decent-sized crop harvested in good conditions. I have hundreds of notes.
Ch Lafite Two bottles recently, both with good levels and excellent long corks: medium-pale, prettily coloured, mature; rich, exquisite bouquet; sweet entry, delectable flavour, perfect weight and balance. Fading gracefully. *Last noted Dec 2005* ★★★★★ *But don't wait.*
Ch Latour Very good wine, more complete and better balanced than the '52 and '53. Most recently, still deep, surprisingly intense and youthful looking; a fully evolved bouquet, classic, cedary, fragrant and ageing a little, but faultless on the palate. *Last tasted Feb 2001* ★★★★★ *Will go on, and on.*
Ch Margaux A lovely wine, with characteristic fragrance and charm. Showing consistently well. Harmonious, fragrant; sweet, perfect weight, delicious flavour. Most recently, a soft, gentle bouquet and flavour, fading a little. *Nov 2000. At best* ★★★★★

Ch Mouton-Rothschild Spectacular, probably at its best in the 1980s. Most recently: medium-deep, richly coloured; sweet, fully evolved bouquet; rich, yet a touch of leanness, very spicy flavour, dry finish. *Last tasted Nov 2003* ★★★★★

Ch Haut-Brion A wide spread of good notes. Latterly, a refreshing but raw-edged bottle with, initially, a lovely singed-bracken bouquet, and, most recently, alas, a bad bottle. *Last noted Feb 2001. At best* ★★★★

Ch Pétrus Still impressively deep; lively bouquet, touch of liquorice; a very rich mouthful, faultless but unexciting. *Last tasted March 2003. A grudging* ★★★★★

Ch Canon-la-Gaffelière Rich, positive bouquet; amazingly sweet; faultless. *April 2006.* ★★★★

Ch Cos d'Estournel Not a brilliant '55. *Oct 2004* ★★★ *(just).*

Ch Léoville-Las-Cases Rich, scented, ripe, chocolatey nose; sweet, soft, good mellow flavour and length. Dry finish. *Dec 2003* ★★★★

Ch La Mission Haut-Brion Most recently, an astonishing spicy bouquet, eucalyptus, raspberries. Very exciting wine, crisp fruit but a bit tart on the finish. *Last noted June 2000. At best* ★★★★★ *Should still be very good.*

Ch Montrose From the château: curious nose and taste, the former quickly opening up, fragrant, crystallised violets settling down to a classic 'stably' bouquet; dry, lean but very flavoury. Fragrant aftertaste. *Sept 2005* ★★★★

SOME OF THE BEST '55S LAST TASTED IN THE 1990S **Ch Cheval Blanc** still being shipped in hogsheads to British merchants, some excellent Berry Bros' bottlings drinking beautifully at 30 years of age: rich, soft, earthy, completely rounded – no sharp edges, a touch of iron (from the soil) on the finish but noted as *à point*. Most recently, a good but not flawless magnum: more meaty, more chewy but refreshing. *At best* ★★★★★; **Ch Ducru-Beaucaillou** magnum: richly mature; harmonious bouquet, cedar, 'warm tiles'; sweet, perfect flavour, weight and balance, though its aftertaste hinted at fatigue. *At best* ★★★★; **Ch Gruaud-Larose** several good bottlings, including an overripe and deliciously drinkable jeroboam. *At best* ★★★★ *but risky now*; **Ch Lafleur** fragrant, 'warm'; perfectly balanced, lively, holding well ★★★★; **Ch Pichon-Lalande** fully mature: 'soft, rich, perfect now'. *At best* ★★★★ *Still good if well cellared*; and **Ch Talbot** most recently, bottled by Nicolas, Paris, its appearance now a bit weak, but the sort of bouquet that flaunts all its charm. Harmonious, soft, sweet. Held well in the glass. *At best* ★★★★★

1957 ★

'The coldest August on record'. Unripe grapes picked in an early October heatwave resulted in mainly aggressive, astringent wines.

Ch La Mission Haut-Brion The best of all the '57s, thanks to the Woltners' skill and Woltner provenance. Most recently, rich fruit, peppery, tannins. *June 1990* ★★★★ *Worth looking out for.*

1958 ★★

A pleasant, late, easy vintage. The best wines lasted far longer than predicted but most are now fading or faded.

Ch Lafite Curiously attractive nose and taste. *March 1996* ★★ *Drink up.*

1959 ★★★★★

A great vintage, following a very favourable growing season and hugely popular with the British wine trade. Speedily proclaimed by the pundits as 'the vintage of the century' and as *très grands vins* by the Bordelais. The optimists were right, despite some talk of lack of acidity.

Ch Lafite One of the best-ever Lafites, quite different from the more delicately fragrant '53s, and keeping well. Most recently, a magnum: very deep, with dark cherry core; nose at first holding back, unreleased fragrance, touch of iron; sweet, glorious mouthfilling flavour, great length, spicy, with teeth-gripping tannins. For Lafite, mammoth. And superb. *Last tasted July 2006* ★★★★★ *And more to come.*

Ch Latour Glorious. It just goes from strength to strength, showing no signs of flagging, its opacity merely prefacing its beautifully developed bouquet, sweetness, richness, excellent flavour and perfect balance – perfect enough to keep on maturing for another quarter century. *Last noted June 2007* ★★★★(★★) *(6 stars)!*

Ch Margaux A lovely warm, rich, well-tempered, complete, harmonious bouquet; sweet, full, rich and rounded. However, looking back, of my 29 notes, about half a dozen have been disappointing, mainly due to less-than-good levels and poor corks. *Last tasted Dec 2001. At best superb* ★★★★★

Ch Mouton-Rothschild With the exception of one disappointing bottle in 2002, the last seven notes have been equally ecstatic. Most recently, its spicy, clove-like nose almost a caricature of itself, reminding me of the '45 and of Heitz's Martha's Vineyard eucalyptus. Overall sweet, audacious, lovely. Dry finish. *Last tasted Nov 2005. At frequent best* ★★★★★★ *(6 stars).*

Ch Haut-Brion Thanks to the vineyard's deep Graves gravel, the wine is distinctively different to its peers further north in the Médoc in appearance, nose and taste – yet it also has elegance and finesse. Very distinctive nose, tobacco-like, earthy fragrance, surging out of the glass; full of fruit yet concentrated. Most recently: a wonderful gradation of colour; showing age but sweet and mellow, with a lovely edge-of-honeycomb scent after an hour in the glass. A positive, sweet entry, soft yet assertive. Above all, all the component parts working in harmony. *Last tasted June 2000* ★★★★★

Ch Cheval Blanc Back on form. Hot, difficult vinification but the end result was a superb wine. Most recently: fairly deep; very fragrant; very sweet, very rich with fabulous flavour and aftertaste. Powerful, perfect tannin and acidity. Outstanding. *Last tasted April 2002* ★★★★★

Ch La Mission Haut-Brion The Woltners at their peak. The wine took 20 years to shrug off some of the tannin. Most recently, a superb bottle: deep, tinged with cherry red; earthy, 'cheese rind', singed tobacco, pebbly, its crisp fruit opening up richly; crisp, aggressive, convincing, with excellent tannin and acidity. *Last tasted June 2000* ★★★★★ *And will keep.*

Ch Montrose Very popular with British merchants at this period. Outstanding – still fairly deep and velvety though fully mature: bouquet opened up deliciously, fabulous fragrance, crystallised violets, yet a certain fragility; sweet, fairly full-bodied, glorious rich flavour, soft yet still tannic. *Last tasted Sept 2005* ★★★★★

Ch Palmer Classic, cedary bouquet; superb sweetness and ripeness, lovely flavour, gloriously rich and harmonious. *Last noted Feb 2001* ★★★★

Ch Pichon-Lalande A superb jeroboam: still youthful; whiff of mocha; sweet, soft, lovely. *Last tasted May 2005* ★★★★★

THE BEST '59S LAST TASTED IN THE 1990S **Ch Ausone** very fragrant, opening up richly. Extraordinarily sweet and rich, chunky, chewy, yet still tannic ★★★★; **Ch Pétrus** a big, rich wine, fully mature ★★★★★; **Ch Beychevelle** a good château-bottling. *At best* ★★★★ *but fading now;* **Ch Calon-Ségur** a superb jeroboam: sweet, full-bodied, concentrated and very tannic. *At best* ★★★★; **Dom de Chevalier** a most excellent magnum, blackberry-coloured, nose restrained yet rich and fruity, opening up superbly in the glass. Full-bodied, fragrant, very tannic ★★★★; **Ch Cissac** demonstrating what a relatively minor Médoc can do in a vintage like '59. Sweet, full, rich, tannic ★★★★; **Ch La Conseillante** limpid, with shades of cherry; lovely fragrance; rich, silky Pomerol texture ★★★★; **Ch Cos d'Estournel** autumnal colour, overripe bouquet, good flavour, still tannic ★★★★★ *but past its best;* **Ch L'Église-Clinet** Belgian-bottled in 1961, with very distinctive nose and flavour, opening up, finally delicious. *At best* ★★★★; **Ch Figeac** impressively deep but browning rim; idiosyncratic bouquet, open, grassy, tea and mothballs; sweet, with a touch of iron from the soil and a hot spicy finish. A roller coaster of a wine ★★★; **Ch Grand-Puy-Lacoste** a big, serious, tannic, slow-maturing wine, at its zenith in the mid-1990s. Superb classic cedary nose, opening up sweetly. On the palate, well clad though leaner than expected, yet with good fruit. Complete ★★★★ *will still be good;* **Ch Gruaud-Larose** though fully mature-looking, sweet and spicy on the nose; dry, severe and tannic ★★★★ *will still be good;* **Ch Langoa-Barton** I would have expected the '59 to be made of sterner stuff but it had a wonderful fragrance ★★★★; **Ch Latour-à-Pomerol** very deep. As often, with even top Pomerols, the palate more interesting than the nose. A classic fullness and flavour. Complete, and for the palate only, a grudging ★★★★★; **Ch Léoville-Poyferré** a soft, sweet, complete and delicious flavour. In short, Poyferré approaching its very best ★★★★; **Ch Lynch-Bages** mature, orange-tinged; its bouquet fully evolved, in fact with the typical high-toned, spicy Pauillac Cabernet nose hurtling out of the glass. Lovely and will keep ★★★★; **Ch Malartic-Lagravière** a deep, uplifting, delicious red Graves. Now living dangerously ★★★★; **Ch Malescot-St-Exupéry** a rich, ruby-tinged bottle, with wonderful mulberry-like fruit. Dry finish. *At best* ★★★★; **Ch Trotanoy** impressively deep; good fruit; sweet, very good flavour but a surprising touch of rawness ★★★; and **Vieux Ch Certan** nose better than palate, for, despite showing its age, it was rich and fragrant. Dry, somewhat austere, though opening up to leave a sweet impression. *At best* ★★★★

1960–1979

This period saw some of the best and some of the worst-ever claret vintages. It was a transitional period in wine, with changes of emphasis, though Bordeaux continued its dominant role. The early 1970s was a terrible period for red Bordeaux: an overheated market, poor weather, a severe recession and, finally a major wine scandal. By the mid-1970s a gradual recovery was taking place, and the next decade, the 1980s, as will be seen, took the Bordeaux market to greater, and more stable heights.

Vintages at a Glance
Outstanding ★★★★★ 1961
Very Good ★★★★ 1962, 1964, 1966, 1970, 1971
Good ★★★ 1975, 1976 (v), 1978

1960 ★

A light, relatively inexpensive wine to drink while waiting for the '59s to mature. Few tasted in recent years. Now rarely seen.

1961 ★★★★★

A great vintage often compared to the 1945, for the two have several things in common. First of all, nature did the pruning: frosts severely reducing the potential crop in 1945 and heavy rain washing away the pollen in 1961. A drought in August was followed by a very sunny September, which resulted in small, thick-skinned, well-nourished grapes in turn producing deep-coloured, ripe but concentrated, tannic wines. The risk is that the tannin will outlive the fruit. Nevertheless some fabulous wines were made. With well over a thousand individual notes, I have had to be ruthless in my selection.

Ch Lafite A magnum: medium depth, fully mature; sweet, rich, lovely bouquet; much sweeter on the palate from start to finish. Delicious flavour. Perfect balance. *Last tasted Nov 2005* ★★★★★

Ch Latour High percentage of Cabernet Sauvignon (75%). In magnum: still very deep with hint of ruby; classic, fragrant, harmonious bouquet; surprisingly sweet, glorious flavour, perfect balance. Years of life. *Last tasted Oct 2006* ★★★★★(★) (6 stars).

Ch Margaux Another splendid '61. Indeed, 5 stars appear with monotonous regularity in over 30 notes. Two recent notes, first, a less than perfect, yet delicious, magnum, 'slightly depraved' flavour, fragrant but fading. A month later, in bottle, level upper shoulder, excellent, very long, cork. Colour 'warm tiles', sweet, fragrant, glorious bouquet; very sweet, delicious flavour, perfect tannin and acidity. *Last tasted Nov 2006. At best* ★★★★★

Ch Mouton-Rothschild Glorious, deep, velvety appearance, still with youthful plummy colour; at first sniff, almost a 'clone' of the '45, spicy, whiff of tobacco. Fairly sweet, very spicy, crisp, great length, dry finish. Delicious. Dramatic but not overdone. *Last tasted Nov 2005* ★★★★★ *Time in hand.*

Ch Haut-Brion Several notes, most recently in magnum: lovely rich colour; fully evolved bouquet, 'hot tiles', mocha; sweet, very distinctive smoky, earthy Graves flavour with hint of tobacco. Elegant. Long life. *Oct 2006* ★★★★★

Ch Cheval Blanc High percentage of Cabernet Franc (59%): medium deep, rich, velvety, mature; exuberant fragrance; sweetish, perfect body, rich and lively on the palate, silky leathery tannins. Delicious. *Last tasted, in magnum, Oct 2006* ★★★★★

Ch Pétrus Merlot 95%. Star of the sale room. Several notes. A luscious mountain of a wine. Very good, soft, fairly deep; bouquet a complexity of fruit, vegetal whiff, *charnu*; more complete on the palate than previously: sweet, crisp fruit, wonderful flavour, great length. *In magnum, Oct 2006* ★★★★★ *Take care, provenance vital.*

Ch Ducru-Beaucaillou A superb '61. Now showing its age but delicious. Extended flavour, still with tannin and acidity. *Last noted July 2001* ★★★★★

Ch L'Evangile Beautiful, herbaceous, spicy, fruit-packed. Most recently, an impressive, more malty, almost too sweet, velvety magnum. *Oct 2006. At best* ★★★★★

Ch Figeac High Cabernet Sauvignon content noted in the 1960s, a Burgundy-like opulence in the 1980s. Most recently, just one note: 'magnificent'. *Last tasted June 2003* ★★★★★

Ch La Gaffelière-Naudes Two notes, the most recent bottled by Lovibonds. Despite mid-shoulder level and oxidation, a rich '61 colour and sweet, rich, ripe, remarkable flavour. Very tannic finish and amazing tarry aftertaste. The survival of the unfittest! *Dec 2002. At best* ★★★

Ch Lafleur Two lovely magnums, its mulberry and raspberry scent indicative of its unusually – unique? – high Cabernet Franc (50%), sweet; delicious, beautiful, distinctive. *Last tasted Oct 2006* ★★★★★

Ch Latour-à-Pomerol Opaque core; rich, fragrant and floral; sweet, high extract, perfect condition. Three slightly variable bottles and magnums. *Last noted, in magnum, Oct 2006. At best* ★★★★★ *Provenance and condition are all.*

Ch Léoville-Las-Cases Followed for nearly four decades: pretty impressive. Most recently: mature; ripe, forthcoming old oak and mocha bouquet; showing its age. Touch of end acidity. *Last tasted Dec 2003. At best* ★★★★★ *but on the decline.*

Ch Lynch-Bages Over 30 notes. Château-bottled: losing its depth of colour though still fairly intense; good nose; dry, taut, crisp, excellent flavour, great length. *Last tasted April 2003* ★★★★★ *At peak.*

Ch La Mission Haut-Brion Several notes, monumental, multi-dimensional. Most recently a mellow-looking magnum; rich, original, mocha, medicinal; dramatic, powerful, tobacco, rustic character, very tannic. Masculine as opposed to the elegant Haut-Brion. *Last tasted Oct 2006* ★★★★★

Ch Montrose An archetypal Montrose. Two recent notes the same month. The first, from the château: not as deep as expected; an extraordinary, uplifting, crystallised violets fragrance; surprisingly delicate flavour, delicious. The second: good ripe bouquet; very flavoury but with a slightly tart finish. *Last tasted Sept 2005. At best* ★★★★★

Ch Palmer One of the top wines of the vintage and unquestionably the greatest ever Palmer. Well over two dozen notes, all noting its fleshiness and extra dimensions. Two recent notes: appearance still fairly deep with a 'warm' mature mahogany rim; superb bouquet, its perfume exceptionally fragrant and penetrating, mulberry-ripe fruit, sublimely rich and totally unmistakable; on the palate sweet, fleshy yet lean, soft fruit flavour, rich, perfectly balanced. *Last tasted May 2006* ★★★★★★ *(6 stars).*

Ch Palmer Bottled by Berry Bros. A couple of notes. Sweet, fully evolved, harmonious, bricky bouquet; sweet, soft, fleshy – mulberry ripe fruit, drying out a little, delicious but – is it my imagination – perhaps lacking the intensity and immediate impact of the château bottling? *Last tasted Oct 2006* ★★★★

Ch Rausan-Ségla Most recently: medium, mature; classic bouquet opening up richly in the glass; good flavour, weight and length. *Last tasted May 2005* ★★★★

Ch Smith-Haut-Lafitte Medium-deep, mature, open, with orange tinge; sweet, rich old flavour, excellent acidity. *Last tasted April 2003* ★★★ *Drink soon.*

Ch **Trotanoy** Very deep, intense; dense, subdued nose, rich though, and slightly malty; sweet, impressive, touch of molasses, teeth-gripping tannin. Impressive magnum but not my style. *Oct 2006. A grudging* ★★★★

THE BEST '61S LAST TASTED IN THE 1990S Ch **Ausone** rich but mature; the familiar (to me) 'dried leaves, brown paper' bouquet but with great depth; positively and surprisingly fleshy and rich despite its unremitting tannin and acidity ★★★★; Ch **Batailley** bottled by Justerini & Brooks: intensely deep; muted blackberry; full of fruit and flavour ★★★★; Ch **Beychevelle** many highly complimentary notes, including some excellent Berry Bros' bottlings, but very variable. *At best* ★★★★ *but be wary now;* Ch **Calon-Ségur** a deliciously cedary flavour and good length. *At best* ★★★★; Ch **Canon** ruby-tinged magnum with harmonious bouquet and a full, rich flavour masking its tannin. Faultless ★★★★; Dom **de Chevalier** gaining extra dimensions; the bouquet becoming sweeter, tea-like, smoky, very tannic though ★★★★; Ch **Grand-Puy-Lacoste** a first-rate classic though understated Pauillac. Still tannic ★★★★★ *plenty of life left;* Ch **Gruaud-Larose** one of the most attractive '61s. Just under 20 notes over a 30-year span. All except the last, which was a bit below par, showing well. *At best* ★★★★★; Ch **Malescot-St-Exupéry** once popular, and now taking on a new lease of life. Recent notes exhibiting Malescot's distinctive fragrance; very deep, very 'Cabernet'; concentrated, complete, with a glorious, spicy flavour ★★★★ *will continue;* Ch **Pichon-Lalande** crisp, fragrant bouquet; mouthfilling, complete, very tannic. *At best* ★★★★★; and Ch **Talbot** consistently good. Intriguing bottle-aged bouquet, *gibier,* liquorice and, after 90 minutes, a delicate, floral fragrance; sweet, nice weight, good acidity, masked tannin. A charmer ★★★★★

1962 ★★★★

An underrated vintage particularly successful in Pomerol. Many wines are still drinking well.

Ch **Lafite** Fully mature; classic bouquet that opened up fragrantly; medium-sweet, rich yet peppery, slightly raw but refreshing. *Last tasted June 2004* ★★★★

Ch **Latour** Very deep, still youthful; very good nose and excellent flavour. A touch of pure Cabernet, and agreeable 'bite'. *Last tasted Feb 2004* ★★★★★

Ch **Margaux** Ruby-coloured; a fragrant, biscuity bouquet of considerable depth; lean, flavoury, but with a touch of tartness. *Last tasted Nov 2000* ★★★★

Ch **Ausone** Very good; excellent, harmonious, smoky, somewhat autumnal bouquet; sweet, delicious flavour; perfect weight and balance. Despite some teeth-gripping tannin and acidity, virtually faultless. *Last tasted Aug 2003* ★★★★★

Ch **Cheval Blanc** Relaxed, open, mature; rich, classic bouquet; 'complete', good length, dry finish. *Last tasted Feb 2003* ★★★★

Ch **Palmer** Several notes, consistently attractive. Still quite deep though autumnal; cedary fragrance and a flavour to match, retaining fruit but drying out a bit. *Last noted Jan 2007* ★★★★

Ch **Pichon-Baron** Fairly deep but mature; ripe, vegetal nose; glorious fruit, pronounced blackcurrant flavour, exciting. *Feb 2005* ★★★★

THE BEST '62S LAST TASTED IN THE 1990S Ch **Mouton-Rothschild** still quite richly coloured, deliciously fragrant; sweet, crisp fruit ★★★★; Ch **Haut-Brion** my 19th recorded note: still fairly deep and youthful with typical earthiness and Haut-Brion elegance. Slightly acidic but refreshing and not obtrusive ★★★★; **Ch Pétrus** consistently good notes. Hint of ruby though mature; lovely, rich bouquet; drier than expected, a touch of end acidity but very attractive ★★★★; **Ch Beychevelle** a slow starter which developed beautifully. Rich, spicy 'almost 1961 quality' ★★★★; **Ch Calon-Ségur** well developed with a particularly lovely nose, excellent body, extract and flavour, yet still youthful ★★★★; **Ch Figeac** as always, full of fruit and character yet some rusticity. A minty, fragrant bouquet with a whiff of caramel. Lovely, lively, excellent finish ★★★★; **Ch Gruaud-Larose** from the start, one of my favourite '62s. Most recently, a marvellously sweet and fleshy mouthful ★★★★; **Ch Léoville-Las-Cases** an outstanding '62. Only one recent note: a well-nigh perfect magnum: soft ruby; harmonious, bricky bouquet; with sweetness, weight, flavour and balance. As good as they come. Just starting to dry out ★★★★★; **Ch Pichon-Lalande** an attractive jeroboam, good for its age; good flavour, nice weight. Crisp, dry, acidic finish ★★★★; and **Ch Talbot** reassuringly reliable. Overall, cedary, quite complex, flavoury, with '62 piquancy ★★★★

1964 ★★★★

A very good vintage. Heavy but localised rain in the middle of the harvest, mainly in Pauillac and St-Estèphe, caught out some major châteaux. The best '64s were made to the south of the Médoc, and in the Graves. On the Right Bank there were some outstanding Pomerols and St-Émilions. I have several hundred notes on over 250 châteaux.

Ch Latour Vying with Ch Pétrus as the finest '64. The harvest was completed before heavy rains. Now variable. The most recent: colour still fairly impressive; overripe and slightly corky nose; medium-sweet, gamey, 'on the verge' and with dull aftertaste. *Last tasted Dec 2005. At best* ★★★★

Ch Margaux Deep, convincing, sweet, rich, chewy and holding well. *Last tasted Nov 2000* ★★★

Ch Haut-Brion Fully mature with tawny-orange rim; earthy, 'ashy'; very rich, smooth, delicious to drink. A very good '64. *Last tasted Dec 2006* ★★★★

Ch Cheval Blanc One of the loveliest of all the '64s. Most recently, a red tinge hinting at volatile acidity; ripe, bricky; sweet, rich, good fruit, still some tannin and a bit of a bite. *Last noted April 2002. At best now* ★★★★

Ch Pétrus Impressively deep and still youthful; low-keyed but harmonious and complete nose. A glorious mouthful and mouth feel. Deep, rich yet not over-powering. *Last tasted Dec 2000* ★★★★★

Ch Canon-La-Gaffelière Delicious, absolutely at its peak. A lovely mouthful. *Last tasted April 2006* ★★★★

Ch La Conseillante Surprisingly deep though mature rim; very fragrant; sweet, delicious flavour, perfect balance, very lively for its age. *July 2003* ★★★★

Ch Malartic-Lagravière Fairly deep; full, rich, earthy Graves nose, well-evolved, good fruit; medium-sweet, good flavour and dry finish. *April 2003* ★★★★

Ch La Mission Haut-Brion Tarry, spicy-nosed, very 'gravelly' flavour and dry finish. *Last noted Oct 2000. At best* ★★★★

Ch Montrose Picked before the rain. Montrose at its sturdiest best. Richly coloured, fully mature; a really interesting nose, fragrant, almost creamy, rich but rustic; positive, delicious flavour, harmonious. *Last tasted Sept 2005* ★★★★

OTHER GOOD '64S LAST TASTED IN THE 1990S **Ch L'Angélus** a
spectacular jeroboam said to be the best ever made. A glorious mouthful and
fully mature ★★★★; **Ch d'Angludet** faultless: soft, mature, lovely ★★★★; **Ch
Beychevelle** remarkably sweet, soft, superb. *At best* ★★★★; **Ch Canon**
harmonious, fragrant; fullish, rich, lovely ★★★★; **Ch Pichon-Lalande** warm
rosehip colour; instantly forthcoming bouquet, soft, lovely, gently singed, cedary;
reasonable touch of sweetness with a crisp dry finish. Holding up ★★★★ *but
drink soon*; and **Vieux Ch Certan** a lovely, soft, rounded magnum at its best
★★★★

1966 ★★★★

One of my favourite vintages: a 'lean, long-distance runner'. I have several
hundred notes on well over 200 châteaux; the following are the best tasted
recently. Many of the minor wines are well past their sell by date.

Ch Lafite Not all the notes have been brilliant. Refreshing but with fading
fruit. Most recently, alas, a poor sample, murky. *Sept 2005. At best* ★★★★ *but now
past its best.*

Ch Latour The slowest maturing of all the '66s. Most recently: still fairly deep,
good colour; cedar, 'oaky' bouquet; excellent flavour, balance and length. *July 2005*
★★★★★ *Lovely now. Time in hand.*

Ch Margaux On the two most recent occasions it was interesting to see how
well its inimitable fragrance developed – about 45 minutes to reach perfection.
Both bottles were in good condition with fine flavour, texture and length. *Last
tasted Nov 2000* ★★★★ *Time in hand.*

Ch Mouton-Rothschild A typically dramatic Mouton. Most recently:
bouquet of great richness and depth, slight whiff of tar, evolving superbly; very
good fruit and flavour. On the lean side and a bit of an end bite. *Last tasted Dec
2002* ★★★★ *More than ready.*

Ch Haut-Brion A remarkably good double magnum at Christie's in 1996 to
celebrate Christie's Wine Department's 30th anniversary. Alas, two less than good
bottles since then. The most recent, what can be summed up as the look of a very
tired youth, let down by a cork. Just drinkable but … *Last tasted Dec 2006. At best*
★★★★

Ch Cheval Blanc To drink I have always preferred this to the great '47, for
though the latter is hugely impressive, the '66 is the epitome of elegance. Many
delectable notes. Most recently: glorious fragrance; medium-dry, still crisp and
youthful. A superb wine. *Last tasted Oct 2003* ★★★★★

Ch Beychevelle This time a magnum to celebrate the 40th anniversary of
Christie's Wine Department and an equally good bottle at my retirement lunch in
Christie's boardroom. Still pretty deep, showing its age but holding well (I refer to
the wine). *Last tasted May 2007* ★★★★

Ch Calon-Ségur A superb Averys of Bristol bottling: lovely colour, bouquet
and flavour. Soft, *à point*. A perfect claret. *Last noted Oct 2001* ★★★★★

Ch Léoville-Las-Cases A string of mainly very good notes. An impressive,
hefty 'masculine' wine. Most recently, faultless. *Last tasted Feb 2000* ★★★★★

Ch Lynch-Bages With inimitable verve and spiciness, Lynch-Bages and 1966
were pre-destined to be ideal partners. On the whole they were, and, most
recently, still showing well: medium-deep, rich, velvety, still youthful, long 'legs';

classic nose; a sweetish, lovely mouthful, with good extract and length. A near faultless magnum. *Last tasted Dec 2003* ★★★★★

Ch Palmer Exceptionally good though not in the same league as the '61. Many mainly excellent notes. Still fairly deep with a shade of youthful cherry red; crisp, fragrant; dry, delicious flavour, still tannic. *Last tasted Nov 2005. At best* ★★★★

OTHER GOOD '66S LAST TASTED IN THE 1990S **Ch Pétrus** enormously impressive. Still deep, the wine's extract almost visible. An equally rich nose, almost malty yet developing a lovely fragrance. Sweet, full-bodied, yet tannic ★★★★★ *long life;* **Ch Batailley** always dependable, certainly very good, possibly at its very best because its fruity style enriches the leanness of the vintage. A leafy arboreal nose; rich and moderately mouthfilling, with an attractive Cabernet touch to the finish ★★★★; **Ch La Conseillante** a wonderful wine. Perfect body and lovely texture ★★★★★ *still tannic;* **Ch Cos d'Estournel** extremely good: mellow for a '66, lovely fruit, delicious. Claret at its best ★★★★★; **Ch Ducru-Beaucaillou** silky texture, fine flesh, a wine with class yet a bit tight-lipped. *Still* ★★★(★); **Ch Figeac** typical Manoncourt wine, full of fruit and character, most distinctive, its fragrance reminding me of privet ★★★★★; **Ch Lafleur** a beautiful wine. Still deep and fairly youthful looking; one of the loveliest of all Pomerol scents; good flesh, balance, its richness masking considerable tannin ★★★★★; **Ch Gazin** a jeroboam: amazingly sweet nose, the ripe raspberry-like Cabernet Franc oozing out. Good fruit, flesh, complete. Drinking deliciously ★★★★; **Ch Grand-Puy-Lacoste** a well-developed, characteristically sinewy classic ★★★★ *and still developing;* **Ch Gruaud-Larose** a most attractive bottle, stylish, mature, drinking well ★★★★; **Ch La Lagune** consistent notes, the most recent a deeply impressive double magnum. Good shape, fruit and finish: a perfect wine ★★★★; **Ch La Mission Haut-Brion** the last great wine of the Woltners and tasted on 20 occasions. They called it 'a no problem' vintage. One of the great '66s. Most recently, showing its age, with rich 'legs' but watery rim; nose creaking, mocha and iron, slightly stewed tobacco. Lots of grip, lovely fruit and length. Refreshing. *Should be* ★★★★★ *but really hard to justify more than* ★★★; **Ch Montrose** an old-fashioned classic. Every early note mentioned tannin. Most recently, a perfect example ★★★(★★); **Ch Mouton-Baron-Philippe** in magnums: a sheer delight. Elegant, delightful flavour ★★★★; **Ch La Pointe** drinking perfectly ★★★★; **Ch Rausan-Ségla** delicious, fairly sweet, good texture, 'vinosity' and perfect state of maturity. A most stylish '66 and very Margaux ★★★★; and **Ch Talbot** consistently lovely, sweet, rich and ready ★★★★

1969

An unripe and acidic vintage due to very uneven weather conditions. Some quite flavoury wines in its early days. Few recent notes. Best to avoid.
Ch Margaux Fairly pale, fully mature, orange-tinged; surprisingly good, fragrant nose; light easy style, flavoury, noticeable but refreshing acidity. *Last tasted Nov 2004* ★★

1970 ★★★★

A highly important vintage in many ways: its quality (initially overrated and its 'perfect balance' was not all that it seemed) and its timing provided a jump start to the wine boom which was simmering during the dreary 1967–69 vintages. The weather conditions were conducive: a long, hot, ripening period leading to a large and successful harvest which began in early October. Unusually, all the major grape varieties – Cabernet Sauvignon, Cabernet Franc, Merlot (usually the first) and Petit Verdot (usually the last) – ripened fully around the same time. But with such a big crop it was tricky to get all the grapes fermented concurrently and 'housed'. All the vats were full.

Ch Lafite Now palish, fully mature, slightly orange-tinged colour; very mature, cheesy, medicinal Pauillac bouquet; surprisingly sweet, attractive, with very noticeable tannin and acidity. *Last noted Sept 2005. At best* ★★★★ *and now on the decline.*

Ch Latour An immensely impressive wine. Even making allowances for its tannic grip, it refuses to budge. Tasted and drunk – more like chewed – in every conceivable circumstance. One can just detect a touch of maturity; its nose is almost impossible to describe because it hardly shows its head above the parapet. It needs days of decanting time and hours in the glass. Most recently: classic, old cedar bouquet; sweet, full-bodied, harmonious, masked tannin. Many more years in hand. *Last tasted June 2007* ★★★★(★) *Now–2040.*

Ch Margaux A big wine but, unsurprisingly, much more approachable than the Latour. Most recently, medium-deep, a lovely colour; nose low-keyed but harmonious, sweet, good fruit, slow to open up; medium sweetness and body, rich, good fruit, grip and balance, its sustaining tannins and acidity under control. *Last tasted Nov 2000* ★★★★ *Drink or keep.*

Ch Mouton-Rothschild I think Mouton '70 is flawed. I first started to note a certain leanness and austerity in the late 1970s. In the 1990s, and since, noticeable bottle variation with fragrant but higher than usual volatile acidity. Most recently, richly coloured; appealingly decadent, oaky nose; edgy, verging on sour taste; despite tattered edges, good length but below the standard expected. *Last tasted May 2006* ★★★ *but do not keep longer.*

Ch Haut-Brion Not excessively deep or exaggerated in any way, though consistently exhibiting its characteristic smell and taste: gravelly, iodine, tobacco, caramel occasionally, smoky. Most recently a ghastly, raw bottle followed by a fully mature, mocha-nosed, refreshing, teeth-gripping bottle. I think it was at its best in the mid-1980s. *Last tasted May 2006* ★★ *variable. At its best* ★★★★

Ch Cheval Blanc More than first rate. Elegance and perfect balance are dotted through my notes. *Not* a blockbuster. Now mature. Most recently, on the verge of corkiness; disappointing, correct weight but something lacking. *Last tasted Feb 2004. At best* ★★★★★ *Drink soon.*

Ch Pétrus Lovely colour, fully developed, rich, exuding power; fleshy, lovely texture, good length. *April 2004* ★★★★

Ch La Conseillante Over the years my favourite and most consistent Pomerol. The '70 displaying youthfulness despite full maturity; all the component parts present and correct. Lovely wine. *Oct 2006* ★★★★

Cos d'Estournel Bruno Prats' first vintage at Cos. A mass of notes, all good, though tannin very much in evidence. Most recently, an *impériale*, rich, fairly complex, nice weight, drinking well and 'as good as it will ever be'. *Last tasted Oct 2000* ★★★★

Ch Ducru-Beaucaillou One of the best of the '70s. Three recent though variable notes. Deep; harmonious; sweet, rich, perfect balance and condition. Most recently: not very clear cut, but good. *Last tasted March 2005. At best* ★★★★★

Ch Giscours A most un-Margaux-like wine. No feminine charm or delicacy. Nonetheless, very impressive. Still astonishingly opaque, concentrated, dry, full, peppery, tannic. I added 'a great '70'. *Last tasted March 2001, the sort of wine I am impressed by but do not much like. If* you *do, then* ★★★★★

Ch Grand-Puy-Lacoste Another serious wine, this time from Pauillac. Yet though a devotee, I have been disappointed with the '70. On the last four occasions, it was almost port-like and well past its best, cracking up in the glass, leaving it high and dry. Some bottles quite good. Most recently, and extraordinarily, the end of the cork blew out! Level upper shoulder. Despite good mature colour, disappointingly raw and edgy. *Last tasted Dec 2002. Drink up.*

Ch Lynch-Bages Deep, rich, mature; rich, almost rustic; dry, singed, tarry taste, heady, powerful – softened with air. Good but don't wait. *Last tasted April 2003. At best* ★★★★

Ch La Mission Haut-Brion Many notes. Exciting in its youth but neither a good La Mission nor a good '70. Unbalanced, high volatility – though flavoury. The most recent bottle rusty-rimmed, unclean, oxidized. *Dec 2006. Avoid.*

Ch Montrose The sort of vintage suited to Montrose. Deep, excellent colour; sweet and 'broad'; distinctly sweet on the palate, still tannic. A good '70. *Last tasted Sept 2005* ★★★ *Drink soon.*

Ch Palmer A very good '70 and a top vintage for this château. Though now showing some maturity it is a lovely, rich, well-balanced wine and drinking superbly. *Last noted May 2001* ★★★★★

Ch Talbot Chunky, usually leaner and more masculine than Gruaud. A ripe though borderline '70: deep; rustic, dry finish. *Last tasted Sept 2000* ★★★

SOME INTERESTING '70S LAST TASTED IN THE 1990S Ch Ausone plummy colour. Good 'legs' though, and its own strangely attractive scent, vanilla, strawberry, an earthy touch; singed, soft yet austere, lacking length ★★★; **Ch Pétrus** a double magnum, fairly full, chunky, austere but lacking length ★★★; **Ch Batailley** classic claret, excellent flavour and balance ★★★★; **Ch Beauséjour-Bécot** slightly jammy fruit; sweet, soft, chewy, very agreeable, yet still tannic ★★★★; **Ch Beychevelle** fully evolved, perhaps lacking definition and character ★★★; **Ch Brane-Cantenac** lots of flavour and good fruit but with rustic, overripe character ★★★; **Ch Calon-Ségur** distinctly sweet, sound, drinking well ★★★; **Ch Canon** consistently good notes. Rich, well knit, well balanced, crisp, very attractive ★★★★; **Dom de Chevalier** very good. Classy and classic nose which arose gracefully, good texture, length, fruit ★★★★; **Ch Figeac** an excellent '70: almost rumbustious, very earthy, touch of iron and supporting tannin ★★★★★; **Ch La Fleur-Pétrus** a serious wine. On the last two occasions a touch of malt or caramel on the nose which then opened up spicily. A fairly sweet, fleshy, chunky mouthful ★★★★; **Ch Gruaud-Larose** dozens of notes. Sweet, still full of fruit and drinking well. *At best* ★★★; **Ch Haut-Bailly** never less than delicious. Soft, harmonious bouquet and flavour. Spicy finish. Drinking well ★★★★; **Ch Haut-Batailley** now fully fledged, mature-looking, rich bouquet and good depth ★★★★; **Ch Lafleur** amazingly fresh and fragrant; full-bodied, concentrated fruit, very impressive, powerful. No new wood used ★★★★★; **Ch Léoville-Las-Cases** a gentlemanly classic.

Typical cedary nose, very good balance and flavour ★★★★; **Ch Magdelaine** lovely colour; fabulous bouquet; sweet, delicious ★★★★; **Ch Pavie** never a big '70 but drinking perfectly ★★★; **Ch Pichon-Lalande** very drinkable ★★★; **Ch Rausan-Ségla** firm, fleshy, good fruit. Still tannic ★★★; **Ch St-Pierre-Sevaistre** chewy, full of fruit, still tannic, squeeze of tangerine, drinking well ★★★★; and **Ch Trotanoy** bouquet faultless and palate perfection. Velvety. Very fleshy ★★★★(★)

1971 ★★★★

A relatively small but good quality, very high-priced vintage. Originally over-rated by the Bordelais and fairly considerably underrated by the British. Many wines have turned out better than the '70s. The weather conditions appeared to favour producers on the Right Bank, especially Pomerol, and in the Graves. Some top growth Médocs have turned out poorly, yet they were the most expensive wines of the period.

Ch Latour More than 20 notes. Totally different in weight and style to its first-growth Pauillac neighbours. More substance, better balanced but simply not inspiring. Most recently: surprisingly deep colour; attractive cedary bouquet, very slightly smoky; dryish, lean, quite a bite, tannic. *Last tasted July 2005* ★★★ *just. Perhaps will benefit from more time.*

Ch Margaux Distinctly more attractive than Lafite or Latour. Now fully mature-looking with a ruddy amber colour and a nowhere-to-go orange rim. Initially an attractive 'leaf mould' nose which opened up richly. Fairly sweet, nice weight and shape, lean yet fleshy. *Last tasted Nov 2000* ★★★ *No need to wait.*

Ch Cheval Blanc The star of '71. Every note virtually identical: sweet, fragrant, elegant, stylish, lovely. Most recently: very deep, opaque core; slightly bricky with typical whiff of iron, then mocha and liquorice; surprisingly soft, well endowed, good fruit, alcohol 13.5%. Still lovely. *Last tasted Jan 2006* ★★★★★

Ch Pétrus Lovely colour; perfect fragrance, opened up richly; sweet, fleshy, delicious flavour, dry spicy finish. *Last tasted, immaculate provenance, April 2004* ★★★★★

Ch L'Église-Clinet Rich, whiff of toffee; sweet, high extract, impressive. *March 2001* ★★★★

Ch Lascombes Sweet, attractive nose; silky/leathery tannic texture, good length. *Sept 2001* ★★★

Ch Palmer Most recently: château-bottled but with Berry Bros labels. Fine mature colour; very ripe, very fragrant, almost scented; seemed to sweeten in the glass, whiff of tar, extended dry finish. *Last tasted Dec 2002* ★★★★

OTHER GOOD '71S LAST TASTED IN THE 1990S **Ch Mouton-Rothschild** fragrant. Full of flavour and surprisingly rich, chunky fruit and good length ★★★★; **Ch Haut-Brion** rich, meaty, gravelly bouquet; sweet, elegant, distinctive, good length ★★★★; **Ch Ausone** a fairly intense colour; rich, unmistakable bouquet. Fairly sweet, powerful, burnt brown paper taste but drinking well ★★★★; **Ch Beauséjour-Bécot** a fleshy wine, quite substantial. Sweet, very distinctive and attractive, nice flavour and grip ★★★★; **Ch Beychevelle** elegant, well rounded, fully mature ★★★; **Ch Canon** lovely wine. Fragrant, sinewy for Canon, lively and interesting ★★★★; **Ch Cantemerle** the sort of vintage that suits Cantemerle. Delicious fragrance, lovely flavour, well clad. Almost exotic ★★★★; **Ch Certan-de-May** one of those maltily rich Pomerols. Certainly lots of fruit and flesh. For those who like the style ★★★★; **Ch La Dominique** rich, silky, tannic ★★★★; **Ch L'Enclos** another successful Pomerol. Sweet, rich ★★★★; **Ch L'Évangile** and another, this one very tannic ★★★(★); **Ch Figeac** one of Thierry Manoncourt's favourite wines. Typically exuberant ★★★★ *drink up*; **Ch La Fleur-Pétrus** rich, appealing and lots of grip ★★★★; **Ch Grand-Puy-Lacoste** crisp, lean, good ★★★★; **Ch Gruaud-Larose** rather tannic but quite stylish ★★★; **Ch Haut-Bailly** very good indeed. A rich, harmonious, earthy Graves, drinking well ★★★★ *should be perfect now*; **Ch Lafleur** youthfully tinged; fabulous bouquet; rich, lissom and lovely, well sustained by its tannin and acidity ★★★★★; **Ch Latour-à-Pomerol** fragrant, rich, attractive ★★★★; **Ch Léoville-Las-Cases** slow to evolve. Good flavour and texture ★★★; **Ch La Mission Haut-Brion** much better than the '70: fragrance, harmony, length. Lovely ★★★★; **Ch Pape-Clément** demonstrating the superiority of '71 Graves over Médocs. Now mature, distinctive ★★★★; **Ch Pichon-Lalande** open knit, fully mature, still very attractive ★★★; **Ch Trotanoy** mature-looking; lovely nose; perfect harmony, flavour, balance. *Last noted Jan 1998* ★★★★★; and **Vieux Ch Certan** rich but a lighter style than some of the big guns. Silky tannin. Delicious ★★★★

1972

A poor vintage yet prices were out of all proportion. In combination with other problems, it broke the market. One of the latest vintages ever with a fairly large crop of immature grapes of uneven quality. Avoid.

Ch Margaux It at least tried. Palish, weak-rimmed; nose and flavour better than expected. Some sweetness, a dash of fruit, tolerable acidity. *Last tasted Nov 2000* ★★ *(just)*.

1973 ★★

Although the growing season was quite good, there was neither the incentive, nor cash, to work hard in the vineyards. This resulted in an abundant crop of wines that were not bad but could have been better; and by 1974, there was no market. Instead of blaming the growers, we should sympathise.

Ch Margaux It was a bit odd on the nose. Better on the palate. Sweet, light, acidic, drinkable. *Last tasted Nov 2000* ★

THE BEST OF DISMAL '73S LAST TASTED IN THE 1990S **Ch Latour** lacking fruit but light and easy for Latour ★★; **Ch Pétrus** attractive colour; honeyed nose; touch of caramel, dry finish ★★ *A fairly good '73 but will not improve*; **Ch Cos d'Estournel** pleasant, easy drink despite tingle of acidity ★★; **Ch Ducru-Beaucaillou** quite attractive but lacking stuffing ★★; **Ch Lafleur** light, crisp, attractive, lacking length but refreshing ★★★; **Ch Gruaud-Larose** one of the top '73s. Latterly, fleshy but a bit dull ★★; **Ch Malescot-St-Exupéry** bland but well chaptalised and still a very pleasant drink ★★★; **Ch La Mission Haut-Brion** flavoury, fragrant, fairly light for La Mission. Pleasant, easy, short ★★; **Ch Palmer** pleasant, some charm ★★; and **Ch Talbot** fairly pale; fragrant; easy but piquant ★★

1974

Bordeaux was at its lowest ebb, and the wines seemed to reflect this. The quantity of wine was prodigious, its quality mediocre. About the most dismal set of notes in my entire collection and no recent good ones.

1975 ★★★ (just)

The wines are controversial because of their high tannins. Initially, I was impressed, but over the past two decades I have noticed an imbalance between both the châteaux and the wines. The heat and dryness of the summer, while raising the sugar content, thickened the skins, giving wines of good fruit, high alcohol, dark colour and high tannins. Astringent.

Ch Lafite Richly coloured, fully mature; pronounced iodine, seaweed nose; very strong – dare I say fishy? – flavour, sweet yet drying out. Very tannic. *Last tasted Nov 2005. An acquired taste. At best* ★★★

Ch Margaux Some Margaux charm but very tannic. Most recent note: tea leaves, slightly sour but not unattractive. Better than expected. Fair fruit masking tannin. *Last tasted Nov 2000* ★★★

Ch Mouton-Rothschild Two fairly recent notes, the first, a magnum from the château; deep, mature, orange-tinged (a recognisable feature of many '75s); rusty, tannate of iron; loads of flavour but unbalanced. Another magnum, similar appearance; somewhat medicinal nose; sweet, rich, seaweed and fruit. Very tannic. *Last tasted Oct 2002* ★★★ *just.*

Ch Haut-Brion One of the best '75s. Most recently, in magnums: fully mature, orange-brown rim; highly distinctive bouquet and flavour – smoky autumn leaves. Fairly sweet, some softness, good body, richness masking tannin. *Last tasted June 2005* ★★★★

Ch Cheval Blanc A relatively elegant '75 though by no means immune to the ever-present '75 tannin. Most recently, soft, mature, cherry-tinged rather than rusty orange. Low-keyed, slightly varnishy, but opened up richly; better on palate, lean fruit, dry finish. *Last tasted Nov 2001. At best* ★★★★

Ch La Fleur-Pétrus Most recently, deep; gloriously sweet, uplifting bouquet; full-bodied, very rich, almost perfect – but very tannic. *April 2006* ★★★(★★)

Ch Lafleur Highly rated in some quarters. Most recently at a La Fleur vertical: impressive, almost opaque; old oak, sweaty tannin; surprisingly sweet, taut fruit, full, dry finish. Not my style of wine and not worth the price. *Sept 2004* ★★

Ch Léoville-Barton Lovely translucent colour; ripe, sweaty (tannic) rustic nose; showing more maturity on palate. Lean, crisp, iodine, clean tannin and acid finish. *Last tasted Oct 2005. At best* ★★★

Ch Léoville-Las-Cases Rich, mature appearance, bouquet and flavour. Extract helping to mask tannin. A very good '75. *Last tasted March 2005* ★★★★

Ch Léoville-Poyferré Uneven. Medicinal, iron nose; fairly sweet, quite rich but edgy. *Last tasted Nov 2003* ★★ *just.*

Ch La Mission Haut-Brion As distinctive as always. Rich, crisp, surprisingly sweet finish and aftertaste despite more than a touch of astringency. *Last tasted June 2000* ★★★★

Ch Montrose Two recent notes: fully mature, tinge of rusty-orange; crisp fruit that developed fragrantly in the glass; full-flavoured, good length, softening but still tannic. Needs food. *Last tasted Oct 2005* ★★★

Ch Pichon-Lalande Consistently good notes. Very deep; very sweet, full of fruit, tannin submerged. *Last tasted Nov 2005* ★★★★

THE BEST OF OTHER '75S LAST TASTED IN THE 1990S **Ch Latour** fragrant, a bit leathery but with good fruit and flavour. Still tannic of course ★★★ *might well improve;* **Ch Ausone** distinctive idiosyncratic nose and taste. Quite good length – but *tannic* ★★★; **Ch Pétrus** still impressive: thick, velvety, full of fruit, chewy ★★★★★; **Ch Cantemerle** soft ruby matching soft fruit. Fragrant. Fleshy. Harmonious despite noticeable tannin ★★★; **Ch Cos d'Estournel** soft, harmonious bouquet but, though good flavour, in the end too tannic. *Allowing for tannin* ★★★; **Ch Ducru-Beaucaillou** good colour; classic cedary nose; fruit and extract almost succeeding in masking its silky-leathery tannin ★★★; **Ch Gruaud-Larose** slow to evolve. A tinge of orange; excellent nose; surprisingly sweet entry leading to a very dry astringent finish by way of attractive fragrance and flavour ★★★★; and **Ch Trotanoy** impressively rich from the start. Fairly sweet, its rich fruit masking high tannin ★★★★

OTHER PASSABLE 75S LAST TASTED IN 1995 – most were noticeably tannic: **Ch Batailley** its usual easy fruity style ★★★; **Ch Calon-Ségur** classic nose; surprisingly sweet, nice weight and length. Tamed tannin ★★★; **Dom de Chevalier** very flavoury. Attractive, good length, noticeable acidity ★★★; **Ch La Conseillante** lovely bouquet; full, rich, touch of liquorice, astringent ★★★; **Ch Duhart-Milon** attractive, fragrant ★★★?; **Clos L'Église** sweet, good fruit and grip ★★★★; **Dom de l'Église** almost exotic, meaty bouquet. Very sweet, rich but touch of astringency ★★★; **Ch La Grave** Elevated bouquet; elegant, silky tannins but some astringency ★★★; **Ch Latour-à-Pomerol** rich but not very distinctive. Chunky, chewy fruit. Touch of astringency ★★★; **Ch Rausan-Ségla** distinctive. Nice firm flavour and weight, with '75 grip ★★★; **Ch Smith-Haut-Lafitte** very fragrant and flavoury but with teeth-gripping tannins ★★; **Ch Talbot** good nose, ripe flavour – but astringent; ★★★ and **Vieux Ch Certan** sweet, fullish, good fruit, attractive ★★★★

1976 ★★ to ★★★

A vintage of undoubted charm; after 30 years most wines well past their best but many are still delightful. The earliest harvest of the decade, beginning on 15 September. A lack of rain resulted in a lack of flesh, the wines being more lean than supple. But they were undoubtedly attractive, well timed and reasonably priced.

Ch Lafite Once a charmer, nearly always a charmer though now verging on transparent. Most recently, a magnum: soft yet lively appearance; bouquet fully developed, ivy and iron, opening up fragrantly, harmonious; some sweetness, very agreeable flavour, a lovely drink. *Last tasted Nov 2005* ★★★★ *At its peak.*

Ch Margaux A very mature, open appearance with '75-like orange tinge. Bouquet fragrant, with a certain decayed charm. *Last tasted Nov 2000* ★★★

Ch Haut-Bailly Sweet, rich, with a long dry finish. *June 2005* ★★★★

Ch Léoville-Las-Cases Fully mature; good nose; attractive, drinking well. *Last tasted March 2005* ★★★★ *Drink soon.*

Ch Lynch-Bages Fully mature; still flavoury, but packing only half a punch, dry finish. *Last tasted Dec 2001* ★★ *Drink up.*

OTHER '76S LAST TASTED IN THE 1990S **Ch Latour** fully evolved; the sweetness of ripe grapes and fairly high alcohol. A really delicious mouthful ★★★★; **Ch Mouton-Rothschild** I would have expected more from this. Medium-deep, browning rim; a sweet, lively Cabernet nose. Faded but fragrant bouquet; dry, crisp, lean, pleasant enough but no more ★★; **Ch Haut-Brion** an earthy tobacco-like nose and flavour, its dry finish now tinged with a touch of bitterness. Needs food ★★★★ *drink soon;* **Ch Cheval Blanc** still very stylish with some charm but beginning to dry out. Attractive though ★★★★ *drink soon;* **Ch Pétrus** though drinking well, with good weight and flavour, its bouquet, initially pleasing, faded in the glass. My most recent note a bit corky and austere. *At best* ★★★?; **Ch Batailley** mature. Good nose and flavoury. Soft. Well balanced ★★★; **Ch La Dominique** an old favourite. Fully mature. Fairly sweet ★★★; **Ch L'Église-Clinet** luminous, mature; incredibly sweet blossoming of fragrance; as good as it looked. Rich, fruity, dry finish, *à point* ★★★★; **Ch Latour-à-Pomerol** distinctive. Very attractive. Good. Dry. Sound ★★★; **Ch Montrose** an uncompromising sort of wine. Good fruit, good grip, silk-clad tannins. Now mature; slightly sweaty tannin on the nose but sweet and rich ★★★★ *will continue;* **Ch Pichon-Lalande** drinking well ★★★★; and **Ch Talbot** ripe, stylish, flavoury, drinking well though acidity catching up ★★★★ *drink soon*

1977

The worst vintage of an uneven decade. Rain throughout the summer followed by the driest September on record. Few tasted. Avoid.

1978 ★★★

Almost the mirror image of 1976. Appalling growing season. At the end of August châteaux owners were in despair. Disaster loomed. Then, suddenly, in September the weather improved, with cloudless skies and unbroken ripening sunshine through to the start of the harvest in October. But could a last-minute reprieve make up for the previous miserable conditions? Well, up to a point it did, though I have always had my doubts about the balance of the wines. The best are very good but most are in decline.

Ch Lafite Magnum, a lovely colour, soft, with brown-edged maturity; characteristic, attractive, oyster-shell bouquet on the verge of cracking up; lean, flavoury, pleasant, needs drinking. More than just interesting. *Last tasted April 2006. At best* ★★★ *Drink soon.*

Ch Latour Several notes. Despite its open, relaxed, luminous appearance and sweetness, the least good vintage in a vertical of Latour. Nose of cedar and old oak. Tired. *Last tasted June 2007. At best* ★★★ *but ageing.*

Ch Margaux Very consistent notes, quite good nose, a sort of static fragrance. Some sweetness, medium-full body and a tingle of end-acidity. *Last tasted Nov 2000* ★★★ *Good wine but past its best.*

Ch Mouton-Rothschild Variable notes. Lacking the usual panache though quite stylish and drinking agreeably. *Last tasted April 2004. At best* ★★★

Ch Haut-Brion Very variable. Distinctive Graves nose and flavour. Most recently: medium-deep, a touch of ruby; mocha fragrance; soft, tarry, tobacco-like aftertaste. *Last tasted May 2002. At best barely* ★★★

Ch Ausone Another distinctive and idiosyncratic wine. Last tasted at a rare Ausone vertical, in magnums: medium-deep, open, mature amber rim; nose fully evolved, sweet, harmonious, floral; sweet and easy on the palate, drinking well despite showing age. A good '78. *Jan 2005* ★★★★

Ch Pétrus I am convinced this is not all that good. Certainly peculiar – exotic fruit combined with a curious meatiness. Even so, it is fragrant and attractive in its wilful way. Recent notes: drinking quite well. *Last noted Dec 2000* ★★★

Ch Cos d'Estournel Many variable notes. Most recently: medium-deep, a touch of ruby; nose indiscernible; on the palate some sweetness and flesh, quite good flavour but tannic and acidic. *Last tasted March 2003. At best* ★★★ *Drying out.*

Ch Ducru-Beaucaillou Fully mature, orange-tinged; initially sound but creaking a little by the time it was served. Quite a treat, in its way. Decent length, very dry tannic finish. *Last tasted Nov 2002. At best* ★★★ *but drink up.*

Ch Giscours Substantial, well endowed with everything but finesse and charm. Most recently, a surprisingly good drink. A good '78. *Last tasted Jan 2004* ★★★

Ch Langoa-Barton This rarely achieves the class and sheer perfection of Léoville-Barton, but it had a good try in '78. Several consistent notes, the last three all in magnums. Most recently: medium-deep, mature but a plummy sheen; harmonious nose; touch of sweetness, drinking well. *Last tasted Jan 2005* ★★★

Ch Léoville-Las-Cases An outstandingly successful '78. Still very deep; rich, fascinating, cedary nose; delicious flavour and length. *Last tasted Oct 2002* ★★★★

Ch Palmer A lovely wine and a very good '78. Most recently: sweet, attractive, quite good length and residual tannin and acidity. Otherwise *à point. Last noted Feb 2001* ★★★★ *Best to drink soon.*

Ch Pichon-Baron Marvellous components but perhaps a trifle coarse. Rich, ripe, mature appearance; old, oaky nose; flavoury but tart. On the downward slope. *Last tasted Dec 2001. At best* ★★★

Ch Pichon-Lalande May de Lencquesaing's first vintage. Most recently: surprisingly deep; richness and spice in an elevated but unknit bouquet; touch of tar, raw finish. Disappointing. *Last tasted May 2005. At best* ★★★ *(just).*

Vieux Ch Certan Medium-deep, mature; good nose and flavour. Nice weight. A decent, drinkable '78. *Sept 2005* ★★★

A HANDFUL OF '78S LAST TASTED IN THE 1990S **Ch Cheval Blanc** one of the most satisfactory '78s. Still very fragrant and distinctive, though a trace of acidity which would not have been noticeable if drunk with food ★★★★; **Ch Gruaud-Larose** the characteristic Gruaud fruit omnipresent though, in this vintage, uncharacteristically lean and raw. However, most recently, its nose ripe and rustic. Drinking quite well ★★★; **Ch La Lagune** a very dependable '78. Still surprisingly deep in colour; sweet, soft – yet highish alcohol ★★★; **Ch La Mission Haut-Brion** at 20 years of age, in magnums: still very deep, almost opaque; sweet fruit, with almost youthful fragrance; full, fleshy, with characteristic tobacco-like flavour. A great wine ★★★★★; and **Ch Montrose** deep but with a surprising amber-coloured rim. Very good. At or a little past its best, finishing very dry ★★★

1979 ★★

An abundant crop, the biggest since 1934, small, thick-skinned grapes resulting in a very tannic wine, lacking flesh. The wines were generally at their best in the mid-1980s, particularly those from the Right Bank, but since then the paucity of fruit, flesh and extract has left the tannin high and dry.

Ch Lafite Most recently, in magnums: very deep, velvety; good nose; hefty, still tannic. A good '79, but… *Last tasted June 2005. A grudging* ★★★

Ch Latour Very deep, still youthful-looking; bouquet reminding me of privet; dry. Little fruit to mask excessively raw tannin. Frankly, unpleasant. *Last tasted May 2003* ★ *It will not improve with keeping.*

Ch Margaux Sweeter than expected, good flavour, but lean and with leathery tannic texture. *Last tasted Nov 2000* ★★★ *I doubt if it will change much.*

Ch Haut-Brion Deep, dark cherry-red tinge, rich 'legs'; alas, unexciting except for the high acidity hinted at by the redness just noted. A touch of liquorice, opening up with a whiff of caramel; surprisingly sweet on the palate, but spoiled by its astringency. *Last noted Dec 2001. At best* ★★

Ch Beychevelle Still fairly deep; good nose; dry, medium body, lean. A fairly good '79. *Last tasted Oct 2003* ★★★

Ch Certan de May Medium-deep, ruby sheen; classic nose; perfect weight and attractive, whiff of citrus, gravelly, spicy finish. However, still very tannic. *Feb 2003* ★★★★

Ch Lafleur Initially a good '79. Now with an unconvincingly weak rim; strange smell, tannic, showing its age; dry, better than most Médocs, but a shadow of its former self. *Last tasted Sept 2004. A generous* ★★★

OTHER INTERESTING '79S LAST TASTED IN THE LATE 1990S

Ch Cheval Blanc one of the best '79s. Most recently, a magnum: very mature-looking; noticeable vanillin on nose; surprisingly pleasant, with leathery-harsh silk texture ★★★★; **Ch Pétrus** crisp fruit on nose and palate, 'classic', tannic – it was better with food ★★★★; **Ch Giscours** packing a punch, rich, assertive yet elegant. More recently: nose needed coaxing, but within minutes opened up well ★★★; **Ch Gruaud-Larose** still richly coloured; very good, slightly caramelly nose; good fruit, curious 'mucked-out stables' endtaste exposing raw tannins. Needs food. *At best* ★★★; **Ch Kirwan** a good '79, nice weight and flavoury. Very refreshing ★★★; **Ch Lynch-Bages** still deep; tannic; not bad. Holding well ★★★(★); **Ch Palmer** continuing its run of well above average wines. Consistent notes: fleshy ripe fruitiness on both nose and – for a '79 – on palate. Endorsed by a more recent note though its tannin now laid bare – a lean, attenuated, spicy, teeth-gripping finish. Good length. Needs food ★★★; **Ch Pavie** a very good '79. Crisp fruit; rich extract masking sustaining tannins and acidity ★★★★; and **Ch Pichon-Lalande** very deep, still youthful-looking; nose hard to get to grips with; sweet enough flavour, lean and tannic; palate more interesting than nose but lack of balance. *At best* ★★★ *drink soon.*

1980–1989

Unquestionably this was a great decade, matching the 1920s for the number of high-quality vintages. On the whole the weather was kind and there was a renewed demand for *en primeur* wines, especially from private customers. In the USA and further afield the 1982 vintage hit the button. Higher prices meant châteaux owners could afford better care in the vineyard, and in the *chais* they could afford the selection of just the best vats for the *grand vin*.

VINTAGES AT A GLANCE

Outstanding ★★★★★ 1982, 1985, 1989
Very Good ★★★★ 1986, 1988
Good ★★★ 1981, 1983

1980 ★

Not a good start to the decade. A very late harvest resulted in an average-sized crop of less than average quality. **Ch Cheval Blanc** one of my best notes (★★★) but unlikely to improve.

1981 ★★★

A good claret vintage, the sort that the British buy for drinking rather than for investment. The weather conditions were advantageous. Few tasted in the present decade and some less than good bottles. Drink up.

Ch Margaux Medium-deep, mature; strange earthy nose, whiff of vanilla and also a whiff of oxidation. Tart finish. *Last tasted Sept 2005. At best* ★★★ *Now fading.*

Ch Mouton-Rothschild By the end of the 1990s lean, flavoury, acidic. Alas most recently, a corked bottle. *Last tasted May 2003. At best* ★★★

Ch Certan de May Medium-deep, ruby tinge; very good nose, citrus whiff; surprisingly assertive, vegetal, a lovely mouthful. Perfection. *Feb 2003* ★★★★

Ch Grand-Puy-Lacoste A good example of this class of wine in this rather lean vintage. *Last tasted Sept 2001* ★★★

Ch Gruaud-Larose Interesting to see how well a fleshy fruity Gruaud can cope with a lean vintage like 1981. Most recently, despite its good, rich, mature, soft cherry colour, spoilt by corkiness. *Nov 2004. At best* ★★★ *Drink soon.*

Ch Léoville-Las-Cases Most recently merely noted as 'austere'. *Last tasted Sept 2000. At best* ★★★ *but drying out.*

Ch Lynch-Bages A stream of admiring notes. Most recently: agreeable 'biscuity' nose, completely mature and showing quite well. *April 2004* ★★★★

Ch Magdelaine Having, out of curiosity, bought a case of this St-Émilion *1er cru classé* in the spring of 2003, six notes – so far. Always decanted and pretty consistent. Good colour, fully mature; residual richness though showing its age; better on palate: sweet, soft, interesting texture. Drinking well. *Last tasted, and more to come, Sept 2005* ★★★

Ch Palmer Fully mature in appearance, nose and taste. Some sweetness, rich, but with quite a bite. *Last tasted May 2001* ★★★ *Drink soon.*

OTHER '81s LAST TASTED IN THE 1990s Ch Lafite it encapsulated the vintage, at least for the Médoc. More recently, mature, open appearance; fully developed nose, cedary, fragrant; nice weight, crisp, delicious flavour. Later, its dryness and leanness noted ★★★ *drink up;* **Ch Latour** neither big nor charming; in fact, rather pedestrian by Latour standards. Will probably have opened up and softened a little ★★(★★)?; **Ch Haut-Brion** a very good '81, in its own way. Elegance and vinosity come to mind. Most recently, outshining some other top '81s, with excellent flavour, good length, tannin and tolerable acidity ★★★★; **Ch Ausone** definitely a good wine. Touch of malt, tobacco, dried ferns, earthy. Distinctively different ★★★; **Ch Cheval Blanc** an impressive *impériale*: opaque core; sweet, perfect weight, good flavour with hint of Cheval Blanc's iron. Dry finish ★★★★; **Ch Pétrus** sweet, delicious ★★★★; **Ch Canon** good. Perfectly evolved, sweet, harmonious, nice fruit, delicious ★★★★ *drink soon*; **Ch Chasse-Spleen** just shows how good husbandry and winemaking pay off: light but attractive. More appealing than the classed growths alongside ★★★ *drink up*; **Dom de Chevalier** closed on the nose; firm, dry, spicy and surprisingly tannic. *At best* ★★★; **Ch Cos d'Estournel** considerable charm, with lip-licking acidity. Very attractive ★★★★ *drink soon*; **Ch La Croix du Casse** deliciously sweet and *à point* ★★★; **Ch L'Église-Clinet** this demonstrated that the leanness of the vintage seeped through to the Pomerols. Also, like some other leading Pomerols, not very interesting on the nose, but lots of grip. Hopefully a long life ahead ★★★(★)?; **Ch Figeac** Distinctive, flavoury, but variable ★★; **Ch Giscours** managing to be a sweet, chunky wine with none of the '81 leanness. Most recently, quite good flavour and extract, with a sort of Médoc-medicinal taste that I had noticed on previous occasions ★★★ *sound but totally lacking charm or finesse*; **Ch Lafleur** a bit dry and raw for a top Pomerol ★★(★)?; **Ch Latour-à-Pomerol** fairly deep; drinking well. Good tannins. Neither lean nor particularly fleshy ★★★ *will continue*; **Ch La Mission Haut-Brion** fairly deep; rich, arboreal, oaky nose with touch of iron; some sweetness, full-bodied, fairly well equipped with tannin and acidity. Typically masculine ★★★(★); **Ch Montrose** by the mid-1990s its bouquet seductive, sweet and meaty; similarly on the palate, though the tannin not sublimated by its extract. A more recent tasting endorsed this view ★★★★; **Ch Pichon-Baron** despite its rather peppery nose, both surprisingly sweet and not lean for an '81 ★★★; **Ch Pichon-Lalande** still rich and ripe; full-flavoured, masked tannin. More to come. A very good '81 ★★★★ *worth looking out for*; **Ch Talbot** though still deep, a mature mahogany rim; singed, sweet, harmonious bouquet with that curious Talbot ripe smell, iodine this time. Hefty, alcoholic, slithery tannins; very dry finish ★★★★; and **Ch La Tour Haut-Brion** rich, earthy and on that occasion better than the La Mission tasted alongside ★★★ *will keep*.

1982 ★★★★★

A milestone. The combination of richness and perceived quality matched the economic climate. It was the first really important, and well-timed, *vin de garde* since 1970. Ideal growing conditions. Flowering early and even. Hot and dry summer, harvest from 14 September in great heat, the early-ripening Merlot having very high sugar content. There was then a change, two days of heavy rain, but then sun and fresh breezes enabled the Cabernets to ripen well. Rich tannic wines resulted. It should not be surprising that after a quarter of a century most '82s are more than fully mature and virtually all the lesser clarets should have been consumed. The best, however, are superb.

Ch Lafite Many notes. Most recently, in magnum: very deep, velvety colour; needs air and patience, once aroused, fragrant and delicious. Fairly substantial, not immediately impressive – give it time. *Last tasted July 2006* ★★★★(★)

Ch Latour Richly coloured; very fragrant, classic, cedar bouquet; very good fruit, flavour of sugared almonds, tannic, impressive. *Last tasted July 2005* ★★★★(★)

Ch Margaux Consistently top of the class at several major tastings in the late 1990s, with power but less elegance. Nevertheless superb with its very fragrant 'hot vintage' scent, sweetness, body, extract and very dry tannic finish. *Last tasted Nov 2000* ★★★★(★)

Ch Mouton-Rothschild Consistently good. Half a dozen recent notes which can be summarised: still fairly deep, rich, dark cherry, positive but mature rim; sweet, glorious fragrance, distinctive Cabernet aroma, great depth, touch of mocha and mild ginger; very sweet entry, great length, dry finish with lashings of fruit and flesh in between. A great classic, dramatic Mouton. *Last tasted Nov 2005* ★★★★★

Ch Haut-Brion Impressive colour; sweet, rich, velvety, fleshy, 'iron fist in velvet glove'. *Last tasted Oct 2005* ★★★★★

Ch Ausone Low-keyed, sweet, harmonious nose; some bottle variation, full of fruit and idiosyncratic 'autumn leaves' taste, leathery tannins. *Last tasted Jan 2005* ★★★★

Ch Cheval Blanc Superb. Medium-deep, lovely colour; distinctive style, harmonious; touch of earthiness and iron, very distinctive, silky texture, perfection. *Last tasted July 2002* ★★★★★

Ch Pétrus Picked in one day by a large team at the end of a very hot harvest. Most recently, still deep and richly coloured; bouquet harmonious and complacent; full, rich, certainly impressive but if one is to be overcritical, a bit obvious and lacking the zest and drama of the top Médocs. But this will not deter the world's richest. *Last tasted Oct 2000* ★★★★★

Ch Batailley Fully mature, its bouquet unravelled deliciously; sweetish, chewy, good length, dry finish. *April 2001* ★★★★

Ch Beychevelle Most recently: opened up slowly but fragrantly, on nose and palate. A bit stolid and lacking finesse. *Last noted Nov 2001* ★★★

Ch Brane-Cantenac Chewy, fleshy, good enough. *Last tasted April 2003* ★★★

Ch Chasse-Spleen Living up to its reputation. Most recently: sweet, rich, tannic finish. *Nov 2003* ★★★

Ch Cissac A superb '82 for its class. Most recently in an *impériale*: deep and still remarkably youthful appearance; chunky, ripe, touch of rusticity; fairly sweet and full-bodied, rich, still tannic. *Last tasted April 2004* ★★★ *and will keep.*

Dom de Chevalier A double magnum: touch of plumminess, maturing nicely; very distinctive Graves nose; very nice despite a touch of coarseness. Dry finish. *May 2005* ★★★

Ch Clerc-Milon Dark cherry core, still youthful; ripe bouquet, good depth; fairly sweet, full rich flavour. *Last tasted July 2003* ★★★★

Ch Cos d'Estournel My best and most recent note: mature red-brown rim; well-nigh perfect bouquet, gentle, harmonious; surprisingly sweet though finishing dry, good fruit. Attractive. *Last tasted March 2000* ★★★★

Ch Ducru-Beaucaillou A rather unshowy, unfleshy '82. Most recently: classic cedar cigar box

My top 1982s
Cheval Blanc, La Conseillante, L'Église-Clinet, Haut-Brion, Lafite, Latour, Léoville-Barton, Lynch-Bages, Margaux, Montrose, Mouton-Rothschild, Pétrus, Le Pin

nose that opened up deliciously, touch of liquorice; rich but tannic. *Last tasted Sept 2003* ★★★★ *just, but drying out.*

Ch Figeac Fragrant fruit and iron; sweet entry, dry finish. Attractive. *Last tasted July 2003* ★★★★

Ch Grand-Puy-Lacoste Still very deep; not yet fully developed, tannic. Demands food. *Last tasted April 2002* ★★★(★) *A pity, none left in my cellar.*

Ch Haut-Batailley Rather lean and without the customary elegance, but dependable as always. Crisp. Refreshing. *Last tasted March 2001* ★★★

Ch La Lagune Slight yet noticeable bottle variation despite being brought up from a good country house cellar. The best of four bottles had pleasing sweetness, good body, some flesh though still tannic. *Last tasted Jan 2002. At best* ★★★★

Ch Langoa-Barton Still very deep and intense though showing maturity; first whiff rustic, farmyard, unknit; surprisingly sweet, good fruit, still tannic. Characterful, a bit coarse, lacking charm. *Last tasted Oct 2003* ★★★ (*just*).

Ch Léoville-Barton Rich, ripe, floral nose; perfect weight and flavour. Still tannic. *Last tasted Nov 2004* ★★★★★

Ch Léoville-Las-Cases Most recently, maturing but still deep with a rich core; surprisingly low-keyed, somewhat muffled nose; more positive on the palate, fairly sweet, full, rich, chewy, good extract. Delicious, but for the tannin. *Last tasted Dec 2003* ★★★(★★) *if it ever comes round.*

Ch Léoville-Poyferré A slightly tarry flavour, sweet but very tannic. *Last tasted Jan 2000* ★★(★) *Not a great '82. I doubt if it will shed the tannin.*

Ch Lynch-Bages A deliciously flavoury mouthful. Most recently: a magnificent, ripe, rustic nose; sweet, full-flavoured, *à point. Last tasted April 2003* ★★★★(★)

Ch Montrose A serious combination, Montrose and the 1982 vintage. And so it proved to be. Most recently: less deep than expected with surprisingly relaxed open rim; superbly evolved bouquet, uninhibited, rich, fragrant, spicy, harmonious; sweet, very distinctive, hint of eucalyptus, great length. Tannic of course. A great wine. *Last tasted Sept 2005* ★★★★★

Ch Palmer Most recently (cork pulled 5.15pm, decanted and tasted 5.30pm, served at 8.45pm): good nose; sweet, delicious flavour, touch of astringency. *Last tasted Dec 2004* ★★★★ (*just*).

Ch Pichon-Baron Consistent. Now mature; rich bricky nose; surprisingly sweet and soft yet with a searingly dry finish. *Last tasted Nov 2006* ★★★★

Ch Pichon-Lalande Many consistent notes. A lovely wine. Spicy fragrance; full flavour and richness masking tannin. Good length. Firm dry finish. *Last tasted May 2006* ★★★★

Ch Le Pin Little did I think that the rich, fruity half-bottle sample tasted in November 1983 was going to be one of the shooting stars of the saleroom; nor did Jacques Thienpont anticipate, when he first experimented with a tiny parcel of land, that Le Pin would become a 'cult wine', upstaging even Pétrus. Most recently: glorious nose, very fruity, very distinctive; sweet, soft, velvety, full of fruit. Fragrant. *Last tasted April 2001* ★★★★(★)

Ch Talbot Deep, velvety, sweet and chunky. *Last tasted April 2000* ★★★★ *Drink soon.*

Ch Trotanoy Very good. No signs of 'baking' (there was tropical heat at vintage time). Just a perfectly rich drink. *Last tasted Dec 2000* ★★★★

SOME OF THE BEST AND MOST INTERESTING '82S TASTED IN
THE MID- TO LATE-1990S

Ch Branaire-Ducru Ruby, intense; fragrant, spicy, eucalyptus nose; sweet,
mouthfilling, glorious flavour. *Last tasted April 1998* ★★★★

Ch Calon-Ségur A good colour with '82 density; a *mélange* of oak, liquorice,
even camphor. A Calon of the old style, nice fruit, not caring too much about
pleasing, still tannic. *Last tasted April 1997* ★★★

Ch Canon An attractive magnum; herbaceous, rich, then meaty; ripe sweetness,
very good fruit and extract masking its considerable tannin content, leaving a
slightly bitter finish. *Last noted April 1997* ★★★★

Ch Cantemerle Good, rich flavour, texture and length. Tannic; lacking charm
and elegance. *Last tasted Nov 1995* ★★★

Ch Certan-de-May Harmonious nose of the sort which gets more
interesting as one goes back to it. Sweet, fleshy, excellent consistency (texture),
complete. Soft, chewy. *Last noted March 1999* ★★★★ *Lovely now.*

Ch La Conseillante A magnificent wine. My last bottle, sheer perfection.
Why try to describe it? *Last tasted Dec 1999* ★★★★★

Ch L'Église-Clinet A sweet, ripe-nosed almost creamy magnum; fairly full-
bodied, very fruity. Tannic. *Last tasted Sept 1998* ★★★★(★) *Needed more time.*

Ch L'Evangile A lovely fleshy Pomerol with distinctive fragrance, crisp fruit,
good grip. Quite punchy, good length. *Last tasted Dec 1997* ★★★★

Ch Le Gay A fearsomely opaque magnum; youthful fruit still, and peppery.
Spoiled for me by its raw, bitter, biting finish. *Sept 1998* ★★★? *A bruiser.*

Ch Giscours Strangely low alcohol for an '82 (12%). Most recently: well-
developed fruit but with a raw tannic finish. *Last tasted Sept 1998* ★★

Ch Gruaud-Larose It started off well, with the usual fruit, flesh and
excitement, but several of my latest notes have included the word 'stodgy'. Good,
but... *Last tasted Dec 1997. At best* ★★★

Ch Lafleur A noticeably ripe raspberry-like Cabernet Franc aroma; good fruit,
great length, lean tannic finish. *Last tasted, a magnum, Sept 1998* ★★★(★)

Ch Latour-à-Pomerol Medium-deep; very sweet, meaty, almost chewy
bouquet; dry, well constructed, tannic. *April 1997* ★★(★)

Ch Magdelaine Meaty on the nose; very sweet, lovely fruit, slight touch of
iron. Delicious. *Last tasted June 1995* ★★★★

Ch Malescot-St-Exupéry Deliciously fragrant; very sweet, soft, chewy fruit,
well balanced, dry finish. *Last tasted Dec 1998* ★★★★

Ch La Mission Haut-Brion Predictable depth of colour though its amber-
brown rim hinting at maturity; also a typically earthy, tobacco-like, slightly malty
nose and taste. Laden with tannin. *Last tasted April 1997* ★★★(★)

Ch Mouton-Baronne-Philippe Fully developed Cabernet fragrance; dry,
lean for an '82. Drinking well. *Last tasted Oct 1999* ★★★★

Ch Pavie Mature; bouquet nicely evolved. Sweet, soft, attractive. *Last noted April
1997* ★★★★ *Drink soon.*

Ch Petit-Village Fully developed, familiar Pomerol Merlot fragrance. Sweet,
fairly substantial. Delicious to drink by itself. *Last tasted Jan 1996* ★★★★ *(just).*

Vieux Ch Certan I found its finish marred by bitter, teeth-gripping tannin.
By its own standards and '82 Pomerols, comparatively mean and pinched.
Disappointing. *Last tasted Jan 1996* ★(★)?

1983 ★★★

The 1983 and '81 vintages certainly have quite a bit in common, in style and weight for example. Both were considered to be classic claret vintages but with a few notable exceptions, the wines of both years are past their best; even the '83 classed growth Médocs were showing distinct signs of fatigue by 2000. The weather conditions were quite good and the harvest took place in ideal conditions resulting in a large crop of decent quality wines. Perhaps too large a crop, too diluted: the most successful district was Margaux.

Ch Lafite Most recently: fairly deep; fair fragrance; surprisingly sweet, not bad fruit. Faint praise. Perhaps unfair. *Last tasted May 2005* ★★★ *Not a great Lafite.*

Ch Latour Not a massive wine, in fact very drinkable. Medium-deep, mature; sweet, 'chewy', oaky nose which opened up richly; sweeter than expected, extract masking tannin. Good but by no means great. *Last tasted Sept 2003* ★★★

Ch Margaux Unquestionably the wine of the vintage: beautiful colour, medium-deep and still youthful; the inimitable Margaux fragrance soaring out of the glass; sweet, soft and rich. It fills the mouth with flavour and seems to last for ever. Most recently: richly coloured; classic bouquet; delicious fruit and balance. A beautiful wine. Long life. *Last tasted Dec 2005* ★★★★★

Ch Mouton-Rothschild Unquestionably a most attractive wine, its tannin and acid finish not out of line. Tantalising flavour. I added 'more or less ready' for drinking. *Last tasted March 1998* ★★★★

Ch Haut-Brion Most recently, an open, mature, orange-brown rim; a fully developed, slightly smelly, stalky vegetal nose, showing its age, and, I thought, drying out. *Last tasted Jan 2000* ★★★ *Not a great Haut-Brion. Needs drinking.*

Ch Ausone A good Ausone. At ten years of age fully mature, rather weak-rimmed; its bouquet fully evolved, sweet, soft, vanillin, reminding me of curling autumn leaves. Sweet, soft texture, open knit, chewy. *Last tasted June 1993* ★★★★

Ch Cheval Blanc A really beautiful wine: beyond description. A sweet, lovely, melting charm. *Last tasted Sept 1998* ★★★★★

Ch Pétrus An impressive double magnum with crisp and agreeable fruit on nose and palate, good texture but very dry finish. *Last tasted Sept 1995* ★★★★

Ch Beychevelle Curious but on the whole, good. In fact 'sweet, delicious, drinking well', though drying out. *Oct 2006* ★★★

Dom de Chevalier Very good nose; drinking well. *Sept 2003* ★★★ *Drink soon.*

Ch Cos d'Estournel Fully mature colour, nose and taste. Some sweetness, drinking fairly well, a touch astringent. Undistinguished. *Last tasted April 2005* ★★

Ch La Dominique Magnum. Distinctly sweet, very mature, still tannic yet delicious. *April 2003* ★★★ *Drink soon.*

Ch Ducru-Beaucaillou A very good '83. Most recently: attractive flavour, nice weight, holding well. *Last tasted April 2004* ★★★★ *But drink soon.*

Ch Duhart-Milon A lean but always fragrant style. Most recently: drinking well but its tannin and acidity upstaging the fruit. *June 2000* ★★★ *Drink up.*

Ch Giscours I have been so accustomed to the dark and chewy Giscours that it came as a surprise to find the '83 so delicious. Most recently, a double magnum: fairly deep; very good nose; ideal sweetness and weight, lovely flavour, drinking well. A good Giscours and a good '83. *Last tasted June 2005* ★★★★

Ch Grand-Puy-Lacoste Still fairly deep; a ripe, mature, immediately forthcoming bouquet; sweet, flavoury, charming, and with a lovely aftertaste, *à point*. *Last noted May 2000* ★★★★

Ch Gruaud-Larose Most recently: typically fruity and flavoury but with quite an end bite. *Last noted Oct 2001* ★★★ *Lively but drink soon.*

Ch Haut-Bailly Rich, mature-looking; with the difficult-to-describe earthy, mocha, cigar leaf bouquet and flavour. It seemed to get sweeter in the glass. *Last noted April 2002* ★★★★ *Lovely now.*

Ch Kirwan Not the best period for this château. Fully mature, but not a very interesting nose or taste. *Last tasted April 2000* ★★

Ch La Lagune Seemed at its ripest best, ready for drinking, in 1990. Most recently, very disappointing, drying out. *Last tasted Oct 2000* ★★

Ch Léoville-Las-Cases Still youthful; nose seemed faded at first but opened and held well; sweet, good flavour, fruity but raw. Nevertheless a good '83. *Last tasted Dec 2003* ★★★★

Ch Pichon-Lalande A jeroboam: plummy coloured; rich, slightly mocha nose; sweet entry, rich extract, dry finish. *Oct 2001* ★★★ *Drink soon.*

Ch Rausan-Ségla Fully mature, weak rim; fully developed; medium sweetness and body, good acidity. *Last tasted April 2004* ★★★ *Needs drinking.*

OTHER '83S LAST TASTED IN THE MID- TO LATE 1990S The following are the best: **Ch Batailley** ★★★; **Ch Brane-Cantenac** ★★★; **Ch Canon** ★★★★; **Ch L'Église-Clinet** ★★★, *possibly* ★★★★; **Ch Figeac** ★★★★; **Ch Haut-Batailley** ★★★★; **Ch Labégorce-Zédé** ★★★★; **Ch Lafleur** ★★★★; **Ch Lascombes** ★★★★; **Ch Léoville-Poyferré** ★★★; **Ch Lynch-Bages** ★★★; **Ch La Mission Haut-Brion** ★★(★★)?; **Ch Montrose** ★★(★)?; **Ch Talbot** ★★; and **Vieux Ch Certan** ★★★★

1984 ★ to ★★

The failure of the Merlot crop resulted in serious problems; rot was a major problem too. The weather, as always, was largely to blame. As well as a dismal ripening, a wet October was rudely interrupted by Hurricane Hortense. Pomerol was particularly badly affected. Merlot's failure in the Médoc was less catastrophic because it is very rarely the dominant variety. But it did result in an even higher than usual percentage of Cabernet Sauvignon. The wines lack balance and I have few recent notes.

Dom de Chevalier A rare – good – '84. Most recently, in magnums: good colour; surprisingly good flavour, drinking well. *Last tasted June 2005* ★★★★

1985 ★★★★★

My favourite vintage of this splendid decade and typifying claret at its best. Despite spring frost damage in some districts, there was an early and successful flowering which anticipated an early and substantial crop. Following a long, hot summer, the harvest took place in ideal conditions. Only the unlucky or incapable made a mess of their '85s. One of the most ideal vintages, both for drinking now and for keeping.

Ch Lafite Still deep, fairly intense, velvety; very fragrant bouquet, slightly bricky, cedar, oyster shell; medium sweetness and body, good length, dry finish. Classic. Double decanted to speed evolution, opening up in the glass. Perfect weight. Many layers. A constant delight. *Last tasted Nov 2006* ★★★(★★) *Now–2025.*

My top 1985s
Cheval Blanc, L'Église-Clinet, L'Évangile, Grand-Puy-Lacoste, Gruaud-Larose, Haut-Bailly, Haut-Brion, Lafite, Lafleur, Latour, Léoville-Barton, Léoville-Las-Cases, Léoville-Poyferré, Lynch-Bages, Margaux, La Mission Haut-Brion, Mouton-Rothschild, Pétrus, Pichon-Lalande, Vieux Château Certan

Ch Latour Well spread-out notes beginning just before fining in 1986. Most recently, more open, less deep and more relaxed than expected; good classic Médoc Cabernet, cedar box nose, slightly medicinal; understated but very good, cedar again, good length, balance, life. Very dry finish. *Last tasted April 2006* ★★★★(★) *Now–2030.*

Ch Margaux Fairly deep, impressive, black cherry core yet mature; typically appealing, forthcoming bouquet; sweet and soft, wonderful flesh and flavour, good finish. Easy to drink by itself. *Last tasted April 2006* ★★★★★ *Now–2020.*

Ch Mouton-Rothschild Deep, black cherry, quite intense though showing maturity; 'very Mouton', exciting, dramatic, distinctive spicy, almost eucalyptus bouquet; sweet entry, good fruit, touch of citrus, good length, tannin. Glorious now but long life. *Last tasted April 2006* ★★★★(★) *Now–2025.*

Ch Haut-Brion Medium-deep, ripe mulberry, open, relaxed rim, long 'legs'. Looks ready. Lovely, earthy, pebbly, 'warm tiles' Graves nose and flavour. Good tannin and acidity, though noting a touch of harshness. A lovely wine. *Last tasted April 2006* ★★★(★★) *Now–2020.*

Ch Ausone Always the odd man out, so distinctive, something of an acquired taste. Most recently, in magnums: a pleasantly mature colour; sweet, rich, whiff of gravy, sweaty tannins. But don't be put off. Sweet, modest weight (12.4% alcohol), agreeable flavour. Ready and undeniably attractive. *Last tasted Jan 2005* ★★★★

Ch Cheval Blanc One of my absolute favourite wines. For me, perfection. Most recently: lovely colour, open, inviting, mature rim; low-keyed at first though very fragrant, whiff of iron; sweet, perfect weight, flavour, balance and finesse. A beautiful wine. *Last tasted April 2006* ★★★★★ *Now–2026.*

Ch Pétrus Now mature-looking, rich, complete. *Last tasted April 2000* ★★★★★ *Perfect now. Another 20 years of life.*

Ch Beychevelle By now less deep, more open and relaxed; extraordinarily vivid fruit; sweeter and softer than expected and an unexpected touch of rusticity. Nice though. *Last noted April 2000* ★★★★ *Drink soon.*

Ch Calon-Ségur Most recently: fully mature in appearance, nose and taste. Lovely, soft, ready, but showing its age. *Last tasted May 2000* ★★★★ *Drink soon.*

Ch Canon Deeper than expected; lovely, ripe, gentle bouquet; some sweetness, soft, fully mature yet 'years of life'. Delicious. *Last noted Oct 2005* ★★★★

Ch Cantemerle Seemed to have regained (after 30 years) its form. Most recently, fully mature, attractive colour and nose; dry, pleasant fruit but on the lean side. Drinking well, but drink soon. *Last tasted Nov 2004* ★★★

Dom de Chevalier An excellent '85. Evolving well. Most recently: medium-deep, warm, mature; harmonious, slightly spicy bouquet. A most agreeable mouthful. *Last noted March 2001* ★★★★ *Good now. Will keep.*

Ch Cissac A superb *impériale*: deep, more intense than expected; very good nose; sweet, soft, a certain delicacy. Lovely, *à point*, a dependable *bourgeois* Médoc at its very best. *Last tasted March 2004* ★★★★ *Good now.*

Ch La Conseillante Lovely colour, more youthful red than expected; very fragrant, whiff of citrus, rich, mature; sweet, soft, perfect body and flavour. Exquisite, irresistible. *Last tasted Oct 2006* ★★★★★

Ch Cos d'Estournel Surprisingly deep and youthful; mammoth (for an '85), lacking charm and the style of the vintage. *Last tasted April 2005. At best* ★★★★? *Drink now or keep 5 years.*

Ch Ducru-Beaucaillou Not up to standard. Pedestrian, and some poor bottles. Even so, showing quite well when last tasted. *Last noted Oct 2001. At best* ★★★ *Drink soon.*

Ch L'Église-Clinet Very deep; beautiful developed bouquet but static; fairly sweet, lovely flavour, fig-like fruit, some charm, sitting smugly in the glass. *Last tasted Nov 2006* ★★★★★ *Lovely now. Long life.*

Ch L'Évangile A charmer. Deep, velvety appearance; good fruit, bouquet expanding in the glass; sweet, rich, ripe, silky tannins. Complete. *Last noted April 2000* ★★★★★ *Drink now or keep.*

Ch de Fieuzal I am very fond of red Graves. They make easy and attractive drinking in a vintage like 1985. This was good from the start. More recently: a bouquet and flavour with the sweet, warm, earthy glow of mature Graves. Crisp. Holding well. *Last noted April 2000* ★★★★ *Ready now.*

Ch Figeac Most recently, 'under a microscope' (at a Christie's masterclass): fully mature, distinctive, bouquet reminiscent of autumnal dried leaves and soft leather; initially sweet, good flavour, passing its peak of maturity, 'on the verge' and, in the end, drying out, tantalising but a bit disappointing for Figeac and for an '85. *Last tasted Oct 2005* ★★★ *Drink soon.*

Ch Grand-Puy-Lacoste Many notes tracing its evolution. Most recently: double-decanted. Surprisingly deep; lovely, fragrant, spicy, crisp fruit; sweet, soft, delicious. Good length and enough tannin to take it effortlessly into the next decade. *Last tasted Aug 2006* ★★★★(★)

Ch Gruaud-Larose Deep, dark cherry and garnet, perfect gradation to mature rim; fully evolved, with Gruaud's cedary fruit, and a whiff of singed heather; sweet, fleshy, delicious. *Last tasted Aug 2004* ★★★★(★)

Ch Haut-Bailly Consistently good. Most recently: soft, harmonious nose; well-nigh perfect weight, balance and flavour. *Last tasted April 2003* ★★★★★

Ch Haut-Marbuzet Deep, intense yet mature; fully developed, rich, lovely, discreetly oaky; sweet, good fruit and acidity for its class. Perfect. *Nov 2003* ★★★★

Ch Lafleur At a Lafleur vertical vying with the '89 as the very best. Lovely gradation of colour; soft, lovely, harmonious bouquet; sweet, silky texture, perfect weight (12.5% alcohol), attractively tamed tannins, dry finish. *Last tasted Sept 2004* ★★★★★ *Drink now or keep.*

Ch La Lagune Most recently: distinctive, attractive, very Graves-like, chocolate nose and flavour. A bit of a bite on the finish. *Last tasted June 2003* ★★★

Ch Langoa-Barton One of the best – and easiest – Langoas I can recall. Developing well. Relaxed, mature; flavour to match, dry finish. Delicious. *Last tasted Jan 2005* ★★★★

Ch Lascombes Sweet, agreeable weight, flavour and balance. *Last noted Sept 2001* ★★★

Ch Léoville-Barton Despite three less than admiring notes, a classic. Most recently: perfect weight and balance. Lovely texture and flesh. At its best, the perfect claret. *Last tasted May 2007. At best* ★★★★★ *Good now but will keep.*

Ch Léoville-Las-Cases A serious wine with extra dimensions. Showing maturity; good nose. Not my idea of a lovely '85 but decidedly good. *Last tasted Jan 2005* ★★★(★★)

Ch Léoville-Poyferré A 'cedar pencil', singed, earthy nose which opened up after only 20 minutes: lovely, harmonious. A wonderfully sweet approach, good mid-palate and mouth-drying astringency. *Last tasted March 2001* ★★★★(★)

Ch Lynch-Bages Two, recent, variable bottles. Both very sweet but one below par (storage?). The best with characteristic Cabernet Sauvignon aroma, touch of vanilla; sweet, good flavour, soft tannins, perfect acidity. Delicious. *Last tasted June 2006. At best* ★★★★★

Ch La Mission Haut-Brion Meaty, tannic but harmonious nose; sweet entry, crisp, lovely flavour. Top class. Distinctive. *Last tasted Dec 2006* ★★★★(★)

Ch Montrose Most recently, three badly corked. All were direct from the château so one must query the storage conditions. The good bottles at each tasting can be summarised: now medium-deep, lovely, fully mature colour; very good toasted mocha nose; distinctly sweet entry, perfect flavour, balance, length. Dry finish. *Last tasted Sept 2005. At best* ★★★(★)

Ch Palmer The palest of its classed-growth peers; fully developed nose; touch of tar; light, easy style. Very drinkable but not good enough for château and vintage. *Last tasted Aug 2004* ★★★

Ch Pavie Mellow, bricky, weak rim; lovely warm nose; soft, sweet, slight touch of iron. An agreeable enough drink. *Last tasted Aug 2004. A grudging* ★★★ *Drink up.*

Ch Pichon-Lalande Most recently, 8 days apart, almost identical notes. Still deep and fairly youthful; glorious bouquet, rich, with extra dimensions; sweet, rich, fleshy, delicious. *Last tasted Sept 2003* ★★★★★ *Now–2020.*

Ch Le Pin Not very deep, mature, relaxed; a high-toned scent of crystallised violets. Ripe Cabernet Franc? Finish a bit raw. *Last noted April 2000* ★★★(★)

Ch Rausan-Ségla Glorious fragrance, crisp, but a touch of rawness. Needs air, and time. *Last tasted April 2000* ★★(★★). *Say 2010–2015.*

Ch Tertre-Rôteboeuf A relatively new 'cult' wine. Impressive but not my type. On both occasions 'unknit' noted, one in relation to its nose, the other to its palate. Rich. Alcoholic; too spicy; thick, with coarse tannic finish. *Last tasted May 2000* ★(★★★)? *Needs time though I am not prepared to wait.*

Ch Trotanoy A soft, milky sort of bouquet and gentle fruit which, after 20 minutes, exploded with an extraordinary Cabernet Franc fragrance. Powerful. A bit inky. *Last noted April 2000* ★★★(★) *2010–2020.*

Vieux Ch Certan Soft, gentle yet rich to look at, smell and taste. Fragrant. A lovely wine. *April 2000* ★★★★★ *Now–2015.*

OTHER '85S SHOWING WELL IN THE MID- TO LATE 1990S

Ch Batailley Most recently, a perfectly pleasant fruitiness, perhaps slightly 'tarry', which I have noted in some Pauillacs. *Last tasted June 1997* ★★★

Ch Chasse-Spleen Definitely overdue for re-classification, the '85 being a prime example. Most recently: still surprisingly deep in colour, with good nose, weight, flavour and balance. *Last noted Oct 1996* ★★★

Ch Feytit-Clinet Attractive, pleasant flavour, drinking well. *June 1999* ★★★

Ch Haut-Bages-Libéral A lovely wine, perfectly balanced. *Last noted June 1998* ★★★★ *Drink soon.*

Ch d'Issan Bouquet surging out of the glass, somewhat loose knit, but drinking well. *Last noted June 1997* ★★★★ *(just). Drink soon.*

Ch Mouton-Baronne-Philippe Most recently: good, but upstaged by the *grand vin. Last noted March 1998* ★★★★ *Now–2010.*

Ch Pichon-Baron Two most recent notes, one disastrously corked, the other sweet with rich fruit; soft, a rather hefty '85, though well balanced. Delicious. *Last tasted Sept 1998. At best* ★★★★ *Now–2010.*

Clos René Velvety, very rich, harmonious. Full, fruity, dry finish. *Last noted Jan 1996* ★★★★ *Drink up.*

Ch Talbot I have a love-hate relationship with Talbot. It has such a rustic farmyard character, mainly on the nose. But I can't help liking the '85. I thought it had reached its plateau, an easy, charming drinkability: deep, velvety-looking; soft, sweet, ripe. *Last tasted May 1999* ★★★★ *Now–2010.*

OTHER '85S SHOWING PROMISE IN THE EARLY TO MID-1990S (far too many to note in detail): **Ch d'Angludet** ★★★; **Ch L'Arrosée** ★★★★; **Ch Beauregard** ★★★; **Ch Beauséjour-Duffau-Lagarosse** ★★★; **Ch Brane-Cantenac** ★★★★; **Ch Canon-La-Gaffelière** ★★★; **Ch Certan-de-May** ★★★; **Ch La Croix-de-Gay** ★★★(★); **Ch L'Enclos** ★★★; **Ch La Fleur-Pétrus** ★★★★★; **Clos Fourtet** ★★(★); **Ch Gazin** ★★★★; **Ch Gloria** ★★★★; **Ch Haut-Batailley** ★★★★★; **Ch Lafon-Rochet** ★★★; **Ch Larmande** ★★★; **Ch Larcis-Ducasse** ★★★★; **Ch Moulinet** ★★★; **Ch Prieuré-Lichine** ★★★★; **Ch du Tertre** ★★★; and **Ch La Tour-Carnet** ★★★

1986 ★★★★

Could the most prolific crop since World War Two produce wines of real quality? The summer was hot and dry until the latter part of September when a violent storm dumped 10cm of rain on the city of Bordeaux and nearby. The harvest began in late September and continued into October in glorious weather. On the whole, these are hard, tannic wines which at best, given time, should turn out well. But I would not bank on it, except for Mouton and just one or two others. They are of course good 'food wines' and are unlikely to go 'over the hill' without plenty of notice.

Ch Lafite Impressively deep; very good nose, considerable depth and more to come; unexpectedly sweet and ready though will keep well. *Last tasted March 2006* ★★★(★)

Ch Latour I expected this to be mammoth and undrinkable, but from the start, though clearly a long-haul wine, it had lovely fruit and flesh. Most recently: very deep, intense and still youthful-looking; crisp fruit, touch of ginger, slightly 'sweaty' tannic nose; good flavour, lively, touch of iron and a bit of a bite. Needs more time. *Last tasted June 2004* ★(★★★) *2010 and beyond.*

Ch Margaux A masculine Margaux. Most recently, still opaque and youthful-looking: crisp fruit, opening up beautifully; sweet, lovely fruit, attractive but very tannic. *Last tasted Nov 2000* ★(★★★)? *Give it lots of time.*

Ch Mouton-Rothschild Reputed to be outstandingly the best '86. Time will tell. Certainly a spectacular wine. Two very recent notes: still immature; crisp fruit, taut, bricky; full-bodied, slightly raw but spicy, rich, chewy. Good length, hard tannins. Not ready. *Last tasted Nov 2005. Hopefully* ★(★★★★) *2010–?*

Ch Batailley Usually dependable but the most recent tasting showed some coarseness. Very tannic. *Last tasted Dec 2000* ★★★? *Clearly context comes into this. Nevertheless, it has a future.*

Ch Beychevelle Contradictory notes. In 1997 surprisingly sweet, good fruit, yet astringent and teeth-gripping. Next, still youthful-looking, softer than expected. Most recently: fully mature appearance, 'gravy' nose and taste (poor cellarage). *Last tasted June 2004. At best* ★★(★)

Ch Chasse-Spleen Yet again top of its class. Well made. Medium-deep, rich; sweet, chewy, tannic. *Last tasted Nov 2003* ★★(★) *Now–2010.*

Ch Cos d'Estournel A magnum: opaque core; uninteresting nose; sweet, crisp, fairly dry finish. Not thrilled. *Last tasted March 2005* ★★(★) *Now–2012.*

Ch Ducru-Beaucaillou Very impressive, intense, dark cherry, rich 'legs'; good fruit, cedar and whiff of medicinal Médoc; a very satisfactory mouthful. Still hard. Needs food. *Jan 2006* ★★(★★) *Now–2015.*

Ch Duhart-Milon Deep, velvety, intense; very Pauillac, whiff of sea air; good fruit and extract, perfect weight (12.5%), tannic. *March 2004* ★★★(★) *Now–2012.*

Ch Figeac More advanced than most '86s, deep enough but showing maturity; very fruity; sweet, chewy, distinctive character – a style I happen to like – refreshing, delicious. *Last tasted May 2005* ★★★★ *Now–2012.*

Ch Grand-Puy-Lacoste An impressive '86, in fact one of the best if you are prepared to wait for this sinewy wine to mature. Convincing colour, starting to mature; fresh, interesting nose with a column of fruit round a hard core. An exciting wine, crisp, fruity with good, drying tannins. *Last noted March 2000* ★★(★★) *2010–2020.*

Ch Gruaud-Larose Fairly deep, maturing; good nose and flavour, fairly sweet and fleshy. An amenable and agreeable '86. *March 2004* ★★★★ *Now–2012.*

Ch Haut-Bailly Unusually, 100% Cabernet Sauvignon as the Merlot completely failed in 1986. Most recently, an *impériale*: soft, fragrant; sweet, very good flavour and grip. A most attractive '86. *Last tasted June 2005* ★★★★ *Now–2012.*

Ch d'Issan Showing well. *May 2000* ★★★

Ch Kirwan A somewhat specious new style. Still very deep and youthful; certainly fragrant; sweet and very 'new-oaky'. *Last tasted March 2001* ★★(★)

Ch Léoville-Las-Cases Deep; crisp fruit; sweeter than expected but a long hard, dry, very tannic finish. A good '86. Needs time. *Dec 2003* ★★(★★) *Now–2018.*

Ch Montrose From the château: deep, fairly intense and still youthful; taut, crisp, spicy nose and flavour. Good length but a touch of hard rawness. Needs time. *Last tasted Sept 2005. At best* ★★(★★) *Now–2012.*

Ch Les Ormes-de-Pez Dependable, as ever. A 'copybook' mature Médoc nose; sweet, rich, good flavour, agreeable weight, dry finish. *April 2003* ★★★ *Now–2010.*

Ch Petit-Village A lightish, mature-looking ruby; almost Graves-like, earthy character with a touch of tar on the nose. Sweetish, soft, ready. *April 2000* ★★★ *Drink soon.*

Ch Pichon-Baron Deep though maturing; vegetal nose; restrained though interesting flavour, touch of liquorice, dry finish. *Feb 2005* ★★(★) *Now–2010.*

Ch Pichon-Lalande Good, rather high-toned fruit. Rich, 'touch of molasses' nose; crisp, lean, dry, drinking well. *Last noted Oct 2000* ★★★(★) *Now–2012.*

Ch Rausan-Ségla Impressive, very intense though mature rim; well evolved, cigar-box nose; very sweet, brambly fruit, swingeing tannic finish. A blockbuster that lacks finesse. *March 2003* ★★(★★)? *Now–2016.*

Ch Talbot Most recently: mature, brown rim; at first a typical ripe, rustic nose which in the glass became less noticeable over time, more honeyed; initially sweet, soft rich fruit, dry finish. Ready for drinking. *Last tasted Jan 2006* ★★★★ *Now–2012.*

THE BEST AND MOST SIGNIFICANT '86S LAST TASTED IN THE LATE 1990S

Ch Haut-Brion Most recently: opening up, but a smelly, iodine nose. I thought it was cracking up. On the palate, earthy, thick-textured and a bit raw. In limbo. *Last tasted Sept 1998* ★★? *I am sure it will pull round but when?*

Ch Cheval Blanc Most recently: very deep, fairly intense but 'only thinking about' maturing; fragrant but somewhat peppery on nose and palate. Good firm fruit though, and went well with the beef. *Last noted March 1997* ★★(★★) *Should turn out well – 2010–2020.*

Ch L'Angélus Fairly impressive, a touch of '86 leanness, but substantial. Tannic. *May 1999* ★★(★) *A mid-term wine.*

Ch Canon Most recently, looking fairly mature; caramelly-chocolatey nose; spicy, lean and quite a bite. *Last tasted March 1996* ★★(★)?

Ch L'Évangile Most recently: deep, fairly intense; good rich fruit and flesh. More advanced than the '86 Médocs. *Last noted Sept 1998* ★★★★

Ch de Fieuzal Most recently: medium-deep, maturing, a sweet, earthy Graves nose; good flavour, but with gripping, leathery, tannins. 'Still some way to go.' *Last noted March 1998* ★★(★) *Now–2012.*

Ch Lafleur Sweet fruit; fairly full-bodied, rich, fleshy. *Sept 1998* ★★★(★) *Now–2015.*

Ch Lascombes Most recently: fragrant nose; good fruit and spicy aftertaste. Masked tannin. *Last tasted Jan 1996* ★★★

Ch Léoville-Barton Most recently: still virtually opaque; a nose of 'iron'; good fruit, but tight-lipped, lean and tannic. *Last noted Sept 1998* ★★(★★)

Ch Lynch-Bages Most recently: packed with flavour, its vigour and fruit taking one's mind off the tannins. Impressively deep colour though a misleadingly mature rim; fleshy, ripe, leathery, cedar and 'cheese rind' bouquet – quite exciting; nice fruit but a lean touch. An agreeable drink despite its teeth-gripping finish. *Last tasted Oct 1998* ★★(★★) *Now–2016.*

Ch Palmer Most recently: nose a bit hard but quite nice fruit, refreshing, not over-tannic. *Last tasted Sept 1999* ★★★ *Now–2015.*

THE FOLLOWING '86S were all tasted, or last tasted, in the early to mid-1990s: **Ch Pétrus** Very impressive in 1990: crisp ruby; sweet nose, opening up beautifully; very sweet, rich, full-bodied, caramel flavour and aftertaste. *Then* (★★★★★), *but should be very drinkable now. Long life*; **Ch Brane-Cantenac** good fruit and flavour ★★★; **Ch Cantemerle** attractive ★★★; **Ch Clerc-Milon** 'syrup of figs' nose. Good fruit but austere, tannic ★★(★); **Ch Durfort-Vivens** impressively deep yet fairly mature; sweet, spicy, attractive bouquet; dry, lean, quite good fruit. Tannic ★★(★); **Ch Lagrange** (St-Julien) a lovely, rich, velvety colour; harmonious bouquet; surprisingly sweet, good fruit, lovely texture and flavour. Complete ★★★★; **Ch Léoville-Poyferré** 'a touch of vanilla'; some sweetness, taut, lean but attractive and quite a lot to it ★★★(★);

Ch Lafon-Rochet opened up deliciously; more fruit and more interesting than expected ★★★; **Ch Malescot-St-Exupéry** chunky fruit; agreeable enough, reasonable balance. Not as exotically flavoured as usual ★★★; **Ch La Mission Haut-Brion** a good '86, its glorious fruit suppressed by its tannins ★★★★; **Ch Mouton-Baronne-Philippe** not the usual feckless charmer. Good firm fruit, but very tannic ★(★★); **Ch Le Pin** an extraordinary, sweet, velvety, mulberry-rich character; fullish and fleshy ★★★★; **Ch Pontet-Canet** unknit, but interesting bouquet; surprisingly sweet, full and fruity. Very tannic ★★(★); **Ch de Sales** good fruit; chunky, maturing pleasantly. ★★★; and **Ch Sociando-Mallet** deep colour; a 'classic Cabernet nose'; dry, crisp fruit, good length, complete but *very* tannic ★★★

1987
Climatically deficient. An average-sized crop producing sound-enough wines but these are now just faded curiosities. **Ch Haut-Brion** and **Ch Cheval Blanc** were the best of my more recent notes.

1988 ★★★★
The first of a trio of very good vintages. Rather like the '86s, with which, at one time, they seemed to be level pegging, I now think that the '88s, initially somewhat overrated, are just about coming into their own as serious long-term clarets. Following a late harvest in satisfactory conditions the grapes were ripe and thick-skinned, resulting in deep colours and high tannins. In the end, however, time and tannin will probably be jostling for supremacy.
Ch Lafite Still very deep, intense, opaque core but on the verge of maturity; high Cabernet Sauvignon noticeable though overall subdued; on the palate, sweet, almost chewable, with a good, long, dry finish. *Last tasted March 2006* ★★★(★★) *Now–2020.*
Ch Latour Most recently: not as deep as expected but with a rich core; 'cheese rind' nose with very sweaty tannins; dry, rich, fruit-packed, lovely flavour but very tannic. *Last tasted Oct 2005* ★★(★★★) *2012–2020.*
Ch Margaux Still pretty deep; crisp and fragrant, its nose this time reminding me of thoroughbred stables. Softer than I had expected, though lean and astringent after the '89. Still, a very good wine with considerable length and future. *Last tasted Nov 2000* ★★(★★) *Possibly 5-star when fully mature. Say 2010–2020.*
Ch Mouton-Rothschild Most recently: f:airly deep, plummy-coloured; sweet, rather rustic, unspectacular nose, good extract and fruit. An hour after decanting, a whiff of charred tar and mocha, opening up better later that evening. Touch of sweetness, perfect weight (12.5% alcohol), full of fruit, good length and sustaining tannin and acidity. *Last tasted April 2007* ★★★(★★) *Could do with more time, say 2010–2020.*
Ch Haut-Brion Opaque; a relatively low-keyed 'hot pebbles' yet floral, citrus-like nose. A silky, tannic texture and mocha-like flavour. Very positive character, but teeth-gripping tannin and acidity. *Last tasted Dec 2006* ★★(★★) *Good wine but needs to shed its astringency.*
Ch Cheval Blanc Showing some maturity; very good, firm, good length, dry finish. Overall a sweet and lovely wine. *Last tasted April 2006* ★★★★(★) *Now–2015, or beyond.*

SOME OF THE OTHER BEST AND MOST INTERESTING '88s TASTED IN THE LATE 1990s

Ch Ausone Medium depth, touch of cherry red; extraordinarily sweet and nutty. I gave it a very high mark. Excellent body, flavour, balance and length. *Last noted Jan 1999* ★★★★ *2005–2015*.

Ch Pétrus Fairly intense; very attractive, ripe, mulberry-like fruit. A very good mouthful with hot, alcoholic finish and totally lacking in charm and finesse. *Last tasted July 1998* ★★★(★) *Perhaps I am being mean.*

Ch L'Angélus A relatively new state-of-the-art St-Émilion. Most recently, fairly deep ruby; well endowed with fruit and extract, but the tannins and acidity levels very high. *Last noted June 1997* ★★(★) *I felt it was trying too hard in an unsympathetic vintage. Probably drinking well now.*

Ch Beychevelle Medium-deep; a lovely 'old oak', slightly cheesy bouquet; fairly sweet, soft, chewy. A good '88. *Last tasted May 2001* ★★★ *Now–2010*.

Ch Branaire-Ducru Attractive colour and gradation; a whiff of varnish; lovely, crisp fruit with a touch of chocolate and tar. Surprisingly sweet for an '88, yet thick and tannic. In the end, I didn't like it, for I had added 'ugh'. *Last tasted March 1997* ★★ *Interesting. But I doubt if it is going anywhere.*

Ch Batailley Misleadingly mature, brown-rimmed; medicinal, sea breeze Pauillac with a whiff of mocha; lean, still hard with masked tannin and acidity. Very untypical. Needs time. *Last tasted April 2006* ★(★★) *hopefully*.

Ch Beauséjour-Bécot Fennel scent. Delicious. *Sept 1998* ★★★

Ch Calon-Ségur Very deep, rich 'legs'; good nose. Surprisingly sweet entry, good body, fruit and flavour. Tannic. *Last noted Dec 1998* ★★★(★) *Now–2015*.

Ch Canon Curious nose, slightly tea-like, but easy on the palate. Dry finish. *Last tasted May 2001* ★★★ *Forget the tannin. Drink soon.*

Ch Canon-La-Gaffelière Most recently, a magnum: medium-deep; fully developed, harmonious nose; despite its power, sweet, soft, delicious. *Last tasted April 2006* ★★★(★) *Now–2015*.

Carruades de Ch Lafite Soft cherry red; fragrant, cedary; attractive weight, flavour and flesh. Elegant perhaps, but, being an '88, lacking Carruades charm. *Last noted Dec 1998* ★★(★) *Now–2012*.

Ch Clerc-Milon Deep, plummy coloured but maturing nicely; delicious fruit; fairly sweet, soft for an '88, fullish body, richness masking bitter tannic finish. *Last tasted June 2004* ★★(★) *Now–2012*.

Ch Clinet I am not a great Clinet fan, yet I noted it as 'crisp, lean and elegant', 'a very good '88'. *Last tasted April 1997* ★★★ *Now–2012*.

Ch Cos d'Estournel Still very deep and still youthful; good nose and very good flavour. Still tannic but a classic '88. *Last tasted April 2005* ★★★(★) *Now–2016*.

Ch La Croix-de-Gay Consistently good. Mature-looking; its original 'ensemble of cherries and raspberries' (the ripe Cabernet Franc) 'spiced up with new oak', noted as merely sweet and attractive, with taste to match. Delicious and easy, though not without tannin. *Last noted April 1996* ★★★★ *Now–2012*.

Ch Ducru-Beaucaillou Most recently: intense with a touch of purple at the rim; typical St Julien 'cigar box' nose; good flavour, hard core, still with a touch of tannic bitterness. *Last tasted Jan 2006* ★★(★) *Now–2015*.

Ch Duhart-Milon Deep, still intense and unready; very Pauillac aroma; powerful, punchy. A long-distance runner. *Last tasted Sept 1998* ★(★★) *2010–2020*.

Ch L'Église-Clinet An *impériale*, rich as the maestro's arias. Good fruit and flesh masking the tannins. *Last tasted Sept 1998* ★★★(★) *Now–2015*.

Ch de Fieuzal 'Rustic' nose, fairly sweet, 'an agreeable '88'. Drinking well. *Last tasted April 1997* ★★★ *Drink soon*.

Ch Figeac Despite its nice, crisp fruit, its oakiness very noticeable, as was the very dry, slightly bitter finish. *Last noted July 1997* ★★★ *I hope the fruit survives*.

Ch Grand-Puy-Ducasse Well made but still tannic. *April 2004* ★★(★)

Ch Grand-Puy-Lacoste Deep, richly coloured; good, classic, bricky nose; good fruit but unyielding flesh. Needs time, food – and patience. *Last tasted Oct 2004* ★(★★★) *2010–2020*.

Ch Gruaud-Larose Bouquet rich, ripe and spicy, complete but very tannic. *Last noted Jan 1997* ★★(★★) *Now–2015*.

Ch Haut-Bailly Deep, velvety; rich bricky Graves. Fleshy, earthy, extract masking tannin. A very good '88. *Dec 1998* ★★★★ *Now–2015*.

Ch Haut-Batailley Medium-deep, mature brown rim; medicinal Pauillac aroma, whiff of citrus and mocha; good flavour but lean, hard tannin and noticeable acidity. *Last tasted April 2006* ★★(★) *Now–2016*.

Ch Lafleur Full of rather raw fruit. Crisp. Short dry finish. *Aug 1998* ★(★★) *Now–2012*.

Ch Langoa-Barton Fair fruit; but tart and tannic. Quite a bite. Good pedigree but worth keeping? *Aug 2002*. *Potential* (★★★)?

Ch Léoville-Barton Masculinity noted; but a fine wine. *Last tasted Dec 1998* ★★(★★) *Now–2016*.

Ch Léoville-Las-Cases Despite its youthful appearance, showing some age on the nose; fleshy, tannate of iron finish. *Last noted April 2001* ★(★★★)

Ch Lynch-Bages Most recently, not 'sweet and sour' but sweet and soft, yet tannic. Still finding its way. *Last noted March 2001* ★★(★★) *I live in hope*.

Ch Malescot-St-Exupéry Magnum: ripe, rustic; surprisingly sweet, firm, fullish, good fruit and well endowed with tannin and acidity. *April 2004* ★★(★)

Ch Mouton-Baronne-Philippe Maturing nicely; lovely aroma on decanting, 'warm', singed; medium-sweet, soft chewy fruit, masked tannins but dry finish. *Last tasted May 2004* ★★★(★) *Now–2012*.

Ch Palmer Richly coloured; soft, 'brown sugar' scent which opened up attractively. Sweet, good fruit, hot, slightly bitter finish. Pleasant to drink, but not living up to its 'super second' reputation. *Last noted July 1998* ★★★ *Drink soon*.

Ch Pape-Clément Medium-deep, maturing; sweet, 'sweaty' tannin nose; attractive but beginning to show its age. *April 2003* ★★★ *Now–2010*.

Ch Pavie On the last two occasions, though deep, already showing some maturity. Vanillin nose. Dry, attractive but very tannic. *Last tasted June 1998* ★(★★)

Ch Pichon-Lalande Mahogany-rimmed maturity; sweet, fleshy. A good ripe '88. 'Delicious now'. *Last noted Oct 2001* ★★★★ *Now–2012*.

Ch Pichon-Longueville (The name was officially changed from Pichon-Baron to -Longueville in 1987.) Maturing; crisp, ripe berry, whiff of farmyard; good length, rusty nails tannic grip. *Last tasted Sept 2006* ★★(★★) *Needs time*.

Ch Le Pin Just one half bottle. Dry, oak, with citrus-like acidity. Crisp fruit. Not a bad drink. *Nov 1995* ★★★★

Ch Prieuré-Lichine Very deep, intense but mature-looking; distinctive Médoc Cabernet aroma; crisp, raspberry-like taste, great acidity, drying tannins. A delicious '88 and a very attractive Prieuré. *Last tasted Nov 2003* ★★★★ *Drink soon.*

Ch Rausan-Ségla Impressively deep, still youthful, rich 'legs'; good Cabernet aroma though still hard and peppery; sweet, plenty of fruit though a bit unyielding, lovely yet astringent. *Last tasted March 2003* ★★(★★) *2010–2020.*

Vieux Ch Certan A spectacular *impériale*: deep, with youthful edge; fragrant; lean, very tannic, but loads of flavour. *Last noted May 2000* ★★(★★) *Now–2016.*

OF THE MANY OTHER '88s LAST TASTED IN THE LATE 1990s, most of the Médocs and Graves can be summed up in four words: 'good fruit, lean, tannic', the Right Bank tending to be fleshier but – as has been noted – also very tannic. The following had good potential: **Ch d'Angludet** ★★(★★); **Ch Brane-Cantenac** ★★★; **Ch Chasse-Spleen** ★★★; **Dom de Chevalier** ★★★(★); **Ch Durfort-Vivens** ★★(★); **Ch L'Évangile** ★★(★★); **Ch Gazin** ★★★(★); **Ch Giscours** ★★(★★); **Ch Labégorce-Zédé** ★★(★); **Ch Lafon-Rochet** ★(★★); **Ch La Lagune** ★★(★); **Ch Lynch-Moussas** ★★★; **Ch Malartic-Lagravière** ★★★; **Ch La Mission Haut-Brion** ★★(★★); **Ch Montrose** ★(★★★); **Ch de Pez** ★★(★); **Ch La Pointe** ★★★; and **Ch Talbot** ★★(★★)

1989 ★★★★★

Unquestionably a great vintage and one which brought a successful decade to a resounding close. First, the weather: an early flowering in excellent conditions, followed by the hottest summer since 1949 and the earliest harvest since 1983. The grapes were fully ripe yet the tannins were not. Later-picked grapes did have softer tannins, but at the expense of acidity. When youthful, the wines were extraordinarily appealing, but what seems to have happened is a sort of reversal of roles, the tannin becoming more noticeable, turning the '89 into a much longer-haul vintage than anticipated. Nevertheless, many superlative wines.

Ch Lafite A warm, rich colour with a tinge of orange at the rim; gloriously fragrant bouquet yet with impenetrable depth and concentration; an extraordinary 'attack', very rich entry, nice weight, good fruit, plenty of tannin and acidity. *Last tasted May 2002* ★★★(★★) *2010–2030.*

Ch Latour Deep, medium intensity, still youthful; nose low-keyed at first but opened up pleasantly, very sweet, rich, cedary; dry, crisp, high extract though modest weight (12.5% alcohol), crisp, still peppery, tannic finish. A very good mouthful needing plenty of ageing. *Last tasted Nov 2005* ★★(★★★) *2012–2030.*

Ch Margaux Most recently, from a jeroboam: very deep, almost opaque, cherry-tinged but maturing; singed, spicy bouquet; drier than expected, stern, firm but with very good flavour. *Last tasted Oct 2001* ★★★★(★) *2010–2025.*

Ch Mouton-Rothschild Very bright and appealing, opaque core but maturing; immediately fragrant, well developed harmonious bouquet, rich, whiff of mocha; medium-sweet, good fruit, perfect weight (12.5%), firm, silky tannins. A lovely wine. *Last noted Dec 2005* ★★(★★★) *2010–2030.*

My top 1989s
Cheval Blanc, La Conseillante, Grand-Puy-Lacoste, Haut-Bailly, Haut-Brion, Lafite, Lafleur, Latour, Léoville-Barton, Léoville-Las-Cases, Léoville-Poyferré, Margaux, Montrose, Mouton-Rothschild, Palmer, Pétrus, Pichon-Lalande, Le Pin

Ch Haut-Brion Wonderful. A double magnum: rich, fruity but with a slightly astringent finish. *Last tasted Nov 2001* ★★★(★★) *2010–2025.*

Ch Ausone Most recently, in magnums: open, mature; sweet, pleasant fruit, fragrant; beginning to show its age, lean, lacking the vigour and sap of the '89 Médocs. *Last tasted Jan 2005. At best* ★★★★ *Now–2012.*

Ch Cheval Blanc The earliest harvest since the early 20th century. Very deep yet with mature rim; bouquet curiously reluctant at first, complex, smoky, bricky, a whiff of mint and liquorice; sweet, full fruit, lovely flavour – liquorice noted again, silky tannins. Needs time. *Last tasted Jan 2006* ★★★★(★) *Now–2020.*

Ch Pétrus Most recently, a double magnum: still virtually opaque; good fruit, truffles; fairly full-bodied, a touch of austerity, rich texture, great length. *Last noted Nov 2001* ★★(★★★) *2015–2030.*

Ch L'Angélus Fairly deep; very ripe; a very good mouthful. Dry finish. *June 2003* ★★★(★) *Now–2015.*

Ch Batailley Good, rich ruby; fleshy, high-toned, savoury bouquet; a wonderful mouthful, good flesh, flavour, and somewhat hard finish. *Last tasted April 2006* ★★★(★) *Now–2016.*

Ch Beychevelle The words 'fleshy' and 'spicy' used both in 1990 and in its tenth year. Sweet, ripe, attractive. *Last noted March 1999* ★★★ *Now–2012.*

Ch Branaire-Ducru One of the two Médoc châteaux to start picking in August. Most recently, still deep but maturing; bricky, cedar pencils nose, the new oak assimilated; fairly dry, good length. *Last tasted March 2003* ★★★

Ch Calon-Ségur Once a great British wine trade favourite. Pleasantly maturing; very good nose and totally delicious. *June 2005* ★★★★ *Now–2015.*

Ch Canon Good nose; soft, chunky fruit, easy style, delicious. *Last noted March 1996* ★★★★ *Now–2012.*

Ch Cantemerle Still deep; good fruit and flesh, but unready. *Last noted Oct 1997* ★★(★) *Now–2015.*

Ch Cantenac-Brown Touch of coffee on the nose; good texture, a refreshing citrus squeeze. Surprisingly attractive. *Last tasted April 1999* ★★★ *Now–2010.*

Ch Chasse-Spleen A dependable 'club claret'. Just about right. Good fruit. Drinking well. *May 1998* ★★★ *Drink soon.*

Dom de Chevalier Medium-deep, maturing nicely; low-keyed nose; good flesh, mouthfilling, earthy Graves character, tannic. *March 2004* ★★★(★) *Now–2015.*

Ch Clinet Not my favourite style of wine. Deep, medium intensity, a bit smelly (tannins?); unusual, distinctive flavour, hefty, rich, raw, tannic. *Sept 1998* ★(★★) *Probably better now.*

Ch La Conseillante Opulent in its youth; an attractive wine. Rich, mature appearance; 'secretive', distinctive bouquet that took time to evolve; more of a bite than the '90, firm, medium-full body (13% alcohol), delicious flavour, good length and acidity. *Last tasted Oct 2006* ★★★★(★) *Now–2015.*

Ch Cos d'Estournel Reasonably substantial body (13% alcohol). Mixed notes. Frankly disappointing. Though fairly deep, rather weak rimmed; a strange nose and, despite its age, lacking maturity. Not warranting its 'super second' reputation. *Last tasted Nov 2004* ★★(★)? *Uncertain future. Wait and see.*

Ch Ducru-Beaucaillou Mixed reviews here, too. Most recently: fairly intense mulberry, lovely gradation of colour; 'soft fruit' Médoc; an attractive mouthful though lots of tannin. *Last tasted Jan 2006* ★★★(★) *Now–2016.*

Ch Duhart-Milon Deep; attractive fruit; positive, ideal weight, good flavour but very tannic. Needs air, and beef. *June 2005* ★★(★★)? *Now–2016.*

Ch Durfort-Vivens Agreeably matured, its masked tannin at last unmasked. Sweet, soft, flavoury, mildly gripping. *Last tasted April 1997* ★★★ *Drink soon.*

Ch L'Église-Clinet In magnums: deep, plummy; scent of privet, a slightly smelly, overripe nose; sweet, soft, fleshy to the point of opulence (no new oak used). On balance, a delicious mouthful. *Last tasted Sept 1998. A wine for hedonists* ★★★(★) *Now–2012.*

Ch Figeac Luscious colour; glorious fruit, evolved, rounded; a full, fleshy mouthful with masked tannin. By no means flawless, but irresistibly rich and fragrant with good length and spicy finish. *Last noted Oct 2001* ★★★★ *Ready.*

Ch La Fleur-Pétrus Mature-looking; rich yet, somehow, lean, with silky, Pomerol texture and lovely flavour. Good. *Nov 1999* ★★★★ *Now–2015.*

Clos Fourtet Soft, sweet, rather Graves-like nose; very attractive flavour, fully mature yet good grip. *Last tasted Sept 2004* ★★★ *possibly more to come. Now–2012.*

Ch Le Gay Ripe mulberry, a hint of mint; very distinctive, full of fruit, some finesse and elegance, spicy tannic finish. *Last noted Sept 1998* ★★★★ *Now–2025.*

Ch Gazin Deep, velvety; a rich, 'meaty' nose; sweet and pretty massive. *Last noted April 1998* ★★★(★) *Now–2015.*

Ch Grand-Puy-Lacoste Consistently good. Deep, velvety colour; rich, singed, nose-filling bouquet of distinctive character; fairly sweet, fleshy, good extract, full-flavoured, its richness masking tannins. Outstanding. *Last tasted Sept 2006* ★★★★★ *Now–2020.*

Ch Gruaud-Larose A vintage tailor-made for Gruaud. A rich, now mature appearance and ripe, spicy bouquet, yet with surprising grip and tannin. *Last noted Oct 2001* ★★★(★) *Now–2020.*

Ch Haut-Bailly Most recently: impressively deep; very sweet, rich yet perfect weight. A typically lovely '89. *Last noted April 2002* ★★★★(★) *Now–2025.*

Ch Lafleur Most recently, equal top marks with the 1995 in a Lafleur vertical: deep, richly coloured, mature rim; completely harmonious on nose and palate. Glorious fruit. Superb. *Last tasted Sept 2004* ★★★★★ *Now–2015.*

Ch Lagrange (St-Julien) Fairly deep; rich; chewy, touch of coarseness but good extract, tannins and acidity. *March 2001* ★★★ *Now–2015.*

Ch Léoville-Barton Most recently: deep, velvety; perfect, subtly scented, classic nose; excellent fruit and length, still tannic. Somewhat fleshier than usual. Extra dimensions, body, fruit, texture, length. *Last tasted March 2007* ★★★(★★) *Now–2020.*

Ch Léoville-Las-Cases Richly coloured, moderately intense; good nose, sweet, slightly chocolatey; full, rich, well-endowed with dry finish. *Last tasted Dec 2003* ★★★(★★) *2010–2025.*

Ch Léoville-Poyferré Back on form. Deep, rich, velvety, mature; good, harmonious, classic cedar cigar box bouquet soft, sweet, delicious, touch of pepper and whiff of freshly peeled mushrooms. *Last tasted April 2005* ★★★★★ *Now–2016.*

Ch La Louvière Rich fruit and extract. Most recently, maturing well; soft, fleshy, *à point* yet some grip. Delicious. *Last noted Oct 2001* ★★★★ *Now–2015.*

Ch Lynch-Bages Usually outperforming its *5ème cru classé* status, invariably packed with exciting fruit and flavour. Most recently, a jeroboam: almost opaque, still youthful; spicy; full of flavour, quite a bite. *Oct 2001* ★★★(★) *Now–2020.*

Ch Magdelaine Sweet, rich, but with quite a bite. Good wine. *June 2003* ★★★(★) *Now–2012.*

Ch Montrose Deep, medium intensity, mature; very distinctive nose, almost creamy; a lovely mouthful, sweet, richly flavoured, well balanced, very fragrant, its tannic austerity masked. *Last tasted Nov 2005* ★★★★(★) *Now–2020.*

Ch Mouton-Baronne-Philippe More flesh than usual but tight-knit and tannic. *Last tasted Dec 1996.* ★★(★★) *Now–2015.*

Ch Palmer Rich, ripe (52% Merlot in '89), open, biscuity; sweet, delicious fruit and flavour. Still tannic. *Last noted in Oct 1999* ★★★★(★) *Now–2016.*

Ch de Pez A consistently good St-Estèphe *cru exceptionnel*, fruity and tannic. *Last noted April 1996* ★★(★) *Now–2010.*

Ch Pichon-Lalande Deep, still youthful; very good, rich yet crisp fruit, Pauillac iron; fleshy, even plump, soft tannins yet very dry finish. *Last tasted April 2006* ★★★★(★) *Now–2015.*

Ch Pichon-Longueville Most recently: very deep, opaque core, velvety; rich ripe fruit; medium dryness and body, fleshy, high extract, masked tannin. The 'Baron' at his best. *Last tasted Sept 2006* ★★★★(★) *Now–2015.*

Ch Le Pin A 'mystery' magnum served blind: very sweet, mocha-like, rather unsophisticated; powerful, rich, tannic. *Sept 1998* ★★★(★★) *2010–2030.*

Ch La Pointe Fully mature; pleasant, slightly minty nose; very sweet, easy, good acidity. Short. *Last tasted Sept 1998* ★★★ *Drink soon.*

Ch de Sales A sweet, easy, wine with decent fruit and a touch of liquorice. Drinking pleasantly. *Nov 2003* ★★★ *Drink soon.*

Ch Sociando-Mallet Magnums: deep, velvety; peppery nose; fairly sweet, rich, touch of tar, rustic but impressive. A newly acquired reputation to live up to. *Sept 2004* ★★★★ *Now–2010.*

Ch Talbot Cedary, 'old oak' (trees not casks); a fairly rich mouthful. *Last tasted March 1997* ★★★ *(some might rate it more highly). Now–2015.*

Ch Tertre-Rôteboeuf Deep, rich, intense; unusual, curiously sweaty (tannic) nose; sweet, delicious, rich texture. Not really my style of claret, more like vintage port. *Last noted March 2001* ★★★ *Now–2010.*

Vieux Ch Certan Fairly deep; extraordinarily sweet, chocolatey nose; sweet and fleshy on the palate. Very good. *May 2002* ★★★★ *Now–2012.*

SOME OF THE OTHER TOP '89S LAST TASTED IN THE LATE 1990S: **Ch d'Angludet** ★★★; **Ch d'Armailhac** ★★★(★); **Ch Le Bon-Pasteur** ★★★★; **Ch Canon-La Gaffelière** ★★★(★); **Ch Clerc-Milon** ★★★(★); **Ch La Dominique** ★★★(★); **Ch La Gaffelière** ★★★; **Ch La Grave-Trigant-de-Boisset** ★★★; **Ch Haut-Batailley** ★★★(★); **Ch d'Issan** ★★★★; **Ch Labégorce-Zédé** ★★★; **Ch Langoa-Barton** ★★★(★); **Ch Latour-à-Pomerol** ★★★(★); **Ch La Mission Haut-Brion** ★★★(★★); **Ch Pape-Clément** ★★★(★); **Ch Pavie** ★★★; **Ch Prieuré-Lichine** ★★★; **Ch Rausan-Ségla** ★★★(★); **Ch Siran** ★★★; and **Ch La Tour-de-By** ★★★

1990–1999

A very uneven decade, with only one outstanding vintage at its beginning and one very satisfactory vintage in the middle. But also notable was the increasing trend – weather permitting – towards a more 'uniform' style of wine: impressively deep, fleshy, easy to taste, lacking finesse.

VINTAGES AT A GLANCE
Outstanding ★★★★★ 1990
Very Good ★★★★ 1994 (v), 1995, 1996 (v), 1998 (v), 1999 (v)
Good ★★★ 1991 (v), 1993 (v), 1994 (v), 1996 (v), 1997 (v), 1998 (v), 1999(v)

1990 ★★★★★

An important vintage and an excellent start to the new decade or, if linked with its twin 1989, the end of an era. The 1990s started with impressive, well constituted, well balanced wines and with all the components for a long haul, whereas the initially precocious, fleshy, immediately appealing 1989s have now swapped places: the 1990s are developing more quickly than I anticipated, while some magnificent 1989s are closing up for a long haul.

The crucial flowering phase was uneven and prolonged. July was excessively hot, hindering maturation. August was warm and dry. A well-timed sprinkling of rain in September enabled the grapes to be harvested mid-month. The Merlots were very successful with some of the highest sugar levels ever recorded. The later-ripening Cabernet Sauvignons were small and thick-skinned, with deep colour and concentration.

Ch Lafite Consistently good notes: very deep, virtually opaque core, rich, velvety, still youthful; bouquet slow to evolve but developing fragrant spiciness, touch of cedar and typical 'medicinal' whiff; medium-sweet, perfect weight (12.5%) good flavour, balance, length and excellent finish. A classic Lafite. *Last tasted March 2000* ★★★(★★) 2010–2030.

Ch Latour Very good, luminous but less deep than expected; nose reminiscent of freshly picked mushrooms, harmonious, complete; rich, good body, flavour and balance. This was not the anticipated blockbuster. *Last tasted June 2007* ★★★★(★) 2010–2020.

Ch Margaux Plummy, deep core but starting to mature; very fragrant bouquet; lovely flavour, excellent balance but very tannic – needed food to accompany it, and more time. *Last tasted May 2005* ★★★(★★) Now–2020.

My top 1990s
Ausone, Cheval Blanc, La Conseillante, Grand-Puy-Lacoste, Lafite, Latour, Léoville-Barton, Léoville-Las-Cases, Lynch-Bages, Margaux, La Missiion Haut-Brion, Montrose, Palmer

Ch Mouton-Rothschild An *impériale* in 2005, completely harmonious, spicy. Most recently: lovely soft red, maturing; rich, 'singed', fruit and depth; medium-sweet, deliciously rich flavour, flesh masking tannin. Refreshing. Ready. Very good but not great. *Last tasted July 2006* ★★★(★) *Now–2016.*

Ch Haut-Brion Lovely colour; bouquet very forthcoming, harmonious, soft, rich; curious, very distinctive, 'old autumn leaves', soft, earthy, unmistakably Graves flavour. *Last tasted Oct 2005* ★★★(★) *Now–2015.*

Ch Ausone Superb. Most recently: mature-looking; low-keyed, attractive bouquet; a soft, sweet entry, crisp, fragrant and a very dry 'autumnal' finish. *Last tasted June 2000* ★★★(★★) *Now–2015.*

Ch Cheval Blanc A bit of a shooting star. Now with fully mature colour, nose and taste. Bouquet almost gamey, very mocha; distinctly sweet, soft, rounded, muffled tannin, delicious. Not a classic Cheval Blanc. *Last tasted Jan 2006* ★★★★★ *Drink soon.*

Ch Pétrus Still very deep; thick, chunky, fleshy nose but one could smell the sweaty tannins; fairly sweet, full, rich, complete but with a dry, rather coarse finish. A matter of taste. *Last noted June 2000* ★(★★★)? *2010–2020.*

A SMALL SELECTION OF THE BEST '90S TASTED SINCE 2000:

Ch d'Armailhac (Note the change of name from Mouton-Baronne-Philippe.) Medium-deep, a soft, lovely colour with mature rim; an immediacy of bouquet, ripe, rich, leaping out of the glass; crisp, refreshing fruit, still sweet though finishing dry. *Last tasted Nov 2001* ★★★(★)

Ch Batailley As dependable and consistent as always. Richly coloured; good fruit; touch of sweetness, fullish, rounded, unobtrusive tannins. Drinking well. *Last tasted Nov 2002* ★★★★ *Now–2012.*

Ch Beauséjour-Bécot New generation. Modern style. Still youthful-looking; very good fruit, unusually sweet, attractive. *Last tasted April 2006* ★★★ *Drink soon.*

Ch Beauséjour-Duffau-Lagarosse A brief but good note in the cellars of La Gaffelière where guests waited for the floods to subside after the destructive 'twister'. *June 2003* ★★★ *Drink soon.*

Ch Beychevelle Plummy colour; whiff of asparagus; sweet, good fruit and flavour, slightly coarse texture. But a decent Beychevelle. *Last tasted July 2006* ★★★ *Drink soon.*

Ch Canon-La-Gaffelière Almost opaque, intense; modern St-Émilion; full, fruity, tannic, impressive. Trying too hard? *Last tasted March 2005* ★★(★★) *Now–2012.*

Ch Chasse-Spleen Magnum: impressively deep; rich, well developed; ripe sweetness, excellent extract, holding well. *Last tasted April 2006* ★★★ *Now–2010.*

Ch Clerc-Milon Still ruby; touch of fragrant 'Pauillac iron'; sweet, attractive, fair body (13% alcohol), drinking well. *Last tasted Aug 2003* ★★★ *Now–2012.*

Ch La Conseillante Mature, relaxed; attractive, floral, sweet; bricky, opening up richly; very sweet, delicious, very quaffable but will keep. *Oct 2006* ★★★★★ *Now–2015.*

Ch Cos d'Estournel Still very deep, immature, opaque, intense; lively aroma; still hard and tannic. Modern style of red Bordeaux. *Last tasted Nov 2005* ★★(★★)? *Now–2012.*

Ch Ducru-Beaucaillou Crisp. Drinking well. No signs of TCA infection (1956–1993). *Oct 2006* ★★★?

Ch de Fieuzal Still youthful; distinctive, a whiff of tangerine. Very good but desperately needs food. *Last noted April 2001* ★★★(★) *Now–2015.*

Ch La Fleur-Pétrus Glorious colour, fully mature; fragrant, whiff of tea; fairly sweet, lovely texture, well balanced. *Last tasted April 2004* ★★★★ *Now–2012.*

Ch Grand-Puy-Lacoste Several notes, two very recent: deep, velvety, shapely 'legs'; on decanting, very medicinal, iron and Pauillac oyster shells, after three hours, extraordinary complex development, coffee, mocha, liquorice; surprisingly sweet, full-flavoured, ideal weight (12.5% alcohol), richness masking tannin – but after all this I added, lamely, lacking finesse? *Last tasted Nov 2006* ★★★★(★) *2010–2020.*

Ch Gruaud-Larose Medium-deep, soft cherry red, maturing; rich, ripe nose, distinct whiff of blackcurrants, sweaty tannins; dryish, ideal weight, chunky fruit, tannic. Dependable as always and very drinkable. *March 2004* ★★★(★) *Now–2015.*

Ch Haut-Bailly Starting to show maturity, but a rich, thick concentration of colour; lovely tarry, earthy Graves bouquet; full-flavoured, a dry, cutting finish. Sweet, spicy, touch of leanness. *Last tasted April 2002* ★★★(★) *Now–2015.*

Ch d'Issan Deep, opaque core; attractive nose; touch of sweetness, good length leading to masked tannins. Still quite a bite. *Jan 2005* ★★(★★) *Now–2016.*

Ch La Lagune Deep and youthful; nose of mocha and iron, more Graves than Médoc; distinctly sweet, rich, distinctive and rather original flavour. Very drinkable. *Last tasted July 2005* ★★★ *Now–2012.*

Ch Larcis-Ducasse Rich, wholesome, crisp, delicious. Drinking well. *Last noted March 2001* ★★★ *Ready now.*

Ch Lascombes Showing some age; drinking well but unexciting. *Last noted April 2000* ★★★ *Drink up.*

Ch Léoville-Barton Deep, velvety, mature-looking; classic, harmonious, cedar cigar box nose, evolving richly; rich yet lean, very good flavour, perfect weight (12.5%) and balance. Copybook claret. *Last tasted May 2007* ★★★★(★) *Now–2016.*

Ch Léoville-Las-Cases Wonderfully deep, rich but mature. Noted its fragrance and silky texture. Restrained but harmonious; a powerful, fleshy wine, tannins both silky *and* swingeing. *Last noted March 2001* ★★★★(★) *2010–2030.*

Ch Léoville-Poyferré Deep, rich, with a fully mature brown rim; very fragrant, a bit tannic and peppery, a lot to it; fairly sweet, crisp, 13% alcohol, touch of mocha, delicious, too good to spit. *Last noted July 2005* ★★★★ *Now–2016.*

Ch La Louvière Richly coloured; mature nose; sweetish. Soft, attractive, *à point. Last noted March 2001* ★★★ *Drink soon.*

Ch Lynch-Bages Fairly deep, open yet still youthful; delicious bouquet that opened up fabulously, held well and developed further in the glass; fleshy yet lean, exciting flavour. *Last tasted July 2004* ★★★★(★) *Now–2016.*

Ch Malartic-Lagravière Open rim; very good, typically Graves nose and flavour though a bit loose-knit. Dry finish. *April 2003* ★★★ *Now–2010.*

Ch La Mission Haut-Brion Though fairly deep and intense, looked ready; very distinctive nose, seaweed, 'wet leaves', sea air, relaxed, ripe and attractive; dramatic up front, sweet, rich, mouthfilling, great length. Sweet tannins, no hard edges. Lovely drink. *Last tasted Dec 2006* ★★★★★ *Now–2020.*

Ch Palmer Great potential. Still fairly deep and intense, with rich 'tears' or 'legs'; nose noted, twice, as 'cheesy', rich, chocolatey; 'incredibly sweet' on the palate, lots of fruit, spice. *Last noted Feb 2001* ★★★★(★) *Now–2015.*

Ch Pape-Clément Opaque core, fairly intense; brambly fruit, touch of tar; sweet, fleshy, powerful, oaky. *Last tasted April 2003* ★★★(★)? *Now–2016*.

Ch Pichon-Longueville Soft cherry, velvety; mocha and new oak nose; round, soft, rich palate. Attractive. *Last tasted Sept 2006* ★★(★★) *Now–2016*.

Ch Pichon-Lalande Fairly deep, soft cherry; distinctive coffee, ginger and 'wholemeal' nose with flavour to match. Lovely but still tannic. *Last noted Sept 2000* ★★★★(★) *Now–2015*.

Ch Rausan-Ségla A distinctly mature brown tinge; smooth, harmonious nose gaining extra dimensions in the glass; sweet, rich, touch of coffee. A lovely mouthful but tannic finish. *Last tasted March 2003* ★★★(★) *Now–2015*.

Ch Siran Very pale for a '90; nice weight, soft texture, pleasant, more tannic than expected. *July 2004* ★★★ *Now–2012*.

Ch Smith-Haut-Lafitte An impressive magnum. Spicy, scented; sweet, mouthfilling, with good fruit and extract. *Last noted June 2000* ★★★(★) *Now–2012*.

Ch Sociando-Mallet A newly fashionable *bourgeois* Médoc. Certainly rising well above its class, in a rather modern way, but I prefer real Médocs to Pomerol-style Médocs. *Last noted Oct 2001* ★★★(★)

Ch Talbot Attractive. Relaxed, rich, mature-looking; lovely fruit, 'arboreal'; very distinctive, clean cut, perfect weight, mature. *Last tasted April 2006* ★★★★ *Now–2012*.

Ch La Tour-de-By Since the 1983 vintage I have been a loyal follower of this consistently well made and reasonably priced Médoc. Still fairly deeply coloured, mature; sweet, mellow nose that opened up richly and ripely; sweet entry, good flavour, body, length and masked tannins. *Last tasted Feb 2003* ★★★★ *for its class. Drink up (alas none left in my cellar but look out for the excellent 2005).*

Ch La Tour-Carnet A chronically underperforming classed growth but quite a good '90, its sweet nose better than palate. Modest (12% alcohol). *Last tasted Feb 1998* ★(★) *Might as well drink up.*

OTHER GOOD 4- AND 5-STAR '90S LAST TASTED IN THE MID- TO LATE 1990S: Ch Brane-Cantenac; Ch Calon-Ségur; Ch Canon; Ch Cantemerle; Dom de Chevalier; Ch Certan-de-May; Ch Clinet; Ch L'Église-Clinet; Ch L'Évangile; Ch Figeac; Ch Le Gay; Ch Gazin; Ch Labégorce-Zédé; Ch Lafleur; Ch Latour-à-Pomerol; Ch Petit-Village; Ch Le Pin; Ch Prieuré-Lichine; Ch Tertre-Rôteboeuf; and Ch Trottevieille.

1991 ★ to ★★★

The weather during the growing season ultimately dictates the timing, quality and size of harvest. In 1991 a severe frost during the nights of 21st and 22nd April, with temperatures plummeting to -8°C which froze the vines, destroyed new shoots overnight and seriously reduced the potential crop. Then, cold weather caused a late and extended flowering which, in turn, resulted in uneven development and a delayed harvest. An extremely hot and dry August, the hottest since 1926, raised hopes of a small harvest of concentrated grapes: a repeat of 1961. Alas, eight days of heavy rains before the harvest destroyed these hopes.

Ch Lafite Magnums: fully mature; lovely, fragrant, cedary nose; touch of sweetness, 'decent flavour' and a light, refreshing bite. *Last tasted July 2006* ★★★ *Now–2010*.

Ch Latour Cedar and fruit; sweet, very pleasant flavour; ready now despite its grip. *Last noted Sept 1998* ★★★ *Now–2015*.

Ch Margaux Starting to mature; nose initially chocolatey but opened up fragrantly, but after two hours in the glass, completely faded. Decent flavour, reasonably complete, drinking well enough. *Last tasted Nov 2000* ★★★ *(just)*.

Ch Mouton-Rothschild Lean and dry, spicy and somewhat astringent, displaying a luminous cherry red; singed, biscuity, mocha nose; crisp, flavoury, food needed to counter its tannin and acidity. *Not tasted since June 1997* ★★ *Drink soon*.

Ch Grand-Puy-Lacoste Deeper than expected, plummy, mature rim; rich, chewy, chaptalised nose; sweeter and chunkier than expected. Drinking well. *Last tasted May 2003* ★★★ *Drink up*.

Ch Pichon-Lalande Ruby; more classic and cedary than expected; drinking well though a touch of iron and tannin. *Last noted March 2001* ★★★ *Now–2010*.

OTHER '91S SHOWING WELL IN THE MID- TO LATE 1990S (ALL 3-STAR WINES): **Ch Beychevelle**; **Ch Brane-Cantenac**; **Ch Ducru-Beaucaillou**; **Ch L'Église-Clinet**; **Les Forts de Latour**; **Ch Giscours**; **Ch Gruaud-Larose**; **Ch Haut-Bages-Averous**; **Ch d'Issan**; **Ch Langoa-Barton**; **Ch Léoville-Las-Cases**; **Ch Pavie**; **Ch Le Pin**; and **Ch Talbot**

1992 ★

The worst vintage of the decade. Execrable growing and harvesting conditions: the wettest summer for over half a century, rainfall roughly double the average and the fewest hours of sunshine since 1980. Few tasted. Avoid.

Ch Margaux Un-notable appearance and nose; dryish, lean, slightly pasty flavour and raw finish. *Nov 2006. Oh dear!*

1993 ★★ to ★★★

Variable, mediocre to not bad, the results depending less on good luck than on good management. The problem once again was rain: 160 days out of the 365, despite the first three months being abnormally dry. Yet the vines were in much better shape than might have been expected, the Merlots in particular being almost perfectly ripe by mid-September. The effect of rain is juice dilution, and the later-ripening Cabernet Sauvignons were susceptible. Care and selection were crucial.

Ch Lafite Surprisingly deep and velvety; fragrant, 'medicinal' nose. A lightish, flavoury drink with a somewhat tart finish. *Last tasted Dec 2004* ★★ *Drink up*.

Ch Latour Deep, velvety, intense; very fragrant; good flavour. Nice wine. *Last tasted Dec 2003* ★★★ *Now–2012*.

Ch Margaux Soft fruit noted as before, on nose and palate; a slightly watery, chaptalised character, but drinking quite well. Not a very notable Margaux. *Last tasted Nov 2000* ★★ *Drink soon*.

Ch Mouton-Rothschild An *impériale*: still deep; characteristic minty, eucalyptus fragrance; dry, lean, refreshing though an edgy, slightly astringent, finish. *Last tasted July 2005* ★★★ *Better sooner than later*.

Ch Haut-Brion Open-rimmed, maturing; nose a rich *mélange* of coffee and fruit; distinct citrus character, easy style but dry finish. *Jan 2000* ★★ *Drink soon*.

Ch Cheval Blanc Medium, maturing, watery rim; attractive nose, whiff of iron, mellow yet shallow, lightish style, nice weight, refreshing acidity. *Last tasted Jan 2006* ★★★ *Now–2010.*

Ch L'Angélus Deep and intense; a comparatively hefty style, showing well. *Last tasted April 2004* ★★★

Ch Clinet Nose tarry and oaky; sweet, rich, moderate alcohol. Not my favourite style but good in its way. *Last tasted Nov 2003* ★★★ *Now–2016.*

Ch Ducru-Beaucaillou Maturing nicely but not very distinctive or memorable. *Last tasted April 2004* ★★

Ch Duhart-Milon Sweet (chaptalised) nose; 'chewy', a pleasant drink. *Last tasted Nov 2000* ★★★ *Drink soon.*

Ch Durfort-Vivens Surprisingly deep; sweet, soft, agreeable nose and taste; some sweetness, lightweight (12% alcohol), tannic finish. *Sept 2005* ★★★ *Now–2010.*

Ch L'Évangile Surprisingly easy and open on the palate, a fleshy wine, drinking well. *Last noted May 2000* ★★★ *Now–2014.*

Ch Figeac Considerable maturity of colour, nose and palate. Attractive, light tannins, pleasant acidity. Drying out a little. *Last tasted April 2003* ★★★ *Drink soon.*

Ch Grand-Puy-Lacoste Still youthful-looking with a good, rich nose and fine with food. *Last noted Dec 2000* ★★★ *Now–2012.*

Ch Gruaud-Larose Rustic, farmyard character. Ripe, rich fruit, complete and compelling. Very drinkable. *Last tasted April 2001* ★★★★ *Now–2012.*

Ch Kirwan Rather an uneven performer. Thick fruit; so-so, drying on palate. Unenthusiastic. *Last noted March 2001* ★(★) *Drink up.*

Ch Lafleur Still fairly deep; strange, low-keyed, whiff of vanilla, 'macerated' fruit; better than expected on the palate, good flavour and texture. *Last tasted Sept 2004* ★★★ *Now–2012.*

Ch Léoville-Barton Moderately deep and youthful still, quite intense but with mature rim; a classic, singed Bordeaux *brûlée* nose; sweet, soft yet crisp, a somewhat coarse, dry finish. *Last tasted Dec 2003* ★★(★) *Now–2012.*

Ch Léoville-Poyferré Maturing, a slight prickle of CO_2; fragrant, whiff of spearmint, opening up richly; nice weight, good flavour, dry finish. A good '93. *Jan 2006* ★★★ *Now–2012.*

Ch Lynch-Bages In the late 1990s, delicious crisp Cabernet nose; sweet, soft, overall tannic. Most recently, a disappointing bottle in distracting company. *Last noted June 2000.* At best ★★(★) *Now–2011.*

Ch Montrose Translucent; sweet, quite nice fruit, tannic; better than expected though with a curious flavour and touch of coarseness. *March 2004* ★★ *Now–2010.*

Ch Pavie Good colour; lovely nose, touch of strawberry and pepper; chunky fruit, mouth-drying tannins. Better than expected. *Last tasted July 2001* ★★★

Ch Pichon-Lalande Impressive, mature; rich 'brown paper and brown sugar'; very distinctive, good fruit, fleshy, specious, lovely to drink. *Last tasted May 2007* ★★★★ *Now–2012.*

Ch Smith-Haut-Lafitte Spicy, lean, very flavoury. *Last tasted June 2000* ★★★ *Now–2010.*

SELECTED NOTES ON THE MANY '93S TASTED IN THE MID- TO LATE 1990S: **Ch d'Angludet** fragrant, soft yet refreshing ★★★ *drink soon;* **Ch d'Armailhac** lovely, smooth, minty, eucalyptus nose, 'with nice trajectory across the palate'. Firm. Medium length ★★(★) *now–2010*; **Ch Batailley** substantial fruit and good flavour ★★★ *now–2010*; **Ch Beychevelle** sweet, sweaty, rustic nose, not bad flavour but unimpressive ★★ *drink rather than keep*; **Ch Branaire-Ducru** quite good fruit and weight. Tannic grip. Lacks length ★(★) *now–2012*; **Ch Brane-Cantenac** piquant; specious, attractive. Fairly well developed and easy ★★★ *now–2010*; **Ch Canon** soft, rich, full and fleshy *At best* ★★(★★) *now–2010*; **Ch Cantenac-Brown** well developed, with its characteristic chunky, chocolatey character, attractive, easy *A generous* ★★★ *but get on with it*; **Ch Chasse-Spleen** as usual, a cut above its class. Touch of sweetness, crisp, clean, agreeable, with refreshing acidity ★★★ *now–2010*; **Dom de Chevalier** forthcoming nose; sweet, attractive, 'charm' and 'pleasing weight' (only 12% alcohol) ★★★ *now–2010*; **Ch Clerc-Milon** good cedary-iodine nose; soft yet with firm, dry finish. A food wine ★(★★) *now–2012*; **Ch Cos d'Estournel** sweet, soft but sweaty (tannins); stylish, crisp fruit, very attractive, sweet yet lean with a tannic finish ★★(★) *now–2015*; **Ch La Dominique** crisp, raspberry-like, mouthwatering fruit; on the sweet side, full of fruit and flavour yet only 12% alcohol. Soft tannins, fleshy ★★★★ *now–2012*; **Ch L'Église-Clinet** rich nose, depth; slightly sweet, good fruit and flesh. Crisp, dry finish ★★★★ *now–2012*; **Ch Ferrière** lots of fruit, sweet, attractive ★★★ *drink soon*; **Ch Feytit-Clinet** certainly impressive, its nose dense, wholesome, lovely after an hour in the glass, then developing in the mouth. But very tannic. Needs time and/or food ★(★★) *worth pursuing*; **Ch de Fieuzal** soft and sweet on the nose; simmering down, relatively easy and attractive ★★(★) *(just) drink up*; **Ch La Fleur-Pétrus** fairly deep; crisp fruit, spicy; good flavour and bite ★★(★) *now–2012*; **Ch Haut-Bailly** a pleasing richness, nice weight and flavour ★★★(★) *now–2010*; **Ch Labégorce-Zédé** consistent notes: fairly deep, soft, velvety cherry red; very fragrant, sweet, distinctive nose; crisp fruit, touch of leanness, quite a bit of tannin, good acidity ★★★ *now–2010*; **Ch Lafon-Rochet** black cherry; good nose, touch of menthol, tannic; raw, hard, the sort of tannic finish which reminds me of concrete (★★) *now–2012*; **Ch Langoa-Barton** its initial cedar and crisp fruit opened up beautifully and on the palate it also showed its class: shapely but tannic ★★★(★) *now–2012*; **Ch Léoville-Las-Cases** fragrant, cedary; firm, convincing fruit ★★(★) *now–2012*; **Ch Magdelaine** exceptionally attractive fruit, flavour and style ★★★★ *drink soon*; **Ch Les Ormes-de-Pez** good fruit, well made, hard tannins ★★★ *drink up*; **Ch Palmer** very attractive. Distinctly sweet, complete. Rather thick-set, plummy colour; low-keyed, soft, fleshy nose and 'wonderful depth'; rich fruit, a good mouthful despite its modest alcohol content (12%) ★★(★★) *now–2010*; **Ch Pavie-Decesse** rich though restrained ★★★ *drink up*; **Ch Pichon-Longueville** showing some maturity, good fruit, extra dimensions, chewy ★★★(★) *now–2012*; **Ch Pontet-Canet** good fruit. Convincing ★★★ *drink soon*; **Ch Rausan-Ségla** a seriously good '93. Suave, quite a bit of new oak; complete, impressive ★★(★★) *now–2010;* **Ch Siran** ripe fruit, lean, elegant, good texture ★★★ *drink soon*; **Ch Talbot** its nose becoming less floral and more rustic, with a touch of astringency ★★(★) *now–2010*; **Ch Trotanoy** nose forthcoming, ripe and harmonious; very sweet, full of fruit, delicious. Also tannic ★★(★★) *now–2010*; and **Vieux Ch Certan** lovely, sweet, harmonious bouquet; soft, nice texture, good finish. Very attractive ★★★★ *drink up.*

1994 ★★ to ★★★★

Distinctly uneven. Disappointments yet some surprises. A heavy spring frost across the whole region reduced the potential average crop by about 50%, in some plots from 70 to even 100%. Warm weather in May encouraged re-budding and a heatwave in June and July induced a rapid flowering. The warm weather continued through August. Everything was set for a fine, early harvest but from 7 September, heavy rains soused the region. The early-picked Merlot and Cabernet Franc were of good quality, the later-picked Cabernet Sauvignon uneven.

Ch Lafite Two magnums, double decanted: very slight variation but neither particularly praiseworthy, unknit, slightly stalky, whiff like new-sawn timber; flavoury, crisp fruit but raw. *Last tasted July 2006* ★★ *Drink up, no future.*

Ch Latour Fairly deep, richly coloured; cedary, tannic nose; sweet yet with rough tannin and edgy acidity, unbalanced, hard finish. *Last tasted April 2006* ★★ *Little point in keeping.*

Ch Margaux Still youthful-looking. A high mark for fragrance. Despite its omnipresent tannin, quite attractive. *Last tasted March 2001* ★(★★) *Now–2015.*

Ch Mouton-Rothschild Fragrant, leathery and lacking Mouton's flair. *Last tasted March 2001* ★(★★)? *Time will tell. But why bother?*

Ch Cheval Blanc The best '94. A well developed, sweet and chocolatey nose and flavour. I did not note any excess tannin. Clear evidence of the Right Bank's success in 1994. *Last tasted March 2001* ★★★(★) *Now–2012.*

Ch Pétrus Deeper than Cheval Blanc, its nose rather hard and uninteresting though a good flavour, its tannin masked. *March 2001* ★★(★) *Now–2010?*

Ch L'Arrosée Deep, intense, still youthful; surprisingly sweet though with raw finish. Needs cheese. *Nov 2003* ★★ *Drink up.*

Ch L'Église-Clinet Quite fragrant; some charm but grippingly tannic. *Last tasted March 2001* ★(★★) *Now–2010.*

Ch L'Enclos Beautiful, honeyed, mellow nose evolving sweetly, like wholemeal biscuits; shapely, elegant, no harsh edges until its teeth-gripping tannic finale. *Last noted March 2000* ★★(★★) *Now–2010.*

Ch Grand-Puy-Lacoste Having shed its youthful appeal, rather stern and unyielding. Needs time. *Last tasted Nov 2001* (★★★) *Now–2012.*

Ch Haut-Bailly Very earthy Graves nose; some sweetness, good fruit but tannin uppermost. *Last tasted June 2001* ★★(★) *Give it a bit more time.*

Ch Lafleur Plummy but weak; vanilla, a whiff of mocha and liquorice; lean, coarse finish, laden with tannin and acidity. A 'poor' Lafleur. *Sept 2004* ★★

Ch Léoville-Barton Deeper and richer than the '93; dry, oaky and firm noted yet again. A good '94. *Last tasted Oct 2001* ★★★(★) *Now–2012.*

Ch Léoville-Las-Cases Still plummy-coloured; low-keyed nose; nice fruit, the tannin on the raw side. Needs food. *Last noted Jan 2000* ★★(★★) *Now–2012.*

Ch La Louvière Chocolatey, smoky, oaky nose; first sip sweet but finishing dry. Fair-enough soft fruit mid-palate. Well made. *Last noted Oct 2000* ★(★★) *Drink soon.*

Ch Malescot-St-Exupéry Distinctive Cabernet nose and piquant flavour. Agreeable. *Last noted March 2001* ★★★ *(just). Drink soon.*

Ch Palmer Fleshy, soft fruit, no harsh edges, floral and fragrant; soft, ripe Merlot uppermost. Perfectly agreeable. *Last tasted Nov 2003* ★★★★ *Drink soon.*

Ch Pichon-Lalande Opening up with an almost farmyard animal richness. Surprisingly sweet. A good '94. *Last tasted Oct 2000* ★★★★ *Now–2012.*

Ch Rauzan-Ségla (Note the change of spelling, from 'Rausan' to 'Rauzan' from the '94 vintage.) Crisp fruit, restrained at first but intriguingly evolved after an hour; nice flesh and fruit, well made, excellent flavour but still very tannic. *Last tasted Sept 2000* ★★(★★) *Now–2012.*

Ch Talbot Medium-deep, maturing; unknit but quite good bricky scent; slightly sweet entry to very dry tannin finish but good fruit, crisp, needs time. *Last tasted April 2000* ★★(★) *Drink soon.*

THE BETTER '94S TASTED IN THE LATE 1990S mainly ready for drinking; some will keep but there is not much incentive: **Ch L'Angélus** laden with thick, hefty fruit. Impressive, a good '94 but not my style ★(★★); **Ch Batailley** very fragrant; sweet, positive fruit. A very drinkable '94 ★★★; **Ch Calon-Ségur** very evolved in appearance, nose and taste. Surprisingly sweet. Chunky. Firm. Attractive ★★★; **Ch Canon-La-Gaffelière** fleshy, attractive ★★★; **Ch Certan-de-May** fairly good fruit and depth though too oaky ★★(★); **Ch Clerc-Milon** immediately appealing, fragrant, mouthwatering Cabernet aroma; dry, lean, crisp, stylish ★★★; **Ch Clinet** deep, crisp, very tannic ★★★; **Ch La Conseillante** herbaceous, fragrant, oaky, very attractive ★★★(★); **Ch Cos d'Estournel** deep colour, quite good fruit, some flesh. A respectable '94 ★★(★); **Ch Duhart-Milon** richly coloured; positive fruit; very attractive ★★★; **Ch L'Évangile** very good fruit, depth, length and bite ★★(★★); **Ch Figeac** surprisingly only one note. Spicy nose; sweet, attractive, touch of bitterness ★★(★); **Ch La Fleur-Pétrus** good, crisp fruit ★★★; **Ch Gazin** meaty nose; rich fruit, attractive ★★★; **Ch Gruaud-Larose** fragrant, rich; very sweet, enough fruit, not over-tannic. An early developer ★★★; **Ch Kirwan** rich, biscuity nose and flavour. Much oak. Sweet, crisp tannin and acidity ★★★; **Ch Lagrange** (St-Julien) hard nose though with pleasant sweetness to moderate the tannin ★★★; **Ch La Mission Haut-Brion** luminous; stalky fruit opening up well; positive, attractive, tannic. Good wine ★★(★★); **Ch Pape-Clément** opening up pleasantly, sweet, very attractive, with smoky, oaky finish ★★(★); **Ch Pichon-Longueville** developing well; forthcoming, 'medicinal' Pauillac nose and flavour, tight Pauillac fruit on the palate ★★★; **Ch La Pointe** surprisingly deep; some sweetness and depth, shapely, complete ★★★; **Ch Pontet-Canet** dense; hard; full and richer than expected ★★★; **Ch Siran** rich fruit, extract, tannin and acidity ★★★; **Ch Trotanoy** Very good. Cherry-like fruit; sweet, attractive ★★★(★); and **Vieux Ch Certan** nice, mouthwatering fruit; quite good flavour and length. A convincing wine ★★(★).

1995 ★★★★

After the previous less inspiring four vintages, 1995 was welcomed by trade and consumers alike. It has turned out well, to the extent that I am tempted to add an extra star. The growing season started well. Budbreak was regular, with rapid flowering before the end of May. The driest summer for 20 years; unusually hot too, up to 30°C. All was set for an exceptional vintage. Picking started early, on 11 September, but was almost immediately interrupted by heavy rain which then subsided into light showers. These lasted until the 20th, after which most châteaux resumed picking in increasingly warm weather, ending with an Indian summer. Some Merlots were caught by the early rains but Cabernet Franc and Cabernet Sauvignon were very successful, the latter achieving almost unheard-of sugar levels. Overall, the wines are ripe, firm, with considerable charm and a good future.

Ch Lafite Firm, elegant, good future. *Last noted Nov 2001* ★★(★★★) *Now–2025.*

Ch Latour The nose somewhat chocolatey, also a whiff of tar; sweet, ripe, very dry but seeming less oppressively tannic. A fine wine. *Last tasted March 2001* (★★★★★) *2020–2030 or beyond.*

Ch Margaux Fairly deep but mature appearance; very fragrant, very pleasant fruit; dry, lean for Margaux but crisp and lovely, good length, good future. *Last tasted Oct 2005* ★★★(★★) *Now–2025.*

Ch Mouton-Rothschild Rich, dark cherry, maturing; deep, rich, slightly singed fragrance, very Pauillac 'medicinal' spiciness, crisp fruit; fairly sweet, rich, high extract, perfect weight, dry finish. *Last tasted July 2006* ★★★(★★) *Now–2025.*

Ch Haut-Brion Equal top mark at a blind tasting of first growth '95s. Well evolved yet surprisingly low-keyed, opened up, harmonious; soft, good fruit, very Graves, very attractive. *Last tasted Dec 2006* ★★★(★★) *Now–2020.*

Ch Ausone The first year with Alain Vauthier in control. Fairly deep, maturing nicely; classic Ausone 'dried leaves', rich, biscuity, singed mocha; dry, very good flavour and flesh but austere, tannic finish. Very good, archetypal Ausone. *Last tasted Jan 2005* ★★(★★★) *Now–2025.*

Ch Cheval Blanc Medium depth and intensity; fragrant, ripe bouquet that opened up richly, lovely, refined, harmonious; medium-sweet, lean yet soft (65% Merlot), a touch of iron, perfect tannin and fresh acidity. Delicious. *Last tasted April 2006* ★★★★★ *Now–2020.*

Ch Pétrus Medium deep, lovely colour; good nose, a bit stalky at first but a class act; sweeter than expected, good flavour, extract and assimilated tannin. *Tasted March 2001* ★★★(★★) *Now–2020.*

Ch L'Angélus Fairly deep, opaque core; rich, ripe, vegetal bouquet; medium-sweet, fullish, heady (13.5% alcohol), good flavour, length and finish. *Last tasted March 2004* ★★★★ *Now–2012.*

Ch d'Angludet Deep, rich, intense, convincing; most agreeable, harmonious bouquet. Sweet, rich, lovely wine. The best Angludet I can recall. *June 2004* ★★★★ *Now–2012.*

Ch d'Armailhac Ruby; high-toned, fragrant, light style though good depth of fruit; lean, delicious flavour, dry tannic finish. A charmer. *Last tasted April 2006* ★★★(★) *Now–2015.*

Ch Batailley 'A copybook Batailley' from the start. Surprisingly deep, richly coloured; perfect, slightly scented, high-toned Médoc nose; sweet, soft, ripe, well balanced, nice texture. Delicious mouthful. *Last tasted April 2006* ★★★★ *Now–2015.*

Ch Beychevelle Middle of the road colour, touch of mahogany, trying to mature; fragrant, refreshing, 'cedar pencils' nose; rich fruit, agreeable body, a touch of grittiness mid-palate, dry finish. *Last tasted March 2000* ★★★(★) *Now–2015.*

Ch Branaire-Ducru Thick core, long 'legs', slightly weak rim; fragrant, crisp, mouthwatering fruit; touch of sweetness, 13% alcohol, dry finish. An easy 'food wine'. *Last noted March 2000* ★★★(★) *Now–2015.*

Ch Calon-Ségur Medium-deep, maturing; very good nose; drinking well. *Last tasted June 2005* ★★★★ *Now–2015.*

Ch Canon-La-Gaffelière Deep, 'modern' style; good, fleshy fruit; ripe-grapes sweetness, typical and impressive, full-bodied, good finish. I have to confess that though I like Stéphan von Neipperg and admire his achievement, I am in two minds about his recent wines. Time will tell. *Oct 2006* ★★(★★★)?

Ch Cantenac-Brown Fairly deep colour and intensity; sound nose; agreeable. Curious finish. *Last tasted – briefly – March 2003* ★★★ *Drink soon.*

Ch Chasse-Spleen Maturing nicely; very rich, chocolatey nose; lean but shapely. Well made, as always. *Last tasted Aug 2004* ★★★★ *Now–2010.*

Ch Clerc-Milon Black cherry, velvety, maturing; sweet, rich, brambly fruit, whiff of mocha; a bitter-sweet wine, full of fruit, slightly pasty texture, masked tannin but raw finish. Needs food. *Last tasted March 2006* ★★(★★?) *Now–2016.*

Ch La Conseillante Ripe, well developed nose; very sweet, mouthfilling, 12.9% alcohol, good balance, length, tannic and refreshing acidity. *Oct 2006* ★★★(★) *Now–2020.*

Ch Dauzac Very deep, velvety, intense; fragrant, some oakiness; agreeable weight, flavour, consistency and flesh. *Oct 2001* ★★★(★) *Soon–2015.*

Ch Ducru-Beaucaillou 'Thick', singed, whiff of petrol, mocha and toast; sweet, rich, very good mid-fruit, 13% alcohol, toasted, oaky tannic finish. *Last tasted March 2000* ★★(★★) *Now–2015.*

Ch Duhart-Milon Lively colour, good 'legs', scarcely any sediment; vanilla, oak, mocha; fairly sweet, chunky soft fruit, touch of iron. Attractive but lacking finesse. *July 2006* ★★★ *Drink soon.*

Ch Durfort-Vivens Medium-deep, maturing; dry, quite flavoury, iron/tannic finish. *Last tasted Sept 2000* ★★★ *Now–2012.*

Ch L'Église-Clinet Very deep, immature appearance; nose slow to emerge from the glass but enormously impressive on the palate, full and rich. *Last tasted March 2001* ★★(★★) *Now–2015.*

Ch L'Enclos Deep, red-brown rim; delicious soft fruit scent which rises to meet one halfway; sweet, silky texture, fleshy fruit, dry finish. *Last tasted March 2002* ★★★(★) *Now–2010.*

Ch L'Évangile Deep; rich, singed, 'stably' nose that arose and then sat, unmoved, in the glass; sweet, rich, assertive, powerful yet only 13% alcohol. Impressive. *Last tasted March 2004* ★★★(★) *Now–2012.*

Ch La Fleur-Pétrus Convincing, maturing; harmonious – a bouquet of real quality; rich, full-bodied (13.5% alcohol), soft, fleshy fruit, extract masking tannin. Lovely wine. *Last noted July 2001* ★★★(★) *Now–2020.*

Ch Figeac Still fairly deep; well evolved crisp fruit; rich, singed, still tannic. *Last tasted March 2003* ★★★(★) *Now–2012.*

Ch La Gaffelière Rich ruby; good nose; pleasing sweetness, soft, agreeable. *March 2003* ★★★★ *Now–2012.*

Ch Giscours Not bad fruit, leaner than expected, *assez bien*. *Last tasted March 2003* ★★★ *Now–2012?*

Ch Grand-Puy-Lacoste A leisurely developer. Soft red, velvety; rich, crisp, touch of iron; good fruit, dry tannic finish. Given air and decanting time, drinking well but needs more bottle age. *Last tasted June 2006* ★★(★★★) *2010–2020.*

Ch Gruaud-Larose Starting to mature; rich, minty, its nose opening up beautifully; soft, fleshy fruit, peppery finish. Very typical Gruaud mouthful. *Last tasted March 2000* ★★★(★★) *Now–2015.*

Ch Haut-Bailly Very fragrant, sweet, shapely, lovely. *Last noted April 2002* ★★★★ *Now–2012.*

Ch Haut-Batailley Still youthful; understated yet fragrant; dry, good flavour and finesse, excellent balance. Needs time. *Aug 2003* ★★(★★) *Now–2016.*

Ch Lafleur Very pleasing colour; complex nose, slightly medicinal at first, after an hour 'squashed strawberries'; sweet, rich, good fruit, full body and flavour, some elegance. Very good texture. *Last tasted Sept 2004* ★★★(★) *Now–2012.*

Ch Lagrange (St-Julien) Beautiful colour, touch of mauve; lovely, cedary nose, fragrant, quite a lot of oak; dry, good wine, a tannic bite on the finish but not harsh. Needs food – and time. *Last tasted March 2000* ★★(★★) *Now–2016.*

Ch La Lagune Deep ruby; sweetish, soft, very oaky, agreeable. *Last tasted March 2001* ★★★ *Now–2012.*

Ch Léoville-Barton Classic, archetypal St-Julien. Rich, dense, mouthfilling yet exuding charm. Fragrant, harmonious; very oaky but good flesh. Drinking deliciously. *Last tasted May 2006* ★★★(★★) *Now–2020.*

Ch Léoville-Las-Cases No harsh edges, harmonious nose; mouthfilling, smooth, its natural sweetness and rich extract masking the tannin. *Last tasted March 2001* ★★★(★★) *Now–2020.*

Ch Léoville-Poyferré Convincing, mouthfilling despite a certain leanness and austerity. Opaque core, velvety sheen, impressive; lovely, spicy cedar, evolving beautifully in the glass; sweet entry, good fruit, dry finish. A very good Poyferré. *Last tasted April 2005* ★★★(★★) *Now–2020.*

Ch La Louvière Deep, velvety; sweet, very pleasant nose and flavour. Good fruit, ideal weight, a rich mouthful. Graves at its best. *July 2004* ★★★★ *Drink up.*

Ch Lynch-Bages Still deeply coloured; fragrant, zestful; sweet, delicious flavour though still tannic. *Last tasted April 2006* ★★★(★★) *Now–2016.*

Ch Lynch-Moussas Mature; fairly sweet, attractive, complete, drinking well. *Last tasted March 2004* ★★★ *Drink soon.*

Ch Maucaillou Very dependable *cru bourgeois* Moulis. Fairly deep; good nose which evolved in the glass; well made wine; tannic but approaching pleasant drinkability. *Sept 2002* ★★(★★) *Now–2010.*

Ch La Mission Haut-Brion Very deep; distinctive, spicy, earthy nose; masculine, still a bit raw and tannic. Good future. *Feb 2006* ★(★★★) *2010–2020.*

Ch Montrose Deep, luminous, maturing; mellowing, pleasant spicy oak; some sweetness, perfect weight, good shape, delicious. An elegant Montrose. *Last tasted March 2004* ★★★(★★) *Now–2020.*

Ch Palmer Worthy of its 'super-second' reputation. Still very deep, dark cherry, youthful; reluctantly rich, ripe nose; distinctive flavour and texture, firm, good wine. *Last tasted Nov 2005* ★★★(★★) *Now–2016.*

Ch Pape-Clément Plummy-coloured, maturing; high-toned, earthy, almost rustic; some sweetness, good, ripe but firm flavour and weight, well made, still tannic. *Last tasted March 2004* ★★★(★) *Now–2016.*

Ch Petit-Village Low-keyed but pleasant nose; sweet, agreeable but curiously coarse tannins which will doubtless ameliorate. *March 2003* ★★(★) *Now–2012.*

Ch Pichon-Longueville Fleshy nose that developed well; nicely balanced, drinking well but really needs more time. *Last tasted Sept 2006* ★★(★★) *Now–2016.*

Ch Pichon-Lalande Distinctive, scented; sweet, rich, gingery, almost gamey. Lovely but specious. *Last tasted May 2007* ★★(★★) *Now–2020.*

Ch Prieuré-Lichine A bit rustic; some sweet fruit but overall dry, lean, a touch of coarseness. Disappointing. *April 2003* ★★ *Drink up, don't keep.*

Ch Rauzan-Ségla Immensely impressive, velvety yet intense; very distinctive, 'almost chewable', raspberry-like fruit; sweet, chunky, crisp, lots to it. *Last tasted March 2003* ★★★(★) *Now–2016.*

Ch Smith-Haut-Lafitte Certainly well made and attractive. Surprisingly sweet, good mid-fruit and dry finish. *Last tasted March 2001* ★★★(★) *Now–2015.*

Ch Talbot Fragrant, more cedary than the familiar *fermier* rusticity, 'coffee' noted; crisp fruit, interesting texture. *Last tasted May 2005* ★★★(★) *Now–2016.*

Ch Tertre-Rôteboeuf Fairly deep, well developed; extraordinarily meaty, malty nose; sweet, full-flavoured, fruit-packed, rich, chewy, but very tannic. Very good in its way but not 'claret'. *Last tasted March 2004* ★★★★ *Now–?*

Vieux Ch Certan Magnums: good colour, classic nose and flavour. Some sweetness but an end bite. Attractive. *June 2006* ★★★(★)? *Now–2015.*

BRIEF NOTES ON OTHER GOOD '95s TASTED AROUND 2000: **Ch Beauséjour-Duffau-Lagarosse** ★★★; **Ch Brane-Cantenac** loose-knit, coffee bean flavour ★★★; **Ch Canon** sweet, spicy; delicious though tannic ★★★(★); **Ch Cantemerle** sweet, gingery; good flavour and weight ★★★; **Ch Certan-de-May** unusual flavour and style ★★★?; **Ch Cos d'Estournel** sweet, mocha nose and almost 'New World' taste ★★★(★); **Dom de Chevalier** lively, dependable ★★★?; **Ch Clinet** opaque; idiosyncratic, tarry; fairly sweet, concentrated. Very good in its way ★★★; **Ch Gazin** chocolatey; attractive, lighter style ★★★; **Ch Kirwan** lots of new oak but richness and flesh to compensate ★★★(★)?; **Ch Labégorce-Zédé** a touch of stalkiness; rich, full of fruit ★★(★); **Ch Lafon-Rochet** typically hard, oaky, lean but good flavour ★★(★); **Ch Magdelaine** very distinctive. Sweet. Good length ★★★; **Clos René** lovely, harmonious nose; beguiling, fleshy, soft tannins ★★★(★); **Ch Roc de Cambes** rich, unusual, very distinctive ★★★; **Ch de Sales** easy, agreeable ★★★; **Ch Troplong-Mondot** good fruit and grip ★★★; and **Ch Trotanoy** sweet, fruit-laden ★★★★★

1996 ★★ to ★★★★

Though upstaged by the attractive '95s, this vintage is better than first thought, and improves on acquaintance. Indeed, I think it is seriously underrated. Growing conditions: budbreak was delayed until mid-April; flowering was quick and even; a very hot June and July; August started cool but ended with hot sun and cold nights. Pre-harvest rain affected the early-ripening Merlots, which diluted and reduced the crop size in Pomerol and St-Émilion. The Médoc fared better. The late-picked Cabernets were of high quality, resulting in rich, fairly concentrated wines.

Ch Lafite Very deep and intense, with opaque core but showing signs of maturity at its rim; very good nose, cedary, subdued – will need air and coaxing; surprisingly sweet, good firm fruit, almost chewable, and long dry finish. As so often, this is a wine that needs time and patience, particularly in a vintage like '96. *Last tasted May 2007* ★★(★★) *2016–2030.*

Ch Latour Fairly deep, intense; high-toned, ripe Cabernet Sauvignon aroma, crisp, developed well in the glass; full-flavoured, attractive, on the lean side, very tannic, crisp acidity. A long-haul wine. *Last tasted June 2007* ★(★★★) *2016–2030.*

Ch Margaux An outstanding wine and, as so often, a joy to taste from the start. A high percentage (85%) of Cabernets Sauvignon and Franc. Totally different style to the '95, leaner, spicy, taut fruit, finesse. Good nose, dumb at first but developed lovely fragrance; good flavour and length but tannic and unready. *Last tasted June 2003* ★★(★★★) *2010–2030*.

Ch Mouton-Rothschild Very deep and intense; very fragrant, crisp fruit, whiff of mocha and chocolate; sweet, fleshy; touch of liquorice and black pepper, delicious flavour, leathery tannins. *Last tasted Sept 2005* ★★(★★★) *2012–2030*.

Ch Haut-Brion Soft black cherry; nose packed with fruit, whiff of raspberries, harmonious; lovely flesh and texture, soft, sweet, richness masking tannin. Preferred to the '95. *Last tasted Dec 2006* ★★(★★) *Now–2025*.

Ch Ausone Very forthcoming nose; medium dryness and body. Once such an uneven performer, Ausone has taken on a new lease of life without losing its distinctive character. *Last tasted Nov 2000* (★★★★) *Now–2020*.

Ch Cheval Blanc A lovely wine. Very fragrant 'soft raspberries'. Perfect balance. 'A charmer'. Developing well. *Last tasted March 2001* ★★★★ *Now–2018*.

Ch L'Angélus Some colour loss though still pretty deep; hefty, fruit-laden on nose and palate. Impressive. *Last noted Nov 2000* (★★★★) *Now–2015*.

Ch d'Armailhac Fairly deep, with a thick midriff; lively, interesting nose; crisp fruit, refreshing, still a bit raw. *Last noted July 2001* ★★★(★) *Now–2012*.

Ch Batailley Lovely colour, good depth and intensity; distinctive cherry-like fruit, whiff of asparagus; shapely but more astringency than expected. Good flavour, though, and grip. *Last tasted April 2006* ★★★(★)?

Ch Brane-Cantenac Plummy colour; fairly sweet, rich, with crisp fruit. *Last tasted Nov 2000* ★★(★★) *Now–2012*.

Ch Calon-Ségur A pleasant-enough, sweet, easy sort of wine though with a touch of coarseness. *Last tasted Nov 2000* ★★(★) *Now–2012*.

Carruades de Lafite Attractive, flavoury, nice texture. Delicious drink. *Last tasted April 2006* ★★★★ *Now–2012*.

Ch Chasse-Spleen Deep, immature; very sweet, soft; delicious flavour, complete, tannic. *Last tasted Jan 2005* ★★★ *Now–2012*.

Dom de Chevalier Impressively deep; sweet, fleshy, classy nose, whiff of new-sawn wood; fruity sweetness, nicely rounded despite teeth-gripping tannin, modest weight (12% alcohol), very distinctive. *Last tasted July 2002* ★★★(★) *Now–2016*.

Ch La Conseillante Completely satisfactory flavour, weight, balance. Excellent tannin and acidity. *Last tasted Nov 2000* ★★★(★) *Now–2016*.

Ch Cos d'Estournel Deep and plummy; sweet, sweaty, tannic nose; nice flavour, style, weight, tannic texture; rich and rustic. An interesting mouthful. *Last noted fleetingly, Oct 2001* ★★★(★) *Now–2015*.

Ch La Croix-de-Gay Suave, harmonious nose; silky texture, soft, drying finish. *Last noted July 2001* ★★★(★) *Now–2015*.

Ch Duhart-Milon Deep, stylish, easy, save for tannic finish. *Last tasted June 2005* ★★(★) *Now–2012*.

Ch L'Église-Clinet Of Médoc first growth quality but with silky Pomerol tannins. *Last tasted March 2001* ★★★(★) *Now–2016*.

Ch de Fieuzal Crisp, refreshing. *Last tasted June 2003* ★★★(★) *Now–2012*.

Clos Fourtet Fragrant; good length; very attractive; 'a great improvement over the old days'. *Last tasted Nov 2000* ★★(★★) *just. Now–2016*.

Ch Giscours A change in style from the big and beefy wines produced in the 1970s. Opening up nicely: sweet, easy, an early developer. *Last noted Nov 2000.* ★★★ *Now–2010.*

Ch Grand-Puy-Lacoste Fairly deep, velvety; delicious bouquet; distinctly dry but very good weight, shape and balance. Uncompromisingly slow to evolve but the perfect beverage. *Last tasted Dec 2006* ★★★(★★) *Now–2020.*

Ch La Grave Trigant-de-Boisset Medium, relaxed; very attractive wine, light grip. *Oct 2001* ★★★(★) *Now–2015.*

Ch Gruaud-Larose Richly coloured; very good, multi-dimensional nose and flavour. Richness masking tannin. *Last tasted March 2003* ★★★(★★) *Now–2020.*

Ch Haut-Bages-Libéral Crisp, harmonious; deliciously sweet, brambly fruit, substantial, chewy, good long dry finish. *Last tasted July 2002* ★★★ *Now–2012.*

Ch Haut-Bailly Rich, velvety; distinctive Graves character and style; fairly rich, though still tannic. Certainly a fine wine. *Last tasted June 2005* ★★★(★) *Now–2016.*

Ch Haut-Batailley Richly coloured; ripe; rich yet tannic. Stylish. Needs time. *Oct 2001* ★★(★★) *Now–2015.*

Ch Kirwan The new style of Kirwan. Most recently: still impressively deep; masses of new oak spice and tar; certainly rich and tannic, but I noted 'dried fruit'. A past underperformer now undergoing an over-performing renaissance. *Last tasted March 2003. Hard to place.*

Ch Labégorce-Zédé Now fairly mature; soft, slightly chocolate nose; sweet, chewy, leathery tannins. Nice wine. *Last tasted April 2005* ★★★ *Now–2012.*

Ch Lafon-Rochet Most recently, confirming a change from the old, rather stern, rustic, tannic style. Surprisingly sweet and fleshy on the palate. Nice wine. *Last tasted March 2004* ★★★ *Now–2012.*

Ch Léoville-Barton Mature yet ruby-tinged; classic, cedar pencil, Cabernet character; crisp fruit, lean, perfect weight; good tannin and acidity. *Last tasted May 2007* ★★(★★) *Now–2016.*

Ch Léoville-Las-Cases Deep, intense; curious, slightly singed, arboreal, chocolatey nose; sweet, chewy, good depth, tannic, oaky finish. *Dec 2003* ★★★ *Now–2016.*

Ch Léoville-Poyferré Fairly deep but well on its way to maturity; good nose, opening up interestingly, tea and mocha; crisp, moderately full-bodied, tamed tannin, easy drinking. *Last tasted April 2005* ★★★ *Now–2015.*

Ch Lynch-Bages Still surprisingly deep; nose low-keyed, taking time to open up and lacking its usual varietal fragrance; sweet, good fruit, a lovely mouthful though coarse textured with 'thick' tannins. *Last tasted Nov 2005* ★★(★) *Now–2012.*

Ch Malescot-St-Exupéry Low-keyed, fragrant, pleasant enough fruit and flavour. *Last tasted Nov 2002* ★★★ *Now–2012.*

Ch La Mission Haut-Brion Fine deep colour; very fragrant; almost medicinal, good depth, distinctive tobacco; distinctive character and flavour, high-toned, crisp but biting tannin and acidity. *Dec 2006* ★(★★★) *Needs time.*

Ch Monbrison A *cru bourgeois* Margaux that has taken on a new lease of life. Two very good notes within a month: deep, intense, impressive; sweet, well constructed, harmonious, agreeable nose; very good flavour, soft fruit, deliciously flavoury. *Last tasted Dec 2003* ★★★ *Now–2010.*

Ch Montrose Top of the St-Estèphes and exceptionally rich for Montrose and a '96. Sweet, ripe, cedary nose; very flavoury, good fruit, yet a trifle lean and tannic. *Last tasted Sept 2005* ★★★(★★) *Now–2025.*

Les Ormes-de-Pez Maturing; soft, slightly chocolatey; sweet, soft fruit, masked tannin, good acidity. *Jan 2005* ★★★ *Now–2012.*

Ch Palmer Though it had a lot to offer, I found it very tannic, with a citrus-like touch of acidity. Will doubtless get its second breath. *Last tasted Feb 2001* ★★(★★) *Now–2018.*

Ch Pape-Clément Frankly variable but undeniably Graves. Peppery, earthy, rustic; an extraordinary rusty iron, smoky tobacco taste and a hard, raw, tannic finish. *Last tasted Nov 2005* ★(★★)? *Now hard to say.*

Ch de Pez Deservedly one of 'Crus Bourgeois Exceptionnels': good colour; sweet, chunky fruit; perfect weight, crisp. *March 2005* ★★★ *Now–2012.*

Ch Phélan-Ségur Earthy, whiff of chocolate; good fruit and extract, very tannic yet drinking well. *Last tasted Feb 2005* ★★(★) *Now–2012.*

Ch Pichon-Lalande Scent of coffee beans and brown sugar; sweet, fruity, good length, silky leathery tannins. As so often, speciously attractive, deservedly well liked. *Last tasted May 2007* ★★★★ *Now–2016.*

Ch Pichon-Longueville Very flavoury, spicy, new oak. Still deep and immature; whiff of coffee; good length but, somehow, not inspiring. *Last tasted Feb 2005* ★★(★) *Now–2012?*

Ch La Pointe Fleshy, Merlot-dominated Pomerol. Drinking well. *Last tasted Nov 2003* ★★★ *Drink soon.*

Ch Rauzan-Ségla Consistently good notes. Dominated by Cabernet Sauvignon, which comes out in the nose and taste. Positive, firm, good flavour and grip. *Last tasted June 2007* ★★★(★) *Now–2016.*

Ch Siran Maturing pleasantly. Richer, higher extract than expected. Soft, masked tannin, agreeable fruity finish. *Last tasted Jan 2005* ★★★ *Now–2014.*

Ch Smith-Haut-Lafitte Settling down now, good fruit, good flavour. *Last tasted April 2003* ★★★ *Now–2014.*

Ch Sociando-Mallet Outperforming its class. Impressive: rich, mature; hefty but sweet and delicious despite tannin. *Oct 2001* ★★★(★) *Now–2012.*

Ch Talbot Very dependable in style and quality. Always a touch of rusticity, ripe and fleshy for a '96. Most recently: still impressively deep; good fruit and flavour, perfect weight, tannic. *Last tasted Sept 2003* ★★★(★) *Now–2015.*

Ch La Tour-Carnet Once one of the dreariest of the Médoc classed growths, now – under new ownership – vastly improved. Sweet and surprisingly attractive on nose and palate. Tannic of course. *May 2003* ★★★ *Now–2012.*

Ch La Tour-de-By A consistently well made *cru bourgeois* Médoc. Lovely colour; pleasant fruit; sweeter than expected, floral, refreshing acidity. *Last tasted May 2005* ★★★ *Now–2010.*

Ch Trotanoy Rich and fragrant. Complete. Good length. Excellent wine. *Last tasted Nov 2000* ★★★★ *Now–2020.*

Ch Trottevieille Not too enthusiastic. Fairly mature; strange, rich, meaty, brambly, fruit; touch of coarseness, tannic yet drinking quite well. *Last tasted March 2005* ★★★ *Now–2012.*

Vieux Ch Certan Glowing colour; harmonious and more to come; vigorous, tannic, good texture and future. *Last noted Nov 1999* ★★★★

BRIEF NOTES ON MAINLY 3-STAR WINES TASTED AROUND 2000: **Ch d'Angludet** curious *mélange* of fruits; rich texture and flavour; **Ch Belgrave** (St-Laurent) undergoing renaissance under Michel Rolland – dense; good, rich fruit, full and spicy; **Ch Beauregard** (Pomerol) not a very deep colour; slightly chocolatey, appealing, easy-going; **Ch Beauséjour-Bécot** still youthful; rich nose but far too oaky on the palate; **Ch Branaire-Ducru** attractive ruby colour; crisp, fragrant nose and taste. Oak very noticeable, as always. Lean. Raw tannins; **Ch Canon-La-Gaffelière** good fruit; a substantial wine. *Possibly 4 stars:* **Ch Les Carmes-Haut-Brion** a fragrant immediacy about the nose; distinctive, quick maturing. Touch of Graves 'tobacco', good flesh. Nice wine; **Ch Clerc-Milon** showing well. Fullish, complete; **Ch Clinet** less deep, lower-keyed than expected though more punch on palate. For a change, a Clinet I like; **Ch Cos Labory** surprisingly sweet, ripe fruit, yet lean and tannic; **Ch Coufran** fragrant, spicy, nice texture. Crisp fruit (virtually 100% Merlot); **Ch Croizet-Bages** initially pure cassis. Irresistible; **Ch Dauzac** improvements here. Rich, ripe, piquant fruitiness; fairly sweet, fleshy, distinctive, attractive – yet something missing; **Ch La Dominique** good wine; **Ch L'Évangile** fruit and flesh. Good length; **Ch Figeac** mellow, light style, attractive but unconvincing; **Les Forts de Latour** restrained; surprisingly sweet, fruit and grip; **Ch La Gaffelière** attractive nose; sweet, slightly harsh tannins. Needs time; **Ch Gazin** deep, rich; sweet, fragrant finish; **Ch d'Issan** crisp fruit. Attractive; **Ch Lagrange** (St-Julien) crisp, fragrant, agreeable; **Ch La Lagune** very deep; full of rich, chunky fruit; **Ch Larcis-Ducasse** a fairly quick-maturing, easy-drinking wine; fragrant enough; sweet, soft fruit – I suspect much Merlot – pleasant but a little unconvincing; **Ch Larrivet-Haut-Brion** opaque core; good fruit, opened up well; crisp, nice wine, overall dry; **Ch Latour-Martillac** soft, sweet and easy; **Ch Lynch-Moussas** impressively deep; fragrant, spicy; distinctive, citrus touch, good ripe fruit. Oaky; **Ch Malartic-Lagravière** deceptively big though initially understated, settling into a light, easy style; **Ch Marquis de Terme** well made. Broad, soft, fleshy; **Ch Olivier** distinctive. Surprisingly good sweetness, flavour and length; **Ch Pavie** scent of box hedge; lightish style, charm; **Ch Pontet-Canet** very good – tempted to say surprisingly good. Attractive nose; lovely crisp fruit, lean but lissom; **Ch Prieuré-Lichine** still fairly deep; sweet, good fruit. A good Prieuré; **Ch Rauzan-Gassies** good nose, rich, spicy; positive on palate; crisp, touch of coarseness and slight astringency; and **Ch La Tour Haut-Brion** sweet, distinctive; much softer and sweeter than expected.

1997 ★★ to ★★★

A useful vintage, for pleasant-enough drinking while giving more time for the '95s, even the '89s, to mature further and, of course, before the better, younger, vintages. The hottest spring for half a century caused premature but prolonged budbreak and uneven conditions. Flowering was also very early – but this was also extended and uneven. May was cool and wet which caused *coulure* and *millerandage*, both reducing potential crop size. Hot and sunny for the second half of August and through the unusually early but prolonged harvest, late-picked Cabernet Sauvignon being particularly successful. Do not keep the wines too long.

Ch Lafite One of the best '97s. Most recently, a magnum: fragrant; soft, agreeable, drinking well. *Last tasted Aug 2003* ★★★ *Drink soon, before it loses its charm.*

Ch Latour Virtually opaque; good cedary fragrance; sweet, lean with rough texture. Otherwise showing well. *Last tasted Nov 2005* ★★(★) *Now–2012.*

Ch Margaux A difficult year – strict selection for the *grand vin*. Most recently: cherry-like fragrance; dry, touch of coffee/mocha. Attractive. *Last tasted Nov 2001* ★★(★★) *Now–2012.*

Ch Mouton-Rothschild A small crop, 55% selected for the *grand vin*, the smallest percentage ever. Most recently: fragrant, crisp, dry finish. *Last noted Nov 2001* ★★(★★) *Now–2016.*

Ch Haut-Brion Showing very well: soft, attractive fruit, good length. *Nov 2001* ★★★ *Now–2015.*

Ch Ausone Good crisp fruit but still very tannic. A very good Ausone. *Last noted Nov 2001* ★★★(★) *Now–2016.*

Ch Cheval Blanc An *impériale*: deep, velvety; sweet, not very clear-cut but attractive nose; sweet, fleshy, fair extract, with some of Cheval Blanc's irresistible charm but lacking finesse. *Last tasted March 2005* ★★★★ *Now–2012.*

Ch Pétrus Plummy-coloured; better flavour than nose to which I had given my lowest points. Better on palate, medium-sweet, rather coarse fruit. *Last tasted March 2001* ★★(★) *Now–2015.*

Ch L'Angélus Bright cherry; *mélange* of fruit and new oak; fairly rich, full, nice weight, attractive. *Last tasted April 2004* ★★★ *Now–2012.*

Ch d'Angludet Deep; attractive, soft, very fruity aromas (coffee and caramel); sweet, soft fruit and tannin, delicious. *Last tasted Nov 2003* ★★★ *Now–2010.*

Ch d'Armailhac Good early notes but most recently, sadly oxidised, a poor bottle. *Last tasted April 2003. At best* ★★★ *Now–2012.*

Ch Batailley Impressively deep; intense yet mature; particularly good Cabernet fruit showing its class; sweet, mouthfilling, good fruit throughout. *Last tasted Dec 2003* ★★★ *Now–2010.*

Ch Clerc-Milon I like the crisp, fruity style. Most recently, a stab at elegance, lean, flavoury. *Last tasted Jan 2004* ★★★ *Now–2012.*

Ch La Conseillante Sweet, fragrant, whiff of mocha on nose and palate. *Last tasted April 2002* ★★★★ *Drink soon.*

Ch Cos-Labory Still youthful; herbaceous; crisp fruit, drinking quite well. *Last tasted May 2003* ★★ *Now–2010.*

Ch Coufran Impressively deep; fragrant; noticeably sweet, good fruit and flesh. Tannic. *April 1999* ★★★ *Now–2010.*

Ch Duhart-Milon In magnums: mature-looking; very fragrant, blackcurrants nose; very distinctive flavour, lean, chewy, touch of coarseness. *Last noted April 2006* ★★★ *Now–2012.*

Ch Figeac Fragrant, light style, delicious, forward. *April 1999* ★★★★ *Now–2015.*

Ch La Fleur-Pétrus Richly coloured; good nose, whiffs of tar and raspberry; good fruit, firm, stylish, refreshing acidity. *Nov 2001* ★★★ *Now–2012.*

Ch Grand-Puy-Lacoste Bought for drinking, and drinking well. Most recently: plummy, mature; rich, chewy, chaptalised, fruit; sweeter and chunkier than expected, agreeable, ready. *Last tasted Sept 2006* ★★★ *Now–2012.*

Ch Gruaud-Larose Good fruit, leaner than usual but drinking well. *Last tasted Jan 2004* ★★★ *Now–2012.*

Ch Langoa-Barton Opaque; good fruit; complete, tannic. Drinking quite well. *Last tasted Sept 2003* ★★★ *Now–2016.*

Ch Larcis-Ducasse Forward; chaptalised sweetness; ripe, rustic, but drinking well. *Last tasted April 2002* ★★ *Drink soon.*

Ch Léoville-Barton Soft red-brown, tailing away; better than appearance suggests, mellow, sweaty tannins, agreeable and ready. *Last tasted Nov 2006* ★★★ *Drink up.*

Ch Léoville-Poyferré Improvements at the château evident, particularly in vintages like 1997. Most recently: deep, intense, velvety; crisp, refreshing Cabernet aroma; more 'modern' style, lean, tannic, needed food. *Last tasted March 2005* ★★(★★) *Now– 2016.*

Ch Lynch-Bages From the start one of the most attractive of the '97s. Most recently: typical lively Cabernet Sauvignon aroma and flavour. Refreshingly attractive. *Last tasted April 2004* ★★★★ *Now–2012.*

Ch La Mondotte An astonishing wine. Opaque, the appearance of a great vintage; equally massive and rich on the palate, and tannic. Very good indeed. A new hand on the tiller. *Last tasted April 2006* ★★(★★) *Now–?*

Ch Palmer Most recently: a chocolatey-mocha nose. A touch of leanness yet chunky, and very dry finish. Nevertheless, a wine of ssome charm. *Last tasted March 2002* ★★(★) *Drink up.*

Ch Pavie Very fragrant and attractive. *April 1999* ★★★ *Now–2010.*

Ch Pichon-Longueville Sweet, easy, very drinkable. *Last tasted Feb 2005* ★★★ *Now–2010.*

Ch Rauzan-Ségla Most recently: attractive, soft-fruit nose; sweet, stylish, but lean and tannic. A good '97. *Last tasted Sept 2003* ★★(★) *Now–2012.*

Ch Troplong-Mondot Maturing; good, fragrant Merlot aroma; touch of sweetness, fleshy yet very dry finish. Drinking well. *Last tasted March 2005* ★★★ *Now–2010.*

Vieux Ch Certan Very distinctive mocha-like nose; good fruit, attractive, silky tannins yet a somewhat raw finish. On balance, a good '97. *Last tasted Oct 2002* ★★(★) *Now–2010.*

OTHER MAINLY 3-STAR '97S TASTED AROUND 2000 and ready to be drunk soon unless otherwise indicated: **Ch Beauséjour-Bécot**; **Ch Beychevelle**; **Ch Branaire** (formerly Branaire-Ducru); **Ch Brane-Cantenac**; **Ch Calon-Ségur**; **Ch Canon**; **Ch Canon-La-Gaffelière** ; **Ch Cantenac-Brown**; **Carruades de Lafite**; **Ch Chasse-Spleen**; **Dom de Chevalier**; **Ch Citran**; **Ch Clinet** ★★★★ *now–2012*; **Ch Cos d'Estournel** ★★(★★) *now–2012*; **Ch La Croix-de-Gay**; **Ch Croizet-Bages**; **Ch Dassault**; **Ch La Dominique**; **Ch Ducru-Beaucaillou**; **Ch L'Église-Clinet** ★★★★ *now–2020*; **Ch L'Évangile**; **Ch Gazin** *now–2015*; **Ch Haut-Batailley**; **Ch Kirwan**; **Ch Lafon-Rochet** *now–2012*; **Ch Lagrange** *now–2015*; **Ch La Lagune** ★★; **Ch Larmande** *now–2012*; **Ch Larrivet-Haut-Brion** *now–2012*; **Ch Léoville-Las-Cases** ★★★★ *now–2016*; **Ch Lynch-Moussas**; **Ch Magdelaine**; **Ch Marquis de Terme**; **Ch La Mission Haut-Brion** *now–2015*; **Ch Montrose** ★★★(★) *now–2015*; **Ch Pape-Clément** *now–2012*; **Ch Pavie-Decesse**; **Ch Petit-Village**; **Ch Pichon-Lalande** ★★?; **Ch Pontet-Canet**; **Ch Rauzan-Gassies**; **Ch Siran** *now–2012*; **Ch Smith-Haut-Lafitte**;

Ch Talbot; **Ch Tertre-Rôteboeuf**; **Ch La Tour-Carnet** ★★; **Ch La Tour Haut-Brion**; and **Ch Trotanoy** ★★★(★) *now–2012*.

1998 ★★ to ★★★★

Variable, like so many recent Bordeaux vintages; but, as always in less than perfect weather conditions, so much depends on the foresight and skill of individual château proprietors and/or their winemakers. Though consultant enologists provide useful advice, particularly in difficult vintages, they can have a noticeably unifying effect on the style of wine produced.

The spring was dry, sunny and warm, encouraging early budbreak. April was cold and wet, May beneficial (one of the earliest flowerings of the decade), June erratic and August was too dry and too hot with scorching temperatures which shrivelled the leaves and grilled the grapes, inhibiting sap rise. September was a roller coaster: good weather, storms and sunshine in the second half. The early-ripening Merlot was picked before heavy rains in October, Pomerol and St-Émilion benefiting. The Médocs were uneven with high Cabernet tannins. Overall, the second largest crop this century.

Ch Lafite Plummy-coloured; good fruit, waxy, 'honeycomb' nose that sweetened in the glass; agreeable though with tooth-gripping tannin. Good future. *Last tasted March 2006* (★★★★) *2010–2025*.

Ch Latour Opaque; dumb at first then lovely fruit; dry, full-bodied, on the lean side, good length. I preferred the '97 but time will tell. *March 1999* (★★★) *2010–2025?*

Ch Margaux Fairly deep, plummy-purple; sweet entry, dry finish, good fruit. More recently: similar description though; given time in the glass, a great whoosh of fruit and oak, within an hour a touch of caramel, after three hours positively exotic. Crisp, dry and fruity. *Last tasted Nov 2000* (★★★★) *2010–2025*.

Ch Mouton-Rothschild Dark; fragrant, full of potentially exotic fruit; touch of sweetness, crisp, fine flavour, very tannic. Interesting, long haul. *Last tasted June 2007* (★★★★) *2010–2025*.

Ch Haut-Brion Very deep; classic, unready. Seriously good. *Last tasted June 2007* (★★★★) *Now–2020*.

Ch Ausone Opaque core, still a youthful purple; low-keyed, soft, fairly fleshy; dry, firm; despite appearance a relatively light style, good length, silky, leathery tannins. *Jan 2005* ★★★(★) *Now–2016*.

Ch Cheval Blanc Impressively deep; herbaceous, vegetal nose, 'thick' cherry, later very pronounced mocha; sweet, soft, crisp, mouthfilling yet still raw and very tannic. Not exactly a charmer – yet. *Last tasted Jan 2006* (★★★★) *Now–2016*.

Ch d'Armailhac Deep, velvety; oaky; lean, flavoury, overall dry, crisp fruit, softer tannins. *Last noted June 2007* ★★(★) *Now–2015*.

Ch Batailley Healthy, relaxed, open appearance; one bottle corky, the second with pleasant, vanillin, 'wholemeal biscuit' nose; good flavour, perfect weight. Dependable as always. *Last tasted April 2006* ★★★ *Now–2012*.

Ch Clerc-Milon Fragrant, oaky; sweet, fleshy, attractive. *June 2007* ★★★(★) *Now–2012*.

Ch La Conseillante Most attractive fruit and flavour, well put together, good texture and elegance. *Last tasted Oct 2006* ★★★(★) *Now–2015*.

Ch Duhart-Milon Plummy-coloured; scent of very strong coffee; surprisingly sweet, flavoury and soft, despite its tannins. Coffee, or mocha, omnipresent. *Last tasted June 2005* ★★★(★) *Now–2012?*

Ch L'Enclos Good. Rich, stylish. *Last tasted Feb 2006* ★★★(★) *Now–2012.*

Ch Feytit-Clinet Impressively deep, plummy, starting to mature; delicious bouquet, sweet, ripe, exceptionally attractive fruit; good fruit and flesh, refreshing acidity, lovely wine. *Last tasted Oct 2003* ★★★★ *Now–2010.*

Ch Fombrauge Advanced maturity; not very distinctive nose; some sweetness, attractive, quick developer. *May 2003* ★★★ *Now–2010.*

Ch Gruaud-Larose One of the best '98s: full, rich, fragrant, fairly sweet. Easy drinking yet still tannic. *Last tasted Aug 2001* ★★★(★) *Now–2020.*

Ch Haut-Bailly The best-ever crop of Merlot (41% in the final blend). Interesting texture, drinking well. *Last tasted April 2006* ★★(★★) *Now–2015.*

Ch Lafleur Plummy-coloured; sweet, meaty, developing after an hour an extraordinary explosion of ripe mulberries; medium-sweet, chocolatey, chewy, texture a little coarse for a top Pomerol. *Sept 2004* ★★(★★) *Now–2015.*

Ch Léoville-Barton Always a class act. Most recently: rich purple robe; initially subdued but opened up, rich, with almost butterscotch sweetness on palate and finish. Tannic, oaky. *Last tasted Oct 2001* ★★(★★) *Now–2020.*

Ch Léoville-Las-Cases Deep, intense colour; spicy, oaky nose, whiff of mocha; dry, impressive, but fairly austere and very tannic. *Dec 2003* ★(★★★) *2010–2020.*

Ch Léoville-Poyferré Still deep, intense but maturing; Merlot fleshiness on nose and palate. Sweet, good flavour, but lacking length. *Last tasted April 2005* ★★(★) *Now–2012?*

Ch La Mission Haut-Brion Youthful; fragrant, good fruit and depth, became more tarry in the glass; substantial, full of fruit, oak, good length, dry finish. *Oct 2001* ★★(★★) *2010–2025.*

Ch Montrose Deep; sweet, rustic, then developing delicious fruit; dry, well-structured, spicy, attractive. A good '98. *March 2004* ★★(★★) *Now–2016 or beyond.*

Ch Nenin Lovely chestnut-shaded colour; distinctive, attractive bouquet; sweet entry, fleshy, elegant, silky Pomerol tannins. *April 2005* ★★★(★) *Now–2012.*

Ch Pavie Over the top, too tarry. Scarcely drinkable. *Last tasted June 2003. Not for me. Possibly* ★★(★★) *for some.*

Ch Phélan-Ségur Impressively deep, starting to mature; sweet, soft fruit aromas; good flavour but touch of stalkiness, fairly tannic. *Last tasted March 2005* ★(★★) *Now–2012.*

Ch Pichon-Lalande A total contrast to the Pichon-Longueville. Good fruit, very agreeable, still tannic of course. *Last tasted Oct 2000* ★★★(★) *Now–2016.*

Ch Pichon-Longueville Still very deep and youthful-looking; high-toned nose; crisp fruit, lean, very flavoury, but lacking charm. *Last tasted Feb 2005* ★★(★) *Now–2012.*

Ch Pontet-Canet Still with distinctive whiff of tar on the nose but rich, complete, good wine. ★★★(★)? *Now–2015.*

Ch Rauzan-Ségla Dark, core like black treacle; sweet, sweaty (tannins) cheese rind nose, developing a spicy, curranty, scent; a perfect food wine, richly flavoured, tannic, mouth-drying finish. *Last tasted March 2003* ★★(★★) *Now–2016.*

Ch du Tertre Very sweet, very oaky nose; curious tarry taste. Hard. Uncompromising. *Last tasted March 2004* (★★) *Might it come round?*

Ch Tertre-Rôteboeuf I cannot help admiring François Mitjavile and his concentrated, fruity 'cult' wine. *March 2001* ★★(★★) *Now–?*

Ch La Tour-Carnet Under new ownership this wine has much improved. Fairly deep, youthful; touch of iron and new oak; flavoury but still raw. *Last tasted May 2003* ★(★★) *Now–2012*.

Ch La Tour-de-By My favourite (Bas) Médoc wine for everyday drinking. Most recently: fragrant, almost raspberry-like fruit; rich, chunky, masked tannin, doing well. *Last tasted May 2005* ★★★ *Now–2010*.

SELECTED '98s LAST TASTED IN 1999, 2000 AND 2001 – all 3-star, unless otherwise stated: **Ch Angélus** (this was the year the L' was dropped from the name.) Very deep; a spicy, oaky, tannic wine but full of fruit. *Now–2012*; **Ch d'Angludet** deep, distinctive, crisp, flavoury. Still tannic, with oaky aftertaste. *Now–2015*; **Ch Beauséjour-Bécot** deep, velvety; attractive fruit and sweet, light style. *Now–2010*; **Ch Beychevelle** fragrant, cedary; lean, firm, positive yet unexciting. *Time will tell*; **Ch Branaire** touch of liquorice, cedar, rich, chunky, oaky, tannic (★★★★); **Ch Brane-Cantenac** curiously fragrant; attractive, lean, spicy, silky tannins (★★★★) *Now–2015*; **Ch Canon** fragrant; good flesh and length. Very tannic. *Now–2012*; **Ch Canon-La-Gaffelière** deep velvety-purple in its youth; fascinating nose, sweet touch of violets. Nice weight. Lean and aristocratic (★★★★) *Now–2015*; **Ch Cantemerle** *Now–2015*; **Ch Cantenac-Brown** fragrant, spicy; good fruit, crisp, a touch lean. *Now–2015*; **Ch Cap de Mourlin** very deep, velvety; rich, forthcoming nose; open-knit, good fruit and flesh. *Now–2010*; **Ch Carbonnieux** normally light, firmer than usual. Good. *Drink soon*; **Ch Chasse-Spleen** always dependable, interesting, good fruit and grip. *Now–2012*; **Dom de Chevalier** distinctive, stylish; fairly sweet and rich, flavoury, tannic ★★★(★) *Now–2015*; **Ch Citran** fruit, flesh, lean but good flavour and length *Now–2012*; **Ch Clinet** rich, malty, tarry; full, rich, spicy. Very tannic. Impressive but not my style. *Now–2012*; **Ch Cos Labory** unusually deep and impressive. *Now–2012*; **Ch Coufran** Merlot fruitiness, well made, complete. *Now–2012*; **Ch Croizet-Bages** dependable Cabernet Sauvignon fruit and flesh. *Now–2012*; **Ch La Dominique** rich 'legs'; distinctive fragrance, slightly metallic; fruity, chewy, good flesh, tannic ★★★(★) *Now–2012*; **Ch Durfort-Vivens** rich, chewy, tannic. *Now–2015*; **Ch Ferrière** recent improvements noticeable. Very oaky, fragrant, attractive. *Now–2012*; **Ch Figeac** distinctive, flavoury and fragrant as always; sweet, easy, some delicacy and charm ★★★(★) *Now–2012*; **Clos Fourtet** fragrant, complete, good texture. *Now–2012*; **Ch La Gaffelière** classic. Complete. Oaky, spicy. *Now–2012*; **Ch Gazin** curious, tea-like, minty nose; soft fruit, silky textured. *Now–2015*; **Ch Giscours** fragrant, spicy (cloves), touch of tar and mandarin; very sweet, rich, dominated by a lean, dry, oaky finish. Needs time. ★★(★★) *Now–2020*; **Ch Greysac** one of the most dependable of the (Bas) Médocs. Good flavour, early drinking. *Now–2009*; **Ch Kirwan** some might say 'renaissance', certainly new style and impressive: deep; oaky, concentrated; sweet, full of fruit, chewy. More masculine assertiveness than Margaux feminine charm ★★★(★)? *2009–2015*; **Ch Lafon-Rochet** much more amenable than the austere style which used to remind me of its concrete cellar. Curious privet-like nose but attractive flavour. *Now–2012*; **Ch Lagrange** (St-Julien) curious fragrance; very oaky, astringent. *Now–2015*; **Ch Langoa-Barton** fragrant; good fruit and grip. ★★(★★) *Now–2015*; **Ch Larcis-Ducasse** sweet fruit and oak. Attractive. *Now–2010*; **Ch Larmande** very fragrant, fruity, spicy. *Now–2010*; **Ch Larrivet-Haut-Brion** opaque; full, rich, fruity, soft, yet raw finish. *Now–2010*; **Ch Latour-Martillac** good fruit but austere. *Now–2010*; **Ch Lynch-Bages** very deep; rich, brambly Cabernet Sauvignon aroma; full of fruit and character, but new oak rather intrusive. Need to give it breathing space. ★★(★★) *Now–2016*; **Ch Lynch- Moussas** sweet, soft, open-knit, early developer. ★(★) *Now–2010*; **Ch Magdelaine** soft, chewy, easy. *Now–2010*; **Ch Malescot-St-Exupéry** distinctive blackberry-like Cabernet Sauvignon, austere, tannic. *Now–2015*; **Ch Monbrison** deep, rich, crisp fruit, tannic, good length. *Now–2012*; **Ch Les Ormes-de-Pez** reliably attractive. *Now–2012*; **Ch Palmer** deep, plummy; spicy, chocolatey; sweet, rich, approachable. *Now–2015*; **Ch Pape-Clément** with the distinctive taste of tar and tobacco associated with wines from the Talence commune. Fragrant. Once again making good wine ★★★(★) *Now–2015*; **Ch Pavie-Decesse** nose like brown sugar, fragrant in its way; attractive flavour and weight but very tannic. *Now–2012*; **Ch Petit-Village** rich, soft texture, attractive. *Now–2015*; **Ch La Pointe** rich, very flavoury, good texture, loose knit. *Now–2012*; **Ch Prieuré-Lichine** deep; sweet scented; not as lean as in the past but still a touch of piquancy. Good fruit, flavoury. *Now–2012*; **Ch Rauzan-Gassies** big improvement. For so long underperforming. Fragrant, attractive, some leanness and astringency. *Now–2015*; **Ch Siran** good mouthful, positive, spicy oaky flavour and aftertaste. *Now–2012*; **Ch Smith-Haut-Lafitte** redolent of mocha, chocolate, tobacco; rich extract. *Now–2012*; **Ch Talbot** very much in the customary Talbot style, rich but rustic; very attractive fruit, flesh, silky, leathery tannins. Good wine. ★★(★★) *Now–2015*; and **Vieux Ch Certan** sweet, soft, spicy; somewhat light character, attractive, dry finish. *Now–2012*.

1999 ★★ to ★★★★

Over the past few years far more attention has been given to vine management for, as they say, good wine can only be made from good grapes. That good grapes could be produced at the end of a growing season like 1999 is little short of a miracle. For some it was one of the most difficult years in memory. Budburst took place in abnormal heat. April and May were also very hot, but humidity necessitated advanced spraying. Exceptional heat in the latter part of May encouraged premature flowering. The first part of June was stormy and caused some *coulure*, but was very hot right through to the end of July. August was variable, delaying the *véraison*, but the three weeks which led up to 5 September were ideal – dry and warm. This was rudely interrupted by a severe thunderstorm and a swathe of devastating hail from Libourne to St-Émilion. Who managed to make good wine this year? In short, those who sprayed in time, green pruned, sorted the grapes and selected the best vats.

Ch Lafite Sweet, fleshy, youthful aroma; dry, undemonstrative with but good mouthfeel and silky tannins. An attractive future. *Last tasted May 2006* (★★★★) *2015–2030*.

Ch Latour Classic Latour. Impressively deep, opaque core; fragrant; sweet, full-bodied, rich 'mocha' new oak, very tannic. *Last tasted May 2003* (★★★★★) *2015–2025*.

Ch Margaux Sadly, just a swift but still appreciative taste; fragrant, sweet, chewy. *Last noted Oct 2005* (★★★★) *2015–2025.*

Ch Mouton-Rothschild An *impériale*: lovely colour, deep of course; very distinctive, ripe Cabernet/blackcurrant aroma, sweet, harmonious; fairly sweet on the palate, mouthfilling flavour, touch of tar, lip-licking acidity, masked tannin. *Last tasted July 2005* (★★★★) *2012–2025.*

Ch Haut-Brion Considered the best since the '89s and '90s. Fragrant, touch of sweetness, silky tannins, good acidity. *Last tasted Sept 2003* (★★★★) *Now–2025.*

Ch Ausone Plummy colour, opaque core; rich, slightly singed biscuity/dried leaves nose; sweet, soft, notably rich, fullish flavour, ripe, tannic finish. Good wine. *Jan 2005* (★★★★) *Now–2020.*

Ch Cheval Blanc Unusually deep, virtually opaque; low-keyed, but fragrant and oaky on nose and palate. Ripe, fleshy, dry finish. Impressive. *April 2000* (★★★★) *2010–2030.*

Ch d'Agassac One of the prettiest moated châteaux in the Médoc. Very deep but an early developer; not very distinctive nose; sweet, open-knit, crisp fruit. *Last tasted Oct 2004* ★★(★) *Now–2012.*

Ch Batailley Deep black cherry, lovely nose, good fruit, touch of cedar, no harsh edges; soft entry, nice weight, crisp, brambly fruit; refreshing, impressive. *Last tasted April 2006* ★★(★★) *Now–2012.*

Ch Beauséjour-Bécot Consistently making one of the most agreeable and stylish St-Émilions. Good flavour, length and tannins. *Last tasted Aug 2004* ★(★★) *Now–2012.*

Ch Beychevelle Medium, luminous; very rich, complex nose and flavour. Sweet, 'mocha', fruity. *Last tasted Aug 2004* ★★★ *Now–2015.*

Ch de Camensac Deep; good fruit; pleasing, nice flesh, dry, slightly astringent finish. *Last tasted April 2006* ★(★★) *Now–2012.*

Ch Clerc-Milon Sweet, fleshy fruit. Attractive and refreshing. *Last tasted March 2006* ★★★ *Now–2012.*

Ch Coufran Deep but maturing; delicious, raspberry-like soft fruit nose; Merlot softness and sweetness, good body and balance. *Last tasted May 2004* ★★★ *Now–2012.*

Ch Durfort-Vivens Rich, dark cherry; sweet nose, sweaty tannins; good flavour, flesh, chunky fruit, oaky, meaty, tannic finish. *Last tasted April 2004* ★★(★) *Now–2012.*

Ch Feytit-Clinet Rich colour, showing some maturity; very agreeable, distinctive, tar, liquorice nose; sweet entry, good fruit, firm mid-palate, dry finish. *Last tasted June 2004* ★★(★) *Now–2012.*

Ch Gruaud-Larose Deep but not intense, signs of early development; good, distinctive fruit; lovely flavour, fleshy fruit and style. Ready now – at least, with food. *Last tasted April 2005* ★★(★★) *Now–2016.*

Ch Léoville-Poyferré Once again approaching the style and elegance of the days of former glory. Most recently: impressively deep though quietly maturing, a soft 'conker' colour; lovely nose. Sweet, soft fruit and tannins; very sweet on the palate, good length, dry finish. A delicious wine. *Last tasted April 2005* ★★(★★) *Now–2016.*

Ch La Mission Haut-Brion Opaque, intense, still immature; singed, earthy nose with whiff of coffee, yet soft and fruity; delicious, similar notes to nose but swingeingly tannic. Needs food – and more time. *Last tasted Sept 2004* (★★★★) *2010–2020.*

Ch Paveil-de-Luze Very deep; crisp fruit; sweet, agreeably soft and pleasant early drinking. *March 2004* ★★★ *Drink up.*

Ch Pichon-Longueville Medium-deep, showing some advanced maturity; 'mocha' nose, low percentage of Cabernet Sauvignon for a Pauillac (just 58%); sweet, soft for a '99, touch of rusticity and tannins. *Last tasted Feb 2005* ★★(★) *Now–2015?*

Ch Rauzan-Ségla Continuing its renaissance. Impressively deep ruby; harmonious, low-keyed nose, firm, good fruit; sweet, ripe, pleasing texture, very dry finish. *Last tasted March 2003* ★★★(★) *Now–2016.*

Ch Talbot Sweet, singed, very oaky; fairly rich, fullish, chunky chewy fruit, slightly coarse texture. Tannic. *Last tasted April 2006* ★★(★) *Now–2012.*

SELECTED '99S LAST TASTED IN 2002 OR EARLIER:

Ch Angélus Packed with fruit and flavour. Very tannic. (★★★★) *Now–2012.*

Ch d'Angludet Very distinctive; good flesh and fruit. Silky leathery tannins. ★★(★) *Now–2012.*

Ch d'Armailhac Deep, cedary, fleshy; very good fruit. A deliciously flavoury wine with flair. *Last tasted March 2001* (★★★★) *Now–2015.*

Ch Bouscaut A fragrant, sweet and easy Graves. (★★★) *Now–2012.*

Ch Branaire Blackberry-like fragrance. Good fruit. A bit lean. Very tannic finish. Most recently, holding back but good power. *Aug 2001* (★★★) *Now–2015.*

Ch Brane-Cantenac Style continuously evolving. Full of fruit, oak and tannin. (★★★★) *Now–2015.*

Ch Canon A sweet, easy style ★★★ *Now–2012.*

Ch Canon-La-Gaffelière Extraordinarily high-toned, unusual scent, touch of tea; sweet, good flavour, but lean, no more than a hint of elegance but certainly impressive ★★(★) *possibly* ★★★★ *in due course. Now–2015.*

Ch Cantemerle Attractive but lacking its former elegance ★★★ *Now–2015.*

Ch Cantenac-Brown Sweet fruit; oak and tannin ★(★★) *Now–2015.*

Carruades de Lafite A forthcoming, cedary nose; soft ripe fruit; stylish ★★★ *Now–2012.*

Ch Chasse-Spleen Good fruit, and with the length so often lacking in *bourgeois* Médocs ★★★★ *Now–2012.*

Dom de Chevalier An easy style, lighter than expected, also (tasted blind recently) a bit lean, good but with a touch of astringency. Time will tell. *Aug 2001* (★★★) *Now–2015.*

Ch Citran Fruit, good follow-through and finish ★★★ *Now–2012.*

Ch La Conseillante Not deep in colour, not overladen with extract, much easier yet with refreshing tannin and acidity ★★★(★) *(just) Now–2012.*

Ch Dassault Impressive ★★★ *Now–2012.*

Ch Dauzac Very sweet, fruit, extract and lashings of oak ★★★ *Now–2012.*

Ch Ducru-Beaucaillou Hard to pin down in its early days in cask yet showing class. Elegant future predicted (★★★★) *Now–2020.*

Ch Duhart-Milon Very fragrant, saplings and greengages; ripe fruit and grip. *April 2000* (★★★) *Now–2012.*

Ch de Ferrande A somewhat underestimated Graves. Attractive ★★★ *Now–2010.*

Ch de Fieuzal Good, crisp, flavoury Graves. *April 2000* ★★★ *Now–2010*.

Ch Figeac Some problem here. Strange overtones which, hopefully, will wear off. *Must retaste.*

Les Forts de Latour Forthcoming; sweet, soft, already developing attractively. *March 2001* ★★★ *Now–2012*.

Clos Fourtet Once such a dull wine, now fragrant, fruity and soft ★★(★★) *Now–2010*.

Ch La Gaffelière Fragrant, fruity, singed and sooty. Sweet. Soft with that touch of acidity which, over the years, I have often noted ★(★★) *Now–2010*.

Ch Gazin Deep, velvety; sweet, attractive, forward ★(★★) *Now–2010*.

Ch Giscours Richly coloured, sweet, attractive. Citrus-tinged acidity. Fair potential ★★(★) *Now–2015*.

Ch Haut-Bailly A consistently well made, stylish wine, one of my favourite Pessac-Léognans – no exaggeration, no speciousness, just extremely good. *Last tasted June 2001* ★★★★ *Now–2016*.

Ch Haut-Batailley The most consistently elegant and charming of the Borie family's Pauillacs, exemplified by their '99. *April 2000* ★★★★ *Now–2016*.

Ch Kirwan Rich, tarry, black treacle nose. Sweet, fleshy, intense. Very good in its way but a bit over the top (★★★)? *Now–2015?*

Ch Lafon-Rochet Mint and privet; soft, fruity, oaky, tannic ★(★★) *Now–2015*.

Ch Lagrange (St-Julien) Interesting flavour, crisp fruit, very dry finish. Needs time. *Aug 2001* ★(★★) *Now–2015*.

Ch La Lagune The '99 no longer as idiosyncratic as in the past. Will make an attractive bottle ★(★★) *Now–2015*.

Ch Langoa-Barton Unyielding in its youth. A wine of substance yet a touch of leanness, and very dry (★★)? *Now–2016*.

Ch Larcis-Ducasse I have woken up to this slightly neglected St-Émilion château. Like many others tasted from the cask in the spring after the vintage, wines with young fruit can have winning ways ★(★★) *Now–2015*.

Ch Larmande The results of new outside investment are plain to see – and taste. Now impressively rich. An agreeable mouthful ★★★ *Now–2010*.

Ch Lascombes Certainly a very positive wine, with lots of grip but a touch of rawness which, I hope, will wear off (★★★)? *Now–2015*.

Ch Léoville-Barton A superb '99. Very good, rich mocha nose and flavour. Good flesh, very oaky and tannic. *Last tasted Oct 2001* ★★★★ *2010–2020*.

Ch Lynch-Bages One is rarely disappointed; indeed I usually have a tingle of anticipation. Typically spicy fruit. *Last tasted May 2001* ★★(★★) *Now–2020*.

Ch Lynch-Moussas Deep, mature rim; taut but fragrant, scent of Pauillac 'oyster shells'; straightforward, dry finish. *Last noted Aug 2001* ★★(★)? *Now–2010*.

Ch Malescot-St-Exupéry 'Very Malescot' blackcurrant aroma; somewhat specious fruit but a lot of flavour. Very tannic (★★★) *Now–2014*.

Ch Palmer Half the crop declassified. The *grand vin* gloriously velvety; intensely fragrant; surprisingly sweet, spicy. *April 2000* ★★★(★) *Now–2020*.

Ch Pape-Clément Once again, one of the stars of Pessac-Léognan. Very ripe yet high strength ★★(★★) *Now–2015*.

Ch Pavie Opaque; tarry, liquorice; fairly powerful, concentrated, singed with a finish of tar and tannin. It will be most interesting to see how this turns out (★★) for me, (★★★★) for some.

Ch Pichon-Lalande A higher percentage of Merlot (47%) than Cabernet Sauvignon (37%) – unusual for a Pauillac wine – soft, yielding fleshy fruit which masked considerable tannin and acidity. *Last tasted Aug 2001* (★★★★) *Now–2016.*
Ch Pontet-Canet Good fruit but extremely tannic (★★★) *2009–2020.*
Ch Prieuré-Lichine Change of style (new winemaker). Very deep, opaque core; spicy fruit, minty fragrance; surprisingly rich and positive, chewy. A turn for the better? *Last tasted March 2001* ★★★(★)? *Now–2012.*
Ch Rauzan-Gassies Changes continue here too. At first I disliked the tarry, molasses nose, but the following year I thought it had simmered down. Crisp. Very tannic ★(★★) *Now–2012.*
Ch Valandraut Opaque, intense, velvety; very good fruit; sweet, impressively highish alcohol (13.5%). Unfined, unfiltered, unwanted (by me) though I can see its attractions. *Nov 2005* ★★★★ *in its way. Now–?*
Vieux Ch Certan Very good wine, soft ruby; very rich, fragrant nose; sweet, surprisingly easy despite tannin. Good length ★★★ *Now–2015.*
Ch Yon-Figeac Rich nose, extract, oak, touch of rusticity; medium sweetness and body, full fruit flavour, chewy, soft, tannic, oaky finish. *Aug 2002* ★★★ *Now–2010.*

2000–2005

This was certainly an interesting period: a satisfactory millennium vintage, an atypical (2003), ending with an almost perfect but very high-priced 2005. The demand from the world's super rich for Bordeaux's first growths and the fashionable 'super-seconds' seems inexhaustible. This leaves a plethora of less well-known châteaux of perfectly accessible vintages like 2001 and 2002 of excellent value, and the 2004, initially a bargain, for serious drinkers to lay down, now being more fully appreciated. Another ongoing trend is 'to move with the times' by producing even top quality wines for the global market: deeply coloured, packed with ripe fruit, high alcohol and soft tannins. Blockbusters instead of finesse.

VINTAGES AT A GLANCE
Outstanding ★★★★★ 2000 (v), 2005
Very Good ★★★★ 2000 (v), 2002 (v), 2003, 2004
Good ★★★ 2000 (v), 2001, 2002 (v)

2000 ★★★ to ★★★★★
Unsurprisingly, the 2000 vintage was eagerly awaited with a combination of hope and anxiety; merchants anticipated substantial trade to mark the millennium. In the event, most people were reasonably satisfied.

The growing season, as always in Bordeaux, was by no means straight-forward. The New Year and spring were mild, with above-average temperatures in March, resulting in early budbreak. However, though the warmth continued in April and May, it was wet, flowering starting at the end of the month. The damp conditions continued through a depressingly cloudy and humid June and July. What saved the day was almost unbroken sunshine without rain from August through September, resulting in fine ripening conditions favouring the Merlot and, for those who waited and timed it right, Cabernet Sauvignon. Unquestionably, this was a very good year, fairly uniform in quality with some really outstanding wines.

Ch Lafite Impressive depth and colour, velvety sheen, long 'legs'; very sweet, delicious, fragrant aroma; fairly sweet on the palate, very crisp, perfect weight (12.5%), attractive. Great future. *Last tasted March 2006* ★(★★★★) 2010–2023.

Ch Latour Lovely colour, deep, velvety; delicious nose, sweet, spicy, forthcoming, almost caramelly richness packed with fruit; lovely flavour and balance, tannic. Great future. *Last tasted May 2006* (★★★★★) 2012–2030.

Ch Margaux Fairly deep, relaxed; very good, fragrant, whiff of coffee; medium-sweet, attractive but very tannic. *Last tasted May 2006* ★★★(★★) 2016–2020.

Ch Mouton-Rothschild Although deep, the most mature-looking of the first-growth Médocs; fully evolved, distinct, 'mocha', chocolatey, lovely but 'unclassic' Mouton nose; dry, very flavoury, touch of vanilla, crisp Cabernet Sauvignon taste, quite a bite. *Last tasted Oct 2005* ★★(★★★) 2010–2025.

Ch Haut-Brion Richly coloured, showing some maturity; slightly singed, earthy, very sweet – almost brown-sugar nose; full flavoured but dry, lean, fine tannins, great length. *Last tasted May 2006* ★★(★★★) 2010–2020.

Ch Ausone Alain Vauthier's 'dream vintage'. Very deep, velvety; initially dumb, finally opening up fragrantly, whiff of bramble and eucalyptus; seemed dry at first but, second time round, sweeter and richer. A superb Ausone. *Last tasted Jan 2005* ★★(★★★) Now–2018.

Ch Cheval Blanc Very successful vintage. Most recently: fairly deep, plummy rim; brambly fruit, whiff of vanilla and spice; perfect balance and constitution, touch of coffee (oak) and dry finish. Lovely future. *Last tasted Jan 2006* ★★(★★★) Now–2020.

Ch Pétrus Distinctive, almost unique in its character and flavour. Richly coloured, maturing; nose initially muffled, low-keyed, but harmonious and fleshy; surprisingly dry, more severe than its appearance, good length, very 'hot', dry finish. *Last tasted June 2004* ★★(★★★) 2010–2020.

Ch d'Agassac Very deep; fragrant; good for its class. *Last tasted July 2002* ★★(★) Now–2010.

Ch Batailley Dark cherry core, open rim; lovely fruit, harmonious; sweet, perfect weight, pleasant, easy flavour, masked tannins. *April 2006* ★★(★★) Now–2016.

Ch Beauséjour-Bécot Very mature appearance; oaky nose and taste. Good but drying out. *Last tasted April 2006* ★★★ Now–2010.

Ch Cantemerle Medium-deep, maturing; pleasant, slightly spicy nose; chewy fruit, easy style but dry, tannic finish. *July 2004* ★★(★★) Now–2016.

Ch La Conseillante Merlot a high 86% of the blend. Very deep, intense, rich, velvety; sweet, slightly peppery nose that opened up amazingly; medium dryness and body (13.5% alcohol on label – actual strength 13.2%), lovely and lively, delicious flavour, touch of sharpness on tongue. *Last tasted Oct 2006* ★★★(★) *Now–2015*.

Ch Haut-Batailley Many notes. Still deep, violet-rimmed; an immediacy of perfume, yet with depth, lovely ripe fruit; lean, elegant and stylish but gathering itself well for a fairly long haul. *Last tasted June 2007* ★★(★★★) *Soon–2016*.

Ch Léoville-Barton Impressive, intense, dark cherry; sweet, wholesome, mouthwatering; a serious wine, lovely fruit, perfect weight, good acidity, mouth-drying tannins. *Last tasted May 2007* ★★(★★★) *2010–2020*.

Ch Léoville-Poyferré Poyferré back on form. Impressive, intense, purple rim; rich, ripe fruit, fleshy, opening up delightfully; rich, good fruit and length. A wine with extra dimensions. *Last tasted April 2005* ★★(★★★) *2010–2020*.

Ch Malartic-Lagravière Still opaque; very sweet, fragrant Graves nose; rich, 'mocha', very tannic yet very drinkable. *Last tasted April 2003* ★★★(★) *Now–2012*.

Ch Malescot-St-Exupéry Two notes. Initially lean but flavoury. Most recently: ripe, meaty rather than varietal aroma; sweet, fairly full-flavoured, very oaky, spicy aftertaste. *Last tasted March 2004* ★★(★)? *Just possibly* ★★★(★).

Ch La Mission Haut-Brion Great future predicted. Very deep, plummy-coloured, rich 'legs'; tight and peppery at first, then earthy, mocha, developing caramel-like sweetness; on the palate, good fruit, full-flavoured, whiff of volatile acidity, good grip, masked tannin. *Last tasted June 2004* ★★★(★★) *2010–2020*.

Ch Monbrison A new Margaux star. Deep, intense, velvety, immature; very good nose, fragrant, with sweaty tannins; substantial, good fruit, hard tannic finish. Give it time. *Last tasted April 2005* (★★★★) *2010–2015?*

Ch Montrose Deep purple; good fruit, slightly scented; delicious flavour, length and finish. Very tannic. *Last tasted May 2006* ★★(★★★) *2010–2020*.

Ch Pichon-Longueville Still deep, velvety; good rich nose and flavour. Attractive wine. Good future. *Last tasted Feb 2005* ★★(★★) *2010–2020*.

Ch Rauzan-Ségla Continues its successful run of stylish, well-made wines. Very forthcoming aroma, good fruit, sweaty tannin underlay; fairly sweet, excellent weight with fragrant, slightly bitter tannin, oaky finish and aftertaste. *Last tasted May 2006* ★★(★★★) *2010–2020*. *A good, long-term wine*.

SELECTED WINES NOTED MAINLY AT THE OPENING TASTING OF 2000S IN SPRING 2001. Most of these wines have good mid-term prospects of 8–15 years unless otherwise suggested: **Ch Angélus** intense, very oaky, appealing violets scent; sweet, full, rich, concentrated fruit and oak. Out to impress, and it does. But where is the finesse? (★★★) *now–2016?*; **Ch d'Angludet** very deep; fragrant, distinctive, almost floral; a good wine (★★★) *now–2015*; **Ch d'Armailhac** immensely deep, almost black; aroma of bramble and coffee; full, fleshy but very tannic (★★★★) *2010–2015*; **Ch Belair** (St-Émilion) medium depth and intensity, sweet, fragrant fruit; similar on palate. Lean. Very dry, hard finish. *June 2001* ★★(★★) *now–2016*; **Ch Beychevelle** startling Cabernet and oak nose, bramble and spice; very positive flavour, good fruit, attractive ★★(★★) *now–2016*; **Ch Branaire** pleasant, straightforward, whiff of raspberry, opening up with pronounced vanillin scent; good fruit, nice weight, piquant finish ★★(★★) *now–2016*; **Ch Brane-Cantenac** medium-deep; good flavour and length ★★★(★) *now–2016*; **Ch Canon-La-Gaffelière** rich 'legs': fragrant, spicy; very sweet, fruity, rich but not overconcentrated. Very tannic (★★★★); **Ch Cantenac-Brown** silky tannins, chewy, very good length

★★(★★) *soon–2016;* **Carruades de Lafite** good, fresh, crisp fruit ★★(★★) *now–2018;* **Dom de Chevalier** rich, toasted oak, mocha nose and flavour; medium- to full-bodied, rich, good length ★★(★★) *now–2016;* **Ch Clerc-Milon** distinct Cabernet aroma, curious fragrance, sweaty tannins; dry, good fruit but hard tannic finish (★★★) *2010–2015;* **Ch Clinet** opaque, intense; sweet, fig-like richness and oak; fairly sweet, certainly rich, almost 'pressed', concentrated fruit and very tannic. I can see the attractions, but I have rarely liked the style. *For me* (★★★), *for admirers of Clinet* (★★★★); **Ch Cos d'Estournel** subtle, fragrant but low-keyed and harbouring sweaty, leathery tannins; sweet, almost fruit salad – delectable. Tannic of course ★(★★★) *2010–2020;* **Ch La Croix-de-Gay** deep, velvety; low-keyed, hard, slightly stalky; sweet, flavoury but taut and tannic. Impressive ★(★★★) *now–2015;* **Ch Dassault** lovely violet rim; intense, taut, brambly fruit; sweet, full-bodied, attractive flavour ★★★ *now–2012;* **Ch La Dominique** rich, brambly, sweaty tannins; fairly sweet, full, rich, loaded with all the right components ★★(★★) *now–2012;* **Ch Duhart-Milon** low-keyed, hard, unyielding; dry curious tarry/iron flavour, very tannic (★★★)? *Now–2012;* **Clos L'Église** concentrated nose and palate, sweet, packed with fruit, masked but bitter tannins ★(★★★) *now–2012;* **Ch de Fieuzal** deep, fairly intense; slightly toasted oaky nose but overall scented and attractive; rich, plenty to it, dry finish ★★★(★) *now–2012;* **Ch Figeac** very deep, though medium intensity; soft, fragrant fruit, scent of raspberry and violets; sweet, amenable, attractive, dry finish. Original and very flavoury as always ★★★(★) *now–2015;* **Ch La Fleur-Pétrus** deep, richly coloured; taut fruit, citrus whiff, opened up beautifully; sweet, lovely fruit, very tannic. *June 2001* ★★(★★★) *now–2016;* **Ch Fonplégade** Armand Moueix's last vintage. One of his best, too: very attractive fruit and depth ★★★★ *now–2012;* **Les Forts de Latour** medium intensity; crisp, a bit stalky but opened up well; surprisingly sweet, moderate flesh, but overall lean and very tannic (★★★★) *2010–2015;* **Clos Fourtet** a dry, powerful wine with good fruit and bitter tannic finish ★(★★) *Now–2012;* **Ch La Gaffelière** lean – for St-Émilion – spicy nose; dry, very distinctive, drying finish. *June 2001* ★★(★) *now–2012;* **Ch Gazin** sweet, open-knit, blackberry-like fruit; sweet, broad, open style, good fruit, oaky finish. *June 2001* (★★★★) *now–2012;* **Ch Giscours** low-keyed but good fruit; medium sweet, fleshy. Quite a lot to it ★★(★★) *now–2016;* **Ch Grand-Puy-Lacoste** lovely dark velvety core, fairly intense; very fragrant, ripe, very Pauillac Cabernet aroma; medium-dry, firm, loads of fruit and tannin (★★★★★) *a long-haul wine, say 2015–2030;* **Ch La Grave** (formerly La Grave-Trigant-de-Boisset) medium intensity; sweet fruit, whiff of raspberry (ripe Cabernet Franc, though only 15%). Sweet, amenable, attractive. *June 2001* ★★(★) *now–2016;* **Ch Gruaud-Larose** vivid mauve rim; interesting aromas of spicy fruit; very distinctive flavour, flesh and fruit ★★(★★★) *now–2020;* **Ch Haut-Bailly** only 50% of crop used for the *grand vin.* Very deep; good young fruit; dry, oaky, spicy. *June 2001* ★★★(★★) *now–2015;* **Ch Haut-Bages-Libéral** almost opaque; strange style, slightly cheesy fruit, opening up, touch of tar; medium-dry, impressive, ripe fruit and extract, very flavoury, perhaps lacking a little length ★★(★★) *now–2012?;* **Hosanna** (formerly Ch Certan-Guiraud) entrancing delicious crisp fragrance; sweet palate and most agreeable fruit. Very tannic. *June 2001* ★★(★★★) *soon–2015;* **Ch d'Issan** mauve rim; curious, as yet unknit, soft, spicy (cloves), better on palate, oaky, attractive, citrus touch ★★★ *now–2015;*

Ch Kirwan Virtually opaque; rich, brambly fruit, distinct vanillin as it opened up; rich, chocolatey, a touch of coarseness on the palate, plenty of new oak. A Michel Rolland-inspired renaissance. Is it still Margaux, though? ★★(★★) *soon–2015?*; **Ch Lafon-Rochet** medium intensity, rich 'legs'; high-toned, whiff of citrus and tar; medium-sweet, bramble-like fruit, very flavoury. A good Lafon ★★★(★) *now–2015*; **Ch Lagrange** (St-Julien) initially hard, earthy, then mocha-like; dry, very toasted mocha flavour, hefty, chewy texture ★★(★) *now–2012*; **Ch La Lagune** deep, velvety, mauve edge; initially hard and dusty but good fruit emerged; sweet, rich, fruity, easy, dry finish ★★★ *now–2012*; **Ch Langoa-Barton** opaque, intense; vivid; fragrant, slightly stalky, then a touch of tar and black treacle, opening up sweetly, almost caramelly; medium dryness and weight, straightforward fruit and oak ★★(★★) *now–2015*; **Ch Larcis-Ducasse** very forthcoming fruit and oak; attractive but lean, very oaky, bitter finish. Needs time to settle down (★★★) *now–2012*; **Ch Larrivet-Haut-Brion** deep; firm, very toasted Graves nose and taste, complete, sweet, impressive ★★★(★) *now–2012*; **Ch Lascombes** low-keyed, hard edge but interesting fragrance; very distinctive, slightly medicinal-Médoc flavour, taut dry finish ★★(★★) *2010–2015*; **Ch Latour-à-Pomerol** fairly sweet, good fruit, with typically silky texture and leathery tannic finish. *June 2001* ★★★(★★) *now–2015*; **Ch Léoville-Las-Cases** aroma of deep bramble and cedar, touch of raspberry (ripe Cabernet Franc); surprisingly sweet, ripe fruit, good length, fragrant, tannic and acid finish. Fabulous wine (★★★★★) *2010–2020*; **Ch La Louvière** harmonious, good fruit on nose and palate, sweet, slightly toasty, fleshy, well-balanced, dry tannic finish ★★★(★) *now–2012*; **Ch Lynch-Bages** good fruit but not the characteristic overt Cabernet Sauvignon aroma, though opening up with a candy-like fragrance; sweet, very attractive. Dry finish ★★★(★★) *now–2016*; **Ch Lynch-Moussas** sweet – too sweet, attractive, rather specious fruit ★★★ *drink soon*; **Ch Magdelaine** deep, fairly intense; sweet, agreeable fruit and flesh. *June 2001* ★★★(★) *now–2012*; **Ch Marquis de Terme** plummy purple; nose of newly sawn wood, very oaky, attractive fruit and flesh but searing dry finish ★(★★) *now–2012*; **Ch Les Ormes-de-Pez** opaque; curious mixture of citrus and meat on nose and palate. Very flavoury ★★(★) *now–2012*; **Ch Palmer** deep, velvety; low-keyed, mainly spicy oak; raw fruit but with good flesh and length, fairly high acidity. *Two notes in 2001* (★★★★★) *2010–2020*; **Ch Pape-Clément** the very characteristic, tobacco-like Pessac nose, refreshing citrus fruit. Very rich, flavoury, but with a very oaky end taste. Impressive though ★★(★★) *now–2015?*; **Ch Pavie** very deep, velvety; tobacco-like, sweaty tannins; sweet, full-bodied, charred and tarry taste. Impressive – but I much preferred the late Jean-Paul Valette's Pavie, which was so much more drinkable. *For me* ★★, *for wine competitions and our American cousins* (★★★★★) *drink now if you want*; **Ch Pavie-Decesse** concentrated, tarry; fairly sweet, full-bodied, good flavour but overextracted ★★★?; **Pavillon Rouge de Ch Margaux** sweet, fragrant, fleshy with Margaux charm. More dense, and totally different from previous Pavillon vintages ★★(★★) *now–2015*; **Ch Petit-Village** opaque; very distinctive, lean, oaky, fragrant, with charm; sweet, citrus-like refreshing fruit, very drying finish ★★★(★) *now–2012*; **Ch Pichon-Lalande** an unusually high percentage of very ripe late-picked Cabernet Sauvignon. Sweet, good, crisp, ripe fruit ★★★(★★) *now–2016*; **Ch Pontet-Canet** a touch of 'tar' on nose and palate. A rich, well-constituted wine with depth and length ★★(★★) *now–2012*; **Ch Prieuré-Lichine** very deep, intense; spicy, minty fragrance; not the usual lean fruit but surprisingly rich, with chewy Cabernet character ★★★(★) *now–2015*; **Ch Rauzan-Gassies** the improvement continues. Elegant fruit on the nose, touch of orange rind, then fragrant, tea-like; sweet, chewy Cabernet mid-palate. Nice wine ★★(★★) *now–2015*; **Ch Siran** virtually opaque; positive, attractive fruit; pleasant sweetness, texture, stylish richness, oaky finish. Deserves to be more highly regarded (★★★★) *almost 5-star .Now–2012*; **Ch Smith-Haut-Lafitte** sweet, very toasted oaky nose and flavour. Rich, fairly full-bodied, very tannic (★★★★); **Ch Talbot** very oaky, citrus whiff, sweet bramble; good fruit and weight. Oak very noticeable and a touch of tartness on the finish. Needs to settle down (★★★★) *2010–2015*; **Ch La Tour Haut-Brion** the mature vines have certainly produced a slightly less aggressive La Tour. Now fragrant, with lovely flavour and aftertaste. One of the best that I can recall ★★★(★) *now–2016*; **Ch Troplong-Mondot** freshly sawn wood; sweet, interesting, rich fruit, masked tannin ★★(★) *now–2017*; **Ch Trotanoy** very deep, opaque core, intense; rich blackberry and cedar nose of considerable depth; sweet, chewy fruit. As magnificent as expected. *June 2001* ★★★(★★) *now–2015*; and **Vieux Ch Certan** deep, velvety; sweet, relatively easy yet, of course, tannic. A sample, from a half bottle, before fining, was quite different, richer, with excellent soft tannins. *June 2001* ★★(★★) *now–2015*.

2001 ★★★

A moderately good, 'useful' vintage for mid-term drinking. From the moment the 2000 harvest had ended, it rained almost continually until April, which helped replenish the water table but made Bordeaux's clay soils soggy. Budbreak was early and a cool April slowed growth. Flowering was successful, short and regular. July was cold and wet and August alternated between hot and cool, pushing the harvest back. Crop-thinning and deleafing were imperative but expensive – doubling the usual hours of work in the vineyard.

Ch Lafite Very deep but not intense; distinct mocha nose; good flavour and length but tannic. Good enough food wine. *Oct 2005* ★(★★) *Now–2012*.

Ch Latour Opaque but not intense; low-keyed; some sweetness, fleshy, velvety/leathery tannin. *April 2003* ★(★★) *2010–2020*.

Ch Margaux Deep, richly coloured; distinctive young nose; amazingly sweet, fleshy, almost succulent, with silky and leathery tannin. *April 2003* ★★(★) *Now–2016*.

Ch Ausone Very deep but open-rimmed; spicy, singed, medicinal nose which became soft and brambly after cupping the glass with one's hand to reduce the chill and bring out the aromas; dry, good flavour and length. Very dry finish. *Jan 2005* ★★(★) *Now–2015*.

Ch Cheval Blanc Very deep, opaque core; interesting nose – bricky, whiff of iron, then mocha and liquorice; surprisingly soft entry and good fruit. 13.5% alcohol. An attractive, early-maturing '01. *Jan 2006* ★★(★) *Drink soon.*

Ch d'Angludet Deep, velvety; little nose as yet; nor very distinctive on the palate. Very tannic. *Nov 2003* (★★)? *Wait and see.*

Ch Batailley Fairly deep; soft fruit and pleasant flavour. A good '01. *Nov 2003* ★★(★) *Soon–2012*.

Ch Beauséjour-Bécot Deep, velvety, rich, soft black-cherry core, good 'legs', immature; delicious fruit; fairly sweet, chewy fruit, dry finish, delicious. *Last tasted April 2005* ★★(★★) *Now–2015*.

Ch Belair Good colour; touch of tar; good, positive fruit and oak. *April 2002* ★(★★) *Now–2012*.

Ch Bouscaut Fairly deep; touch of tar; very sweet, easy, masked tannin. An agreeable Graves for drinking early. *Nov 2003* ★★★ *Drink soon*.

Ch Canon Fairly deep, plummy purple, fairly open rim; curiously sweaty nose; pleasing, spicy. *Nov 2003* ★(★★)? *Early drinking?*

Ch Canon-La-Gaffelière Opaque core; very pronounced fruit and oak; positive, distinctive, very oaky. *Nov 2003* (★★★) *Now–2015*.

Ch Certan-de-May Fairly deep, plummy; demonstrative, iron-tinged nose; dry, good length. Modern style. *May 2005* ★★(★) *Now–2012*.

Ch Chasse-Spleen Very deep, richly coloured, almost opaque core; fragrant, whiff of tobacco and refreshing citrus edge, very oaky; sweet, light character (though 13% alcohol), crisp, stylish, good length and finish. Performing well above its class. *Jan 2005* ★★(★★) *Now–2010*.

Dom de Chevalier Medium-deep, lively, ruby colour; toasted, touch of Graves rusticity; very tannic. Worth holding a bit longer. *Aug 2004* (★★★) *Now–2015*.

Ch Cos d'Estournel Deep, rich 'legs', developing; sweet, sweaty tannins, coffee; lean, austere fruit, very tannic. *March 2004* (★★★) *2010–2016*.

Ch Dauzac Seriously deep; spicy, oaky, herbaceous; well made but austere. *Nov 2003* (★★★) *Now–2015*.

Ch Feytit-Clinet Fairly deep, youthful; whiff of coffee; medium-sweet, rich, fullish body (13.5% alcohol), good fruit. *June 2005* ★(★★) *Now–2010*.

Les Forts de Latour Deep, rich, plummy; delicious fruit; medium-sweet, fleshy, flavoury. *April 2003* ★(★★) *Now–2010*.

Ch Grand-Puy-Ducasse Deep plummy purple; tight knit, fragrant; sweet, soft and easy. *Last tasted July 2004* ★★★ *Now–2010*.

Ch Grand-Puy-Lacoste Medium-deep, maturing; crisp fruit; sweet, relatively easy for a change. Not a long-distance runner. *June 2005* ★★★ *Now–2010*.

Ch Gruaud-Larose Very deep, rich, plummy; fruity, spicy nose and flavour. Fullish body, good extract, complete. *Nov 2003* ★★(★★) *Now–2015*.

Ch Haut-Bailly Medium-deep, rich, impressive colour; good nose, whiff of chocolate; sweet, fleshy, chewy, tannic. *Aug 2004* ★(★★) *Now–2012*.

Hosanna Deep; low-keyed; touch of tar; medium-sweet, good crisp fruit and spicy aftertaste. *April 2002* ★★(★★) *Now–2012*.

Ch Kirwan Fairly deep, velvety; not very distinctive, nor as over top as recent vintages; very tannic. *Nov 2003* (★★) *2010–2015?*

Ch Lafon-Rochet New label for a new look. Opaque; good, touch of spice; a great improvement in style, and drily. *Nov 2003* ★★(★★) *Now–2015*.

Ch Léoville-Barton Most recently: deep, black-purple, fairly intense; new oak and bramble; good flavour, flesh, touch of mocha, perfect weight; oaky. *Last tasted Nov 2003* ★★(★★) *2010–2016*.

Ch Léoville-Poyferré Most recently: deep, impressive; delicious classic nose, nice fruit; sweet, good length, tannic. A good '01. *Last tasted April 2005* ★★(★★) *Now–2015*.

Ch Lynch-Bages Deep, plummy; oaky; lean but very flavoury, leathery tannins. *Nov 2003* ★★(★★) *Now–2016.*

Ch Malartic-Lagravière Very deep; fragrant fruit and oak; sweet, attractive. *Nov 2003* ★★(★) *Now–2012.*

Ch Monbrison Fairly deep, rich 'legs'; low-keyed; sweet, delicious. *Nov 2003* ★★★(★) *Now–2012.*

Ch Les Ormes-de-Pez Deep, plummy; sweet, rich extract; with whiff of strawberry and agreeable oakiness; sweet, fairly full-bodied rim, chewy, good fruity finish. *Jan 2005* ★★(★★) *Soon–2020.*

Ch de Pez Fairly deep, velvety, youthful yet early maturing, good 'legs'; unfamiliar style but sweet, chunky fruit; fairly sweet on the palate, perfect weight, mocha chocolatey flavour and tannin. *March 2005* ★★(★) *Now–2012.*

Ch Phélan-Ségur Opaque; low-keyed, light style, pleasant fruit; more positive palate, rich fruit and extract, well made. A very pleasant young wine. *Last tasted Feb 2005* ★★(★) *Now–2010.*

Ch Pichon-Lalande Deep; agreeable; remarkably sweet and easy, fruit-laden, but very tannic. *Last tasted Nov 2003* ★★(★★) *2010–2016.*

Ch Pichon-Longueville Impressively deep colour; tar, oak, tannin; distinctive, lovely fruit, hard tannins, tarry aftertaste. *Last tasted Feb 2005* (★★★) *Now–2011.*

Ch Prieuré-Lichine Very deep, opaque core; oaky, fairly sweet, very flavoury, easier than expected from its appearance, new style of Prieuré. *Nov 2003* ★(★★) *Now–2012.*

Sanctus A new St-Émilion *grand cru*. Impressively deep, velvety colour, youthful rim, good 'legs'; unusual, high-toned fruit, oaky; fairly full-bodied (13.5% alcohol), quite a lot of fruit, some bitterness, dry citrus, tannic finish and tarry aftertaste. *Jan 2004* ★(★★) *Now–?*

Ch Siran Dark cherry; sweet, floral, lovely brambly fruit; pleasant fruit and flavour, decent weight and length, touch of rawness on the finish. *Jan 2005* ★(★★) *Now–2012.*

Ch Smith-Haut-Lafitte Very deep, fairly intense; crisp fruit; good extract, slightly tarry finish. *Dec 2003* ★★(★) *Now–2012.*

Ch Talbot Medium-deep; spicy fruit, fragrant; agreeable flavour, some charm, distinctly oaky. *Nov 2003* ★(★★) *Now–2010.*

2002 ★★★ to ★★★★

Until I assembled my notes, I had not realised how much I liked these '02s. It was a much better vintage than had been feared. A small crop but, because of a dismal market, the wines were moderately priced and are still good value. A claret drinker's vintage, not for investment.

For the growers, the conditions were nerve-wracking. After normal budbreak the vital flowering period was catastrophic – cold, wet, erratic and prolonged. *Coulure* throughout the region was followed by *millerandage* and the potential crop was halved. Merlot was particularly badly affected. However, not unlike the 1978 vintage, sun and warmth from around 10 September followed by an Indian summer saved the day. After severe selection of the grapes some were excellent wines made. It was decidedly a 'Left Bank' year.

Ch Lafite Opaque core, plummy purple; low-keyed, undeveloped; dry, medium body (12.8% alcohol), good length, bitter tannin and touch of iron on finish. A serious, quite impressive wine. *April 2004* (★★★★) *2010–2018.*

Ch Latour Still very deep and fairly intense; sweet, spicy nose, touch of ginger; sweet on palate, very good flavour and texture. Very tannic. Good future. *Last tasted March 2004* (★★★★) *2012–2020.*

Ch Margaux Merlot crop seriously affected by poor summer. Highest-ever percentage of Cabernet Sauvignon in blend (86%). More recently, also in cask: plummy purple, attractive fruit and spicy new oak; very flavoury and relatively easy. *Last tasted March 2004* (★★★★) *2010–2020.*

Ch Mouton-Rothschild At the château: black core, intense, velvety sheen; dumb, unyielding nose; surprisingly sweet, soft and ripe on the palate, silky tannin, oak and end grip. *April 2003* (★★★★) *2010–2020.*

Ch Haut-Brion High percentage of Merlot (51%), Cabernet Sauvignon 40%, Cabernet Franc 9%. Opaque, intense; low-keyed but rich aromas and considerable depth; fairly sweet, rich, full-flavoured, suave, long, fragrant, oaky aftertaste. Lovely wine. *April 2003* (★★★★★) *2010–2018.*

Ch Ausone Deep, youthful, fairly intense; spicy, floral, whiff of citrus; dry, rich, very oaky flavour and aftertaste, leathery tannic texture. *Jan 2005* (★★★★) *2010–2015.*

Ch Cheval Blanc Smallest vintage since 1991. Good Merlot, very good Cabernet Franc. Rich, velvety; very crisp, oak not yet integrated, very dry finish. Wait. *March 2003* (★★★★)? *Now–2015.*

Ch Angélus Very deep; substantial fruit, very impressive; medium-sweet, fleshy, good extract but raw tannic finish. *Last tasted Aug 2004* (★★★) *Now–2015.*

Ch d'Angludet Less deep, easing, lovely gradation; crisp Cabernet aroma, sweaty tannins, will develop further; medium-dry, substantial (13.5% alcohol), good mid-palate, very attractive and very tannic. *Last tasted April 2006* ★(★★) *Soon–2012.*

Ch d'Armailhac Deep, spicy, soft, chewy, attractive. Early developer. *Last tasted Oct 2004* ★★(★) *Now–2010.*

Ch Batailley Medium-deep; nice fruit; sweet, rich, good fruit, agreeable flavour. *Oct 2004* ★(★★) *Now–2012.*

Ch Cantenac-Brown Very deep; fruit and newly-sawn timber; chewy, chocolatey, easy. *Last tasted Oct 2004* (★★) *Drink soon.*

Ch Cos d'Estournel Still very deep; low-keyed, oak, cedar; attractive, positive flavour, spicy tannic finish. A good '02. *Last tasted March 2004* ★(★★★) *2010–2015.*

Ch Feytit-Clinet Very deep; touch of tar, brambly fruit; overall dry, spicy, new oak, touch of coffee, tannic. *June 2005* ★(★★) *Soon–2010.*

Ch Figeac Very distinctive; sweet, easy, attractive. *Oct 2004* ★★★ *Soon–2012.*

Ch Grand-Puy-Ducasse Deep, rich; sweet, toasted coconut nose; fruity, chewy, oaky, marked tannin and acidity. *Last tasted Oct 2004* (★★) *Now–2012.*

Ch Grand-Puy-Lacoste Good fruit, sweet, soft, oaky, tannic. *Last tasted June 2005* (★★★) *2010–2016.*

Ch Haut-Bailly Fairly deep ruby; lovely nose, highish-toned fruit and oak; good taut fruit and flesh, very tannic. *Last tasted Nov 2004* ★(★★★) *2010–2015.*

Ch Langoa-Barton Impressively deep, intense; nose of freshly sawn timber;

very flavoury, fragrant oak, interesting texture. *Last tasted Sept 2003* ★★(★★) *(just) Now–2015.*

Ch Léoville-Barton Still deep; lovely soft fruit nose and palate. *Last tasted Oct 2004* ★★(★★) *2010–2016.*

Ch Léoville-Poyferré Good flavour but upstaged by the Barton (see above). *Oct 2004* ★(★★) *Now–2015.*

Ch Lynch-Bages Already less deep; fleshy, good fruit, attractive. *Last tasted Oct 2004* ★★(★★) *Now–2015.*

Ch Lynch-Moussas Less deep than usual; sweet, good fruit, early developer. *Oct 2004* ★(★★) *Now–2012.*

Ch Monbrison Holding back a little; sweet, rich wine, dry finish. *Last tasted Oct 2004* ★★(★) *Now–2010.*

Ch Montrose Virtually opaque, intense, immature; mocha, crisp fruit, opened up fragrantly; dry, fleshy but crisp, a bit raw, very tannic. *Sept 2005* ★(★★★) *2010–2016.*

Ch Pichon-Lalande Richly coloured; sweet, fruity nose; good, complete, dry finish. *Last tasted Oct 2004* ★★(★★) *Now–2011.*

Ch Pichon-Longueville Rich fruit, new oak; crisp, good flavour and length. Tannic grip. *Last tasted Feb 2005* ★★(★★) *2010–2016.*

Ch Pontet-Canet Spicy, rich, attractive nose; sweet, soft, very fleshy. Great improvement on yesteryears. *Last tasted Oct 2004* ★★(★★) *Now–2015.*

Ch Prieuré-Lichine Initially opaque; taut, hard, brambly fruit, opening up fragrantly. New style of Prieuré. *Last tasted Oct 2004* ★(★★) *Now–2012.*

Ch Rauzan-Gassies Still a bit hard and stalky but huge improvement. *Last tasted Oct 2004* ★★(★) *2010–2015.*

Ch Rauzan-Ségla Flawless fruit; very satisfactory mouthful, good length. *Last tasted Oct 2004* ★★(★★) *2010–2016.*

Ch Siran Ruby-coloured; distinctive but very deep; nice fruit, touch of citrus; similar on palate, elegant, early developer? *Last tasted Oct 2004* ★★★ *Now–2012.*

Ch Yon-Figeac Pleasant, young, brambly, spicy nose; medium sweetness and body, crisp fruit but a bit raw and sharp. Dry finish. *Aug 2005* ★★(★) *Now–2012.*

WINES NOTED ONLY AT THE OPENING TASTING OF 2002S in April 2003, unless otherwise stated: **Ch Beauregard** (Pomerol) nose of freshly sawn timber and fruit; sweet, pleasant fruit, oak ★(★★) *now–2010;* **Ch Beauséjour-Bécot** deep, intense, velvety, ruby core; as yet unknit oak and fruit, sweet, whiff of tar; good flavour, length, silky, tannic finish (★★★) *now–2012;* **Ch Beychevelle** mauve; very pleasant, fragrant nose; dry, crisp, querying its length, tannic and very oaky aftertaste (★★)? *now–?;* **Ch Branaire-Ducru** deep purple; taut, fragrant, Cabernet aromas and fruit; attractive flavour, very tannic (★★★) *now–2015;* **Ch Brane-Cantenac** deep; mild fruit, light oak; good flavour, length (★★★) *(just) now–2012;* **Ch Canon** very deep; low-keyed, oaky; fairly sweet, soft, nice flesh, tannic finish (★★★) *now–2012;* **Ch Canon-La-Gaffelière** opaque core; new oak, whiff of sourness, lightly scented; sweet, loose-knit, attractive flavour, tannic ★(★★) *now–2012;* **Carruades de Lafite** virtually opaque, intense, velvety; very good, fragrant, refined oak nose; dry, lean fruit, very good flavour ★(★★) *now–2012;* **Ch Les Carmes-Haut-Brion** attractive, high-toned fruit, touch of liquorice and tar; good flavour, silky/leathery tannins ★(★★) *now–2012;* **Ch Chantegrive** opaque, intense, violet; sweet, youthful, fragrant, forthcoming; very flavoury, spicy, tannic finish. Minor Graves but major new winemaking (★★) *now–2012*; **Ch Chasse-Spleen** opaque; very flavoury, fairly intense fruit ★(★★) *now–2010*; **Dom de Chevalier** very deep, rich 'legs'; low-keyed, touch of strawberry and oak, developed fragrantly; very sweet, agreeable fruit and oak. Nice wine ★★(★) *soon–2012*; **Ch Clerc-Milon** opaque; dumb; sweet, good fruit, very flavoury, tannic grip (★★★) *now–2015*; **Ch Clinet** opaque, plummy; too sweet, very oaky. 'New World' sweetness on the palate, lashings of oak, very flavoury. Specious ★(★★) *now–2010*; **Ch La Conseillante** opaque core, rich 'legs'; forthcoming minty fruit, spicy oak; soft entry, pleasant fruit, dry finish. Very good wine ★★(★★) *Now–2015*; **Ch Cos Labory** very deep; fresh fruit and oak; sweet, easy, attractive, slightly raw finish ★(★★) *now–2016*; **Ch Croizet-Bages** deep; good fruit, very pleasant nose; medium-sweet, good body and fruit, complete. Uncomplicated wine ★(★★) *soon–2012*; **Ch Dauzac** opaque, velvety; oaky; very tannic. Needs time (★★★)?; **Ch La Dominique** deep, plummy; 'broad', leafy fruit; curious raspberry flavour (Cabernet Franc?), dry finish ★★ *soon–2010*; **Ch Ducru-Beaucaillou** high percentage of Cabernet Sauvignon (81%). Rich, velvety; cedar; fairly sweet, rich, lovely flavour, very oaky, good length (★★★★) *now–2016*; **Ch Duhart-Milon** opaque; dry, hard, slightly peppery, serious (★★★) *2010–2015*; **Ch Fieuzal** plummy; mulberry-like fruit; medium-sweet, chewy, tannic. Attractive ★(★★) *soon–2010*; **Ch Fombrauge** opaque; quite good fruit; fairly condensed, very oaky ★★(★) *soon–2010*; **Les Forts de Latour** opaque, intense; good fruit; some sweetness, lean, flavoury (★★★) *now–2015*; **Clos Fourtet** intense, prickle of CO_2; quite attractive fruit, nose and taste. Fleshy, good length. Tannic ★(★★) *soon–2012*; **Ch La Gaffelière** opaque, intense, rich 'legs'; good fruit, fragrant, arboreal; attractive, crisp fruit but very oaky and very tannic (★★★) *now–2015*; **Ch Gazin** opaque, velvety core, purple rim; low-keyed, sweet, whiff of caramel; dry, crisp fruit, straightforward, tannic ★(★★) *soon–2016*; **Ch Giscours** intense; low-keyed; sweet, attractive fruit (★★★) *now–2015*; **Ch Gruaud-Larose** very deep; minty fruit; curious, distinctive flavour, herbaceous. Certainly interesting (★★★) *now–?*; **Ch Haut-Batailley** bright purple; good, rich, oaky nose; lean but fruity, slightly stalky, tannic finish (★★★) *now–2015*; **Ch La Lagune** violet; low-keyed; good fruit, assertive, tannic (★★★) *now–2015*; **Ch Larmande** fragrant, oaky; sweet, soft texture, very flavoury ★★★ *now–2010*; **Ch Latour-Martillac** virtually opaque; good nose, whiff of oak and tar; good fruit and length, slightly raw, tannic finish ★(★★) *now–2012*; **Ch Léoville-Las-Cases** opaque, intense violet rim; dumb, slight whiff of tar; fairly sweet, full rich fruit, good length, very dry finish, lovely end taste ★★(★★) *2010–2018*; **Ch Malescasse** deep; herbaceous, agreeable. *Oct 2003* ★★ *drink soon*; **Ch Malescot-St-Exupéry** opaque; very spicy, very oaky; sweet, distinctive flavour ★(★★) *now–2012*; **Ch La Mission Haut-Brion** very deep, not intense, violet rim; low-keyed fruit and oak; fairly sweet, full, rich, good fruit, lean, slightly raw dry finish (★★★) *now–2015*; **Ch Nenin** intense, violet rim; nose not very distinctive; remarkably sweet, full of fruit, masked tannin though very dry finish ★★(★) *now–2012*; **Ch Olivier** fruit, oak, citrus whiff, good depth; sweet, nice fruit. Good wine ★★★ *now–2012*; **Les Ormes-de-Pez** very deep; touch of mocha and bramble; dry, good fruit, positive grip ★★(★) *now–2012*; **Ch Pape-Clément** very deep, velvety; very fragrant fruit and oak; medium-sweet, delicious flavour and spicy oaky aftertaste.

Attractive wine. *Last tasted May 2003* ★★(★★) *now–2015*; **Ch Pavie** opaque, intense; low-keyed at first, then fragrant, oaky, hint of mulberry; medium-sweet, rich, crisp fruit, oaky, masked tannin ★★(★) *now–2012*; **Ch Pavie-Decesse** opaque, intense; fragrant, spicy, oaky, biscuity nose; sweet, silky tannic texture, dry finish ★★(★) *now–2012*; **Pavillon Rouge de Ch Margaux** bright ruby; refreshing raspberry-like aroma; fragrant, flavoury ★★★ *now–2010*; **Ch Petit-Village** opaque; very spicy oaky nose; fairly sweet, fleshy fruit, yet lean. Pleasant finish ★★★ *now–2012*; **Ch Phélan-Ségur** very deep, velvety; herbaceous; dry, taut fruit, hard ★(★) *now–?*; **Ch La Pointe** opaque, intense; very strange nose, fudge, fruit and sawn wood; fairly sweet, full of fruit. Early drinking ★★★ *now–2010*; **Ch Potensac** distinctive cedar and oak; notably sweet, pleasant fruit, good grip and aftertaste ★(★★) *now–2012*; **Ch Poujeaux** deep; good fruit, flesh and oak ★(★★) *now–2010*; **Ch Smith-Haut-Lafitte** rich, tarry, good fruit, already well evolved; rich fruit, chewy, tarry oak and touch of stalkiness. Overall good ★★(★) *now–2012*; **Ch Talbot** medium-deep; curious appley aroma, fragrant but unfamiliar; dry, flavoury, individual as always ★★(★★) *now–2015*; **Ch du Tertre** deep, velvety; distinctive, good fruit and flavour. Big investment and improvements here ★★(★★)? *now–2015?*; **Ch La Tour-Carnet** for long an underperforming classed growth Médoc but improvements now showing. Very deep, opaque core; fragrant fruit, lightly toasted oak; fairly sweet, distinctive flavour, oak dominated ★(★★) *2010–?*; **Ch La Tour-de-By** deep; rich, fragrant; good flavour and fruit, very oaky aftertaste ★(★★) *now–2012*; **Ch Troplong-Mondot** deep, plummy; very distinctive nose and taste. Fairly sweet, silky tannin texture ★(★★) *now–2012*; and **Vieux Ch Certan** very deep; strange, 'green', sappy nose but very fragrant; sweet, full, rich, not as impressive as expected ★(★★) *now–2012*.

2003 ★★★★

'The year of the heatwave. Untypical reds entirely due to the exceptionally hot summer and early harvest. The early part of the growing season was unexceptional, satisfactory flowering predicting an appropriately early harvest. However, temperatures in August were up to 40°C compared to 'normal' Bordeaux heatwaves of around 34–35°C. This resulted in an unusually precocious harvest, producing a low volume of small, concentrated, very ripe grapes with thick skins.

Some great wines were made but several were disappointing. On the whole these are attractive wines. I tasted a very extensive range, mainly noted as *en primeur* wines in the spring of 2004. In the following notes the depth of colour not commented on unless unusually deep or pale.

Ch Lafite Very deep, virtually opaque, intense; cedar and oak, hard but fragrant; overall dry, lean, some fleshy, spicy, very oaky, tannic of course, long dry finish. *March 2004* (★★★★) *2015–?*

Ch Latour Very high Cabernet Sauvignon (81%). Opaque core, intense; fragrant, whiff of violets, citrus, opening up richly, biscuity, good depth; medium-sweet, rich, full flavour and body (13.0% alcohol). More dynamic than the '02 and more fleshy than Lafite. *March 2004* (★★★★★) *2015–2030*.

Ch Margaux Three months prior to bottling: appearance already losing its youthful garb, opening up; nose low-keyed, touch of coffee and soft sawn wood;

sweet, high extract, soft, very rich yet firm. Sweet tannins. Attractive. Relatively early development? *Last tasted May 2005* (★★★★) *2013–2023*.

Ch Mouton-Rothschild Very deep, rich 'legs'; spicy, meaty nose which quickly opened up fragrantly with 'biscuity' fruit; sweet, rich, chewy, substantial (12.87% alcohol) extract, semi-masked tannins. *March 2004* (★★★★) *Now–2025*.

Ch Haut-Brion High percentage of Merlot (58%). Very deep, intense, ruby; fruit, oak, whiff of strawberry, scented, attractive; medium-dry to dry finish, good flesh and length. *March 2004* (★★★★) *2013–2023*.

Ch Cheval Blanc 56% Cabernet Franc. Wonderfully deep, fairly intense; difficult to smell in the *chai* but sweet and sweaty (tannins); sweet on the palate, soft, touch of tar. Attractive. Relatively early developer. *April 2004* (★★★★) *2010–2020*.

Ch Chasse-Spleen Pretty impressive. *Last tasted Aug 2004* ★★(★) *Now–2012*.

Ch L'Evangile Not very deep; singed fruit, distinctive, rich, chewy, very tannic. *Oct 2006* (★★★★) *2010–2020*.

Ch Haut-Bailly Sweet, copybook Graves nose; rich, tannic. Good wine. *Last tasted June 2005* ★(★★★) *Now–2016*.

Ch Labégorce-Zédé Deep; very rich chocolatey nose; fairly sweet; very ripe fruit and extract. *Aug 2004* ★(★★★) *2010–2015*.

Ch Malescot-St-Exupéry Richly coloured, maturing; delicious flavour but perhaps lacking length. But there is now serious new winemaking here. *Last tasted April 2006* ★(★★★) *2010–2016*.

Ch Montrose Attractive nose, touch of liquorice; rich, quite an attack, tannin more noticeable. *Last tasted Sept 2005* (★★★★) *2012–2020*.

Ch Pichon-Lalande Soft dark cherry, fairly intense; wholesome spice and fruit on nose and palate. Fairly sweet, delicious flavour. Slightly rough tannic texture. *Last tasted May 2007* (★★★?) *2010–2015*.

Ch Pichon-Longueville Before bottling in June: lovely sweet, blackcurrant aroma and flavour. *Last tasted Feb 2005* ★(★★★) *2010–2016*.

Ch Pontet-Canet Very deep, fairly intense; rich, fragrant; fairly sweet, chunky fruit, decent mouthful. Immensely impressive. *Last tasted Aug 2004* ★(★★★) *Now–2016*.

Ch du Tertre Attractive fruit, sweet, rich, cloves-like spiciness. *Last tasted Aug 2004* (★★★) *Now–2015*.

THE FOLLOWING '03S WERE TASTED IN THE SPRING OF 2004. The wines all have the normal depth of colour of any young red Bordeaux unless otherwise noted: **Ch Angélus** hard, straw and bramble; dry, tough, lean, oaky, dry tarry tannic finish (★★★) *not my style. 2010–*; **Ch d'Angludet** initially opaque; distinctive, 'meaty' nose; rich, interesting flesh and texture; very good flavour, minerally, dry finish ★★(★★) *2010–2018*; **Ch d'Armailhac** sweet, pleasant fruit, vanilla; distinctly sweet on the palate, easy yet with rasping tannic finish (★★★) *2010–2015*; **Ch Batailley** very oaky, spicy, crisp fruit and flesh, positive, tannic. Nice wine. ★(★★) *2010–2016*; **Ch Beauregard** (Pomerol) closed but fragrant nose; sweet, good fruit, interesting flavour, slightly coarse ★(★★) *2010–2015*; **Ch Beauséjour-Bécot** very deep; fruit and oak, sweet, brambly; lean, very oaky, very dry. Needs bottle age (★★★) *2010–2015*; **Ch Branaire** sweet, oaky nose; fairly sweet, nice fruit, slightly cardboardy finish ★★? *Ought to improve;* **Ch Brane-Cantenac** curious spicy fruit, whiff of mocha and citrus; medium-sweet, unusual and interesting flavour, dry finish (★★★) *2010–2016*; **Ch Canon** lean, very tannic, strange appley nose; dry, good flavour, decent length. Lacking the richness of old? ★★ *now–2012*; **Ch Canon-La-Gaffelière** citrus whiff; sweet, unusual, distinctive flavour. Expected more ★★? *drink soon*; **Ch Cantemerle** raw fruit but fragrant; rich, chunky, pleasing texture, very tannic (★★★★) *2010–2011*; **Ch Cantenac-Brown** curious nose, 'old apples'; better on palate, complete ★★ *possibly* ★★★ *in time*. Say *2010–2015*; **Carruades de Lafite** light, spicy oaky nose; pleasant enough, dry finish ★★★ *now–2012*; **Ch Chantegrive** attractive, fragrant, raspberry-like fruit, vanilla; crisp fruit. Delicious. Continuing its renaissance ★★★ *now–2012*; **Ch Citran** chunky, rich, spicy nose, whiff of mocha; fairly sweet, good fruit, nice texture, easy yet tannic (★★★) *now–2015*; **Ch Clerc-Milon** sweet, chewy fruit nose and taste. Soft yet teeth-gripping finish (★★★) *2010–2015*; **Ch Clinet** deep, velvety; attractive, rich, mulberry; very positive and distinctive, tar and mocha, tannic. Good but a style I have never taken to ★(★★) *or* ★★★★ *for aficionados 2010–2016*; **Ch La Conseillante** most attractive fruit and oak; sweetish, soft. Lovely flavour ★(★★★) *2010–2018*; **Ch Cos d'Estournel** opaque, intense, rich 'legs'; fragrant but very oaky, whiff of mocha; medium-dry, rich, soft, spicy, mouthfilling. Highish alcohol (13.5%), masked tannin, long 'warm' finish (★★★★) *2010–2020*; **Ch Cos Labory** low-keyed, spicy, whiff of citrus fragrance; medium-dry, crisp, short ★★ *now–2012*; **Ch Croizet-Bages** pleasant aroma; medium-sweet, very fruity, almost speciously attractive ★(★★) *now–2015*; **Dom de Chevalier** light, fragrant, slightly tarry Graves nose; sweet, soft, chewy fruit, agreeable, richly flavoured, quite good length ★(★★★) *now–2015*; **Ch Coufran** very attractive, soft fruit nose and taste ★(★★) *now–2014*; **Ch Croizet-Bages** deep; very fruity aroma and flavour. Attractive. A bit obvious ★(★★) *now–2015*; **Ch La Dominique** flowery, slightly scented, attractive nose; interesting flavour, some softness, silky leathery tannins. Nice wine. ★★(★★) *2010–2014*; **Ch Ducru-Beaucaillou** very good nose; sweet; rich, crisp flavour. Correct tannin and acidity. A lot to it ★(★★★) *2010–2016*; **Ch Duhart-Milon** very deep, intense; cedar; lean, flavoury, a bit austere (★★★) *2010–2015*; **Ch Ferrande** immediately forthcoming, piquant, raspberry-like fruit; fairly sweet, a *mélange* of raspberry and ripe mulberry, full-flavoured. Taking itself seriously. *Worthy of* ★(★★★) *now–2015*; **Ch Figeac** brambly fruit; dry, austere, oaky tannic finish. Lacks the rich idiosyncratic character I expect ★★? *now–2012*; **Ch de Fieuzal** deep; crisp fruit and oak; sweet, soft, rich fruit, chewy, masked tannin. Attractive ★(★★★) *now–2012*; **Ch Fombrauge** opaque, intense; tight tannin and oak, whiff of ginger; very sweet, touch of liquorice. New style. Agreeable ★★★ *now–2012*; **Clos Fourtet** very deep, intense; indistinct fruit; more interesting on palate, good flavour and length ★★★ *now–2015*; **Ch La Gaffelière** light but fragrant; medium-sweet, coarse tannin but attractive ★(★★) *now–2014*; **Ch Gazin** attractive but unknit fruit, scent of grape skins; good Pomerol texture but rasping dry finish (★★★)? *2010–?*; **Ch Grand-Puy-Ducasse** crisp fruit and oak; sweet, not bad fruit, raw tannin (★★) *2010–2016*; **Ch Grand-Puy-Lacoste** low-keyed, brambly fruit; sweet, plenty of fruit, leathery tannic texture. Good wine (★★★★) *2012–2020*; **Ch Gruaud-Larose** crisp, citrus-edged fruit; fairly sweet, rich, attractive ★(★★★) *2010–2020*; **Ch Haut-Batailley** new oak; very sweet, a lot of fruit, very oaky. Tannin and more acidity than expected ★★(★★) *2012–2016*; **Ch**

Kirwan thick tarry nose, attractive fruit and flavour. Very tannic. The new *régime* toned down a little ★(★★★) *2010–2016*; **Ch Lafon-Rochet** fairly intense, rich 'legs'; low-keyed; fairly sweet, fleshy, good fruit and length (★★★) *2010–2015*; **Ch Lagrange** (St-Julien) crisp fruit, very positive, raw tannic finish (★★★) *2010–2015*; **Ch La Lagune** good, ripe fruit on nose and palate. Fairly sweet, soft, good extract. Very attractive wine ★(★★★) *now–2015*; **Ch Langoa-Barton** distinctive, oaky fragrance; sweet, fruity, fleshy, chunky, tannic. A very amenable Langoa ★★(★★) *2010–2016*; **Ch Larrivet-Haut-Brion** very deep, plummy; very deep, citrus and vanilla; lean, flavoury, piquant fruit and tannin ★★★ *now–2012*; **Ch Léoville-Barton** classic cedar nose, muffled oak, good depth; fairly sweet, full-flavoured, good fruit, delicious flavour, grip and good length ★★(★★★) *2012–2020*; **Ch Léoville-Las-Cases** opaque, intense, purple; low-keyed, cedar, very slight whiff of tar; extraordinarily sweet yet dry tannic finish. Mouthfilling ★(★★★) *2010–2020*; **Ch Léoville-Poyferré** very fragrant, oak, citrus-edged nose; fairly sweet, rich, some softness, mouth-drying tannin and oaky aftertaste. Different style to the Barton (★★★★) *2012–2018*; **Ch La Louvière** opaque, velvety; rich, slightly jammy fruit and vanilla; medium-sweet, firm fruit, very tannic (★★★) *2010–2015*; **Ch Lynch-Bages** good fruit and new oak; soft, pleasant chunky flavour, tannic (★★★★) *2010–2020*; **Ch Lynch-Moussas** ripe fruit; fairly sweet, crisp, tannic (★★★) *2010–2016*; **Ch Malartic-Lagravière** fragrant, piquant fruit and flavour. Flavoury. Tannic. Nice wine ★(★★) *now–2012*; **Ch La Mission Haut-Brion** very deep, opaque core, fairly intense; very scented, oaky nose, then very tarry and spicy; medium-sweet, at this stage dominated by spicy, clove-like oak. Mouthfilling. Impressive ★(★★★★) *2012–2018*; **Ch Monbrison** low-keyed yet fragrant and attractive nose; medium-sweet, interesting flavour, good length ★★★ *2010–2015*; **Ch Nenin** very deep, velvety; blackberry/bramble aroma; whiff of citrus; very sweet, soft fruit, masked tannin ★★(★) *now–2012*; **Ch Olivier** rich, modest fruit; medium-sweet, crisp fruit, oaky ★(★★) *now–2012*; **Ch Les Ormes-de-Pez** scent of newly sawn wood; medium-sweet, fleshy, quite good fruit ★(★★) *2010–2015*; **Ch Palmer** all oak and spice; sweet, rich, modest alcohol (12%), good aftertaste. Nice wine (★★★★) *2010–2016*; **Ch Pape-Clément** opaque, intense; brambly fruit, touch of tar; fairly sweet, fleshy, oaky, powerful. Impressive ★(★★★) *2010–2018*; **Ch Pavie** very deep; extraordinary, fishy, tarry nose; fairly sweet, full-flavoured, powerful, dense, tarry. Impressive – but not for me ★★ to ★★★★ *depending on how it develops*; **Ch Pavie-Decesse** very deep, opaque core, intense, purple; similar type of nose to Pavie; medium-dry. Full, hot, dense, powerful finish. Same owner and winemaker. Totally untypical St-Émilion. Frankly, a matter of taste; **Ch Pavie-Macquin** opaque, intense; pleasant fruit on nose and palate; sweet, attractive ★★(★) *now–2012*; **Ch Petit-Village** deep, velvety; curious, slightly fishy, sweaty tannic nose; yet attractive fruit and flavour. Good mouthfeel, tannic ★(★★★) *2010–2016*; **Ch La Pointe** pleasant fruit, slightly spicy, gingery; medium-sweet, agreeable and easy, as usual ★★★ *(just) drink soon*; **Ch Potensac** opaque; brambly fruit; very sweet, soft, rich fruit, attractive ★★★ *now–2012*; **Ch Prieuré-Lichine** very deep; attractive fruit, whiff of meatiness; some sweetness, lean but flavoury, tannic ★(★★) *2010–2015*; **Ch Rauzan-Gassies** attractive fruit; medium body and weight, fruit-laden, very dry tannic finish (★★★) *2012–2016*; **Ch Rauzan-Ségla** low-keyed, new oak, scent of violets; medium-sweet, good fruit, flesh and texture. Elegant ★(★★★) *2010–2016*; Ch Siran low-keyed, lean, oaky; sweetish, straightforward fruit, tannic (★★★) *2010–2015*; Ch Smith-Haut-Lafitte light, pleasant, refreshing citrus-like nose; sweet, agreeable fruit ★(★★★) *now–2015*; Ch Talbot good fruit and oak; medium-sweet, newly sawn wood, Cabernet fruit, very tannic ★(★★★) *2012–2018*; Ch La Tour-de-By dense, oaky, young fruit; pleasant sweetness and flesh, good extract ★★★ *now–2010*; Ch La Tour-Carnet touch of tar; very good. New look ★(★★) *now–2014*; Ch La Tour Haut-Brion low-keyed, spicy, gentle vanilla scent, opening up, sweet and fleshy; interesting texture, a touch of the usual coarseness but an attractive La Tour ★(★★★) *2010–2015*; Ch Trottevieille soft, spicy, brambly fruit; medium-sweet, pleasant flavour and texture ★★(★) *now–2014*; and Ch Vieux Ch Certan citrus edge to good fruit; fairly sweet, distinctive flavour, complete. Good wine ★(★★★) *2010–2016*.

2004 at best ★★★★

A useful, agreeable, underrated and relatively reasonably priced vintage; these are wines for future drinking not investment. Careful selection is needed as by no means all the properties could afford the vital and expensive green-pruning and crop selection to avoid unripe grapes with raw tannins.

The weather was conducive, the flowering taking place in perfect conditions, even and speedy, the absence of *coulure* and *millerandage* ensuring a large crop and, all being well, an early harvest. The summer was warm, with refreshing showers. However, August was very wet and temperature levels declined. A big crop of large bunches made full ripening and dilution a problem. Properties on the Left and Right Banks had similar successes – and failures, mainly due to the affordability of severe crop-thinning and selection. One thing in common: high tannin levels, the best soft, the least successful harsh.

A SELECTION OF '04S TASTED IN OCTOBER 2006:

Ch d'Armailhac Deep; distinctive, some sweetness but lean style. ★★(★) *2010–*

Ch Batailley Opaque core; good fruit, hard edge; sweet, chewy, good flavour, tannic. ★★(★) *2010–*

Ch Beychevelle Fragrant; very sweet, delicious flavour, masked tannins. ★★(★★) *2010–2016*.

Ch Branaire Good fruit, sweet, oaky, good length. ★(★★) *2010–2016*.

Ch Brane-Cantenac Opaque core; mocha, slightly stalky; very sweet, easy, some charm. ★(★★) *Soon–2016*.

Ch Canon Very deep; good fruit and 'sweaty' tannins; sweet, delicious, good acidity. ★★(★★) *Now–2015*.

Ch Canon-La-Gaffelière Opaque core; very good fruit, fragrant; most agreeable. ★★(★★) *Soon–2015*.

Dom de Chevalier Fairly deep, plummy; hard, undeveloped nose; some sweetness, extract, tannic. (★★★) *2012–2020*.

Ch La Conseillante Richly coloured; good fruit; sweet, easy, attractive. ★★(★) *Now–2015*.

Ch Figeac Sweet, very oaky, tannic. (★★★) *2010–2016*.

Ch La Gaffelière Impressively deep; distinctive. ★(★★) *2010–2016*.

Ch Giscours Rich nose and flavour. Touch of mocha (new oak). Tannic. ★★(★) *Soon–2016*.

Ch Gruaud-Larose Not as deep as expected; very fruity but pronounced mocha on nose and palate. Tannic. (★★★)

Ch Haut-Bailly Impressively deep, velvety; low-keyed, very Graves; sweet, very good flavour, well balanced. (★★★★) *2010–2018*.

Ch Kirwan Seems to have settled down after excesses excessive wines of previous years. Attractive. Silky/leathery tannins. ★(★★) *2010–2016*.

Ch Léoville-Barton Still youthful; very distinctive, slightly 'medicinal'; sweet, delicious. A class act. ★★(★★) *2012–2020*.

Ch Léoville-Poyferré Impressive; low-keyed but fragrant; very sweet, oaky, good flavour. Very tannic. ★★(★)

Ch Lynch-Bages Impressive colour; very typical Cabernet aroma and oak; sweet, delicious flavour. ★★(★★) *2010–*

Ch Pichon-Lalande Rich; good fruit, almost peppery new oak; very flavoury, tannic. ★★(★★)

Ch Pichon-Longueville Very distinctive Cabernet Sauvignon aroma; harmonious, developing well, good fruit. ★★(★★)

Ch Rauzan-Gassies Very deep; sweet, rich nose and palate, lots of fruit, extract, tannic. Great improvement. At last becoming worthy of *2ème cru* classification. ★★(★★) *2010–2018*.

Ch Rauzan-Ségla Rauzan-Gassies' next door neighbour is now a serious competitor! Good fruit, positive style, good length, dry finish. ★★(★★) *2010–2018*.

Ch Talbot Good fruit and depth; sweet, characteristic, distinctive, tannic. ★★(★) *2010–*

OTHER '04S TASTED ALSO IN OCTOBER 2006, all 3-star: **Ch Clerc-Milon**; **Ch Ferrière**; **Ch Gazin**; **Ch Grand-Puy-Ducasse**; **Ch Larose-Ducasse**; **Ch Malescot-St Exupéry**; **Ch Siran**; **Ch Smith-Haut-Lafitte**; **Ch La Tour-de-By**; **Ch La Tour-Carnet**; and **Ch Trottevieille**.

2005 ★★★★★

A vintage much heralded and achieving considerable acclaim from almost the moment the grapes were picked following well-nigh ideal growing conditions. The sort of year in which, unless the grower and winemaker were incompetent or suffered some misfortune, there was no excuse for making a poor wine. The following notes, which must be regarded as preliminary, were made in Bordeaux in April 2006.

Before preparing my notes for publication, I was inclined to think that this was probably an over-hyped, overrated vintage. Having assembled them, however, it is perfectly apparent that 2005 is unquestionably a vintage of the highest and, on the whole, most uniform quality. More than usual I have rated many wines 5- and 4-star; and few, in fact, hardly any, below 3-star. In short, thanks to beneficial growing conditions and uniformly ripe grapes, sound winemaking and selection have made Bordeaux once again attractively drinkable – but at a price, not just at a high selling price but at the cost of individual character. If not 'all the same', there are insufficient contrasts. Too few faults and aberrations are, of course, welcome. But where is the drama, the excitement and undemonstrative finesse?

Ch Lafite Very high percentage of Cabernet Sauvignon: 88% (Merlot 12%, no Cabernet Franc or Petit Verdot in the *grand vin*). Opaque, intense; low-keyed but harmonious nose; medium sweetness and body (12.9% alcohol), good Cabernet-dominated flavour and flesh. Seemed to become sweeter in the glass, excellent length and finish. *April 2006* (★★★★★) *2020–2040*.

Ch Latour *Grand vin* blend: Cabernet Sauvignon 87%, Merlot 12%, Cabernet Franc and Petit Verdot 1%. Very deep, velvety sheen, fairly intense purple; low-keyed but distinctive, newly sawn wood and mocha; sweet, full-bodied (13.5% alcohol), very fleshy, good length, teeth-gripping, mouth-drying tannin. *April 2006* (★★★★) *2020–2035*.

Ch Margaux *Grand vin*: high percentage of Cabernet Sauvignon (85%), unusually low percentage of Merlot (8%), the latter due to the exceptionally rich and high alcoholic content which would unbalance the blend. Deep, lovely colour but not as intense as expected; even by youthful Margaux standards, an extraordinary aroma, exquisite crystallised violets and mint. Totally unique: no other '05 matches this scent. On the palate, very crisp, alcohol a reasonable 13%, good length of course, and tannic. *April 2006* (★★★★★) *Tempted to say 2015–2030 but Margaux has the tendency to be hard and unyielding aged 10, so from 2020.*

Ch Mouton-Rothschild *Grand vin*: Cabernet Sauvignon 85%, Merlot 14%, Cabernet Franc 1%. Unsurprisingly dramatic in every aspect: intensity of colour; the immediacy of its varietal aromas, great depth, opening up richly and sweetly in the glass; spicy, cloves (new oak), an exotic wine with fair strength (13.1% alcohol), silky, leathery tannins and great length. *April 2006* (★★★★★) *2020–2040*.

Ch Haut-Brion When the much revered Jean Delmas, the now retired *régisseur* or director, comments that the '05 vintage is one of the best he has ever experienced (and likened it to his '61), then one must take this as high praise indeed. Note the high percentage of Merlot in the blend (56%), with Cabernet Sauvignon at 39% and Cabernet Franc 5%. Impressively deep, of course; very distinctive and harmonious from the start; sweet, fleshy, soft tannins, in short – glorious. *April 2006* (★★★★★) *2015–2030*.

Ch Ausone Alas not tasted, but it has a high reputation.

Ch Cheval Blanc *Grand vin* blend: 55% Cabernet Franc, 45% Merlot. Fairly deep, velvety sheen, medium intensity; low-keyed, then developing a rich, biscuity, spicy, gingery nose; leaner than expected, highish alcohol (13.7%), somewhat bitter tannins, good length. A classy wine. *April 2006* (★★★★) *2015–2025*.

SELECTED WINES FROM A VERY WIDE RANGE TASTED IN APRIL 2006:

Ch Angélus Sweet, good fruit, oak-dominated and very tannic finish. I do not share the admiration for this state-of-the-art estate. (★★★) *2012–2018*.

Ch d'Angludet Fairly intense; 'tight', interesting fruit aroma and flavour. Crisp. Distinctive. Good wine. ★★(★★) *2012–2018*.

Ch d'Armailhac Rich core; fragrant brambly fruit, crisp new oak; surprisingly sweet, rustic fruit, full flavour, delicious. ★★(★★) *Now–2020*.

Ch Batailley Opaque, fairly intense; low-keyed, yet rich, new oak; rich, lively fruit, nice wine. (★★★) *2010–2016*.

Ch Beauséjour-Bécot Touch of coffee; quite simply, a very good wine. ★(★★★) *2010–2016*.

Ch Belair Muffled fruit; interesting mid-palate, full-flavoured, soft texture, decent length. Attractive. ★(★★★) *2010–2016*.

Ch Beychevelle Fairly deep; straightforward, undramatic, moderate fruit; medium-sweet, lacking flesh, easy. ★(★★) *2010–2016*.

Ch Bourgneuf-Vayron Low-keyed; sweet, nice fruit, teeth-gripping tannins. (★★★★) *2012–2018*.

Ch Bouscaut Deep, velvety; dramatic fruit; good flavour and balance. ★★(★★) *Now–2012*.

Ch Branaire Opaque; forthcoming, blackberry and new oak; medium-sweet, good flesh and fruit. Tannic. ★★(★★) *2012–2018*.

Ch Brane-Cantenac Spicy fruit; interesting flavour, good depth and length. Great improvement on its old, rustic style. (★★★★) *2010–2018*.

Ch Calon-Ségur For some time now formidably good but not as fashionable as Montrose or Cos. Good colour but not opaque; sweet fruit, whiff of strawberry; very sweet, full of fruit, laden with tannin – as all good St-Estèphes should be, and delicious. An outstanding Calon. (★★★★★) *2015–2030*.

Ch Camensac Highish-toned fruit; citrus whiff; sweet, agreeable fruit and flavour, teeth-gripping dry finish. A little-known classed growth now benefiting from new and more enlightened ownership. ★(★★) *on verge of* ★★★★ *2010–2020*.

Ch Canon Slightly scented fruit; sweet, delicious flavour, long, oaky, dry finish. (★★★★) *2010–2018*.

Ch Canon-La-Gaffelière High-toned, whiff of strawberry; interesting and unusual flavour, very spicy oak. (★★★★) *2012–2018*.

Ch Cantemerle Virtually opaque, intense; certainly different, well evolved crisp fruit, slightly minty; surprisingly sweet, nice flesh, fruit, weight and finish. A very good Cantemerle, reminded of its style and quality in the mid-1950s. (★★★★) *2010–2020*.

Ch Cantenac-Brown Plummy purple; crisp, tight fruit, opening up attractively though a bit 'jammy'; fairly sweet and soft yet tannic finish which seems to be both velvety and raw. (★★★) *2012–2018*.

Carruades de Lafite Crisp fruit, good tannin and acidity. ★★(★★) *2012–2018*.

Ch Certan-de-May-de-Certan A mouthful of a name! Firm, deep, rich appearance; whiff of coffee; crisp, good fruit and future. (★★★★) *2010–2018*.

Ch Chasse-Spleen Nice fruit; soft, ripe, tannic. ★★(★★) *2010–2016*.

Dom de Chevalier Deep, fairly intense; low-keyed, vanilla; more positive on palate, very good but not spectacular. Tannic. ★(★★★) *2010–2015*.

Ch Clerc-Milon Opaque; low-keyed, medicinal, touch of iron; very sweet, high alcohol (14.4%), fairly lean, delicious flavour. ★★(★★) *2010–2020*.

Ch Clinet Fruit and whiff of caramel; sweet, rich texture, touch of tar, nice wine. (★★★★) *Now–2016*.

Ch La Conseillante Medium-deep, confident yet relaxed appearance; equally amenable nose, distinctive, 'tea leaves'; fairly sweet, good flavour, easy and approachable, good length. ★(★★★) *Now–2016*.

Ch Cos d'Estournel Opaque, fairly intense; scented, touch of mocha; fairly sweet, fleshy, full-flavoured, mouthfilling. ★★(★★★) *2012–2025*.

Ch La Croix de Gay Taut, hard, brambly; fairly full-bodied. Good but not very interesting. ★(★★★) *(just)*. *2010–2016*.

Ch Croizet-Bages Attractive Pauillac Cabernets, whiff of greengage; sweet, lots of fruit, delicious flavour, masked tannin. (★★★★) *Now–2020*.

Ch Dauzac Virtually opaque; good fruit, spicy new oak, 'peppery' (alcohol); sweet, attractive extended fruit, dominant oak, tannic finish. (★★★★) *2010–2020*.

Ch La Dominique Low-keyed, whiff of tar; sweet, distinctive and interesting flavour; tar noted again. Good wine. (★★★★) *2010–2018*.

Ch Ducru-Beaucaillou Deep, intense; nose difficult to define; dry, good length, ripe tannins yet a slightly bitter finish? Classic Ducru. Needs time to sort itself out. (★★★★) *2015–2025?*

Ch Duhart-Milon Very deep, intense; whiff of cedar and Cabernet Sauvignon; medium-sweet, pleasant refreshing fruit, touch of greenness. ★★(★★) *2014–2024*.

Ch Durfort-Vivens Very straightforward, lean, very tannic. (★★★★) *(just)*. *2012–2018*.

Ch Ferrière Impressive; taut but good depth; fairly sweet, fleshy, lovely flavour. (★★★★) *Now–2015*.

Ch de Fieuzal Almost opaque core; straightforward, hard; sweet, delicious flavour, oaky. ★★(★★) *2010–2015*.

Ch Figeac Deliciously fragrant nose with whiff of violets; fairly sweet, soft fruit flavour, distinctive but not as idiosyncratic or characterful as in more challenging years. ★(★★★) *2010–2018*.

Ch La Fleur-Pétrus Richly coloured; sweaty, tannic nose; sweet, complete, delicious. (★★★★) *2010–2025*.

Forts de Latour Taut, newly sawn wood; crisp fruit, sweetened up in the glass. Very good. ★★(★★) *2012–2018*.

Ch Gazin Opaque; good fruit, dry, lean, very tannic. Change of style, more 'modern'. (★★★★) *(just)*. *2010–2020*.

Ch Giscours Opaque, velvety, rich 'legs'; tight bramble and oak; good crisp fruit, new oak uppermost. Fair length. (★★★) *possible* ★★★★ *development*.

Ch Grand-Puy-Ducasse Purple; distinctive, rich fruit and good depth; sweet, rich body, good fruit, very dry finish. A great Ducasse. ★(★★★) *2015–2025*.

Ch Grand-Puy-Lacoste Distinctive, interesting fruit; sweet, crisp fruit; delicious flavour, grip. A high-quality, fairly long-haul wine. ★★★(★★) *2018–2030*.

Ch La Grave Richly coloured; whiff of mocha; fairly sweet and rich on the palate, and quite an attack. Very dry finish. (★★★★) *2012–2024*.

Ch Haut-Bailly Very good, classic nose, sweaty tannins; medium-sweet, delicious fruit and flavour. ★★(★★) *2010–2020*.

Ch Haut-Batailley Impressive; low-keyed, fragrant, distinctive; sweet, crisp, nice texture, delicious flavour. ★★(★★) *2012–2020*.

Hosanna Sweet, leathery tannic nose and taste. Excellent but exceptionally tannic. (★★★★) *2015–?*

Ch Kirwan Deep, velvety, rich 'legs'; good tight bramble and oak, sweet fruit, tannin; medium-sweet, impressive, distinctive fruit, very dry finish. A much toned down and more agreeable style than the 'over the top' Kirwan of the late 1980s. (★★★★) *(just)* *2010–2018*.

Ch Lafon-Rochet Hint of caramel, a bit unyielding; medium-sweet, lean, attractive fruit, good length. ★(★★★) *2015–2025*.

Ch Lagrange Whiff of liquorice and tar; overall dry, good crisp fruit. ★★(★★) *2012–2020*.

Ch La Lagune The 'odd man out' of the Médoc. The vineyard lies on a swathe of Graves soil that rings Bordeaux, which accounts for its distinctive style, in the past referred to as the Burgundy of Bordeaux. In 2005, due to weather, uniform ripeness and vinification, its novel characteristics subdued. Rich fruit on nose and palate, very varietal, refreshing citrus element. ★(★★★) *2010–2020*.

Ch Langoa-Barton Very forthcoming, brambly fruit, slightly stalky; overall sweet, positive, good fruit. (★★★★) *2015–2025*.

Ch Larcis-Ducasse Opaque; well evolved, flowery nose; sweet, good texture, delicious flavour and aftertaste. Deserves to be better known. ★(★★★) *Now–2016*.

Ch Larrivet-Haut-Brion Virtually opaque; very good wine. ★(★★★) *2010–2018*.

Ch Lascombes Very deep, very purple; neutral, oaky; medium-sweet, distinctive flavour, raw tannins. (★★★) *2012–2018*.

Ch Latour-à-Pomerol Very good fruit, sweet, assertive. (★★★★) *2012–2020*.

Ch Latour-Martillac Impressive colour, virtually opaque; good, slightly medicinal nose; sweet, rich, good flavour and length. ★★(★★) *2010–2018*.

Ch Léoville-Barton Opaque, intense; brambly fruit and oak, considerable depth; fairly sweet, good extract, classic, distinctive Cabernet flavour, long dry finish. Outstanding. (★★★★★) *2018–2030*.

Ch Léoville-Las-Cases Opaque, intense purple; whiff of fresh walnuts, sweaty (tannins), cheesy; medium-sweet, good flesh and body (13.2% alcohol), complete. (★★★★★) *2015–2030*.

Ch Léoville-Poyferré Low-keyed, a touch of meatiness; more positive on palate, fairly sweet, good weight and texture. Elegant. (★★★★) *2015–2025*.

Ch La Louvière Crisp fruit, new oak; dependable style, and good length. ★★(★★) *2010–2020*.

Ch Lynch-Bages Opaque, intense; distinct spicy blackcurrant; sweet, delicious fruit, complete. (★★★★★) *2015–2030*.

Ch Lynch-Moussas Impressively deep, opaque; piquant, metallic, fragrant, highish tone, powerful; fulsome, lean, austere, fruit-laden, very dry finish. (★★★★) *2015–2030*.

Ch Malartic-Lagravière Curious peppery fruit; medium-sweet but very dry bitter tannic finish. (★★★) *potential* (★★★★)? *2012–2018*.

Ch Malescot-St-Exupéry Rich 'legs'; interesting scent, spicy oak, good depth; fairly sweet, soft, fleshy, very attractive, tannic finish. (★★★★) *2010–2020*.

Ch Marquis de Terme Deep, velvety; good, brambly, spicy new oak; fairly sweet, full-flavoured, masked tannin. ★★(★★) *2010–2018*.

Ch La Mission Haut-Brion Harmonious; impressive, tannic grip. A superb classic La Mission. (★★★★★) *2015–2030*.

Ch Monbrison Velvety sheen; sweet, harmonious, good extract and oak; nice fruit, flesh, length. (★★★★) *2010–2018*.

Ch Montrose Nose neither easy nor obvious – needs time and air; much more dramatic on the palate with sweet, intense fruit and flavour, touch of iron, silky/leathery tannins and great length. '*Puissance exceptionelle*' – I quote Monsieur Charmolüe who, a few days later, sold his legendary château. ★(★★★★) *2015–2030*.

Ch Nenin Fragrant, blackberry, new wood, 'rather exciting' aromas; good fruit, high strength (14.19% alcohol), tannin and acidity. ★(★★★) *2010–2018*.

Ch Olivier Good fruit and depth; fairly sweet, fullish, flavoury, delicious.
★(★★★) *Now–2015*.

Les Ormes-de-Pez Low-keyed, taut, fragrant, citrus; pleasant sweetness and
fruit, good flavour, masked tannin. ★(★★★★) *2011–2016*.

Ch Palmer Impressively deep, intense; dumb – as yet; huge wine, very tannic.
(★★★★) *2015–2025?*

Ch Pape-Clément Very good colour, nose and flavour, fruit and new oak in
balance. ★(★★★) *2010–2018*.

Ch Pavie Opaque, very intense, 'modern'; extravagantly, almost explosively
positive and distinctive nose; very sweet, full, rich, good texture and length but
very tannic. Though impressive and concentrated, it was far less tarry than in the
previous vintages I had so disliked. Frankly, not my idea of St-Émilion. I still
prefer the drinkable and good-value Pavies made by the previous owner.
(★★★★★) *2015–?*

Ch Pavie-Decesse Similar appearance but whiff of tar and iron mingled with
the fruit; punchy, 'modern' style, lean fruit, good length, oaky and very tannic. A
grudging (★★★★) *2015–?*

Ch Pavie-Macquin Virtually opaque; attractive, unexaggerated,
straightforward and agreeable. ★(★★★★) *Now–2016*.

Ch Petit-Village Slightly chocolatey; sweet, good fruit and flavour, nice
exture. ★★(★★) *Now–2016*.

Ch Phélan-Ségur Opaque core; touch of tar; sweet, soft, full fruit, attractive.
(★★★★) *2015–2025*.

Ch Pichon-Lalande Deep, velvety; distinctive fruit and oak; very sweet on
the palate, delicious flavour, good tannin and acidity. ★★(★★★) *2012–2025*.

Ch Pichon-Longueville Fairly intense, velvety; charred, hefty fruit; fairly
sweet, good length, fruity dry finish. (★★★★) *2015–2030*.

Le Pin 100% Merlot. Minute production, and a very rare opportunity to taste
from the cask. Medium – not deep; very good, slightly spicy; unostentatiously
natural, nice weight (13% alcohol). Simply delicious. ★(★★★) *2010–2016*.

Ch La Pointe Lovely colour, deep, velvety; very fragrant, very oaky; sweet,
rich, easy, perhaps somewhat specious. A good drink. ★★(★) *Now–2015*.

Ch Pontet-Canet Opaque; fragrant, high-toned; very sweet nose and palate,
delicious fruit and flavour, good tannin and acidity. Best ever? ★★(★★★) *2010–2030*.

Ch Potensac Strange, unknit, vegetal; sweet, attractive, lip-smacking
tannin/acidity. For its class (★★★★) *2010–2015*.

Ch Prieuré-Lichine Low-keyed, good fruit; medium-sweet, soft, good fruit
and flesh. Different to the lean, crisp style of old. (★★★) *2010–2015*.

Providenc Like Hosanna, another idiosyncratic Mouiëx name. Fragrant, good
flavour and length. Hard to pin down. (★★★) *Possibly underrated. Now–?*

Ch Rauzan-Gassies Curious metallic nose, distinctive; better on palate, fairly
sweet, soft fruit, attractive, very dry finish. A good Gassies. (★★★★) *2010–2018*.

Ch Rauzan-Ségla Good brambly fruit, spicy new oak; good flavour, length,
very tannic. (★★★★) *2015–2025*.

Ch Smith-Haut-Lafitte Velvety, opaque core; curious, arboreal nose, whiff
of liquorice; sweet, soft, distinctive. ★(★★★) *2010–2020*.

Ch Talbot Very forthcoming, 'broad', rich fruit, whiff of tea; medium sweetness?
and body, well constituted fruit and flavour. ★(★★★) *2012–2025*.

Ch du Tertre Sweet, sweaty tannins and oak on nose and palate. Good fruit. (★★★) *2010–2020*.

Ch La Tour-Carnet In the mid-1970s arguably the worst classed growth of the Médoc, now transformed and ultra-modernised – perhaps trying too hard. Opaque, intense; deep, pronounced Cabernet Sauvignon aroma, new oak; medium-sweet, full, rich, brambly fruit, new oak. Almost 'New World'. I admire it, but prefer a less aggressive style. (★★★) *2015–2020*?

Ch La Tour Haut-Brion Opaque, intense; good nose, flavour and length. Tannic but less abrasive masculine than so often. (★★★★) *2012–2014*.

Ch Troplong-Mondot Strange, meaty, but fragrant. Good fruit and texture, dry finish. Good wine. (★★★★) *2010–2016*.

Ch Trotanoy Low-keyed but sweet and fleshy on the nose, also sweaty tannins; sweet, powerful, strength and length. By any standards a superb Pomerol, vying with Pétrus for top place. (★★★★★) *2015–2030*.

Ch Trottevieille Attractive, interesting nose and flavour. Rich brambly fruit, straightforward, punchy, very tannic. (★★★★) *2010–2016*.

Vieux Ch Certan Vintage saved by rain. Very deep; fairly sweet, touch of tar and tobacco, very oaky, good length, tannic. (★★★★) *2012–2020*.

Ch Le Vray-Croix-de-Gay Opaque; fruit-laden; sweet, delicious flavour, tannic of course. (★★★★) *2012–2018*.

Dry White Bordeaux

Most dry white Bordeaux wines, like most other dry whites, are best drunk young and fresh. However, a few top châteaux, from the Pessac-Léognan appellation, are capable of producing outstanding whites which, with bottle age, take on extra dimensions, lasting for over 20 years or so, and on occasion up to 50 years. Unlike Sauternes, vintages for good dry white Bordeaux wines do not need botrytis – in fact the opposite; rot of any kind is to be avoided. Although vintages vary in quality from year to year it is rare for a dry white Bordeaux not to be made.

Outstanding vintages
1928, 1937, 1943, 1945, 1971, 1976, 1978, 1989, 1990, 2005

Classic older vintages: 1926–1979

Both before and after World War Two almost all dry white Bordeaux wines were cheap and of low quality. At the top end some superb wines were made, albeit uneconomically, for a limited number of connoisseurs and the better French restaurants. Those of major vintages kept well.

VINTAGES AT A GLANCE

Outstanding ★★★★★ 1928, 1937, 1943, 1945, 1971, 1976, 1978
Very Good ★★★★ 1926, 1929, 1934, 1947, 1949, 1955, 1959, 1961, 1962, 1975
Good ★★★ 1927, 1933, 1935, 1940, 1942, 1948, 1952, 1953, 1966, 1970, 1979

1928 ★★★★★
The best vintage of the century for dry whites. Firm, distinguished wines which held well. **Pavillon Blanc de Ch Margaux** was still good, after 60 years, with excellent length and acidity.

1929 ★★★★
Some wines still good if well kept.
Ch Laville Haut-Brion Faultless. Harmonious honeyed bottle-age bouquet, excellent flavour, flesh, balance. *From the Woltner cellars, June 1999* ★★★★

1934 ★★★★
An excellent vintage.

Ch Laville Haut-Brion Virtually faultless. *June 1990* ★★★★★
Ch Olivier Blanc Pale gold; sound nose that opened up fragrantly; medium-dry, waxy Sémillon flavour; good flavour, dry acidic finish. *Dec 2002* ★★★
SPECIAL NOTE A range of vintages of **Ch Laville Haut-Brion** from the Woltner family cellars were tasted in 1990 and are noted in *Vintage Wine*. Particularly good were the 1935 and the wartime years 1940, 1941, 1942 and 1943 (also for **Ch Haut-Brion Blanc**). Of the post-war vintages the following were outstanding 1945, 1949, 1955, 1959, 1961 (last tasted in 1997), 1966, 1970, 1971 (great). If cellared well, they will range from interesting to excellent.

1976 ★★★★★

Excessive heat and drought. Low in acidity. Most aged quickly.
Ch Laville Haut-Brion Glorious gold colour; softly fragrant lanolin Sémillon; dry, fairly full-bodied, adequate acidity, lovely flavour. *April 2003* ★★★★ *Drink up.*

1978 ★★★★★

Successful vintage but most wines tiring now. **Ch Haut-Brion Blanc** and **Dom de Chevalier Blanc** still good when last tasted in the late 1990s.

1980–1999

In the 1980s the making of dry whites improved enormously: much of the credit is due to Professor Denis Dubourdieu of Bordeaux University. However, I believe that the pendulum began to swing too far, from the drab, heavy-handed Graves of old to the fresh, lean, fruity and acidic. In my view Sauvignon Blanc and new oak are not compatible bedfellows: too much of either one is superficially attractive but specious. Balance is all.

VINTAGES AT A GLANCE

Outstanding ★★★★★ 1989, 1990
Very Good ★★★★ 1983, 1985 (v), 1994, 1995
Good ★★★ 1981 (v), 1982, 1985 (v), 1986, 1996, 1997, 1998, 1999

1982 ★★★

Successful vintage. The top wines are certainly worth pursuing.
Ch Haut-Brion Blanc Though still fairly pale, a magnificent bouquet, fragrant, nutty, opening up in the glass like a great Montrachet, pineapple, vanilla, peaches. Medium-dry, with delicious flavour and length. *Last noted Jan 1999* ★★★★(★)
Ch Laville Haut-Brion Still pale; low-keyed though harmonious nose; dry, somewhat austere, good flavour and acidity. *Last noted April 1999* ★★★(★)

1983 ★★★★

This top Sauternes vintage was also an excellent one for dry whites.

Ch Haut-Brion Blanc Very pale for its age with lime and gold highlights; equally fresh smelling, at first lemon and vanilla (charred oak), opening up with astonishing scent; bone dry, mouthfilling, depth and power, teeth-gripping acidity. *Last noted Nov 2005* ★★★★ *Will keep.*

Ch Laville Haut-Brion Earlier notes: pale; fragrant; firm, lean, austere. Most recently: had gained colour, now straw yellow; rich but tiring. '83 acidity. Very disappointing. Poor bottle? *Last tasted June 2006. At best* ★★★★ *Needs downgrading?*

Ch Malartic-Lagravière Blanc Distinctive yellow; mature Sémillon; dry, positive flavour, remarkably good. *April 2003* ★★★

1985 ★★★ to ★★★★

Some nice wines and with staying power.

Ch Haut-Brion Blanc Still pale; fragrant; dry, nutty flavour, considerable body and good finish. But I expected better. *Last tasted Feb 1999* ★★★

Ch Laville Haut-Brion Curious scent of camphor, pure vanilla and face powder! Overall dry and lean, with good acidity. Interesting. *April 2000* ★★★

Dom de Chevalier Blanc Fragrant; ideal weight, balance and lovely flavour. *Last tasted Sept 1990* ★★★ *Should still be good.*

1986 ★★★

A successful vintage for early pickers, but risky now.

Dom de Chevalier Blanc Pale for its age; dry, delicious flavour, excellent acidity. *Last tasted Nov 2005* ★★★

1989 ★★★★★

An extraordinary year and some astonishing wines. Because of the intense summer heat the grapes ripened precociously, with too much natural sugar and too little acidity. The grapes were picked early to achieve balance.

Ch Haut-Brion Blanc Palish, highly polished light gold; its puppy fat and oak very noticeable; rich, assertive, stylish but hefty. Good but showing bottle age. *Last tasted Nov 2002* ★★★ *But drink soon.*

Ch Laville Haut-Brion Lovely colour, bright lemon yellow; strange, vanillin, almost Chenin Blanc-like aroma; good, but now lacking the earlier creamy aromatic character. *Last tasted Dec 2004. At best* ★★★★★ *now* ★★★★

Dom de Chevalier Blanc Still very pale, enticingly lime-tinged; touch of vanilla, bottle age noted; dry, good flavour and acidity. *Last tasted Jan 2006* ★★★ *Now at peak.*

Pavillon Blanc de Ch Margaux Oaky, ripe attractive nose; medium-dry, assertive. *March 2001* ★★★★

1990 ★★★★★

Despite the hot summer the dry whites turned out to have a better balance of acidity and alcohol than the '89s. All except the top growths should have been consumed by now.

Ch Haut-Brion Blanc Good colour; waxy, touch of vanilla; firm dry finish, a bit four-square. *Last noted June 1997* ★★★(★) *Needed more bottle age.*

Ch Laville Haut-Brion Still a very distinctive yellow colour and equally distinctive flavour and body. Very good. Perhaps needing a little more bottle age. *Last tasted Sept 2003* ★★★★ *Probably at its peak now.*

1991, 1992, 1993 forgettable vintages

1994 ★★★★

Highly favourable growing conditions. The grapes for the dry whites were mainly picked before the start of the mid-September rains.

Ch Laville Haut-Brion Very pale; light, subdued nose; medium-dry, on the lean side and surprisingly oaky. *June 2000* ★★(★)?

Pavillon Blanc de Ch Margaux Palish, slightly green tinge; fragrant, spearmint; pleasantly aromatic with slightly spicy finish. *Nov 2000* ★★★

1995 ★★★★

Good conditions for the dry whites. The top wines have class and stamina for further ageing. Most of the rest will have passed their best by now.

Ch Haut-Brion Blanc Attractive nose, whiff of vanilla and touch of peach kernels on the palate. Good length and aftertaste. *June 1999. Then* ★★★(★) *Drink soon.*

Dom de Chevalier Blanc Very pale; low-keyed, some spicy oakiness; dry, complete, all-of-a piece, firm. *April 2000* ★★★ *Now–2010.*

Ch Smith-Haut-Lafitte Blanc Very fragrant; medium-dry, spicy, touch of melon and pineapple. *Last tasted June 2000* ★★★ *Drink soon.*

1996 ★★★

Good but not exceptional. The best fresh, aromatic, with good acidity. For early drinking.

Ch Haut-Brion Blanc Not impressive. *Last tasted April 2005* ★★

Dom de Chevalier Blanc A whiff of new oak and 'arboreal' piquancy; still distinctly dry of course, Sauvignon very apparent, attractive, acidic. *April 2000* ★★★

Ch Malartic-Lagravière Blanc Sémillon-dominant; fairly dry, very pleasant flavour, good balance and condition for its age. *April 2003* ★★★

1997 ★★★

Sauvignon Blanc grapes with a high sugar content lacked acidity. The later-ripening Sémillon tended to dominate, giving the blends a broader style with good depth of fruit but lacking vivacity.

Ch Haut-Brion Blanc Delicious, spicy, sweet and soft; ripe grapes and alcohol resulting in surprising sweetness. Full-bodied, attractive, touch of astringency. *April 1998. Then* ★★★(★) *Drink soon.*

Ch Laville Haut-Brion Good colour; young pineapple aroma and flavour; rich but drier than Haut-Brion. Oaky. Dry finish. *April 1998* ★★★(★) *Drink now.*

Dom de Chevalier Blanc Very pale; a vivacious aroma; attractive, perhaps lacking a little length. *Last tasted April 2000* ★★★ *Now–2010.*

1998 ★★★

Because of the excessive heat in August, fully ripe grapes were picked early.
Ch Haut-Brion Blanc A hefty, stolid but very rich, full-bodied wine.
Impressive. *Oct 2001* ★★★(★) *Now–2015.*
Ch Latour-Martillac Dry, lean and far too oaky. *March 2001* ★★★
Ch Laville Haut-Brion Very pale, limpid; medium dryness and weight,
distinctive flavour, well balanced. Very good finish. Superb. Drinking well. *Last
tasted Nov 2005* ★★★★ *Now–2010.*

1999 ★★★

A satisfactory year. The early harvest took place in great heat. Sauvignon
Blanc was picked first, as usual. However – paradoxically – the Sauvignon
Blanc provided the power and the later-picked Sémillon the fruit, both
attaining natural alcohol levels over 12%.
Ch Haut-Brion Blanc Fairly pale, starbright; slow to open up but very
good; fairly dry; perfect flavour, balance and weight. Probably at its optimum. *Last
tasted June 2003* ★★★★ *Now–2010.*
Ch Laville Haut-Brion Delicious crusty, nutty nose with whiff of peach
kernels; medium-dry, fairly substantial, very good texture. *Last tasted Oct 2005*
★★(★★)
Dom de Chevalier Blanc Showing bottle age and frankly unsure whether
this is 'complex' or merely 'unknit'. Dry lean lemon and vanilla. *Last tasted Oct 2005*
★★★?
Ch Pape-Clément Blanc Pale; with Sauvignon aroma, pineapple and
'tomcats'; touch of sweetness, flavoury. New broom identifiable. *Last tasted May
2003* ★★★ *Drink soon.*

2000–2005

The past few years have been a period of stability, with many
châteaux, including a surprising number of many hitherto minor ones,
producing distinctly better dry white wines. These attractive wines are
now showing plenty of freshness and acidity. If anything there is a bit
too much new oak and a too liberal use of Sauvignon Blanc. Only the
top classic wines are reported below.

VINTAGES AT A GLANCE

Outstanding ★★★★★ 2005
Very Good ★★★★ 2000, 2001, 2002, 2003
Good ★★★ 2004

2000 ★★★★

Dry whites more successful than Sauternes. Growing conditions almost as
good as for the magnificent reds. The top whites have plenty of life ahead.

Ch Haut-Brion Blanc Though still slightly hazy, the wine showed considerable character and depth. Not the often austere style. Attractive. Considerable potential. *March 2001* (★★★★) *Now–2010*.

Ch Laville Haut-Brion Slightly hazy; fragrant nose, youthful pineapple and oak; dry, very good. But I missed the excitement of the almost overpowering '89. *March 2001* (★★★)? *Now–2012*.

Ch Smith-Haut-Lafitte Blanc Pale; good nose; dry, very good flavour and balance. *June 2007* ★★★ *Now–2010*.

THE BEST OF OTHER WINES NOTED AT THE OPENING TASTING IN MARCH 2001: **Dom de Chevalier** (as usual); and **Ch Pape-Clément** (a wine to look out for).

2001 ★★★★

A good vintage. Cool conditions suited the early-ripening Sauvignon Blanc and Sémillon, resulting in fresh, aromatic dry whites with good levels of acidity.

Ch Haut-Brion Blanc Very pale; low-keyed, developed attractive fragrance; better on palate, dry, crisp, very good acidity. *Oct 2005* ★★★(★★) *Now–2012*.

Ch Laville Haut-Brion Medium-pale, limpid; excellent, opened up in the glass; fairly dry, medium–full-bodied, lovely, slightly smoky flavour, good balance and acidity. *Feb 2006* ★★★(★) *Now–2010*.

2002 ★★★★

The uneven and dismal summer was saved by a perfect September. These are attractive wines with good aroma and fresh acidity. Only the top growths will benefit from keeping any longer.

Ch Haut-Brion Blanc Yellow gold; deliciously forthcoming, rich vanilla and youthful pineapple fragrance; medium-dry, very rich, soft texture, great length, fresh acidic finish and oaky/spicy aftertaste. Superb. *April 2003* ★★(★★★) *Now–2016*.

Ch Laville Haut-Brion Yellow; low-keyed at first but soon opened up, pineapple and vanilla; medium-dry, complete, attractive, very good positive dry acidic finish. *April 2003* ★★(★★) *Now–2012*.

Ch Smith-Haut-Lafitte Blanc Fairly pale; attractive aroma; dry, drinking well. *Last tasted June 2005* ★★★ *Drink soon*.

THE BEST OF OTHER WINES NOTED AT THE OPENING TASTING IN APRIL 2003: **Ch Bouscaut** youthful, pineapple, acidic ★(★★); **Ch Carbonnieux** raw Sauvignon Blanc (★★); **Dom de Chevalier** fragrant, fair length ★(★★); **Ch de Fieuzal** ★(★★); **Ch La Louvière** mild, soft ★★★; and **Ch Pape-Clément** distinctive ★★(★★)

2003 ★★★★

This was one of Bordeaux's hottest vintages ever, with extreme heat in June, July and August. The early harvest produced somewhat untypical dry whites, rich but with low acidity. They are attractive but are wines mainly for short term drinking as they will evolve more speedily.

Ch Haut-Brion Blanc Youthful, spicy pineapple; rich, full-flavoured and very attractive wine. *April 2004* ★★★★ *Now–2016*.

Ch Laville Haut-Brion Distinctive palish yellow; vanillin dominates the nose; not sweet, certainly not dry, with the richness of ripe grapes, yet leaner than expected, and oaky. *April 2004* ★★★★ *Now–2015.*

Ch Chantegrive Typical of the new breed. One of the rising stars of the Graves, though frankly I found it unexciting. Dry, well made, pleasant enough for early drinking. *June 2005* ★★ *Drink soon.*

Dom de Chevalier Blanc Very pale; floral, vanilla; pleasant ripe entry, medium weight, dry finish. Good wine. *Last tasted May 2007* ★★★★ *Now–2012.*

Ch Smith-Haut-Lafitte Blanc Pale colour; refreshing, distinctive Sauvignon Blanc aroma; dry but ripe, drinking well. *Last tasted June 2005* ★★★ *Drink up.*

2004 ★★★

After the excesses of 2003, this was a more normal vintage, unexceptional in the Graves with rain and warm weather in August, and a lacklustre market. As I was unable to attend the opening tastings in the spring of 2005 I have few first-hand notes.

Pavillon Blanc de Ch Margaux Fairly pale with distinctly youthful green tinge; 100% – and very ripe – Sauvignon Blanc, the fragrance of poire Williamine; touch of sweetness, flavour of raw pineapple. Regarded as one of the best ever Pavillon Blancs, but not remotely in the class of Ch Margaux's *grand vin* reds. *Assez bien* but not inexpensive. *May 2005* ★★★ *Drink soon.*

Ch Smith-Haut-Lafitte Blanc Pale, greenish tinge; fresh minty aroma, medium-dry, medium–full-bodied (13% alcohol), flavoury, Sauvignon Blanc dominated. *April 2006* ★★★ *Now–2010.*

Of the châteaux tasted by my colleague, Steven Spurrier at the spring tastings, the most highly rated include **Ch Chantegrive, Ch Bouscaut, Ch La Louvière, Ch Malartic-Lagravière** and **Ch Pape-Clément**, all drinking well now but will hold well for a further 5 years or so.

2005 ★★★★★

This was an impeccable growing season, even though this was the second year of drought in a row. The summer was hot but not excessively so and a little rain at the end of August helped soothe the vines. Ch Haut-Brion, the first to harvest, started picking on 24 August. Sauvignon Blanc and Sémillon, the traditional white varieties, achieved a rare balance of fruit and acidity. The top dry whites, mainly from the Pessac-Léognan appellation, have a promising future.

Ch Haut-Brion Blanc The *cépage* mix in 2005: 52% Sauvignon Blanc, 48% Sémillon. Lovely nose, great depth; sweet, excellent flavour and length. Beautiful wine capable of excellent mid-term, even long-term, development. *April 2006* ★★(★★★) *2010–2015.*

Ch Laville Haut-Brion High percentage of Sémillon (78%) much in evidence. Rich, almost fat; medium-sweet, lovely flavour. The quality and ripeness of the '89 but leaner, more elegant. *April 2006* ★★★(★★) *Now–2015.*

Dom de Chevalier Blanc Very pale; pronounced Sauvignon Blanc, spicy, 'tom cats' and gooseberries; fairly dry, floral, very attractive, good acidity. *April 2006* ★★(★★) *Now–2015.*

Ch de Fieuzal Blanc Very pale; distinctive, arboreal, privet; medium – not dry, ripe sweetness, attractive. *April 2006* ★★(★★) *Now–2010*.

Pavillon Blanc de Ch Margaux 100% Sauvignon Blanc. Pale; very fragrant, lime blossom, honey, youthful pineapple; medium-dry, ripe, full-bodied (14.5% alcohol), impressive. *April 2006* ★★(★★) *Now–2012*.

Ch Smith-Haut-Lafitte Blanc Pale; the usual, distinctive and vivacious Sauvignon Blanc 'tom cats'; also distinctive touch of ripe sweetness, very attractive, pronounced floral character. *April 2006* ★★★(★) *Now–2010*.

Sauternes

The Sauternes *appellation* covers a compact area in the southern part of the Bordeaux region. In certain years, thanks to a unique microclimate, autumn morning mists arise which are then burned off by the warm, ripening, afternoon sunshine. The mist encourages the formation of botrytis or 'noble rot' fungus (*pourriture noble* in French). This attacks the ripening grapes, reducing the potential juice and concentrating their natural sugar content. In some years Sauternes can be made without the onset of botrytis but, though sweet, lack the extra dimension. The principal grapes are Sémillon, a dependable variety happily susceptible to botrytis, and the more acidic Sauvignon Blanc which adds zest. Sometimes a small percentage of the grapey, aromatic Muscadelle is used. Sauternes is always sweet. Dry white wine from here is sold as straightforward Bordeaux AC.

A visit to Ch d'Yquem will show you at once why the wine is so special. The ancient château sits in a commanding position with its vast rows of vines spreading down the slopes below: a perfect combination of site, soils, drainage and *cépages*. Equally dominant, since the 18th century, is its wine, both in quality and price. From 1785 until 1999, the château was owned and run by the Lur Saluces family. Yquem, along with Tokaji Aszú Eszencia and the finest madeira, develops well in bottle and is famed for its longevity. For over two centuries it has been the pride of connoisseurs and collectors.

Drink Sauternes by itself, with ripe nectarines or cheese; avoid serving it with sweet pastry confections.

1784–1899

Sweet wines from late-picked grapes were being made in the Sauternes district in the 18th century; and the reputation of Yquem was well established long before the end of that century. The full provenance of several of these old vintages is not known and I have described their condition and, to a necessarily limited extent, their colour, smell and taste, as I have found them. As can be seen, many of these ancient wines appear to have been remarkably well preserved and, by any standards, are most lovely wines.

Outstanding vintages
1784, 1802, 1811, 1831, 1834, 1847, 1864, 1865, 1869, 1875, 1893, 1906, 1921, 1929, 1937, 1945, 1947, 1949, 1955, 1959, 1967, 1971, 1975, 1983, 1989, 1990, 2001

Vintages at a Glance

Outstanding ★★★★★ 1784, 1802, 1811, 1831, 1834, 1847, 1864, 1865, 1869, 1875, 1893

Very Good ★★★★ 1787, 1814, 1820, 1825, 1828, 1841, 1848, 1858, 1871, 1874, 1896, 1899

Good ★★★ 1818, 1822, 1851, 1859, 1861, 1868, 1870

1784 ★★★★★

The most renowned vintage of the late 18th century and well documented thanks mainly to the original copies of the letters of Thomas Jefferson.
Ch d'Yquem Bottled at the château in January 1788. Sloping-shouldered bottles with contemporary wheel engraving '*Ch d'Yquem Th J 1784*'. Most recently with short, crumbly, original cork, the level of the wine mid-shoulder: a warm mahogany-amber colour with pronounced yellow-green rim. After 15 minutes settled down to reveal a remarkably rich, tangy, honeyed scent, and after a further 30 minutes opened up sweetly, like black treacle. Medium sweetness and body. Lovely old flavour and good finish. *Last noted Sept 1998* ★★★★

1802 ★★★★★

Ch Yquem Labelled '*Château-Yquem, Perrault, Chalon s/Saône*'. Good colour for its age; slightly maderised with shades of caramel and vanilla. Better flavour than expected. Rich yet dry finish. Good acidity. *Aug 1998* ★★★

1811 ★★★★★

The most famous 'comet' vintage.
Ch Yquem Contemporary mould blown bottle, labelled '*Château Yquem, Marquis A M de Lur Saluces, 1811, Grand Vin Sauternes*'; sweet scent; considerable depth and length. Dry finish. *Last tasted Sept 1998* ★★★★

1814 ★★★★

Ch Yquem Labelled '*Château Yquem, Lur Saluces, 1814*'. Original cork. Level upper shoulder. Lovely colour; rich, peachy, perfection – almost too good; chocolatey flavour, fragrant aftertaste. Delicious. *Last tasted Sept 1998* ★★★★★

1818 ★★★

Ch Yquem Original dried-out cork. Level into neck. Nose showing its age, singed but fragrant; sweet, full, fat, tangy, with positive raisiny flavour. *Sept 1998* ★★★★

1820 ★★★★

Ch Suduiraut Half bottle, from the château. Original cork, good level. Rich, deep amber; amazing scent, apricot and old honey; still very sweet, glorious *crème brûlée* flavour, concentrated, wonderful acidity and aftertaste. *May 2004* ★★★★★

1825 ★★★★

Ch Yquem Most recently, with lead capsule embossed '*1825 G Paillère & Fils,*

Ch Yquem
From 1789–1855 the wine was known as 'Yquem', and as 'd'Yquem' before and after this period. In the 1855 classification of Bordeaux's top sweet white wines Yquem was classed as Bordeaux's only Premier Grand Cru Classé château and the d' was reintroduced.

Bordeaux'. Original cork, level top-shoulder. Sadly, unclean nose, grubby, oily, dried-out. *Last noted Sept 1998. At best* ★★★★

1831 ★★★★★
Ch d'Yquem In magnum: pale for its age; spicy apricot, light caramel, glorious; medium-sweet, rich, fantastic flavour, dry finish yet lingering sweetness. *Aug 2005* ★★★★★

1834 ★★★★★
Ch Yquem Similar label to the 1814, but with '*Sauternes*' added. Short capsule, wizened cork. Level top-shoulder. Beautiful colour; rich, fragrant bouquet of great depth; very rich, attractive. *Sept 1998* ★★★★

1847 ★★★★★
Unquestionably the greatest-ever Sauternes vintage.
Ch Yquem A superb bottle with short gold capsule and original cork: faultless bouquet, harmonious, glorious evolution in the glass; very rich, excellent flavour, perfect acidity, length and finish. *Last tasted June 2001* ★★★★★★ *(6 stars)*

1848 ★★★★
Ch Yquem Most recently, original cork branded '*Yquem Grand Vin*'. Good level. Rich colour, gold highlights; slightly varnishy nose, but rich, with great depth. Powerful, full-bodied, complete, good acidity. *Last tasted Sept 1998* ★★★★

1851 ★★★
Ch Yquem Original cork. Good level. Orange-amber; honeyed, caramelly, fragrant bouquet; drying out, singed barley sugar flavour, good acidity. *Sept 1998* ★★★★

1858 ★★★★
Ch d'Yquem Excellent vintage. Several notes: various bottlings and in variable condition, from oxidised to deliciously rich and concentrated. Most recently, drab, dried out. *Last tasted Oct 2004. At best* ★★★★

1861 ★★★
Ch d'Yquem Original cork. The colour of black treacle, bouquet and flavour to match. High sugar content, low alcohol, very high acidity keeping maderisation at bay. *Last tasted Sept 1998* ★★★★

1864 ★★★★★
One of the greatest Bordeaux vintages, both for reds and whites.
Ch d'Yquem Two notes, one well-nigh perfect. Most recently, dried out, not very clean. *Last noted Sept 1998. At best* ★★★★★

1865 ★★★★★
Another great pre-phylloxera vintage for both red and white Bordeaux.

Ch d'Yquem Recorked at the château in 1992, showing its age on the nose, caramelised yet somehow correct. Dried out. *Last tasted Sept 1998. At best* ★★★★★

1868 ★★★

Ch d'Yquem Most recently, Bordeaux-bottled, ethereal, acidic. *Last tasted Sept 1998. At best* ★★

Ch Coutet Bottled in London, perfectly preserved in an ideal country house cellar. Sheer perfection. *Last tasted Sept 1977* ★★★★

1869 ★★★★★

Ch d'Yquem Most recently, with an oily original cork, a Cruse label and brass-wired bottle: warm amber with orange-gold highlights; enticing, *crème brûlée* and orange blossom bouquet that opened up, exotically. Sweet, assertive, raspberry-vanilla flavour, very fragrant but with a bite. *Last tasted Sept 1998* ★★★★★

1871 ★★★★

Ch d'Yquem Good level; amber-coloured; rich, toasty nose; sweet, powerful, concentrated. *Last noted Feb 1988. At best* ★★★★

1874 ★★★★

A very good pre-phylloxera vintage.

1875 ★★★★★

A vintage noted for its delicacy and elegance.

Ch d'Yquem Bottled in Bordeaux by Cruse: palish amber-gold; quite good bouquet; rich, assertive. *Last tasted Sept 1998. At best* ★★★★★

1876 ★★

Ch d'Yquem Original branded cork. Low-keyed nose; creamy, good flavour, no signs of age, dry finish. *Sept 1998* ★★★

1886

A lean period and mildew now serious throughout the region.

Ch d'Yquem Original cork, high level. Rather drab appearance; rich, high-toned but varnishy; very sweet, surprisingly positive and attractive. *Sept 1998* ★★★

1890 ★★

Ch d'Yquem Rich colour; caramelised almost sickly sweet nose; sweetish, old barley sugar flavour. *Last tasted (a magnum) Sept 1998. At best* ★★★

1893 ★★★★★

One of the hottest summers on record. Superb Sauternes.

Ch d'Yquem Tasted three times, all memorable, two (in 1995 and 1996) warranting 6 stars, both with glorious, glowing, orange-amber colour; deep, rich, honeyed bouquet – ripe apricots, peaches; very rich, powerful, high alcohol and noticeable volatile acidity. Most recently, recorked at the château in 1996, disappointing; whiff of varnish; bitter aftertaste. *Last noted Sept 1998. At best* ★★★★★

1896 ★★★★
Ch d'Yquem Provenance unknown: pale amber; bouquet of old apricots and honey; pure caramel flavour, excellent acidity. *Last noted Jan 2000. At best* ★★★★★

1899 ★★★★
Ch d'Yquem Warm amber; pleasant, sweet nose that started to fade; medium-sweet, good flavour and acidity. Dry finish. *Last tasted Sept 1998. At best* ★★★★
Ch Coutet Medium-deep amber; very rich, barley sugar and *crème brûlée*; no longer sweet yet very rich. Excellent in its way. Dry finish. *March 2002* ★★★

1900–1929

The nadir during this period was the wartime vintage of 1915 but the end of the 1920s were triumphant. Any wine of high quality and unimpeachable provenance in my 4- to 5-star range should still be excellent. A practical tip: levels of ullage up to 7cm below the cork are not abnormal for wines of this age: the wine can still be sound, unlike old red Bordeaux wines with an equivalent level.

VINTAGES AT A GLANCE
Outstanding ★★★★★ 1906, 1921, 1929
Very Good ★★★★ 1900, 1904, 1909, 1926, 1928
Good ★★★ 1914, 1918, 1920, 1923, 1924

1900 ★★★★
The second of the very good *fin de siècle* twin vintages.
Ch d'Yquem Four notes, variable depending on condition, provenance and level. Most recently, a bottle recorked in 1990: fragrant; good flavour, assertive but dried out and a bit tart. *Last noted Sept 1998. At best* ★★★

1903 ★★
Ch d'Yquem Recorked in 1996. Green tinge; caramel, peaches, blossom; still sweet, good flavour, strength and length. *Aug/Sept 1998* ★★★

1906 ★★★★★
A classic Sauternes vintage, still good if kept well.
Ch d'Yquem Most recently, original but poor cork. Deep amber-brown; high-toned, madeira-like nose. Immensely sweet and powerful, good grip but slightly maderised. *Last noted Aug 1998. At best* ★★★★★

1909 ★★★★
Ch d'Yquem Recorked in 1995. Despite a lovely colour and fragrance, dried out. *Last tasted Aug 1998. At best* ★★★★

1914 ★★★

Ch d'Yquem Most recently, recorked in 1994. Lively and lovely colour; curious, highish tone, chocolatey nose, then sickly vanilla; equally odd peach-skin taste. Very dry finish. *Last noted Aug 1998. At best* ★★★★

1918 ★★★

Shortages of materials as well as labour.

Ch d'Yquem A late harvest ending three days before the Armistice. Pale green wartime bottle. Recorked in 1993. Astonishingly pale, with a fine bitty sediment; attractive, fragrant bouquet; fairly sweet, on the light side, good flavour, dry finish. *Aug 1998* ★★★

Ch Climens Lovely colour; heavily botrytised nose; rich *crème brûlée* bouquet and flavour. Very sweet. Penetrating aftertaste. *Last tasted Dec 1995* ★★★★

Ch Lafaurie-Peyraguey Lovely lime-shaded amber; glorious bouquet and flavour. Still sweet, soft with good length and fragrant aftertaste. *Sept 1990* ★★★★

1920 ★★★

A first-rate Sauternes vintage though upstaged by the great '21.

1921 ★★★★★

Unquestionably the greatest Sauternes vintage of the 20th century. The hottest summer since 1893: the grapes had a very high sugar content which, after fermentation, led to high levels of alcohol and residual sugar.

Ch d'Yquem A colossus. Perhaps the richest Yquem of all time, certainly since the towering 1847. Do not be put off by the dark colour. This is correct. I have had the pleasure of tasting the wine over 30 times, from magnums as well as bottles. Not all have warranted 5 stars for, as always, provenance, storage, and state of the cork has a bearing. But most have been unforgettable. The differences are more due to bottle variation rather than the wine's evolution which, for the past 30 or so years, seems to be relatively stable.

Most recently, probably the best ever. Old Yquem always looks its richest in a decanter, this time a 'ruddy' old gold, deep with brush of brown, almost red highlights and open apple-green rim; its bouquet both easy and, in truth, difficult to do justice to: the anticipated *crème brûlée*, old apricots, honeyed, whiff of caramel and unplumbable depth; medium-sweet, drying out a little after 85 years, gloriously rich, intense and persistent flavour, perfect sustaining acidity and lingering aftertaste. Sheer perfection. *Last tasted April 2006* ★★★★★★ *(6 stars)*

1924 ★★★

Wet summer saved by glorious ripening September sun. Underrated.

Ch d'Yquem Recorked in 1996: its bouquet opened up well but not for long. Better on the palate – in fact, quite rich. *Last tasted Sept 1998. At best* ★★★★

Ch Guiraud Remarkably good. Deep colour; caramelised but delicious. Still fairly sweet, ripe, rich, tangy. Good length. *Last tasted June 1997. At best* ★★★★

Ch de Rayne-Vigneau Original cork. Good level. Lovely golden colour; lanolin-like bouquet which opened up sweetly in the glass; in excellent condition, a touch of tangerine, good length and aftertaste. *New Year's Day 1994* ★★★★

1926 ★★★★
Ch d'Yquem A bottle recorked in 1996: too pale, little nose, poor flavour, short. Most disappointing. *Last tasted Sept 1998. At best* ★★★
Ch de Rayne-Vigneau Rich and lovely. *Last tasted Nov 1990. At best* ★★★★

1927
Appalling growing season, though Sauternes enjoyed an Indian summer.
Ch d'Yquem Good upper-shoulder level: very deep amber; sweet, raisiny, toffee-like but harmonious nose; medium-sweet, surprisingly rich with good aftertaste, preserved by its acidity. *Last tasted Feb 2003. At best* ★★★

1928 ★★★★
The first of two excellent vintages, of different weight and style.
Ch d'Yquem Tasted well over a dozen times over the last 35 years, almost all 5-star though colour variation noted, from lemon gold to rich warm amber. Most recently, a magnum: an amazing colour, bright gold with apple-green rim; bouquet of dried apricots, honey and butterscotch; sweet, not cloying nor overwhelming. Delicious flavour. Firm, crisp '28 acidity. *Last tasted Aug 2005*
★★★★★
Ch Caillou A delightful magnum, surprisingly full, rich, tangy, with excellent acidity. *Sept 1996* ★★★★
Ch Climens Most recently: a gorgeous amber-gold; intriguingly complex botrytis nose that unravelled in the glass; still fairly sweet, with '28 crispness and acidity giving it a dry finish. *Nov 1998* ★★★★
Ch de Rayne-Vigneau Very rich, tangy, but a bit tired. *Last noted Nov 1998. At best* ★★★★
Ch Suduiraut Orange-tinged, amber-gold; fabulous bouquet, crisp, fragrant, dried apricots; still sweet, immense depth and complexity. *Last tasted Nov 1998* ★★★★★

1929 ★★★★★
Magnificent. The finest Sauternes vintage between 1921 and 1937. As in these two vintages, the wines were deep in colour.
Ch d'Yquem Several notes, all superb except two bottles recorked at the château. Most recently: medium-deep rich amber with distinct apple-green rim; perfect *crème brûlée* bouquet; still fairly sweet, very rich with glorious flavour and excellent acidity. *Last tasted Feb 2004. At best* ★★★★★
Ch Climens Though not tasted recently, this is unquestionably one of the greatest vintages of one of the most consistently well made Sauternes (*premier cru* Barsac to be more precise). Perfection. *Last noted March 1983* ★★★★★

1930–1949

The world depression hit Bordeaux as elsewhere. Weather conditions in the 1930s were equally disastrous, only the '34s and, in particular, the '37s having real quality. Well-kept Sauternes of these two vintages can still be in remarkable condition, if they have been well cellared. The miracle of the great post-war vintages cannot be explained, merely appreciated.

VINTAGES AT A GLANCE

Outstanding ★★★★★ 1937, 1945, 1947, 1949
Very Good ★★★★ 1934, 1942, 1943
Good ★★★ 1935, 1939, 1944

1934 ★★★★
There were encouraging signs of recovery even though it was still a very lean time for Sauternes.
Ch d'Yquem Two encouragingly consistent notes. Original corks. Both 'medium-deep, warm looking'; bouquet fragrant, 'classic, honeyed', opening up in the glass. Fairly sweet, full body and flavour, rich. *Last noted Sept 1998* ★★★★

1935 ★★★
Ch d'Yquem Recorked in 1996: rich colour; fragrant, with a high-toned, crystallised violet bouquet (as in a refined old Sercial madeira). Good flavour, sweet entry leading to a distinctly dry finish. *Last tasted Sept 1998. At best* ★★★

1937 ★★★★★
One of the great Sauternes vintages, on a par with the top pre-phylloxera years and 1929, but not as monumental as the 1921. The high acidity which resulted in many astringent reds was of great benefit to the sweet whites.
Ch d'Yquem If well cellared, then certain still to be superb. Fairly deep colour, less so than the '21 and '29. Most recently: a fairly deep warm amber with green rim; very distinctive nose, fragrant, complex, harmonious yet with a refreshing, piquant citrus scent; sweet, very rich, mouthfilling, soft, gentle caramel flavour, excellent '37 acidity giving it a dry finish. Superb. *June 2003* ★★★★★
Ch Coutet A fairly deep old gold which, in the decanter, looked almost like a red wine; old nose, apricot skins and caramel; medium-sweet, a good rich flavour, quite powerful, with a hot alcoholic finish and crisp acidity. *June 2000* ★★★★

1939 ★★★
Ch d'Yquem Most recently, a resin-like overtone to its quite rich caramel and raisiny character. Still sweet, fleshy. *Last tasted Sept 1998. At best* ★★★★

1942 ★★★★
Very good weather conditions, but wartime production problems.

Ch d'Yquem Original cork and level into neck: fairly deep colour; very rich, heavily honeyed, toffee-like nose. Holding its sweetness with attractive raisiny flavour. *Last tasted Sept 1998. At best* ★★★★

1943 ★★★★
The most satisfactory wartime vintage.
Ch d'Yquem Most recently, with an original cork, very good level: hefty old-fashioned style, sweet, good length and acidity. *Last noted Sept 1998. At best* ★★★★
Ch Climens Waxy buttercup yellow; fragrant, honey and vanilla; some sweetness loss but fine flavour and excellent condition. *Last noted April 1996* ★★★★

1944 ★★★
Good but now variable.
Ch d'Yquem Three good notes: amber-gold, orange-tinged, vivid apple-green rim; lovely 'honeyed bouquet', 'lanolin', 'orange blossom' repeated; very attractive flavour, good length, dry fragrant finish. *Last tasted Sept 1998* ★★★★

1945 ★★★★★
A small crop produced in difficult post-war conditions but of superb quality.
Ch d'Yquem Deep, with rich golden highlights; rich, 'singed' nose; very sweet yet crisp, with glorious flavour and length. High volatile acidity which gave the wine added vibrancy and piquancy. *Last tasted 2003* ★★★★★
Ch Rieussec Glorious colour and flavour, its superb acidity keeping the 55-year-old Sauternes alive. *Feb 2000* ★★★★★
OTHER GOOD '45S NOTED IN THE LATE '90S: **Ch Doisy-Daëne** rich with excellent length and finish, though drying out a touch. *At best* ★★★★★;
Ch Lafaurie-Peyraguey bouquet assertive, very rich, singed raisins. Perfect flavour, weight and counterbalancing acidity ★★★★★

1947 ★★★★★
Hot summer with the harvest beginning early in intense heat on 15 September. Superbly ripe, rich wines.
Ch d'Yquem Tasted 15 times. Never a poor bottle. Perfect, glowing amber-gold with apple-green rim; totally harmonious bouquet; still remarkably sweet, mouthfilling with a singed hot-vintage character. It looks the purest glowing gold in a decanter by candlelight. *Last noted June 1998* ★★★★★
Ch Climens One of the most magnificent of all Climens vintages. A glowing amber, shot, like taffeta, with pure gold highlights; despite its richness, crisp, minty, ripe nectarines, *crème brûlée*; perfect flavour, weight and balance with creamy texture and infinite aftertaste. *Last noted Jan 1995* ★★★★★
Ch Coutet At best, full, fat, rich and soft. *Last noted Dec 1995. At best* ★★★★
Ch Rieussec Glorious colour in decanter, 'sheer perfection, creamy yet crisp'. *May 1994* ★★★★★
Ch Suduiraut Rich amber; glorious fragrance, pure *crème brûlée*; sweet, rich, powerful. Perfect condition. *Feb 2005* ★★★★★

1949 ★★★★★
A great vintage, still superb.

Ch d'Yquem Most recently, at the château, recorked: bright, medium-deep amber with shades of orange-tawny; very rich, deep, harmonious bouquet, soft, fragrant, perfect; sweet, full, rich yet not hefty, drying out a little, its extract masking its acidity. *Last tasted June 2003* ★★★★★

1950–1969

This was a difficult period for Sauternes, which had gone out of fashion. Nevertheless, there were some superb vintages, and several are still glorious to drink. The marvellous Sauternes vintages of this decade – 1953, 1955 and (best of all) 1959 – went largely unnoticed at the time.

VINTAGES AT A GLANCE

Outstanding ★★★★★ 1955, 1959, 1967
Very Good ★★★★ 1953, 1962
Good ★★★ 1950, 1952, 1961, 1966

1950 ★★★
Ch d'Yquem Several notes. Leaner than the previous post-war vintages but flavoury. 'Peach kernels' nose. Not my favourite. *Last tasted Sept 1998* ★★
OTHER CHÂTEAUX SHOWING WELL IN THEIR HEYDAY: **Ch Climens** ★★★★; **Ch Doisy-Védrines** ★★★★; and **Ch Gilette 'Crème de Tête'** ★★★★

1953 ★★★★
Lovely wines, the best still drinking well.
Ch d'Yquem Nine notes, first in cask, 1955. Though always on the pale side it was taking on a shade of mahogany with age and a sort of hefty fragrance, good length, sweet. Still one of my favourite Yquems. *Last noted Sept 1998* ★★★★

1955 ★★★★★
A perfect growing season and well-nigh perfect Sauternes. Still lovely.
Ch d'Yquem From an English country cellar: extraordinarily deep, like amber-gold, unpolished brass buttons; fully evolved, glorious bouquet, *crème brûlée* and orange blossom; sweet, very rich, tangy. *Last tasted April 2005* ★★★★
OTHER GOOD '55S LAST TASTED IN THE MID- TO LATE 1990S: **Ch Climens** ★★★★; and **Ch Lafaurie-Peyraguey** ★★★★

1958 ★★
Good summer, late harvest. Wines *assez bien*.
Ch d'Yquem Most recently, singed caramel nose and taste. Some fat, hot finish. *Last tasted Sept 1998. At best* ★★★

1959 ★★★★★

A long hot summer with some rain just before the harvest to flesh out the grapes, which retained their high sugar content. Monumental wines.

Ch d'Yquem Many notes. Most recently: old gold; glorious bouquet and flavour; very sweet, full, rich, magnificent. *Last tasted Nov 2005* ★★★★★

Ch Climens A lovely, medium-pale, orange-yellow with an open, lime-shaded edge; showing its age on the nose, a whiff of caramel; fairly sweet, powerful yet lean with a touch of vanilla and good acidity. *Last noted March 2002* ★★★

Ch Rieussec Most recently, almost onion skin colour; sweet, soft, with rich old apricots flavour and finish. Lovely wine. *Last tasted Dec 2004* ★★★★

Ch Sigalas-Rabaud 'Apricots' on nose and on taste. A lovely, fairly substantial wine. Vanilla and barley sugar noted. *Last tasted April 1999* ★★★★

Ch Suduiraut One of Suduiraut's best. Many notes. Still fairly deep amber-gold; glorious bouquet; sweet, rich, full, perfect. *Last tasted Feb 2005* ★★★★★

OTHER '59S SHOWING WELL IN THE MID-1990S: Ch Doisy-Daëne ★★★★; Ch Gilette 'Crème de Tête' ★★★★; Ch Guiraud ★★★; Ch Clos Haut-Peyraguey ★★★★; Ch Lafaurie-Peyraguey ★★★★; and Ch La Tour-Blanche ★★★★★

1961 ★★★

Poor flowering, drought in August and sunny September reduced the size of the crop. Good but lacking the lusciousness of the '59s.

Ch d'Yquem Not a top Yquem. Frankly a mixed bunch of notes, with considerable bottle variations. *Last tasted Sept 1998. At best* ★★★

Ch Climens Many notes. Soft, fragrant, drying out a little but very good. *Last tasted July 1995* ★★★★

Ch Coutet Not a heavyweight but lovely from the start. Most recently: sweet, honeyed, soft, harmonious, fleshy. *Last tasted May 1994* ★★★

Ch Doisy-Védrines Averys' bottling, a lovely amber-gold; bouquet of chocolate and barley sugar, touch of caramelisation; tangy. Good acidity. *Jan 1998* ★★★

Ch Rieussec Most recently, sweet, soft, curiously caramelly with a trace of peach kernels which I never like. *Last noted Aug 1999. At best* ★★★

1962 ★★★★

Far superior to the '61s: superb, elegant, but lacking the richness and body of the great '59s. A delayed but successful flowering. After a warm, fairly dry summer, a sprinkling of rain and sun ripened the grapes and encouraged noble rot for a successful Indian summer harvest.

Ch d'Yquem Most recently, at Yquem, recorked: medium-amber, paler than expected, open lime rim; very fragrant orange blossom, melon, caramel; medium-sweet flavour, some softness yet dry finish. Crisp and lovely. *June 2003* ★★★★

Ch Climens Perfect, harmonious, creamy bouquet; sweet, fullish, apricots; wonderful acidity. *Last tasted Jan 1993* ★★★★

Ch Coutet Pale gold with shade of orange; fragrant honey and apricot bouquet; drying out a little though retaining pleasant sweetness, lean not plump, very good flavour but beginning to show its age. A good Coutet with finesse. *Last tasted May 2006* ★★★★ Drink soon.

Ch Doisy-Védrines Full, rich, remarkably good though a touch of coarseness alongside Ch d'Yquem. *Feb 1997* ★★★★

Ch Guiraud Orange amber; lovely barley sugar nose; still sweet, good flesh, almost fat, with orange blossom flavour and marvellous acidity. *Jan 1995* ★★★★

Ch Sigalas-Rabaud Glorious colour; sweet, silky, harmonious bouquet; rich, powerful. Just a little four-square, lacking finesse. *Last tasted April 1990* ★★★★

Ch Suduiraut Though an old note (1982), superb and worth looking out for. ★★★★(★)

1963, 1964 and 1965

Three disastrous years in Sauternes.

Ch d'Yquem Prematurely aged with oily nose and taste. In 1963 it should never have been put on the market – it was not good. Some English buyers dumped their stock. *Last tasted Sept 1998. 1964 Yquem ruined by torrential rain; 1965 variable. Below standard. Avoid.*

1966 ★★★

A return to better times, vintage-wise, but still a difficult Sauternes market. An unusually cool dry summer with no real warmth until September, resulting in wines with lean, firm and sinewy character.

Ch d'Yquem Surprisingly deep orange-amber colour; caramelised barley sugar bouquet; rich flavour. *Sept 1999* ★★★★

Ch Climens Medium-gold; lovely, fragrant bouquet with whiff of vanilla; sweet, light style, delicious. *Last tasted Nov 2005* ★★★★ *Should keep well.*

Ch Sigalas-Rabaud Startlingly bright yellow and surprisingly dry. Good acidity. *March 1997* ★★

1967 ★★★★★

A superlative vintage, the best since 1959. The crucial flowering period was late, which always leads to a late harvest. After a wet September, sunny conditions, together with beneficial botrytis, were doubly favourable, resulting in stylish wines. The best are still superb.

Ch d'Yquem Tasted over 50 times! Never less than lovely. However, many variations of colour and taste, the former from mid-gold to deeper 'burnished gold', partly due to the ageing progress. Its bouquet I have described as 'ambrosial', 'mint and muscat', 'orange blossom, lime blossom and ripe peaches', and, like all great wines, it unravels and displays extra dimensions. Though rich and ripe, with a welcome element of finesse. Most recently: medium-gold; lovely, classic, *crème brûlée* bouquet; sweet, glorious flavour. *June 2005. At best* ★★★★★

Ch Climens Medium-deep yellow-gold, lime rim; strangely unknit nose, slightly minty, creamy, touch of resin, then opened up, fragrant barley sugar. Fairly sweet, very distinctive, spicy, dry finish. Charming but not great. *Oct 2001* ★★★

Ch Guiraud Brassy colour; 'old gold' nose and flavour. Drying out a bit but rich with very good acidity. *Last noted May 2001* ★★★★ *Past its best.*

Ch Sigalas-Rabaud Most recently: very fragrant, perfection; medium-sweet, good length, excellent acidity. *Last noted March 1997* ★★★★

Ch Suduiraut One of my favourite Sauternes, one of the most successful '67s and one of the best-ever Suduirauts. Most recently: superb amber-gold; bouquet

of apricots, cream, botrytis and honeyed bottle age; medium-sweet, rich yet crisp, lovely flavour and condition. *Last tasted May 2007* ★★★★★
OLDER NOTES, WORTH LOOKING OUT FOR: Ch de Fargues ★★★★; Ch Lafaurie-Peyraguey ★★★★ and Ch Rieussec ★★★★

1969 ★

Dismal weather. Growers in Sauternes were saved by the Indian summer.
Ch d'Yquem Pale; light style, not very sweet, highish acidity. Better than expected but not good enough. *Last tasted Sept 1998* ★★
Ch Climens Medium gold; peach and apricot nose; very sweet, delicious flavour, excellent acidity. A very good '69. *Last tasted April 2006* ★★★

1970–1989

The 1970s started reasonably well; then came the oil price hike, instant recession and a complete collapse of the Bordeaux market. Prices for Sauternes remained uneconomically low. The next decade was more successful for Bordeaux reds than the sweet whites, both in quality and market value, though the '83 Sauternes were, and still are, excellent. The end of the 1980s was blessed with the first two of an outstanding trio of vintages.

VINTAGES AT A GLANCE

Outstanding ★★★★★ 1971, 1975, 1983, 1989
Very Good ★★★★ 1976, 1985 (v), 1986, 1988
Good ★★★ 1970, 1978, 1979, 1985 (v)

1970 ★★★

A turn for the better but with ripe grapes more generous in alcohol than acidity. An Indian summer increased the grapes' sugar content but inhibited the development of botrytis. An overrated vintage with some stodgy, four-square wines lacking the richness and zest of the '71s. Drink soon.
Ch d'Yquem Fairly deep, amber-gold with orange highlights; fragrant 'apricots and cream'; sweet, fairly hefty, good 'dry caramel' flavour and adequate acidity. *Last tasted July 2003* ★★★
Ch Doisy-Védrines Flowery, vanilla, whiff of mint; medium-sweet, good flavour; typical Barsac, fairly dry finish. *June 2007* ★★★
Ch Rieussec Still sweet. Lovely flavour. *Last noted Dec 1995* ★★★★
Ch Suduiraut Warm gold; rich, honeyed bottle age bouquet; very sweet, rich, but lacking extra botrytis dimension, good length. *Last tasted June 2007* ★★★★

1971 ★★★★★

A pleasant, sunny summer, ideal ripening conditions and botrytis.
Ch d'Yquem The best vintage between 1967 and '75. Richly coloured; barley

sugar and caramel nose; sweet and rich, a glorious powerhouse of a wine with perfect counterbalancing acidity. *Last tasted Sept 1999* ★★★★★ *Time in hand*.

Ch Climens Ambrosial. In the class of '29 and '49. Grapes with perfect noble rot. Most recently: now a warm gold with green rim and orange and lime highlights; an amazingly rich, almost too rich, buttery bouquet, lanolin, fudge (the soft caramel type), great depth; very sweet, full body and glorious flavour, richness and depth. *Last tasted Oct 2001* ★★★★★ *Will continue to enchant for another quarter of a century*.

Ch Coutet, Cuvée Madame The top *cuvée* marketed only in great years. Unquestionably good: golden colour; a bouquet of sweet ripe peaches that leaps out of the glass; sweeter than the standard blend, wonderful style and life, great length, superb aftertaste. *March 1992* ★★★★★ *Will still be excellent*.

Ch de Fargues Yellow-gold, orange highlights; risking yawns I must repeat the well worn honey, *crème brûlée* description; sweet of course, excellent flavour, body and acidity. Well-nigh perfect. *April 1998* ★★★★★

Ch Filhot Medium-deep, highly polished gold; beautiful honeyed fragrance; medium-sweet, now drying out a little, excellent acidity and aftertaste. A surprisingly good Filhot. *Last tasted April 2003* ★★★★

Ch Sigalas-Rabaud Bright buttercup yellow; glorious, fragrant bouquet but less sweet than expected. Good length. *March 1997* ★★★

Ch Rieussec Old note (1984) but worth looking out for. ★★★★

1975 ★★★★★

An outstanding vintage, one of the finest of the decade. Hot dry summer, some welcome rain in September, followed by good harvest conditions including excellent botrytis and sustaining acidity.

Ch d'Yquem A lovely wine. Most recently: surprisingly deep amber-gold with very bright orange highlights; glorious fragrance, orange blossom, lanolin and *crème brûlée*; very sweet, very rich, exquisite flavour, good length, 'hot' acidic finish. *Last tasted May 2005* ★★★★★ *Long life*.

Ch Climens Almost up to the '71 in quality, combining power with finesse. Most recently: medium-gold; floral, honeyed bouquet, wonderful richness and depth revealing extra dimensions; sweet, full-bodied, wonderful concentration and length. *Last tasted Oct 2001* ★★★★★ *Another 20 years in hand*.

Ch Coutet Most recently: fairly deep bright amber; lovely rich, crusty caramel bouquet; sweet, full, rich, excellent masked acidity. *Last tasted Oct 2003* ★★★★

Ch Guiraud Fairly deep colour, orange gold; honeyed bottle age and botrytis bouquet; very agreeable flavour. *Last noted Dec 1999* ★★★

Ch Lafaurie-Peyraguey Lovely colour; cream of *crème brûlée* bouquet; sweet, rich, hefty, with hot alcoholic and acidic finish. Attractive though. *Last noted Nov 1998* ★★★

Ch Rieussec Unmistakably and eccentrically deep amber; classic bouquet of apricots, honey and caramel; fairly sweet, delicious flavour with mouth-drying acidity. *Last tasted July 2003* ★★★★

Ch Sigalas-Rabaud Most recently: fresh, forthcoming, with a touch of meat, lemon curd, peaches and 'the smell of a new tennis ball' (really!). Good flavour though lacking intensity and with a hot, hard, dry finish. *Nov 1998* ★★

Ch Suduiraut A superb wine from start to whenever it will finish. Half a

dozen admiring notes. Most recently: old gold; lovely, discreetly caramelised, great length; still perfection. *Last tasted Feb 2005* ★★★★★
THE BEST OF THE OLDER NOTES: **Ch Doisy-Védrines**; **Ch de Fargues**; **Ch Haut-Peyraguey**; and **Ch Rabaud-Promis**, all of which should still be very good.

1976 ★★★★

A year of excessive heat and drought; very ripe grapes, well-nigh perfect in Sauternes. Lovely wines from the outset but only the best will stay the pace.
Ch d'Yquem Many notes. Most recently: touch of orange, viscous; heavy, caramelly, whiff of old apricots; fairly sweet; rich, substantial mouthful, good enough acidity, considerable depth. Fully mature. *Last tasted Oct 2006* ★★★★ *Now–2015.*
Ch Climens Beautiful grapes, but no botrytis. Large crop with fairly high alcohol (14.3%) and very high residual sugar (114g/l). Most recently: lovely, fragrant, though lighter than expected. *Last tasted March 2003* ★★★★ *Drink soon.*
Ch Coutet Colour golden, but not deep; herbaceous, grassy, cress-like; lovely flavour, its acidity both propping it up and adding vivacity. Enjoyable, good but by no means great. *Last noted Oct 2000* ★★★ *Drink up.*
Ch Rieussec Nearly a dozen notes, its characteristic and very recognisable depth of colour throughout, also its almost exotic bouquet and flavour. Very rich, some caramel, over the top but most enjoyable. *Last tasted Jan 1997* ★★★★
Ch Suduiraut Glorious gold with lime-green tinge; deep, perfect *crème brûlée*, barley sugar nose; still sweet, very rich, perfect flavour and balance. *Last tasted Oct 2006. At best* ★★★★★ *Now–2012.*
OTHER '76S DRINKING WELL IN THE 1990S: **Ch Doisy-Védrines**; and **Ch Lafaurie-Peyraguey**. *Both* ★★★ *Drink soon.*

1978 ★★★

Wet summer, followed by a long sunny autumn that ripened the crop but did not allow the development of noble rot.
Ch d'Yquem Not up to standard. Short and clumsy. *Last tasted Sept 1998.*
Ch Climens Once again rising to the occasion. Most recently, slight bottle variation: the first harmonious, waxy, touch of meatiness and peach kernels, the other more creamy. Both still fairly sweet, crisp, with good flavour, the second cleaner. *Last noted Oct 2001. At best* ★★★ *Drink up.*
Ch Rieussec Something of an aberration. Fairly deep orange gold; surprisingly good nose and taste; sweet, apricot, good acidity. *Last tasted Feb 2004* ★★★★

1979 ★★★

A cold, showery growing season, but a dry late harvest saved the day.
Ch d'Yquem A pure yellow gold; sweet, creamy bouquet and taste. Nice flesh. Dry acidic finish. *Last tasted Sept 1998* ★★★
Ch Sigalas-Rabaud Showing well. *Last tasted March 1997* ★★★ *Drink up.*

1981 ★★

Hot, dry summer produced good grapes; autumn rainfall and an Indian summer encouraged the development of noble rot.

Ch d'Yquem Not a typical Yquem. Refreshing, better than expected. *Last noted Sept 1998* ★★
Ch Coutet Very attractive nose and flavour. *July 1989* ★★★
Ch Doisy-Daëne Half bottles. 'Tutankhamen' gold; curious 'sand and gravel' honeyed nose; medium-sweet, crisp, good flavour, dry finish. *Jan 2006* ★★★
Ch Lafaurie-Peyraguey Fragrant, creamy, barley sugar and pineapple. Sweet. Some fat and flesh. *Last tasted July 1990* ★★★
Ch Rieussec As usual, old gold; good nose, sweet, honeyed, but 'cress' noted too. Sweet and unusually good for an '81, a lovely emerging flavour. Assertive. Most recently, showing well. *Last tasted May 1997* ★★★★
Ch Sigalas-Rabaud Fragrant; good flavour and acidity. Some delicacy. *March 1997* ★★★

1982 ★★

After a sunny summer and hot September botrytis forming on fully ripe grapes was washed away by torrential rain at the end of the month.
Ch d'Yquem A very small and difficult crop. Most recently, scarcely better than the below-par '81. *Last tasted Sept 1998* ★★
Ch Climens A big crop of better than expected quality. Most recently: medium pale; low-keyed at first, then fragrant, floral; still sweet, touch of peach kernels, but hard and lacking charm. *Last tasted Oct 2001* ★★★ *No improvement likely, so drink up.*
Ch Suduiraut, Cuvée Madame Though an old note, richer, more powerful than the regular blend. Wonderful flavour and harmony. *June 1988* ★★★★★ *Should still be drinking well.*
OTHER GOOD '82S LAST TASTED IN THE EARLY TO MID-1990S:
Ch Raymond-Lafon ★★★; **Ch Rieussec** ★★★; and **Ch Suduiraut** ★★★★

1983 ★★★★★

The best vintage between 1975 and '89. A wet spring was followed by hot dry weather in June and July. Rain in August and early September caused some anxiety but misty mornings and warm days proved ideal for botrytis.
Ch d'Yquem Tasted many times, notes as glowing as the wine itself. Most recently, some bottle variation: a deeper old-gold colour and 'old apricot skins' bouquet; sweet. Well-nigh perfect. *Last tasted Nov 2006. At best* ★★★★★ *Now–2040.*
Ch Climens Superb. On a par with the '71. Most recently: pale gold; glorious floral bouquet, honey, ripe 'apricots and cream'; still fairly sweet, lovely flavour, rich yet firm, perfect weight and acidity. *Last tasted Nov 2006* ★★★★★ *Now–2050 or longer.*
Ch Coutet Gaining some colour, fully developed, soft and rich with a touch of caramel on the end taste. *Last tasted June 1998* ★★★
Ch Doisy-Daëne Pale; tropical fruits; sweet, light style, crisp. *Feb 1993* ★★★★ *Drink up.*
Ch Doisy-Védrines Yellow-gold; crisp, lightly honeyed; fairly sweet, high acidity, good length. *Last tasted June 2006* ★★★ *Drink soon.*
Ch Filhot Very sweet, lovely flavour and flesh, citrus-like acidity, noting 'not a great '83 but a very good Filhot'. *Last tasted Jan 2000* ★★★

Ch Guiraud Sweet, fairly pronounced flavour of apricots and honey, good extract and acidity. *Last tasted March 2004* ★★★

Ch Lafaurie-Peyraguey Amber-gold; lovely apricot bouquet; excellent flavour and acidity. *Last tasted Feb 2004* ★★★★★ *Will keep.*

Ch de Rayne-Vigneau Low-keyed, rather cress-like nose; better on the palate, deliciously sweet, creamy without being unctuous. Lovely wine. *Last tasted Dec 2004* ★★★★

Ch Rieussec Usual deep colour, amber shaded with orange, both nose and flavour being almost exotic. Sweet, rich, complete. *Last tasted April 2005* ★★★★

TWO DISAPPOINTMENTS: **Ch Suduiraut** lean and lacking; and **Ch La Tour Blanche** not bad, not good enough. Drink soon.

1984 ★ to ★★

Erratic weather. Fine summer followed by heavy rain in September which delayed the harvest, botrytis helping to save the day. Not for keeping.

THE BEST OF A NOT VERY GOOD BUNCH: **Ch d'Yquem**; **Ch de Fargues**; and **Ch Suduiraut**.

1985 ★ to ★★★★

Fine and dry weather throughout, September one of the driest on record. In Sauternes the drought resulted in high concentrated sugar levels but there was insufficient moisture to encourage widespread noble rot. Variable.

Ch d'Yquem Amber-gold (in decanter, paler of course in the glass), with hint of lime and rich 'legs'; bouquet of apricots and honey with a whiff of caramel, attractive flavour, noticeable acidity. Good but by no means great. *Last tasted April 2006. At best* ★★★★ *Drink soon.*

Ch Climens Magnums from the château. Perfect bouquet, floral, with richly honeyed botrytis; sweet, perfect flavour, weight, balance and very good acidity. *Last tasted Oct 2002* ★★★★★ *Long life.*

IN THE EARLY 1990s: **Ch Guiraud** harmonious, powerful ★★★; and **Ch Rieussec** pure gold, sweet, very attractive ★★★★

1986 ★★★★

Successful flowering and perfect summer. Heavy rains came at harvest time, followed by humid conditions which encouraged botrytis. Variable quality.

Ch d'Yquem Still very pale for Yquem; medium-sweet, firm, very good flavour and acidity. *Last noted June 2003. But an unenthusiastic* ★★★

Ch Climens A rather hard though honeyed nose; sweet, firm, some flavour, finishing caramelly and dry. Disappointing. *Last noted Oct 2001* ★★

Ch Doisy-Védrines Sweet, attractive flavour, good acidity. *Last noted June 2006* ★★★

Ch Liot Showing pretty well: attractive, medium-pale gold; fragrant, orange-blossom nose; fairly sweet, good flavour. *Last tasted Jan 2005* ★★★

Ch de Rayne-Vigneau One of the best '86 Sauternes. Beautiful colour, 'Tutankhamen' gold with a touch of lemon; mature waxy Sémillon bouquet, honeyed, mouthwatering Sauvignon, and considerable depth. Sweet entry with the vital counterbalancing acidity. Good. Slightly minty flavour, still very fresh, nice length. *Last tasted March 2002* ★★★★

Ch Rieussec Ranging from pale yellow to warm orange, the paler wines crisp and fresh. All sweet, with good acidity. *Last noted Jan 2002. At best* ★★★
SHORTER NOTES FROM THE EARLY TO LATE 1990S: **Ch Coutet** quite good ★★★; **Ch Doisy-Daëne** lovely but tails off ★★; **Ch Filhot** assertive but unknit ★★; **Ch Guiraud** sweet, unexciting ★★; **Ch Lafaurie-Peyraguey** delicious, one of the best ever ★★★; **Ch Nairac** delicate fruit. Delicious ★★★; **Ch Sigalas-Rabaud** light style; good enough ★★★ (*just*); and **Ch Suduiraut** fragrant, floral, fleshy yet delicate ★★★★

1987 ★

Summer generally warm and dry but the harvest was marred by heavy storms in early October. Few tasted. Best to ignore.
Ch d'Yquem Most recently, to my surprise, at this tasting in 1998 about the best vintage in the 1980–1987 'flight'. Unknit but sweet, with surprisingly good weight and flavour. *Last tasted Sept 1998. At best* ★★★ (*just*).

1988 ★★★★

The first of an unprecedented trio of highly successful Sauternes vintages. The early autumn weather, following a hot summer with storms, encouraged the spread of *pourriture noble* and provided ideal harvesting conditions.
Ch d'Yquem Most recently, well-nigh perfect bottles, developing an amber tinge; bouquet of honey and apricots, enhanced by volatile acidity; fairly sweet, intensely rich, glorious flavour. *Last tasted Nov 2005. At best* ★★★★★ *Beginning to show its age but still superb.*
Ch Climens Heavily botrytised grapes picked in perfect autumn sunshine. Fragrant; sweet, rich, almost creamy, harmonious though a slight whiff of peach kernels. Good acidity. *Last tasted July 2005* ★★★★ *Will keep.*
Ch Coutet Most recently, a half bottle: buttercup-tinged, with orange-gold highlights; low-keyed but fragrant bouquet; fairly sweet, surprisingly fleshy, mouthfilling, marred by clumsy finish. *Last tasted May 2006* ★★★
Ch Doisy-Védrines Whiff of caramel and peach skins; sweet, firm. *July 2006* ★★★ *Now–2010.*
Ch Guiraud Yellow-gold; lovely, scented, orange blossom bouquet; sweet, very good indeed. *Last tasted Nov 2001* ★★★★
Ch Lafaurie-Peyraguey Yellow-gold; vanilla, touch of honey, whiff of grapes; sweet, fullish, assertive flavour, very good acidity. Still a bit harsh on the finish. *Last noted Nov 2001* ★★★(★)
Ch de Rayne-Vigneau Pure gold with tinge of lime; lovely, honeyed bouquet, apricots and whiff of lychee; sweet, high extract, dry finish. Delicious and will continue to evolve. *Last tasted Nov 2003* ★★★★★
Ch Rieussec Relatively pale for Rieussec; fully evolved, harmonious nose; very rich, touch of caramel and peach kernels. Positive, tangy. Dry finish. *July 2005* ★★★★
Ch Suduiraut Consistent notes. Bright yellow-gold; lovely, fragrant, honey and apricots bouquet; fairly sweet, rich enough, crisp, light style, excellent flavour, length and acidity. *Last tasted Oct 2005* ★★★★
LAST TASTED IN THE MID- TO LATE 1990S: **Ch de Fargues** better flavour than nose ★★★; **Ch Filhot** very sweet, good fruit, flesh and acidity.

An exceptionally good Filhot ★★★★; **Ch Liot** dependable. Fragrant, spicy, harmonious and considerable charm. Excellent for its class ★★★(★); **Ch de Malle** fragrant, lean and light ★★; **Ch Rabaud-Promis** touch of malt, but sweet, full, rich ★★★; and **Ch La Tour-Blanche** curious nose; very sweet, fat, rich but need to retaste ★★★?

1989 ★★★★★

Extremely hot summer assured full ripeness and very high sugar levels. Mild, misty mornings in September provided ideal conditions for the development of the highly desirable botrytis or 'noble rot'. Magnificent Sauternes. The best vintage of the decade.

Ch d'Yquem Medium yellow-gold with visibly rich 'legs'. High-toned, honey, peaches, apricots; very rich, full-bodied, complete, quite a bite to it and extended flavour. Perfect. *Last tasted Sept 1998* ★★★★★ *Long life.*

Ch Bastor-Lamontagne A large, relatively minor château capable of producing some very attractive and inexpensive wine, making the most of a great vintage. An impressively rich appearance, an attractive bouquet variously described as ripe peaches, vanilla, milk chocolate, a whiff of gooseberry; waxy, lanolin, pure honey; sweet, slightly grapey flavour, not insubstantial, fleshy, high alcohol (14.5%), good counterbalancing acidity. *Last tasted Nov 1996* ★★★

Ch Climens Magnificent. One of the highest levels ever of alcohol and residual sugar (14.5% and 123g/l). Glorious bouquet, white chocolate, apricots and honey; delectably sweet, perfect acidity, glorious aftertaste. A lovely wine. *Last tasted May 2005* ★★★★★

Ch Coutet Amber-gold; slightly caramelised, though sweet soft bouquet and flavour. *Last tasted Sept 2003* ★★★★ *Perfect now.*

Ch Doisy-Daëne Most recently: pure 'Tutankhamen' gold; delicious honeyed nose with sweet, mouthwatering acidity. Sweet, of course – 'a charmer'. *Last noted May 1998* ★★★★

Ch Doisy-Védrines Most recently: paler than expected for year and age; ripe rich bouquet; sweet, soft, delicious. *Last tasted April 2004* ★★★★

Ch Lafaurie-Peyraguey Most recently: pale gold, rich, tangy bouquet; 'sweet and lovely'. *Last noted May 1999* ★★★★

Ch Rieussec Typical Rieussec colour; very rich orange blossom bouquet; delectably sweet, full body and flavour, dryish finish. *Last tasted May 2005* ★★★★★

Ch Suduiraut Many notes. Consistently superb. Most recently: bright gold; deliciously fragrant; retaining elegance despite its richness and sweetness. Perfection. *Last tasted Feb 2005* ★★★★★

Ch Suduiraut, Crème de Tête Cork branded *'Madame de Suduiraut'*. Orange-gold; orange scented bouquet and candied orange flavour. Powerful yet soft. Extra dimensions. Superb. *Sept 1998* ★★★★★

OTHER SAUTERNES TASTED IN THE 1990s: **Ch Brouset** distinctive, flowery ★★★; **Ch Guiraud** lighter than expected, crisp ★★★; **Ch Liot** honeyed melon; crisp, fleshy, herbaceous ★★★★; **Ch de Malle** rich ★★(★)?; **Ch Nairac** very sweet, fleshy (for Nairac) and quite good ★★★; **Ch de Rayne-Vigneau** attractive, a certain delicacy of flavour. Good length, and potential ★★★★; **Ch Sigalas-Rabaud** very fragrant; very sweet, crisp, oaky ★★★; and **Ch La Tour-Blanche** very sweet, fat, rich ★★★

1990–1999

This was a roller-coaster decade for Sauternes. Happily, but controversially, those producers in Sauternes who installed the expensive cryoextraction equipment were able to avoid complete disaster in the poor years of the early 1990s.

VINTAGES AT A GLANCE

Outstanding ★★★★★ 1990
Very Good ★★★★ 1995, 1996, 1997 (v), 1998, 1999
Good ★★★ 1997 (v)

1990 ★★★★★

The third of the outstanding Sauternes trio of vintages and the best Sauternes vintage for decades. A hot dry summer brought the grapes to full ripeness (overall the highest sugar levels since 1929). The worry that it was too dry for botrytis to set was remedied by adequate rain in August and September, inducing early evidence of noble rot and well-nigh perfect conditions for the production of great sweet wines. Virtually no-one made a poor wine and even the habitual underperformers did well.

Ch d'Yquem Bottled in 1994. The biggest crop since 1893. Most recently, at Yquem: bright amber-gold with orange highlights; sweet, rich, orange blossom fragrance becoming increasingly caramelly; medium-sweet, rich texture, nutty flavour though lacking the opulence and rich sensuality of the '89. *Last tasted Aug 2006* ★★★★(★) *Long life.*

Ch Climens Amber-gold; deep, ripe, rich, harmonious nose and flavour. Very sweet of course, lovely fruit, complete. *Last tasted Oct 2001* ★★★★★ *Glorious, but better to give it another five to ten years. Almost infinite life.*

Ch de Fargues Pale gold; fragrant, lanolin and mint leaf; sweet but on the lean side, delicious vanilla and honey flavour. *Last noted Nov 2001* ★★★(★)

Ch Guiraud Attractive colour, nose and taste. Amber-gold; deep, rich, old apricots nose; very sweet, rich, touch of caramel, delicious. *Dec 2005* ★★★★

Ch Rieussec Palish gold; touch of honey, citrus, apricots; sweet, good flavour, noting caramel and a 'hot' high alcohol finish. *Last tasted Dec 2002. At best* ★★★★

Ch Suduiraut Most recently, at a Suduiraut vertical: fairly deep yellow-gold colour and 'outrageously rich' bouquet; medium-sweet, full-bodied and powerful. *Last tasted Feb 2005* ★★★★(★)

OTHER '90s TASTED MAINLY IN THE MID- TO LATE 1990s:
Ch Coutet full, rich, unusually fleshy and fat ★★★★★; **Ch Lafaurie-Peyraguey** good colour, flavour and balance ★★★★; **Ch de Malle** amazingly rich, apricots and peaches. One of the best de Malles ★★★★; **Ch de Rayne-Vigneau** very sweet, honeyed, high acidity. Great future ★★★★(★); and **Ch La Tour-Blanche** retaining its pristine flesh, fat and sweetness ★★★★

OTHER BRIEFER, OLDER NOTES: Ch d'Arche harmonious and very good ★★★★; **Ch Bastor-Lamontagne** very sweet and intense. *For its class* ★★★★★; **Ch Broustet** lovely, honeyed, lightish style and delicious. *For its class*

★★★★; **Ch Doisy-Daëne** harmonious nose, sweet, hefty, dry finish ★★★; **Ch Doisy-Védrines** touch of orange; sweet, suave; 'hefty' ★★★; **Ch Filhot** very fragrant, sweet, distinctive, its dryness embodying fairly high volatile acidity, otherwise very good ★★★; **Ch Clos Haut-Peyraguey** fragrant, assertive, hot finish ★★★; **Ch Lamothe-Guignard** richly coloured, sweet, powerful ★★★★; **Ch Nairac** very sweet, botrytis, fat on finish ★★★; and **Ch Sigalas-Rabaud** very sweet, rich, powerful with spicy, honeyed bouquet ★★★★

1991, 1992 ★ and 1993

Three disastrously wet years for Sauternes. Avoid these wines.

1994 ★★

At last a better season, though the harvest was prolonged and hazardous. The weather eventually improved but it was a battle between botrytis and ruination. Those who harvested late did best.

Ch d'Yquem An *impériale*: warm amber verging on old gold; somewhat medicinal nose; medium-sweet, some richness but lacking fat, caramel and apricot flavour and, unsurprisingly, good acidity. *Last tasted July 2005* ★★ *A bit of a freak.*
Ch Climens Distinctly pale; a light, fragrant but superficial nose; fairly sweet, strange barley sugar flavour, lacking length. *Oct 2001* ★★ *Drink soon.*
THE FOLLOWING PASSABLE '94S were noted in the mid-1990s: **Ch Doisy-Védrines** ★★; **Ch Lafaurie-Peyraguey** better than expected, sweet, a touch of fat ★★; **Ch de Malle** surprisingly attractive, mint and honey, touch of caramel ★★; **Ch Nairac** medium-sweet, not bad ★★; **Ch de Rayne-Vigneau** creamy, positive, rich, good acidity, hot finish. One of the best '94s ★★★ *(just)*; **Ch Suduiraut** bright; attractive; fairly sweet, assertive, good acidity ★★★; and **Ch La Tour-Blanche** good colour; creamy, vanilla; very sweet, rich. Developed quite well in the glass ★★★

1995 ★★★★

A return to better times. Beneficial growing conditions until mid-September, then blessed with an Indian summer after the rains ceased on 20th.

Ch d'Yquem At the château: amber-gold; spicy, lime blossom, settled down harmoniously, whiff of caramel on nose and finish; soft, rich, powerful. *Last tasted June 2003* ★★★★ *2010–2025.*
Ch Climens Pale gold; honeyed yet 'green' and unknit; fairly sweet, moderate extract and length. Disappointing. *Oct 2001* ★★★?
Ch Coutet Lovely nose; curious flavour, good length. *Last tasted Nov 2004* ★★★
Ch Doisy-Védrines Definite buttercup yellow; very fragrant, honey, cress, gooseberry-like; sweet, delicious flavour, good acidity. *Dec 2003* ★★★★ *Now–2010.*
Ch de Rayne-Vigneau Pure gold; scents of honeycomb, *crème brûlée* and 'calf's foot jelly'; sweet, lovely flavour, good acidity, length and aftertaste. *March 2005* ★★★★ *Now–2015.*
LAST TASTED IN THE LATE 1990S: **Ch Lafaurie-Peyraguey** very good ★★★(★) *good future*; **Ch Liot** remarkably good for its class: fragrant; opened up nicely ★★★ *drink soon*; **Ch de Malle** pale; fragrant, flowery; medium-sweet, crisp. Attractive ★★★ *drink soon*; **Ch Rabaud-Promis** pale; minty, grassy style; sweet from start to finish ★★★(★)? *now–2015*; **Ch Rieussec** good colour; rich

bouquet; slightly odd flavour, but good potential ★★★(★)? *now–2015*; **Ch Sigalas-Rabaud** green-gold colour; very fresh, attractive, forthcoming; good honey-peachy flavour but a hot, hard, dry finish ★★★(★) *now–2015*; **Ch Suduiraut** bouquet particularly attractive, very fragrant, scented, orange blossom; light style but flavoury with somewhat hard dry finish. Needs more time ★★★(★) *now–2020*; and **Ch La Tour-Blanche** bright yellow-gold; honey and cress; fairly sweet, crisp, appealing flavour, lively acidity ★★★★ *now–2015*.

1996 ★★★★

Particularly successful in Sauternes due to fortuitous conditions. Long, slow ripening produced wines with wonderful aromas, particularly the Sauvignon Blanc picked before the inevitable September rains. After a final burst of botrytis on 17 October the last grapes were picked in perfect conditions, resulting in richly constituted wines.

Ch d'Yquem Medium-pale gold; orange blossom fragrance slow to evolve; sweet, crisp, very acidic – piquant volatile acidity. Good flavour. Needs time. *June 2003* ★★(★★) *2010–2020?*

Ch Climens (100% Sémillon) Very attractive 9-carat gold; honey, tempered with refreshing acidity, a touch of peach kernels lurking beneath; fairly sweet, full-bodied. Perfect balance. Lovely wine. *Last tasted March 2004* ★★★★ *Now–2020*.

Ch Coutet Pale gold; creamy, minty nose; sweet, rich, youthful flesh, excellent length and aftertaste. A very good Coutet. *Last tasted March 2006* ★★★★ *Now–2012*.

Ch Doisy-Védrines Medium-pale gold; very good honeyed bouquet; sweet, good flavour, flesh and acidity. *Nov 2004* ★★★ *Now–2012*.

Ch Guiraud 'Dark citrine', polished brass; scent of drab apricots and caramel; not as sweet or rich as it should be. Too caramelly. *Dec 2004* ★★ *Drink soon*.

Ch Lafaurie-Peyraguey Glorious yellow-gold; fragrant, floral, orange blossom; sweet, full-bodied, minty, touch of caramel but excellent acidity. *Last tasted Sept 2002* ★★★★ *Now–2015*.

Ch Liot Lovely colour, buttery yellow, shades of green and gold; minty, honeyed nose with mouthwatering acidity; sweet, nice weight, delicious flavour, refreshing acidity. *Last tasted Oct 2000* ★★★ or ★★★★ for its class. *Now–2010*.

Ch de Malle Bright 'Tutankhamen' gold; delectable scents, cress, mint, honey, lime, apricots; sweet, deliciously fresh floral flavour, good length leading to dry, acidic finish. One of the best Malles. *Last tasted Oct 2003* ★★★★ *Now–2012*.

Ch Myrat Following on from some dismal vintages for Ch Myrat. Very good bouquet; sweet, lightish style, very pleasant. *Oct 2003* ★★★ *Drink soon*.

Ch Nairac Golden; honeyed botrytis evident on nose; sweet, lovely, very good finish. *Last tasted March 2001* ★★★★ for its class. *Now–2010*.

Ch Rieussec Yellow-gold; gentle honey and apricots; very sweet, excellent flavour and balance, rich, good acidity. *Last tasted Dec 2003* ★★★★★ *Now–2020*.

Ch Sigalas-Rabaud Bouquet creamy with touch of mint, honeycomb edge. Sweet, good acidity. *Last noted Nov 1998* ★★★★ *Now–2015*.

Ch Suduiraut Most recently: minty, grassy, agreeably evolved nose; medium-sweet; lean, elegant, with good acidity. *Last tasted Sept 1998* ★★★(★) *Now–2015*.

THE FOLLOWING GOOD '96S LAST NOTED IN 1997: **Ch d'Arche** sweeter and fatter than expected ★★★; **Ch Bastor-Lamontagne** pale; minty; on the lean side but a pleasant flavour ★★★; **Ch Clos Haut-**

Peyraguey very sweet, full, powerful but not too assertive, finished richly.
★★(★★); **Ch Doisy-Daëne** delicious, very sweet, fragrant, on the lean side
★★★★; **Ch Filhot** fresh, young, grassy nose; sweet enough, assertive, lean and
hard ★(★★); **Ch Lamothe-Guignard** honey and mint; sweet, plump, touch
of caramel. Attractive ★★★; **Ch Rabaud-Promis** medium-sweet, high-toned,
noticeably acidic ★★(★); **Ch de Rayne-Vigneau** flowery nose; sweet,
powerful, richly honeyed. Good flavour and grip ★★★(★★) *will be excellent.*
now–2020; **Ch Suau** sweet, straightforward, youthful acidity, good potential ★★★;
and **Ch La Tour-Blanche** fairly powerful yet elegant, with good length and
potential ★★(★★)?

1997 ★★★ to ★★★★

A roller-coaster of a year, as in the rest of Bordeaux, with the hottest spring
for 50 years. Very variable from then on. The harvest was difficult, the good
and rotten grapes being dotted around each vineyard, making selection
labour-intensive and time-consuming, and yields were especially low.

Ch d'Yquem Pure gold; delicious fragrance, rich but as yet 'unknit' lanolin,
honey, whiff of caramel; very sweet, very rich, orange blossom and peaches, lip-
licking acidity, very dry finish. *Last tasted June 2003* ★★★ *Now–2012.*

Ch Bastor-Lamontagne Most recently: lime with gold highlights; nose that
conjured up milk chocolate; very sweet, quite attractive with some flesh and fat.
Clearly quite good. *Last tasted April 2000* ★★★ *Now–2010.*

Ch Climens Medium-pale yellow-gold; very forthcoming nose, with rich,
spicy, clove-like new oak fragrance; medium-sweet, very peachy-nutty flavour and
aftertaste. Considered *'un très grand millésime'*. *Oct 2001* ★★★★ *Now–2020.*

Ch Coutet Lovely nose; curiously attractive flavour, good length and potential.
Last tasted Nov 2004 ★★★ possibly ★★★★ *Now–2015.*

Ch Doisy-Védrines Honeyed, grapey, well balanced, fragrant. Most recently:
attractive. Good wine. *Last tasted Sept 2003* ★★★ *Now–2012.*

Ch de Fargues Palish gold; good nose; sweet, packed a punch. Impressive.
April 2007 ★★★ *Now–2015.*

Ch Filhot Beautiful green-gold; extraordinary bouquet, touch of peach-like
honey, caramel and refreshing acidity; sweet, lacking a little flesh and fruit, and a
somewhat hard finish. But overall delicious. *Last tasted June 2004* ★★★ *Now–2012.*

Ch de Rayne-Vigneau Medium-gold; slightly woody (Sémillon), *crème
brûlée*, apricot and caramel, with touch of fresh pineapple; unquestionably sweet,
very good flavour, good acidity and hot finish. *Last tasted March 2004* ★★★★
Now–2015.

Ch Rieussec Good bright yellow gold; peachy, creamy nose and taste. *Last
noted, hastily, but much liked, Sept 2003* ★★★ *Now–2015.*

Ch Suduiraut Several good notes. Very fragrant, floral, *passerillé* (no botrytis),
sweet and lovely. *Last tasted Feb 2005* ★★★★ *Now–2015.*

THE BEST OF THE FIRST GROWTH SAUTERNES tasted in April 1998,
or as otherwise stated: **Ch Guiraud** curious apricot and peach skin flavour and
bite. *April 1999* ★★(★) *Time will tell*; **Ch Clos Haut-Peyraguey** hazy but
good botrytis, grapey-minty nose; assertive, still harsh, good potential ★(★★)
now–2015; **Ch Lafaurie-Peyraguey** pale, sweet, creamy, good grip. *Last tasted
April 1999* ★★(★★) *now–2020*; **Ch Rabaud-Promis** fragrant, grapey; fairly

sweet, quite attractive but unexciting. Good acidity ★(★★) *now–2015*; **Ch Sigalas-Rabaud** impressive: fragrant; very sweet, full-bodied, good finish, attractive ★★(★★) *now–2015*; and **Ch La Tour-Blanche** honeyed botrytis, creamy, vanilla, mint and oak. Not as sweet as some, but good body, flesh and taste ★★(★★) *now–2020*.

THE BEST OF THE SECOND GROWTH AND LESSER WINES tasted in April 1998, or as otherwise stated: **Ch Brousset** very minty, herbaceous, sweet, assertive ★★★ *drink up*; **Ch Caillou** good, straightforward. Should turn out quite well ★★★ *now–2010*; **Ch Doisy-Daëne** classic, spicy; very sweet, full-bodied, good flavour. Oaky aftertaste ★★★ *possibly* ★★★★ *now–2015*; **Ch Lamothe** some charm. Interesting flavour ★★★ *now–2010*; **Ch Lamothe-Guignard** a hefty style of wine, very sweet, somewhat caramelly ★★★? *now–2012*; **Ch de Malle** fairly sweet, fat for de Malle, touch of caramel ★★★ *(just)*. *Now–2010*; **Ch de Myrat** fragrant botrytis; medium-sweet, initially hard ★★(★)? *Now–2010*; **Ch Nairac** positive colour; fragrant; very sweet, full, fat, dry finish. Good ★★★ *now–2012*; and **Ch Romer du Hayot** nice weight and style, barley sugar flavour ★★★ *now–2012*.

1998 ★★★★

The fourth very good vintage in a row, making up for the disheartening harvests earlier in the decade. The best wines were made from the very ripe, botrytis-infected first waves of picking or tries carried out between 16 and 29 September and again from 10 October, well after the worst of the heavy rains in early October.

Ch d'Yquem Yellow, touch of gold; honeyed Sémillon, vanilla and mint; medium-sweet, good straightforward flavour, somewhat hard end. Will doubtless benefit from more bottle age. *Last tasted June 2003* ★★(★★) *2010–2020*.

Ch Climens Fragrant orange blossom, after 1½ hours in the glass, like a sweetshop; very sweet, very rich, slightly chewy confectionery, spicy (cloves, new oak), good length and aftertaste. *Last noted Oct 2001* ★★(★★) *2010–2025*.

Ch Coutet Pale; floral; sweet, firm, touch of almond kernels. *Last tasted Nov 2004* ★★★ *Now–2014*.

Ch Doisy-Védrines Honeyed Sémillon and refreshing Sauvignon aromas; sweet, delicious. *Last tasted April 2004* ★★★(★) *Now–2012*.

THE BEST OF THE FIRST GROWTH WINES not tasted since the Sauternes opening tasting on April Fool's Day, 1999. Many wines still cloudy: **Ch Clos Haut-Peyraguey** very good nose, opening up attractively. Reminded me of privet. Very sweet, rich, honeyed, good length and acidity. Just slightly cloying; but good future ★★(★★) *Now–2015*; **Ch Lafaurie-Peyraguey** a complex, minty, botrytis nose with tangerine-like acidity. Sweet, powerful. Impressive ★(★★★) *Now–2015*; **Ch Rieussec** the best of the young wines at the opening tasting. Distinctive yellow-gold; sweet, creamy, vanilla, classic; very sweet, very rich, honeyed botrytis flavour. ★(★★★) *Now–2020*; **Ch Sigalas-Rabaud** rich, honeyed; very sweet, lovely flavour, classic ★(★★★) *Now–2015*; **Ch Suduiraut** very sweet, crisp, attractive. Queried its finish. Need to retaste. *Probably* ★(★★★); and **Ch La Tour-Blanche** barley sugar botrytis nose and taste. Firm. Good length ★(★★★) *now–2015*.

THE BEST OF THE SECOND GROWTH AND LESSER WINES briefly noted 1 April 1999 (for drinking now–2012): **Ch d'Arche** good weight and flavour ★★★; **Ch Bastor-Lamontagne** ★★; **Ch Broustet** very sweet, teeth-gripping acidity ★★; **Ch Doisy-Daëne** rich, good depth; touch of toffee, rich, lacks the deft touch of Védrines ★★; **Ch Lamothe** rich, some depth, hefty style ★★★; **Ch de Malle** despite high percentage of Sémillon, very much a Sauvignon Blanc aroma; very sweet, light style, crisp, grapey flavour. Good acidity ★★★; **Ch de Myrat** floral, attractive; sweet, hefty style ★★★ (*just*); **Ch Nairac** not ready for tasting. Unusually rich nose yet lean on the palate. Youthful acidity ★★, *possibly* ★★★; and **Ch Suau** pure gold colour, more appealing than nose or taste ★★

1999 ★★★★

A satisfactory and uniform growing season. An Indian summer induced excellent botrytis which helped produce the fifth very good Sauternes vintage in a row. A small harvest with excellent potential.

Ch d'Yquem Palish; not very distinctive; medium sweetness and body. Alas, unimpressive. *June 2005* ★(★★)? *Time will tell how this will develop.*

Ch Climens Most recently, youthful aroma still unknit, but fresh, floral, very attractive with mouthwatering acidity; sweet, very fragrant, still very oaky, very pleasant flavour, good length and future. *Last tasted Oct 2001* (★★★★) 2010–2025.

Ch Guiraud Most recently: a whiff of mandarin on the nose; very sweet, very rich mouthful. Hot finish. *Last tasted May 2001* ★★(★) *Now–2020.*

Ch Lafaurie-Peyraguey Most recently: slightly grassy nose; sweet, quite good, 'hot', needs time. *Last tasted Aug 2004* ★★(★★) 2009–2015?

Ch de Rayne-Vigneau Very sweet, assertive, lovely. A limpid pale gold, its early promise confirmed. *Last tasted May 2001* ★★★(★) *Now–2025.*

Ch Nairac Colour of a Tokaji Aszu; rich, very caramelly; sweet, assertive, lemon-acid finish. One of the best Nairacs. *Last tasted Nov 2003* ★★★ *Drink soon.*

Ch Rieussec Slightly spicy, creamy, *crème brûleé* nose; sweet, good flavour, complete, good length and aftertaste though quite a bite, highish acidity. *Last tasted Nov 2006* ★★(★★) *Needs time.*

Ch Suduiraut Pale, orange highlights; rich though not fully harmonious, sweet, fullish body and flavour, hot acidic finish. *Last tasted Feb 2005* ★★★ *Now–2020.*

Ch La Tour-Blanche Pure gold; honeyed; very sweet, powerful, delicious. *Last tasted Nov 2004* ★★(★★) *More time needed.*

THE FOLLOWING FIRST GROWTH WINE tasted only on 1 April 2000: **Ch Clos Haut-Peyraguey** unusual spearmint scent and flavour. Attractive (★★★)?

THE FOLLOWING SECOND GROWTH AND LESSER WINES tasted only in April 2000, unless otherwise stated: **Ch Bastor-Lamontagne** vanilla, ripe melon, lanolin; nice fruit and grip. *May 2001* (★★★); **Ch Broustet** very sweet, clove-like spiciness – new oak (★★); **Ch Caillou** quite good (★★); **Ch Doisy-Daëne** not very sweet, crisp (★★); **Ch Doisy-Védrines** showing very well: good colour; sweet buttery Sémillon, botrytis; rich, mouthfilling, complete. *May 2001* (★★★★); **Ch Lamothe-Guignard** Sémillon uppermost, sweet, some flesh (★★★); **Ch de Malle** quite good depth; very sweet, attractive

(★★★★); **Ch de Myrat** caramelly nose; surprisingly dry, full-bodied (★★); and **Ch Romer du Hayot** very minty, Sauvignon Blanc uppermost; medium-sweet, quite a bite. Should improve (★★★)

2000–2005

Anyone who cares about the future of Sauternes will understand the disappointment, in some cases despair, following a poor harvest, and its financial implications, and will join in the welcome relief provided by the good enough 'millennium' vintage of 2000, the truly magnificent 2001 and its variable successors. It is worth stressing that at the otherwise excellently organised opening tastings, most wines are presented far too early; the unreadiness is particularly noticeable with the youthful Sauternes, which frequently look hazy or cloudy. Skill and a little imagination are needed to judge their potential.

VINTAGES AT A GLANCE

Outstanding ★★★★★ 2001
Very Good ★★★★ 2003, 2004, 2005
Good ★★★ 2000 (v), 2002

2000 variable, at best ★★★

The 'millennium' vintage was something of a damp squib. Results were very mixed, with Ch Nairac, for example, unable to make any wine. The opening tasting was in March 2001, far too early. For example, wines from 12 of the 20 châteaux ranged from hazy to cloudy, only six being bright; the 'nose' varied from unfinished to creamy and fragrant. All were sweet, some very sweet. The potential was there, but by the time follow-up tastings were due, the 2000s were completely upstaged by the magnificent 2001s. For this reason, I have tasted only one mature 2000 Sauternes and one just before the final *assemblage*.

Ch Doisy-Védrines Lovely medium-gold colour; good 'cress-like' nose; very sweet, rich, delicious. *April 2005* ★★★★ *2010–2020*

Ch Climens The various components were tasted just before the final blend. All were fragrant and spicy, medium-sweet, lovely flesh and 'should turn out well'. *Oct 2001* (★★★★)

THE BEST FIRST GROWTH WINES NOTED only at the opening tasting in March 2001: **Ch Lafaurie-Peyraguey** grapey; very sweet, mouthfilling, lovely (★★★); **Ch de Rayne-Vigneau** excellent (★★★★); **Ch Rieussec** astonishing colour, like unpolished brass; but equally amazingly sweet, fat and full (★★★★); **Ch Sigalas-Rabaud** good though on the lean side (★★★); and **Ch Suduiraut** good enough (★★★)

THE FOLLOWING SLIGHTLY LESSER WINES WERE GOOD (★★★): **Ch Bastor-Lamontagne**; **Ch Brousset**; **Ch Filhot**; and **Ch de Malle**.

2001 ★★★★★

A great vintage. Ideal weather conditions with rain and unseasonably high temperatures at the end of September producing perfect botrytis, the best since 1989.

Ch d'Yquem Pale; *crème caramel*, vanilla; sweet, caramelly, excellent body and acidity. Great wine. *May 2007 ★(★★★★) Long life.*

Ch Bastor-Lamontagne Palish; extraordinary fragrance, mandarin orange on nose and palate, plus grapefruit. Sweet. *Nov 2003 ★★★ Drink soon.*

Ch Climens Exquisite finesse. Great wine. Great future. In the same league as the '29 and '89. *Last tasted Oct 2005 ★★★(★★) 2010–2040.*

Ch Doisy-Daëne Medium-pale, faint green tinge, starbright; sweet nose and flavour, rich flavour, delicious. *Nov 2003 ★★★★ Now–2020.*

Ch Doisy-Védrines Pale; light yet high-toned; citrus-like acidity; medium-sweet, crisp, touch of caramel and acidic finish. *Nov 2003 ★★★ Drink soon.*

Ch de Fargues Barrel sample. Peachy fragrance; very sweet, rich, citrus flavour and finish. Attractive. *Nov 2003 ★★★ Soon–2015.*

Ch Guiraud Highly polished yellow-gold; gloriously evolved bouquet, apricots, honey; sweet, luscious, fleshy, good length and aftertaste. Clearly a very good Guiraud. *Last tasted April 2006 ★★★★★ Now–2025.*

Ch de Rayne-Vigneau Complex aromas, peaches, grapefruit; sweet, rich but firm, very good acidity, length and aftertaste. *Nov 2003 ★★★(★★) Soon–2020.*

Ch Rieussec Palish gold, yellow highlights; slightly caramelly, incredibly rich nose of great depth; immensely sweet, fleshy, peachy flavour, good acidity and length. *Oct 2005 ★★★★(★) Now–2025.*

Ch Suduiraut Very pale; adding youthful pineapple, melon and honey to the nose; very sweet, delicious flavour, very good acidity, great length, lovely aftertaste. Suduiraut on top form. *Last tasted Feb 2005 ★★★★★ Soon–2030.*

Ch La Tour-Blanche Pleasing colour, lovely bouquet and flavour. 'Very very good'. *April 2006 ★★★★ Soon–2020.*

2002 ★★★

Light vintage with little botrytis.

Ch Climens Two notes. Remarkable transformation from first tasting. Superb, the best wine at the London tasting of '02s. *Last tasted Oct 2004 ★★★★*

Ch Suduiraut Most recently: more vanillin noted on the nose and 'early developing'. *Last tasted Feb 2005 ★★(★★)*

THE FOLLOWING WINES WERE THE BEST MAINLY 3-STAR WINES NOTED AT THE OPENING TASTING IN MARCH 2003. At that time, which is not unusual for sweet wines of this youthfulness, the colours ranged from pale to yellow-gold and from starbright through hazy to cloudy. I have only noted here the more distinctive elements and extremes: **Ch d'Arche** youthful pineapple supported by richness and ripeness; sweet, spicy ★★★; **Ch Broustet** unknit, unready; very sweet, yet lean and attractive. Hard finish (★★★); **Ch Clos Haut-Peyraguey** pure 'Tutankhamen' gold; steely, then a whiff of mint and cress, opening up fragrantly; very sweet, full, rich, powerful grip. ★★★★; **Ch Coutet** unknit, raw, immature pineapple; very sweet, rich, spicy, assertive ★★★?; **Ch Doisy-Védrines** youthful pineapple, whiff of mint; very sweet, lovely peachy honeyed flavour and good length (★★★★); **Ch de Fargues** golden with shades of orange; rich, honeyed, hefty style developing rich, peachy aromas; sweet, rich, full-bodied, fairly assertive, hard finish. Impressive. Good future (★★★★); **Ch Filhot** lemon-gold; light, fragrant, whiff of melon; sweet, attractive, touch of oak, good acidity (★★★); **Ch Guiraud** a hard steely edge to the nose, metallic, slightly spicy, improved in the glass; sweet, powerful, high alcohol, good length, 'hot' finish (★★★); **Ch Lafaurie-Peyraguey** good colour; positive, rich, peachy, classic nose; very sweet, very rich, soft, curious, slightly spicy flavour. Showing its class and suggesting its potential (★★★★); **Ch Lamothe-Guignard** youthful pineapple, rich and ripe; extremely sweet, soft, luscious (★★★); **Ch de Malle** straightforward, well-supported aromas, a bit hard; very sweet, soft, full, oaky (★★★); **Ch de Myrat** pleasant, youthful pineapple and melon, soft and ripe; very sweet, rich. Continuing its renaissance (★★★); **Ch Rabaud-Promis** yellow-gold, orange highlights; soft, *crème brûlée* nose, minty, opening up fragrantly, considerable depth; very sweet, full, rich flavour, quite a tang, good aftertaste (★★★★); **Ch de Rayne-Vigneau** palish lemon-yellow; curious nose, hint of melon, then displaying its youthful pineapple aroma and, after a short while in the glass, peachy; extremely sweet, creamy, rich lovely flavour. Just queried its length (★★★★); **Ch Rieussec** richly coloured with orange-gold highlights; honeyed, fudge-like nose; sweet, rich, assertive, good length, yet lighter style than usual (★★★★); **Ch Romer du Hayot** fruity, minty, quite good aromas; sweet, rich, good peachy flavour, hard (highish alcohol) finish. (★★★); **Ch Sigalas-Rabaud** rich gold; attractive, harmonious nose; sweet, good flavour, length and balance though powerful (★★★★); **Ch Suau** melon and mango; very sweet, rich, full-flavoured, good grip (★★★); and **Ch La Tour-Blanche** indefinable nose; better on palate. Very sweet, assertive, yet creamy ★★?

2003 ★★★★

Very hot vintage, early ripening, the Sauternes harvest completed early and speedily within a relatively short period. Happily, in addition to the naturally high sugar content, there was a very rapid development of noble rot.

Ch Broustet Very pale; rich, whiff of kernels; very sweet, very rich, delicious flavour, complete. A good *2ème cru* Barsac. *April 2004* (★★★)

Ch Climens Great potential. *Barrel tastings in April 2004* (★★★★★)

Ch Doisy-Védrines Unusually pale; curious overtone; very sweet, soft. Attractive. *April 2004* (★★★)

Ch Lafaurie-Peyraguey Fairly pale; hefty style, sweet, straightforward. Good wine. *Aug 2004* (★★★★) *2010–2020.*

Ch Suduiraut Pale yellow, gold highlights; good fruit, attractive; medium-sweet, lovely flavour, apricots and honey, 'hot' finish. *Aug 2004* (★★★★)

2004 ★★★★

A very good vintage which can be summed up as fresh and fruity. A long period of harvesting under ideal weather conditions, morning mist yielding to hot sunshine resulted in excellent *pourriture noble*. Only a small selection of wines tasted, alas, as I missed the opening tastings in the spring of 2005.

Ch Guiraud Palish, slight green tinge; very floral plus pineapple and peaches; fairly sweet, 'hot', dry finish. *Oct 2006* (★★★) *2010–?*

Ch Lafaurie-Peyraguey Rich, floral, whiff of Muscadelle (2%); sweet; delicious, hard finish but fragrant aftertaste. Needs time. *Oct 2006* (★★★★)

Ch de Malle Pure gold; very good nose and flavour. The '04 floral style. *Oct 2006* (★★★) *Soon–2012*.

Ch de Rayne-Vigneau Floral, glorious; yet curious flavour and finish. *Oct 2006. Must retaste*.

Ch Sigalas-Rabaud Palish; delicious, peaches and cream. Good flavour and acidity. *Oct 2006* (★★★★) *2012–2020*.

Ch Suduiraut Very pale, faint green tinge; exuberant, floral, 'greengage' aromas; sweet, not a blockbuster but lovely flavour. *Oct 2006* (★★★★) *2010–2020*.

Ch La Tour-Blanche Floral bouquet, peaches, apricots, greengage and privet; very sweet, honeyed, attractive. *Oct 2006* (★★★★) *2012–2025*.

2005 ★★★★

The second driest vintage after 1897, on a par with 1921 and 1989, both great Sauternes vintages. From June to October it was the fifth hottest vintage in 110 years (after 2003, 1949, 1921 and 1899). The growing conditions were favourable with good, even flowering in June. Towards harvest time, there was a welcome sprinkle of rain.

THE FOLLOWING '05S WERE ALL TASTED IN APRIL 2006:

Ch d'Yquem Six *tries* or waves of picking the botrytised grapes resulted in a diversity of aromas and flavours. Medium-gold; floral, honeyed bouquet; sweet of course, rich, fleshy, lovely flavour, nice weight, good length and good future. Not a heavyweight. Easier to judge when it has gained bottle age. (★★★★★)

Ch d'Arche Hazy; low-keyed nose; medium-sweet, straightforward, slightly 'hot' finish (★★★) *(just)*.

Ch Bastor-Lamontagne Pale, faint green tinge; low-keyed but crisp; medium-sweet, positive and attractive flavour, good acidity (★★★)

Ch Broustet Floral nose, trace of honey and touch of caramel; sweet but acidic (★★?)

Ch Caillou Very bright pure gold; sweet, open, floral, refreshing, touch of caramel; very sweet, soft, rich, good acidity (★★★★)

Ch Coutet Interesting, slightly minty, deep, honeyed, spicy nose; sweet, adequate flesh and some creaminess, good acidity, 'hot' finish (★★★★)

Ch Doisy-Daëne Hazy; positive, crisp, acidic nose with hint of lime blossom; fairly sweet, lean, lightish style, fragrant, with very dry acidic finish (★★★ to ★★★★)

Ch Doisy-Védrines Cloudy; very distinctive floral nose, lightly honeyed; fairly sweet, very pleasant flavour, nice weight and acidity (★★★★)

Ch de Fargues Slightly hazy; rich, honeyed, floral nose with touch of caramel; very sweet, flavour of caramelised honey, rich, good acidity (★★★★)

Ch Filhot Positive lime blossom fragrance, honey, harmonious; medium-sweet, curious spirity spearmint flavour and 'hot' acidic finish (★★)

Ch Guiraud Medium-gold; curious 'hot', spicy, honeyed nose; medium-sweet, very positive, 'hot' dry finish (★★★)

Ch Haut-Peyraguey Straightforward, not very distinctive but attractive nose; sweet, good flavour and length, very dry finish. A bit of a bite (★★★)

Ch Lafaurie-Peyraguey Palish, still hazy; somehow not very convincing, minty, honeyed nose; much more positive on the palate. Sweet, fat, positive, good flavour (★★★★)

Ch Lamothe Still hazy; straightforward, lightly honeyed, floral nose; sweet, good flavour and length. (★★★)

Ch Lamothe-Guignard Orange highlights; creamy, crisp and honey, with a whiff of mint; sweet, good flavour, assertive, a bit of a bite on the finish (★★★)

Ch de Malle Slightly cloudy; immediately forthcoming, intensely honeyed, with touch of mint and considerable depth; sweet, crisp, powerful. A very good de Malle with potential (★★★★)

Ch de Myrat Slightly hazy; faded old gold; distinctive, fragrant, herbaceous, touch of lime and honey; fairly sweet, positive flavour, a bit of a bite. An attractive Myrat (★★★★)

Ch Nairac Hazy; touch of mint; medium-sweet, quite a bite but fragrant (★★)

Ch Rabaud-Promis Medium-gold, orange highlights; deep, full, positive, rich, peachy, very spicy, clove-like nose; very sweet, rich, oaky/cloves end taste (★★★★)

Ch de Rayne-Vigneau Palish, touch of green; floral, oaky, clove-like spiciness; very sweet, very spicy, too oaky. Needs time (★★★ *to* ★★★★)

Ch Rieussec Hazy; low-keyed at first but opened up richly, slightly scented, apricots; very sweet, very rich, creamy, complete. Lovely wine (★★★★★)

Ch Romer Slightly hazy; pale, touch of green; low-keyed, slightly grassy; sweet, creamy but touch of woodiness (★★)?

Ch Romer du Hayot Palish, very bright; strange, buttery, slightly earthy nose; sweet, crisp, quite good flavour, 'hot' finish (★★)?

Ch Sigalas-Rabaud Yellow-gold; forthcoming, attractive, floral; very sweet, minty flavour, good acidity. Quite a youthful bite (★★★)

Ch Suau Hazy; straightforward, refreshing nose; very sweet, rich, interesting flavour, crisp finish. The best Suau I have tasted for some time (★★★★)

Ch Suduiraut Palish; muffled nose opening up, slightly smoky, honeyed, harmonious, floral, herbaceous; sweet, very good flavour, power and length (★★★★★)

Ch La Tour-Blanche Good colour; curious, slightly clumsy nose; sweet, very assertive. Time will tell (★★★)

Red Burgundy

Unlike Bordeaux, with its maritime climate and range of grape varieties, Burgundy, 400 miles or so to the north-east, has a continental climate and, for the reds, uses just one grape variety, Pinot Noir. The other principal difference is the subdivision of the land. The heart of Burgundy, the Côte d'Or, consists of blocks and strips of vines tended by many owners, some grand, mostly modest. The way the owners tend their vines and make and look after their wines makes for infinite variations on a theme.

Outstanding vintages
1865, 1875, 1906, 1911, 1915, 1919, 1929, 1937, 1945, 1949, 1959, 1962, 1969, 1978, 1985, 1988, 1990, 1999, 2002, 2005

By the mid-19th century there was an official classification of the Côte d'Or vineyards, beginning at the top with *grand cru* and followed in descending order by *premier cru*, village, regional and generic Bourgogne appellations. For example, 'Chambertin' is a *grand cru*; 'Gevrey-Chambertin, Clos St-Jacques' is a *premier cru*, 'Gevrey-Chambertin' alone is a village wine. But it is not enough to know the village and vineyard names; more important in Burgundy is the name and reputation of the producer. And this is what makes the region so challenging and fascinating. There can be some disappointments en route, but burgundy at its best is sublime, unbeatable.

The wines in this chapter are grouped by vintage year and in alphabetical order, by appellation, not producers, regardless of their hierarchy, with one exception – the wines of the Domaine de la Romanée-Conti (DRC) are listed first in each vintage, not just because they epitomise – arguably – red burgundy's best, but more importantly because they provide a benchmark of the character, quality and state of development of a given vintage.

Classic older vintages: 1864–1969

Burgundy was not immune to the dreaded louse phylloxera, but it arrived later than in Bordeaux and was first recognised in the Côte de Beaune in 1878. It caused havoc. It was not until 1887 that grafting onto American rootstock was reluctantly accepted as the only solution. It is a pity that the British upper classes of the time were not as appreciative of the fine wines of Burgundy as they were of

Bordeaux. This had more to do with history and custom than with quality and ability to age. The few 19th-century burgundies I have tasted have come mainly from France, from Burgundy itself, or from patrician cellars in the United States.

In the early decades of the 20th century most burgundies were shipped *en barrique* for bottling by wine merchants. In Burgundy itself the trade was dominated by *négociants* in Beaune and Nuits-St-Georges, few individual domaines being known by name. Most of the burgundies I have tasted from this period have emanated from France, most notably from the incredible Barolet cellar, the first part of which was auctioned at Christie's in December 1969. The rest of the Barolet stock was subsequently recorked and marketed in the 1970s.

In 1935 the *Appellation d'Origine Contrôlée* (AOC) laws were enacted. Domaine-bottling was pioneered by a few major growers, a step not popular with the local *négociants* who were, however, in no position financially to do much about it. Following a series of miraculous post-war vintages, the 1950s were taken up with the replanting and regeneration of old vineyards. In parallel, however, the AOC laws were being sidelined by the 'stretching' of *le vrai* burgundy with wine transported by road tanker from the Rhône, the Midi and elsewhere. Around this time only about 15% of burgundy was domaine-bottled. The trade was dominated by the *négociants*, who provided the importer with what the latter and his wine merchant customers wanted: well known names at commercially acceptable prices. British wine merchants, skilled and experienced bottlers, were not immune to 'stretching' and blending. By and large, one got what one paid for and there were few complaints.

I have listed the classic older vintages in order to give a historical perspective, even though my recent notes only cover a few of these years. As these wines were bought for drinking, rarely for ageing and never as an investment, hardly any survive. Of vintages since World War Two the 1952s and '59s are particularly well worth looking out for, as are the '62s, '64s, '66s and '69s. Any wine of high quality and unimpeachable provenance in the 4- to 5-star range could still be excellent.

Vintages at a Glance

Outstanding ★★★★★ 1865, 1875, 1906, 1911, 1915, 1919, 1929, 1937, 1945, 1949, 1959, 1962, 1969

Very Good ★★★★ 1864, 1869, 1870, 1878, 1887, 1889, 1904, 1920, 1923, 1926, 1928, 1933, 1934, 1943, 1947, 1952, 1953, 1961 (v), 1964, 1966

Good ★★★ 1858, 1877, 1885, 1886, 1893, 1894, 1898, 1914, 1916, 1918, 1921, 1924, 1935, 1942, 1955, 1957, 1961 (v)

1865 ★★★★★

A magnificent vintage producing deep, firm, flavoury wines.
Romanée-Conti Labelled '*S. Guyot, Masson & fils & J. Chambon Petits fils de J.M. Dufault-Blochet*'. Warm amber with a ruddy core; low-keyed, virtually faultless bouquet despite showing a bit of age, opening up fragrantly; medium-dry, good length and acidity. In remarkable condition. *March 2002* ★★★★★
Volnay, Santenots Bouchard Père Surprisingly deep; rich bouquet; very good flavour, complete, excellent tannin and acidity. *Last noted Nov 1995* ★★★★

1889 ★★★★

Romanée-Conti S Guyot, Masson & fils and J Chambon/Petits fils de J M Dufault-Blochet Original cork. From a 'patrician' American cellar. Medium-pale, warm, ruddy amber; low-keyed at first, sweet, faultless, whiff of age then noticeable yet very fragrant, held well in the glass; fairly dry, good length and refreshing acidity. In remarkably good condition. *Feb 2004* ★★★★★

1906 ★★★★★

Great vintage. Perfect growing season, the hot summer harvest was early.
Chambertin, Clos de Bèze Faiveley Jeroboam: many-layered, slightly piquant fruit; medium-sweet, rich, soft yet tangy. Excellent for its age. *Sept 1996* ★★★★★
Romanée-St-Vivant Dufouleur An amazingly good half bottle. Rosehip tawny; lovely, fragrant, old beetroot-like Pinot bouquet; sweet, beautiful smoky flavour, good length and intensity, excellent finish. *April 1990* ★★★★

1919 ★★★★★

Great vintage. Small crop of magnificently ripe wines.
Chambolle-Musigny Dr Barolet One of the most beautiful and dependable of all Barolet burgundies. Medium-pale, healthy glow; sound nose and flavour, holding well. Remarkably good. *Last noted Nov 2000* ★★★★
Musigny de Vogüé Medium-pale, pink-cheeked; a most extraordinary fragrance, cherries and *poire Williamine*; sweet, delicately flavoured, with cherry-like fruit, positive, good length and aftertaste. A lovely wine. *March 2002* ★★★★★

1921 ★★★
Exceptionally hot summer. Early harvest.
Romanée-Conti Labelled *'de Villaine & J Chambon Petits fils de J.M. Dufault-Blochet'*. Impressively deep; nose a bit dusty at first, with a touch of cork or wood, evolved richly; very sweet, very good flavour, considerable power though showing some decay. Extended finish, more acidity than tannin. *March 2002. For its age* ★★★

1923 ★★★★
A small but high-quality vintage.
Pommard, Epenots Moillard Original cork, lovely colour for age; amazing, faultless bouquet and flavour. Sweet. Lovely. From Monsieur Moillard's private cellar. A delightful surprise. *Nov 2006* ★★★★★
Savigny, Hospices, Cuvée Fouquerand Dr Barolet Lovely colour; distinguished bouquet; refined flavour and texture. One of the best wines in the remarkable Barolet sale. *Dec 1969* ★★★★
SEVERAL OLDER NOTES: the most interesting tasted in 1984 **Romanée, La Tâche** (*sic*) **Berry Bros Label** Original cork; fragrant, vanilla, old oak; high extract, good flavour. On the edge.

1924 ★★★
Despite inclement weather, some pleasant wines were made.
Corton-Maréchaudes Seguin-Manuel Medium-pale, open, warm, ruddy colour; sound, light, spicy; sweet, very good despite a touch of old age and hint of acidity on the finish. *Jan 2005* ★★★ *(just)*.

1928 ★★★★
High-quality, sturdy, dependable and long-lived wines.
Romanée-Conti Recorked at the Domaine. Similar label to the 1921. Lively colour with cherry and ruby highlights and tawny rim; harmonious bouquet, rich, almost meaty; excellent, crisp taste, touch of spice resembling iodine, very good flavour which seemed to get sweeter in the glass. *March 2002* ★★★★★
Clos de Vougeot Pasquier-Desvignes *'aux domaine du Marquisat depuis 1420'* Fair depth and intensity; a demonstrative but sound nose; sweet, complete, touch of meatiness but surprisingly good flavour. *March 2002* ★★★

1929 ★★★★★
A glorious vintage, both abundant and high quality. Refined, ripe, elegant wines, some of which, if well cellared, have stayed the course.
Richebourg DRC Excellent level. Soft, mature red; remarkably good nose, whiff of vanilla; sweet, very rich and concentrated, good length. *Feb 2004* ★★★★
Vosne-Romanée, Les Gaudichots DRC Palish, little red, nevertheless richly coloured; rich, sound, tangy bouquet, an hour later, perfection; sweet, very rich and powerful, good length and grip. Superb. *Feb 2004* ★★★★★
Chambertin J Drouhin *'Tirage d'Origine'*, *'Vin des Anciens celliers des Rois de France et Ducs de Bourgogne'*. Sweet, fragrant, touch of meatiness; also sweet on the palate, crisp, flavoury, flowery, attractive but acidic. Originally shipped from the Belgian importer's cellar and recently removed from a New Jersey mansion. *March 2002* ★★★

Charmes-Chambertin Boyer Lovely colour; good bouquet that opened up well; fairly sweet, slightly singed flavour, good tannin and acidity. *Feb 2004* ★★★

Musigny Boyer The bottle had a very good level: palish hazelnut colour, very little red, open orange rim; appearance misleading because it had a rich, fragrant Pinot nose and flavour; very rich, slightly 'stewed', very good in its way. *Feb 2004* ★★★

Clos St-Denis Seguin-Manuel Ruddy colour; hint of fungi; better on the palate; fairly sweet, very attractive flavour, good, tannic and acidic grip. *Jan 2005* ★★★★

Romanée-St-Vivant Marey-Monge Lively warm rosehip colour; showing its age initially but quickly settled down, sweet, soft, scented, then after 30 minutes the tanginess of a thoroughbred stables; very sweet, a lovely, rich, chocolatey flavour, good length and acidity. Complete. *Nov 1995* ★★★★★

Clos Vougeot Boyer Lovely glow; singed bouquet that held well; very sweet on the palate, rich, slightly 'cheesy' flavour but good length and bite. *Feb 2004* ★★★

1933 ★★★★

A very good but very small vintage. Stylish, elegant wines but only one tasted since the 1980s, an ullaged and oxidised **Richebourg DRC** in 2003.

1934 ★★★★

Perfect growing conditions. The biggest vintage of the decade; ripe, well-constituted wines. Exceptional heat during the vintage caused some fermentation problems. What could have been great was merely very good. The small growers were anxious to make up for lost time and money by selling as much as possible to merchants who, in turn, needed to have decent stocks of wine for a slowly reawakening market.

Romanée-Conti A magnificent wine. Two virtually identical notes. Both bottles had excellent levels. Superb colours – rich, mature, warm, hazelnut tawny; both with rich, fragrant complex bouquets, each with a slight whiff of caramel and black treacle; incredibly sweet on the palate, rich, ripe, but no signs of decay yet, concentrated, glorious flavour. *Last tasted Feb 2004* ★★★★★★ *(6 stars).*

La Tâche Berry Bros & Rudd A most interesting bottle from the cellar of a Vanderbilt mansion in upper New York State. Bottled by Berry Bros: good classic nose, whiff of lemon; very sweet, delicious flavour and finish. In their archives this was listed in 1937 as *'La Tâche Romanee'*. *March 2002* ★★★★★

Grands-Echézeaux DRC Also from the same Vanderbilt cellar as the wine above, with *'Berry Bros & Co'* pictorial label: low-keyed, meaty nose; full, rich, singed flavour, with power and length. *March 2002* ★★★★

Chambolle-Musigny Poulet A slightly chocolatey, pre-war commercial burgundy in very good condition, not classy but pleasant. *Feb 2001* ★★★

Chambolle-Musigny, Les Amoureuses Dr Barolet Palish, pleasant colour; gentle, harmonious bouquet; touch of sweetness, perfect weight, crisp, delightful flavour. Virtually faultless. *Last tasted Sept 2001* ★★★★

Chambolle-Musigny, Les Amoureuses Seguin-Manuel Palish, hint of rose; meaty and touch of sourness; better on palate, medium-sweet, rich, tawny, very good flavour. *Jan 2005* ★★★

Grands-Echézeaux Seguin-Manuel Tawny, rosehip colour, rich 'legs';

gentle, low-keyed bouquet; sweet, very sound, good tannin and acidity. Delicious. *Jan 2005* ★★★★

Romanée-St-Vivant J Drouhin A ripe but low-keyed bouquet; rich, meaty, fractionally malty, good length, clean finish. Enjoyable. *March 2002* ★★★★

Romanée-St-Vivant 'Quancard Collection' Good colour; very good, rich bouquet; sweet, rich, perfect flavour and balance. *July 2003* ★★★★

1937 ★★★★★

Looking back this is now close run by the '34 vintage, but unquestionably this is the outstanding vintage in this difficult decade. Growing conditions were near to ideal thanks to warm weather from May throughout the summer but a welcome sprinkling of rain in September was insufficient to swell the grapes. The crop was small, roughly half that of the '34 and the grapes more concentrated and tannic which enabled the best wines to keep extraordinarily well. Few recent notes.

Romanée-Conti A great wine. Five notes. Most recently, from a private American cellar, originally imported by '*Bellow & Company Inc*', New York. Excellent level. Original cork. Very good colour, warm, open, mature; very sweet bouquet, vanillin, whiff of caramel and black treacle; amazingly sweet on the palate, ripe, no signs of decay, glorious flavour. Superb. *Last tasted March 2003. At best* ★★★★★★ *(6 stars)*

Richebourg DRC Original capsule, long cork, very good level, with added slip labels. '*Red Burgundy wine*'; '*Imported by National Wine & Liquor Importing Company*'. Rich mature mahogany rim; bouquet excellent, with a citrus note, after 2 hours still good but fading a little; extraordinarily sweet, rounded, perfect flavour, richness masking supportive tannins, great length. *March 1999* ★★★★★

'Côte de Beaune' bottled by **Matthew Gloag, Perth** Just to demonstrate an indestructible example of a '*bonne cuisine*', a wine skilfully blended (in Burgundy) and efficiently bottled (in the UK): lovely soft cherry colour; 'very British' Pinot; sweet, good flavour and condition. A good drink. *May 2004* ★★★

1943 ★★★★

The best wartime vintage. If well kept, the wines should still be remarkably good. No recent notes.

1945 ★★★★★

A great vintage. Though the war in Europe had ended in May, labour problems and material shortages continued. Severe frosts in March and April reduced the potential crop, though the unaffected vines benefited from a beautiful spring. The summer was hot and dry. The result of 'nature's pruning' and low rainfall was a small crop of high-quality, concentrated grapes.

Romanée-Conti From the last of the ungrafted vines. Most recently: ullage a not serious 4.5cm. Richly coloured; amazingly sweet bouquet, after 10 minutes black truffles and a whiff of liquorice, and after 30 minutes glorious (fresh raspberry crumble); sweet, firm, spicy, richly textured, perfect crisp fruit, great length. *Last tasted March 2002* ★★★★★★ *(6 stars)*

La Tâche Two old notes but worth recording as the wine was superb, more than perfection. Most recently unlike most red burgundies, unusually deep in colour; endlessly unravelling scents; rich, great length with the DRC hallmark, a glorious 'peacock's tail' of flavour spreading and lingering in the mouth. *Last tasted, unforgettably, May 1983* ★★★★★★ *(6 stars)*

Richebourg DRC Medium-deep; deliciously ripe, earthy bouquet that was still excellent after 2½ hours; a sweet powerhouse of a wine, lots of grip, tannin and acidity. Just the slightest touch of sour old age. *March 2002* ★★★★★

Chambertin Jean Thorin Variable bottles, mine drinking well: medium-pale; sound though ageing; touch of sweetness, nice weight and old flavour. Lacking the breathtaking quality of a DRC or de Vogüé, but *assez bien. Jan 2005* ★★★

Charmes-Chambertin Seguin-Manuel Very little red, a touch of tawny; initially, the nose indefinable, but opened up attractively, good fruit, whiff of strawberry; richer on the palate, full-flavoured, good length, tannin and acidity. *Jan 2005* ★★★★

Ch Corton-Grancey L Latour From Nicolas in Paris: soft, rosy-cheeked; sweet, rich, ripe; dry, touch of mocha, singed but enjoyable. *Last noted March 2002* ★★★★

Pommard, Rugiens François Gaunoux Very good bouquet; touch of ripe sweetness, deliciously crisp flavour, dry finish. *March 2002* ★★★★★

1947 ★★★★

A wonderfully rich vintage following an excellent growing season: warm summer, fully ripe crop picked early, from 16 September, and fermented in very hot weather. I was fortunate to have started my wine trade career in the early 1950s when these '47s were imported, mainly *en barrique*. The quality of wine and of merchants' bottling in the UK was reassuringly high, allowing for some commercial 'stretching' at either end. Few recent notes.

La Tâche Most recently, succumbed to its 18-cm ullage: *gibier*, rich but decayed nose, banana skins on palate. *Last tasted April 1998. At best* ★★★★

1948 ★★

Fairly good, somewhat idiosyncratic wines. Largely bypassed by the British trade. Variable weather conditions, the late spring and early summer too cold and wet though it was good from mid-August to the early October harvest.

Grands-Echézeaux DRC Recorked at the Domaine in 2003. Lovely colour; low-keyed, sweet, ripe, earthy-vegetal Pinot character; very sweet, rich, slightly singed flavour, very good acidity. Complete. *Nov 2003* ★★★★

Both **DRC's La Tâche** and **Richebourg** were immensely impressive in their youth, 'big and black' even at ten years of age, the La Tâche being perfect in 1980. If well cellared these wines should still be richly mouthfilling.

1949 ★★★★★

The most perfect end to the decade. Flowering took place in worryingly unsettled rainy conditions but thereafter warm and dry with sufficient rain to swell the grapes prior to picking. Elegant, well-balanced wines, the best the epitome of burgundy. Alas, few tasted recently.

La Tâche Soft ruby core with autumnal rim; rich, smoky bouquet and flavour, good medium fruit, quite a bite, showing its age on the finish. *April 1998* ★★★

Chambertin A Rousseau Great wine: rich, fully evolved, vegetal Pinot, penetrating, sinus-clearing nose; very powerful and penetrating, amazing texture, flavour and aftertaste. *Nov 1995* ★★★★★ *Will still be excellent.*

Chambolle-Musigny, Les Charmes Doudet-Naudin Most recently: typical Doudet-Naudin chocolatey nose; agreeable sweetness and body and, predictably, reliably sound if lacking finesse. *Last tasted Nov 2000* ★★★

1952 ★★★★

One of my favourite red burgundy vintages of the decade; these were firm, well structured, dependable wines. It would have been a great vintage had it not been for a cool September. Fairly late harvest. Most of my notes are now too old.

Romanée-Conti By 1945, the production from the ungrafted old vines had become uneconomic and a decision was finally made to uproot and replant with American rootstock. 1952 was the first major vintage to be harvested from the young vines. Spicy, slightly minty, soft, harmonious bouquet which soon developed a meaty, gravy-like smell and after an hour had become degraded. Initially very sweet, very 'warm', very rich, yet it was showing some age and the finish was twisted and slightly sour. A less than good bottle? *March 2002* ★★

Richebourg DRC Autumnal colour and bouquet, the latter opening up dizzily with many facets; on the palate sweet, firm, excellent flavour, balance, length and finish. Showing its age yet full of life. *Last tasted Oct 2001* ★★★★★

1953 ★★★★

A most attractive vintage. August and September were warm and dry, producing a satisfactory harvest of ripe grapes. Less sturdy but with more charm than the '52s, the wines were instantly appealing and very popular. At their best in the mid-1970s to mid-1980s.

La Tâche Most recently, its best feature being its sweet, rich bouquet. Strangely assertive. Not as inspiring as expected. *Last tasted April 1998. At best* ★★★★

Romanée-St-Vivant Marey-Monge bottled by Bourré for Averys. Pure amber; very scented bouquet; delicious flavour. *July 2003* ★★★★

Pommard Jules Belin Very good colour; nondescript nose; a good example of a slightly jammy, fairly sweet village wine for the English market, doubtless 'stretched' but still agreeable, drinkable. *Nov 2005* ★★

1955 ★★★

Unquestionably good, the best wines with finesse, but lacking the masculinity and staying power of the '52s and ripe charm of the '53s. Well-ripened grapes were picked early October 'in the best conditions for 20 years'. I have described it as 'the Indian summer of English bottling', the bottling being reliable, indeed, more dependable than the wines that emanated from Burgundy, where 'stretching' and the blatant abuse of village names were commonplace. With notable exceptions, the wines were not suitable for laying down, the Côte de Nuits lacking length and flesh, the Côte de Beaune reds light and at their best in the mid-1960s.

Romanée-Conti Fully mature; singed, hot vintage smell, very rich, vegetal (beetroot) nose; very sweet on the palate, with a delicious earthy, tangy flavour and great length. *Nov 2003* ★★★★★

1959 ★★★★★

At last, a top-class vintage. Ideal blossoming in June; July and August hot and dry followed by some rain to swell the grapes prior to an early harvest in hot weather. A record crop of high quality wine. I have more notes on this vintage than on any other except 1964.

Romanée-Conti Most recently: richly coloured; harmonious nose, rich fruit, almost jammy – strawberry, raspberry – great depth, faultless; lovely flavour, still with excellent tannin and acidity, typical Romanée-Conti persistence of flavour. *Last tasted March 2002* ★★★★★ *Perfect now, yet years of life left.*

La Tâche Medium-pale; very fragrant; very everything; intense, flavoury, dry finish. A lovely wine. *July 2003* ★★★★

Corton Dom du Ch de Beaune Better on nose than palate: ripe, singed, mature bouquet; 'sweet and sour', very drinkable but a bit edgy. *March 2002* ★★★

Ch Corton-Grancey L Latour Magnums at Latour's bicentenary dinner: fine, deep colour; surprisingly gentle nose, earthy root-like Pinot; rich and powerful, full of fruit and vigour. *Last tasted June 1997* ★★★★ *Years of life ahead.*

Grands-Echézeaux Colette Gros Richly coloured; ripe, singed, harmonious nose; dry, lean, quite good flavour though a little tart on the finish. *March 2002* ★★★

Le Musigny L Jadot Dark cherry, mature rim; scented nose developing a bit of caramel; sweet, meaty, hot, peppery, still tannic, good in its way but only just above '*bonne cuisine*', the sort of burgundy the English used to prefer. *March 2002* ★★★

La Romanée Dom du Ch de Vosne Romanée Palish, open; ripe, meaty, sweet vegetal nose; sweet on palate, attractive, quite an end bite, with the charm of an old *roué*. *March 2002* ★★★

Clos Vougeot Seguin-Manuel Healthy glow; fairly rich, meaty nose; medium sweetness and body, good, rich flavour, very tangy. Sound. *Jan 2005* ★★★★

1961 at best ★★★★

The crop was well below average and the quality, though better than first anticipated, was simply not of an overall level of excellence to achieve prices 50% above those of the magnificent '59s. Few notes since 1990.

Romanée-Conti Only one note: deep in colour with noticeably thick 'tears' or 'legs'; a marvellously rich, brambly, harmonious Italianate nose which was evolving after nearly an hour in the glass; sweet, a big wine. *Nov 1995* ★★★★

La Tâche DRC Attractive, dry, with some delicacy, despite being upstaged by the '69. *Last noted Sept 2000* ★★★ or, at a squeeze, ★★★★ depending on the context.

Romanée-St-Vivant Marey-Monge/J Drouhin Rich, mature; very sweet, harmonious, vanillin scent; very sweet also on the palate, rich, rounded, lovely flavour. Delicious, at its peak. *April 2004* ★★★★

1962 ★★★★★

Unquestionably a superior vintage to 1961. A cool spring with good flowering conditions in June, followed by a fair July, fine and warm August and some welcome September rain. A late harvest of sound, fully ripe grapes.

Romanée-Conti Fairly deep, fully mature; bouquet harmonious, with great richness and depth; sweet, excellent flavour, good 'grip' – inadequate words for a wine of this stature and complexity. *Last tasted Feb 2002* ★★★★ and more to come.

La Tâche Most recently: beginning to lose its redness and showing some age on nose and palate. Yet its flavour penetrating, developing and holding well. *Last tasted Sept 2005. At best* ★★★★★★ *(6 stars) A great and rare experience.*

Richebourg DRC In its youth, misleadingly pale and seeming to lack substance, yet developed steadily. The odd man out of the DRC range. Most recently: deeply coloured; an urgent and immediate rush of bouquet; rich, round, mouthfilling. *Last tasted Sept 1997* ★★★★★

Grands-Echézeaux DRC Seven notes. Most recently: full and forthcoming, sweet, old-Pinot root-like bouquet; ripe and rich, tangy, considerable power and great length. *Last noted March 2002* ★★★★★

Bonnes-Mares de Vogüé Rich colour; crisp, fine, mature bouquet; excellent flavour, mature fruit, body, length and elegance. Sweet finish. *March 2002* ★★★★★

La Romanée Leroy Lovely colour; initially not very clear-cut, a mild 'beetroot' aroma, opening up fragrantly but showing its age; better on the palate, sweet and soft, yet with quite a bite, good length, dry finish. *Sept 2005* ★★★★

1964 ★★★★

Very good vintage: rich, meaty and fairly substantial wines of a contrasting style to the '62s and '66s. A perfect flowering in June and a hot, almost too hot, summer though perfect ripening weather, alternating rain and sun, led to an excellent harvest from 18 September. It was immediately recognised as a first-rate vintage with record prices reached at the Hospices de Beaune auction.

Romanée-Conti On the pale side of medium, fully mature-looking; nose undemonstrative but good; fairly sweet, full-bodied, rich, powerful, tangy, still with silky tannins. *Last noted July 1996* ★★★★ *Should continue to please.*

La Tâche Rich colour; nose of freshly picked mushrooms; sweet, very rich, good flavour, but also slightly mushroomy, and good length. Lovely aftertaste. *Last tasted Nov 2003* ★★★★

Grands-Echézeaux DRC Recorked at the Domaine in 1996: attractive, mature appearance; sweet, low-keyed, somewhat vegetal nose; sweet on the palate, delicious flavour, soft, its richness masking the tannins. *Last tasted Nov 2003* ★★★★

Beaune, Clos des Mouches J Drouhin Soft, pale autumn colour; showing its age, fully mature nose; drying out, remnants of flavour, sound. *April 2005* ★★★

Chapelle-Chambertin Leroy Very fragrant bouquet; sweet, soft, very rich, good length. Delicious. *March 2002* ★★★★ *Drink up.*

Corton, Hospices, Cuvée Charlotte Dumay Leroy Medium-pale, touch of cherry; initial whiff of age which soon cleared, slightly singed '64 heat, sweet fruit; good, rich, nutty flavour. Dry finish. *March 2002* ★★★

Musigny J Drouhin The first of seven '64 Musignys tasted blind: medium-pale, pinkish hue, open, mature rim; sweet, attractive, gently fragrant, opening up spicily and holding well (for 2½ hours); fairly sweet on the palate, fair body (13% alcohol), slightly gritty texture, dry finish. *March 2002* ★★★ *Drink soon.*

Musigny Faiveley Sweet, very attractive, fully mature, eventually strawberry-like; agreeable sweetness and flavour, rich, straightforward. *March 2002* ★★★

Musigny Leroy (labelled '**Le Roy**') Good colour; touch of sourness at first, low-keyed yet within 45 minutes an exotic strawberry jam scent completely contradicted by its dry, somewhat coarse and short palate. *March 2002* ★★★

Musigny, Vieilles Vignes Coron Fairly high-toned 'boiled beetroot' Pinot; dry, stern, fair body, a touch of tartness but delicious flavour. *March 2002* ★★★

Musigny, Vieilles Vignes de Vogüé Attractive colour; distinctly floral bouquet, slightly singed, developing an almost Cabernet Franc raspberry scent; dry, most delightful flavour and great length. *March 2002* ★★★★ *Drink soon.*

Pommard, Epenots Leroy Fragrant though not very forthcoming; initially sweet and showing its age but good flavour, tannin and acidity, rather lean and with a slightly raw, dry finish. Quite a good drink. *March 2002* ★★ *Creaking a bit.*

Clos de la Roche Leroy Palish, soft; good fruit, 'sweet and sour', classic flavour, lean, dry, good length. *March 2002* ★★★

Romanée-St-Vivant Leroy Attractive, vanillin nose, opening up, mocha-like; very sweet on the palate, chewy, slightly singed, lovely aftertaste. *March 2002* ★★★★

Volnay, Clos des Chênes Ropiteau Palish, soft, mature, rosehip, orange-tawny; distinct whiff of stewed beetroot, *le vrai Pinot*; sweet, pleasant, fully mature, flavour verging on *gibier*, good acidity, attractive. *March 2000* ★★★

1965

A washout. The worst-ever post-war vintage. Late pickers, such as **DRC**, managed to salvage some grapes during a brief Indian summer.

Romanée-Conti Slight bottle variation. Rich yet very pale, a touch of green on the open rim; very slight mushroom whiff; surprisingly sweet, rich, still with quite a bite. Remarkably good for the year. *Nov 2003* ★★★

1966 ★★★★

Good quality and quantity. Not great wines but stylish nevertheless. My sort of wine. The summer was not particularly good but September was sunny and balmy, with a little rain to swell the grapes and growers were able to harvest at the end of the month in exceptionally fine conditions.

Romanée-Conti Medium, mature; glorious, perfection; lovely flavour and length, mouthfilling, high alcohol and an end bite. Superb. *Last tasted Oct 2003* ★★★★★ *Ready but will keep.*

La Tâche Opulent yet elegant. *Last tasted Feb 1997* ★★★★

Romanée-St-Vivant Marey-Monge/DRC Medium-deep, mature; fragrant, 'refined beetroot' nose; sweet, ripe, lovely flavour but still quite a bite. *Last noted Oct 2001* ★★★★

Grands-Echézeaux DRC A recorked bottle: ruddy, tawny, mature; an extraordinary 'fish skin' Pinot nose that opened up fragrantly; full-bodied, very sweet, excellent length, tannic. *Last noted July 1996* ★★★★(★) *Will continue to evolve.*

Echézeaux DRC Very fragrant, distinctive, forthcoming bouquet and flavour. Perfect weight and state. Dry finish. *Last noted June 1999* ★★★★

1967 ★★

From the sublime to the not so hot. It could have been a good vintage but ten days of rain fell in September, with disastrous results, though good weather returned in time for the vintage in early October. Variable quality and some wines were particularly high in alcohol. Few recent notes.

Grands-Echézeaux DRC Medium, mature, soft 'warm' red; extraordinarily meaty nose; sweet, powerful but lean. Tannic, quite a bite. *July 2004* ★★

1969 ★★★★★

It took a little time to realise that this was by far the finest vintage of the period, thanks to the excellent acidity which made, and has sustained, the '69s. A cold, rainy spring, followed by late flowering was happily made up for by very fine ripening weather in July and August which enabled well-developed grapes to survive a cold, wet September. A late harvest with a small, sound, ripe crop.

La Tâche Initially a vegetal whiff but developed a lovely citrus-like fragrance; dry, lean, austere but with a delicious and distinctive flavour and unusually disposed tannin and acidity. Perfection. *Last tasted July 2003* ★★★★★

Romanée-St-Vivant DRC Rich colour; complete, harmonious nose; fairly sweet, full-bodied, firm, very good, refreshing and life-sustaining acidity. Fine wine. *Last noted Nov 1995* ★★★★(★) *A long, immaculate life ahead.*

Grands-Echézeaux DRC Mature brown tinge; 'singed' nose. Lean, elegant, very characteristic beetroot-like varietal aroma; a touch of decay, dry finish. Good but slightly disappointing. Drying out. *Last tasted March 2003* ★★★

Bonnes-Mares de Vogüé Lovely colour; the real thing – a beautiful ripe, elegant 'beetroot' Pinot; excellent flavour, great length though with a curious upturned tannic finish. Very refreshing. *Feb 1999* ★★★★

Echézeaux Leroy An open, fully mature rim; somewhat 'stewed' Pinot nose; fairly sweet, attractive flavour, good acidity. *Feb 1998* ★★★

Musigny, Vieilles Vignes de Vogüé The old Comte de Vogüé's favourite wine. Most recently: an attractive colour; very rich varietal nose; very sweet on the palate, glorious in its way but now almost over-mature and 'almost tart'. *Last noted Sept 1997* ★★ *Possibly there are better bottles.*

Romanée-St-Vivant Bottled in Burgundy for Averys Lovely warm colour; very vegetal nose; medium-dry, very unusual, root-like Pinot, harmonious, all components 'present and correct'. *Last tasted July 2003* ★★★

1970–1999

If not exactly a turbulent period, it was certainly one of great contrasts: economic, stylistic and in quality. The 1970s started off well, but the almost unhealthily buoyant market quickly evaporated. This coincided with poor growing conditions, which had a disastrous effect on the '73s, '74s and '75s. The atrocious 1977 vintage obliged the best estates to select carefully. Fermentation control in difficult conditions was only mastered in the 1980s. Importantly, domaine-bottled wines were beginning seriously to bypass the *négociants*, though the vast majority of the growers did not have the necessary incentive or ability to market their wines.

Looking back, the decade of the 1980s was not as successful as in Bordeaux. However, there was considerable improvement in overall quality and commerce, with two of the most appealing vintages of recent times: 1985 and 1988. What was noticeable also was a sea change in attitudes, particularly among growers. The younger generation of *vignerons* tended to be not only more qualified technically, but also more innovative and conscious of quality.

The 1990s was surely one of the best decades yet in Burgundy. Better still, there was fuller awareness of quality among both the producers and consumers. The price paid for good burgundy – and the best has never been available in substantial quantities – was more directly based on quality and genuine, not speculative, demand.

Vintages at a Glance

Outstanding ★★★★★ 1978, 1985, 1988, 1990, 1999
Very Good ★★★★ 1971, 1986, 1989, 1993, 1995, 1996, 1997, 1998
Good ★★★ 1972, 1976, 1979, 1980 (v), 1983 (v), 1987, 1992

1970 ★★

A vintage sandwiched between the superior '69s and '71s. The wines lacked grip and, though initially attractive, also lacked stamina. Many tasted, few recently. Most not worth pursuing.

Romanée-Conti Rich, mature appearance; sweet, earthy, vegetal nose; rich but raw, powerful but with a bitter finish. *Nov 2003* ★★★ *Time will tell.*

La Tâche Most recently: fragrant bouquet; flavoury but a hot alcoholic finish. *Last tasted Sept 1999* ★★★ *Drink up.*

Grands-Echézeaux DRC Only one not very up-to-date note: fairly deep; spicy; impressive. *Jan 1990.* ★★★(★) *Probably still drinking well.*

1971 ★★★★

The firmest and, judging by my own notes, infinitely the most dependable of the '69, '70 and '71 trio, for though it has had the reputation of being somewhat hard, unyielding and 'untypical' it is these very factors which have so effectively developed the best over the past 35 years. There was some unevenness at the time of flowering and a severe hailstorm in August, affecting in particular the Côte de Beaune, otherwise the growing season was satisfactory. The first half of September was lovely and a small crop of ripe grapes was harvested from the 16th. The major estates and top *négociants* produced wonderful wines which are still delectable.

Romanée-Conti Most recently: medium-deep, warm, soft, open; restrained but very good, with a true classic Pinot character opening up fragrantly; very sweet, very rich and complete – all the components fully represented and in place, extract masking tannin. Outstanding. *March 2002* ★★★★★

La Tâche Good colour; gloriously fragrant, sustained Pinot bouquet, sweet, superb balance. *Last tasted April 1998* ★★★★★ *Plenty of life left.*

Richebourg DRC It always astonishes me to note how different these DRC wines can be despite the proximity of the vineyards on the slope above Vosne-Romanée and the same winemaking in the same cellars. Most recently, a magnum: still richly coloured but showing some maturity; glorious bouquet; sweet ingress, flavour of violets, great length. *Last tasted Sept 1990.* ★★★★(★) *Doubtless perfection now.*

Grands-Echézeaux DRC A magnum: brownish, mature rim; very sweet, fully ripe 'boiled beetroot' nose of great depth and which held magnificently. Sweet entry, lovely flavour but a fairly dry finish. *Last tasted March 2002* ★★★★

Romanée-St-Vivant DRC I have always had a soft spot for the St-Vivant, yet of all the DRC 'stable', it does not command quite the same attention as the others. Most recently: very attractive colour, rich 'legs'; fully evolved bouquet surging out of the glass, sweet, fragrant, singed, great depth; now very sweet on the palate, full-bodied (14% alcohol), rich flavour, touch of citrus zest and still tannic. *Last noted Nov 1995* ★★★★★ *Will still be excellent.*

Beaune, Grèves Moillard Fully mature, hardly surprising; very ripe, meaty, yet grapey; slightly sweet, fairly high alcohol (14%), vegetal Pinot flavour, good length and aftertaste. *Nov 2006* ★★★★

Bonnes-Mares, Vieilles Vignes Clair-Daü Mature; nose both earthy and flowery, vegetal and violets, opening up marvellously; sweet, full, soft yet assertive, rich yet dry finish. *Jan 1990* ★★★★★ *Should still be good.*

Bonnes-Mares G Roumier Correct, open, mature rim; lovely, well-developed Pinot opening up sweetly; soft, sweet, attractive texture, very dry finish. *March 2002* ★★★★ *Now–2010.*

Volnay, Les Taillepieds Dom de Montille Fully mature, open rim; sweet, ripe 'beetroot' varietal nose opening up and holding fragrantly; sweet, rich, excellent flavour. *March 2002* ★★★★ *Now–2012.*

OTHER VERY GOOD '71S last tasted in the 1990s. These and other leading '71s should be lovely to drink now – and good value: **Beaune, Grèves, Vignes de l'Enfant Jesus, Bouchard Père** lovely wine ★★★★; **Corton, Clos des Fiètres E Voarick** luminous; hint of strawberry, delicious ★★★; **Echézeaux Leroy** soft, spicy, good flavour, dry finish ★★★; **Clos Vougeot Hudelot** rich, roasted, powerful, assertive yet harmonious ★★★★

1972 ★★★

This year was considered a good vintage in Burgundy but, with a wine slump and '72 Bordeaux in mind, it was spurned by the British trade. It was an unusual growing season: a warm spring, but a cold and dry summer. A warm rainy September saved the day and a huge crop, well over the permitted yield, was a problem. Despite this there was no let up in prices. The habitually late-picking Domaine de la Romanée-Conti wines were outstandingly the most successful. Few other wines are now worth looking out for.

La Tâche More recently, tasting it alongside the '69, '70 and '71, I felt it had run its course: medium-deep, luminous, slightly singed nose, slightly caramelly taste, not bad but edgy. *Last noted April 1998* ★★ *Hanging on (just).*

Grands-Echézeaux Engel Magnum: medium, weak rim; distinctly sweet vegetal nose. Fairly sweet on the palate, crisp, flavoury, dry finish. *Oct 2003* ★★★

Musigny, Vieilles Vignes de Vogüé Good colour; scented Pinot aroma; dry, crisp, fruity. Good acidity and grip. *Last tasted Jan 1990* ★★★ *Probably still holding on.*

Pommard, Rugiens, Tasteviné Gaunoux Palish, fully mature; good ripe Pinot smell which reminded me of a shoe repair shop; sweet, earthy, with refreshing acidity. *Jan 1998* ★★★

1973, 1974, 1975 and 1977
All poor. Avoid.

1976 ★★★
Despite its considerable attractions, this vintage produced unbalanced wines, over-endowed with tannin from the start, and they still are. Will these impressively constituted but still very tannic wines become more amenable, or will they continue to dry out?

Romanée-Conti Most recently: rich, harmonious nose; sweet, full, very rich and powerful. *Last tasted Feb 1992* ★★★★ *Though an old note, a survivor.*

La Tâche Most recently: two bottles, the first with an attractive colour; inimitable La Tâche fragrance with whiff of liquorice, olives, strawberry Pinot; medium-dry, flavour of dried berries, very tannic, austere finish. The second bottle, slightly paler; softer nose, harmonious, forthcoming, spicy, cherry-like; less aggressive, lovely fruit, very dry finish. *Last tasted Nov 2005. At best* ★★★★★

Richebourg DRC Pure varietal Pinot; sweet, delicious flavour, soft, despite its tannic finish. *Last tasted April 2004* ★★★★

Romanée-St-Vivant DRC Through the 1980s, opening up with silky texture and fragrance but with abrupt astringent finish. *Last tasted Feb 1992* ★★★

Grands-Echézeaux DRC Most recently: warm, mature colour; ripe, elegant, slightly scented 'squashed cherry bouquet'; pure Pinot flavour, good texture, dry finish. *March 2002* ★★★★ *Drink soon.*

Bonnes-Mares Dujac Medium-deep, soft colour, open, mature; classic, fragrant, whiff of soy sauce; initially sweet, very tannic and high acidity. Now fleshy, soft, very Pinot aroma, dry finish. *Oct 2005* ★★★

Chambertin A Rousseau Palish, open, rosy-hued; sweet, mature, slightly smoky aroma; sweet, rich, but by no means hefty. The '76 tannin present but merely leading to a good, dry finish. *Last tasted May 1999* ★★★

Chambolle-Musigny Thomas-Bassot Medium-deep, mature; good commercial wine, yet with character and flavour. *Jan 2005* ★★★

Echézeaux Dujac Mature; glorious soft 'beetroot' vegetable bouquet and flavour. '76 tannin very noticeable. *Nov 2005* ★★★

THE BEST OF OTHER '76S last tasted in the 1990s: **Beaune, Grèves, Vignes de l'Enfant Jésus Bouchard Père** good ripe nose and flavour. ★★★; **Corton, Clos du Roi Voarick** two contrasting bottles, both good in their way. Harmonious, crisp, tannic and the other sweeter, fuller ★★★ *hard to predict;* **Corton, Hospices, Cuvée Dr Peste** Dark; meaty; fairly sweet, full-bodied, rich, concentrated though with somewhat coarse tannic finish ★★★; **Corton, Hospices, Cuvée Charlotte Dumay** soft, harmonious, vanillin nose; a good rich mouthful but stubbornly tannic ★★★★ *worth keeping;* **Musigny J Drouhin** at 14 years old, a lovely wine, fabulous flavour, assertive, good length, relatively unobtrusive tannin ★★★★ *should still be delicious;* **Clos de Tart** tart the operative word. Highish volatility, enlivening colour, elevating bouquet, bringing out the flavour. Perverse but I enjoyed it ★★★ *risky now.*

1978 ★★★★★

At last, a great vintage. Yet weather-wise it was touch and go: spring and early summer cold, retarding vegetation and flowering. Around the third week in August, the sun came out and superb weather through September and into October saved the vintage, resulting in a small but healthy crop of aromatic wines with good colour and alcoholic content. Thanks to high extract and tannins, the best are still drinking well.

Romanée-Conti Magnificent. Medium-pale, yet lively-looking, yellow-amber rim; rich, lovely fragrance, pure mature 'beetroot' varietal bouquet that opened up in the glass, soft fruit, whiff of raspberry; sweet on the palate, full-bodied (yet a moderate 13% alcohol), interesting texture, peppery acidity and an almost spritz finish. *Last tasted March 2002* ★★★★★ *Now–2012.*

La Tâche A ripe and lovely nose which gushed out of the glass; soft, beautiful flavour, good length, dry finish. *Last noted Sept 2000* ★★★★★

Grands-Echézeaux DRC Some colour loss, tailing off to a somewhat weak rim; almost sickly sweet, jammy even, on the nose yet the finish dry and a bit raw. The bottle? Should have been finer. *Last noted Sept 2000. At best* ★★★★★

Romanée-St-Vivant DRC Bouquet fully evolved, surging out of the glass; sweet entry, dry finish, elegant. True burgundy. *Last tasted Sept 2000* ★★★★★

Beaune, Cent Vignes Ch de Meursault Very good, mature Pinot; sweet, good fruit, flavour and weight. Ready. *April 1998* ★★★★ *Drink now.*

Bonnes-Mares J Drouhin Still very deep, with a dark cherry core; glorious bouquet, with a sort of cherry-like fruit; perfect sweetness, fairly hefty yet not obtrusively so, lovely flavour, with mulberry-ripe fruit. All the component parts perfectly balanced. *Last noted Oct 2001* ★★★★★

Mazis-Chambertin Leroy Autumnal, very mature; tea-like, fragrant, developing penetrating Pinot, whiff of treacle; lovely wine, mature, uplifting flavour, high alcohol, still tannic. *March 2003* ★★★★★ *Now–2010.*

Nuits-St-Georges, Les Perrières Seguin-Manuel Fully mature, ruddy colour; sweet, rich, meaty; pleasant 'tangy' nose and taste, rich but surprisingly tannic. *Jan 2005* ★★★ *Now–2010.*

Richebourg J Drouhin Rich, mature; equally rich, ripe nose expanding in the glass; sweet, mouthfilling, great to drink though still tannic. *May 1990* ★★★★★ *Should be perfect now.*

Clos de la Roche Dujac Superb. Most recently: medium-deep, mature; scented 'beetroot' Pinot, glorious fragrance; lovely flavour, touch of leanness and quite a tannic bite. *Last noted Nov 2000* ★★★★

Clos de la Roche A Rousseau Sweet, hefty, mature Pinot; sweet, rich; delicious. *May 1999* ★★★★

Vosne-Romanée, Aux Brûlées Henri Jayer In magnum: deep, richly coloured, velvety, maturing in its own time; bouquet expanded in the glass; fairly sweet, powerful (yet 13% alcohol on label), concentrated, marvellous flavour, balance, grip, tannin and acidity. A supreme example of the late Henri Jayer's genius. *Last tasted Nov 2002* ★★★★★ *Now–2015.*

Vosne-Romanée, Cros Parantoux Henri Jayer Deep, hefty, richly coloured and bouquet to match. Laden but not inhibited by its extract, the nose opening up wonderfully; amazingly sweet, concentrated, glorious length and aftertaste, still tannic. *Dec 1995* ★★★★★ *Years of life.*

Clos Vougeot Noëllat Still fairly deep; a classic, ripe Pinot nose and flavour. *April 2000* ★★★★

1979 ★★★

A good, prolific vintage. Apart from three major hailstorms, the most severe in June cutting swathes in the vineyards in the Côte de Nuits between Nuits-St-Georges and Chambolle-Musigny, the summer weather was favourable and a large harvest of healthy grapes took place around the end of September. Though less well-balanced than the '78s, there were some attractive wines which will be holding well.

Romanée-Conti Only one note, but memorable, a jeroboam: medium, expansive but open and fully mature in its 15th year; a sensational, indescribably glorious bouquet; sweet, full of vigour and power, fabulous flavour, length and aftertaste. *Sept 1994* ★★★★★ *Will still be superb.*

La Tâche A palish, pretty coloured wine; very distinctive fragrance with a touch of malt; very sweet, very rich, meaty character, great length, very dry finish. *Last tasted March 1998* ★★★★

Romanée-St-Vivant DRC Not much red left but a 'lovely DRC' bouquet and flavour, powerful, scented. *Last tasted Sept 1997* ★★★★ *(just).*

Richebourg DRC Palish, fully mature; initially sweet, singed, chocolatey nose, vegetal and prolonged fragrance; very rich and chocolatey on the palate, mouthfilling, touch of butterscotch. *At the Domaine, Nov 2003* ★★★★ *Now–2010.*

Vosne-Romanée, Cros Parantoux Henri Jayer Although an old note, an exceptional wine. Medium, with ruby at its centre; showing some age but glorious bouquet, ripe, exciting; medium-dryness and body, still very crisp, fragrant, dry finish (some minor bottle variation). *Tasted Sept 1994* ★★★★

GOOD '79S last tasted in the 1990s, all ready for drinking: **Beaune, Clos des Mouches J Drouhin** fully evolved ★★★ **Beaune, Clos des Ursules L Jadot** ripe, lean, attractive ★★★; **Chambertin, Cuvée Héritiers Latour L Latour** good but lean and very tannic ★★★(★)?; **Corton, Clos des Cortons Faiveley** rich, full, complete ★★★★; **Ch Corton-Grancey L Latour** fully mature, good flavour and grip ★★★★; **Clos de Tart** fragrant, sweet, harmonious ★★★

1980 ★★ to ★★★

Uneven quality and the market still in recession. An extended and uneven flowering in June. Summer temperatures, August in particular, were above average and continued into September. There was some rain before the harvest, which started early October. Late pickers fared best. Few recent notes. Of little interest now.

La Tâche Late picked. Most recently, and surprisingly, a glorious burst of fragrance; slightly lean, light style yet heady. Lovely flavour. *Last noted March 1999* ★★★ *Drink while the going is good.*

Romanée-St-Vivant DRC Also late picked. Surprisingly good: a surge of fragrance, sweet, soft fruit, iodine, then a shut down followed 15 minutes later by another burst of fragrance; very sweet, complete, fully evolved, rich, slightly chocolatey. A very attractive wine. *Last noted Nov 1995* ★★★★ *Drink soon, before it touches down.*

Beaune, Clos des Mouches J Drouhin A fully evolved nose, opening up beautifully. Firm, a touch of hardness, good acidity, dry finish. *Last tasted Oct 1990* ★★★ *Drink soon.*

Gevrey-Chambertin, Clos St-Jacques A Rousseau Glorious Pinot scent, fragrant; sweet, medium weight, very flavoury and with a most attractive 'peacock's tail'. *March 1995* ★★★★ *Drink soon.*

Clos de la Roche Dujac Crisp and fresh for its age, scents of violet, privet; attractive flavour, arboreal, privet again, plenty of tannin and acidity. Unfiltered. Needs decanting. *Oct 2005* ★★★ *Drink soon.*

1981 ★★
A poor vintage in Burgundy. Avoid.

1982 ★★
What went wrong? Was it overproduction and a bumper crop resulting in lack of concentration? The very noticeable feature of the '82s is that they scarcely qualify as red burgundy as they are often so pale, with little red and a weak rim. Many old notes. Not worth pursuing

La Tâche In its youth, fragrant, harmonious, developing quickly. Alas, most recently, it was corked and 'screwed up'. So judgment must be reserved. *Last noted April 1998* ★★★? *Probably best to drink soon.*

Romanée-St-Vivant DRC Most recently: appearance open, already fully mature; soft, fragrant, slightly singed nose. On the palate sweet, very characteristic, very burgundian, but with a chaptalised character and, though with tannic grip, lacking length. *Last tasted Nov 1995* ★★★ *(just).*

Bonnes-Mares G Roumier Decent colour; attractive, ripe, varietal nose and flavour. Drinking pleasantly. *Oct 2000* ★★★ *Drink soon.*

Musigny, Vieilles Vignes de Vogüé Tasted alongside the '81, its nose far more evolved; sweet, rich, ready. *Jan 1999* ★★★ *Drink soon.*

1983 ★★★ (variable)
A difficult and highly controversial vintage, the growing season punctuated by disasters – frost, hail, excessive heat, wet and rot; excessively hard and tannic wines; with hindsight, crass premature marketing and a scandalous report on the DRCs in a major American wine journal. Those who picked late and highly selectively did best. Undoubtedly, the two major problems were rot and excessively harsh tannins. Difficult to say when to drink these wines.

Romanée-Conti Most recently, a magnum: its initial depth of colour now softening, rim maturing; very meaty, fragrant nose which opened up gloriously, tangy, fragrant, blackberry; fairly sweet, rich, mouthfilling, very good flavour and texture, spicy, still tannic. Not an easy wine, needing far more bottle-ageing. *Last tasted Nov 2003* ★★(★★★) *2010–2030?*

La Tâche Most recently: medium-deep, attractive colour, maturing; a flowery varietal nose, with, I thought, a whiff of rot but not on the palate. Sweet, soft, chewy, with a dry, citrus-like finish. *Last tasted April 1998* ★★★(★) *(just).*

Romanée-St-Vivant DRC Ruddy coloured; rich, singed nose, harmonious, then, after an hour sagging a little; distinctly sweet, interesting, lovely, still quite a bite. *Last tasted Nov 1995* ★★(★) *2010–2020.*

Grands-Echézeaux DRC Rich nose, fullish; very appealing. I did not notice any rot or excessive tannin. *Last noted April 1992* ★★★(★) *Now–2015.*

Echézeaux DRC The weakest of the range. Most recently, bottle variation: nose initially sweet and appealing though one bottle a bit corky – or was it rot? Sweet, soft, dry finish. *Last tasted April 1992* ★★? *Drink up or avoid.*

Chambertin A Rousseau By now fully mature; subtle, complex nose, almost too sweet; good flavour, power, length, tannin and acidity. *Last noted March 1995* ★★★★ *Should be excellent now.*

Chambertin, Clos de Bèze A Rousseau Harmonious; fairly sweet, full-bodied. An expanding flavour. *March 1995* ★★★★ *Good life predicted.*

Charmes-Chambertin A Rousseau The biggest *grand cru* vineyard in Gevrey and one of the biggest in Burgundy. Lovely colour, gentle gradation; equally gentle, harmonious nose, more scented than varietal; some sweetness, elegant, crisp, good tannins. *March 1995* ★★★★ *Now–2015.*

OTHER VERY GOOD '83S not tasted since the mid-1990s: **Chambertin, Cuvée Héritiers Latour L Latour** fully mature, lovely flavour ★★★★; **Corton, Hospices, Cuvée Dr Peste Rossignol** sweet, powerful, very tannic ★★(★★)?; **Gevrey-Chambertin, Les Cazetiers A Rousseau** Beautiful varietal aroma; sweet, assertive, very tannic ★★★(★★)? **Gevrey-Chambertin, Clos St-Jacques A Rousseau** aggressive, swingeingly tannic (★★★★) *future depends on tannin amelioration;* **Clos de la Roche A Rousseau** not exactly a charmer. Impressive but teeth-gripping tannins ★★(★★)?; **Ruchottes-Chambertin A Rousseau** rich, lovely fruit ★★★(★)

1984
One of the most lacklustre vintages of the decade in Burgundy. Avoid.

1985 ★★★★★
One of my favourite burgundy vintages and certainly some of my most consistently glowing notes. Delayed flowering; June and July were fairly normal but, from the first week in August, heat and drought, then hailstorms. From 1 September constant sunshine. A ripe, healthy crop and one of the best vintages in most growers' memories. Now fully mature.

Romanée-Conti Alas, only one note: concentrated nose; very sweet, rich, multi-dimensional. *Feb 1996* ★★★★★ *Now–2025.*

La Tâche Most recently: beautiful in all respects. At its most gloriously fragrant best. *Last noted August 2006* ★★★★★ *yet more to come.*

Richebourg DRC Most recently: still deeply coloured; 'hefty' to which I added 'glorious'; a massive wine with loads of grip. Tannic. Superb but needing time. *Last noted April 2000* ★★(★★★) *Now–2015.*

Grands-Echézeaux DRC Most recently: excellent, mature Pinot Noir bouquet and flavour. Great length, marvellous fragrance. *Last noted Nov 1999* ★★★★★ *Drink soon.*

Romanée-St-Vivant DRC Exuberantly fragrant, soft mocha, then walnuts and autumnal berries; expanded quickly in the mouth, glorious flavour and finish. Very sweet, rich, delicious. *Last tasted Feb 1996* ★★★★★ *Drink now.*

Echézeaux DRC Mature; delicious fragrance and flavour. Lovely wine. *Last tasted Oct 2003* ★★★★ *Now–2010.*

Beaune, La Mignotte Leroy Ruby and still then youthful-looking for a mature '85; good fruit; soft, fleshy, penetrating flavour. *Nov 1999* ★★★★ *Now–2015.*

Bonnes-Mares Dujac Bright, mature. Two bottles, the first on verge of corkiness, singed, tannic. The second softer, more earthy nose; delicious flavour, complete. *Oct 2005. At best* ★★★★★ *Drink up.*

Chambertin Leroy Attractive colour, mature, but not a great Chambertin. Some sweetness, showing age on the palate yet still tannic. Disappointing. *March 2003* ★★★ *Drink up.*

Chambertin A Rousseau Lovely colour, mature rim; excellent bouquet; magical, highly sensitive fruit, elegant, perfect condition. *Last noted Aug 2000* ★★★★★ *Now–2020.*

Corton J Drouhin Harmonious bouquet, gentle, touch of spice; medium-sweet, matching flavour, smooth, lovely. Perfection. *Jan 2001* ★★★★★ *Drink soon.*

Corton Tollot-Beaut Sweet, fudge-like (soft toffee); sweet, rich, easy, very agreeable. *Nov 2000* ★★★ *Drink soon.*

Ch Corton-Grancey L Latour Sweet, good fruit, nicely evolved. *Last tasted March 1998* ★★★★ *Ready now.*

Echézeaux Dujac Classic, ripe Pinot, very meaty, glorious, great depth, showing some age; almost too sweet, delicious flavour. *Oct 2005* ★★★★★ *Drink soon.*

Echézeaux Henri Jayer Extraordinary strawberry-like fruit, very rich but, alas, corked. *Nov 2003. Potential* ★★★★★ *Now–2015.*

Echézeaux Thomas-Bassot Fairly pale, rosy-hued, very mature appearance but better flavour and more bite than expected. *March 1999* ★★★ *(just). Drink soon.*

Gevrey-Chambertin, Combe aux Moines P Leclerc Mature; fragrant; attractive fruit. Very drinkable. *March 1999* ★★★ *Drink soon.*

Latricières-Chambertin L Ponsot Glorious fragrance; excellent flavour, body and balance. *Nov 2000* ★★★★ *Fully evolved now.*

Musigny, Vieilles Vignes de Vogüé Good but not great. *Aug 1998* ★★★★

Nuits-St-Georges Leroy Should have been decanted. Well made, lots of flavour, ready. *Feb 1998* ★★★ *Now–2015.*

Richebourg Grivot Ripe, classic, *merde*; very attractive, quite a bite for an '85. *July 2003* ★★★★ *Now–2010.*

Richebourg J Gros Meaty Pinot Noir nose; sweet, attractive. *Nov 2000* ★★★ *Drink now.*

Richebourg Henri Jayer Fairly deep, rich 'legs'; fabulous, most extraordinary bouquet, blackcurrant, boiled sweets, three hours of Pinot aroma; fairly sweet, glorious flavour, 13.5% alcohol, length and finesse. *Nov 2003* ★★★★★ *Now–2015.*

Clos de la Roche Dujac Crisp, earthy nose that developed beautifully; medium-dry; firm, good flavour, length and finish. *Oct 2005* ★★★★ *Now–2010.*

Clos St-Denis Dujac Mature, luminous; fragrant, whiff of oak, undemonstrative but good; better on palate, lovely, DRC-like Pinot flavour, crisp, dry but gentle finish. *Oct 2005* ★★★★★ *Now–2010.*

Savigny-lès-Beaune, Les Lavières R Ampeau Not much red left; true Pinot aroma, subtle, soft, harmonious; almost a caricature of Pinot. Verging on liquorice. Very good in its way. *Feb 1998* ★★★★ *Drink soon.*

Volnay, Santenots du Milieu Comtes Lafon Glorious, rich, uplifting

Pinot; a lightish, leanish '85 but with excellent flavour. Perfect now. *Sept 2003* ★★★★ *Now–2010*.

Clos de Vougeot Hudelot-Noëllat Lovely colour; very ripe varietal 'boiled beetroot' nose, very fragrant after an hour and a half; sweet, delicious flavour, touch of bitterness on the finish. *April 2002* ★★★★ *Now–2010*.

GOOD TO VERY GOOD '85S not tasted since the mid-1990s. The wines will be mainly at peak now. Drink soon: **Corton Dom Sénard** brambly fruit; powerful, tannic, good potential ★★★(★); **Echézeaux Jacques Cacheux et Fils** fully mature; fairly sweet, good crisp fruit ★★★; **Gevrey-Chambertin, Clos St-Jacques A Rousseau** fully evolved; exciting surge of fragrance; gorgeously lush flavour. Pinot at its best ★★★★★; **Mazis-Chambertin J Faiveley** full, lovely flavour ★★★★; **Mazis-Chambertin, Hospices, Cuvée Madeleine-Collignon Leroy** fragrant, a light rein, delicious ★★★★; **Nuits-Meurgers Henri Jayer** surprisingly deep; almost brambly fruit; lovely flavour, good grip ★★★★; **Clos de la Roche A Rousseau** rich varietal nose and flavour, fairly sweet and full-bodied, nice weight and balance ★★★★; **Romanée-St-Vivant, Les Quatre Journaux L Latour** rich vanillin; very sweet attractive fruit ★★★★ (*just*); and **Volnay, Clos des Chênes Lafarge** rich ruby; crisp, delicious; flavour lively and lovely, perfect acidity ★★★★

1986 ★★★★

I was tempted to demote this vintage to 3 stars but felt this would be unfair, particularly in the light of so few recent notes. The growing season was reasonably satisfactory and there was a late harvest in good weather. Late pickers made the best wines. This has turned out to be a largely forgotten vintage, but I for one will look out for any '86s that come my way.

La Tâche Mature, singed, spicy Pinot, seeming unknit at first but opened up fragrantly and the small amount left in my glass holding well for over four hours. Good, firm, fullish, flavoury. *Last noted April 1998* ★★★★ *Now–2010*.

Richebourg DRC A soft, autumnal red-brown; lovely, gentle, open nose; silky, leathery tannins. *Last tasted Jan 1990*. ★(★★★★) *Ready now.*

Grands-Echézeaux DRC Fairly deep yet browning at rim; rich, soft, harmonious, but still very tannic. *Last tasted Nov 1991*. (★★★★) *But ready now.*

Romanée-St-Vivant DRC Surprisingly pale, open, weak-rimmed, orange-tinged; a fully evolved, singed, mature nose, fragrant, vegetal. Rich but no development though settled down harmoniously; medium-dry, attractive flavour and style, lean, dry, tannic finish. *Last tasted Nov 1995* ★★★ *Now–2010?*

Chambolle-Musigny, Les Amoureuses Mounier Ripe bouquet; very fruity, fragrant, a touch lean and tannic. *July 2003* ★★★(★) *Now–2012*.

1987 ★★★

Good, but not as good as the early reports indicated, for though it was indeed a small crop of grapes with a high ratio of skin to juice, there was a good deal of chaptalisation. Chaptalised wines are often very attractive when young, but do not retain their appeal. Late pickers, as so often, fared best.

La Tâche Not for the first time, a 'contrary Mary'. Most recently: pale, 'unconvincing'; sweet, slightly singed, fully developed nose; richer and more body than its colour led one to anticipate. *Last noted May 1999* ★★★ *But unenthusiastic.*

Romanée-St-Vivant DRC Bottle variation. One bottle dry, lightish, clearly chaptalised and with a short, coarse, dry finish. The second was horribly sweet, also coarse and tannic. Both came from the DRC cellars. *Last tasted Nov 1995* ★★

So WHAT IS ONE TO THINK OF THE DRC '87S? I have not tasted the rest of the range since the early 1990s.

Romanée-Conti Pale; low-keyed but genuinely complex; assertive, considerable length, tannin, acidity. *Feb 1990* (★★★)?

Richebourg It seemed sweeter, more flowery for Richebourg than usual though it was good, rich and meaty round the waist. Dry finish. *Last noted May 1992* (★★★★)

Grands-Echézeaux Chocolatey (chaptalised), slightly stewed nose; soft fruit, adequate tannin and acidity. *Last tasted Jan 1991* ★★★ *An early developer.*

Echézeaux Surprisingly sweet, a whiff of strawberry; overall drier and more powerful than expected. *Last noted April 1992* ★★★ *Drink soon.*

THE BEST OF THE FEW '87S tasted in the mid-1990s:

Vosne-Romanée, Champs Perdrix Perrin-Rossin Palish, maturing; slightly vegetal nose; medium sweetness and body, quite good flavour. *April 1996* ★★★

1988 ★★★★★

With the '85, one of the two best vintages of the decade. But while the '85s had an easy – misleadingly easy – charm, the '88s were less flattering, firmer, tannic and are now, in my opinion, superior. The important feature of the growing season was an exceptional summer: hot and dry from the end of July through to October, happily interspersed with refreshing showers. The result of this heat was thick skins, ripe and concentrated flesh, deep colour, fairly substantial alcohol and a great deal of tannin. The intrinsic richness, the extract and complexity have made these wines a rare pleasure to drink through the first two decades of the 21st century.

Romanée-Conti Old note: a powerhouse with great future. *Last tasted March 1991* (★★★★★) *Now probably* ★★(★★★) *2012–2030.*

La Tâche Showing some maturity; vegetal Pinot aroma, sweet, like caramel with an upturned edge; sweaty tannins; but after an hour rich, great depth, and after four hours in the glass, strawberry-like fruit, later still, spicy. Fairly sweet, assertive, piquant fruit and some astringency. *Last tasted April 1998* ★★(★★★) *Now–2020.*

Richebourg DRC A full, chunky, tannic wine, dry with silky textured tannins, fragrant aftertaste. Great future. *Last tasted March 1991* (★★★★★) *Say 2010–2020.*

Romanée-St-Vivant DRC Medium-deep, bright, open, rich 'legs'; sweet, harmonious nose with whiff of vanillin, its initial harsh edge softening and opening up. Almost sickly sweet after an hour or two in the glass. Medium-sweet entry leading to a very dry, tannic finish, full-bodied, crisp, firm. Fine wine, needs time. *Last tasted Nov 1995* ★(★★★★) *Now–2020.*

Grands-Echézeaux DRC Packed with fruit, wonderful fragrance, stylish, lovely aftertaste. Great future. *Last tasted March 1991* ★★★(★★) *Now–2020.*

Echézeaux DRC Pink-tinged; crisp fruit; dry, firm, very tannic. Should develop well. *Last tasted Oct 1991* (★★★) *Now–2010.*

Beaune, Montrevenots J-M Boillot Medium-deep, cherry red with maturing rim; very fragrant, spicy, lovely scent, 'true burgundy'; powerful and complete. Very well made. *Last tasted Feb 1998* ★★(★★) *Now–2012.*

Beaune, Clos des Ursules L **Jadot** Most recently: some colour loss, attractive nose and taste. Drinking fairly well but I was not as enthusiastic as I thought I should have been. *Last noted Sept 1997* ★★★ *Drink soon.*

Beaune, Toussaints **Mathouillet-Besancenot** Pretty impressive: fairly deep; a lovely, soft, fragrant Pinot; richly flavoured but with quite a bite and slightly bitter, tannic finish. *July 2000* ★★(★★) *2010–2015.*

Bonnes-Mares **de Vogüé** Fairly deep; glorious nose; medium-sweet, fullish (13.5% alcohol), 'warm', soft tannins; excellent finish. *Jan 2005* ★★★★ *Now–2015.*

Le Chambertin A **Rousseau** Lovely scent, perfect harmony; soft, lovely flavour, surprisingly tannic. Excellent wine. *April 2004* ★★★★(★) *Now–2015.*

Chambertin, Clos de Bèze L **Jadot** Dry, powerful, lots of fruit, great length, the tannin a bit metallic. More recently just noted 'very tannic'. *Last tasted Sept 1997* ★(★★★) *Now–2016.*

Chambolle-Musigny J-F **Mugnier** Medium, mature; ripe, 'sweaty' nose; very sweet, very fragrant, delicious. *July 2003* ★★★★ *Now–2012.*

Le Corton **Dom du Ch de Beaune** Minerally, slightly medicinal nose; a big wine, meaty, with plenty of tannic grip. *Last noted Nov 1995* ★★(★) *Now–2015.*

Corton, Bressandes **Chandon de Briailles** Slightly scented nose; lovely Pinot flavour, quite a bite. *Last noted Jan 1995* ★★★(★) *Should be fine right now.*

Ch Corton-Grancey L **Latour** Most recently: fairly pale and fully mature-looking; pure Pinot Noir nose; leaner and drier than the '90 or '85, crisp, good flavour but very dry, tannic finish. *Last noted March 1998* ★★★(★) *Approaching its best but still tannic.*

Echézeaux **René Engel** Fairly well developed; rich, meaty Pinot; tannic, impressive. *March 1999* ★★★(★) *Now–2012.*

Echézeaux **Henri Jayer** Lovely crisp fruit on nose and palate; very distinctive, ripe, firm but tannic. *Nov 2003* ★★★(★★) *Now–2015.*

Gevrey-Chambertin, Cazetiers **Faiveley** Medium, hint of cherry red; low-keyed; better flavour than nose, crisp fruit. *May 1999* ★★★ *Drink soon.*

Gevrey-Chambertin, Clos St-Jacques A **Rousseau** Soft, earthy, slightly smoky, harmonious; good flavour, crisp, with a citrus-like acidic touch to accompany its tannins. An attractive wine. *March 1995* ★★★(★) *Should be drinking well now.*

Nuits-St-Georges, Clos de la Maréchale **Faiveley** Low-keyed nose; dry, considerable grip, needs time. *May 1999* ★★(★★) *Now–2015.*

Nuits-St-Georges, Vaucrains H **Gouges** Most recently: Pinot Noir aroma and flavour. Fair tannin and acidity. *Last tasted Nov 1996. Then* ★★(★) *Doubtless drinking well now.*

Pommard, Grands Epenots L **Jadot** Medium-deep, rich 'legs'; good fruit, considerable depth; medium sweetness and body, fragrant, as rich as it looked, opening up gloriously in the glass, spicy, dry finish. *Oct 1999* ★★★★(★) *Now–2010.*

Clos de Tart Most recently: soft cherry; lovely, ripe, hen droppings' scent; sweet, delicious flavour, the end bite – more than a peck – very noticeable. *Last noted Sept 2001* ★★★(★) *Perhaps overrated, but an enticing drink.*

Clos Vougeot **Méo-Camuzet** Rich 'legs'; understated nose and flavour. Medium sweetness, soft, good length. *March 1998* ★★★ *Holding its own quite well.*

1989 ★★★★

Not as tannic as the '88s but well constructed and, on the whole, very satisfactory wines, the best and best-kept drinking well now. A long hot summer resulted in an early harvest of healthy ripe grapes picked in perfect conditions from mid-September.

Romanée-Conti Fairly deep, lovely, soft, vanillin nose; intense, assertive, great length – earning an exceptionally high mark. *Maddeningly my most recent note misindexed* ★★★(★★)

La Tâche Less intense, more open than expected, a somewhat chocolatey fragrance which after a long time in the glass took on a strawberry-like fruitiness, still spicy after six hours. Fairly sweet, full, still assertive, notably tannic and with a long, piquant, fruity extension. *Last tasted April 1998* ★★★(★★) *Now–2020.*

Richebourg DRC Soft, lovely nose; (surprisingly) elegant, stylish, good flavour and length. *Not tasted since June 1992. Then* ★(★★★★) *Should be lovely now.*

Romanée-St-Vivant DRC Still fairly deep, dark cherry; vegetal nose, 'broccoli'; sweet, rich, high alcohol, assertive and more grip than the '90. *Last noted Oct 2001* ★★★(★★) *Could still do with more bottle age.*

Grands-Echézeaux DRC A high mark on the palate, soft fruit yet well endowed with tannin and acidity. *Last tasted June 1992. Then* ★★(★★★) *Now–2020.*

Echézeaux DRC Though its nose was ripe it seemed unready. A fairly big wine, with touch of tannic bitterness. *Last noted Sept 2000* ★★(★★) *Give it time.*

Bonnes-Mares de Vogüé Medium-deep, lovely soft mature colour; sweet, ripe, rich bouquet and flavour. Dry finish. A most delicious wine. *Last tasted June 2006* ★★★★★ *Perfect now. Will keep if cellared well.*

Chambertin, Clos de Bèze L Jadot Deep, still youthful; not very distinctive at first, root-like Pinot emerged; better in the mouth, full, rich, complete. *Sept 2003* ★★★★ *Now–2010.*

Charmes-Chambertin, Les Corbeaux Denis Bachelet Delicious. *Nov 2003* ★★★★ *Now–2010.*

Ch Corton-Grancey L Latour Curious nose; crisp fruit, full, notable grip and tannin. *Last noted June 1997* ★★★ *Now–2015.*

Echézeaux Henri Jayer Nutty at first, after an hour, lovely fruit, a whiff of raspberry; sweet, soft, rich, full – though alcohol a reasonable 13%. Mulberry, raspberry, fabulous 'peacock's tail' length and aftertaste. *Nov 2003* ★★★★★ *Now–2015.*

Musigny J-F Mugnier Medium-deep, rich, still plummy-coloured; unfamiliar nose and curious flavour. Dry finish. *Nov 2003* ★★?

Musigny, Vieilles Vignes J-F Mugnier Medium, open rim; fuller, richer and more to it than the above. *Nov 2003* ★★★ *Now–2012.*

Musigny, Vieilles Vignes de Vogüé Most recently: medium-pale, positively glowing, fully mature; very sweet meaty nose showing its age; very rich, lovely flavour but more than ready for drinking. *Last tasted June 2006* ★★★★★ *Drink soon.*

Pommard, Fremiers (*sic*) **de Courcel** Two years in new wood and bottle age accounted for its relatively pale colour, though a lovely, soft gradation and luminosity; smoky vanillin nose; sweet and soft on the palate too, yet with a tannic finish. *Feb 1998* ★★★(★) *Now–2015.*

Clos de la Roche Ponsot Well developed Pinot aroma; sweet, positive, very good. *Nov 2003* ★★★★ *Now–2010.*

La Romanée Dom du Ch de Vosne-Romanée Palish colour; sweet, vanillin, soft fruit; rich, rounded yet with good grip. *Nov 1995* ★★★(★) *Now–2015*.

Romanée-St-Vivant, Les Quatre Journaux L Latour Nice wine. Touch of bitterness. *Jan 1997* ★★★ *Now–2012*.

Clos de Vougeot, Tasteviné Fairly deep, rich and very attractive. *Nov 1995* ★★★★ *Now–2012*.

SOME OTHER VERY GOOD '89S tasted in the early to mid-1990s, with potential rating at the time of tasting: **Beaune, Clos de la Chaume, Gauffroy Hippolyte Thévenot/Guyon** ★★★; **Beaune, Clos des Mouches Drouhin** (★★★★); **Beaune, Clos des Ursules Jadot** (★★★★); **Chambertin, Clos de Bèze Jadot** (★★★★★); **Chambertin, Clos de Bèze A Rousseau** ★★★★(★); **Chambertin, Cuvée Héritiers Latour** (★★★★); **Chambolle-Musigny, Amoureuses de Vogüé** (★★★★); **Chambolle-Musigny, Haut-Doix Drouhin** (★★★★); **Le Corton, Dom du Ch de Beaune Bouchard Père** (★★★★); **Corton, Bressandes Chandon de Briailles** ★★★★ *(just)*; **Corton, Clos du Roi Chandon de Briailles** ★★★; **Epenottes Drouhin** (★★★★); **Gevrey-Chambertin, Vieilles Vignes Bachelet** ★★★; **Richebourg Méo-Camuzet** ★★★(★★); **Clos de la Roche Dujac** (★★★★); and **Clos de Tart** (★★★★)

1990 ★★★★★

A superb vintage, drinking yet keeping well. Flowering was later than usual and the potentially large crop was reduced by *coulure* and *millerandage*. The summer was hot and too dry, with near drought conditions. Nevertheless, ripening was advanced and the harvest began early. The grapes were small and healthy with thick skins, resulting in concentration of flesh and high sugar levels, good colour extraction and tannins.

Romanée-Conti After 13 years, still nowhere near full maturity; nose rich, fairly tangy and deep, quickly opened up; rich, creamy 'chocolate cream', harmonious and complete after an hour; on the palate distinctly sweet, powerful, lovely, mouthfilling, still tannic. *Nov 2003* ★★★(★★) *2010–2030*.

La Tâche Medium-deep, open rim; superb, slightly singed bouquet; fairly sweet, lovely perfumed flavour, great length. Glorious wine. *Last tasted Oct 2006* ★★★★★(★) *(6 stars)*. *Now–2025*.

Richebourg DRC Lovely colour; rich 'legs'; fragrant, whiff of tar, well evolved, great depth; very positive entry, fairly powerful, immediately mouthfilling, high extract masking tannin and acidity. *Nov 2003* ★★★★(★) *Now–2025*.

Romanée-St Vivant DRC Fairly deep, still plummy; very good, fragrant, 'beetroot' Pinot nose; full of fruit, lovely flavour, excellent dry finish. *Last tasted Oct 2006* ★★★(★) *Now–2020*.

Beaune, Clos des Mouches J Drouhin Never a very deep colour, now fully mature with a touch of orange at the rim; surprisingly little nose, slightly jammy; sweet, good fruit but a bit raw. Disappointing. The bottle? Storage (at Drouhin cellars in Beaune)? I suspect it would have been in better shape if it had come from a good cold British cellar. *Last tasted Oct 2001. Benefit of the doubt* ★★★(★) *Drink now.*

Beaune, Clos des Ursules L Jadot Still a dark cherry red; good fruit, rich extract, brambly, touch of tar; sweet, complete, masked tannin, good length. *Last tasted Oct 2001* ★★★★ *Now–2012.*

Beaune, Hospices, Cuvée Dames Hospitalières Most recently: sweet, harmonious nose, good flavour and length, but still pretty tannic. *Last noted Oct 1995* ★★★★ *Now–2012.*

Bonnes-Mares de Vogüé Fairly deep, impressive. Alas not in good condition. Whiff of oxidation. Should be better than this. *June 2006. Potential* ★★★★★?

Le Chambertin A Rousseau Very good fruit, brambly Pinot Noir, persistent; medium sweetness and body, firm flavour. A classic Chambertin. *Oct 2003* ★★★(★★) *2010–2020.*

Chambertin, Clos de Bèze Faiveley Most recently, still firm and tannic. *Last noted June 2001. The jury is out. It should be first rate.*

Chambertin, Clos de Bèze A Rousseau Needed more time to shake off its tannic overcoat. *June 1996* ★★(★★)?

Chassagne-Montrachet, Clos de la Boudriotte Ramonet Delicate, fragrant, delicious; fairly full and sweet, lovely flavour, length and aftertaste. *June 1996* ★★★★ *Ready now.*

Corton Bonneau du Martray Sweet, harmonious, varietal; soft, rich, fleshy and fragrant. *Oct 1995* ★★★★★ *Lovely now.*

Corton, Clos des Cortons Faiveley Good varietal aroma; medium-sweet, fairly full-bodied, rich, rather jammy flavour. *June 2003* ★★★ *Now–2012.*

Corton, Hospices, Cuvée Dames Hospitalières Lovely wine, 'will keep'; and the **Cuvée Dr Peste** deep; scent of violets; full, tannic, magnificent. *Jan 1995 Both* ★★★★★ *Now–2015.*

Corton, Clos Rognet Méo-Camuzet Appealing fruit, depth, fragrance; very sweet, lovely fruit and flavour. *June 1996* ★★★★ *Drink soon.*

Ch Corton-Grancey L Latour Most recently: a light tawny edge tinged with orange; perfect harmony; rich, complete, oaky aftertaste. Despite its mature appearance, it has time in hand. *Last tasted July 2000* ★★★★ *Now–2010.*

Echézeaux Henri Jayer A superb note in November 2003: crisp, nutty, then slightly singed, smoky, good ripe nose, very fragrant even after three hours in the glass; sweet, full, soft, ripe, very rich, glorious fruit, crisp tannin and acidity. Superb. Most recently: a disappointing cabbagey, oxidised and very tannic bottle. What a shame. *Last sniffed Oct 2006. At its best* ★★★★★ *Now–2020.*

Gevrey-Chambertin, Combottes Leroy Deep; very good bouquet and flavour. *Nov 2000* ★★★★ *Drink soon.*

Gevrey-Chambertin, Clos St-Jacques L Jadot Good rich appearance; vegetal, opened exotically; full-flavoured, excellent fruit, length and aftertaste. Very tannic. *June 1996. Then* ★★★(★) *Now–2015.*

Gevrey-Chambertin, Clos St-Jacques A Rousseau Deliciously ripe 'very Rousseau' bouquet; lovely, perfect balance, wonderful future. *Oct 2006* ★★★★(★) *Now–2025.*

Gevrey-Chambertin, La Perrière Dom Heresztyn New to me. Still a touch of cherry red; crisp fruit, rich, harmonious, slightly tangy; dry, good flavour, weight, grip, depth and acidity. *April 2006* ★★★★ *Now–2015.*

Le Musigny J-F Mugnier Fairly deep; whiff of cork on nose; sweet, fragrant flavour, good length, still quite a tannic bite. *Oct 2006. At best* ★★★(★) *2010–2020.*

Musigny, Vieilles Vignes de Vogüé Medium-depth, luminous. Lovely

colour, bouquet and flavour. Combines delicacy and power. Good length.
Glorious. *June 2006* ★★★★★ *Perfect now, will keep.*

Nuits-St-Georges, Ch Gris Lupé-Cholet Fragrant; crisp fruit – not
blatantly Pinot Noir, nor speciously burgundian, but pretty good. *March 1999* ★★★
Drink soon.

Pommard Coste-Caumartin Very deeply coloured; good fruit; impressive,
very dry. *March 1995* ★★★ *Drink soon.*

Pommard, Clos des Epeneaux Comte Armand Fairly deep, rich core;
soft, fruity yet distinctly tannic; rich, powerful, very tannic coating the mouth, a lot
to it – in time. *Last tasted Oct 2005* ★(★★★) *2010–2020.*

Pommard, Rugiens Gaunoux A traditional estate. The wines are given
bottle-ageing before release. Deep, rich, impressive; one could smell the warmth of
the summer, wonderful but restrained fruit, an old-fashioned burgundy nose
opening up gloriously. Sweet, fullish, delicious. *Feb 1997* ★★★★(★) *Now–2010.*

Clos de la Roche Dujac Good colour though with orange-tinged maturity;
soft, harmonious, varietal nose; full, complete, rich, perfect balance. *Oct 2001*
★★★★★ *Lovely now.*

Romanée-St-Vivant Leroy Deep ruby; brilliant fruit; lovely wine, still
tannic. *Oct 1996* ★★★(★) *Now–2010.*

Volnay, Taillepieds Marquis d'Angerville Dark cherry; low-keyed fruit;
good flavour, silky tannins. *June 1996* ★★★ *Now–2012.*

Vosne-Romanée, Beaumonts Leroy Almost opaque; very fragrant,
extraordinary in its way; sweet, its fruit a bit too scented, almost artificial. *June 1996*
★★★★ *Drink soon.*

Vosne-Romanée, Les Beaux-Monts Clavelier Brosson Good colour;
nose holding back but not on the palate: sweet, firm, high extract, loads of fruit,
marvellously complete. *Feb 1998* ★★★★★ *Drink soon.*

Vosne-Romanée, Cros Parantoux Henri Jayer Very deep, richly
coloured; strangely sweet, then fragrant, spicy; very sweet, marvellous fruit and
flavour, very distinctive. *June 1996* ★★★★ *Drink soon.*

A SUPERB RANGE OF '90S tasted in 1994, mostly ready for drinking:
Chambolle-Musigny Michèle et Patrice Rion ★★★; **Corton,
Bressandes Tollot-Beaut** ★★★(★); **Les Echézeaux Jean Mongéard**
★★(★★); **Morey-St-Denis Dujac** ★★★(★); **Nuits-St-Georges, Vignes-
Rondes Daniel Rion** ★★(★); **Richebourg Anne et François Gros**
★★★(★★); **Savigny-Lès-Beaune, Serpentières J Drouhin** ★★★;
Volnay, Clos du Verseuil Y Clerget ★★★; **Vosne-Romanée Méo-
Camuzet** ★★★; **Clos de Vougeot Méo-Camuzet** ★★★(★); and **Clos
Vougeot, Musigni** (*sic*) **Gros Frère et Soeur** ★★★★

1991 ★★ very variable

Not a very inspiring vintage and, apart from the extraordinary DRCs and
one or two others, best forgotten. The growing conditions could not have
been more difficult. Growers who were selective were able to make wines
with fair colour and concentration.

Romanée-Conti Medium-deep, soft colour, touch of orange; subdued but
rich (after three hours in a burgundy glass); dry, massive, concentrated, tightly knit.
Impressive for a '91. *Feb 1994* ★★★★? *Hard to predict.*

La Tâche Most recently, a jeroboam: still fairly deep; rich, slightly singed, fragrant, almost cherry-like Pinot nose; medium body, lovely mouthfilling flavour, lissom rather than fleshy, extended taste. *Oct 2005* ★★(★★) *2010–2025*.

Richebourg DRC Most recently: medium-deep, soft, very mature; low-keyed nose; very sweet, completely mature, lean but lovely flavour, good tannin and acidity. 'Remarkable'. *Last tasted July 2003* ★★★ *Now–2015*.

Romanée-St-Vivant DRC Already fully mature-looking with faint touch of orange at the rim; ripe, rustic Pinot; sweeter than expected, dramatic Pinot flavour but fairly acidic finish. Needed food. *Last tasted Nov 2002* ★★(★) *Now–2012*.

Grands-Echézeaux DRC Appearance and nose soft and rich; distinctly sweet, good fruit, tannin present but not overt. *Feb 1994. Then* ★★★ *Now–2010*.

Echézeaux DRC Hard and closed when first poured but had opened up nicely after three hours; assertive, lean, spicy new oak, very dry tannic finish. *Feb 1994* ★★★ *Drink soon*.

Echézeaux Henri Jayer Nose fruity then a surge of smoky, slightly singed fragrance, high-toned; medium-sweet, comparatively light weight and style, eliciously crisp and flavoury but with very dry acidic finish. Even Jayer cannot do better in a vintage like this. *Nov 2003* ★★ *Drink, don't keep*.

Gevrey-Chambertin, Clos St-Jacques A Rousseau Ruby; rich, brambly nose, opening up agreeably, touch of raspberry; medium-sweet, crisp, good grip and attractive. *March 1995. Then* ★★★ *Drink soon*.

Musigny, Vieilles Vignes de Vogüé A difficult vintage. Picked grape by grape. Surprisingly deep; smell of warm mushrooms and bramble; equally surprisingly sweet, rich and mouthfilling (13.5% alcohol) and with a modest future. *Jan 2003* ★★★ *Now–2012*.

Nuits-St-Georges, Les Pruliers H Gouges Low-keyed, vanilla, slightly earthy, pleasant fruit; dry, crisp; refreshing, touch of bitterness. *June 1997* ★★★

Clos de la Roche Dujac Palish, soft ruby; an intriguing scent of *merde* and *betterave* (beetroot); boiled beetroot flavour and good, dry finish. *Oct 2001* ★★★

1992 ★★★

A vintage that was acceptable, commercial and drinking well in its own decade. I would rate it 'good' overall but have the feeling that it has since lost its lustre. August was hot and sunny which advanced ripening, leading to an early harvest, which was mainly completed before the rains set in.

Romanée-Conti Fairly pale, not much red left, very mature, touch of orange at rim; low-keyed, sweet, vegetal nose and flavour. Developed a rich, tangy fragrance; open-knit on palate, subdued fruit, leathery tannic finish. *Nov 2003. A generous* ★★ *Drink, don't keep*.

La Tâche Just one note: medium-deep, forward – already looked fairly mature; light, vegetal Pinot aroma speedily opening up, fragrant, crisp and, even after four hours in the glass, still a charmer; dryish, relatively light body and style but with teeth-gripping acidity. *April 1998* ★★★ *But just misses. Drink soon*.

Romanée-St-Vivant DRC Most recently: open, mature; when first poured, a very vegetal nose, stewed beetroot, cabbage, but after less than 30 minutes, very fragrant and sweet; firm fruit, lean, fair length, dry, somewhat astringent finish. *Last noted Oct 2001. By DRC standards* ★★, *by other yardsticks* ★★★ *Drink up*.

Grands-Echézeaux DRC Maturing; sweet, very vegetal aroma but opened up deliciously and held well; flavour to match, crisp, fairly lean, a relatively soft, easy drink. *Nov 2003* ★★★ *Drink soon.*

Echézeaux DRC Late-harvested. Very fragrant; lovely entry and mid-palate, good length, acidity rather than tannin noted. Delicious. *Last tasted Nov 1995* ★★★ *Drink soon.*

Beaune, Clos des Mouches J Drouhin Ruddy coloured, open rim; jammy, strawberry Pinot nose and taste, nice fruit. Pleasant enough. *Last tasted Oct 2001* ★★★ *Drink soon.*

Beaune, Clos des Ursules L Jadot Mature; sweet, chaptalised nose, hint of raisins; soft, quite rich, brambly tangy taste. Relatively easy style though with refreshing grip. *Oct 2001* ★★★ *Drink soon.*

Chambolle-Musigny, Les Amoureuses de Vogüé Soft cherry, open rim; very meaty, vegetal, whiff of straw; sweet, quite a grip despite its open arms. Not bad for the vintage. *Jan 2005* ★★★ *(just). Drink soon.*

Corton Bonneau du Martray Very sweet, very good, rich, crisp Pinot nose and flavour. An excellent '92. *April 1998* ★★★★ *Drink now.*

Ch Corton-Grancey L Latour Still pink-tinged, weak about the rim; very forthcoming, ripe, varietal nose; far more punchy than its colour led one to expect and with a hot, hard finish. *Last noted July 2000* ★★(★) *Should soften a little.*

Echézeaux Georges Jayer My most detailed note made in 1997: only 13% alcohol though it seemed higher. Heady, spicy, and a deft use of oak. A misleadingly unconvincing appearance, but a lovely wine. The real thing. *Last noted Nov 2001* ★★★★ *Alas I have none left.*

Mazis-Chambertin Good colour; attractive vanillin scent; sweet, crisp, fragrant and positive. *Last noted June 1997* ★★★(★) *Should be fully evolved now.*

Volnay, Vendanges Sélectionnées Lafarge 'A blend from mainly *1er cru* vines, all older than 30 years'. Fragrant with fabulous fruit. Not great, but drinking well. *Last noted Jan 1999* ★★★ *Drink soon.*

Volnay, Hospices, Cuvée Général Muteau Bottled by Jadot A most attractive wine. *April 1995* ★★★★ *Ready now.*

Vosne-Romanée, Cros Parantoux Méo-Camuzet Rich, spicy, delicious ★★★★ *Jan 1994*; and his **Richebourg** lovely but an outrageous price *Jan 1994* ★★★★

1993 ★★★★

These were and still are attractive wines. The growing season began well: early budding and successful flowering. However, the summer was warm and wet with mildew threats. Happily, August was hot and dry, with good ripening conditions which thickened the skins – fortuitously, as the grapes needed protection from the effects of fairly heavy rains in the third week of September. Most wines are ready but the most tannic ones still have a little way to go.

Romanée-Conti A very flowery and surprisingly soft nose; on the palate, full, packed, good length. Totally unready of course. *March 1996* (★★★★) *2010–2020.*

La Tâche Fairly deep; an immediately forthcoming nose, very rich, fragrant Pinot, sweet, vanillin, then a touch of caramel, still rich after four hours, and even after six hours in the glass, a strawberry-like fruitiness. I liked it. *Last noted April 1998* ★★★(★) *Evolving well, good mid-term. Say 2010–1015.*

Richebourg DRC Very forthcoming, fragrant, flowery nose; a substantial wine with a long, dry finish and good aftertaste. *March 1996.* Then ★(★★★) *Now–2015?*

Romanée-St-Vivant DRC Deepish, plummy; bottle variation, one chocolatey, the other cherry-like; sweet, crisp, mouthfilling, tannic. *Last noted Oct 2001* ★★(★★) *Now–2015.*

Grands-Echézeaux DRC Very singed, fragrant, flowery nose; sweet, rich, flavourful. *March 1996* ★★(★★) *Now–2015.*

Echézeaux DRC Bright ruby; an open-topped sort of nose, lovely fruit, opened up well. Crisp, tannic, refreshing. *March 1996* ★★★ *Drink soon.*

Beaune, Clos des Mouches J Drouhin Less deep; pleasant raspberry-like aroma; relatively high acidity noted but good fruit and sustaining tannins. *Last tasted Oct 2001* ★★★ *Drink soon.*

Beaune, Clos des Ursules L Jadot Dark cherry, some intensity, still immature (at 8 years old); thick, chocolatey, rich, brambly nose with hard edge; sweet, powerful, distinctly tarry taste, mouthfilling and fairly well endowed with tannin and acidity. *Oct 2001* ★★★ *Needs time, but not much.*

Bonnes-Mares de Vogüé Lovely, luminous colour; rich, whiff of raisins; lovely flavour, crisp, full-bodied. *June 2006* ★★★★ *Now–2013.*

Chambolle-Musigny de Vogüé Village wine but including some wine from the *1er cru* Fués. Spicy varietal nose, rather Italianate, touch of straw then a gentle cherry-like fragrance; curious individual flavour and end taste, hot alcoholic finish. Certainly interesting. *Jan 2005* ★★★ *Drink now or keep 5 years.*

Corton Bonneau du Martray Fairly deep; very fragrant, good fruit; sweet, attractive, nice texture, length and aftertaste. Tannic. *June 1999* ★★★(★) *Now–2012.*

Gevrey-Chambertin, en Matrot Denis Mortet (Monopole). His first vintage. Fairly mature; good earthy, root-like varietal aroma; medium-dryness and weight. Nice wine. *Jan 2004* ★★★ *Now–2012.*

Gevrey-Chambertin, Clos St-Jacques A Rousseau Medium-deep and still youthful, with an open, mauve tinge; lovely scent, copybook Pinot Noir; sweet, rich, crisp fruit, delicious flavour. *Oct 2001* ★★★(★) *Now–2015.*

Musigny, Vieilles Vignes de Vogüé Good colour; harmonious, fragrant; delicious flavour, crisp fruit, fairly full-bodied, tannic. *June 2006* ★★★★ *Now–2013.*

Nuits-St-Georges, aux Chaignots Alain Michelot Medium-deep; ripe farmyard Pinot; rich, attractive wine, good finish. *July 2003* ★★★ *Now–2012.*

Clos de la Roche Dujac Mature; ripe, soft, harmonious Pinot; fairly sweet, lovely, silky tannins. *Oct 2000* ★★★★ *Drink soon.*

Clos de Tart Mommessin Good, ripe, varietal aroma that opened up gloriously; spicy Pinot, surprisingly tannic, excellent aftertaste. *Oct 1999* ★★★(★) *Now–2010.*

Volnay, Clos de la Bousse d'Or Dom de la Pousse d'Or Medium-deep, rather weak-rimmed, fairly mature; soft, ripe, classic vegetal (beetroot) Pinot; a lovely, very mature and flavoury mouthful, dry tannic finish with touch of bitterness – needs food. *Sept 2003* ★★★★ *Now–2012.*

A RANGE OF GOOD '93S noted in the mid-1990s: **Chambertin, Clos de Bèze Faiveley** ★★★★; **Corton, 'Clos des Cortons' Faiveley** ★★(★); **Ch Corton-Grancey L Latour** ★★★; **Latricières-Chambertin Faiveley** ★★★★; **Mazis-Chambertin Faiveley** ★★★★; **Musigny J Drouhin** ★★★(★); **Savigny-Lès-Beaune Simon Bize** ★★★; Vosne-

Romanée J Gros ★★★; **Clos Vougeot Jean-Jacques Confuron ★★★★**; and **Clos Vougeot D Rion ★(★★★)**

1994 ★

Some domaines made a fairly spectacular start but my most recent notes are less than enthusiastic. Frankly, avoid this vintage. Late pickers fared best. I shall just list the DRC wines.

Romanée-Conti Most recently: surprisingly forward; still dumb but rich, easing itself out of the glass reluctantly; assertive, tannic. *Last noted Feb 1997 ★(★★)? Now–2015.*

La Tâche Fairly deep colour; its nose almost a caricature of Pinot – 'boiled beetroot'. It opened up, vanilla, meaty, then a touch of caramel. After over four hours in the glass, fragrant, and after six hours, an astonishing explosion of fruit. On the palate (tasted just after it was poured), very dry, tannic, slightly astringent. This is a wine that needs time and air to bring out its flavour. *Last tasted April 1998 ★(★★)? Hard to assess.*

Richebourg DRC Not as deep as expected; a broad, meaty, spicy nose, good depth; powerful, intense, penetrating flavour, long, dry, tannic finish. *Last noted Feb 1997 ★(★★)? Time will tell.*

Romanée-St-Vivant DRC Initially chocolatey, fruit and oak, then a *mélange* of strawberry and liquorice; medium-sweet, lean, loose-knit, dry, slightly raw finish. It had lost its bloom of youth without showing any of the benefits of maturity. *Last tasted Oct 2001 ★★?*

Grands-Echézeaux DRC Rich, spicy; fairly sweet and full-flavoured, good fruit and length. Distinctly tannic. *Last tasted Feb 1997 (★★)? Slow start, early decline?*

Echézeaux DRC Gentle fruit. But in freshly poured glass a bit smelly. Sweet, flavoury, but harsh, very tannic finish. *Last tasted Feb 1997 (★★) Not liked.*

1995 ★★★★

Unquestionably an attractive vintage but possibly over-endowed with tannin. Overall: small vintage, high quality. The summer was hot and the grapes matured speedily. Rain during the first half of September threatened rot though the weather improved for a satisfactory end of vintage. Yet again, late pickers fared best. There is a fair consistency of quality and style and this is certainly a vintage to keep an eye on.

Romanée-Conti Not as deep as expected; initially low-keyed, brambly, opening up, very vegetal but a nose of great complexity and richness, a touch of caramel after two hours, then floral fragrance; sweet, rich, complete, wonderful flavour, silky, leathery tannins, excellent aftertaste. Multi-dimensional. Hidden depths, revelations. *Nov 2003 ★★★(★★) 2015–2030.*

La Tâche Fairly deep, very attractive colour, striving to mature; rich, rounded, sweet, vegetal, sweaty tannin, spicy – endless revelations; rich, yet dry-as-dust tannic finish. Innate fruit and a tantalising glimpse of softness. *Nov 2003 (★★★★★) 2015–2030.*

Richebourg DRC Fairly deep, starting to mature; complex nose, at first vegetal, spicy, slightly metallic, developing a more earthy, tangy character with a whiff of liquorice; sweet, rich, complete, attractive, tannic. *Nov 2003 ★★(★★★) 2010–2030.*

Romanée-St-Vivant DRC Good colour; harmonious, good fruit; beautifully complete, crisp, quite a bite. *Last tasted March 2006* ★★★(★★) *2012–2025*.

Grands-Echézeaux DRC Medium depth, open rim, signs of maturity; immediate fragrance, touch of iron, considerable depth; dry, vegetal, relatively light style, leathery tannins. Attractive wine. *Last tasted Nov 2003* ★★★(★★) *2010–2025*.

Beaune, Clos des Mouches J Drouhin Soft garnet; vanillin, good fruit; attractive flavour, flesh, body (13% alcohol), but with highish tannins. *Last tasted Oct 2001* ★★★(★) *Drink soon*.

Beaune, Clos des Ursules L Jadot Very small crop, very slightly chaptalised. Good colour, still youthful; sweet, discreet touch of vanillin, lovely brambly Pinot aroma; sweet, soft, fair flesh, good length. Complete but very tannic finish. *Oct 2001* ★★(★★) *Now–2010*.

Chambertin A Rousseau Rich 'legs'; sweet, harmonious brambly nose; a big wine in every sense, colourful, characterful, fairly full-bodied. Rich extract, well modulated tannins and acidity. *Last tasted Oct 2001* ★★★★(★) *Lovely now–2012*.

Chambolle-Musigny G Roumier Fairly deep; very good varietal nose and taste. A very appealing 'village' wine. *Nov 2003* ★★★ *Now–2015*.

Corton L Jadot Deep, rich, maturing; slightly scented, singed, brambly; very sweet, rich, full-bodied (yet only 13% alcohol), fairly tannic but under control. *April 2001* ★★★(★) *Now–2012*.

Corton, Bressandes Ch de Citeaux, Philippe Bouzereau Good colour; harmonious; fairly sweet, fleshy, attractive flavour, crisp dry finish – in fact a noticeable end-bite. *Oct 1998* ★★★(★) *Now–2010*.

Corton, Grèves L Jadot Very deep, velvety; singed, tarry nose; sweet, rich, full-bodied, very good flavour, tannin and acidity. *April 2002* ★★(★★) *Now–2015*.

Corton, Clos du Roi Remoissenet Touch of cherry; scented, well evolved; delicious flavour, 13.5% alcohol, excellent bite and acidity. *Nov 2006* ★★★ *Now–2015*.

Ch Corton-Grancey L Latour Most recently: mature; lovely ripe bouquet; very sweet, 'warm' – totally delicious. *Last tasted March 2001* ★★★★ *Now–2010*.

Musigny de Vogüé Half bottle. Medium-deep, mature rim; extraordinary fragrance, slight whiff of *cèpes*; medium-sweet, a seriously big wine for Musigny, 'luscious in cask, now closed down'. *Oct 2005* ★★(★★★) *2010–2020*.

Nuits-St-Georges, Les Porets-St-Georges Faiveley Curious, slightly meaty nose; sweet, soft, berry-like flavour, dry finish. *April 2001* ★★★ *Drink up*.

Nuits-St-Georges, Les Saint-Georges Faiveley Good colour, nose and taste; touch of sweetness, excellent flavour and weight. *June 2003* ★★(★★) *Now–2015*.

Savigny-lès-Beaune, Les Vergelesses Simon Bize Palish; good, fresh, acidic Pinot aroma; dry, crisp fruit but astringent. *Feb 2002* ★★ *Drink soon*.

A RANGE OF GOOD '95S tasted in 1997. The tannins will have ameliorated by now and the wines should be drinking well: **Beaune, Grèves Tollot-Beaut** ★★★; **Corton Bonneau du Martray** ★★(★★); **Corton, Bressandes Tollot-Beaut** ★★(★★★); **Chambertin, Clos de Bèze Bruno Clair** ★(★★★); **Chambolle-Musigny, Les Fuées Ghislaine Barthod** ★★(★); **Chambolle-Musigny, Vieilles Vignes Perrot-Minot** ★★★; **Echézeaux** excellent **Mugneret-Gibourg** ★★(★★★); **Gevrey-Chambertin, Cazetiers Bruno Clair** ★★★; **Nuits-St-Georges, Les**

St-Georges R Chevillon ★★(★★); **Nuits-St-Georges, Vaucrains R Chevillon ★★(★★)**; **Pernand-Vergelesses, Ile de Vergelesses Rollin ★★★**; **Volnay, Champans Marquis d'Angerville ★★★(★)**; **Volnay, Clos des Ducs Marquis d'Angerville ★★(★★)**; and **Volnay, Santenots Vincent Girardin ★★★**

1996 ★★★★

A good vintage, quantity and quality, but hardness and astringency noticed. The growing conditions could hardly have been better: cool spring and wet May which forestalled late frost problems; June was warm with an ideal quick and early flowering. The summer was long, cool rather than hot but with ripening sunshine and a refreshing north wind to help maintain acidity levels. The harvesting of healthy grapes took place in bright, but not warm, conditions in late September and early October. The overall lack of real warmth was responsible for the hard tannin and acidity which verges on astringency. Frankly not my favourite vintage.

La Tâche Fairly deep; multi-part fragrance, earthy, root-like, rustic with slightly hard edge, then vegetal, whiff of tar, rich, spicy, opened up and held well for two hours in the glass; mouthfilling, complete, very good flavour, lean, firm, good length, touch of austerity, tannin and crisp acidity. *Nov 2003* (★★★★) *2012–2025*.

Richebourg DRC Starting to mature; cheesy, sweaty (tannin) yet harmonious nose; distinctly sweet but, even after ten years, quite a bite and slightly rasping tannin and acidity. A class act but needs to develop further. *March 2006* (★★★)? *2012–2025*.

Romanée-St-Vivant DRC Medium-deep, trying to mature; crisp, lean, firm fruit, complete, silky-leathery tannins, great length, powerful finish. Plenty of tannin. *Oct 2001* (★★★★) *2010–2020*.

Grands-Echézeaux DRC Medium, open rim, attractive colour; initially hard-edged and minerally, dense and tannic, sweet, whiff of caramel, medicinal, developing a sweet, fully-evolved bouquet after two hours in the glass; overall dry from start to finish, touch of severity, lean but creamy flavour and aftertaste. Crisp and flavoury. Not an easy wine to assess. *Nov 2003* (★★★★) *2012–2020*?

Beaune, Grèves Bouchard Père Good colour, nose and taste. Medium dryness and body. Drinking well with food. *June 2004* ★★★ *Now–2012*.

Beaune, Grèves, Tasteviné (At a Clos Vougeot dinner.) Medium-deep, good nose but with '96 bite will it ever soften? *Oct 2005* ★★(★)?

Beaune, Clos des Mouches J Drouhin Medium, pink-tinged; good nose, harmonious, slightly smoky; sweet, lean but attractive flavour, decent fruit, its riginally high acidity simmering down. *Oct 2001* ★(★★) *Now–2012*.

Beaune, Clos des Ursules L Jadot Deep, richly coloured; whiff of raisins, sweet, opened fragrantly; sweet, rich yet lean and with good flesh. Crisper than the '95. Extended and very dry finish. *Oct 2001* ★★(★★) *Drink soon*.

Beaune, Hospices, Cuvée Guigone de Salins Deep; very tannic, typical '96. *Nov 2003* ★(★★) *2010–2015*.

Charmes-Chambertin A Rousseau 'The easiest of the Gevrey *grands crus*' according to Charles Rousseau. Touch of privet and caramel; hard, thanks to thick skins – and quite unready. *Oct 2001* (★★★) *Now–2016*.

Chassagne-Montrachet, Vieilles Vignes Colin-Deléger Italianate brambly Pinot which developed a lovely fragrance; moderately sweet; pleasant fruit, good texture, a citrus touch. *Nov 2000* ★★★ *Now–2012.*

Corton Bonneau du Martray Medium-deep, mature appearance; nose dumb (cold cellar), highish acidity; dry, crisp, berry-like flavour, good tannin and acidity. *Nov 2003* ★★(★) *2010–2015.*

Ch Corton-Grancey L Latour Low-keyed but complete, tannic. Quite a bite. *Last tasted July 2000* ★★★(★) *Now–2010.*

Pommard, Clos des Epeneaux Comte Armand Good colour; good but not very varietal nose; powerful wine, tannin coating the mouth, very acidic. Time will tell. *Oct 2005* (★★★) *2010–* ?

Richebourg A F Gros Good cherry-ruby colour; an immediacy of fragrance settling down to a serious nuttiness; a mouthfilling wine with the extra dimensions of a *grand cru*. Very dry finish. *Jan 2002* ★★(★★) *Now–2015.*

Clos St-Denis Dujac Distinctive, rich, slightly 'stewed' Pinot aroma, which opened up astonishingly, the scent of a *crème brûlée* crust; good flavour, teeth-gripping tannin and acidity; touch of bitterness. *Oct 2005* (★★★) *2010–2015.*

Volnay, Cuvée Sélectionnée Lafarge Fairly deep; good nose and flavour. Overall dry, lean but shapely. Refreshing acidity. *Oct 2001* ★★(★) *Now–2010.*

Volnay, Les Caillerets, Clos des 60 Ouvrées Dom de la Pousse d'Or. (Monopole) Good flavour, length, crisp dry finish. *Oct 2000* ★★(★) *Now–2010.*

Vosne-Romanée, Aux Réas A F Gros Pleasant sweetness, good body and length. A full, rich, stylish wine. Still tannic. *Jan 2002* ★★★(★) *Now–2010.*

THE FOLLOWING '96S tasted in 1998 and 1999 were above average: **Beaune, Clos des Mouches Chanson** ★★★; **Pommard, Les Chanlains Parisot** ★★★; **Santenay, Clos de Malte Jadot** ★★★ *(just)*; **Volnay-Champans Bichot** ★★★; and **Vosne-Romanée, Les Chaumes Daniel Rion** ★★(★)

1997 ★★★★

The third very good vintage in a row and one that has given me much pleasure. Apart from a cold and wet July, growing conditions were favourable. August, however, was hot, with no rainfall though there was some worrying humidity. Apart from a sprinkling of rain, which conveniently stopped before the early harvest, September was also hot. A smaller crop than in 1996.

Romanée-Conti Often I am more seduced by La Tâche, but this had a rich immediacy on the nose and was fuller and sweeter, its hallmark being multi-dimensional and relatively concentrated. A mouthfiller. Good fruit. *Feb 2000* ★★(★★) *Will last well into the second decade of the 21st century.*

La Tâche A pronounced, brambly Pinot Noir aroma; drier than expected, lean, firm, flavoury, teeth-gripping tannin but delicious end taste. *Feb 2000* (★★★★) *Now–2016.*

Richebourg DRC Medium-deep, relatively open rim, forward; rich, round, meaty; fairly sweet, broader character – as always – powerful, good length, very dry, tannic finish. *Feb 2000* (★★★★) *For the long haul.*

Romanée-St-Vivant DRC Most recently: the wine appeared less deep than on previous occasions. But it was still mauve-edged; sweet, slightly singed, raisiny nose which opened up beautifully, sweet, honeyed; crisp fruit, lightish in style but well endowed with tannin and acidity. *Last tasted Oct 2001* ★★(★★) *Good life ahead.*

Grands-Echézeaux DRC Fairly deep, purple-tinged; the initial impact was somewhat disappointing but it opened up, deep, rich, mulberry-like; good concentration and length, oak, quite a bite, well endowed with tannin and acidity. *Feb 2000* (★★★★) *2010–2020.*

Echézeaux DRC A misleadingly palish, open appearance; very fragrant; crisp, very oaky, very spicy, delicious flavour. Dry finish but refreshing acidity. *Feb 2000* ★★(★★) *Now–2010.*

Beaune, Clos des Mouches J Drouhin Most recently: showing traces of purple; combination of oak and fruit; the sweetest Mouches of the 1990s decade, character almost overripe, low acidity, very oaky. *Last tasted Oct 2001* ★★★ *Drink up.*

Beaune, Clos des Ursules L Jadot Very deep though maturing; sweet, brambly aroma, good depth, showing well; fairly sweet, perfectly ripe (as in 1996, no need to chaptalise), crisp fruit, very tannic. *Oct 2001* ★★★(★) *Now–2010.*

Beaune, Vignes-Franches L Latour Medium, maturing; very sweet, soft toffee nose and flavour. Delicious. *April 2001* ★★★ *Drink up.*

Bonnes-Mares Dom Drouhin Lovely, soft colour, warm, open, mature rim; very attractive scented Pinot; a bit on the lean side, some elegance, dry finish. More than just agreeable. *Oct 2003* ★★★★ *Now–2010.*

Bonnes-Mares, Tasteviné Fairly deep; good classic nose; drinking well at the Tastevin dinner, Clos Vougeot. Still tannic. *Oct 2005* ★★★(★) *Now–2012.*

Chambolle-Musigny G Roumier Decent colour; good, rich, varietal aroma and flavour, almost spritz finish. *May 2002* ★★★ *Now–2010.*

Chambolle-Musigny, 1er Cru de Vogüé Young vines (under 25 years old, but not the youngest) from the Musigny *grand cru*. Glorious bouquet, very 'meaty', rich; fairly sweet, very spicy, fullish body (13.5% alcohol). *Jan 2005* ★★★★ *Now–2010.*

Charmes-Chambertin J Drouhin Most recently: nice wine though lightish style, dry. *Last noted Jan 2002. Giving it the benefit* ★★★★ *Drink up.*

Echézeaux Christian Clerget Medium-deep; crisp Pinot aroma; dry, fragrant, fairly full-bodied, dry finish, still tannic. *Nov 2003* ★★★★ *Now–2010.*

Nuits-St-Georges, Clos de la Maréchale Faiveley Scented beetroot; sweet, soft, attractive fruit, agreeable weight, dry finish. *April 2001* ★★★ *Drink up.*

Clos de la Roche Dujac Ripe Pinot-beetroot nose; sweet, most attractive varietal flavour and good dry finish. *Oct 2001* ★★(★★) *Now–2012.*

Volnay Arnaud Ente Fairly deep ruby; dry, interesting flavour, touch of bitterness. *Nov 2003* ★★★ *Drink soon.*

Vosne-Romanée, en Orveaux Sylvain Cathiard Medium-deep, lovely colour, mature rim; arboreal Pinot; fairly sweet and full-bodied, rich, moderately endowed with tannin and acidity. *Good wine. Dec 2003* ★★★★ *Drink soon.*

A RANGE OF OTHER GOOD '97S last tasted in 1999 and 2000: **Beaune, Belissand Jean Garaudet** ★(★★★) *now–2016;* **Beaune, Clos des Fèves Chanson** ★★(★) *possibly 4 stars when fully evolved, now–2010;* **Beaune, Grèves, Vignes de l'Enfant Jésus Bouchard Père** ★★★ *drink soon;* **Bonnes-Mares de Vogüé** ★★★(★) *now–2015;* **Chambolle-Musigny, Les Sentiers R Groffier** ★★★(★) *now–2015;* **Ch Corton-Grancey L Latour** ★★(★) *now–2012;* **Echézeaux D Bocquenet** ★★(★★) *now–2012;* **Gevrey-**

Chambertin R Groffier ★★(★★) *now–2010*; Gevrey-Chambertin
Dom Humbert ★★★★ *drink up*; Gevrey-Chambertin, Combes aux
Moines Chanson ★★★ *drink up*; Gevrey-Chambertin, Estournelles-
St-Jacques J-P Marchand ★★★★ *drink up*; Richebourg Anne Gros
★★★(★) *now–2015*; Savigny-Lès-Beaune, Les Pimentiers Maurice
Ecard ★★(★★); Savigny-Lès-Beaune, Narbartons Maurice Ecard
★★(★★); Volnay, Clos des Chênes Fontaine-Gagnard ★★★★ *drink
now*; Vosne-Romanée, Cros Parantoux E Rouget ★★★★ *now–2010*;
Vosne-Romanée, Les Chaumes Méo-Camuzet ★★★? *drink soon*;
and Vosne-Romanée, Les Hautes Maizières R Arnoux ★★★(★)
now–2010

1998 ★★★★

A remarkable year. The best are very good which really makes this run of
vintages in the mid- to late 1990s quite exceptional. Astonishing how the
growers managed to juggle with such varying conditions. Early May saw sun
and high temperatures, which resulted in an explosion of growth. Flowering
started early, but was unevenly spread over three weeks. By early June, all was
on course but the second week was cool, and unwelcome oidium appeared.
July swung between spells of cool and very hot weather (up to 38°C on the
14th). There was a second heatwave in August. Dryness and heat stressed the
vines and singed the grapes: there was welcome rain in the first half of
September, then sun for a week, and rain again. But the grapes were healthy
and the harvest successful.

Romanée-Conti Not a very impressive colour, but DRC wines are often
misleading and actually gain colour in bottle. The nose of the wine that had been
in a large burgundy glass for three hours had opened up and was lovely, whereas
freshly poured in a tasting glass it was tighter and harder. So always give DRC
wines plenty of air before drinking. On the palate fairly sweet, a full, rich wine
with abundant fruit and length. As always, multi-dimensional. *Feb 2001 (★★★★) A
long-haul wine.*

La Tâche In the open glass, flowery, lovely. Surging with fragrance and fruit
when freshly poured; medium-sweet, full, rich, a powerful statement, glorious
flavour and length. Spicy aftertaste. *Feb 2001 (★★★★) 2010–2030.*

Richebourg DRC Freshly poured, I found it reclusive, low-keyed though
complete; more interesting on the palate, fairly sweet, fleshy, rounded, shapely.
Richness masking considerable tannin. *Feb 2001 (★★★★) 2010–2020.*

Romanée-St-Vivant DRC Most recently: an attractive colour, soft and with
medium intensity; when first poured out, Italianate, with brambly fruit that
opened up spicily and, in the end, had a touch of honey; on the palate relatively
harsh, immature, tannic finish. *Last noted Oct 2001 (★★★★) Needs time.*

Grands-Echézeaux DRC Distinctive fruit; surprisingly sweet, fullish, rich,
complete, good length. *Feb 2001 (★★★★) Now–2016.*

Echézeaux DRC Medium, mauve rim; delightful, fragrant and lovely in the
previously-poured glass but hard, spicy, comparatively unyielding when freshly
poured. Sweet, soft entry, crisp, very spicy, oaky flavour, finish and aftertaste. *Feb
2001 ★★(★★) Very good but will not have the extra dimensions and long life of the five
senior DRC wines above. Now–2012.*

Beaune, Grèves, Vignes de l'Enfant Jésus Bouchard Père Still virginal pink; sweet, gently stewed nose and flavour. Light grip. Pleasant enough. *March 2001* ★★★ *Early drinking.*

Beaune, Clos des Mouches J Drouhin Youthful mauve-purple; pronounced varietal aroma and oak; very good flavour overcoming the initial tannic impression. Nice wine, good future. *Oct 2001* ★★(★★) *Now–2010.*

Beaune, Clos des Ursules L Jadot Medium-deep, open-rimmed, early maturing; open-knit, slightly chocolatey (chaptalised), vanillin nose that opened up attractively; sweet, brambly fruit, easy, very sweet finish. *Oct 2001* ★★★ *Drink now.*

Corton, Clos des Cortons Faiveley Still mauve-tinged; crisp, brambly nose and taste. Sweet. *April 2001* ★★★ *Very agreeable mid-term drinking. Now–2010.*

Morey-St-Denis, La Riotte, Vieilles Vignes Henri Perrot-Minot Agreeable colour, rich 'legs'; good, not very varietal nose; very good flavour and weight, dry finish. A pleasant discovery. *Feb 2006* ★★★ *Now–2012.*

Nuits-St-Georges, Les Cailles Bouchard Père Gentle fruit; sweet, very attractive, some grip. *April 2001* ★★★ *Now–2010.*

Nuits-St-Georges, Porrets-St-Georges H Gouges Soft, luminous cherry red; good, slightly vegetal Pinot nose and flavour. Drinking well. *Nov 2002* ★★★ *Now–2012.*

Pernand-Vergelesses, Ile de Vergelesses, Tasteviné (Enjoyed at a Clos Vougeot dinner.) Crisp, attractive and had the right acidity to cope with the traditional poached eggs in rich brown gravy. *Oct 2001* ★★★ *Drink up.*

Savigny-lès-Beaune, Les Peuillets Jacques Girard Ruby sheen; agreeable, undemonstrative scent and taste. *Aug 2002* ★★★ *(just). Drink up.*

Clos Vougeot René Engel Fairly deep, mature rim, rich 'legs'; ripe barnyard Pinot; fairly sweet, good texture, firm tannic grip, touch of bitterness. Classic. Needs time. *Sept 2003* ★★(★★) *2010–2020.*

OTHER GOOD '98s last noted in January 2000: **Beaune, Grèves Tollot-Beaut** delicious upfront fruit on nose and palate, good length, very oaky ★★(★); **Corton, Bressandes Tollot-Beaut** powerful, very tannic and very oaky (★★★★). Of the three **Marquis d'Angerville Volnay** wines: **Champans** unknit but very attractive, with lots of grip ★★(★★); **Taillepieds** nutty, hard, very tannic ★(★★★); and **Clos des Ducs** more forthcoming, good length ★★(★★)

1999 ★★★★★

A great vintage and, for ripeness and finesse, exceeding even the 1990. And also one of the biggest ever. This vintage is a must for lovers of red burgundy.

It also demonstrates the unpredictability of the weather, for the year started miserably with an unusually wet spring, raining almost incessantly. The wet conditions continued through April and May, though the first half of June was brilliantly hot and sunny with unusually high temperatures, which provided perfect flowering conditions. The weather during the rest of June and through July was variable. The crucial ripening periods, August and September, were both hot and dry, 'luxuriant' leaves responsible for a substantial sugar content. The moisture reserves resulting from the earlier heavy rains prevented any ill-effects of drought, particularly vital when temperatures soared to 37°C for the first three days in August, almost as high toward the end of that month, and 36°C from 9 to 15 September for the main harvest which followed.

Romanée-Conti Deep, though showing more development than expected; initially low-keyed but rich and very distinctive, opening up cautiously, touch of liquorice and surprisingly toffee-like but great depth; sweet, rich, massive concentration and intensity, mouthfilling flavour, great length and magnificent aftertaste. Fleshy, tremendous power. *July 2003* (★★★★★★) *(6 stars)* 2015–2030.

La Tâche Low yield. Very deep, immature purple rim; rich, spicy, essence of Pinot, minty, arboreal, great depth; fairly sweet, very distinctive, full-flavoured, silky leathery tannins. 'Iron fist in velvet glove' – and surely one of the greatest-ever La Tâches. *Last tasted July 2003* (★★★★★★) *(6 stars)* 2015–2030.

Richebourg DRC Deep, fairly intense, purple rim; relatively undemonstrative, deep, rich, meaty, impeccable nose; lovely flavour, mouthfilling, great length, spicy, tannic finish. Its 'second breath' seemed sweeter, surprisingly fleshy, open yet very tannic. *Last tasted July 2003* (★★★★★) 2012–2030.

Romanée-St-Vivant DRC Medium-deep, fairly open, light purple rim; broad, evolved floral nose, singed; sweet, lovely spicy, fruit and length, good tannin and acidity. *Last tasted July 2003* (★★★★★) 2015–2030.

Grands-Echézeaux DRC Most recently, a magnum: on opening, a whiff of ripe *merde*, deep, rich, Pinot, after an hour displaying deep fragrance; assertive, beautiful flavour, refreshing acidity, tannic. Magnificent but needs time. *Last tasted Oct 2005* (★★★★) 2012–2025.

Echézeaux DRC Still fairly youthful; delicious varietal fragrance; soft yet touch of leanness and penetrating flavour. A very good Echézeaux. *Last tasted Oct 2005* ★(★★★) 2010–2020.

Vosne-Romanée, 1er Cru, Cuvée Duvault-Blochet DRC Due to the overripeness of the crop in 1999, a second wine was produced using grapes from young vines from all of the Domaine's *grand cru* sites. Most recently: now a medium-deep ruby; slightly singed with minty fragrance; modest body (12.5% alcohol), fairly dry, touch of sharpness, and unready. *Last tasted March 2006* ★(★★★) 2010–2015?

Beaune, Les Chardonnereux Rossignol-Fevrier Medium-deep; good varietal aroma; touch of sweetness, attractive flavour, a bit of an acidic bite. Well paired with grouse. *Sept 2003* ★★★ *Now–2010.*

Beaune, Montrevenots Bouchard Père Still youthful; rich, brambly Pinot Noir aroma; medium-sweetness and body, drinking well. *July 2005* ★★★ *Now–2010.*

Bonnes-Mares de Vogüé Medium-deep, lovely colour; good nose, rich, complete, developing whiff of coffee; sweet, rich, high extract, mouthfilling, masked tannins. *Last tasted June 2006* ★★(★★★) 2009–2016.

Chambolle-Musigny J-F Mugnier Shade of cherry; even cherry-like fruit; dry, crisp, delicious flavour. *Oct 2002* ★★★★ *Now–2010.*

Chambolle-Musigny de Vogüé Medium-deep, rich, luminous; slightly stalky, Pinot aroma; sweet, soft yet full-bodied (13.5% alcohol), very good flavour but with teeth-gripping tannin. *June 2006* ★★(★★) *Now–2012.*

Chambolle-Musigny, 1er Cru de Vogüé Fairly deep, rich, touch of ruby; corky, alas not correct; nevertheless very rich, full-bodied, tangy taste but raw. *June 2006* (★★★★)

Chambolle-Musigny, Les Amoureuses de Vogüé Medium-deep, fairly intense; good fruit, fragrance and depth, 'crushed red and black fruit'; elegant, feminine, fine-boned. Lovely wine. *Jan 2005* ★★(★★★) *Now–2015.*

Chambolle-Musigny, Clos des Avaux L Jadot Medium-deep ruby; excellent nose, flavour and balance. *Nov 2002* ★★★(★) *Now–2012.*

Charmes-Chambertin A Rousseau Medium-deep; classic Rousseau, not overtly varietal – just the smell of the real thing; excellent flavour and length. *May 2006* ★★(★★★) *2010–2020.*

Chassagne-Montrachet, Les Chaumés J-N Gagnard Medium-pale; lovely scent, flavour, balance and acidity. *Oct 2003* ★★★(★) *Now–2015.*

Gevrey-Chambertin Confuron-Cotétidot Medium, open, youthful rim; sweet, beetroot-like, earthy, Pinot Noir aroma with flavour to match. Modest weight (12.5% alcohol), fairly good length and finish. *Nov 2004* ★★★ *Now–2015.*

Gevrey-Chambertin Dupont-Tisserandot Attractive, luminous; good crisp Pinot aroma and flavour. Dry, a bit lean, but another decent drinkable 'village' wine. *Nov 2002* ★★★ *Drink soon.*

Gevrey-Chambertin, Clos St-Jacques A Rousseau Soft ruby with pink-purple edge; sweet, vibrant fruit, firm, spicy, scent of violets; medium-sweet, full flavour, moderate strength (13% alcohol), delicious but needs more time. *May 2006* ★★★(★★★) *2010–2015.*

Clos des Lambrays Dom des Lambrays Relaxed appearance; lovely scent, harmonious, no harsh edges; medium-dry, medium-full body (13.5%) delicious flavour, tannin and acidic finish. *March 2004* ★★★★(★) *Now–2015.*

Musigny, Vieilles Vignes de Vogüé Medium-deep, relaxed open rim, attractive colour; distinctly sweet, lovely flavour, complete, good length, tannin and acidity. *June 2006* ★★★(★★) *Now–2015.*

Pernand-Vergelesses, Les Vergelesses Chandon de Briailles Amazing scent; rich though still tannic. Delicious. *Feb 2005* ★★★(★) *Now–2012.*

Pommard, Clos des Epeneaux Comte Armand Blend of 50-year-old vines and 'young' vines planted in 1978: lovely colour; good flavour, soft tannins. *Oct 2005* ★★(★★) *2010–2018.*

Pommard, Clos des Epenots Ch de Meursault Fairly deep; good, correct but not an obvious varietal aroma; drinking well. *May 2006* ★★★ *Now–2012.*

Savigny-lès-Beaune, Les Serpentières Maurice Ecard Medium-deep, luminous ruby; good varietal aroma; medium-dry, nice weight, crisp, delicious flavour and good tannin and acidity. *May 2004* ★★★ *Now–2012.*

Volnay, 1er Cru, Santenots, Hospices, Cuvée Jehan de Massol Fairly deep colour; good nose and flavour. Drinking well. *Nov 2006* ★★★★ *Now–2012.*

Vosne-Romanée, Reignots Sylvain Cathiard Medium-deep, plummy purple, rich 'legs'; ripe Pinot aroma, crisp fruit which sweetened in the glass; medium-sweet, distinctive flavour, somewhat raw, tannic finish. A 'sweet and dry' wine needing more bottle age. *Sept 2003* ★★(★★) *2010–2015?*

THE FOLLOWING JADOT '99S last tasted in 2001: Beaune, Boucherottes (★★★★); Beaune, Cent Vignes (★★★★); Beaune, Teurons (★★★★); Beaune, Clos des Ursules (★★★★); Bonnes-Mares (★★★★★); Chambertin, Clos de Bèze (★★★★★); Chambolle-Musigny, Les Fuées (★★★★); Corton, Pougets (★★★★★); Echézeaux

(★★★★★); Gevrey-Chambertin, Cazetiers (★★★); Gevrey-Chambertin, Clos St-Jacques (★★★★); Nuits-St-Georges, Chaines Carteaux (★★★★); Savigny-lès-Beaune, La Dominode (★★★); Volnay, Clos de la Barre (★★★★); and Vosne-Romanée, Les Beaux-Monts (★★★★)

OTHER GOOD '99S only tasted in 2001: Beaune, Clos de Mouches J Drouhin (★★★★); Chambolle-Musigny Géantet-Pansiot (★★★★); Chambolle-Musigny Roumier (★★★★); Charmes-Chambertin Géantet-Pansiot (★★★); Chassagne-Montrachet, Clos St-Jean Guy Amiot (★★★★); Chassagne-Montrachet, Clos St-Jean Ch de Maltroye (★★★); Gevrey-Chambertin, Vieilles Vignes Géantet-Pansiot (★★★★); Griottes-Chambertin Dom Fourrier (★★★★★); Nuits-St-Georges, Les Boudots Dom Gagey (★★★★); Clos de la Roche Dujac (★★★★) *possibly 5-star future*; Savigny-lès-Beaune, Les Guettes Dom Gagey (★★★)?; Volnay, 1er Cru Dom de Montille (★★★★); Volnay, Clos des Chênes Jean-Michel Gaunoux (★★★★); Volnay, Taillepieds Marquis d'Angerville (★★★)?; and Vosne-Romanée, Aux Réas A F Gros (★★★★)

2000–2005

Burgundy is continuing to go through a successful period, in terms of the market and of quality (so far this century it has been blessed with vintages that range between good and outstanding). I detect healthy attitudes among the producers and the trade, and a good deal more respect and appreciation by consumers. Moreover, there is an absence of any distorting secondary demand from speculators and 'investors'. The international demand for the small supplies of the very best is another thing altogether. There is no point in complaining, for the finest burgundy has always – historically – been the prerogative of the wealthy and privileged. Below these most exalted levels, burgundy should be honest and good, and it should live up to its reputation. But, in the final analysis, you get what you pay for.

VINTAGES AT A GLANCE

Outstanding ★★★★★ 2002, 2005
Very Good ★★★★ 2003, 2004
Good ★★★ 2000, 2001

2000 ★★★

Although some are bold enough to rate the 2000s as highly, if not more highly, than the excellent '99s, while this certainly applies to the white burgundies, the consensus of opinion is that the reds are more variable and less successful. The season started off well with a mild spring and almost summer-like May. Warmth in June enabled the flowering to be speedy and successful. July, however, was cold and wet though August sun and heat enabled the ripening process to catch up. Rain returned in September with a big storm mid-month, particularly affecting the Côte de Beaune. The later-picked Côte de Nuits reds are the most successful. Quality, as always, depends on the level of pruning and, at harvest time, selection. There were few vinification problems. Generally the ripe tannins are lower than in the '99s.

THE DRC WINES

All six Domaine de La Romanée-Conti reds were tasted in Feb 2003 and July 2004, the four top reds also in Nov 2003. Where consistent within these dates, my notes have been consolidated. Very noticeable was that the nose of the freshly poured wine was, in most cases, astonishingly, almost unrecognisably, different from the same wine, from the same bottle, but which had already spent two hours in a large, broad-based glass. From which I conclude that a speedy first impression, from cask or bottle, can be misleading. Furthermore, a classic capacious burgundy glass is essential when the time comes to drink the wine.

Romanée-Conti DRC Impressive colour but soft, not deep and with a faint tinge of violet; full, rich, beetroot and cobnuts, great depth; as always, extra dimensions on the palate, very sweet, very soft yet mouthfilling, great length, fabulous finish, very tannic, spicy aftertaste. *Last tasted July 2004* ★★(★★★)
Disarmingly lovely now yet criminal to drink too soon. Ideally 2015–2030.

La Tâche DRC Most recently: fairly deep; subdued fragrance in open glass, crisper, more oaky in freshly poured tasting glass, harmonious, sweet, rich, 'beetroot' varietal aroma; surprisingly sweet at first sip, very positive, powerful, stern and very tannic. A complex long-haul wine. *Last tasted July 2004* (★★★★★)
2015–2030.

Richebourg DRC Fairly deep; in the open glass, well developed, soft, almost 'chewy', varietal aroma, crisper fruit and more oak noticeable in the freshly poured glass, harmonious and great depth; also distinctly sweet, full, positive, rich, sturdy, a tannic bite on the finish. Distinctive, broad-shouldered, disarmingly amenable style. *Last tasted July 2004* ★(★★★★) *2010–2030.*

Romanée-St-Vivant DRC Most recently, the same two-stage nose, an earthy, ripe Pinot, then spicy fruit; sweet, full-flavoured, positive, fragrant, good length and dry, tannin and acidic finish. *Last tasted July 2004* ★★(★★★) *2010–2025.*

Grands-Echézeaux DRC Medium, disarmingly pale, soft, open-rimmed; classic ripe Pinot, herbaceous; glorious flavour, shapely, dramatic, good length, very tannic. *Last tasted March 2006* ★★(★★★) *Now – if you must –2025.*

Echézeaux DRC Fairly deep, plummy, open rim; lovely fragrant fruit in open glass; much harder, less demonstrative in freshly poured glass; medium sweetness leading to a dry, slightly bitter, tannic finish, fuller body than expected, crisp fruit. Lacking the length of the 'big five' and reflected in its relatively modest price. *Last tasted July 2004* ★★(★★) *2010–2020.*

THE FOLLOWING WINES WERE ALL TASTED between Oct 2001 and Jan 2002 unless otherwise stated:

Aloxe-Corton, Les Vercots Follin-Arbelet A good colour; nose unknit; better on palate but very dry and raw (★★★)? *Now–2010. Time will tell.*

Auxey-Duresses Comte Armand Cask sample: deep; earthy, raw (★★★)? *Now–2010.*

Beaune, Grèves Tollot-Beaut Medium-deep; sweet, rich, brambly nose; very sweet, delicious ★★★(★) *Drink soon.*

Beaune, Clos des Mouches J Drouhin Medium-pale, touch of cherry red; cherry-like fruit too, and violets; sweet, very attractive, fragrant with pleasant end taste ★★★(★) *Now–2010.*

Beaune, Clos St-Jacques L Jadot Lovely luminous colour; intriguing scents of sapwood, cherry stalk and strawberry; sweet, very spicy, cloves, almost eucalyptus. Attractive wine. *Oct 2005* ★★★(★) *Now–2015.*

Beaune, Clos des Ursules L Jadot (Monopole) Chaptalised 0.5%. Medium-deep, mature, attractive; sweet, fairly rich, chewy, mouthfilling, good length. *Oct 2005* ★★★ *Now–2012.*

Bonnes-Mares J Drouhin Fairly assertive, good length, touch of bitterness and acidity but good potential (★★★★) *2012–2018.*

Bonnes-Mares de Vogüé Medium-deep; rich, floral, nutty nose which opened up deliciously; fairly sweet, distinctly rich and fleshy, oak, glorious flavour, length and aftertaste. *Oct 2002* ★★★(★★) *Now–2015.*

Chambertin A Rousseau Powerful, spicy and tannic ★★(★★) *2010–2016.*

Chambertin, Clos de Bèze Bruno Clair Sweet, oaky nose; good length ★★(★★) *Now–2015.*

Chambertin, Clos de Bèze J Drouhin Fairly deep; good nose; very rich, chewy, powerful, good length, tannin and acidity ★★(★★) *Now–2015.*

Chambertin, Clos de Bèze A Rousseau Cask sample. Very peppery, spicy (eucalyptus-like) aroma; impressive persistence in the mouth (★★★★) *2010–2015.*

Chambolle-Musigny de Vogüé Medium-pale, open rim; sweet, touch of caramel, opening up richly; sweet, soft, moderate body, good flavour and length for a 'village' wine. *June 2006* ★★★ *Now–2012.*

Chambolle-Musigny, 1er Cru de Vogüé Attractive colour, low-keyed; fragrant 'dog rose'; sweet, rich, spicy, oaky fruit. *Oct 2002* ★(★★★) *Now–2012.*

Chambolle-Musigny, Les Amoureuses J Drouhin Touch of meatiness, bramble and cold ashes; sweet, soft fruit yet good tannin and acidity ★★★ *Now–2010.*

Chambolle-Musigny, Les Amoureuses de Vogüé Fairly deep plummy purple; rich, cherry-like fruit, good depth; medium sweetness and body, soft texture, tannic and acidic finish. Good future. *Oct 2002* (★★★★) *2010–2015.*

Chambolle-Musigny, Les Fuées Ghislaine Barthod Sweet, slightly meaty, caramelly nose; sweet, delicious, silky tannins ★★(★★) *Now–2010.*

Chambolle-Musigny, Les Véroilles Ghislaine Barthod Very fragrant, sweet but quite a bite (★★)★ *Now–2010. Time will tell.*

Le Corton J Drouhin Lively, cherry-tinged; powerful, rich, meaty nose; fairly full-bodied, good, 'singed' Corton flavour, dry finish ★★(★★) *Now–2015.*

Le Corton Follin-Arbelet Plummy; low-keyed nose; very dry, powerful, raw (★★★) *2010–2015.*

Corton, Bressandes J Drouhin Sweeter, not as full-bodied, more charm than Le Corton, rich, lovely flavour ★★(★★) *Now–2012.*

Corton, Bressandes Follin-Arbelet Medium-deep; fragrant, nutty; very sweet, richness masking tannin (★★★★) *Now–2012.*

Corton, Bressandes Tollot-Beaut Medium-deep; plummy-coloured; rich, nutty; lovely tangy flavour, very tannic ★★★(★) *Now–2012.*

Echézeaux E Rouget Nose and flavour of great power and depth (★★★★) 2010–2015.

Gevrey-Chambertin, Cazetiers A Rousseau Cask sample. Plummy colour; dry, spicy. Some elegance ★★★ *Now–2010*.

Gevrey-Chambertin, Cuvée Ostréa Dom Trapet From select parcels of old vines. Plummy-coloured; crisp Pinot aroma, opening up richly; good flavour, touch of bramble-like fruit, dry finish. *Dec 2003* ★★★ *Now–2012*.

Gevrey-Chambertin, Clos des Ruchottes A Rousseau (Monopole) Spicy, complex; very rich and powerful ★(★★★) *Now–2012*.

Gevrey-Chambertin, Clos St-Jacques Bruno Clair Nutty, fragrant; lovely fruit, good length ★★★(★) *Now–2010*.

Gevrey-Chambertin, Clos St-Jacques Esmonin Good colour and nose; crisp young Pinot flavour. *March 2005* ★★★★ *Now–2012*.

Gevrey-Chambertin, Clos St-Jacques A Rousseau Cask sample. Good colour, powerful aroma; very tannic. *Oct 2001* ★★(★★) *Now–2012*.

Grands-Echézeaux R Engel Aroma of raspberry and figs; very good flavour and length. Very tannic ★★(★★) *Now–2015*.

Grands-Echézeaux J Drouhin Cherry tinge, open rim; strawberry scent, considerable depth; sweet, good flavour, quite a lot of grip ★★(★★) *Now–2012*.

Griottes-Chambertin J Drouhin Floral, fragrant, harmonious; very sweet, lovely flavour, great length. Sweet throughout ★★(★★) *Now–2012*.

Clos des Lambrays Cask sample. Hard but fragrant, raspberry-like young fruit, touch of bitterness; dry, good length ★★(★★) *Now–2012*.

Mazis-Chambertin Faiveley Palish; not very varietal; lean, unimpressive, immature, sharp. Needs bottle age. *June 2004* (★★★)? *Try again in 2010*.

Mazis-Chambertin A Rousseau Cask sample. An impressive mouthful, needing long cellaring (★★★★) 2012–2015.

Morey-St-Denis Dujac Cask sample. Vanillin; attractive flavour, soft, spicy, good tannins ★★★(★) *Now–2010*.

Musigny J Drouhin Good colour; lower-keyed, more elegant than Drouhin's Bonnes-Mares; also sweeter, softer. Rich, very fragrant, delicious. The most expensive of the range ★★★(★★) *Glorious future. Now–2012*.

Musigny, Vieilles Vignes de Vogüé Medium-pale, faint plummy shade; initially slightly meaty, then a cherry-like fragrance; sweet, full-bodied (14% alcohol), penetrating flavour. *June 2006* ★★★(★★) 2010–2020.

Nuits-St-Georges, Les Corvées Pagets R Arnoux Cask sample. Assertive fruit; very sweet, oak, good length. *Jan 2002* ★★(★★) *Now–2012*.

Nuits-St-Georges, Les Perrières R Chevillon Fragrant; very sweet, spicy, oaky ★★(★) *Now–2010*.

Nuits-St-Georges, Les St-Georges R Chevillon Deep, 'thick' (extract); nutty, Italianate, brambly; sweet, good flavour but dry sandy texture. Very tannic ★★(★★) *Now–2012*.

Romanée-St-Vivant Follin-Arbelet Very nutty, brambly nose; very oaky, immensely sweet with price to match ★★(★★) *hopefully*. *Now–2012*.

Clos de Tart Good colour; spicy oaky nose, crisp fruit, depth; amazing power, very oaky, very tannic ★(★★★) *Now–2015*.

Volnay H Delagrange Medium-deep dark cherry, lively colour; very attractive Pinot aroma and flavour, crisp fruit. *Nov 2003* ★★(★) *Now–2010*.

Volnay Lafarge Touch of cherry; low-keyed; good flavour but lean and quite a bite. A decent 'village' wine from a traditional producer. *Nov 2003* ★★★ *Now–2010*.

Volnay, Vieilles Vignes Nicolas Potel Magnums. Still ruby; good varietal nose and flavour. Still very tannic. *Aug 2004* ★★(★★) *Now–2012*.

Volnay, Champans Marquis d'Angerville Surprisingly pale; soft, fruity, whiff of strawberry; slightly sweet, seems to combine rich fruit and mild character, dry finish. *Oct 2005* ★★★ *Now–2012*.

Volnay, Clos des Chênes J Drouhin Medium-deep colour; pleasant scent; some sweetness.★★(★) *Drink soon*.

Volnay, Clos des Ducs Marquis d'Angerville Fairly deep; sweet, rich, chewy. Attractive wine ★★(★) *Drink soon*.

Volnay, Taillepieds Marquis d'Angerville Fairly deep; 'nutty'; sweet, delicious ★★★(★) *Now–2010*.

Vosne-Romanée R Arnoux Cask sample. Low-keyed nose but good fruit; pleasant sweetness and weight, very good flavour, well balanced ★★(★★) *Now–2012*.

Vosne-Romanée, Aux Brûlées, Vieilles Vignes B Clavelier Cask sample. Extraordinary high-toned nose; very acidic (★★) *Hard to predict how this will turn out*.

Vosne-Romanée, Clos du Château Liger-Belair (Monopole) Medium-deep; pleasant fruit; sweet, good flavour and grip (★★★★) *Now–2010*.

Clos de Vougeot J Drouhin Fairly deep, dark cherry core; rich, a touch of the 'fishiness' I associate more with Chambertin; surprisingly sweet, silky tannins, dry finish (★★★★) *Now–2012*.

Clos Vougeot J Grivot Cask sample. Youthful raspberry-like aroma; lean, crisp, long, very oaky (★★★★) *Now–2012*.

2001 ★★★

Not an easy year but it was particularly good in the Côte de Nuits. The weather was not ideal: it was mainly cold and wet, the flowering was late and extended and humidity caused mildew. Late July was warm, the end of August hot and the first three crucial weeks of September were cold and wet. Late pickers did best. All in all, it was a plentiful crop and some very good wines were made.

Romanée-Conti Never very deep, but paler and browner than expected; completely different from the other DRC '01s; complex, a whiff of liquorice and rose petals; more intense and concentrated than the others, and than its appearance suggested. Good length. Lovely drink. *Last tasted March 2006* ★(★★★) *Now–2015?*

La Tâche Rich, maturing; flowery, whiff of violets, complete, convincing but much more to come; powerful, still on the hard side. *Last tasted March 2006* ★★(★★) *2010–2015*.

Richebourg DRC Not as deep as expected, distinctive character and style on nose and palate, substantial, mouthfilling, masculine, good length and grip. Long life. *Last tasted March 2006* ★★(★★★) *2010–2020*.

Romanée-St-Vivant DRC Intense, thick (extract), starting to mature; lively, good depth; really lovely wine, positive, powerful, very good finish and aftertaste. *Last tasted March 2006* ★★(★★★) *2010–2020*.

Grands-Echézeaux DRC Most recently: appeared lighter and softer; classic ripe Pinot aroma, herbaceous; glorious, dramatic flavour, shapely, good length, very tannic. *Last tasted March 2006* ★★(★★★) *2010–2020.*

Echézeaux DRC Medium-deep; sweet, harmonious nose, touch of strawberry; the least impressive of the DRC '01s though still delicious, with sweet, positive attack and good rich fruit. Tannic and acidic finish. *March 2006* ★★(★) *Now–2012.*

Beaune, Clos des Ursules L Jadot (Monopole) Developing well; decent fruit and tannin in a difficult year. Crisp finish. *Oct 2005* ★(★) *Now–2012.*

Beaune, Clos St-Jacques L Jadot Cherry-like, harmonious nose; fairly sweet, good flavour but a dry, tannic finish, quite a bite. *Oct 2005* ★(★★) *2010–2015.*

Bonnes-Mares de Vogüé Medium-pale, open-rimmed; initially earthy 'vegetal' Pinot aroma, developing a touch of raspberry; sweet, 'singed' flavour. Moderate weight. *June 2006* ★★(★★) *2010–2015.*

Chambolle-Musigny de Vogüé Very scented, 'crushed fresh fruit'; crisp fruit, a vivacious 'village' wine. *Jan 2005* ★★★ *Now–2012.*

Chambolle-Musigny, 1er Cru de Vogüé Medium-pale, open, luminous; attractive fruit, sweet and crisp; very sweet, moderate body, good, rich flavour. *June 2006* ★★★★ *Now–2012.*

Musigny, Vieilles Vignes de Vogüé Medium-pale, advanced; light, fragrant nose; medium-sweet, crisp, lean, elegant. *June 2006* ★★(★★) *Now–2015.*

Pommard, Clos des Epéneaux Comte Armand Pleasant, scented nose; sweet, fullish, delicious flavour, soft tannins, dry finish. *Oct 2005* ★(★★★) *2010–2015.*

Volnay, Champans Marquis d'Angerville Soft, earthy, 'beetroot' Pinot, pleasant scent; sweet, attractive, harmonious, dry finish. *Oct 2005* ★★(★★) *Now–2012.*

2002 ★★★★★

An extremely good vintage with some unquestionably great wines which have good colour, concentration and acidity.

A brief look at the growing conditions: spring was mild, budding early. The weather during the flowering period was uneven: a good start, a pause and then beneficial warmth. The summer was dry but rain at the end of August and early September caused some worries. However, strong northerly winds dried the vines and concentrated the fruit. Thereafter warm (not hot), sunny weather ensured perfect harvesting conditions from mid-September and an 'Indian summer'. The smallest crop since 1988. Ripe grapes, thick skins, good colour, soft tannins and excellent acidity – all the hallmarks of a top vintage.

La Tâche Fairly deep, youthful rim; seemed reluctant at first, touch of stalkiness but opened up fragrantly; more immediate on the palate, sweet, mouthfilling, lean yet well clad, spicy, very tannic. *Nov 2003* (★★★★★) *2015–2030.*

Richebourg DRC Powerful and complex. The deepest of the '02 DRC wines; a surge of fragrance, almost strawberry-like fruit, rich, great depth; initially 'a heck of a bite', but very sweet, very flavoury, tannic. *Nov 2003* (★★★★★) *2015–2030.*

Grands-Echézeaux DRC Medium-deep, trace of cherry red, open rim; immediately forthcoming fragrance, good fruit, very scented; sweet, delicious young fruit, very tannic. *Nov 2003* (★★★★★) *2012–2025.*

Beaune, Clos St-Jacques L Jadot Medium-deep, lovely colour; good varietal scent; most attractive wine. *Oct 2005* ★★(★★) *2010–2016*.

Beaune, Clos des Ursules L Jadot (Monopole) Distinctive, good, oaky nose; soft, delicious flavour, distinct oakiness. Attractive wine. Good mid-term. *Oct 2005* ★★(★★) *2010–2016*.

Bonnes-Mares de Vogüé Medium-deep; very good rich varietal nose of great depth; sweet, rich, full-bodied (14% alcohol), tangy, an elegant Bonnes-Mares with good length. *June 2006* ★★(★★★) *2010–2015*.

Chambolle-Musigny de Vogüé Curious, slightly medicinal, singed, rich; sweet, crisp, fairly full-bodied, good length but still tannic. *June 2006* ★(★★) *Now–2012*.

Chambolle-Musigny, 1er Cru de Vogüé Medium-deep; completely different to the 'village' wine, slightly stalky but good fruit; fairly sweet, full-bodied, very flavoury, dry finish. Very tannic. *June 2006* ★(★★★) *2010–2015*.

Corton Bonneau du Martray From the family's Pinot Noir vines in the middle of their important Corton-Charlemagne vineyard. Deep, dark cherry, fairly intense colour; crisp fruit, some oakiness; medium – some sweetness, fairly full-bodied, crisp, cherry-like fruit, dry finish. *Nov 2003* (★★★★) *2012–2020*.

Musigny, Vieilles Vignes de Vogüé Medium, hint of cherry; good deep fruit but sweaty tannins; medium-sweet, lean, full-bodied (14% alcohol), good flavour, good dry finish. *June 2006* ★★★(★★) *2010–2015*.

Pommard, Clos des Epéneaux Comte Armand A 'brilliant year' for the Domaine. Medium depth of colour; soft, attractive varietal aroma; medium-sweet, full, ripe, rich, complete, with excellent aftertaste. *Oct 2005* ★★(★★★) *Now–2016*.

Volnay, Champans Marquis d'Angerville Harvested by the highly respected Marquis, his 52nd and last vintage. Medium-pale with a pink glow; fragrant, harmonious, whiff of strawberry-like fruit; sweet, easy to taste, good length, dry finish. A 'copybook' Volnay with charm and finesse. *Oct 2005* (★★★★★) *Now–2015*.

2003 ★★★★

The 2003 harvest was the earliest since 1893 and for similar reasons: great heat, exceptional ripeness, low yields – and problems. In the Côte d'Or, picking started on 18 August, virtually unheard of. It is worthwhile following the growing season: early budbreak was in mid-March following an unusually mild period. Development was well advanced by mid-April though Nuits-St-Georges was severely affected by two nights of frost. Flowering early and speedy. From June throughout the summer, the weather was unusually hot and dry, averaging 30°C, up to 40°C in August. The danger was that the grapes, lacking moisture, would be more like raisins. As the natural sugar levels increased, acidity dropped alarmingly, hence the need for an early harvest. Happily for some, there was rain at the end of August and into September. Late pickers made outstanding wines. A small crop of interesting wines which I have found very attractive. On the whole, good mid-term drinking.

The Domaine de La Romanée-Conti are habitually late pickers and in 2003 commenced on 18 September, a full month after the *ban de vendanges*. **Romanée-Conti** Deep, luminous, lovely colour; indescribably complex nose, toasty, intriguing fruit, very slight whiff of vanilla and tea; sweet, rich, mouthfilling;

good length, substantial and hard. *Feb 2006* (★★★★★) *2020–?*

La Tâche Medium-deep, soft-looking; glorious fragrant fruit, depth; very sweet, delicious flavour, leathery tannins, dry finish. *Feb 2006* (★★★★★) *2018–2036.*

Richebourg DRC Fairly deep; an immediate burst of fragrance, slightly smoky Pinot aroma, whiff of tea; sweet, packing a punch, complete, good length and finish. *Feb 2006* (★★★★★) *2018–2036.*

Romanée-St-Vivant DRC Fairly deep, pink, youthful rim; smoky nose; 'super brambly' – herbaceous, blackberry; sweet, positive, delicious flavour, good length, tannic. *Feb 2006* (★★★★★) *2015–2030.*

Grands-Echézeaux DRC Medium, attractive, pale luminous cherry; low-keyed but very fragrant, raspberry-like fruit; sweet, rich, immediate flavour impact, delicious, good length, dry oaky finish. *Feb 2006* (★★★★★) *2012–2025.*

Echézeaux DRC Medium depth; very forthcoming, almost explosive, brambly Pinot; very sweet, very positive impact and flavour, one of the best Echézeaux I can recall. *Feb 2006* (★★★★★) *2013–2025.*

Aloxe-Corton, Les Fournières Tollot-Beaut Cherry red colour; very pronounced cherry-like fruit on nose and palate. Sweet. Very flavoury. *Jan 2005* ★★(★) *Now–2012.*

Beaune, Clos des Couchereaux Héritiers Jadot Medium-pale, open rim; attractive, touch of sweetness, drinking well. *March 2005* ★★★ *Drink soon.*

Beaune, Grèves, Vignes de l'Enfant Jésus Bouchard Père Richly coloured, good 'legs'; mild varietal aroma, singed, touch of tar, extract, complex; medium-sweet, good flavour, dry, teeth-gripping, tannic finish. *July 2005* (★★★) *2010–2015.*

Beaune, Clos des Mouches Drouhin Crisp cherry fragrance and flavour. Good length. *Jan 2005* ★★★ *Drink soon.*

Beaune, Clos St-Jacques L Jadot Fairly deep; stalky young fruit; full, flavour of leather, rich but tannic. *Oct 2005* ★★(★★) *Now–2015.*

Beaune, Les Siziés Dom de Montille Attractive fruit, touch of raspberry; very sweet, light style yet good length and grip. *March 2006* ★★★ *Now–2012.*

Beaune, Clos des Ursules L Jadot (Monopole) Surprisingly deep; sweet, soft, medium-full-bodied, 'chewy', dry finish. *Oct 2005* ★★★ *Now–2012.*

Bonnes-Mares Fougeray de Beauclair Immediately forthcoming, very brambly, almost 'New World' Pinot; medium-sweet, flavour to match. Attractive. *July 2005* ★★(★★)? *Now–2012.*

Bonnes-Mares de Vogüé Fairly deep colour, intense; very varietal aroma, deep, rich, fruity; distinctly sweet, fairly full-bodied, light tannins, delicious. *Jan 2006* ★★(★★★) *2012–2020.*

Chambertin A Rousseau Medium, relaxed open rim; very fragrant bouquet, depth; fairly sweet, lovely flavour, length and grip. *March 2006* ★★(★★) *2010–2020.*

Chambertin Trapet Medium; sweet, rich, oaky nose; rich, full-bodied, good flavour, length, and slightly oaky finish. *Jan 2006* ★★(★★) *2012–2018.*

Chambolle-Musigny de Vogüé Most recently: deep plummy purple; sweet, crisp, cherry-like nose with good depth; distinctly sweet, very positive but medium body (13% alcohol), very attractive. *June 2006* ★★(★★) *Now–2012.*

Chambolle-Musigny, 1er Cru de Vogüé Most recently: impressively deep, fairly intense; lovely fruit, very varietal; amazingly sweet, rich, chewy, also very attractive. *June 2006* ★★(★★) *2010–2015.*

Chambolle-Musigny, Les Fremiets, Vieilles Vignes L Rémy
Attractive, crisp fruit, underlay of violets; fairly sweet, touch of marzipan on the palate. *Jan 2005* ★★? *Drink soon.*

Chambolle-Musigny, Les Fuées Ghislaine Barthod Smoky, cherry-like fruit; delicious. *Jan 2005* ★★★ *Now–2010.*

Chambolle-Musigny, Les Véroilles Ghislaine Barthod Crisp fruit, good depth, smoky; delicious flavour, good length. *Jan 2005* ★★★ *Now–2010.*

Chapelle-Chambertin Trapet Medium-deep; sweet, rich, slight oakiness; rich, medium–full-bodied (13.5% alcohol), good flavour, length and touch of oak on the finish. *March 2006* ★★(★★) *2010–2015.*

Corton Bonneau du Martray Deep; vanillin, rather jammy fruit; medium-sweet, rich, full-bodied, tannic. Impressive. *March 2006* ★★(★★) *2010–2015.*

Corton, Bressandes Chandon de Briailles Paler than expected; indistinctive; sweet, moderately good flavour and grip. *March 2006* ★★? *Drink up.*

Corton, Bressandes Tollot-Beaut Deep; distinctive, slightly meaty, brambly fruit; sweet, attractive, plausible. *March 2006* ★★★ *Now–2012.*

Corton, Clos des Cortons Faiveley Very deep, intense; rich, jammy, port-like nose and taste. Tannic. *March 2006* ★★★ *Now–2013.*

Corton, Clos du Roi Comte Senard Medium-deep; attractive nose, flavour and grip. *March 2006* ★★(★★) *Now–2015.*

Corton, Clos du Roi Prince Florent de Mérode Attractive, smoky, oaky raspberry-like fruit; in short, delicious. Ripe farmyard finish. *Jan 2005* ★★★ *Now–2013.*

Echézeaux Robert Arnoux Very deep; rich, spicy nose; '03 sweetness, rich, delicious flavour, tannic. *Jan 2005* ★★(★★) *2012–2020.*

Echézeaux Jacques Cacheux Not very clear cut, whiff of crystallised violets; raw, tannic finish. *Jan 2005* (★★★)? *2010–2015.*

Gevrey-Chambertin, Cazetiers Bruno Clair Crisp, nutty bouquet, good fruit; fairly sweet, delicious flavour. *Jan 2005* ★★★(★) *Now–2012.*

Gevrey-Chambertin, Clos St-Jacques Bruno Clair Deep; rich, powerful nose and palate, good depth, spicy oak finish and aftertaste. *Jan 2005* ★★(★★) *2010–2015.*

Gevrey-Chambertin, Clos St-Jacques A Rousseau Paler than expected; glorious, very distinctive, floral; lovely wine, comparatively light style and weight (13% alcohol), delicious flavour, very good tannin and acidity. A class act. *March 2006* ★★★(★★) *2010–2016.*

Gevrey-Chambertin, Lavaux St-Jacques René Leclerc Opaque core, broad, rich, plummy, purple colour; low-keyed, brambly nose; sweet, delicious flavour, richness masking tannins. *July 2005* ★★(★★) *Now–2015.*

Grands-Echézeaux René Engel Cask sample. Medium-deep; initially low-keyed but lovely fruit, spicy; glorious flavour of crystallised violets. *Jan 2005* ★★★(★★) *2010–2015.*

Grands-Echézeaux Drouhin Sweet, meaty, tannic nose; very sweet, very attractive, slightly 'hot', very oaky finish. *March 2006* ★★(★★) *2010–2015.*

Clos des Lambrays Cask sample. Fairly deep; rich, strawberry-like fruit and spicy oak; impressive but too oaky. *Jan 2005* ★(★★★)? *Time will tell.*

Latricières-Chambertin L Rémy Fragrant, some delicacy; good flavour and length. *Jan 2005* ★★(★★) *Now–2015.*

Morey-St-Denis Georges Lignier Palish; very distinctive, raspberry-like fragrance; medium-sweet, agreeable, lightly tannic. *Feb 2006* ★★★ *Now–2010.*

Musigny J-F Mugnier Medium-deep; immediate burst of fragrance, rich, oaky; very sweet, delicious flavour. *March 2006* ★★★(★) *2010–2015.*

Musigny, Vieilles Vignes de Vogüé Very small crop. Deep, fairly intense; powerful nose; impressive, complete. *Oct 2005* ★★(★★★) *2012–2020.*

Nuits-St-Georges, Vieilles Vignes Ambroise Opaque, intense; dramatic, brambly nose; good fruit. *July 2005* ★★★ *Now–2012.*

Nuits-St-Georges, Les Cailles Robert Chevillon Most unusual leathery, tannic nose; fairly powerful, not very typical of Pinot Noir. *Jan 2005* ★(★★)? *Drink soon.*

Nuits-St-Georges, Les Chaignots Robert Chevillon Distinctive character. Nutty (walnuts); interesting flavour, quite a bite. *Jan 2005* ★(★★) *Now–2012.*

Nuits-St-Georges, Clos des Porrets-St-Georges Henri Gouges Deep; attractive, overtones of violets; fairly sweet, moderate body (13% alcohol), good flavour and grip. *March 2006* ★★(★★) *2010–2015.*

Nuits-St-Georges, Clos des Pruliers Jean Grivot Deep and fairly intense; sweet, attractive, singed, slightly meaty nose; good crisp flavour, overall dry and tannic. *March 2006* ★★(★★) *2010–2015.*

Nuits-St-Georges, Les St-Georges Henri Gouges Very deep, fairly intense; brambly Pinot; rich, full-bodied (14% alcohol), very tannic. *March 2006* ★(★★★) *2010–2015.*

Nuits-St-Georges, Les Vaucrains Robert Chevillon Fairly deep; crisp, cherry-like fruit, oak; medium-sweet, attractive wine, leathery tannic finish. *Jan 2005* ★★(★★) *2010–2015.*

Pommard, Clos des Epéneaux Comte Armand Spicy, whiff of violets; fairly sweet, rich, soft tannins yet overall dry. *Oct 2005* ★★(★★) *Now–2012.*

Pommard, Clos des Epenots Dom de Courcel Lower-keyed than Fremiets but spicy; medium-sweet, crisp, attractive. *Jan 2005* ★★(★★) *Now–2012.*

Pommard, Les Fremiets Dom de Courcel Very sweet, almost jammy, spicy nose; delicious, very oaky. *Jan 2005* ★★(★★) *Now–2012.*

Pommard, Les Grands Epenots Michel Gaunoux Positive, attractive, arboreal; sweet, rich, full-bodied, good grip. *March 2006* ★★(★★) *Now–2015.*

Pommard, Les Rugiens Michel Gaunoux Medium-deep; floral; rich, positive, fruity, good flavour, tannic. *March 2006* ★★(★★) *2010–2016.*

Pommard, Les Rugiens Dom de Montille Very fragrant, attractive; sweet, delicious flavour, nice weight (13% alcohol), dry finish. *March 2006* ★★★★ *Now–2013.*

Clos de la Roche Dujac Curiously murky; strange, singed nose; very sweet, medium-full-bodied, curious mid-palate, dry finish. Rot? *March 2006* ?

Savigny-lès-Beaune, La Dominode Bruno Clair Cherry-like fragrance; delicious delicacy. *Jan 2005* ★★★ *Now–2010.*

Savigny-lès-Beaune, Aux Vergelesses Simon Bize Already fairly mature; nutty, pleasant fruit; distinctly sweet, full fruit, moderate weight (12.5% alcohol), tannic. *March 2006* ★★★ *Drink soon.*

Clos de Tart Deep; rich, tangy, raspberry-Pinot; glorious flavour, great length. *Jan 2005* ★★★(★★) *2010–2015.*

Volnay, Caillerets, Ancienne Cuvée Carnot Bouchard Père Fairly deep, rich core, plummy; smoky, touch of tar, singed hot vintage nose, opened up sweetly with blackberry-like fruit; sweet, rich, fairly full-bodied (13.5% alcohol), good grip, lovely wine. *Jan 2005* ★★(★★) *2010–2015*.

Volnay, Champans Marquis d'Angerville Picking commenced 25 Aug! Still with youthful appearance; delicious varietal aroma; medium-sweet, rich, lovely. *Last tasted Oct 2005* ★★★(★) *Now–2012*.

Volnay, Clos des Chênes Michel Lafarge Touch of ruby, slightly singed, arboreal; medium-sweet, rich, meaty, slightly rough, tannic finish. *March 2006* ★★(★) *2010–2015*.

Volnay, Les Santenots Girardin Scent of raspberries and candies; good flavour and length (and modestly priced). *Jan 2005* ★★★ *Drink now*.

Volnay, Les Taillepieds Dom de Montille Fairly deep; strange nose, whiff of 'virol', malty and slightly medicinal; meatier than expected, tannic. *March 2006* ★★ *Needs time?*

Vosne-Romanée, La Colombière Liger-Belair Pleasing combination of fruit and delicacy. *Jan 2005* ★★★ *Drink soon*.

Vosne-Romanée, Aux Reignots Liger-Belair Fairly deep; delicious, fragrant, cherry; very distinctive, flavour reminding me of cinders in the hearth, good length. *Jan 2005* ★★★(★) *2010–2015*.

Vosne-Romanée, Les Suchots Jacques Cacheux Attractive fruit with interesting undertone of crystallised violets. *Jan 2005* ★(★★) *Now–2012*.

Vosne-Romanée, Les Suchots Jean Grivot Fairly deep; strange singed nose; attractive flavour and grip. *March 2006* ★★★ *Now–2013*.

Clos de Vougeot Robert Arnoux Deep; low-keyed, whiff of violets, good flavour and length. Very tannic. *Jan 2005* ★★(★★★) *2012–2018*.

Clos de Vougeot Jean Grivot Cask sample. Deep; fruit and tannin; crisp, good flavour, tannic. *Jan 2005* ★(★★★) *2010–2015*.

2004 ★★★★

A good vintage but upstaged by the 2005. The harvest was late and the quantity large. Despite problems, the wines are good overall, some excellent. After 2003 there was a return to normality, which is to say that conditions during the growing season were, as usual, tricky. The spring, however, was mild and budding prolific, no frosts and a successful though late flowering. A large crop was indicated. Problems started in July, the first half of which was cold and cloudy which caused outbreaks of oidium; the second half was warm and cloudy, with some hail and frequent thunderstorms. August was also warm and cloudy. Prudent estates green-pruned to eliminate poor bunches and concentrate the crop. Happily, late August to mid-September, the crucial ripening period, was warm and sunny. However, selection was crucial and, as so often, late pickers fared best. Summing up, major estates made very good to excellent wines, the differences between vineyards being distinctive though not easy to describe.

The following notes, though not as comprehensive as I would ideally have liked, will at least give an idea of the character and style of this vintage. It is essential to taste the 2004s or take good advice, for there are many to be avoided. Alas the DRC '04s not yet tasted.

Beaune, Boucherottes Héritiers Jadot Fragrant; medium-sweet, fairly full-bodied, complete, good flavour and length. *Jan 2006* ★★★(★) *Now–2012.*

Beaune, Grèves, Vignes de l'Enfant Jésus Bouchard Père (Monopole). Medium-deep, fairly intense; curiously medicinal aroma; moderately sweet, rich and attractive. *Jan 2006* ★(★★★) *2010–2012.*

Beaune, Marconnets Bouchard Père Placid, youthful, open-rimmed; developed meaty character; dry, lean but flavoury. *Jan 2006* ★(★★★) *2010–2015.*

Beaune, Theurons Héritiers Jadot Medium-pale, tinge of cherry red and youthful rim; low-keyed, light Pinot aroma; dry, more to it on the palate, crisp cherry-like fruit, good acidity – a bit sharp. *Jan 2006* ★(★★) *2010–2015.*

Beaune, Clos des Ursules Héritiers Jadot Medium-pale though deeper than the four previous vintages, luminous cherry red, youthful rim; attractive, cherry-like fragrance; medium-sweet, lean, crisp, fairly full-bodied, flavoury but quite a bite. *Jan 2006* ★★(★) *2009–2013.*

Bonnes-Mares Drouhin-Laroze Good colour; slightly smoky Pinot; sweet, very rich, good varietal flavour. *Jan 2006* ★(★★★) *2010–2018.*

Bonnes-Mares de Vogüé Hail in August reduced the crop of de Vogüé wines by 30–40%. Only 120 casks produced. In cask; youthful stalkiness; medium-sweet, crisp fruit, quite a bite, vibrant. *Nov 2005* (★★★★) *2012–2018.*

Chambertin, Clos de Bèze Drouhin-Laroze Medium-deep; sweet, powerful wine. Good length. *Jan 2006* ★★(★★★) *2012–2018.*

Chambertin, Clos de Bèze L Jadot Medium-pale, open, youthful rim; low-keyed, very slightly 'medicinal' with underlying fragrance; medium-sweet, full-bodied, assertive, good length and finish. *Jan 2006* ★★(★★★) *2012–2018.*

Chambolle-Musigny de Vogüé In cask. Soft cherry; raspberry-like aroma; dry, crisp, stylish. Touch of bitterness. *Oct 2005* (★★★) *Now–2010?*

Chambolle-Musigny, Les Amoureuses de Vogüé In cask; racked once. Totally different to the 'village' wine above, sweet, fuller and rounder. *Oct 2005* ★★(★★) *2010–2015.*

Chambolle-Musigny, Les Baudes Dom Gagey Medium-pale; distinctive, pleasant varietal aroma; good flavour, full-bodied, lean, overall dry. *Jan 2006* ★(★★★) *2010–2014.*

Chambolle-Musigny, Les Fuées Ghislaine Barthod Medium-dry, delicious flavour, good length, tannic. *Jan 2006* (★★★★) *2010–2015.*

Chambolle-Musigny, Les Véroilles Ghislaine Barthod Good colour; lovely nose; medium sweetness and body, distinctive, smoky, delicious. *Jan 2006* ★★★(★) *Now–2012.*

Corton, Pougets Héritiers Jadot From two parcels in Aloxe-Corton's upper and middle slope adjacent to the Charlemagne. Much paler colour than expected, luminous with open rim; holding back, not very distinctive, Pinot lurking; dry, lean, full-bodied yet not a big meaty Corton. Tannic and acidic finish. *Jan 2006* ★(★★) *or* ★(★★★) *depending on its sustaining acidity. Say 2010–2015.*

Le Corton Bouchard Père Richly coloured; good nose, whiff of violets; medium-dry, full flavour and character, well rounded. *Jan 2006* ★★(★★) *2010–2015.*

Echézeaux L Jadot One of the largest *grands crus* in Burgundy, with variable terroir and multiple ownership. Medium, cherry red; fragrant; full-bodied, good varietal flavour. *Jan 2006* ★★(★★) *2010–2015.*

Gevrey-Chambertin, Les Cazetiers L Jadot One of the two most important *premiers crus* in the important wine village of Gevrey in the Côte de Nuits. Medium-pale, attractive colour, touch of cherry red; fragrant, meaty and spicy; fairly dry, lean but very good flavour, very dry tannic and acidic finish. *Jan 2006* ★(★★★) *2010–2015*.

Gevrey-Chambertin, Clos St-Jacques L Jadot Medium-pale, soft and rich; distinctive Pinot aroma; medium sweetness and body, good 'serious' flavour, almost tangy tannin and acidic finish. *Jan 2006* ★(★★★) *2010–2015*.

Morey St-Denis, La Forge Dom Clos de Tart Medium-pale; very distinctive, sweet, slightly jammy nose; very positive Pinot flavour and very tannic. *Jan 2006* ★(★★★) *2010–2015*.

Le Musigny de Vogüé In cask; fairly deep; scent of privet; rich, positive, full-flavoured, dense, a bit tight. Should develop well. *Oct 2005* (★★★★★) *2010–2018*.

Nuits-St-Georges, Clos de la Maréchale J-F Mugnier Very rich, slightly chocolatey nose; medium sweetness and body, crisp, lovely flavour. *Jan 2006* ★★(★★) *2010–2015*.

Pommard, Clos des Epéneaux Comte Armand Crop reduced by 10–15% due to hail, the 35-year-old vines most affected. I tasted a blend of 50-year old and 'young' (planted in 1978) vines: lovely colour, good flavour, soft tannins. From over 50-year old vines, rich but with a drier, hard finish. *Oct 2005* ★(★★) *2010–2015?*

Pommard, Rugiens L Jadot From two *premiers crus* parcels, in Les Rugiens Hauts and Les Rugiens Bas. Softly coloured, relaxed rim; brambly varietal nose; very positive flavour, full-bodied, crisp yet rich, quite a bite. *Jan 2006* ★(★★) *2010–2015*.

Savigny-lès-Beaune, Les Lavières Bouchard Père Medium, cherry-tinged; strangely meaty, sweaty tannin; more agreeable on the palate, good flavour, moderate body. Good value for early drinking. *Jan 2006* ★★★ *Now–2010*.

Clos de Tart Medium-deep; very good flavour and length, full-bodied, very tannic. *Jan 2006* ★★★(★) *2012–2018*.

Volnay, Les Caillerets, Ancienne Cuvée Carnot Bouchard Père Crisp, rich, slightly singed; pure varietal aroma; some sweetness, rich, full-bodied, positive flavour, good tannin and acidity. *Jan 2006* ★★(★★) *2009–2012*.

Clos de Vougeot Drouhin-Laroze Fairly deep; fragrant, a familiar whiff of violets (new wood ?); full-bodied, good Pinot flavour. *Jan 2006* ★★(★★) *2010–2015*.

Clos Vougeot L Jadot Colour fairly deep; low-keyed, 'meaty' nose, good depth; medium-dry, full-bodied, very good, rich, meaty flavour. Touch of bitterness on the finish. Early days. *Jan 2006* ★(★★★) *2012–2016* ?

2005 ★★★★★

Unquestionably, this was a very good vintage in Burgundy, completely upstaging the good but leaner 2004s.It was a perfect growing season from spring to harvest. A small but representative range tasted from the Chalonnais in the south, through the Côte de Beaune to the Côte de Nuits endorses my first exposure to these lovely reds. It was noticeable that most of these wines were around 13% alcohol, none above 13.5%.

Aloxe-Corton Patrick Javillier Medium, soft red; good, firm, varietal aroma; attractive, refreshing, slightly better tannins. *July 2007* ★(★★) *2008–2012*.

Auxey-Duresses Pierre Matrot Good, not overplayed Pinot aroma; crisp, refreshing, an agreeable uplift of flavour. Lovely drink. *July 2007* ★★(★★) *Now–2012.*

Chambolle-Musigny Dom Taupenot-Merme Plummy, open-rimmed; rich, very good, slightly 'singed' varietal aroma; medium-dryness and body, firm, crisp, quite a bite. *July 2007* ★(★★) *possibly up to 4 stars. 2009–2015.*

Côte de Nuits-Villages Dom Gilles Jourdan Fairly deep, intense; low-keyed nose but fragrant with good fruit; crisp, positive flavour, dry finish. Demonstrating the quality, sheer drinkability (and value) the reds once considered 'off the beaten track'. *July 2007* ★★★(★) *Soon–2012.*

Gevrey-Chambertin Dom Taupenot-Merme An attractive village wine: medium-deep, lovely colour; sweet, fragrant, agreeable nose; medium-dry, good fruit but with a somewhat hard tannic finish. *July 2007* ★(★★) *possibly 4 stars. 2008–2012.*

Gevrey-Chambertin, Clos du Meix des Ouches Dom des Varoilles A flavour as intriguing as its name: fragrant, slightly piquant, delicious scent; sweet, flavour to match, soft yet firm, perfect balance of tannin and acidity. *July 2007* ★★(★★★) *2009–2015.*

Gevrey-Chambertin, 1er Cru, Clos des Varoilles Dom des Varoilles I couldn't resist its 'cousin'. Very fragrant, floral nose; medium-sweet, almost chewy, good length, quite a bite, yet well balanced. Most attractive. *July 2007. A generous* ★★★(★★) *2009–2025.*

Mercury, Les Montots Dom A et P de Villaine So this is what Aubert de Villaine gets up to when relaxing at home after the rigours and responsibilities of DRC: fresh young fruit, appealing whiff of raspberry; delicious flavour, modest alcoholic content (12.5%), yet with a sustaining bite. A weekend 'food wine'. *July 2007* ★★★ *Soon–2010.*

Monthélie Pierre Matrot On the pale side; fairly pronounced, fragrant scented, tangy nose; medium dry – touch of sweetness, soft yet crisp. Easy style. *July 2007* ★★★ *Delicious now.*

Savigny-Lès-Beaune, Les Grands Liards Patrick Javillier Very distinctive, arboreal, slightly singed nose and aftertaste; very sweet. *July 2007* ★(★★) *2008–2011. A matter of taste.*

HOSPICES DE BEAUNE '05S: In October 2005 Anthony Hanson and I were privileged to have a preview tasting in the Hospices de Beaune cellars and we were able to taste a wide range in new oak barriques. Even at this early stage, what was very notable was the depth of colour of most of the reds, ranging from deep and velvety to opaque, and the overall sweetness of the wines. Of the 18 Cuvées tasted I rated highly the **Beaune Grèves, Cuvée Nicolas Rolin**; **Volnay, Santenots, Cuvée Gaudin**; **Corton, Renardes, Cuvée Charlotte Dumas**; and the best of all **Mazis-Chambertin, Cuvée Madeleine-Collignon**.

White Burgundy

Burgundy has long set the standards for the world's dry whites. Burgundy's white grape variety, Chardonnay, has spawned a global flood of lookalikes, ranging from very good indeed to grotesque. Good white burgundy is often understated and subtle, and, at its best, is a wine of finesse and refinement.

There are three main areas for white wines in Burgundy: Chablis, the Côte de Beaune and southern Burgundy (the Côte Chalonnaise and Mâconnais). Chablis lovers might query the comparative paucity of my notes here. The reason is that despite the development potential of *grands crus* in suitable years, most Chablis is consumed young and fresh; southern Burgundy produces good but moderately priced wines such as Montagny, Mâcon-Villages and Pouilly-Fuissé, almost entirely for everyday drinking. Which leaves the principal communes of the Côte de Beaune, in effect those of Corton-Charlemagne, Meursault, Puligny-Montrachet and Chassagne-Montrachet. These are the touchstones for white burgundy; at their best inimitable. Good Meursault and Puligny-Montrachet should be drunk between three and six years; the bigger whites like Corton-Charlemagne and Bâtard-Montrachet from five to twelve years and the intense Montrachet of a good vintage up to 20 years.

Outstanding vintages
1864, 1865, 1906,
1928, 1947, 1962,
1966, 1986 (v), 1989 (v),
1996, 2005

Two important points: do not overchill good white burgundy. As for the top whites, the bouquet evolves fully only when the wine approaches room temperature.

Classic older vintages: 1864–1949

Even if one manages to come across a bottle of white burgundy of an old vintage, it is virtually impossible to judge what it was like in its early days. This section is merely to put white burgundy into a historical perspective. The chart indicates the quality of vintages based on reasonably well-documented reports and fairly arbitrary tastings of old wines. As with pre-phylloxera claret, if they are remarkably good now – for their age – they must have been even better in their youth and heyday.

The condition of bottles of old vintages is likely to be risky, and, even at best, they do not drink like their modern, certainly post-1980s, counterparts. Expect the wine to be deeper in colour, preferably a glowing yellow-gold rather than a drab tawny yellow, with a sweet, honeyed bottle-age bouquet; also sweeter on the palate and more substantial – the light, squeaky clean and lean wines either did not exist or, if they did exist, will not have survived. Old wines can be delicious even if only of passing interest. Provenance – cold cellars – is all important; and the state of the corks.

VINTAGES AT A GLANCE

Outstanding ★★★★★ 1864, 1865, 1906, 1928, 1947
Very Good ★★★★ 1899, 1919, 1923, 1929, 1934, 1937, 1945, 1949
Good ★★★ 1941

1950–1979

Three decades, during the course of which some remarkably good wines were made, but with a big gulf between the relatively few top wines from old-established domaines and the great mass of commercial wines which, at the time, were accepted as the norm. It is worth stressing that splendidly hot years like 1959 and 1964 were marvellous for the red burgundies but far less so for the whites, which tended to suffer from flabbiness. White burgundies thrive on the acidity of cooler vintages.

VINTAGES AT A GLANCE

Outstanding ★★★★★ 1962, 1966
Very Good ★★★★ 1952, 1953, 1955, 1961, 1967, 1969, 1971, 1973, 1976, 1978, 1979
Good ★★★ 1950, 1957, 1959, 1964, 1970

1962 ★★★★★
Excellent vintage. The best wines, such as **L Latour**'s **Corton-Charlemagne**, were superb in the 1980s. The top wines are still worth looking out for.

1966 ★★★★★
Excellent vintage. All the component parts in balance but few to be seen now and only the very best, well kept, will be more than just interesting.

Le Montrachet DRC The first major Montrachet vintage made at the Domaine de la Romanée-Conti (DRC) with the old de Moucheron parcel of vines. For the record: yellow-gold; fabulous bouquet which soared, with an equally amazing expansive and expanding flavour. The most magnificent dry white I have ever drunk. *Last noted, and never forgotten, May 1983* ★★★★★★ (*6 stars*).

1967 ★★★★

Very good, zestful wines (many warranting 4 stars). At best in the mid-1970s.

1969 ★★★★

A very good vintage with firm, well constituted, vibrant wines. They were at their best in the 1970s. I have few recent notes.
Le Montrachet Leroy Lovely colour, medium yellow gold; smoky-oaky nose that reminded me of a bonfire, harmonious, whiff of pineapple. Held well. Very powerful, assertive, good length and delicious flavour. *March 2000* ★★★★
Meursault, Charmes Leroy Very pale for its age; a distinctive, sweet, meaty, nutty, whiff of lime blossom bouquet, with flavour to match. Adequate acidity, dry finish. *March 2000* ★★★★

1970 ★★★

The wines were soft but agreeable, most lacking the acidity to sustain any interesting life beyond the decade. Of those tasted in the 1980s and '90s, few wines warranted more than 2 stars, outstandingly the best being Le Montrachet from the **Domaine de la Romanée-Conti**.

1971 ★★★★

One of the best vintages of the decade and the wines were drinking well through the 1980s. The best survived into the late 1990s. Drink up. No recent notes.
Corton-Charlemagne Ancien Dom des Comtes de Grancey, L Latour Palish gold; very good bouquet, an underpinning of vanilla and crisp fruit; perfect weight and flavour. *Nov 1997* ★★★★★ *Impressive.*
Meursault, Perrières Leroy Golden; buttery, nutty, powerful yet suave. *Oct 1997* ★★★★

1973 ★★★★

At its best, these were delicate, fragrant and attractive wines with sustaining acidity. At their least good, they were unbalanced and too acidic.
Montrachet Baron Thénard Bottled by Remoissenet. Shades of old gold; harmonious bouquet though whiff of caramel; rich, good flavour, but past its best. *Last tasted April 2006* ★★★ *Drink up.*

1976 ★★★★

Very good vintage but the wines are variable due to the excessive heat of the summer, overripeness of the grapes and some lack of acidity. The top wines can still be very good.
Corton-Charlemagne L Latour Still pale for its age; good bouquet; mouthfilling, oaky, glorious flavour and aftertaste. *Dec 1997* ★★★★ *Drink up.*

1978 ★★★★

A good vintage, after the damp and dismal year of 1977. The wines were supple, well constituted and of surprisingly high alcoholic content. I have many notes of the top wines.

Montrachet DRC Most recently, two bottles, one of which was 'dull', the other pale for its age; very sweet, rich, vanilla nose of unplumbed depth; dry, crisp, nutty. Not at all bad! *Last tasted Sept 2000. At best* ★★★★

Montrachet A Ramonet Yellow gold, pendulous 'legs'; nose low-keyed at first, but at room temperature it opened up, sweet, nutty, lemon-curd, classic, oaky-smoky, then further elevation, pineapple and vanilla; medium-sweet, very full-bodied, a mammoth wine, with power, length, excellent life-guaranteeing acidity and '20 years to go', I noted. *Dec 1995* ★★★★★ *Now–2015.*

Bâtard-Montrachet L Latour Two notes, both the same evening: glorious lime gold; rich, meaty bouquet; sweet, full, rich, lovely flavour, excellent acidity. A similar note, 'smoky, nutty' added. *Feb 1997* ★★★★★ *Perfect now.*

Bâtard-Montrachet Leflaive A gusher, rich, buttery, ripe, great length. *Oct 1990* ★★★★★ *Drink up.*

Bienvenues-Bâtard-Montrachet A Ramonet Lovely colour, hint of lime; creamy, rather Sémillon-like nose opening up richly, sweet, blissfully fragrant; fairly sweet, full-bodied, very rich, perfect touch of oak, good length and acidity. Elegant despite its power. Years of life. *Dec 1995* ★★★★★ *Now–2015.*

Corton-Charlemagne Bonneau du Martray Medium-deep gold; very rich, creamy, almost buttery bouquet; medium sweetness, fairly full-bodied, rich, soft, 'double cream'! With sustaining acidity. *Last tasted Nov 2003* ★★★★ *At peak.*

Puligny-Montrachet, Les Pucelles Leflaive Yellow, waxy sheen; deceptively mild, smooth, calm, but very good length and acidity. A fine, understated wine. *Nov 1990* ★★★★

1979 ★★★★

The '79 white burgundies had an early, easy charm yet fine structure. Most wines were at their best by the mid- to late 1980s but the top wines have stayed the course. Drink soon.

Montrachet A Ramonet Lovely colour, pure gold highlights, rich 'legs'; biscuity, spicy, and, after an hour, fabulous, and after nearly two hours in the glass 'honeyed pineapple'; medium-dry, assertive, incredibly powerful, with vanilla flavour and aftertaste, excellent acidity and length. Great wine. *Dec 1995* ★★★★★

Bâtard-Montrachet Bachelet-Ramonet Glorious smoky-oaky nose, hint of lime, toasted coconut and marshmallow; pleasing sweetness, very rich, assertive, fruit-laden. A magnificent wine. *Last tasted Sept 1990* ★★★★★ *Will doubtless have survived.*

Bienvenues-Bâtard-Montrachet Leflaive Lime-tinged; rich, biscuity, smoky; fairly dry, fullish, still powerful but slightly harsh finish. *Jan 1995* ★★★

Beaune, Clos des Mouches J Drouhin Taking on some colour by 1988, nose more buttery, fruit, oak; positive, assertive but with a slightly hard, acidic finish. *Last noted Oct 1990* ★★★★

Corton-Charlemagne Bonneau du Martray Bright yellow; initially hard but opened up, gently honeyed clover; full-bodied, very good flavour, vanilla, appley acidity, years of life. *Sept 1994* ★★★★★

Puligny-Montrachet Robert Ampeau Lovely colour, lemon/lime highlights, oaky/smoky nose, touch of caramel; very good flavour and acidity, excellent for a village wine of its age. *Jan 2006* ★★★★
Puligny-Montrachet, Clavoillon Leflaive Deep, rich, toasty, vinous; medium sweetness, full flavour and body. Rich and lovely. *Nov 1995* ★★★★
Puligny-Montrachet, Les Combettes Robert Ampeau Surprisingly pale; mouthfilling, very good length and acidity but with strong peach-kernel flavour. *April 2005* ★★★?
Puligny-Montrachet, Les Pucelles Leflaive Most recently: fairly pale; very oaky, dry, lean. *Last tasted Feb 1996* ★★★★

1980–1999

A successful period for white burgundy with more than its share of really top class wines. What follows is not a gazetteer, for the complexity of this region makes it impossible to do justice to the wines of just one vintage let alone of a couple of decades. The notes are meant to be illustrative not comprehensive.

VINTAGES AT A GLANCE

Outstanding ★★★★★ 1986 (v), 1989 (v), 1996
Very Good ★★★★ 1982 (v), 1983, 1985 (v), 1986 (v), 1989 (v), 1990 (v), 1995, 1997, 1998, 1999
Good ★★★ 1982 (v), 1985 (v), 1986 (v), 1988, 1989 (v), 1991 (v), 1992, 1993 (v), 1994 (v)

1982 variable, up to ★★★★

To start with it was a ripe and attractive vintage, but if not exactly flaccid, the wines had inadequate acidity to provide zest and a long life. Even though some of my notes are not recent I shall start with the Montrachets as they represent the best of the vintage. Drink soon.
Montrachet L Jadot Lovely, wax-sheened yellow colour; creamy, vanilla, harmonious nose; lovely, full, rich and buttery flavour. *Oct 1995* ★★★★
Montrachet Comtes Lafon Most recently: straw gold; glorious, creamy, almost custardy bouquet; full, fat, rounded, oaky, touch of bitterness. *Last tasted Sept 1989* ★★★★
Montrachet Laguiche/Drouhin High-toned, still youthful pineapple, opening and holding well; some sweetness, 13.5% alcohol, intriguing flavour, decent length, moderately good acidity (3.8g/l). *Oct 1990* ★★★★
Montrachet DRC Fairly deep yellow; 'warm', crusty, toasty bouquet; dry yet very rich, hefty, four-square. *Last tasted April 2004* ★★★ *Alas, past its best.*
Montrachet Ramonet Superb. Palish, appealingly bright; twist of lemon and smoky pineapple on the nose which opened up fragrantly; slightly sweet, perfect mouthfilling flavour, acidity and aftertaste. Elegant. Sublime. *April 2002* ★★★★★

Bâtard-Montrachet E Sauzet Buttery, waxy; richly flavoured, touch of bitterness. *Oct 1990* ★★★★
Corton-Charlemagne Bonneau du Martray Luscious, bread-crust nose; rich, full body and flavour, surprisingly good acidity for an '82. *July 1994* ★★★★
Meursault, Clos de la Barre Comtes Lafon Pale for its age, still lemon-tinged; sweet, crusty, lovely bouquet; medium-sweet, delicious flavour and excellent acidity. *Oct 2000* ★★★★

1983 ★★★★

A very mixed growing season with heaavy rain in September. These were well-endowed whites with body, flesh and good acidity. They were probably at their best in the late 1980s to mid-1990s and most are now fading.
Montrachet Laguiche/Drouhin Distinctive yellow; nose deep, rich, with spicy fragrance after two hours in the glass; sweet, rich, full-bodied, good acidity. Lovely wine. *Oct 1990* ★★★★★ *Now–2010.*
Montrachet DRC Low-keyed nose; far more interesting on the palate, fairly sweet, full of flavour, good fruit and body. Impressive but still hard. *Sept 1995. Then* ★★(★★★) *Probably a fully fledged 5-star now. A long-haul Montrachet.*
Bâtard-Montrachet Leflaive Palish; wonderfully fragrant, nutty, oaky bouquet and flavour. Rich, fullish, yet lean and steely. Lemon-like acidity. Very high mark. *Sept 1995* ★★★★★
Bienvenues-Bâtard-Montrachet H Clerc Touch of gold; ripe, mature, assertive nose and flavour. Very acidic. *July 2003* ★★★ *Too acidic?*
Chevalier-Montrachet Leflaive More recently, in magnums: still pale; very oaky-smoky bouquet; very dry, lean but assertive. *Nov 1997* ★★★★ *Drink up.*
Chevalier-Montrachet, Les Demoiselles L Jadot Bouquet showing some age but good; medium dryness and body, smoky flavour, elegant, ready. *Sept 1994* ★★★★ *Drink up.*
Corton-Charlemagne Bonneau du Martray Good colour; 'fat', 'warm', whiff of peach kernels; remarkably sweet, touch of caramel and showing its age. *Last tasted Nov 2003. At best* ★★★★ *Declining.*
Corton-Charlemagne L Jadot Glorious. Lovely fruit and vinosity. *Oct 1990* ★★★★★ *Should still be excellent.*
Meursault, Poruzots F Jobard Bright yellow; attractive, minty nose and taste. Medium sweetness and body. Touch of lanolin. Good acidity. *Nov 1997* ★★★ *Drink up.*
Puligny-Montrachet L Jadot Astonishingly high alcohol (14.6%) and acidity (4.6g/l). Yellow-hued; very rich bouquet; the sweetness of ripe grapes and substantial alcohol; plump for Puligny. *Oct 1990* ★★★★★ *Drink soon.*

1985 variable, at best ★★★★

This should have been an exemplary vintage and was certainly promising. The harvest was good, if a little late; the grapes were ripe, but on the whole it has not lived up to my high expectations. On balance, drink up.
Montrachet Laguiche/Drouhin Golden sheen; glorious, forthcoming classic bouquet of great depth; glorious flavour, texture, length and aftertaste. *Last tasted June 2006* ★★★★ *Perfect now.*
Montrachet Baron Thénard Most recently: pale, still retaining a hint of

youthful green; fragrant, opening up as it reached room temperature, nutty, vanilla; very good, clean, fresh flavour and length with a lovely lemony, oaky finish. *Last tasted Sept 1998* ★★★★

Montrachet DRC A substantial wine with a convincing appearance; rich, round, soft, bread-like – more dough than crust, with touch of pineapple. Full-bodied, very rich, nutty flavour, good acidity. A lovely wine. *Nov 1995* ★★★★

Beaune, Clos des Mouches J Drouhin At ten years of age, it appeared to have a satin sheen; gloriously evolved bouquet; delicious oaky-Chardonnay flavour, rich, perfect balance and lovely oaky aftertaste. *Last noted July 1995* ★★★★

Bienvenues-Bâtard-Montrachet Remoissenet Surprisingly pale; perfect, harmonious, slightly crusty (bread) nose; rich, full body and flavour, perfect balance, very good acidity. *Feb 1999* ★★★★

Corton-Charlemagne Bonneau du Martray Attractive vanillin bouquet; very good flavour and acidity. Fully mature. *June 2006* ★★★ *Drink now.*

Corton-Charlemagne L Latour Many notes and always disappointing. Most recently: still pale; little nose; dryish, and the least satisfactory of several vintages. *Last tasted Dec 2003* ★★

Montrachet Laguiche Superb wine. Most recently: palish gold; glorious, classic bouquet and flavour of great depth and length. Lovely texture. *Last tasted June 2007* ★★★★★ *Still at peak.*

Puligny-Montrachet, Les Pucelles Leflaive Pale, hint of lime; very forthcoming, smoky-oaky nose and taste. Good length. *Oct 2003* ★★★

1986 variable, up to ★★★★★

This is unquestionably a very attractive and successful vintage: dense, well-structured, firm wines and with excellent acidity. The best are still lovely.

Montrachet Laguiche/Drouhin Only tasted in its youth: nose low-keyed, slow to emerge; medium-dry, medium-full body, good length, teeth-gripping acidity. Needed considerable bottle age to open up and simmer down. *Oct 1990. Then* ★(★★★★) *Probably on its plateau now.*

Montrachet A Ramonet Very pale; rich, toasty bouquet that spread its wings magnificently; distinct sweetness, full-bodied, nutty flavour – what a pathetic, inadequate description; rich, of course, and with very good acidity. *Nov 1997* ★★★★★ *Will keep for ages.*

Montrachet DRC Palish; scent of toasted coconut, opening up beautifully; mouthfilling, in fact quite a bite. *Oct 1997* ★★★★★ *Great. Long life.*

Beaune, Clos des Mouches J Drouhin This is always my vintage yardstick. Of the entire range of white Clos des Mouches from 1979 to 1989 tasted at Drouhin in 1990, I rated this the highest. Most recently: fully mature, medium-gold; freshly picked mushrooms, medium-sweet, perfect weight and flavour. Immaculate balance, fully mature. It blossomed in the glass. *Last noted August 1999* ★★★★★ *Drink soon.*

Bienvenues-Bâtard-Montrachet Leflaive Very pale, lime-tinged; crisp, spicy, lemon-like acidity; fairly dry, fragrant, stylish, acidity flapping in the wind. *Feb 1995* ★★★ *Should be drinking well now.*

Bienvenues-Bâtard-Montrachet A Ramonet Lovely 'smoky' nose and flavour, perfect weight and balance, excellent acidity. Fragrant. *Nov 2002* ★★★★★

Chevalier-Montrachet, Les Demoiselles L Latour Very nutty nose and flavour. Fairly sweet, certainly very rich and developing well. *June 1997* ★★★(★) *Drink now.*

Corton-Charlemagne Bonneau du Martray Very good, positive colour; very rich, minty bouquet; indeed richness the operative word. Perfection. *Last noted Oct 2000* ★★★★★ *At peak.*

Meursault, Charmes Comtes Lafon Lovely gold sheen; smoky, citrus touch; sweet, richly flavoured. *March 1995* ★★★★ *Drink soon.*

1988 ★★★

A good vintage and deservedly popular when it came on to the market. However, yields were high and the wines of those producers who did not prune hard or select diligently tended to lack concentration. Even so, there were quite a few ripe, fresh, well-balanced wines and the finest are still drinking well.

Montrachet DRC Sadly, only tasted in its youth, but even then a very attractive mouthful, good nose, fairly full-bodied, good flesh, fruit and acidity. *Oct 1990.* Then (★★★★) *Doubtless at peak now.*

Montrachet Laguiche/Drouhin Fragrant, lovely. *March 1991* (★★★★)

Chassagne-Montrachet Ch de la Maltroye Palish yellow straw; good nose, Chardonnay with some bottle age; excellent flavour and length. *Nov 1994* ★★★★

Chassagne-Montrachet, Les Chaumées M Colin-Deléger Initially not very distinctive, then nutty; dry, pleasing, good acidity. *Jan 2002* ★★★ *Ready now.*

Corton-Charlemagne Bonneau du Martray Bright pale gold; bouquet good but static, not opening up fragrantly as expected; dry, crisp, discreetly full-bodied. At peak. *Last tasted July 2006* ★★★★ *(just). Drink soon.*

Corton-Charlemagne Coche-Dury Fairly pale; an appealing, fragrant, smoky, vanilla nose that took on a hint of chocolate; fairly sweet, delicious flavour, substantial but not overdone, with a good, clean, dry finish. *June 1998* ★★★★

Corton-Charlemagne L Latour Almost meatily rich, good acidity, oaky aftertaste. Perfect (then) for drinking. *Last noted March 1998* ★★★★ *Drink now.*

Meursault, Charmes Comtes Lafon Smoky, vanilla and a touch of honeyed bottle age; medium-sweet, full-bodied, mouthfilling, firm, even a touch of austerity, high acidity. *March 1995* ★★★ *Drink soon.*

Puligny-Montrachet, Les Folatières H Clerc Touch of gold; strange toasted nose reminding me of Gentleman's Relish and grilled bacon; fairly full-bodied, very oaky, spicy. *Sept 1996* ★★★ *Drink up.*

Puligny-Montrachet, Les Pucelles Leflaive Pale, starbright, lime yellow, making one salivate just to look at it; firm, fresh, lemon and vanilla; surprisingly sweet and still youthful. *Sept 1995* ★★★★ *Now–2010.*

1989 variable, up to ★★★★★

The grapes were ripe and the harvest was early. The wines were immediately attractive. Some of the top wines are still drinking beautifully.

Montrachet DRC Most recently, two bottles, slight variation. The first medium-pale yellow; smoky – like cooling ashes, lemon, vanilla, penetrating bouquet; an astonishing flavour, minty, spicy, tremendous attack, almost biting finish. In the adjoining glass, paler, lemon-tinged; gentle nose but great depth; slightly softer, less pushy, classic. *Last tasted Nov 2005* ★★★★(★) *Long life.*

Montrachet Laguiche/Drouhin Excellent, gently toasted, classic, opening up further; outstandingly the best of a range of top white burgundies at the tasting. *Last tasted Sept 1993. Then* ★★(★★★) *Will be perfect now.*

Montrachet Thénard/Remoissenet Impressive, remarkably sweet, very flavoury but too much oak. *Last tasted May 1999* ★★★★

Bâtard-Montrachet Niéllon Excellent: a most attractive, smoky nose and flavour, soft, rich, long smoky finish. *Oct 1995* ★★★★

Bâtard-Montrachet Leflaive Fairly pale; far too oaky on nose and palate, and not enough fat for a Bâtard of a vintage like 1989. *Sept 1997* ★★★

Chablis, Les Clos Dauvissat-Camus Nose restrained but opened up; dry, positive, good acidity, distinctive. *Oct 2002* ★★★ *Probably at its best now.*

Chassagne-Montrachet, La Boudriotte Gagnard-Delagrange Pale, lime-tinged; a most delicious, smoky, lemony nose and mouthful. Fragrant aftertaste. *Feb 1995* ★★★★★

Chassagne-Montrachet, Les Caillerets A Ramonet Highly polished, pale gold; sweet, smoky-oaky nose and flavour, full-bodied, very good acidity. *Sept 1997* ★★★★

Corton-Charlemagne Coche-Dury Fabulous, and well deserving his starry reputation: indescribably sweet, 'full cream', surging bouquet; fairly sweet, soft, rich. *June 1998* ★★★★★

Corton-Charlemagne L Latour Most recently: a wonderfully sweet, soft, full, rich wine. *Last noted March 1998* ★★★★

Meursault, Charmes Comtes Lafon Showing superbly. Positively opulent on the nose and almost too powerful. *Last noted Nov 1996* ★★★★★

Meursault, Genevrières Bouchard Père Decent colour; unexciting nose; medium richness and body. Rather Napa-like. *June 2003* ★★★

Meursault, Perrières Comtes Lafon Distinctive yellow; a harmonious subtle nose; lovely, full-flavoured, smoky, oaky. *Oct 1994* ★★★★

Puligny-Montrachet, Les Pucelles Leflaive Most recently, drinking well. *Last tasted April 1999* ★★★ *Good but no better that that.*

1990 ★★★★ but variable

I was expecting better from this vintage. The variations in quality are, frankly, surprising to say the least. Yet some of the wines, the top names, are magnificent. The growing season was good, but the heat and drought favoured the red wines. There was a surprisingly large, too large, crop of whites which, while rich, often elegant and mainly well balanced, were best for early drinking.

Le Montrachet J-N Gagnard Medium-pale yellow; lovely, rich, vanilla and all the components in place; sweet, full flavour but modest weight (12.5% alcohol). A glorious mouthful. *July 2003* ★★★★★ *Perfect now but will still keep.*

Montrachet Comtes Lafon Initially rather low-keyed but after 20 minutes in the glass it developed glorious richness; marvellous flavour, great length and aftertaste, with light but tingling acidity. *March 1995. Then* ★★(★★★) *Should be lovely now.*

Montrachet Laguiche/Drouhin Very fragrant, toasty, smoky nose; appeared to be fairly sweet, certainly rich, fat, higher acidity than the '89 but masked. *Last tasted Feb 1996* ★★★(★★) *Lovely now. Will also keep.*

Montrachet Thénard/Remoissenet Most recently: pale, very oaky nose; good flavour and grip. *Last noted May 1999* ★★★★★ *Drink now.*

Bâtard-Montrachet Leflaive Pale for its age; perfect bouquet, harmonious, fragrant, touch of vanilla; slightly sweet, perfect development, just a touch of peach kernels after time in the glass. *Oct 2004* ★★★★★ *At peak now.*

Bâtard-Montrachet Ramonet Lovely, deep, nutty varietal nose; flavour to match, dry, lemon-like acidity, slightly oaky–smoky aftertaste. (Initially served too cold; refreshing but better as it approached room temperature.) *Feb 2003* ★★★★

Chassagne-Montrachet Ramonet Pale; good nose though not distinctive; very satisfactory flavour and acidity. Certainly a classy wine. *July 2000* ★★★★

Chevalier-Montrachet, Les Demoiselles L Jadot Very good indeed. Perfect blend of fruit and oak. *Dec 1997* ★★★★

Corton-Charlemagne Bonneau du Martray Delicious nose, like supercharged vanilla ice-cream; distinctly sweet, a perfect blend of fruit and oak, smoky, elegant, good finish. *Last noted Nov 1999* ★★★★★ *White burgundy can't get much better than this.*

Corton-Charlemagne L Latour Now a waxy yellow-gold; sweet, rich, creamy, very oaky, vanillin bouquet and a wonderfully rich, mouthfilling flavour. Very good acidity. One of the best ever 'LL' Charlemagnes. *Last tasted April 2006* ★★★★★ *Fully developed.*

Meursault, Clos de la Barre Comtes Lafon Full-bodied, good fruit, firm acidity. *March 1995* ★★★★

Meursault, Genevrières F Jobart Palish yellow; fragrant, walnut-like (served too cold); dry, classic. *April 1999* ★★★

Meursault, Genevrières L Latour Developed quite well, butter and oak on nose and taste. Attractive but a bit four-square. *July 1997* ★★★

Meursault, Rugeots Coche-Dury Coche-Dury is a down-to-earth master of Meursault. 'Warm', smoky, plump, vanillin; medium-dry entry, dry yet rich, smoky finish. Very positive flavour, excellent length. *Last tasted Sept 2005* ★★★★

Musigny blanc de Vogüé Decanted. Attractive palish yellow with hint of gold; bouquet and flavour classy, rich but – tasting quickly – not as great as expected. *June 2006* ★★★ *Drink up.*

Puligny-Montrachet Séguin-Manuel Pale, hint of lime; very attractive floral aromas; drinking well. *Jan 2005* ★★★

1991 ★★★ but variable

An appalling growing season. Heavy rain fell from 29 September, the vines were thirsty because of the drought and the leaves came off. The result was wines like the '82s. Take care.

Montrachet Laguiche/Drouhin Good 'legs'; nose relatively low-keyed yet intense and slightly spicy; medium sweetness and fullish body. Rich, rounded, good length and acidity. *Last noted Feb 1996* ★★★ *Drink soon.*

Montrachet DRC Most recently, two bottles, both very consistent: lovely, medium-deep, yellow-gold colour; very rich, waxy, buttery nose, with discreet oak; delicious flavour and fragrant aftertaste. *Last tasted Nov 2003* ★★★★ *Drink soon.*

Montrachet Thénard/Remoissenet Whiff of peach kernels; fairly sweet, very flavoury, oaky, powerful. *May 1999* ★★★ *Drink now.*

Bienvenue-Bâtard-Montrachet Ramonet Pale with a slightly green tinge; oaky, scented vanilla nose, lean, almost sharp; lovely crisp oaky flavour, good length, lemon-like acidity. *Sept 1996, then* ★★★★ *Drink soon.*

Chassagne-Montrachet Niéllon Soft, oaky flavour and 'warm', dry finish *1998* ★★★ *Drink now.*

Chassagne-Montrachet, Morgeot L Latour Nice weight and flavour *2001* ★★★ *Drink up.*

Chevalier-Montrachet Leflaive Curious mintiness; dry, fairly powerful, oaky, cloves-like spice, lean finish. *April 1998* ★★★ *Drink up.*

Corton-Charlemagne Fromont-Moindrot Medium-deep yellow; nose dumb – served too cold; better as it warmed up in the mouth, dry, medium-full body, fairly strong almond kernel flavour, very good acidity. *Feb 2004* ★★★ *Will keep further.*

Meursault, Charmes Comtes Lafon Served too cold but nose opened up well, sweet, vanilla; fullish, assertive flavour, good length for a '91. *Nov 2000* ★★★

1992 ★★★

A remarkably good growing season. Ripening took place under perfect conditions and August temperatures were high. Glorious sunshine lasted virtually throughout the relatively early harvest. The white grapes were fully ripe and rounded, the initial worry being that there would be enough acidity to balance the sweetness and body. The best wines are drinking well now.

Montrachet Amiot Of three bottles, one was corked. The others: positive yellow; rich, nutty bouquet; full-bodied, immensely rich, good length. Lovely wine. *Nov 2006* ★★★★★

Montrachet Laguiche/Drouhin Lovely, bright, pure Tutankhamen gold; nose initially low-keyed though smoky and spicy, but after three hours, what was left in the glass had opened up intriguingly, with scent of privet and vanilla; on entry, medium-dry, lean though fullish body, steely, with good acidity, racy richness and depth. In the context of a great wine dinner perhaps my notes underrated it. *Last tasted Aug 2005. Awarded* ★★★, *perhaps in a different situation* ★★★★ *Drink soon.*

Bâtard-Montrachet Ramonet Lemon-tinged, starbright; lovely, gently scented; glorious flavour, very oaky, but elegant and with excellent acidity. *Last tasted Sept 1995* ★★★★ *Probably at peak now.*

Bienvenues-Bâtard-Montrachet L Latour Very pale for age; deep, rich, oaky nose and flavour. Very mouthfilling. *May 2006* ★★★★ *Drink soon.*

Chablis, Les Clos J Moreau Extremely pale; very fragrant, dry. Light style, touch of oak, very good acidity. Fresh for age. *May 2006* ★★★★ *Drink soon.*

Chablis, Montée de Tonnerre Raveneau Traditional, uncompromising producer. Palish, good for its age; fabulous 'old oak' bouquet; fairly dry, lean, trace of lemon and marzipan. Very distinctive. *Nov 2006* ★★★★

Chevalier-Montrachet Dom du Ch de Beaune Gold colour; touch of oiliness, otherwise very good; dry, interesting texture, some flesh, very slight touches of caramel, kernels and nuttiness. *Jan 2000* ★★★ *(just).*

Chevalier-Montrachet Leflaive Floral; attractive. *Last noted June 1999* ★★★

Meursault, Charmes Comtes Lafon Medium-pale yellow, with touch of lime; gentle, youthful pineapple aroma, becoming pleasantly scented; crisp, good length, glorious flavour. *March 1995* ★★★★ *Doubtless at peak now.*

Musigny Blanc de Vogüé Fairly pale yellow; good but not as spectacular as expected. Dry finish. Fully developed. *June 2006* ★★★ *Drink soon.*

Puligny-Montrachet, Champ Canet E Sauzet Palish; good nose and flavour. Fullish body, quite assertive, slightly 'hot' finish. *July 2003* ★★★ *Ready to drink.*

Puligny-Montrachet, Les Enseignières H Prudhon Distinct yellow; ripe, rich Chardonnay showing some bottle age; medium dryness and body, good flavour. Some bottle variation. *Oct 2005* ★★★ *Drink up.*

Puligny-Montrachet, Folatières J Drouhin Positive colour, good nose and flavour, attractive lanolin and oak. *Oct 1998* ★★★

Puligny-Montrachet, Les Pucelles L Jadot Yellow, touch of gold; very buttery, oaky – almost 'New World', held well; medium-dry, very positive and attractive flavour though lacking a little acidity. *April 2002* ★★★ *Drink now.*

1993 ★★★ variable

A useful vintage, but take great care in selection. The leading producers picked before the rain and made some excellent wines, many not only drinking well now but with more to come. Most overproduced, generic and *négociants'* village wines should have been consumed long ago.

Montrachet Laguiche/Drouhin Crisp, inimitable Montrachet nose, glorious flavour, length and aftertaste. Full-bodied (14% alcohol) and exuding power as well as beauty. *Last tasted Oct 2001* ★★★★★ *Lovely now. Good for another 10 years or more.*

Montrachet Fleurot-Larose Medium-pale gold; lovely, fragrant, fully opened bouquet, touch of vanilla blancmange; medium-sweet, full, rich, oaky, nutty flavour and fragrant aftertaste. *Aug 1998* ★★★★★ *At peak.*

Le Montrachet Leflaive Full, rich, yellow-gold; flowery, whiff of caramel; medium-dry, fullish body, interesting flavour but somehow not settled down. *April 2004* ★★★ *Time will tell.*

Bâtard-Montrachet Ramonet More recently, a Methuselah: smoky, oaky, biscuity bouquet and flavour, rich, substantial. *Sept 1999* ★★★★ *Now–2012.*

Chevalier-Montrachet Leflaive Far better than the '92: vanilla nose; lovely, rich, nutty taste. *June 1997* ★★★★ *Perfect now.*

Chevalier-Montrachet E Sauzet Compared in Riedel glasses, in which it seemed more flowery, and in Baccarat 'Grands Blancs' glasses, the nose appearing rather raw and palate more of a bite. Nice wine, though. *Jan 1998* ★★★ *Ready.*

Corton-Charlemagne Bonneau du Martray Most recently: palish yellow; nutty, walnuts; medium-dry, rich, mouthfilling, good acidity. A whiff and touch of peach kernels. *Last tasted Nov 2003* ★★★ *Should be very good now.*

Corton-Charlemagne Coche-Dury Fairly pale; very good indeed, its nutty vanilla bouquet opening up fabulously in the glass; dry, assertive, a powerhouse. *Nov 2000* ★★★★ *Now–2012.*

Corton-Charlemagne L Latour Served far too cold; it deadened the nose: dry, steely, powerful, impressive. *Last tasted July 2000* ★★★(★) *Now–2012.*

Puligny-Montrachet, Clavoillon Leflaive Sweet and soft vanilla; crisp yet buttery, oak, good length and acidity. I liked its vivacity. *May 1998* ★★★ *Will be excellent now.*

OTHER TOP '93S tasted in 1996: **Chassagne-Montrachet, Boudriotte Ramonet** smoky, rich and powerful ★★★★; **Chassagne-Montrachet, Grande-Montagne Fontaine-Gagnard** spicy, fragrant, tingling acidity ★★★★; **Chassagne-Montrachet, Vergers Ramonet** soft, rich, rounded ★★★★; **Meursault, Clos St-Felix Michelot** substantial, complete ★★★★; **Puligny-Montrachet, Folatières Leflaive** fragrant, lean, acidic ★★★; and **Puligny-Montrachet, Pucelles Verget** crisp Puligny character, good acidity ★★★

1994 ★★★ variable

The weather broke on 31 August, with two weeks of torrential rain. Growers were faced with a classic dilemma: whether to pick early, pick hurriedly at the onset of rain, or hope the weather would clear up enough to pick later? Thanks to careful selection, a certain amount of luck and good winemaking, a few growers did well.

Montrachet Comtes Lafon Palish yellow; forthcoming, open, very rich, smoky bouquet, vanilla with touch of marzipan, opening up extraordinarily in the glass; sweet, rich, fairly full-bodied, oaky vanillin flavour, dry acidic finish. *Nov 2003* ★★★★ *Lovely now.*

Montrachet L Jadot Pale, green-tinged; low-keyed nose, twist of lemon, a smidgen of fruit; more positive on palate, dryish, medium–full-bodied, lean, very acidic. *Sept 1998* ★★★ *Needed more bottle age, but can it aspire to 4-star?*

Montrachet E Sauzet Palish yellow, touch of straw; touch of refreshing, lemon-like acidity; medium-sweet, leaner than Lafon's though full-flavoured and with teeth-gripping acidity. *Last tasted Nov 2003* ★★★(★) *Might soften with time.*

Beaune, Clos des Mouches Blanc J Drouhin Muffled, still youthful, pineappley nose; fairly dry, a bit stolid. *Oct 2001* ★★★ *(at most) Drink up.*

Chevalier-Montrachet E Sauzet Still youthfully minty, acidic; served too cold, dry, firm, oak on finish, acidity verging on tartness. *Last noted Sept 1998* ★★★ *Drink up.*

Corton-Charlemagne Bonneau du Martray Palish yellow; a creamy rather than nutty Corton-Charlemagne. Showing well. *Nov 1997* ★★★★ *Ready.*

Corton-Charlemagne L Latour Slightly caramelised; some sweetness, presumably chaptalised to achieve 14% alcohol, vanilla flavour and raw finish. *Last noted July 2000. At best* ★★★ *Drink up.*

Puligny-Montrachet, Les Champs-Gain Remoissenet Palish; light 'bread basket' nose; touch of sweetness, soft, not too much oak. *Oct 1998* ★★★ *Drink up.*

Puligny-Montrachet, Les Pucelles Leflaive Pale; floral nose, lime and pineapple, lively; medium-dry, lovely flavour, oaky finish. *Jan 1999* ★★★★ *Ready.*

OTHER '94S showing well in 1996: **Montrachet Laguiche/Drouhin** fairly sweet, full-bodied, rich, good acidity and potential ★★★★; **Chassagne-Montrachet Laguiche/Drouhin** surprisingly mouthfilling, very agreeable ★★★★; **Chassagne-Montrachet, Vergers Marc Morey** sweet, good body and flavour ★★★ *should be fully mature now*; and **Chevalier-Montrachet Leflaive** firm, steely, delicious ★★★★ *drink up.*

1995 ★★★★

An attractive and mainly very successful vintage despite the uneven growing season: after a late and difficult flowering the grapes ripened well during the hot summer, but rain and risk of rot during the first half of September hampered an early vintage. Yields were down 30% but a touch of noble rot on the grapes gave the wines more richness and concentration with increased sugar levels and good acidity. The best wines are lovely now.

Montrachet DRC Very pale; poured 8.30pm (too cold), scented by 8.45pm, fully evolved vanilla and touch of caramel by 10pm; amazingly powerful, deft oak, spicy. *Feb 1998* ★★★(★★) *Too young but delicious.*

Montrachet Fleurot-Larose Highly polished; fairly full-bodied, plump, with lip-licking acidity. Rare, good but not exceptional. *Aug 1998* ★★★

Montrachet Laguiche/Drouhin A jeroboam: touch of youthful lemon, almost grapefruit-like; very good indeed, clinging reluctantly, patiently, to the sides of the glass. *Sept 1999* ★★★★(★) *Now–2020.*

Montrachet L Latour Very pale; hefty; taste of peach kernels, disappointing. *Dec 2000* ★★

Montrachet Thénard/Remoissenet A jeroboam: pale; touch of vanilla but shapely, harmonious nose; medium-dry, fairly powerful, good flavour, spicy. *Sept 1999* ★★★(★) *Should be drinking well now.*

Bâtard-Montrachet J-N Gagnard Most recently: rich, fragrant, vanilla, nutty bouquet; fairly sweet and full-bodied, delicious, mouthfilling flavour, very good acidity. As good as it gets. *Last tasted Nov 2003* ★★★★★ *Now–2012.*

Bâtard-Montrachet L Jadot Magnums: palish, starbright; low-keyed – served too cold but opened up well as it approached room temperature; rich entry but overall dry, smoky-oaky finish. Rather lean and ethereal. *March 2000* ★★★(★)

Bâtard-Montrachet Leflaive Fullish, nutty, minty, opening up fragrantly; fairly sweet, full-bodied, good flavour, extract and oak. Starting to spread its wings. *Sept 1998* ★★★(★★)

Bâtard-Montrachet Albert Morey Fabulous mouthful. *Oct 1997* ★★(★★★)

Beaune, Clos des Mouches J Drouhin Medium-pale, rich 'legs'; good vinosity, initially harmonious but then I thought it a bit unknit, with some meatiness; better on the palate, fairly sweet, rich, assertive, full-bodied (labelled 13.5% but alcohol actually 14%). *Oct 2001* ★★(★★) *I think it will pull through.*

Chablis, Les Preuses Simonnet-Febvre Pale; almost meatily rich; a steely, powerful, scented *grand cru. Oct 1999* ★★★★ *Should be at peak now.*

Chassagne-Montrachet, Les Chevenottes J-N Gagnard Fragrant and showing well at the opening tasting in 1997 and drinking well at 10 years of age. *Last tasted Jan 2005* ★★★★ *Ready now.*

Chassagne-Montrachet, Morgeot L Latour Very pale; low keyed; medium-dry, fairly full-bodied. *Nov 2001* ★★★

Chevalier-Montrachet Dom du Ch de Beaune A Methuselah: pale; after 30 minutes floral and fragrant; lean, flavour of vanilla and pineapple, good length and acidity. *Sept 1999* ★★★(★) *Now–2010.*

Chevalier-Montrachet L Latour Very pale; 'a Leflaive lookalike'; medium-dryness and weight, strange flavour, very raw at first – too cold – but later was pleasantly crisp and 'nutty'. *Dec 2000* ★★★

Corton-Charlemagne L Latour Eight consistent notes. Most recently: pale, lemon-tinged; oaky nose, refreshing whiff of lemon-like acidity, pure vanilla after an hour; leaner, drier and more full-bodied (14% alcohol) than the '98. Very good flavour and acidity. One of the best Latour Charlemagnes I have ever tasted. *Last tasted Feb 2004* ★★★★ *Perfect now.*

Puligny-Montrachet, Clavoillon Leflaive Very pale, lime-tinged, starbright; pure, understated Chardonnay, youthful pineapple and vanilla, slightly smoky, mouthwatering acidity; unmistakable lean style, full-bodied yet unobtrusive (13.5% alcohol); delicate, subtle, good acidity. Classic. *March 1999* ★★★(★)

Puligny-Montrachet, Les Combettes E Sauzet Medium-pale yellow; rusty, bread-like nose with touch of honey; fairly dry, fullish body, lovely, slightly flinty flavour, good length and excellent aftertaste. *Last tasted March 2004* ★★★★

Puligny-Montrachet, Les Folatières H Clerc Pale; vanilla, oak; dry enough, straightforward. *Nov 2001* ★★★

Puligny-Montrachet, Les Perrières E Sauzet Pale, bright; crisp, smoky, dry, lean but assertive. *Aug 2000* ★★★★

Puligny-Montrachet, Les Referts Remoissenet Medium-pale yellow; good but rather four-square and unexciting. *May 2005* ★★★

THE FOLLOWING GOOD PULIGNY-MONTRACHETS tasted in 1997: **Garennes E Sauzet** far sweeter than expected, good flavour and aftertaste ★★★★; **Les Folatières Philippe Chavy** good colour; fragrant; crisp, good flavour and acidity ★★★; **Perrières Vincent Girardin** yellow; lean, rapier-like, high acidity, good length ★★★★; and **La Truffière Bernard Morey** nutty; rich, powerful ★★★★

AND THE BEST '95S AT THE OPENING TASTINGS IN 1997, not tasted since, all with a minimum of 4 stars and with excellent potential for drinking now: **Chassagne-Montrachet J-N Gagnard**; **Chassagne-Montrachet, Caillerets J-N Gagnard**; **Chassagne-Montrachet, Les Embrazées Bernard Morey**; **Chassagne-Montrachet, Les Caillerets Bernard Morey**; **Corton-Charlemagne Bonneau du Martray**; **Meursault, Clos Les Perrières Albert Grivault**; **Meursault, Genevrières F Jobard**; **Puligny-Montrachet, Garennes E Sauzet**; **Puligny-Montrachet, Perrières Vincent Girardin**; and **Puligny-Montrachet, La Truffière Bernard Morey**.

1996 ★★★★★

If the '95s were good, the '96s were even better, with extra dimensions, about as good as white burgundy can get. Very good growing conditions with low rainfall, long ripening period, healthy clusters with perfect sugar levels and high levels of acidity following the coldest September on record. Remember to stick to the best *négociants* and serious domaines. The perfect Chablis vintage but mainly best drunk fairly young.

Montrachet Parisot Very fragrant; some sweetness and softness, attractive but a touch of spice and oak. Far too young. *May 1999* (★★★★)?

Montrachet Thénard/Remoissenet Palish, green-tinged, very bright – it actually looked youthfully mouthwatering; nose surprisingly minty, oaky, good but only on the fringes of harmony; medium, fairly full-bodied though on the lean side, raw, pasty, pineappley acidity. *Sept 1998* (★★★★) *possibly 5 stars in due course.*

Bâtard-Montrachet DRC A rarely seen Bâtard from a few DRC-owned vines making a small amount for 'family consumption' (just one barrel). The most beautiful wine, at five years of age showing well. *Oct 2001* ★★★★★

Beaune L Latour A nice surprise: good colour; very attractive, interesting mint and oak nose; positive flavour, good acidity. *Feb 1999* ★★★, *or* ★★★★ *for its class*.

Beaune, Clos des Mouches, Blanc J Drouhin Most recently: still showing well, good palish yellow; deft, lightly oaky nose; medium dryness and body, well balanced, good flavour and acidity. *April 2004* ★★★★ *Now–2010*.

Chablis, Les Clos J-M Brocard Very bright; intriguing raspberry-tinged aroma; dry, good acidity, and, thank goodness, not a speciously oak-laden Chablis. *Feb 1999* ★★★ *Drink now*.

Chablis, Montée de Tonnerre Billaud-Simon Clearly a good vintage in Chablis too: palish; lovely nose; touch of attractive bottle age; dry, mouthfilling, good length. *Jan 2005* ★★★ *Drink soon*.

Chablis, Vaillons William Fèvre A very respectable *premier cru*. Pale yellow; very good nose, flavour and body. *Nov 2000* ★★★ *Drink up*.

Chablis, Valmur J-M Brocard Positively attractive and refreshing nose; not too dry, good flavour and length. *Last noted Aug 2000* ★★★ *Drink up*.

Chassagne-Montrachet Laguiche/Drouhin Bright and appealing, medium-pale yellow; lovely 'copybook' nose; touch of sweetness, fullish body, good, positive, pleasant oaky flavour and good length. *Nov 2004* ★★★★ *Drink now*.

Corton-Charlemagne Bonneau du Martray Gleaming pale gold; rich, fragrant, with very pronounced peach kernel scent; distinctly sweet, mouthfilling; richly flavoured and excellent acidity. *Nov 2003* ★★★★ *Now–2010*.

Corton-Charlemagne L Latour Good old standby. Most recently: showing its best with a lively fragrance; noted again as 'overall dry', firm, crisp, good length and finish. *Last tasted July 2000* ★★★★ *Now–2010*.

Meursault, Les Grands Charrons Michel Bouzereau Remarkably good. Fresh for a 10-year-old. *April 2006* ★★★★ *At peak*.

Puligny-Montrachet L Jadot Good colour, nose and delicious flavour, distinctly oaky, good acidity. *July 2001* ★★★ *Drink up*.

Puligny-Montrachet, Champ Gain L Jadot Low-keyed but good, straightforward flavour, balance and '96 acidity. *Jan 2004* ★★★ *Drink soon*.

A SELECTION OF OTHER GOOD '96 WHITES tasted mainly in their youth and all displaying life-enhancing acidity: **Chablis, Les Clos J-M Brocard**; **Chablis, Valmur J-M Brocard**; **Chablis, Vaillons William Fèvre** all three wines copybook Chablis; **Chassagne-Montrachet, Les Caillerets J-N Gagnard** almost as pale as many '96 Mosels; young, fruity; medium-sweet, lovely flavour, oaky, spicy, excellent weight ★★★★(★); **Mâcon-Clessé Jean Thévenot** idiosyncratic, without any touch of the usual *botrytis*, powerful, complete with good length and acidity; **Puligny-Montrachet L Latour** very good indeed. However, **Montrachet Parisot** and **Thénard** both wines lean and raw, needing at least 10, possibly 12 to 15 years of bottle age.

1997 ★★★★

Another very satisfactory vintage, thanks to a hot summer, riper grapes, somewhat richer wines which, though well balanced, lack the zestful acidity of the 1996s. They are not for the long haul.

Montrachet DRC Almost exotic, ripe and appealing in its youth. Not tasted since. *Nov 2000* ★★★★ *Probably at its peak now.*

Montrachet Ramonet The old master produced a fairly powerful wine with glorious flavour and good acidity. *March 2001, then* ★★★★(★) *Now–2010.*

Montrachet Thénard/Remoissenet Palish yellow; some sweetness, powerful, meaty, good vinosity and length. *Jan 2000* ★★★? *Now–2010.*

Chassagne-Montrachet, Les Chevenottes Marc Morey Pale; rich, meaty nose; full-flavoured and very attractive. *Jan 1999* ★★★★ *Drink up.*

Chassagne-Montrachet, La Maltroie Fontaine-Gagnard Pale yellow; rich, nutty nose and taste. Firm, teeth-gripping. *Jan 1999* ★★★(★) *Needs time.*

Chevalier-Montrachet Leflaive Very pale, lime-tinged; 'classic'; sweeter than expected, refined though still raw and youthful. Very dry finish. Will benefit from bottle age. *Dec 2000* ★★★(★)

Corton-Charlemagne Bonneau du Martray Total contrast to the '96. Pale, starbright, aroma of spearmint, creamy, kernelly; rich, still closed up, with surprisingly dry finish. *Nov 2003* ★★★★ *(just). Drink soon.*

Meursault Coche-Dury A minor masterpiece from a much-revered winemaker. Starbright; smoky-oaky, vanillin with a taste of lemon; delicious flavour, very acidic. Only a village wine? 'Copybook'. *Nov 2002* ★★★ *Drink soon.*

Puligny-Montrachet, Les Enseignières H Prudhon Palish yellow-green; very forthcoming, rich, nutty; refreshing acidity. *Aug 2002* ★★★ *Drink soon.*

1998 ★★★★

Despite a difficult growing season this was a remarkably good vintage for the whites. Some Côte de Beaune producers consider these wines superior to the '97s. Firm, elegant, fragrant wines for mid-term drinking.

Bâtard-Montrachet Sauzet Nutty nose; rich and powerful – as the buyer also has to be (over £1000 per dozen). *Jan 2000* ★★(★★★) *Now–2015.*

Beaune, Clos des Mouches Blanc J Drouhin Good colour, nose, flavour, balance and finish. 'Copybook'. *Jan 2005* ★★★(★) *Good now, more to come?*

Chablis, Les Grenouilles L Jadot Deep yellow; rich, oaky; medium-dry, soft – oak noted again. An astonishing contrast in style. Not wearing its maturity gracefully. *Oct 2006* ★★ *Drink up.*

Chablis, Montmain Louis Michel Very pale; flowery; touch of caramel but drinking well despite its age. *Oct 2006* ★★★ *Drink soon.*

Chassagne-Montrachet, Les Boudriottes J-N Gagnard Most recently: palish yellow; very discreet oak, whiff of lanolin; crisp, fairly dry and full-bodied, lovely flavour that opened up, good length and acidity. *Last tasted July 2006* ★★★★ *Drink up.*

Chassagne-Montrachet, Les Caillerets J-N Gagnard Melon yellow; discreet oak and lanolin; dry, full, positive flavour, length and acidity. Initially served too cold. Better as it reached room temperature. *Last tasted July 2006* ★★★(★) *Drink soon.*

Chassagne-Montrachet, Chevenottes M Colin-Déléger Yellow-gold; classic, understated, glorious fruit; rich, good length and acidity. *Sept 2002* ★★★★ *Drink up.*

Corton-Charlemagne Bonneau du Martray Classic. *Dec 2005* ★★★★ *Now–2010.*

Corton-Charlemagne L Jadot Nutty, spicy nose and flavour but far too oaky, with aftertaste of cloves. *Feb 2004* ★★ *More time?*

Puligny-Montrachet, Les Combettes E Sauzet Most recently: still pale; very fragrant; well balanced oak and acidity. Delicious. *Last tasted Aug 2003* ★★★★ *Drink up.*

Puligny-Montrachet, Les Referts Louis Carillon et Fils One of the oldest wine families in Burgundy, dating back to 1632. Gold highlights; dry, lovely flavour, good length and acidity. *Jan 2006* ★★★★ *Drink up.*

OUTSTANDING '98S tasted only in their youth: **Bâtard-Montrachet J-N Gagnard** expensive perfection (★★★★★); and **Beaune, Clos des Mouches J Drouhin** delicious flavour, perfect balance (★★★★)

1999 ★★★★

Another very good vintage. Burgundy has had a remarkable run of good vintages recently though the whites are perhaps not quite as remarkable as the reds. Thanks to late summer and early autumn sun, the grapes were fully mature with particularly high levels of sugar and, happily, substantial degrees of acidity. Many of the wines are drinking beautifully now and might benefit from further bottle age.

Le Montrachet DRC Medium-pale yellow with light gold highlights; high-honeyed, spicy with twist of lemon, after 30 minutes in the glass displaying indescribable richness and depth; fairly sweet, fullish body (13.5% alcohol), very rich, positive even assertive on the palate. Superb. *July 2003* ★★★★★ *Lovely now but another 10 years of unravelling scents and flavours.*

Montrachet H Boillot Very fragrant; very rich, smoky, vanillin flavour. 'A lot to it'. *Oct 2002* ★★★★ *Now–2010.*

Bâtard-Montrachet Lequin-Colin Very pale; very meaty; rich, tough finish. *Jan 2001* (★★★★) *Needs time.*

Bienvenues Bâtard-Montrachet Leflaive Palish; amazing scent, rarefied, exquisite; glorious flavour, subtle, so distinctive it is difficult to put into words – smoky, nutty, slightly spicy, with wonderful length and aftertaste. One of the most beautiful and original white burgundies ever tasted. Perfection. *April 2007* ★★★★★★ (6 stars). *Now–2015?*

Bienvenues-Bâtard-Montrachet Paul Perrot Rich, tangy nose; fairly sweet, very rich, very powerful. *Jan 2001.* Then (★★★★★) *I have always liked the power combined with elegance of Bienvenues. Probably approaching its peak.*

Chablis, Grenouilles L Jadot Vinified in oak. Palish, attractive colour; still young and appley; surprisingly sweet, full-bodied (13.5% alcohol), touch of blancmange. *Feb 2001* ★★★★ *Drink up.*

Chassagne-Montrachet, Les Caillerets J-N Gagnard Very pale; fragrant; a bit too sweet, fairly full-bodied but light in character, very flavoury but too oaky. *Jan 2004* ★★★ *Perhaps a bit more bottle age might sort it out, say now–2010.*

Chassagne-Montrachet, Les Vergers Ramonet A tiny 0.4-ha vineyard in 'the master's' 18-ha estate. As always, immaculate wine: very pale; lovely, gentle oaky fragrance; dry, fairly full body, excellent flavour and finish. *Sept 2003* ★★★★ *Now–2010.*

Corton-Charlemagne L Latour Fairly high alcohol by French standards – 14%. Most recently, from two jeroboams: palish yellow, shades of lime; very fragrant, classic nose; rich, fairly complex flavour. One of Latour's best. *Last tasted July 2005* ★★★★ *Now–2010.*

Meursault, Genevrière (*sic*) **Bouchard Père** '*Assez bien*' agreeable. *June 2005* ★★★ *Drink soon.*

Meursault, Genevrières Dom Louis Jadot Interesting to compare two major *négociants' premier cru* vineyard wines (see Bouchard above), albeit at a different stage of maturity. Jadot's far superior with rich, lovely flavour, touch of vanillin and glorious aftertaste. *Nov 2003* ★★★★ *Drink up.*

Meursault, Les Narvaux P Bouzereau Well made, undramatic, good length. *Nov 2003* ★★★ *Drink soon.*

Meursault, Perrières M Bouzereau And as a contrast to the Meursaults from the bigger companies above (Bouchard Père and Jadot), a perfect example of a grower producing minuscule amounts. Out of his 11-ha estate, Michel makes a tiny amount from his 0.05ha in the Perrières *premier cru* vineyard. Palish, good nose, flavour and length. Moderate alcohol. *March 2005* ★★★ *Drink now.*

Puligny-Montrachet L Latour A village wine agreeably well made by this well-known *négociant*. *July 2003* ★★★ *Drink now.*

St-Aubin Ramonet To demonstrate what Ramonet can do with one of the lesser villages of the Côte de Beaune: good colour; vanillin nose, almost blancmange; touch of sweetness, a rich, good, positive, flavoury mouthful, with refreshing acidity. *Nov 2003* ★★★ *Perfect now.*

Vougeot Blanc, Clos de Prieuré Dom de la Vougeraie A rarely encountered Côte de Nuits Blanc from a tiny 0.52ha plot. I am surprised but delighted that they bother to make and market the wine. But clearly they had in mind the Worshipful Company of Vintners, for I much enjoyed the wine at their 'Lentern Dinner'. *March 2006* ★★★ *Drink now.*

OTHER 4-STAR '99S noted in 2001: **Corton-Charlemagne Jadot's Dom des Héritiers** surprisingly sweet; full-bodied, rich; **Corton-Charlemagne Rapet** substantial, lovely; **Meursault, Charmes L Jadot** extraordinary, sweet; **Meursault, Genevrières L Jadot** also sweet and fragrant; **Puligny-Montrachet E Sauzet** pale and powerful; and **Puligny-Montrachet, Les Folatières L Jadot** immediately appealing, curiously lovely.

2000–2005

Allowing for the ever variable and unpredictable weather conditions in Burgundy, the future is more rosy thanks to improved quality and the seemingly insatiable demand for the best wines. Although the great growths of the Côte de Beaune are, and will remain, sublime, even more care and attention in the vineyard and more efficient winemaking could improve things further.

Burgundy continues to be let down by the part-time small producers whose vines are almost a sideline; by overproduction; and by the poor commercial wines produced by the large companies which open up the opportunities for New World Chardonnays to step in. Nevertheless, the future is bright.

VINTAGES AT A GLANCE
Outstanding ★★★★★ 2005
Very Good ★★★★ 2001 (V), 2002, 2003 (V), 2004
Good ★★★ 2000, 2001 (V), 2003 (V)

2000 ★★★

Not the easiest of weather conditions – the Mâconnais had the coldest, wettest July for 50 years and there were the usual September rains. The Côte de Beaune whites were picked after the reds (starting on 10 September), the grapes being dried by a cold north wind. Chablis, considerably to the north of the Côte d'Or, usually harvests later, and in 2000 started picking ripe and healthy grapes under a clear blue sky from 24 September. Most of the wines noted below were tasted in their youth but they should be drinking well now. Some classics will benefit from further bottle ageing.

Montrachet Laguiche/Drouhin Cask sample. Very pale, of course; low-keyed but very fragrant; sweet entry, powerful, youthful 'captured pineapple' flavour, teeth-gripping acidity. *Jan 2002*. Then (★★★★), now ★★(★★)

Montrachet L Jadot Almost colourless; nutty; splendid wine, notable persistence of flavour – worth having a stop watch, good acidity. Great potential. *Jan 2002*. Now ★★(★)

Le Montrachet DRC Medium-yellow gold; very fragrant, with oaky, smoky nose and flavour. Sweet, balanced by good acidity, full, rich, dry finish. *Sept 2004* ★★(★★) Now–2016.

Bâtard-Montrachet Blain-Gagnard Basically good flavour, weight and balance. Whiff of peach kernels on the finish. *July 2004* ★★(★) Now–2012.

Bâtard-Montrachet L Jadot Extremely pale; soft mid fruit, masking acidity. Impressive. *Feb 2002*. Now ★★★(★)

Bâtard-Montrachet Vincent & François Jouard Very impressive nose and taste though I did not take to its touch of peach kernels. With Bâtard power. *Jan 2002*. Now ★★★(★) *Should turn out well*.

Bâtard-Montrachet Ch de la Maltroye Assertive, impressive but far too much oak. *Jan 2002*. Now ★★(★)

Beaune, Clos des Mouches Blanc Drouhin Youthful pineapple; touch of sweetness, rich, soft, fullish body and oaky fruit. A nice wine. *Jan 2002* ★★★ *Drink up*.

Bienvenues-Bâtard-Montrachet Paul Pernot (The Pernot family regularly sell their white grapes from a dozen small parcels dotted around the Côte de Beaune to Drouhin.) Lean and nutty. Needs time to show its 'very welcome' charm. *Jan 2002*. Now ★★(★)

Chablis, Grenouilles L Jadot Vinified in oak. Slightly more 'meaty' than Les Preuses, whiff of violets; soft, oaky, lemon-like acidity. Attractive. *Feb 2002* ★★★ *Drink up*.

Chablis, Les Preuses L Jadot Vinified in oak. Almost colourless though with a slight stain of youthful green; an immediacy of fruit and vanilla; pleasantly fruity entry, young but not raw, pineapple and a good deal of oaky vanilla. Good acidity. *Feb 2002* ★★★ *Drink soon*.

Chassagne-Montrachet, Les Caillerets Guy Amiot Tinge of straw; lean, acidity a bit tinny. I queried its length. *Jan 2002* ★★(★)? *Now–2010.*

Chassagne-Montrachet, Les Caillerets J-N Gagnard Lemon gold; sweet, full, rich, buttery nose; rich, chewy, assertive. Dry finish. *July 2004* ★★★(★) *Now–2010.*

Chassagne-Montrachet, Les Champs Gains, Vieilles Vignes L & F Juard Several notes. Lovely, fragrant nose with underlying gooseberry-like acidity; good, rich, mouthfilling flavour with oaky end taste and good acidity. *Last tasted May 2007* ★★★(★) *Now–2010.*

Chassagne-Montrachet, Les Chaumes, Clos de la Truffière Vincent & François Jouard Virtually colourless; dry, good length and acidity. *Jan 2002* (★★★★) *Good future.*

Chassagne-Montrachet, Grandes Ruchottes Ch de la Maltroye Slightly minty, nutty nose and flavour. Medium-dry, good length. *Jan 2002* ★★★ *Ready now.*

Chassagne-Montrachet, Clos du Ch de la Maltroye Ch de la Maltroye (Monopole) Rich nose and flavour, powerful, oaky. *Jan 2002. Now* ★★(★) *2010–2015.*

Chassagne-Montrachet, Morgeot, Clos de la Chapelle Duc de Magenta/L Jadot Jadot bought the Magenta domaine in 1985. Pale, hint of lemon; low-keyed, young, pineappley nose; classic, attractive, oaky, dry finish. Needs bottle age. *Oct 2005* ★(★★)? *2010–2015.*

Chassagne-Montrachet, En Virondot Marc Morey A great whoosh of floral, oaky fragrance; very distinctive, curious flavour, good weight and acidity. *July 2004* ★★★(★) *Now–2010.*

Chevalier-Montrachet, Les Demoiselles Héritiers Jadot Deliciously forthcoming, oaky; medium-sweet – as white wine goes – lean and fit, good acidity. *Feb 2002* ★★★(★) *Now–2010.*

Corton Blanc Chandon de Briailles Unusual, not from the Charlemagne vines but from three other Corton vineyards. Unfiltered and not starbright; rich, 'chewy' nose, touch of lemon and oak; fairly sweet, medium body yet mouthfilling and attractive. *July 2004* ★★★ *Drink soon.*

Corton-Charlemagne Bonneau du Martray Low-keyed; slightly sweet, soft, light style for Corton. Would benefit from more bottle age. *Nov 2003* ★★(★) *Now–2010.*

Corton-Charlemagne J Drouhin Deep, fairly rich, meaty/fruity, unknit; fairly full-bodied, good flavour that needs sorting out. Lovely acidity. *Jan 2002, then* (★★★★) *Now should be well knit* ★★★(★)

Corton-Charlemagne Faiveley Pale; nutty, oaky; very good flavour but on the lean side for Charlemagne, a deft touch of vanillin, dry acidic finish. *Nov 2003* ★★(★) *Now–2012.*

Corton-Charlemagne Héritiers Jadot Very meaty; medium-sweet, full, soft, nutty. What Corton-Charlemagne is all about. *Feb 2002* (★★★★★) *2010–2020.*

Criots-Bâtard-Montrachet Jadot The only *grand cru* vineyard wholly within the commune of Chassagne, its pale stony soil producing a wine with more delicacy than the broad-shouldered Bâtard-Montrachet. Very pale; crusty; very mouthfilling, touch of lemon-like acidity, dry finish. *Feb 2002* (★★★★) *2010–2015.*

Meursault Joseph Matrot A typically good village wine from this relatively extensive family domaine. Palish, starbright; very good nose though whiff of vanillin suggests oak though Matrot does not use new oak for his *1er cru* wines. Attractive flavour and good acidity. *Feb 2005* ★★★ *Drink up.*

Meursault, Blagny Gérard Thomas A perfect summer garden party drink. Extremely agreeable. *Aug 2006* ★★★ *Now–2010.*

Meursault, Charmes Jadot Bought from contract growers from a vineyard with richer and heavier soil than Meursault-Perrières, further up the slope. Pale; touch of lemon and oak; some richness, touch of oak and mouth-drying acidity. *Feb 2002* ★★★ *Should be drinking well now.*

Pouilly-Fuissé, Ch Fuissé Vincent As Pouilly-Fuissé should be drunk young and fresh, it does not usually feature in my published notes. However, Vincent's wines are consistently first rate. This 2000 has an excellent flavour, complete and, though drinking well, will develop further, for up to 10 years. *July 2003* ★★★ *Drink up.*

Puligny-Montrachet, Clavoillon Leflaive Medium-pale yellow; 'meaty' for Puligny, vanillin from roughly ⅓ new oak; medium-dry, fairly full-bodied, some softness and richness – not the usual Leflaive crisp steeliness. Good length. *July 2004* ★★★★ *Drink soon.*

Puligny-Montrachet, Les Enseignières H Prudhon Very pale, lovely sheen; nutty; penetrating, good acidity. *Sept 2005* ★★★ *Drink up.*

Puligny-Montrachet, Les Folatières J Drouhin Very pale; touch of gooseberry-like acidity on nose which translated to grapefruit on the palate. Lovely flavour, good length, smoky-oaky aftertaste. *Jan 2002* ★★★(★) *Now–2010.*

Puligny-Montrachet, Les Folatières L Jadot Almost colourless; broad, open, crusty (bread) nose with a slight whiff of celluloid; rich, well integrated oak, very hard acidic dry finish. *Feb 2002 Potential* ★★★★?

Puligny-Montrachet, Clos de la Garenne Duc de Magenta (Monopole.) Virtually colourless; low-keyed, crisp, vanilla; broader, richer style, very good flavour and length. *Feb 2002* (★★★) *Good wine and needs time.*

Puligny-Montrachet, Les Referts Louis Carillon et Fils Positive yellow; deep, characteristic smoky-oaky nose; medium-dry to very dry acidic finish, crisp, good flavour. *July 2004* ★★(★★) *Now–2020.*

Puligny-Montrachet, Les Referts L Jadot Very pale; deliciously fragrant, crisp, oaky nose, flavour and aftertaste. Soft yet lean. *Feb 2002* ★★★ *Drink soon.*

Puligny-Montrachet, Clos St-Jean Blanc Michel Niéllon A minute 0.15ha parcel, in a small 5-ha estate. Pale gold; sweet, whiff of sulphur?; very sweet, rich yet with acidic finish. *Oct 2005* ★★★ *Lovely now but will keep.*

2001 ★★★ to ★★★★

An irregular vintage, with a wet, cool and cloudy season. After a satisfactory start in the Côte de Beaune the growing season was interrupted by frosts. Howver, the summer was warm ending with considerable heat and thunderstorms in late August. Early September was cool and wet but conditions improved for a satisfactory harvest.

On the whole, the whites were soft and easy and should have been consumed by now. However, the top estates, thanks to hard work in their vineyards, produced attractive and well balanced wines.

Bâtard-Montrachet Leflaive Palish; very good, nutty, characterful; lovely wine. *June 2005* ★★★★ *Now–2010.*

Chassagne-Montrachet M Niéllon Delicious flavour, weight and balance. *Oct 2005* ★★★ *Drink up.*

Chassagne-Montrachet, Morgeot, Clos de la Chapelle Duc de Magenta/Jadot Small crop. Fairly pale; rich, touch of vanillin; medium-dry, good flavour, mouthfilling (never chaptalised, always naturally over 13% alcohol), dry finish, stylish wine. *Oct 2005* ★★★★ *Drink soon.*

Corton-Charlemagne Bonneau du Martray Very pale; lovely, young, pineappley, with underlying cherry, peach kernel nose; sweet, rich, very flavoury, some puppy fat. More exuberant than the 2000. *Nov 2003* ★★★★ *Now–2010.*

Corton-Charlemagne Coche-Dury From the Meursault master's small parcel of vines in the Corton *grand cru*, harvested by 22 pickers making an early start and finishing by 11am! Fragrant, minerally, vanilla (50% new oak) and youthful pineapple; rich, chewy, powerful, good length. *Oct 2005* ★★★(★) *Now–2010.*

Meursault, Clos de la Barre Comtes Lafon Lovely colour; very good nose opening up deliciously in the glass; equally good flavour but needing more bottle age. *Oct 2005* ★★★(★)? *Now–2010.*

Meursault, Les Genevrières, Tasteviné Excellent nose, flavour and refreshing acidity. *At Ch de Clos Vougeot, Nov 2006* ★★★★ *Perfect now.*

Meursault, Perrières Coche-Dury Fairly pale; very distinctive, earthy, meaty style; medium-sweet, mouthfilling, good finish. Higher in alcohol than 2000 or 1999. Typical of vineyard and grower. *Oct 2005* ★★★★ *Now–2010.*

Meursault, Santenots Marquis d'Angerville Medium-pale; lovely sheen; sweet, rich, delicious flavour, excellent acidity. *Oct 2005* ★★★★ *Now–2010.*

Puligny-Montrachet Leflaive Perfect colour; copybook nose and flavour. Effortless. *June 2006* ★★★★ *But drink soon.*

2002 ★★★★

A very good vintage. Even the lesser whites are attractive and the top estates produced wine of real quality with an aromatic vigour, richness and concentration, worthy of bottle ageing.

Le Montrachet Leflaive From just 11 rows of vines purchased in 1991: 290 bottles in two small casks. Cask sample. Very pale, near to colourless; rich, creamy – hard to pin down; fairly sweet, full, rich with touch of lemon on the lips. *March 2003* (★★★★) *2010–2015?*

Bâtard-Montrachet L Latour Hard, minerally nose; positive, still youthful pineappley nose. Hard finish. *May 2006* ★★(★) *Now–2012.*

Bâtard-Montrachet Leflaive Lovely pale yellow; steely yet rich, youthful pineapple, spicy, squeeze of lemon; distinctly sweet, rich, full-bodied (circa 14% alcohol), mouthfilling. Good length and aftertaste. A 'serious' wine with a splendid future. *March 2003* (★★★★) *2010–2015.*

Beaune Blanc J Drouhin An impressive village wine. Hefty style, oak; better on palate, delicious, full-flavoured, highish alcohol, good acidity. *May 2006* ★★★ *Now–2020.*

Bienvenues-Bâtard-Montrachet Leflaive From 40–45 year old vines adjacent to Leflaive's Bâtard. Very pale; initially low-keyed but then noting slightly nutty grapiness and considerable depth; fairly dry, spicy. Interesting contrast of style. *March 2003* ★★★★ *Now–2012.*

Chassagne-Montrachet L Jadot A well made village wine; rich, refreshing aroma; very dry, delicious flavour, good acidity. *May 2006* ★★★ *Drink soon.*

Chassagne-Montrachet, Morgeot, Clos de la Chapelle Duc de Magenta/Jadot Medium sweetness, medium- to full-bodied (13.5% alcohol), touch of bitterness on the finish. Needs bottle age. *Oct 2005* ★★★(★) *Now–2012.*

Chassagne-Montrachet, en Virandot Marc Morey Very pale; fragrant; dry, crisp, delicious. *Dec 2005* ★★★ *Now–2010.*

Chevalier-Montrachet Leflaive Fragrant, touch of lemon, greengage and quince; amazingly sweet, rich, full-bodied (14% alcohol) yet wearing this almost unobtrusively. A stunning future. *March 2003* ★★(★★★) *Now–2015.*

Corton-Charlemagne Bonneau du Martray Very pale; youthful, hard, pineappley, slightly spicy nose. Delicious, slightly spicy flavour. Dry. *Last tasted May 2006* (★★★★) *2010–2015.*

Puligny-Montrachet Leflaive Village wine from the La Rue aux Vaches vineyard and something of a Leflaive novelty. Fragrant vanilla and lemon; surprisingly sweet, good flavour and acidity. *March 2003* ★★★ *Drink up.*

Puligny-Montrachet, Clavoillon Leflaive Metallic, spicy yet delicate; sweet, good length, delicious. *March 2003* ★★★★ *Now–2010.*

Puligny-Montrachet, Les Combettes Leflaive Old vines, very small grapes. Nose reminded me of lemon-meringue; sweet, rich, mouthfilling. *March 2003* ★★★(★) *Now–2012.*

Puligny-Montrachet, Les Folatières Leflaive Very pale yellow; light, fragrant, steely, minerally, then almost creamy; sweet, chewy, assertive, full flavour, moderate weight (13.3% alcohol) yet 'hot' finish. *March 2003* ★★(★★) *2009-2012.*

Puligny-Montrachet, Les Perrières Jomain A good example of the change in marketing. The family used to sell to *négociants*, the two sons now market their wine as domaine-bottled. Medium-pale yellow; smoky-oaky, like a burnt match, held and developed well; dry yet buttery, almost New World. Seemed heftier than the 13% alcohol on the label. *April 2005* ★★★ *Drink soon.*

Puligny-Montrachet, Les Pucelles Leflaive Pale; flowery, but I will not be popular by noting a whiff of kerosene, associated more with Riesling than Chardonnay! Sweet, rich, complete. Lovely wine. *March 2003* ★★★★ *Now–2010.*

2003 ★★★ to ★★★★

Thanks to a very hot summer and a real heatwave in July, July and August the whites are untypical, very rich, almost exotic. The harvest for white burgundy was over by 1 September. The best wines are fairly concentrated, high in alcohol and may well prove to have a long life ahead of them, though the less than best should be drunk soon.

With white burgundies as rich as the '03s, serve them cooler than normal (most top white burgundies are better at, or near, room temperature – never chilled, as with lesser-quality white wines).

Le Montrachet Laguiche/Drouhin Cask sample. Sweet, fabulous flavour and length. *Jan 2005* (★★★★) *2010–2016?*

Bâtard-Montrachet J-N Gagnard Very nutty (walnuts), nose and flavour; medium-sweet, fairly assertive. Promising wine. *Jan 2005* (★★★★) *2010-2015.*

Bâtard-Montrachet Leflaive Still youthful. Delicious nose and flavour, very rich, huge by Leflaive's standards, oaky. *March 2006* ★★(★★) *2009-2012*.

Beaune, Clos des Mouches Blanc Drouhin Very little colour; positive character, sweet, nutty – almost biscuity, delicious. *Jan 2005* ★★★ *Now–2010*.

Chablis, St-Martin Laroche Drinking very pleasantly. Adequate acidity. *July 2006* ★★★ *Drink up*.

Chassagne-Montrachet, Les Caillerets J-N Gagnard Nutty, delicious flavour. *Jan 2005* ★★★ *Drink soon*.

Chassagne-Montrachet, Clos de la Maltroie Michel Niéllon Picked at the end of August. Fairly pale, lemon-tinged; vanillin, almost sickly sweet nose but good depth; medium-dry, on the lean side, minerally, a bit of an end bite. Jury out. *Oct 2005* ★★(★) *Now–2010?*

Chassagne-Montrachet, Morgeot P Colin Overoaked scented nose and palate. 2003 ripeness and softness. Disappointing. *Oct 2006* ★★★ *(just). Drink soon*.

Chassagne-Montrachet, Morgeot, Vieilles Vignes V Girardin Exceedingly pale, usually the sign of very clean, unblemished grapes, but could be CO_2; lightly nutty nose; dry, flowery, spicy, attractive wine. *Jan 2005* ★★(★) *Now–2010*.

Chassagne-Montrachet, Morgeot, Clos de la Chapelle Duc de Magenta/Jadot Still on its lees. Sweet, soft, very rich, oaky, complete. *Oct 2005* ★★(★) *Now–2010*.

Corton-Charlemagne Bonneau du Martray Still hard, rather spicy. Distinctive, more of a New World style. *Last tasted May 2006* ★★★? *Will be interesting to follow its development. Now–2012*.

Meursault, Clos de la Barre Comtes Lafon Very little colour; fragrant, youthful, pineapply aroma and flavour. Distinctly sweet. An attractive wine. *March 2006* ★★(★★) *Now–2012*.

Meursault, Les Charmes V Girardin Slightly steely, not remotely a buttery Meursault; delicious flavour, crisp acidity. *Jan 2006* ★★★★ *Drink soon*.

Meursault, Clos du Cromin Bitouzet-Prieur From a 0.75-ha parcel of vines in a small 1-ha family domaine. Little colour; nose not very distinctive; medium-dry, crisp, adequate. Appropriately modestly priced. *Feb 2006* ★★ *Drink soon*.

Meursault, Les Narvaux V Girardin Spicy, youthful, very slight touch of caramel, quite a lot to it. *Jan 2005* ★★(★) *Drink soon*.

Meursault, Clos des Perrières A Grivault Very pale; positive nose and flavour, crisp, good acidity. *Jan 2005* ★★★ *Now–2010*.

Meursault, Les Perrières Bitouzet-Prieur A tiny parcel (0.27ha). Pale; touch of mint; medium-sweet; fairly rich, full and attractive. Hard finish. Modestly priced but appealing. *Feb 2006* ★★★ *Drink soon*.

Meursault, Les Perrières Yves Boyer-Martenot Another typically small parcel of vines (0.63ha in an 8.5-ha family estate). Flowery; medium-dry, full-flavoured. *Jan 2005* ★★★ *Now–2010*.

Nuits-St-Georges, Jeunes Vignes du Clos de L'Arlot Dom de l'Arlot A rarely seen Côte de Nuits white, from 1ha of vines in the ancient 14-ha Arlot domaine at the southern end of the Côte de Nuits, and enjoying a renaissance. Very pale; immature pineappley aroma; very sweet, delicious flavour, oaky finish. *Jan 2005* (★★★) *Now-2010?*

Pommard, Clos Blanc A Grivault Extremely pale; positive, crisp, good flavour and acidity. *Jan 2005* (★★★) *Now–2010.*

Puligny-Montrachet, Champ Canet Louis Carillon et Fils Pale; oaky-smoky, depth; medium-dry, attractive, ripe, slight whiff of caramel. *Oct 2006* ★★★ *Drink soon.*

Puligny-Montrachet, Les Folatières E Sauzet Lovely young fruit, delicious flavour. *Jan 2005* ★★(★★) *Now–2010.*

Puligny-Montrachet, Clos de La Garenne Duc de Magenta/Jadot Curious, very oaky nose and palate. Fairly dry. Jury out. *April 2006* ★★ *Would like to retaste.*

2004 ★★★★

A total contrast to 2003. A return to normal – variable weather conditions and its attendant problems. A cool spring was followed by a speedy and successful flowering which ensured a potentially large crop. The summer was indifferent and August was cool with heavy rain to swell the abundant, unripe grapes. Happily, a sunny September saved the day, those estates picking late to reduce the malic acid made some excellent wines.

Montrachet L Jadot Pale colour; nutty nose and flavour. Medium-sweet, lovely, crisp, perfect weight; good length and excellent finish. *Jan 2006* ★★(★★★) *2010–2015.*

Bâtard-Montrachet E Sauzet Positive, minerally; classic, powerful, mouthfilling. *Jan 2006* (★★★★★) *2010–2015.*

Chablis, Fourchaume Durup Pleasant surprise: delicious, dry, positive, excellent acidity. *May 2006* ★★★ *Drink soon.*

Chassagne-Montrachet, Abbaye de Morgeot, Clos de la Chapelle Duc de Magenta/Jadot (Monopole.) Though fragrant, still immature with pineapple husk aroma; dry, good flavour, body, length and acidity. *Last tasted Jan 2006* ★★(★★) *Now–2012.*

Chassagne-Montrachet, Clos de la Maltroie Michel Niéllon Lovely colour, bright and appealing; creamy vanilla; fairly sweet, rich style, very agreeable. *Oct 2005* ★(★★★) *Now–2010.*

Chassagne-Montrachet, Clos St-Jean Michel Niéllon Fulsome, almost specious fragrance and flavour. Medium-sweet, positive, acidic finish. Needs time. *Oct 2005* ★★(★★) *Now–2012.*

Chevalier-Montrachet Bouchard Père Pale; stylish, touch of sweetness, good flavour and acidity. *Jan 2006* ★★(★★) *Now–2012.*

Chevalier-Montrachet, Les Demoiselles Jadot A 1.04-ha vineyard bought in 1794 by the first members of the Jadot family to arrive in Beaune from Belgium. Very pale, tinge of lime; immediate fragrance; very good, vibrant flavour and acidity. *Jan 2006* ★★(★★★) *2009–2015.*

Corton-Charlemagne Bouchard Père Planted high, facing the village of Ladoix and grapes mature slowly here. Very fragrant; dry, fairly full-bodied, very good flavour and finish. *Jan 2006* ★★(★★) *Now–2012.*

Corton-Charlemagne Coche-Dury Small parcel of vines between Louis Latour's and Bonneau du Martray's major holdings. Just four barrels made in 2004. A rich, complex aroma; fairly sweet, firm, with lemon-like acidity. *Oct 2005* (★★★★) *2009–2015.*

Corton-Charlemagne Héritiers Jadot Two differing sample bottles, the first pale yellow and slightly cloudy; low-keyed, faintly kernally nose; interesting, correct weight, good length but quite right. The second bottle very pale, bright; fresher nose and lovely flavour. *Jan 2006. At best* ★★★ *Now–2012.*

Meursault, Caillerets Coche-Dury Extremely pale; very minerally; creamy, spicy almost exotic clove-like flavour. *Oct 2005* ★★(★★) *Now–2010.*

Meursault, Charmes François Mikulski The best of a group of (expensive) Meursaults, including Genevrières and Poruzots, from a producer new to me: fragrant but steely for a Meursault; good flavour, acidity and aftertaste. *Oct 2006* ★★(★) *Now–2012.*

Meursault, Chevalières Coche-Dury Nutty; glorious, pure, mouthfilling, perfect balance, lovely wine. *Oct 2005* ★★★★(★) *Now–2012.*

Meursault, Genevrières Coche-Dury Almost colourless; flowery, hazelnuts, distinctive; fairly sweet and very rich, lovely texture, good length, complete. Good examples of the 'Meursault master's' art. *Oct 2005* ★★★★(★) *2009–2015.*

Meursault, Genevrières Louis Jadot Very pale; fragrant; youthful pineapple, lemon and vanilla; medium-sweet, mouthfilling, delicious. *Jan 2006* ★★★★ *Now–2012.*

Meursault, Les Narvaux Coche-Dury Virtually colourless; very 'green', almost Sauvignon Blanc-like acidity, flowery, minerally; medium-sweet entry, lean, steely, fragrant, hard acidic finish. *Oct 2005* ★★(★★) *Now–2012.*

Meursault, Les Bouchères Bouchard Père Extremely pale; nutty; vibrant, delicious *Tasted Jan 2006* ★★★(★) *Now–2012.*

Meursault, Perrières Bouchard Père Rocky limestone soil. Very fragrant, good finish *Tasted Jan 2006* ★★★★ *Now–2012.*

Meursault, Perrières Dessus Coche-Dury Very pale; minerally, exuding glorious fragrance, even creamy vanilla; rich, wonderful texture, spicy, mouthfilling. *Oct 2005* ★★★(★★) *2009–2015.*

Morey-St-Denis Blanc, Mont Luisants Dujac Very pale; distinctive, lovely; good flavour and acidity. *Oct 2006* ★★★(★) *Crisp now, more to come.*

Puligny-Montrachet, Chalumeaux Bouchard Père Dry yet rich and assertive. *Jan 2006* ★★★ *Now–2012.*

Puligny-Montrachet, Champ Gain Dom Gagey/Jadot Youthful pineapple and vanilla; fairly dry, positive, good length. *Jan 2006* ★★(★★) *Now–2012.*

Puligny-Montrachet, Les Folatières Jadot Good nose, flavour and length. *Jan 2006* ★★(★★) *Now–2012.*

Puligny-Montrachet, Les Folatières E Sauzet Extremely pale; good, positive, whiff of vanillin; medium-sweet, attractive, soft yet acidic. *Jan 2006* ★★★★ *Now–2012.*

Puligny-Montrachet, Clos de la Garenne Duc de Magenta/Jadot A 2-ha 'monopole'. Lively, spicy; medium-dry, rich, good flavour and finish. *Jan 2006* ★★★★ *Now–2012.*

Puligny-Montrachet, Rougeots Coche-Dury Marlstone soil, deep roots. Minerally nose, whiff of lemon; steely, lovely long finish. Class act as usual. *Tasted Oct 2006* ★★(★★) *2010–2015.*

Puligny-Montrachet, En Seigneures Dessus Coche-Dury Adjoining Bâtard-Montrachet. Delicious, fragrant, very dry finish. *Tasted Oct 2006* ★★★(★) *Now–2010.*

2005 ★★★★★

A most attractive, well balanced vintage, clearly one of the best for the past 20 years and with much in common with '85. I visited some of the leading estates just after the harvest in October and briefly in November. Without exception, the growers were happy with the growing season and the fledgling quality of their wines but did not want it to be talked up as most producers still had 2004s to sell.

The crucial flowering was under favourable conditions though there was some *coulure* and *millerandage* which has the effect of reducing potential crop yields. The commune of Chassagne and vineyards in its immediate vicinity were hit by a hailstorm in July, severely affecting the crop. Otherwise the summer was well-nigh perfect though dry, as in other parts of France, and the harvest was early and successful. The lesser 2005 white burgundies will provide attractive early drinking, the *premier cru* whites for mid-term, say from now–2012, the *grands crus* from 2010–2017 and Montrachet up to 2025.

Chablis, Vaillons William Fevre Almost colourless; good aroma, flavour and dept. Firm. Classic. Preferred to the Montmain which I found too acidic. *Oct 2006* ★★★ *Now–2010*.

HOSPICES DE BEAUNE '05S: At the end of October 2005 I tasted a wide range of '05s in cask in the cellars of the Hospices de Beaune. The whites were, unsurprisingly, still in a milky state though rich and delicious even in their infancy. I rated highly **Meursault-Genevrières, Cuvée Philippe de Bon; Meursault-Charmes, Cuvée Bahezre de Lanlay; Corton-Charlemagne Cuvée François de Salins; and Corton-Charlemagne, Cuvée Charlotte Dumay; and Bâtard-Montrachet, Cuvée Dames de Flandres.**

Rhône

Describing the Rhône as one single wine region is misleading because there is a geographical and frequently climatic north–south divide. The steep slopes of the Côte-Rôtie *appellation* commence on the right bank of the river at Vienne, not far south of Lyon, whereas way down-river, south of Orange, the vineyards of Châteauneuf-du-Pape spread themselves on a broad plain with a hot, near-Provençal climate. In the North, from Côte-Rôtie south to Hermitage, the reds are usually made from one variety, Syrah, whereas in the South, though Grenache is the dominant red grape, in Châteauneuf up to 13 different varieties are permitted in the blend. The following notes are entirely concerned with red wines – virtually all the Rhône whites are best consumed young and fresh.

Outstanding vintages
1929, 1945, 1949, 1952 (South only), 1959, 1961, 1969 (North only), 1970 (South only), 1971 (North only), 1978, 1983, 1985, 1989 (South only), 1990, 1995 (South only), 1998, 1999 (North only), 2005

A short history

The Romans, invading Gaul, were the first to establish vineyards in the Rhône Valley. An early high period for the wines, much esteemed by the English, was between the mid-18th and mid-19th centuries, Coti Roti (Côte Rôtie) and Hermitage appearing in James Christie's catalogues as early as 1768 and 1773. Hermitage, highly regarded for its quality and reliability, was not infrequently transported in barrels to Bordeaux to prop up weak vintages there. There were even reports of Lafite being 'hermitaged' and as late as 1850 'Hermitage blended with claret' appeared in a Christie's catalogue.

The next century, as far as the British were concerned, was uneventful, if not bleak, as claret increased its hold on the market. Though there were some excellent vintages between World Wars One and Two, notably 1929, 1934 and 1937, interest in good Rhône wines was desultory.

1945–1977

It is significant that though there were some excellent post-war vintages in the Rhône, Côte-Rôtie and the adjacent appellation for white wine, Condrieu, were virtually non-existent because depressed market conditions made grape-growing and harvesting on the steep slopes uneconomical. Well into the 1960s, even the best wines of Hermitage were cheap, and the name of Châteauneuf-du-Pape was as popular, though perhaps not as abused, as 'Nuits-St-Georges' which, for the British, epitomised burgundy. Importantly, until well into the 1970s, few of even the best Rhône wines were bought for keeping.

RED VINTAGES AT A GLANCE

NORTHERN RHÔNE (CORNAS, CÔTE-RÔTIE, CROZES-HERMITAGE, HERMITAGE, ST-JOSEPH)

Outstanding ★★★★★ 1929, 1945, 1949, 1959, 1961, 1969, 1971
Very Good ★★★★ 1933, 1937, 1943, 1947, 1952, 1953, 1955, 1957, 1962, 1964, 1966, 1967, 1970, 1972 (v) (except Côte-Rôtie)
Good ★★★ 1934, 1942, 1976 (v)

SOUTHERN RHÔNE (MAINLY CHÂTEAUNEUF-DU-PAPE)

Outstanding ★★★★★ 1929, 1945, 1949, 1952, 1959, 1961, 1970
Very Good ★★★★ 1934, 1937, 1947, 1955, 1957, 1962, 1964, 1967, 1969, 1971
Good ★★★ 1939, 1944, 1953, 1966, 1972 (v)

1945 ★★★★★
Great vintage, small production. Hermitage was particularly fine. Magnificent in the mid-1970s; but not – alas – tasted since.

1947 ★★★★
Hot vintage, ripe, alcoholic, voluptuous. No recent notes.
Hermitage, Rochefine Jaboulet-Vercherre Seemingly ageless, great charm 1989 ★★★

1949 ★★★★★
Well-nigh perfect growing season throughout the Rhône Valley. The best-kept wines could still be excellent. None tasted recently.
Hermitage, La Chapelle Jaboulet Perfect. *1985* ★★★★★

1961 ★★★★★
A great vintage, on a par with 1945 and, arguably, unsurpassed.
Hermitage, La Chapelle Jaboulet Most recently a magnum. Still fairly deep; very distinctive bouquet, warm, 'autumn leaves'; very sweet, lovely flesh, delicious flavour, modest alcohol (13%), great length. A sensational grand finale at a tasting of great '61 clarets. Extraordinarily modestly priced in the mid-1960s, priceless now. *Last tasted Oct 2006* ★★★★★

1969–1971
Some 5-star wines, especially Hermitage. The best can still be excellent.

1972–1977
All largely mediocre vintages.

1978–1999

The outstanding 1978 vintage gave the Rhône a kick start. One of the pioneer specialist Rhône merchants was the British dentist, Robin Yapp. Then, thanks largely to Marcel Guigal, Côte-Rôtie was revived, its resurgence publicised by the American critic, Robert Parker.

RED VINTAGES AT A GLANCE
NORTHERN RHÔNE (CORNAS, CÔTE-RÔTIE, CROZES-HERMITAGE, HERMITAGE, ST-JOSEPH)
Outstanding ★★★★★ 1978, 1983, 1985, 1990, 1998, 1999
Very Good ★★★★ 1979, 1982, 1988, 1989, 1992, 1995, 1996 (v)
Good ★★★ 1981 (v), 1991, 1997
SOUTHERN RHÔNE (MAINLY CHÂTEAUNEUF-DU-PAPE)
Outstanding ★★★★★ 1978, 1983, 1985, 1989, 1990, 1995, 1998
Very Good ★★★★ 1982, 1999
Good ★★★ 1979, 1980, 1981 (v), 1986, 1988, 1992, 1996 (v), 1997

1978 ★★★★★
Despite the difficult weather conditions during the spring and summer, this was unquestionably a great Rhône vintage, regarded as the best since 1911, especially for Hermitage and Côte-Rôtie in the North and Châteauneuf-du-Pape in the South. It heralded a much-welcomed renaissance for the region's wines.
Châteauneuf-du-Pape, Ch de Beaucastel Perrin Now fully mature, ripe, singed bouquet; sweet, showing its age. *Last tasted May 2001* ★★★★ *Drink soon.*
Châteauneuf-du-Pape, Ch Rayas Medium-deep, soft ruby; singed – mature, hot-vintage bouquet; attractive fruit and flavour. *Tasted May 2001* ★★★★★ *Time in hand.*
Châteauneuf-du-Pape J Vidal Fleury Good level and cork but past its best, nose sweet but cracking up; dry, faded fruit, tart finish. *May 2005. Over the hill.*
Côte-Rôtie, Brune et Blonde Guigal Medium-deep, soft, mature appearance; sweet, slightly singed, harmonious bouquet; sweet, soft, delicious flavour when pre-tasted but less impressive and showing its age at table. *Last tasted Oct 2003. Probably at its* ★★★★ *best in the 1990s.*

Côte-Rôtie, Les Jumelles Jaboulet In magnum, medium-deep and mature; seemed overripe but settled down pleasantly. Rich, full, lovely. *Last tasted Oct 1998* ★★★★★

Côte-Rôtie, La Landonne Guigal First vintage from this 2-ha vineyard. Most recently, from the estate, disappointing with 'cheesy' nose, powerful but tired. *Last tasted Feb 2005. At best* ★★★★★*, now* ★★

Côte-Rôtie, La Mouline Guigal In 1988: close knit, harmonious; rich, complex and concentrated. Tannin laden. Glorious fruit. Alas, I next had the misfortune of tasting this in the wrong order and in the wrong ambience: rather raw and tasteless after Ch d'Yquem. *Last tasted Feb 1997. At its best* ★★★★★

Hermitage Guigal Fairly deep, rich; figgy, smoky; medium-sweet, rich, ripe, still packing a punch. Very good. *Dec 1997* ★★★★

Hermitage, La Chapelle Jaboulet Most recently: soft, mature, almost burgundy-like appearance; ripe, beautiful bouquet; drinking perfectly. What a great classic Hermitage is all about. *Last tasted July 2003* ★★★★★

Hermitage, La Sizeranne Chapoutier Soft, mature, open; harmonious bouquet, opening up fabulously, 'ripe figs'; very sweet, richly flavoured, yet still with peppery grip, dry finish, scented aftertaste. *March 1999* ★★★★★

1979 ★★★★ North ★★★ South

Variable conditions: Côte-Rôtie enjoyed an abundant harvest beginning in late September; rain delayed harvesting in Hermitage until early October. In the South, Châteauneuf wines were successful, fragrant and soft.

Châteauneuf-du-Pape, Ch de Beaucastel Perrin Gently coloured, fully mature; ripe, citrus touch; flavoury, more acidity and looser knit than Ch Rayas. *May 2001* ★★★

Châteauneuf-du-Pape, Ch Rayas Medium-deep, mature; very open; scented; very good flavour and grip. *May 2001* ★★★★

Côte-Rôtie, La Mouline Guigal Fully mature; low-keyed but harmonious; peppery, with teeth-gripping finish through ready for drinking. *April 1998* ★★★

Crozes-Hermitage, Dom de Thalabert Jaboulet Misleadingly youthful appearance; harmonious bouquet; sweet yet very tannic and showing its age. *March 1998* ★★★

Hermitage, La Chapelle Jaboulet Medium-deep; cherry-like fruit; supple, delicious flavour, well balanced. A survivor. *Last noted March 1998* ★★★★

1980 ★★ North ★★★ South

Big contrast between the North and the South, due as usual to the weather conditions. Châteauneuf enjoyed much better weather and the largest crop ever recorded. Early-maturing wines now past it.

1981 ★★ to ★★★

Though rain interrupted both flowering and harvest, some good wines were made in Côte-Rôtie; in the South flowering was also uneven but, after a summer drought, a fairly good vintage of rich, concentrated wines.

Châteauneuf-du-Pape, Ch de Beaucastel Perrin Medium-deep, a shade of pink; mature, slightly singed; less sweet, and with softer texture than Ch Rayas, good length, tannin and acidity. *May 2001* ★★★

Châteauneuf-du-Pape, Ch Rayas Medium but intense; fragrant; sweet, soft, attractive, dry finish. *May 2001* ★★★★

Côte-Rôtie Guigal First-rate range of wines but none tasted recently.

Hermitage Both **Chave**'s and **Jaboulet**'s **La Chapelle** had good potential in the mid-1980s.

1982 ★★★★

Even by Rhône standards, the summer was excessively hot and mainly dry. Despite heavy rains in August, it was an early harvest with sun-baked grapes and reduced acidity. There were some very good wines but they need drinking soon.

Châteauneuf-du-Pape, Dom du Vieux Télégraphe Brunier Deliciously soft and sweet but with an upturned touch of tannic bitterness. *1985* ★★★★ *Probably surviving.*

Côte-Rôtie, Les Jumelles Jaboulet Youthful red though with a mature rim; very meaty, slightly caramelly; sweet, rich, good for its age. *April 2002* ★★★

Hermitage Chave Appearance open and fully mature; a glorious 'old oak', rich, soft, singed bouquet; fairly full-bodied, soft, ripe. Now a bit gamey. *Last tasted May 1999. At its peak* ★★★★ *Now past its best but still a good ripe mouthful* ★★★

Hermitage, La Chapelle Jaboulet Still mouthfillingly attractive. *Last tasted May 1992. Then* ★★★★ *Doubtless fully mature and beginning to tire now.*

1983 ★★★★★

A magnificent summer, one of the hottest and driest on record. The North and South were both successful – the red wines were initially rich and concentrated with hard tannins and are proving long-lived.

Châteauneuf-du-Pape, Ch de Beaucastel Perrin Soft, lovely colour with slightly orange rim; very fragrant, spicy – 'needs air' I was told; pleasant sweetness and weight (12.5% alcohol), a lovely coffee-bean flavour, very good tannin and acidity. *Last tasted Oct 2001* ★★★★

Châteauneuf-du-Pape, Ch Rayas Pleasant, sweet, ripe bouquet; fragrant, attractive, hot finish and quite a bite. *Last noted May 2001* ★★★(★)

Cornas Jaboulet Soft red, almost mahogany; touch of singed caramel but otherwise harmonious and mature; sweet, soft, very agreeable, gentle tannins. Complete. *Jan 1998* ★★★

Côte-Rôtie, Brune et Blonde Guigal Medium-deep, mature rim; rich, ripe, rather earthy nose and flavour. Dry finish. *Dec 2005* ★★★ *Ready.*

Côte-Rôtie, La Mouline Guigal Glorious bouquet, flavour, great length, perfect tannin and acidity. *Feb 2005* ★★★★★★ *(6 stars).*

Crozes-Hermitage, Dom de Thalabert Jaboulet Medium-deep, maturing nicely; lovely fruit, subtle fragrance; sweet, singed, earthy, dry finish. *March 1998* ★★★★

Hermitage, La Chapelle Jaboulet Developing an orange rim; better flavour than nose, good length, somewhat acidic. *Last noted Jan 2002* ★★★ *Drinking quite well, but get on with it.*

Hermitage, La Sizeranne Chapoutier Almost opaque, intense; nose a bit 'stewed', but delicious flavour and balance. *Jan 2006. At best* ★★★ *Drink up.*

1984 ★★
Small crop of mainly mediocre wines.

1985 ★★★★★
Outstanding. A cool spring and late flowering were followed by a hot, dry and sunny summer with no rain in the South until after the vintage. Not many recent notes.

Châteauneuf-du-Pape, Ch de Beaucastel Perrin A touch of ruby; meaty, alcoholic; fairly full-bodied and firm. *Last tasted May 2001* ★★★★★

Châteauneuf-du-Pape, Ch Rayas Fairly deep; lovely mature bouquet; sweet, full-bodied; perfect flavour, balance and condition. Delicious. *Last tasted May 2002* ★★★★★ *Drink soon.*

Cornas Hugely successful but I have few recent notes. Outstanding were **La Geynale** Robert Michel ★★★★★; **A Clape** ★★★★★; and **Jaboulet** ★★★★

Côte-Rôtie, La Landonne Guigal Less deep, shapely with velvet sheen; rich, mocha-like nose; lovely flavour and finish. *Last tasted Feb 2005* ★★★★★ *Perfect.*

Côte-Rôtie, Brune et Blonde Guigal Very good fruit on nose and palate. Sweet. Delicious. *Last noted April 1999* ★★★★(★) *Drinking well but more to come.*

Côte-Rôtie, La Mouline Guigal A fine though more relaxed appearance; mocha-like again; sweet, full-bodied, slightly singed flavour. Still impressive. *Feb 2005* ★★★★★

Côte-Rôtie, La Turque Guigal Less deep than previously; glorious hot year bouquet; sweet, indescribably lovely. *Last tasted Feb 2005* ★★★★★

Hermitage, La Chapelle Jaboulet Still fairly deep; very fragrant; richly textured, substantial. *Last tasted Nov 2000* ★★★★★ *Lovely now but with time still in hand.*

1986 ★★ North ★★★ South
Uneven and difficult vintage. Few recent notes.

1987
The worst weather of the decade.

1988 ★★★★ North ★★★ South
Excellent, particularly in the North. Côte-Rôtie was severely hit by hail during flowering which reduced and concentrated the crop. Humidity problems in the South were countered by spraying and early picking.

Châteauneuf-du-Pape, Ch de Beaucastel Perrin Most recently, in magnums: soft, mature-looking; dried-out nose, dried leaves, old wood(?); better on palate. Sweet, rich flavour, cheesy, soft tannins. *Last noted April 2000* ★★★

Châteauneuf-du-Pape, Ch Rayas Soft, open, mature; sweet, easy, agreeable nose; attractive flavour. Mouth-drying tannin. *May 2001* ★★★★★

Côte-Rôtie, La Landonne Guigal Deep ruby; good nose; a strange Bordeaux style, good flavour, firmness and austerity. *Last tasted May 1999* ★★★(★)

Côte-Rôtie, La Mouline Guigal Most recently, coffee-like nose, softer, more amenable. *Last tasted Feb 2005* ★★★

Côte-Rôtie, La Turque Guigal Still opaque and youthful; tar-like nose; very much a 'Parker 100' style of wine. *Last noted Dec 2000* (★★★★)? *Time will tell.*

Hermitage Chave Lovely crisp fruit; pleasantly sweet and full, soft fruit, lovely flavour. *Last tasted May 1999* ★★★★ *Should still be delicious.*

Hermitage, La Chapelle Jaboulet Now medium-deep; ripe, rich, fruity; despite soft entry, very tannic finish. *Last noted May 2001* ★★★(★) *I am sure it will continue to improve.*

1989 ★★★★ North ★★★★★ South

A drought year, especially in the North. The older vines with a deep and complex root formation coped best – this was particularly noticeable in Côte-Rôtie; Hermitage produced a crop of rich wines. Rich, complete reds in Châteauneuf.

Châteauneuf-du-Pape, Ch de Beaucastel Perrin Delicious flavour, with mouth-drying finish. Lovely wine. *Last tasted May 2002* ★★★★★ *At its peak.*

Châteauneuf-du-Pape, Ch Rayas Open knit, mature; almost over-sweet, mulberry-ripe fruit; sweet, lovely, though dry finish. *May 2001* ★★★★★

Côte-Rôtie, La Mouline Guigal Lovely colour; sweet and soft – and burgundy-like; rich, delicious. *Nov 2000* ★★★★★

Hermitage Chave Medium-deep, rich; very good, slightly meaty and singed nose; medium-sweet, well balanced, lovely flavour. Delicious. *Nov 2000* ★★★★★

Hermitage, La Chapelle Jaboulet In magnums: deep but maturing; gorgeous bouquet; warm, rich – yet still struggling to harmonise, full-flavoured, very good fruit, excellent tannin and acidity. *Last noted April 2000* ★★★★★

1990 ★★★★★

A splendid year throughout the Rhône, despite more drought conditions. Early flowering, hot dry summer and early harvest. Firmer wines, with more power than the '89s.

Châteauneuf-du-Pape, Ch de Beaucastel Perrin Still fairly deep, ripe bouquet, very good flavour but with quite a bite. *Last tasted Jan 2004* ★★★(★) *Probably approaching peak now.*

Châteauneuf-du-Pape, Hommage à Jacques Perrin, Ch de Beaucastel Perrin Very deep, opaque core, intense; low-keyed, great vinosity, slightly malty; enormously impressive. *May 2001* ★★★(★★) *Now–2020.*

Châteauneuf-du-Pape, Clos des Papes Avril Medium-deep; ripe somewhat rustic nose; sweet, good fruit, quite tannic. *Last tasted May 2002* ★★★(★)

Châteauneuf-du-Pape, Ch Rayas Rich, spicy; soft, full, fleshy, with fairly swingeing tannic finish. *Last noted May 2001* ★★★★(★) *Needs more time.*

Côte-Rôtie, La Landonne Guigal Very fragrant; dry, lean, high quality. *Feb 2005* ★★★(★★) *Good future.*

Côte-Rôtie, La Turque Guigal The most dashingly flowery, scented nose, yet below that seeming superficiality, great depth; glorious flavour, heavenly fruit, fragrant aftertaste. *Last tasted Sept 1996* ★★★★★ *Probably at peak now.*

Crozes-Hermitage, Dom de Thalabert Jaboulet Deep; low-keyed, figgy; sweet, big, attractive wine with singed flavour. *March 1998* ★★★★

Hermitage, La Chapelle Jaboulet Still impressively deep; delicious flavour and crisp fruit. *Last tasted May 1999* ★★★★★ *At peak now.*

'Ermitage', Le Pavillon Chapoutier Rich; earthy, distinctive; full-bodied, very good fruit and flavour. *Tasted, blind, June 1996* ★★★★★ *Doubtless at peak now.*

1991 ★★★ North ★★ South

Uneven year. The Rhône was the only major region in France not severely hit by spring frosts; hot, dry summer but mid-September rains spoiled the chance of a top-class vintage. A small crop of light wines in Châteauneuf. More successful in the North for those who picked before the rain.

Côte-Rôtie, La Mouline Guigal Medium-deep, maturing; harmonious; medium-sweet, nice weight, attractive flavour. Charm. *Nov 2000* ★★★ *Drink up.*

Côte-Rôtie, La Turque Guigal Deep, rich, impressive; sweet, soft, burgundy-like; rich, delicious. *Nov 2000* ★★★★ *Drink soon.*

Hermitage, La Chapelle Jaboulet Complete, no harsh edges, a copybook Hermitage. *Last tasted March 2000* ★★★★ *Drink up.*

Hermitage, La Sizeranne Chapoutier Fairly deep, still youthful. Good nose and palate. An agreeable lunchtime wine. *July 1998* ★★★ *Drink up.*

1992 a grudging ★★★★ North, ★★★ South

A moderate year. August was hot but September wet and stormy. Despite all the problems, some quite good wines were made for early drinking.

Hermitage Chave Showing some maturity; lovely, slightly burgundian nose; rich, earthy, distinctive. Most enjoyable. *Last tasted May 1999* ★★★★

1993 ★★

Good summer conditions were washed away by heavy rains from mid-September. Mainly lightish wines. Chaptalisation was widespread. Best to avoid. Of those wines I have tasted since the mid-1990s, few achieved 3 stars.

Hermitage Chave Misleadingly pale; attractive nose; fairly sweet, rich, powerful. A big wine needing time. *Sept 1995* ★★★★ *Probably at its peak now.*

1994 ★★ North ★ South

Once again, high hopes for a good vintage were dashed by heavy mid-September rains. The grapes were not ripe enough, lacked acidity and had to be chaptalised.

Châteauneuf-du-Pape, Ch de Beaucastel Perrin Attractive bouquet; delicious, soft, easy, fully mature and perfect weight. Very good for a poor vintage and waterlogged vineyards. *May 2006* ★★★ *Drink up.*

Châteauneuf-du-Pape, Hommage à Jacques Perrin, Ch de Beaucastel Perrin Fairly intense dark cherry; very distinctive, figgy, tarry nose; fairly sweet and full-bodied, chunky fruit, a touch of raw tannin. *May 2001* ★★(★)

Châteauneuf-du-Pape, Ch Rayas Very sweet. Delicious. *Nov 2003* ★★★ *Drink up.*

1995 ★★★★ North ★★★★★ South

A very satisfactory vintage. In the North *coulure* and *millerandage* during the flowering reduced the potential crop by 20% but the reds were – still are – elegant and charming. In the South the late September mistral wind had a drying effect, resulting in very ripe, fairly concentrated grapes with good levels of tannin and acidity and comparable to the '90s.

Châteauneuf-du-Pape, Ch de Beaucastel Perrin Medium depth and intensity; attractive fruit, very distinctive; a delicious mouthful, good fruit, still tannic and a citrus edge adding to its refreshing acidity. *May 2001* ★★★★(★)

Châteauneuf-du-Pape, Hommage à Jacques Perrin, Ch de Beaucastel Perrin Very deep ruby, intense, still youthful; very sweet, ripe, fig-like fruit; rich, fleshy, dry finish. I queried its length. *May 2001* ★★★(★★)?

Châteauneuf-du-Pape Dom de Pegau Magnum: medium; attractive scent, minty, whiff of asparagus; drinking well though palate drying, with a light end bite. *May 2002* ★★★ *No point in waiting.*

Châteauneuf-du-Pape, Ch Rayas Dark cherry, still youthful; unknit and a bit sharp; sweet, fascinating fruit, good grip. *May 2001* ★★★(★★)

Châteauneuf-du-Pape, Dom du Vieux Télégraphe Brunier Still deep; whiff of bottle age and *un peu de merde*; very rich, slightly singed and chocolatey on palate. *Last tasted Jan 2004* ★★★★ *An exciting wine. Drink soon.*

Cornas, La Louvée Jean-Luc Colombo A single-vineyard wine from 60–70-year-old vines. 100% new oak. Medium-deep, rich core, long 'legs'; rich, plummy fruit, sweet, scented; good fruit and flavour. *May 1999* ★★★(★)

Côte-Rôtie, Ch d'Ampuis Guigal Fairly deep, immature, rich 'legs'; crisp, oaky, spice with deep fig-like fruit; sweet, full, rich fruit, oak flavour and aftertaste. *May 1999* ★★★★★ *Now–2010.*

Côte-Rôtie, La Turque Guigal Made with Syrah from the Côte Brune with 5% Viognier added. Three years' ageing in 100% new oak, unfined and unfiltered. Deep, attractive, rich 'legs'; rich, fig-like brambly fruit; sweetly fruity, concentrated yet soft, soft yet tannic. *May 1999* ★★★(★★) *Long life.*

Hermitage, La Chapelle Jaboulet Fragrant; fairly sweet, attractive, gentle grip. Copybook Hermitage. *Last tasted August 2005* ★★★★★ *Now–2010.*

St-Joseph, Deschants Chapoutier Chapoutier's small but prime vineyard. Still plummy-coloured; pleasant, bramble-like Syrah; drinking well. *Sept 2002* ★★★ *Drink up.*

1996 ★★ to ★★★★ very variable

Similar to 1994, with rain. The season started well with satisfactory flowering. Early August was cool and wet which inhibited sugar development. Happily, in the North late August was sunny and conditions were good until the harvest end, the crop being healthy and abundant. In the South, the rain continued into September though the mistral wind saved the crop from too much rot.

Châteauneuf-du-Pape, Ch de Beaucastel Perrin Medium-deep ruby; a meaty, farmyard smell; medium-sweet, ripe, good fruit, a touch of CO_2, lovely acidity. *Oct 2001* (★★★★) *Needs bottle age.*

Châteauneuf-du-Pape, Les Cailloux Alain Brunet Very good nose; delicious flavour, very pleasant, dry finish. *Oct 1999* ★★★★ *Drink soon.*

Cornas, Dom de St-Pierre Jaboulet Pleasant fruit; nice weight, delicious flavour. Some oak. Refreshing. *June 1999* ★★(★)

Cornas, Dom de Rochepertuis J Lionnat Warm brambly aromas; fairly sweet, agreeable weight, delicious. *Last tasted July 2003* ★★★ *Drink up.*

Côte-Rôtie Jasmin Deep, immature; amazing scent of violets, privet and Persian cats; very distinctive. *Jan 1998* ★★(★★) *How will this develop?*

Crozes-Hermitage, 'Famille 2000' Jaboulet Opaque, tough. Nowhere near ready. *June 1999* (★★★) *Probably drinking well now.*

Hermitage Chave Sweet, bramble-like fruit; good balance and body, crisp fruit, dry finish. Finesse. *May 1999* ★★(★) *Probably at best now.*

Hermitage, La Chapelle Jaboulet Still fairly deep; sweeter than the '95, very rich, complete, tannic. *Last tasted Aug 2005* ★★★ *Now–2012.*

1997 ★★★

A useful and attractive vintage. Both the North and the South experienced early budding and a prompt start to flowering. The summer was relatively cool until a heatwave hit the entire region at the end of August. The Côte-Rôtie experienced a long, hot, late harvest. In the South it was much drier, and the picking was earlier. These wines are easier and suitable for early drinking.

Châteauneuf-du-Pape, Ch de Beaucastel Perrin Richly coloured; very good, raspberry-like fruit; slightly sweet, lovely flavour – delicious. *Jan 2000* ★★★ *Drink soon.*

Châteauneuf-du-Pape, Le Crau, Dom du Vieux Télégraphe Brunier Weak-rimmed, soft cherry; pleasant brambly fruit; fairly sweet, soft and easy but with very dry finish. *Last tasted Aug 2002* ★★★ *Drink soon.*

Châteauneuf-du-Pape, Dom de Mont-Redon Very deep; pleasant fruit; sweet, rich, very drinkable. *Oct 2001* ★★★ *Drink soon.*

Côte-Rôtie, Ch d'Ampuis Guigal Very deep; rich, spicy; sweet, full-bodied, fruit-packed, very tannic yet with a velvety texture. Impressive. *Oct 2001* (★★★★) *Long life.*

Côte-Rôtie, Les Jumelles Jaboulet Fairly deep; sweet, 'warm', lovely fruit; fairly sweet, slightly singed, raisiny flavour. Attractive. *June 1999* ★(★★) *Drink soon.*

Côte-Rôtie, La Mouline Guigal Fairly deep; low-keyed; relatively easy for early drinking. *Feb 2005* ★★★ *Now–2010.*

Côtes-du-Rhône, Coudoulet de Beaucastel, Ch de Beaucastel Perrin Richly coloured, extraordinary nose, like a whiff of fine cognac and crushed raspberry; soft, very fruity and delicious. Perfect for early consumption. *Last tasted March 2000* ★★★ *Drink soon.*

Hermitage, La Chapelle Jaboulet Medium-deep, luminous cherry red; fragrant; sweet, chewy, plenty of tannic grip. *August 2005* ★★★(★) *Now–2012.*

1998 ★★★★★

Great vintage. Uniformly good growing season (except for severe April frosts in Côte-Rôtie). Hot, dry summer, a touch of rain then intense heat in August stressing the vines. Happily, well-timed rain fleshed out the parched grapes followed by dry and sunny conditions. Deeply coloured reds with high sugar content and substantial alcohol levels.

Châteauneuf-du-Pape, Ch de Beaucastel Perrin Fairly deep; very distinctive nose and flavour. Very tannic. *Last tasted March 2006* ★★★(★) *Getting its second breath, now–2012.*

Châteauneuf-du-Pape, Hommage à Jacques Perrin, Ch de Beaucastel Perrin Five grape varieties used, Grenache uppermost (60%). Thick, dense, almost port-like nose; sweet, full fruit flavour, high alcohol (circa 15%), slightly figgy flavour, masked tannin, great length. A great classic in the making. *Last tasted Oct 2001* (★★★★★) *2010–2020.*

Châteauneuf-du-Pape, Cuvée de la Reine des Bois Dom de la Mordorée Deep, plummy, good 'legs'; very sweet, fragrant; almost too sweet though with good grip. Full-bodied. A rich mouthful. *Oct 2001* ★★★(★)

Châteauneuf-du-Pape, Dom du Vieux Télégraphe Brunier Grenache 75%, Syrah 15%, Cinsault and Mourvèdre each 5%. Medium-deep, soft red, maturing, distinctive; sweet, full-bodied (14%) yet elegant. Delicious. 'Slips down easily'. *March 2004* ★★★★★ *Now–2012*. **Châteauneuf-du-Pape, Le Crau, Dom du Vieux Télégraphe Brunier** Light purple rim; a whiff of strawberry and vanilla; dry, crisp fruit; very tannic. *Aug 2002* ★★★★

Châteauneuf-du-Pape, Ch Rayas Medium-pale, open rim, light style; soft fruit; a bit lean, sweet, gamey, curious flavour, very tannic. *May 2001* ★★(★★)?

Côte-Rôtie Guigal's range of wines tasted in cask *Oct 2001*: **Brune et Blonde** 30% new oak. Dark cherry, tannic (★★★★); **La Landonne** opaque, velvety; meaty nose; firm, minerally, peppery finish (★★★★★) *Long life*; **La Mouline** with 12% Viognier added to the Syrah. Opaque, lovely wine, very fragrant, spicy (★★★★); and **La Turque** opaque; blackberry-like fruit; fairly sweet, very distinctive (★★★★★)

Hermitage Chave If Guigal's Côte-Rôties suit the American taste, Chave's Hermitage, for the English, epitomises northern Rhône at its classic best. Not deep. Understated; fairly sweet, perfect balance, lovely flavour, maturing well. *Jan 2004* ★★★★ *Now–2012*.

Hermitage, La Chapelle Jaboulet Medium, relaxed, open; touch of stalkiness; sweet, rich, fairly full bodied though, easy, attractive. Slightly hot finish. Delicious. *Aug 2005* ★★★★★ *Now–2012*.

1999 ★★★★★ North ★★★★ South

It was a particularly successful vintage in the northern Rhône. The grapes in Côte-Rôtie ripened early and reached record sugar levels. It was slightly less successful in Châteauneuf due to heavy rains at the end of September.

Châteauneuf-du-Pape, Ch de Beaucastel Perrin Fairly deep, ruby; crisp, spicy, gamey; lovely young fruit, crisp, good length, tannic. *Oct 2001* (★★★★)

Châteauneuf-du-Pape, Ch La Nerthe Soft ruby; very scented, vanillin; medium-sweet, glorious fruit and flavour. Perfect weight. An enchanting wine. *Nov 2002* ★★★★★ *Now–2010*.

Châteauneuf-du-Pape, Dom du Vieux Télégraphe Brunier Sweet, lovely flavour, stylish. My sort of wine. *Jan 2006* ★★★★ *Now–2010*.

Côte-Rôtie R Rostaing 'Thick', hefty fruit, overripe and smelly; very sweet, interesting flavour, pleasant weight, good length. *Sept 2005* ★★★(★?)

Côte-Rôtie, La Landonne Guigal Still fairly deep; rich, tar-like scent; medium-dry, full-flavoured, very good. *Last tasted Feb 2005* ★★(★★★)

Côte-Rôtie, La Mouline Guigal Rich, singed nose; delicious flavour, good acidity. *Last tasted Feb 2005* ★★★(★★) *Now–2015*.

Côte-Rôtie, La Turque Guigal Moderate weight for Guigal (13.5% alcohol). Deep yet soft appearance; delicious flavour, soft – masked tannins. *Last tasted Feb 2005* ★★★★(★) *Now–2012*.

Hermitage, La Chapelle Jaboulet Very deep, velvety, starting to mature; rich, deep, slightly singed Syrah and sweaty tannins; sweetest of the range, ripe, good fruit, length and tannin. Delicious. *Last tasted Nov 2005* ★★★★(★) *Now–2010*.

2000–2005

In recent years things have certainly changed in the Rhône Valley, and for the better. Syrah has become a popular and successful variety, not only in the Midi of France but also as Shiraz in the New World. It is, however, always consoling for the growers that the soil and climate of the Rhône is rather special. The future bodes well.

Red Vintages at a Glance

Northern Rhône (Cornas, Côte-Rôtie, Crozes-Hermitage, Hermitage, St-Joseph)
Outstanding ★★★★★ 2005
Very Good ★★★★ 2000, 2001, 2004
Good ★★★ 2002 (v), 2003 (v)
Southern Rhône (mainly Châteauneuf-du-Pape)
Outstanding ★★★★★ 2005
Very Good ★★★★ 2000, 2001 (v)
Good ★★★ 2001 (v), 2002 (v), 2003 (v), 2004

2000 ★★★★

A good vintage but not without its problems. It was an abnormally dry spring with, generally, above average temperatures. April to June was wetter than normal and July was exceptionally cool. August was quite the opposite, with very high temperatures and dry. September was more equable, with fine warm days interspersed with occasional showers. Abundant crops in both the North and the South. The wines in the North were ripe and well balanced and in the South the healthy grapes had thick skins and high tannin levels.

Châteauneuf-du-Pape, Dom de Mont-Redon Rich, full-bodied (14.5% alcohol), delicious flavour, mouthdrying tannin. *May 2004* ★★★(★) *Now–2012.*

Châteauneuf-du-Pape, Dom du Vieux Télégraphe Brunier Medium-deep, open, maturing; very slightly singed, raisiny and chocolatey scent; fairly sweet, rich, good fruit and flavour, tannic texture. *Last tasted Sept 2004* ★★★★

Cornas A Clape 100% Syrah. Sweet, distinctive, considerable depth; dry, rich, cherry-like fruit, tannic bite. *May 2006* ★★★★ *Now–2010.*

Cornas, Les Ruchets J-L Colombo Virtually opaque; fragrant, arboreal, bramble, cherry-like fruit; medium-sweet, packs a punch, teeth-gripping. Impressive new style of wine. *May 2006* ★★(★★) *Now–2012.*

Cornas, Dom de la St-Pierre Jaboulet Medium, soft, open-rimmed; maturing; touch of caramel and violets fragrance. Delicious flavour, good acidity. *May 2006* ★★(★★) *Now–2010.*

Côte-Rôtie J-P and J-L Jamet Fairly deep; sweet fruit, distinctive, whiff reminding me of Bual madeira; sweet, rich, moderate weight (12.5% alcohol), delicious flavour, tannic. *May 2006* ★★★(★) *Now–2010.*

Côte-Rôtie Ogier 1%Viognier included with the Syrah, 60% from the Côte Blonde, 40% from the Côte Brune. 18 months in oak. Medium; oaky; rich, touch of tar. *May 2006* ★★★? *Hard to predict.*

Côte-Rôtie, 'Maison Rouge' Georges Vernay 90% Syrah, 10%Viognier. Maturing; very good, rich, whiff of mocha, very fragrant, new oak; a bit too oaky. Moderate weight, delicious. *May 2006* ★★★★ *Now–2012.*

Côte-Rôtie, La Landonne Guigal 100% Syrah. 3½ years in small oak casks! Rich, very deep core, velvety sheen; low-keyed nose, sweet, bramble-like oak, sweet, easier than expected, tannic. *May 2006* ★★★(★) *Now–2012.*

Côte-Rôtie, La Mouline Guigal 89% Syrah, 11%Viognier, 42 months in oak casks. Good colour, soft, relaxed rim; very good indeed, brambly oak; very sweet, full flavour, moderate weight, hot finish. *May 2006* ★★★(★★) *Now–2012.*

Côte-Rôtie, La Turque Guigal 93% Syrah, 7%Viognier. Fairly deep, rich core, maturing rim; bouquet of 'toasted oak', fragrant; very sweet, full, rich flavour, good length, tannic. *May 2006* ★★(★★) *Now–2012.*

Ermitage, 'Le Pavillon' M Chapoutier Matured in 50% new oak for 18–20 months. Bottled without fining or filtration.Very deep, almost opaque, intense; low-keyed fruit and oak; sweet, rich, full-bodied, tannic, complete. Impressive. *May 2006* ★★★(★★) *Now–2015.*

Hermitage Chave 100% Syrah from 7 different *climats*, mainly matured in used oak casks. Rich, deep core, moderate intensity; spicy, good depth; very sweet, excellent flavour and length. Dry finish. *May 2006* ★★★★(★) *Now–2015.*

Hermitage, La Chapelle Jaboulet Medium-deep, open rim; good fruit; sweet, rich, rounded, blackberry-like fruit. *Aug 2005* ★★★★ *Now–2010.*

Hermitage, 'Marquise de la Tourette' Delas 100% Syrah, 14–16 months in barrel, 9% new. Medium, relaxed appearance; fig-like fruit, tangy; sweet, delicious flavour, fragrant, good length. *May 2006* ★★★★ *Now–2010.*

OTHER '00S SHOWING GOOD POTENTIALin 2002, all 4 star:
CHÂTEAUNEUF-DU-PAPE: Bosquet des Papes Boiron; La Nerthe; Clos Val Seille; and Dom de la Vieille Julienne.
CORNAS: Dom de Rochepertuis Lionnet.
CÔTE-RÔTIE: Daubrée; J-M Stephan; and Les Jumelles **Jaboulet.**
ST-JOSEPH: Dom du Mortier.

2001 North ★★★★ South ★★★ to ★★★★

Overall more successful in the North. Though there was great heat in August, there was enough rain to prevent vines becoming too stressed, and harvesting took place before the October rains set in. The reds have good concentration and extract. In the South a week of extreme heat and a very strong mistral in August reduced yields. Uneven, but some excellent wines.

Châteauneuf-du-Pape Jaboulet Fairly deep; good nose; medium-sweet, ripe, fullish. *Nov 2003* ★★★ *Drink up.*

Châteauneuf-du-Pape, Dom du Vieux Télégraphe Brunier Medium-deep, very pleasant, light fruitiness; sweet, easy, excellent flavour and balance. Full-bodied, touch of oakiness. *Last tasted Dec 2004* ★★★(★) *Now–2010.*

Cornas, Les Ruchets J-L Colombo Rich, opaque core; crisp fruit; dry, lovely flesh, concentrated, very tannic. Impressive. *Last tasted March 2005* ★★(★★) *Now–2012.*

Crozes-Hermitage A Graillot Pale; fresh, fragrant; very distinctive, surprisingly acidic. Youthful but drinking well. *March 2003* ★★★★ *Drink soon.*

Hermitage, La Chapelle Jaboulet Open, relaxed; 'green' nose but sweet, mediumweight, attractive. *August 2005* ★★★ *Now–2010.*

Hermitage, 'Ex Voto' Guigal (formerly Grippat's Hermitage) Deep, youthful, full-bodied, impressive. *Feb 2005* ★★(★★) *Now–2012.*

St-Joseph, Vieilles Vignes Tardieu-Laurent Deep; spicy oak; medium sweet, delicious fruit, good tannin and acidity. *Jan 2005* ★★★★ *Drink soon.*

St-Joseph, 'La Pompée' Jaboulet Deep ruby; distinctive; dry, medium-full body, refreshing. *Feb 2006* ★★★ *Drink up.*

2002 at best ★★★

A nightmare year, particularly in the flooded South. It was better on the well-drained slopes of the North where Côte-Rôtie was the most successful. Hermitage of good commercial quality. In Châteauneuf, despite inundated vineyards, the top producers who could salvage their crops managed to make the best of a bad job. Few wines shipped. Drink up.

2003 ★★★ variable

Even for the hot Rhône Valley, 2003 temperatures were abnormally high. Soils were dehydrated and overripe grapes with high sugar content resulted in an early harvest of dense alcoholic wines. Few tasted.

Châteauneuf-du-Pape, Ch de Beaucastel Perrin Medium-deep ruby; ripe; soft entry, attractive, drinking well though in limbo – neither youthful nor mature. *Oct 2006* ★★★(★)

Châteauneuf-du-Pape, Dom du Vieux Lazaret Quiot Nondescript nose; hefty style, full-bodied (14.5% alcohol), fruit and extract. *Nov 2006* ★★★ *A matter of taste.*

Châteauneuf-du-Pape, Réserve R Sabon Immature but sweet and brambly; dry, fairly full-bodied, positive, needs time. *Sept 2005* ★★★ *Now–2010?*

Hermitage, La Chapelle Jaboulet Very deep, virtually opaque, intense; a fruit bomb, powerful, impressive. *August 2005* (★★★★) *2010–2015.*

2004 ★★★★ North ★★★ South

A very satisfactory vintage, not unline the '99s, and a complete contrast to the '03s. A wetter and longer ripening season. The wines of the North, Hermitage and in particular, Côte-Rôtie, have excellent tannin and acidity, described as 'slow burners' and built to last. In the South, the Châteauneuf wines are very good, more amenable but perhaps unfairly upstaged by the '05 vintage. These are wines for the serious Rhône lover. (A 'tip from the horse's mouth': the whites of Condrieu are excellent, Château-Grillet the best ever.)

2005 ★★★★★

Perfect growing season. The reds throughout the Rhône are of outstanding quality, said to be on a par with the great '78s, even the magnificent '61s. Succulent fruit and excellent acidity; one of those rare vintages enjoyable in its youth, yet with the constitution and balance for it to develop over the next 20 years.

Loire

The Loire is France's longest river, wending its way for some 1000 kilometres from almost the western edge of Burgundy to the Atlantic coast in the west. It is hardly surprising that the vineyards on or near its banks offer a vast range of wines; indeed, they have only one thing in common – refreshing acidity. Mainly they are white, from very dry to very sweet. Apart from Muscadet, the grape that gives its name to the dry whites toward the mouth of the Loire, there are two main grape varieties, Sauvignon Blanc and Chenin Blanc. The first, at its most characteristic in the districts of Sancerre and Pouilly-Fumé, produces crisp dry whites for early drinking. Chenin Blanc produces a huge range of wines in its homeland of Anjou-Touraine, from dry, medium-dry, medium-sweet to sweet, and both still and sparkling.

The main Loire red wines, Chinon, Bourgueil and Saumur-Champigny, are made mostly from Cabernet Franc, with some Pinot Noir and Gamay. They tend to be very acidic and only those made in a hot vintage are capable of satisfactory ageing in bottle. They are best drunk on the spot, in a restaurant on the banks of the Loire.

Outstanding vintages
1921, 1928, 1937, 1947, 1949, 1959, 1964, 1989, 1990, 1997, 2003, 2005

The following notes are confined mainly to the medium-sweet and sweet wines of good vintages, particularly ones made from botrytis-affected grapes. Few Loire dry whites other than top-class Savennières will benefit from bottle age.

Sweetness levels of Chenin Blanc wines

*Here is an approximate definition of the levels of sweetness of the wines made from the Chenin Blanc grape in Vouvray and Anjou. **Sec** is dry; **demi-sec**, literally half-dry, can vary according to the vintage; **moelleux**, which sounds pleasingly like mellow, also varies between medium-dry and fairly sweet; and **doux** is definitely sweet though the acidity, a marked feature of all Loire wines, can give it a dry finish. The sweetest of all these wines are often described as **liquoreux**. With their high sugar levels and relatively high acidity virtually all the richer, sweeter whites will keep well for many decades and also develop in bottle.*

Classic older vintages: 1921–1959

The consensus of the period was that the wines of the Loire, light and acidic, 'did not travel'. Visitors to France saw them as local, holiday wines: Muscadet went with seafood in Brittany and Sancerre was the staple white of Paris bistros.

Sweet Vintages at a Glance

Outstanding ★★★★★ 1921, 1928, 1937, 1947, 1949, 1959
Very Good ★★★★ 1924, 1934, 1945
Good ★★★ 1933, 1953, 1955

1924 ★★★★
Le Haut-Lieu, moelleux Huët Distinctive yellow with apple-green rim; soft, sweet, 'calf's foot jelly' with honeyed depth; medium-sweet, very attractive flavour, very good for its age, sustained by its acidity. *May 2004* ★★★★

1928 ★★★★★
A great vintage. Well-structured wines with excellent acidity; a few sweet wines have survived. Now scarce.
Anjou, Rablay Caves de la Maison Prunier A wonderful wine, which I have tasted over a dozen times and it was still going strong on the last occasion. At one time a medium-sweet Loire wine was the traditional accompaniment to grilled Dover sole. Fabulous amber-gold with apple-green rim; lovely, very Chenin Blanc honey, with a refreshing whiff of 'lemon curd' acidity; medium-sweet, glorious flavour, good body and perfect acidity – even better after two hours in the glass. Still gloriously rich on the nose, with perfect acidity. *Last tasted May 2001* ★★★★

1937 ★★★★★
Vying with 1921 and 1928 as the greatest pre-war Loire vintage. No recent notes.

1945 ★★★★
Small crop of excellent wines. No recent notes.

1947 ★★★★★
The greatest post-war vintage. Beautiful wines made and jealously hoarded, yet over the past few years odd bottles have been culled from the original estates, in particular fine, well-preserved Vouvrays. These wines had benefited from a gloriously hot summer and early autumn with perfect conditions for the growth of *Botrytis cinerea* or 'noble rot'.
Vouvray Foreau A brief mention, for I have always regarded this as the best '47. *Last tasted in 1986* ★★★★★
Vouvray Jean-Pierre Laisement Extraordinarily rich bouquet of raisins and old apples; sweet, delicious. *June 1999* ★★★★

Vouvray, Colnot Marc Brédif Though the bottle had an 11-cm ullage and the wine was slightly cloudy, its amber-gold, apple-green rim was glorious in the sunlight; nose sound; now medium-dry – perhaps it had never been *doux* – good body, delicious old-gold taste and crisp, dry finish. *Last tasted Aug 2000* ★★★
Vouvray, Le Haut-Lieu, moelleux Huët Amber, apple-green rim; rather Tokaji-like, rich, honeyed, tangy yet creamy; medium-sweet but very rich, glorious flavour, long finish. *Last tasted May 2004* ★★★★★

1949 ★★★★★

Excellent vintage, not as luscious as '47 but with good fruit and firm structure. No recent notes.

1955 ★★★

The summer lacked heat though botrytis produced some sweet whites.
Chinon, Clos de L'Olive Couly-Dutheuil Translucent pink-tinged red, soft, mature, rich; unusual, very distinctive fragrance; flavour of dried raspberries and *fraises des bois*. Dry, acidic finish. *June 1999* ★★★ *Rare and remarkable.*

1959 ★★★★★

Exceptionally hot summer and magnificent vintage, the best since 1947.
Bonnezeaux Ch des Gauliers/Boivin Golden colour; calf's foot jelly nose; medium-sweet, hefty, excellent acidity, dry finish. *Aug 2000* ★★★
Coteaux du Layon, Chaume Ch de la Guimonière Creamy Chenin nose; fairly sweet and assertive, with lovely flavour and weight. Drinking perfectly and no signs of fatigue. *March 1995* ★★★★ *Will still be good.*
Vouvray Marc Brédif Not starbright, a sliver of sediment, so decanted to enhance its shimmering yellow-gold colour; good nose; medium-sweet, correct weight, original flavour, good acidity. *May 2000* ★★★
Vouvray, Le Mont, moelleux, 1er trie Huët Surprisingly pale for its age and vintage; curious, distinctive, fragrant and floral, developing a delicious spiciness and flavour to match; fairly sweet, though rich, with a touch of syrup and caramel, leaner than expected. *May 2004* ★★★★

1960–1999

With travel and currency restrictions easing after World War Two, the 'Garden of France' became a popular holiday destination for the British, its main attractions being the glorious châteaux and, for me, fresh trout with local wines. But back home the 'local' wines did not taste the same and restaurants offered the same old – or rather young – Muscadet, Sancerre and Pouilly-Fumé. However, the 1990s were blessed with more than their fair share of good vintages and lovely, sweet wines from Anjou-Touraine. At home, particularly in the spring and summer, I enjoy these medium-sweet wines for our 'elevenses' or mid-morning drink.

SWEET VINTAGES AT A GLANCE

Outstanding ★★★★★ 1964, 1989, 1990, 1997
Very Good ★★★★ 1962, 1971, 1976, 1985, 1986, 1988, 1995, 1996, 1998 (V)
Good ★★★ 1966, 1969, 1975, 1978, 1982, 1993, 1998 (V), 1999

1960

A poor start to the decade. In addition. the vintages of 1963, '65, '67, '68, '70, '72, '73, '74, '77, '79, '80, '81, '83, '84, '87, '91 and '92 are now past it.

1961 ★★

At the time best known for its dry wines.
Vouvray, Clos du Bourg, moelleux, 1er trie Huët Palish straw yellow; very intriguing floral fragrance floating above the scent of apples and pears; medium-sweet, attractive flavour, soft and fleshy but leading to a very dry finish. *May 2004* ★★★★

1962 ★★★★

A very good vintage despite being overshadowed by the rich '64s.

1964 ★★★★★

A hot year and best vintage of the decade for the *demi-sec*, *moelleux* and *doux* wines. Most of the sweeter wines were at their peak in the early 1980s.
Bonnezeaux Ch des Gauliers/Boivin Colour had deepened to straw gold; slightly maderised; drying out a little but with good old apricots flavour and supporting acidity. *Last tasted March 1995. At best* ★★★★, *now* ★★
Vouvray, moelleux Marc Brédif Lanolin yellow; lanolin on the nose too. Mature Chenin, reminding me of lemon cheesecake. Now dry but with a lovely flavour. *Nov 1997* ★★★

1966 ★★★

Better for dry wines than for sweet. No point in pursuing.

1969 ★★★

In contrast to 1966, better for sweet than for dry, the acidity providing a good sustaining backbone for the richer Anjou and Vouvray wines. Few wines tasted.

1971 ★★★★

A very good vintage. Stylish, elegant, with zestful and sustaining acidity. The best of the sweet wines are still very good.
Vouvray, Clos du Bourg, sec Huët An unusual opportunity to taste a 26-year-old quality dry wine from a leading producer: remarkably pale for its age and very bright; dry, good length, flavour and acidity. *Nov 1997* ★★★
Vouvray, Clos du Bourg, moelleux Huët Palish; most attractive, honeyed botrytis nose; fairly sweet, lovely flavour, perfect acidity. *Nov 1997* ★★★★

1975 ★★★

Good vintage for dry and sweet. Now mainly *passé*.

1976 ★★★★

An extremely hot summer, a drought year in northern Europe. Early harvest of superripe grapes. Hot years produce the best Loire reds, though the '76s are now hard to find.

Bourgueil, Cuvée Ploquin Dom du Chêne Arrault/Christophe Deschamps Fairly deep, soft, red, rich core; soft yet hefty fruit, showing some age; extremely good for its age on the palate. However, still very tannic. *June 1999* ★★★★

1985 ★★★★

The vineyards of Anjou and Vouvray enjoyed unbroken hot and dry weather from the third week in August to early November. A particularly good year for the reds: Chinon, Bourgueil and Saumur-Champigny.

Vouvray, Clos du Bourg, moelleux Huët Paler and drier than expected; fragrant, creamy; lean but lovely. Good acidity. *Oct 2006* ★★★★ *Perfect for drinking now.*

1986 ★★★★

An ideal year, mainly for the dry whites – the best of the decade.

1988 ★★★★

A very satisfactory vintage for reds and for dry and semi-sweet whites.

Bourgueil Dom de la Closerie Raspberry red, weak rim; aroma of squashed raspberries; medium-dry, soft, earthy, rustic character. *June 1999* ★★★

1989 ★★★★★

Exceptional weather: early budding, flowering was advanced by three weeks followed by a very hot summer. A superb vintage for the semi-sweet and sweet whites, a top Chenin year and on a par with 1947. The Chinon and Bourgueil reds were excellent, the dry whites were too plump, alcoholic and lacked acidity. Many wines bought, many tasted, many consumed. None were less than very good.

Coteaux du Layon, Clos Ste-Cathérine Baumard Surprisingly pale; a very original scent, ripe melon and peach; fairly sweet, good flesh, fabulous flavour, perfect balance and acidity. *April 1997* ★★★★(★)

Jasnières, Les Truffières, moelleux J-B Pinon Medium-pale, waxy yellow; fragrant, classic, grassy, cress-like Chenin Blanc nose; moderate weight (12.5% alcohol), pleasant flavour, adequate acidity, its finish softer and lacking zest. *Last noted Dec 2000* ★★★

Montlouis, Vendanges Tardives Dom des Liards Lovely colour, rich gold with yellow-gold highlights; gentle, slightly minty, 'greengage' nose of great depth; sweet, very rich, powerful yet only 12% alcohol. Try with a nectarine. *June 2006* ★★★★ *Now–2012.*

St-Nicolas-de-Bourgueil, Les Harquerets Dom de la Cotelleraie/ Gérald Vallée Medium-pale, soft red, pink-rimmed; a ripe, appealing raspberry-like (Cabernet Franc) nose; sweeter and richer than normal. Delicious. In a ripe vintage like this Loire reds can be most attractive. *June 1999* ★★★★

Vouvray, doux/liquoreux Daniel Jarry Distinctive yellow with lemon-gold highlights; very good, honeyed, waxy Chenin nose and flavour, with a soft, rich mid-palate and counterbalancing acidity. *July 2000* ★★★★

Vouvray, Clos Baudoin Prince Poniatowski Deep yellow; low-keyed but ripe nose; medium-sweet, lovely flavour and length with crisp, dry finish. Delicious. *Last tasted June 1999* ★★★★

Vouvray, Le Haut-Lieu, moelleux, 1er trie Huët Yellow-gold; harmonious bouquet; delicious flavour, perfect balance. *Last noted May 1999* ★★★★

OTHER VERY GOOD '89s tasted in the early 1990s. Should still be drinking well: **Bonnezeaux, La Montagne Dom du Petit Val** ★★★★; **Coteaux du Layon, Beaulieu, Clos des Ortinières Dom d'Ambinos** ★★★★; **Quarts de Chaume Ch de Bellerive** ★★★★; **Vouvray, Clos du Bourg, moelleux Huët** ★★★★★; and **Vouvray, Cuvée Constance, moelleux Huët** Yield only 5hl/ha, 390g/l sugar in the juice, long barrel fermentation just achieving 10.9% alcohol, leaving 162g/l residual sugar. Even at scarcely two years old, it was a rich, golden colour; pure honeyed botrytis nose and flavour. The most perfect Loire wine I have ever tasted. ★★★★★★ *(6 stars)*. *Will still be lovely.*

1990 ★★★★★

Another excellent vintage for early-picked dry whites, reds and medium-sweet to sweet wines. Early but uneven flowering. Drought and scorching sun tempered by later rains. Early morning mists in October enabled superb sweet wines to be made. Firmer, less luscious than the '89s. Many tasted.

Coteaux du Layon, Ch La Tomaze, Cuvée Les Lys Lecointre A luminous, lanolin and buttercup yellow; curious waxy bouquet, raw apricot and honey, 'powdery blancmange'; but still sweet, fat, full and rich, with very good acidity and finish. *Last noted Jan 2001* ★★★★ *Years of life left.*

Montlouis, Grains Nobles Michel et Laurent Berger A ripe melon-yellow; sweet, peachy, raisiny; lovely fruit and flesh, glorious mid-palate, perfect weight (13% alcohol), richness masking Loire acidity. *July 1999* ★★★★★

Quarts de Chaume Baumard Medium-pale yellow; waxy peach-skin, Chenin nose; medium-sweet, good flavour and acidity. Harsh finish. *Aug 2000* ★★★(★) *Even after ten years, still not fully developed.*

Quarts de Chaume Ch de l'Écharderie Attractive lime-tinged yellow with gold highlights; minty fragrance; medium sweetness and body, attractive but now lacking zest. *Last tasted May 2002. At best* ★★★★, *now* ★★★

Savennières, Roche aux Moines, moelleux Chevalier Buhard Honeyed bottle age; medium-sweet, as long as its title, touch of liquorice on the aftertaste. Lovely wine. Hard to place. Drink by itself or with mild cheese. *June 2006* ★★★★ *Drink soon.*

Vouvray, Le Mont, moelleux Huët Palish amber; immensely rich, honeyed *pourriture*; very sweet, rich, tangy, lovely fruit – still with a touch of youthful pineapple. *May 2004* ★★★★★ *Now–2015.*

Vouvray, Clos Naudin, moelleux Foreau Lovely nose, immensely fragrant; sweet, fat, soft – only 9.5% alcohol – perfect acidity. *Jan 1996* ★★★★★

Vouvray, Clos Naudin, moelleux, Goutte d'Or Foreau Deep amber with warm orange highlights; very fragrant, deep, rich, botrytis bouquet; very sweet, exceptionally rich, lovely peachy flavour, pure honey and golden syrup, modest weight (12% alcohol), perfect counterbalancing and preserving acidity. *June 2005* ★★★★★★ *(6 stars) Now–2020*.

Vouvray, Trie des Grains Nobles Dom des Aubuisières A lovely waxy-sheened gold; gloriously sweet nose and taste, 'honey and flowers'. *Jan 1995* ★★★★★ *Perfection*.

1993 ★★★

The botrytis-affected grapes produced some good sweet wines.

Bonnezeaux, Cuvée Mathilde Mark Angeli Most recently: orange-tinged amber; very good, sweet, honeyed bouquet – bottle age and botrytis; medium-sweet, delicious flavour, with tinglingly acidic finish. *Last tasted Oct 1999* ★★★★

1994 ★★

Very hot summer, then rain. Some late-harvest botrytis wines made. No recent notes.

1995 ★★★★

Successful throughout the Loire. The reds were good and the sweet whites, where there was careful grape selection, were very good indeed.

Coteaux du Layon, Ch la Tomaze Lecointre Fabulous old gold; buttery, harmonious; sweet, lovely peachy flavour, nice acidity, touch of liquorice on finish. *June 2006* ★★★★ *Now–2015*.

Coteaux du Layon, Rablay, Ch la Tomaze, Cuvée des Lys Lecointre Pure gold; slightly honeyed; sweet, rich, delicious flavour, perfect acidity. *Aug 2003* ★★★★★

Vouvray, Clos du Bourg, 1er trie Huët Palish; classic pure cress nose; medium-sweet, relatively lightweight (12% alcohol), delicious flavour, perfect acidity. A seemingly effortless wine from the old Loire master. *June 1999* ★★★★

1996 ★★★★

A good season though the potentially large harvest was curtailed by drought conditions throughout the summer. Welcome September rain swelled the grapes. Some really lovely sweet white wines, which should have survived.

Bonnezeaux, Grand Vin Liquoreux Ch de Fesles Palish yellow; pleasant, grapey aroma; sweet, good flesh, fruit and length. Hard finish. *Last tasted Aug 2003* ★★★

Coteaux du Layon, Beaulieu Pierre-Bise Touch of mint and caramel; fairly sweet, lovely. *June 1998* ★★★(★) *Needed a bit of bottle age*.

Coteaux du Layon, Chaume, Les Julines Ch de Fesles Lovely, honeyed – pure expression of ripe Chenin Blanc; very sweet, rich, fairly powerful (13% alcohol), lovely fruit – youthful pineapple and melon. *Dec 1997* ★★★★★

Coteaux du Layon, Dom de Pierre Blanche Lecointre Pale, lime-tinged; sweet, rich, buttery nose and taste. Some agreeable fat, acidity completely integrated. *March 2002* ★★★(★)

Coteaux du Layon, Les Omnis Dom des Forges/Branchereau
Lovely nose, honey and mint; fairly sweet, lightish style, absolutely glorious flavour
with a lively touch and excellent acidity. *Jan 1998* ★★★★
Jasnières, Dom de la Charrière, Sélection de Raisins Nobles
Joël Gigou Palish yellow; lime highlights; grassy; medium-sweet, pleasant enough,
fair flesh, light end acidity. *March 2002* ★★★ *(just)*.
Quarts de Chaume, Dom du Petit Métro Joseph Renou Very
pronounced brass-gold; honeyed, rich, buttery with refreshing acidity; very sweet,
full, rich flavour, high extract, its fat masking acidity. Good length. *April 2004* ★★★
Vouvray, moelleux Daniel Jarry More *demi-sec* than *moelleux*, a pleasant, soft
ripeness but very dry acidic finish. *April 2001* ★★★
**Vouvray, La Gaudrelle, Réserve Personnelle Alexandre
Monmousseau** Orange-tinged gold; peachy nose; sweet, modest weight (11.5%
alcohol), very attractive honey and apricot flavour. *June 2001* ★★★★
Vouvray, Le Mont, moelleux, 1er trie Huët Floral, honeyed; medium-
sweet, 'warm' character, powerful, very good acidity. *July 2002* ★★★★

1997 ★★★★★

The third remarkably good Loire vintage in a row. Superb wines, honeyed
botrytis much in evidence. Yet there were worrying moments, for despite
good flowering, the end of June was the coolest and wettest for 30 years.
Happily, the summer was long and hot, punctuated by rainstorms which
served to refresh the flagging grapes. Superripe botrytised Chenin Blanc up
to the end of October. It was also an excellent vintage for the reds.
Azay-le-Rideau, moelleux G Pavy Pleasant, young, grassy nose; medium-
sweet, light (10.8% alcohol), quite good fruit, tingling acidity. *July 2000* ★★★
Bonnezeaux Ch de Fesles/Bernard Germain Distinctive buttercup-yellow,
waxy sheen; lovely ripe botrytis nose; sweet, perfect weight and flavour, excellent
acidity. *Last noted Jan 2000* ★★★★(★) *Long life*.
Bonnezeaux, Cuvée Elisabeth H Ch de Fesles/Bernard Germain
Glorious yellow-gold; honey and ripe apricots; sweet, fat, medium-full body (13%
alcohol), delicious flavour. *Aug 2002* ★★★★
Coteaux du Layon, Le Clos du Bois Jo Pithon Straw yellow; fairly
sweet. Delicious. *Jan 2000* ★★★★
Coteaux du Layon, Chaume Ch de la Guimonière Bright yellow;
honey and clover; sweet, lovely flesh and flavour. Very good – and very necessary –
acidity. *Sept 2001* ★★★★★ *A delectable half bottle.*
**Coteaux du Layon, Chaume, Les Aunis Ch de la Roulerie/Ch de
Fesles** Beautiful golden colour; lime blossom; gloriously rich, perfect acidity.
Superb. *Last noted (mid-morning) Feb 2001* ★★★★(★)
Sancerre, La Grande Cuvée Rouge Pascal Jolivet From 40-year-old
Pinot Noir vines. Medium-pale red; very fragrant; light style, very pleasant fruit
and good acidity. *Jan 2000* ★★(★) *Probably excellent now.*
Savennières, Clos de la Coulée de Serrant Nicolas Joly Joly is
renowned for his biodynamic philosophy. This is one of the most remarkable dry
Chenin wines of the Loire, from a tiny vineyard within the Savennières
appellation south of Anjou. An amazing colour, pure yellow-gold with touch of
straw; original bouquet, honeyed walnuts; reminding me of an amalgam of sherry,

Condrieu and dry Tokaji Szamorodni. Dry. Positive entry, full-bodied (14% alcohol), appley flavour, 'white pepper' finish. *Oct 2005* ★★★★

1998 variable. At best ★★★★

A very uneven growing season. The late-harvested wines were more successful than the Sauvignon Blancs. I have tasted a wide range and the best are noted below.

Coteaux du Layon, Chaume, Les Aunis, Grand Vin Liquoreux Ch de la Roulerie/Ch de Fesles Yellow; honeyed Chenin; certainly sweet, slightly raisiny flavour, rich and attractive, good acidity. *Aug 2000* ★★★★

Montlouis, Vieilles Vignes Dom des Liards Medium-sweet; really lovely flavour. Mouthfilling but not heavy (12.5% alcohol). *Aug 2000* ★★★

Vouvray, Le Mont, demi-sec Huët Palish; hard and underdeveloped; more *sec* than *demi*, lightweight (12% alcohol), decent flavour, good acidity. *Dec 2001* ★★★

1999 ★★★

The year started well: an ideal spring, no frosts, successful flowering and a beautifully warm summer. However, the rains came in mid-September, with just ten days break in early October. The early picked dry whites, from Muscadet to Sancerre, fared best but the growers of Chenin Blanc struggled, needing many expensive *tries* through the vineyards to find ripe and botrytised grapes to make their sweet wines.

Coteaux du Layon, Chaume Ch de la Guimonière Sweet, creamy, agreeable body, delicious (especially with cheese). *Feb 2003* ★★★

Coteaux du Layon, Chaume, Les Aunis, Grand Vin Liquoreux Ch de la Roulerie/Ch de Fesles Positive yellow; scented caramel and orange blossom; sweet, rich, grapey taste, attractive with some length and acidity. *Sept 2002* ★★★ *Drink up.*

Coteaux du Layon, Les Clos Dom Leduc-Frouin Ripe Chenin; sweet, assertive (13.5% alcohol), good flavour. A delightful surprise! *July 2001* ★★★

2000–2005

Encouragingly there has been a distinct improvement in overall quality in the Loire. This, I believe, has to do with a new generation of *vignerons* whose aim is simply to produce the best wines of their type, weather permitting.

Sweet Vintages at a Glance

Outstanding ★★★★★ 2003, 2005
Very Good ★★★★ 2001, 2004
Good ★★★ 2000, 2002

2000 ★★★

Plenty of wines of reasonable quality were made but this vintage did not hit the high notes. There was moderately successful flowering in early June. July was cool with mildew-inducing rain. Happily, August was dry and warm. Grapes for the dry wines were picked early; but only a few intrepid growers managed to make sweet wines from grapes picked in late November. For the sweet whites of Anjou and Touraine this was a 'correct' rather than 'outstanding' year.

Bonnezeaux, liquoreux Ch de Fesles/Bernard Germain Medium-brassy gold; sweet, rich, honeyed nose and flavour. Nice weight. Whiff of tea, very good acidity. Most attractive. *Jan 2006* ★★★★ *Now–2015.*

Savennières, Roche aux Moines Dom aux Moines Waxy yellow, rich 'legs'; whiff of papaya and pineapple; characteristically bone dry and austere yet with innate richness and flesh. 12.8% alcohol, a perfect food wine. *April 2007* ★★★★

2001 ★★★★

Growing conditions were overall satisfactory. Strong sunshine in May and June enabled the vital flowering to take place in good conditions; rain followed but the summer was hot with temperatures close to those of 1989 and 1990. Some excellent dry wines for early consumption and well-nigh perfect conditions for the sweet wines in Anjou and Touraine, typified by the three lovely examples below. My sort of wine.

Bonnezeaux, Liquoreux Ch de Fesles/Bernard Germain Grassy, touch of caramel; medium-sweet, good flavour and acidity but on the lean side with a dry, almost bitter finish. *June 2006* ★★ *possible* ★★★ *with more bottle age.*

Coteaux du Layon, Chaume Pierre-Bise Shimmering, pure Tutankhamen yellow-gold; scents of hay, clover and the edge of a honeycomb; sweet, lovely flavour, refreshingly dry finish. *Dec 2004* ★★★★

Coteaux du Layon, 1er Cru, Chaume 'Les Aunis' Dom des Forges Palish gold; lovely nose, minty and with typical botrytis honey; fairly sweet, delicious flavour, good acidity, honeyed aftertaste. *Sept 2005* ★★★★

2002 ★★★

A 'good' rather than 'great' year. Generally the wines are well defined with good purity of fruit. Conditions for flowering were not ideal and there was above average rainfall in August. The vintage was saved by an exceptionally sunny September. Some excellent and well-balanced sweet wines made.

Bonnezeaux, liquoreux Ch de Fesles/Vignobles Germain Totally different to the 2001. Low-keyed, more minerally nose; very sweet, more flesh and fat. Low alcohol (12%) but well balanced. Delicious. *June 2006* ★★★★ *Now–2012.*

Pouilly-Fumé Ch de Tracy An ancient aristocratic estate. A not very positive nose or flavour; just a very pleasant dry wine, with a hint of liquorice added to its crisp, fruity Sauvignon Blanc grapiness. *July 2005* ★★★ *Drink now.*

Vouvray Sec Marc Brédif Palish yellow; low-keyed but fragrant aroma; medium-dry, lovely flavour, excellent acidity. A perfect example of the versatility of the Chenin Blanc grape, in this instance the wine was delightful by itself but would also be delicious with fish or chicken dishes. *June 2004* ★★★★

Vouvray Sec, Coteau de la Biche Dom Pichot/Dom le Peu de la Moriette The New World cannot compete with evocative names like this – or the wine. I always look out for Vouvrays. Very pale, still youthful green tinge; pure 'waxy' Chenin Blanc; not too dry, delicious flavour, good acidity. *May 2006* ★★★ *Delightful now. Don't keep.*

2003 ★★★★★

Incredibly ripe fruit was harvested exceptionally early. The superripe Chenin Blancs of Anjou and Touraine are amazingly rich and powerful but have lower acidity than in many of the great classic vintages. Yields were minimal. Atypical wines. Only time will tell how these will last, long-term.
Bonnezeaux Ch de Fesles/Bernard Germain Sweet, richer, more honeyed nose; very sweet, very rich, 13% alcohol, fleshy, good length and finish. *June 2006* ★★★★ *Now–2015.*
Vouvray Marc Brédif Attractive light gold; lovely 'waxy' Chenin Blanc aroma; medium dryness and body, delicious flavour. *Nov 2005* ★★★★ *Now–2012.*

2004 ★★★★

A classic vintage in the Loire Valley with a long, slow ripening season and an abundant crop. For sweet Chenins, 2004 is perhaps overshadowed by the super-concentrated and short '03s and the benchmark '05s. Nevertheless, some excellent wines were made which should age well.
Anjou Blanc, Coteau du Houet La Ferme de la Sansonnière/Mark Angeli Very small biodynamic production. Bonnezeaux in all but name. Glorious old gold; peachy, floral; sweet, high extract, fleshy, powerful yet only 12% alcohol, great length. *June 2006* ★★★★ *Now–2012.*
Menetou-Salon, Moroques, Le Petit Clos J-M Roger Almost as good as its attractive, intriguing name. Dry, youthful, pleasing. I enjoyed it with *boudin noir* (black pudding). *Nov 2006* ★★★ *For drinking not keeping.*
St-Nicolas de Bourgueil J-C Mabileau Very deep youthful red; initially – and typically – raw, needing food: which is how, in Laon, we enjoyed it. *Nov 2006* ★★(★) *Now–2010.*

2005 ★★★★★

A markedly superior vintage where the grapes achieved a balanced phenolic ripeness over a long growing season. The finished wines exhibit an excellent concentration of fruit underscored by fine acidity, which should see them age well into the long-term. A terrific sweet wine vintage, the wines being very well balanced. *Bien classique.* The best vintage of the decade so far. Few wines yet tasted.
Sancerre Rouge Dom de Carron Fairly deep, youthful; dry enough, some softness from ripe grapes, though characteristically tannic and acidic. Enjoyed with *andouillettes* at a charming restaurant in Troyes. *Nov 2006.* ★★★ *Best drunk young and fresh but will keep – say now–2010.*
Vins de Thouarsais, demi-sec F Gigon Very pale, faded melon; fragrant refreshing, youthful, minty; pineapple; medium-sweet, fresh melon on the palate, white currant, dry acidic finish. Inexpensive because few have heard of the Thouarsais district, south of Anjou. *June 2006* ★★★ *Best drunk young and fresh.*

Alsace

Alsace is an odd man out: the region is most definitely French, yet it has many Germanic overtones. This includes the wines; it is the only classic French wine region producing varietal wines sold under the grape name. The best wines come from four 'noble' varieties – Riesling, Gewurztraminer, Pinot Gris (previously labelled as Tokay-Pinot Gris) and Muscat.

Outstanding vintages
1865, 1900, 1937, 1945,
1959, 1961, 1971, 1976,
1983, 1988, 1989, 1990,
1995, 1997, 2002, 2005

Despite their quality, dependability and reasonable prices, Alsace wines have never achieved the popularity they deserve. It is largely thanks to the efforts of a handful of major firms and gifted winemakers that the fine wine horizons have been widened. The introduction of *grand cru* classifications (in 1985) has led to an increasing awareness of what can be achieved. I make no apologies that my notes cover only a few of the many excellent Alsace producers. The Hugel family are my oldest Alsace friends, dependable, and noted for top-quality Vendange Tardive and Sélection de Grains Nobles wines; the Trimbach family are renowned for their crisp, dry, elegant wines; and Schlumberger for wines with impressive power that blossom with age. Two other excellent family estates are the Faller sisters' Domaine Weinbach and Zind-Humbrecht.

Although I enjoy drinking the many excellent, good-value everyday wines from Alsace, my notes here are devoted to the better, richer, ageworthy wines from the top vintages. With bottle-ageing the high-alcohol Gewurztraminer and Pinot Gris wines achieve the greatest heights of sublimity.

Vendange Tardive and Sélection de Grains Nobles

Vendange Tardive (VT) means 'late harvest' and, in terms of Alsace wines, refers to wines made from late-picked grapes with high natural sugar levels, strictly with no chaptalisation. The wines can vary between seriously dry to very sweet, without there being any indication of the sweetness level on the label. While this can be very irritating, the term is always a measure of good quality. Sélection de Grains Nobles (SGN) wines are made from individually selected, late-ripened, botrytis-affected berries: these wines are invariably sweet, rare and expensive.

Classic older vintages: 1865–1989

Alsace's chequered history left a legacy of very ordinary wine. It was not until the 1930s that producers were encouraged to 'pull their socks up'. The Hugel family were heavily involved in this renaissance and in the tightening up of regulations. They were also the first to introduce two styles of wine now associated with Alsace: Vendange Tardive and Sélection de Grains Nobles. The 1970s and '80s were, on the whole, a successful period but only the best sweet wines will have survived.

VINTAGES AT A GLANCE

Outstanding ★★★★★ 1865, 1900, 1937, 1945, 1959, 1961, 1971, 1976, 1983, 1988 (v), 1989

Very Good ★★★★ 1921, 1928, 1934, 1964, 1967, 1981, 1985, 1986 (v), 1988 (v)

Good ★★★ 1935, 1953, 1966, 1975, 1986 (v), 1988 (v)

1953 ★★★

Good summer. Ripe grapes though the lesser wines were quick maturing.
Riesling Vendange Tardive Hugel In magnum: paler than expected; slightly spicy, then 'smoky'; very dry, slightly peachy flavoured, almost steely, with rapier-like acidity. Remarkable vivacity for its age. *Last noted April 2002* ★★★★

1959 ★★★★★

Hot summer. As in 1953, the richer wines did best.
Gewurztraminer SGN Hugel Still magnificent, still sweet, firm, soft and spicy. *June 1989* ★★★★★
Riesling Vendange Tardive Hugel Pure gold; classic Riesling, almost creamy rich; medium-sweet, full, rich, fleshy with a 'warm', nutty finish. Perfect example of a great vintage with a quarter of a century's bottle age. *Dec 1995* ★★★★

1961 ★★★★★

Very good vintage. Less overripe, better acidity than 1959.
Riesling Vendange Tardive Hugel Old gold; initially low-keyed but opened up, grapey, honeyed; medium-dry, rich, fairly assertive, in excellent condition. *Last noted April 2002* ★★★★

1966 ★★★

Good year. Well-structured whites with good acidity.
Riesling Vendange Tardive Hugel Pale for its age; initially a whiff of bottle age, then minty, opening up vividly with a sort of raw, greengage acidity; very dry, lean. Holding well. *Last tasted April 2002* ★★★

1971 ★★★★★

The smallest crop of the 1970s due to *coulure* in June and, overall, a very dry season. A burst of autumn heat resulted in high-quality, late-harvest wines.
Riesling Vendange Tardive Hugel Seemed to have gained colour, now a brassy gold; rich from start to finish, with whiff of classic kerosene, then smoky, grapefruit; dry yet rich, wonderful extract, full. *Last noted April 2002* ★★★★★

1976 ★★★★★

A great year, particularly for the richer wines. Well-nigh perfect summer, with an occasional shower to flesh out the grapes. An average-size crop picked from early October with ideal conditions for late-harvested wines.
Gewurztraminer Vendange Tardive 'SGN par Jean Hugel', Fût 20 Hugel 'Fût 20' is Hugel's greatest cask. Golden sheen; ambrosial syrup of figs, intensely rich and fragrant. *Last noted Jan 1990* ★★★★★
Riesling SGN Hugel One of Hugel's greatest Rieslings. A brassy touch to its old gold, but very bright; perfectly harmonious, creamy nose; very sweet, lovely texture, peachy flavour, complete, well balanced. *Last noted April 2002* ★★★★★
Riesling Vendange Tardive Hugel Medium-gold, pale for its age; good, classic bouquet with touch of Riesling kerosene and honeyed bottle age. Good flavour and length. *Last tasted April 2004. At best* ★★★★ *Drink soon.*
Tokay-Pinot Gris SGN Hugel Hugel's first Pinot Gris SGN since the superb 1865. Fairly stolid but with a good finish. *Last tasted July 1994* ★★★★

1978 ★★

Small crop though some quite good wines made.
Tokay-Pinot Gris Clos St-Urbain Zind-Humbrecht Possibly the finest made in the '78 vintage: buttercup gold; 'milk and honey' bouquet; fairly dry though rich and substantial. *Tasted Sept 1986* ★★★★ *And will have survived.*

1981 ★★★★

Very satisfactory for both quantity and quality. Good flowering, sunny summer and an early harvest, yet conditions were also perfect for late-harvest wines.
Riesling Réserve Personnelle (now called 'Jubilee') **Hugel** Pale; a ripe bottle-age kerosene Riesling; dry, very good for its age. *Magnum, Jan 2002* ★★★
Riesling Vendange Tardive Hugel Very untypical Vendange Tardive: medium-pale yellow; low-keyed, grassy, minty nose; extremely dry, almost raw, melon-like flavour, lean and acidic. *April 2002* ★★

1983 ★★★★★

Excellent vintage, abundant and of high quality; many of the top wines are still superb. The warmest winter, wettest spring and driest summer on record. There was an extended harvest from early October to mid-November for the late-picked wines.
Gewurztraminer SGN Weinbach/Faller Bright yellow-gold; very distinctive, soft rose cachou fragrance; much drier than expected though very rich and assertive. Impressive. *July 2004* ★★★★

Riesling Vendange Tardive Hugel Even in a good vintage this wine was only 1% of Hugel's production. Only 5% botrytis. Medium-gold colour; subtle, honeyed nose, waxy, spicy, touch of peach kernels; rich but not as sweet as the '89 or '95. Good acidity. A wine to accompany turbot. *Last tasted Nov 1999* ★★★★

Tokay-Pinot Gris SGN Hugel 192° Oechsle, an astonishing 220g/l residual sugar: fairly deep yellow; smoky, harmonious, 'Williamine pears'; fabulous, sweet, rich, fat, fleshy, perfect – and very necessary – acidity. *June 1989* ★★★★★ *Will still be superb.*

1985 ★★★★

An abundant crop of good wines followed a fine and dry summer. There were attractive wines at each quality level.

Muscat Rangen Zind-Humbrecht Splendid combination of good *grand cru*, good year and gifted winemaking. Medium-dry, assertive. *June 1990* ★★★★★

Muscat Rothenberg Vendange Tardive Zind-Humbrecht Rich, spicy. *June 1990* ★★★★★

Riesling TBA Hugel Medium-pale yellow; youthful kerosene Riesling aroma; not as sweet as expected, full body and flavour. Hot finish. *Dec 1995* ★★★★

1986 variable, at best ★★★★

A poor start but by June the weather was ideal for the flowering. Late summer was cold, encouraging rot, followed by ideal weather again. Picking began on 9 October, morning mists and ripening sun encouraging botrytis.

Gewurztraminer SGN Zind-Humbrecht Pure gold; exotic bouquet; fairly sweet, delicious flavour and a fabulous future. *June 1999* ★★★★(★)

Tokay-Pinot Gris Vendange Tardive Hugel Medium-pale gold, waxy sheen; extraordinarily forthcoming, ripe melon fragrance; fairly sweet still, lovely crisp fruit, excellent acidity. Perfect with foie gras. *Oct 2004* ★★★★

1988 ★★★ to ★★★★★

A glorious spring and summer spoiled by heavy rains before the harvest. Hot November and botrytis enabled some high quality late-harvest wines to be made. The best are still superb.

Gewurztraminer Cuvée Anne Schlumberger Harvested mid-November after late-autumn sun. The first to be made from '100% botrytis grapes' since 1976: just one 60-litre cask. Yellow gold; heavenly honeyed botrytis nose; full-bodied. Perfection. *May 1991* ★★★★★ *Now–2010.*

Riesling Vendange Tardive Hugel Medium-yellow gold; touch of lime, green acidity, opening up, more honeyed; surprisingly dry, firm, good acidity but lacked excitement. Will benefit from more ageing. *Last noted April 2002* ★★★(★)

OTHER TOP-CLASS '88s TASTED IN THEIR YOUTH

Gewurztraminer: Zind-Humbrecht's Goldert Grand Cru ★★★★; **Kuentz-Bas' Cuvée Tradition** delicate and fragrant ★★★★; and **Zind-Humbrecht's Clos Windsbuhl** rich and fragrant ★★★★

Riesling: Hugel's SGN astonishing wine: hefty; minty; sweet, crisp, spicy ★★★★★ *will still be superb.*

Tokay-Pinot Gris: Zind-Humbrecht's Clos Jebsal scented; full-bodied;

lovely ★★★★; and **Hugel**'s Vendange Tardive fabulous flavour and fragrance, though hard ★★★★★ *doubtless perfect now*; and their rare Vin de Paille du Jubilee Only 200 half bottles produced. Pale gold; glorious scent – a *mélange* of Muscat, Gewurz and Riesling; slightly sweet, delicate, lovely ★★★★★

1989 ★★★★★

Superb vintage, combining abundance and overall high quality. A hot and dry summer. An unusually early harvest from 29 September, with the largest-ever production of late-harvest and SGN wines.

Gewurztraminer Cuvée Anne **Schlumberger** Bought in 1991, it was so powerful and austere that I put it to one side. After 13 years in my cellar an amazing transformation: palish gold; full, rich, fleshy, spicy; medium-sweet, full-bodied (14.5% alcohol), but neither heady nor clumsy. Lovely flavour and fresh. Perfect with ripe Vacherin. *Oct 2004* ★★★★★ *Leaving my last bottle for another 5 years.*

Gewurztraminer Heimburg SGN **Zind-Humbrecht** Glorious bouquet of scented roses; fairly sweet, very rich. An incredibly beautiful wine. *June 1997* ★★★★★ *Glorious now but will keep and evolve over another 20 years.*

Gewurztraminer SGN **Beyer** Lovely, medium-pale yellow-gold; peachy, rose cachou, honeyed lychee fragrance; sweet, rich, smooth, plump and fleshy, counterbalancing acidity. Superb wine. *Aug 2006* ★★★★★ *Now–2015.*

Gewurztraminer SGN 'S' **Hugel** Now a fairly deep gold; glorious bouquet and flavour. Full, rich, superb aftertaste. *Nov 2000* ★★★★★

Riesling 'Quintessences de Sélection de Grains Nobles' **Weinbach/Faller** Golden colour; immensely rich kerosene Riesling aroma, with a touch of caramel and honeyed botrytis; sweet, rich, perfect weight, length, finish. *Sept 1997* ★★★★★ *Years of life ahead.*

Riesling Grand Cru Schlossberg **Weinbach/Faller** Lovely colour; classic Riesling; medium-dry, fairly full-bodied, excellent flavour, balance and aftertaste. Holding its age well. *Dec 2005* ★★★★ *Drink soon.*

Riesling Vendange Tardive **Hugel** Warm gold; fully evolved, harmonious, slightly scented, honey and mint; medium-dry, hefty, four-square, good acidity, and dry finish. *Last noted April 2002* ★★★★ *Drink soon.*

Riesling Clos Windsbuhl SGN **Zind-Humbrecht** Surprisingly low-keyed nose; sweet, amazingly rich and full for its unexpectedly modest strength (11.9% alcohol). Hot, biting finish. *Nov 1997* ★★★(★★) *Needs more time.*

1990–1999

This ranks as Alsace's most successful decade to date; only one vintage was ranked less than good.

VINTAGES AT A GLANCE

Outstanding ★★★★★ 1990, 1995 (v), 1997
Very Good ★★★★ 1992 (v), 1993, 1995 (v), 1996, 1998
Good ★★★ 1992 (v), 1994 (v), 1999 (v)

1990 ★★★★★

The second of the exceptional twin vintages, similar in style and quality to 1989, but with a considerably reduced volume. The growing season was cold with wet weather during flowering which caused both *coulure* and *millerandage*, reducing the crop by some 25% compared with 1989. Most affected were the more delicate Gewurztraminer, Muscat and Tokay-Pinot Gris vines. Conditions during the rest of the summer were excellent and a crop of healthy grapes was harvested from 4 October. Sugar content was high and many Vendange Tardive wines were made but, because of the lack of botrytis, there were few SGNs. The best were outstanding.

Gewurztraminer Cuvée Anne Schlumberger Fairly sweet, full, rich, scented flavour, excellent finish and aftertaste. *Sept 1996* ★★★ *Now–2010*.

Gewurztraminer SGN Dopff au Moulin Lovely yellow-gold; heavy botrytised nose of considerable depth; sweet, full-bodied, very good flavour. *April 1996* ★★★★

Riesling Clos Ste Hune Trimbach Distinct yellow; very positive classic Riesling aroma plus bottle age; unquestionably dry, mouthfilling, full-bodied (14% alcohol) yet not obtrusively, good length and finish. A beautifully made wine. *July 2005* ★★★★ *Drink soon*.

Riesling Vendange Tardive Hugel Medium-pale gold; glorious, peach blossom; medium-dry; lovely silky texture and flavour, perfect weight and acidity. Partnered langoustines. *Last tasted Oct 2004* ★★★★★

Tokay-Pinot Gris Vendange Tardive Weinbach/Faller Slightly minty, indefinable but good nose; sweet, soft, lovely flavour, full-bodied yet with delicacy and fragrance. *Jan 1996* ★★★★★ *Perfection then and will keep*.

1991 ★★

The decade's one really poor vintage. However, there were some surprises from producers who picked late, risking all to make interesting wine.

Tokay-Pinot Gris Clos Jebsal SGN Zind-Humbrecht Although this is not a new note it shows how a quality producer copes with a poor vintage. A small production from late-picked, selected botrytis-affected berries. Rich gold; gloriously honeyed, peachy, bouquet and flavour. Sweet, rich but with a crisp, acidic touch giving it a refreshing finish. *Oct 1995* ★★★★★

1992 ★★ to ★★★★

Well-nigh perfect conditions. Early budding, frost-free, excellent flowering, followed by a warm, dry summer and the hottest August since 1921. A perfect September, picking commencing on the 30th, avoiding the torrential rains which plagued the rest of France. Other than this Pinot Gris, no other sweet wines have come my way.

Tokay-Pinot Gris Grand Cru Kitterlé Schlumberger Extraordinary colour, medium-deep, amber-gold; very rich, honeyed bottle-age bouquet, almost Gewurz fragrance; medium-dry, full-bodied (14% alcohol), a bit four-square but with excellent flavour. Good length. Very impressive. *Oct 2000* ★★★★★ *Shows how a top-class Pinot Gris will not only keep but take on new dimensions with bottle age.*

1993 ★★★★

The harvest was smaller than the '92 but quality was higher, with ripeness almost reaching the levels of '88 and '89. However, late pickers were hampered by rain and few sweet wines were made.

Riesling Cuvée Frédéric Émile Trimbach Palish; crisp, steely nose; very good, firm, dry and stylish. Excellent flavour and marvellous length. *Dec 1998* ★★★★ *Drink now.*

1994 ★★ to ★★★

A difficult year, starting with a cold, wet spring. The summer was reasonably warm and dry but was followed by 30 days of persistent and heavy rain in September. Widespread rot, Riesling being most affected. The only healthy crop was Gewurztraminer. Growers who took advantage of the later fine weather produced some good ripe Gewurztraminers, both late-harvested and botrytis-affected, and passable Rieslings.

Gewurztraminer Cuvée d'Or Quintessences de SGN Weinbach/Faller Gold; gloriously ripe, honeyed, spicy botrytis; sweet, full (14% alcohol), soft and long. Glorious wine. *Tasted Sept 1997* ★★★★(★) *Now–beyond 2010.*

Gewurztraminer Goldert Vendange Tardive Zind-Humbrecht Luxuriously rich yet a soft and spicy Gewurz; fairly sweet, superb flavour and balance. *Sept 1999* ★★★★ *Lovely then. Will keep.*

Gewurztraminer SGN Rolly Gassmann Slightly hazy straw gold; glorious lychees; fairly sweet, very rich, honeyed botrytis flavour. *Oct 1998* ★★★★

Riesling Clos Windsbuhl Zind-Humbrecht A whiff of almost Muscat-like scent; dry, well made, good acidity. *June 2003* ★★★ *Drink soon.*

1995 ★★★★ to ★★★★★

Late budbreak, damp spring and uneven flowering with *coulure*. September was rainy and cool but there was a long Indian summer. Late pickers did best. Rieslings were perfect and generally better than Gewurztraminers. There were some superlative Pinot Gris. The top sweet wines will last.

Gewurztraminer Grand Cru Furstentum SGN Weinbach/Faller Yellow; opulent aroma, rose cachou, lychees; very sweet, luscious, moderate weight (12% alcohol), richness and fat cut by unusual (for Gewurz) acidity. A brilliant wine. *Sept 1997* ★★★★(★) *Drink soon.*

Riesling Grand Cru Hengst Josmeyer Palish, very bright; very attractive, scented nose; medium-dry entry leading to long, crisp, dry finish. Good flavour and acidity. *Sept 2003* ★★★★ *Drink soon.*

Riesling Vendange Tardive Hugel Pure gold; substantial grapey, grassy, honeyed nose; rich texture and balance. Delicious. *Last noted April 2002* ★★★★★

Tokay-Pinot Gris Altenbourg Cuvée Laurence Weinbach/Faller Palish, bright yellow; hefty, peach and mint nose; fairly sweet, full-bodied (14% alcohol), superb flavour, perfect acidity. *Dec 2001* ★★★★

(Tokay) Pinot Gris Clos Jebsal SGN Zind-Humbrecht Golden colour; gloriously exotic, honeyed botrytis fragrance; very sweet, immensely rich yet not cloying, lovely flavour, great depth, perfect acidity. *June 2001* ★★★★★ *Great now but will continue to dazzle well beyond 2010.*

1996 ★★★★

In many ways this was an ideal vintage. The Rieslings were particularly attractive, the most appealing being noted below. Growing conditions: late spring, budburst uneven. June mainly warm and dry, Gewurztraminer affected by *coulure*. The rest of the summer was warm and dry, the harvest beginning in cool conditions in early October, continuing – for the late-harvest wines – almost to the middle of November though the dry weather prevented the formation of botrytis. The better wines are still delicious.

Gewurztraminer Grand Cru Brand Zind-Humbrecht Highly polished; lovely, copybook rose cachou and lychee scents; medium-dry, full, rich, excellent flavour and very good acidity. *July 2003* ★★★★ *Now–2012.*

Riesling Grand Cru Moenchberg Ostertag A somewhat controversial winemaker in Epfig with a cult following. Showing bottle age and not a typical Riesling aroma, but developed well in the glass; medium-dry, unusual flavour, body and texture. Touch of spearmint. Very good acidity and fragrant aftertaste. *Jan 2004* ★★★★ *Now–2010.*

Riesling 'Les Princes Abbés' Schlumberger Pale; good, fresh, varietal aroma; crisp, delicious, light style and weight. *Jan 2000* ★★★

Riesling Cuvée Ste Catherine II Weinbach/Faller From the lower part of the Schlossberg vineyard. Totally different appearance to the Schlossberg II below: positive yellow; still hard though with considerable depth; sweeter, spicy, higher extract though same strength, good length, 'hot', dry finish. *Sept 1997* ★★★(★★) *Probably at its best now.*

Riesling Grand Cru Schlossberg II Weinbach/Faller Almost colourless; good, light, fragrant Riesling aroma; fairly dry, excellent flavour, pleasant weight (13% alcohol), firm, crisp, long, dry finish. *Sept 1997* ★★★★

Riesling Vendange Tardive Hugel Lovely, honey and orange blossom, almost Pinot Gris-like; swingeingly dry (fully fermented out and no malolactic fermentation) but good penetrating flavour and length. *April 2002* ★★★★

Tokay-Pinot Gris Vieilles Vignes Zind-Humbrecht Yellow gold; good but – for me – always difficult to describe Pinot Gris aroma; medium-sweet, full, rich, soft, lovely. *Nov 2003* ★★★★ *Now–2010.*

1997 ★★★★★

Yet another superb vintage despite some early problems with an uneven budbreak, and *coulure* due to rain in June and July. August and September were hot and sunny, with record overall hours of sunshine, double those of 1995. Fully ripe grapes were harvested from 1 October: Riesling was excellent with very high ripeness levels, but Gewurztraminer, once again hit by *coulure*, suffered crop losses. Early morning mists in October generated some botrytis, but not everywhere. Ideally this is a dry wine vintage and many of the wines should have been consumed while young and fresh. I have quoted a handful of notes to illustrate the richer styles of the three major grape varieties.

Gewurztraminer 'Hommage à Jean Hugel' Hugel Medium-pale, lime-tinged yellow; fragrant, slightly minty Gewurz; medium-sweet, rich, fleshy, typically hard, blunt Gewurz finish. *Aug 2006* ★★★★ *Now–2010.*

Gewurztraminer 'Jubilee' Hugel Medium-pale yellow; lovely mellow lychees and rose cachou; medium-sweet, rich, mildly spicy. *April 2002* ★★★★

Gewurztraminer SGN 'S' (Super Selection) Hugel An astonishing wine. 165° Oechsle, 153g/l sugar, picked at 18% alcohol, bottled at 13.5%. Pure botrytis, rather like a Rheingau TBA. Colour of polished brass, rich 'legs'; glorious bouquet, honey, ripe apricots, lychees; very sweet, very rich, assertive, fabulous flavour and counterbalancing acidity. Great wine. *Last tasted Nov 2005* ★★★★★ *Now–2020.*

Riesling Cuvée du Cinquantenaire A Mann Magnum: positive yellow; lovely, waxy, vanillin nose and flavour. Medium sweetness and body, adequate acidity. More than interesting. *Jan 2006* ★★★★ *Drink soon.*

Riesling Vendange Tardive Hugel Very little botrytis. Palish yellow; harmonious, slightly waxy almost Chenin nose, crisp, grapey; medium-sweet, delicious flavour, fragrant, good finish. *April 2002* ★★★★ *Now–2010.*

Tokay-Pinot Gris Altenbourg Cuvée Laurence Weinbach/Faller Bright yellow; hefty, minty, peachy nose; medium-sweet, full-bodied (14% alcohol), rich, superb flavour and perfect acidity. *Dec 2001.* Then ★★★(★★) *Now–2012.*

1998 ★★★★

The fourth really good – indeed unprecedented – vintage in a row. Yet the weather conditions throughout the growing season were very up-and-down: cool April, hot and dry May, uneventful flowering. July was wet but from early August to mid-September, there was exceptional heat. An early harvest, 25 September, in sunshine but a short, sharp burst of rain put off most picking until early October. The gap between the merely decent and the really good wine in Alsace continues to widen.

Gewurztraminer Grand Cru Goldert Vendange Tardive Zind-Humbrecht Lovely aroma, mint and orange blossom; fairly sweet, still hard. *June 2001* ★★★(★★)

Gewurztraminer Grand Cru Hengst Zind-Humbrecht Pale; glorious scent; medium-dry, rich, very high alcohol (16%), yet subtle, superb. *Last tasted June 2003* ★★★★ *Now–2016.*

Gewurztraminer SGN Cuvée Anne Schlumberger Only the tenth
Cuvée Anne since World War Two, selected from the best SGNs of the vintage.
Pale; honey and mint; sweet, excellent acidity, delicious. *Nov 2004* ★★★(★★)
Now–2015.
Gewurztraminer Vendange Tardive Hugel Pale, lime-tinged; beautifully
scented; medium-sweet, lovely flavour, easy, a touch of blandness. *Jan 2002* ★★★
Riesling Cuvée Frédéric Emile Trimbach Extremely pale; very
distinctive, fragrant 'kerosene' aroma, grassy and minty; bone dry, lovely crisp fruit,
delicious flavour, balance and acidity. *Last tasted Oct 2003* ★★★★ *Now–2009.*
Riesling Schoenenbourg Vendange Tardive Hugel Pale, faint green
tinge; very eager to perform, flowery fragrance, greengages and lime; medium-
sweet, lovely, delicate, crisp, with tingling acidity. *Last noted April 2002* ★★★(★)
Delicious now but will keep and develop further.
Riesling Grand Cru Steinert Rieflé Yellow gold; a surge of fragrance,
minty, whiff of Riesling 'kerosene', refreshing acidity; medium-dry, medium-light
weight, lovely crisp flavour, very good acidity and length. *Nov 2005* ★★★★
Now–2010.
Tokay-Pinot Gris 'Jubilee' Hugel Pale; floral, delicious; medium, neither
dry nor sweet, full-bodied, delicious flavour. *Jan 2002* ★★★(★)
Pinot Gris Réserve Personnelle Trimbach Very pale; fragrant, grapey,
cress-like; medium sweetness and body, lovely wine. *Feb 2003* ★★★ *Now–2009.*
NOTES FROM A TASTING OF ZIND-HUMBRECHT '98S held in 2000:
Gewurztraminer: Heimbourg (limestone soil) relatively low-keyed; fairly
sweet (14.5% alcohol) ★★★(★); **Clos Windsbuhl** spicy; medium, lovely flavour
(14% alcohol), dry finish ★★★★
Riesling: Grand Cru Brand fermented for one year, 14.8% alcohol:
medium-pale; full, ripe melon; dry but very rich, with peachy flavour. Rather like
an Auslese *trocken* from the Rheingau ★★(★★★); **Grand Cru Rangen de
Thann, Clos St-Urbain** low-keyed, ripe melon and honey – touch of
botrytis; medium-sweet, full flavour. Glorious ★★★(★★); **Clos Hauserer** pale;
grapey, greengage acidity; assertive. *Needs time* ★★★(★★); and **Clos Heimbourg**
more melon-like, fragrant; medium-sweet, delicious flavour, good finish ★★★(★)
Pinot Gris: Heimbourg 118° Oechsle. Pale; subtle, honeyed botrytis nose;
medium-sweet, glorious flavour. Drink by itself, also perfect with selected cheeses
★★★(★★) *will gain momentum with bottle age*; **Rothenbourg** unusually for Alsace,
a west-facing vineyard catching the late afternoon sun, favourable for botrytis:
pale; honeyed bouquet; medium-sweet, rich, extra dimensions because of botrytis
★★★★(★); and **Clos Windsbuhl** ripe quince jelly and marmalade scents;
medium-sweet, substantial but not hefty, delectable botrytis ★★★(★)

1999 variable, at best ★★★

The season started well enough with a pleasant spring, hot May and
relatively early flowering which, however, was extended until mid-June
owing to humid conditions. Mildew was a problem exacerbated by mixed
weather to the end of July. August was equally mixed, but from the middle of
the month to the third week in September the weather was hot and dry.
Then came the rain. It lasted for five weeks during what should have been

an ideal harvesting period. It was a question of picking between wet spells, and much selection of the grapes. Yet, overall, growers reported some good wines with racy acidity.

Gewurztraminer Bollenberg Théo Cattin Buttercup yellow; glorious surging fragrance, more rose cachou than lychee; medium-sweet, delicious flavour but with the rather blunt finish so typical of Gewurz. *Dec 2003* ★★★★ *Drink soon.*

Pinot Noir 'Les Neveux' Hugel I have never thought much of red Alsace wines. In the past, not unlike German Pinot Noir or Spätburgunder, they tended to lack definition, with colours ranging from *pelure d'oignon*, a sort of feeble-tinted tawny, to plummy and weak-rimmed. This one was surprisingly deep and impressive; distinct Pinot aroma; dry, full-bodied (14.5% alcohol) and with remarkably good flavour. *Jan 2002* ★★(★) *It would be interesting to see how this ages.*

Riesling Cuvée Frédéric Emile Trimbach As much as I admire Trimbach's pure, uncompromisingly dry Rieslings, I found this '99 a bit too austere, as if stripped of colour, with stern though correct varietal nose, and taut acidity. *Last tasted May 2004. In its way* ★★★ *Not the style to mellow with bottle age.*

Riesling Rangen Zind-Humbrecht Flowery; dry, good flavour and aftertaste. *Tasted June 2001* ★★★ *Drink up.*

Riesling Grand Cru Steinert Rieflé Good nose though not very distinctive; dry, yet richly flavoured and good acidity. *Nov 2002* ★★★ *Drink soon.*

2000–2005

Looking back also helps me to look forward. For over the past decade in Alsace, better and more individualistic wines have been made by a handful of intelligent, diligent – well, brilliant – growers and winemakers setting new standards. In the middle remain the good, well-established merchant growers, while the stubbornly ordinary producers plod along. But it is rare to come across a really poor Alsace wine.

Vintages at a Glance

Outstanding ★★★★★ 2002, 2005
Very Good ★★★★ 2000 (v), 2001 (v), 2003 (v), 2004 (v)
Good ★★★ 2000 (v), 2001 (v), 2004 (v)

2000 a cautious ★★★, a possible ★★★★

A season with uneven weather: early budbreak was followed by a very hot May and June and satisfactory flowering; it was a very cool July, warm and sunny in August and early September. Then came mixed weather. The harvest started in the third week of September. The main problem was not ripening but overproduction. However, some beneficial botrytis formed, and some interesting late-harvest and SGN wines were made, albeit in small quantities.

Gewurztraminer Hugel Very pale, lemon-tinged; fresh, youthful, minty nose with characteristic lychees aroma; medium-dry, delicious, dry finish. *April 2002* ★★★★ *for freshness and charm.*

Gewurztraminer Cuvée Laurence Weinbach/Faller Glorious varietal aroma, but with a hard core; sweet, rich, lovely. *Jan 2002* ★★(★★)

Gewurztraminer Cuvée Théo Weinbach/Faller Pure, starbright, pale Tutankhamen gold; very typical rose petals, face powder fragrance; medium-sweet, hefty style (though only 13.5% alcohol), blunt end yet good acidity, very good flavour. *Sept 2003* ★★★★ *Now–2009.*

Gewurztraminer Herrenberg Zind-Humbrecht Medium-deep gold colour; amazing aroma of lychees, rose petal, cachous; fairly sweet; full-bodied (15% alcohol), a soft knockout drop. Lovely wine. *March 2004* ★★★(★★) *Now–2016.*

Gewurztraminer Vendange Tardive Rieflé Very bright pale gold; rose cachou and honey; fairly sweet, soft, fleshy, very moderate alcohol (12.5%). *Aug 2004* ★★★ *Now–2010.*

Pinot Blanc 'Les Princes Abbés' Schlumberger Pale, touch of honey; medium dryness and weight, good, straightforward. *April 2005* ★★★ *Drink soon.*

Pinot Gris Réserve Trimbach Medium-dry, surprisingly delicious, fragrant aftertaste. *Feb 2003* ★★★ *Drink soon.*

Riesling Grand Cru Schlossberg Cuvée Ste Catherine 'L'Inédit' Weinbach/Faller Very pale; lovely pineappley nose; medium-sweet, rich, soft, 'crusty' flavour. *Jan 2002* ★★★(★)

Riesling Grafenreben Bott-Geyl Decent, dependable producer. Pure, slightly honeyed varietal aroma; fairly assertive, dry, good, straightforward. *April 2007* ★★★

A RANGE OF HUGEL 2000s tasted in 2002, in ascending quality order:

Riesling Vinified from 95% bought-in grapes. Delicious, floral, minty nose; dry, light (11.5% alcohol), still young and raw. Good acidity. Inexpensive. (★★★)

Riesling 'Tradition' Selection by Hugel of the best bought-in grapes. Touch of almond kernels or marzipan on nose and flavour. Dry, fragrant (just 12% alcohol) (★★)?

Riesling Grand Cru 'Jubilee' From Hugel's own *grand cru* vineyard. Medium dry, 12% alcohol, greater length and depth ★★(★★)

Tokay-Pinot Gris 'Jubilee' Slightly nutty, good fruit, gooseberryish acidity; medium-sweet, full-bodied (13.5% alcohol), good melon and grapes flavour ★★(★★)

2001 ★★★ to ★★★★

This was not an easy year though some good wines were made, particularly *grand cru* Rieslings and top Gewurztraminers. As always, it was the weather that created difficulties, particularly at the time of flowering which was protracted. July and August were sunny but rain in September dampened hopes, though these were revived by an exceptionally hot and dry October, enabling some Vendange Tardive wines to be made. All lesser quality wines should have been consumed by now.

Gewurztraminer Cuvée Laurence Weinbach/Faller Palish yellow gold; lovely, richly scented varietal nose; fairly sweet, soft, rich, excellent flavour. *April 2005* ★★★★ *Now–2009.*

Gewurztraminer Furstentum Vendange Tardive Weinbach/Faller
Yellow-gold; sweet, rich, crisp, floral bouquet; medium-sweet, good flesh, moderate weight yet hefty style, fleshy, rather hard 'hot' finish. *Sept 2006* ★★(★★) *2010–2015*.

Gewurztraminer Clos Heimbourg Zind-Humbrecht Pale gold; more earthy, grapey aroma; sweet, soft, moderate weight, delicious. *March 2003* ★★★★ *Now–2010*.

Gewurztraminer Hengst Zind-Humbrecht Palish gold; lovely; classic Gewurz nose; medium-dry, powerful (14.5% alcohol), great depth and length. *March 2003* ★★(★★) *Now–2010*.

Gewurztraminer Herrenberg Zind-Humbrecht Very pale gold; perfect varietal nose; dry, austere, full-bodied (14.5% alcohol), very spicy. *March 2003* ★★(★) *Now–2010*.

Gewurztraminer Sporen Vendange Tardive Hugel Glorious colour, warm gold; substantial, rich, harmonious; sweet, plump, perfect balance, dry finish. *Nov 2005* ★★★(★) *Now–2010*.

Gewurztraminer Clos Windsbuhl Zind-Humbrecht Beautiful aroma; fairly sweet, soft, full-bodied, lovely, spicy and peachy. *March 2003* ★★★★ *Now–2010*.

Pinot Noir Côte de Rouffach Rieflé Soft, red-brown, open, mature rim; slightly jammy, chaptalised Pinot aroma and flavour. Back to the old style, thought I, but the more we sipped the more we enjoyed it. *May 2006* ★★★ *in its way*.

Riesling Ostertag Out of the ordinary and a good understated example of a pure Riesling, well balanced, good acidity. *March 2003* ★★★★ *Drink soon*.

Riesling Grand Cru A Mann Pale; touch of vanillin; dry, good length, agreeable weight. Drinking well. *June 2005* ★★★ *Drink soon*.

Riesling Grand Cru Schlossberg Cuvée Ste Catherine 'L'Inédit' Weinbach/Faller Positive colour with yellow-gold highlights; pure Riesling aroma; drier than expected, scented grapey flavour, good length – nearly as long as the wine's name – and refreshing acidity. *March 2006* ★★★★ *Now–2010*.

Riesling Grand Cru Steinert Rieflé Palish yellow; excellent Riesling aroma; medium-dry, modest alcohol (12%) though seemed higher, perfect flavour and balance. *Feb 2004* ★★★(★) *Now–2010*.

Tokay-Pinot Gris Clos Jebsal Zind-Humbrecht Pale gold; scented, touch of Gewurz-like spice; surprisingly sweet, fairly powerful ★★★ *Now–2010*.

Tokay-Pinot Gris Grand Cru Rangen Zind-Humbrecht Sweet, melon-like flavour, delicious ★★★★ *Now–2010*.

Tokay-Pinot Gris Clos Windsbuhl Zind-Humbrecht Low-keyed but also sweet and fairly powerful ★★★ *Now–2010*.

2002 ★★★★★

A high-quality vintage, the only problem being potential overproduction which the better growers countered with severe green-pruning. The weather conditions: freezing New Year, followed by a sunny and rainy spring; and successful flowering. July and August saw sunshine and showers and September was mainly sunny and warm, continuing through October to early November. There are some excellent Gewurztraminers and other excellent VT and SGN wines.

Gewurztraminer Altenbourg SGN Weinbach/Faller 130g/l sugar, low alcohol (11.5%). Extremely rich yet not heavy-handed, exquisite flavour and acidity. *Last tasted Sept 2006* ★★★★★ *Now–2015.*

Gewurztraminer Furstentum Vendange Tardive Weinbach/Faller 95g/l sugar and high acidity. Exquisite bouquet and flavour, good length and fragrant aftertaste. *Nov 2005* ★★★★★ *Now–2012.*

Gewurztraminer Grand Cru Goldert Vendange Tardive Zind-Humbrecht Buttercup-yellow with pale-gold highlights; rich, gentle, honeyed, harmonious rose petal and lychee fragrance; fairly sweet, rich, assertive, full-bodied (14.5% alcohol), lovely flavour, lip-licking finish but heady. *Jan 2006* ★★★★(★) *Now–2012.*

Gewurztraminer Grand Cru Hengst Zind-Humbrecht Lovely buttercup colour; luscious nose; medium-sweet, high acidity and high alcohol (14.4%), giving it a 'hot' finish. Great future. *Nov 2005* ★★(★★★) *2010–2015.*

Gewurztraminer Schlossberg Vendange Tardive Weinbach/Faller Pale; fairly sweet, pure, clean, crisp, lovely flavour and length. *Nov 2005* ★★★★(★) *Now–2012.*

Gewurztraminer Sporen Vendange Tardive Hugel Lovely colour; classic, rose petal Gewurztraminer; sweet, very rich, delicious. *Nov 2005* ★★★★★ *Now–2012.*

Pinot Gris Altenbourg SGN Weinbach/Faller Colossally sweet, 185g/l sugar. Honeyed fragrance; very sweet, glorious flavour, exquisite nuances, extremely good acidity. Great wine. *Nov 2005* ★★★★★ *Now–2016.*

Pinot Gris Altenbourg Vendange Tardive Weinbach/Faller Light gold; very minty; medium-sweet, modest weight (11.5% alcohol), some fat and flesh, delicious flavour, good length. *March 2006* ★★★★ *Now–2012.*

Pinot Gris Grand Cru Steinert Rieflé Yellow gold; rich, deep, cress-like nose and flavour; medium-dry, fleshy, very positive, moderate weight, dry finish. *Aug 2004* ★★★★ *Now–2010.*

Riesling Grand Cru Brand Zind-Humbrecht Pale gold; lightly honeyed with acidic undertone; medium-sweet, full-bodied, glorious peachy flavour, good length and acidity. *Nov 2005* ★★★★ *Now–2010.*

Riesling Grand Cru Rangen de Thann Clos St-Urbain Zind-Humbrecht Small crop, much botrytis. Palish gold; touch of honey, waxy, harmonious and complete; medium-sweet, delicious, very full-bodied (15% alcohol on label). Magnificent. *Nov 2005* ★★★(★★) *2010–2015.*

Riesling Grand Cru Schlossberg P Blanck Palish; spicy, complex, whiff of greengages; medium dryness and body, delicious flavour, good length and acidity. Vivacious. *Jan 2005* ★★★★ *Now–2010.*

Riesling Grand Cru Schlossberg Weinbach/Faller Crisp, almost grapefruit-like acidity; medium-sweet, fleshy yet still steely; modest alcohol (10.5%). Copybook Riesling. *Dec 2006* ★★★(★) *Now–2015.*

Riesling Grand Cru Steinert Rieflé Palish; very fragrant, minerally, almost Sauvignon Blanc-like acidity; dry, delicate yet positive, refreshing acidity. *Oct 2005* ★★★★ *Now–2010.*

2003 at best ★★★★

A hot year and the earliest vintage in Alsace since 1893. High summer temperatures and low acidity were the main problems but top producers used careful selection to good effect. These are wines with extra dimensions.

Gewurztraminer Hengst Zind-Humbrecht Lovely colour; spicy, cheesy nose; sweet – but no botrytis – fat, plump, exotic, full-bodied, very good aftertaste. *Nov 2005* ★★★★ *Now–2010.*

Gewurztraminer Sporen Vendange Tardive Hugel Palish, slightly green-tinged; young, pineappley, uneven; sweet, soft, fairly powerful, dry, spicy – cloves – finish. *Nov 2005* ★★★★ *Now–?*

Pinot Gris Altenbourg Cuvée Laurence Weinbach/Faller Pale; touch of melon; sweet (50g/l sugar), rich but adequate acidity, powerful (14.5% alcohol). A smooth blockbuster. *Nov 2005* ★★★★ *Now–2012.*

Pinot Gris Grand Cru Steinert Rieflé A perfect year for Pinot Gris and Pinot Noir, harvested at the end of August. Very pale; peach-like nose; medium sweetness, surprisingly modest weight (12% alcohol), soft, ripe; lovely flavour though touch of caramel, adequate acidity. *Oct 2005* ★★★★ *for early drinking.*

Pinot Noir Côte de Rouffach Rieflé A change from old-style Alsace Pinot Noir wines, with their feeble colours and chaptalised style. From grapes grown on chalky limestone soil with a trace of iron. Deep, virtually opaque; with good, 'sweaty' tannic nose and flavour, dry, good finish. *Nov 2005* ★(★★) *Now–2011.*

Riesling Grand Cru Rangen de Thann Clos St-Urbain Zind-Humbrecht Low acid, high ripe tannin. Glorious yellow-gold; initially dumb, touch of youthful pineapple; dry (less than 2g/l residual sugar) a certain softness and flesh, middle weight (just over 13% alcohol). Curious mixture of austerity and richness. *Nov 2005* ★★★★ *Now–2010.*

Riesling Grand Cru Schlossberg Cuvée Ste Catherine Weinbach/Faller Old vines, long roots, mid-slope. Good colour; little nose; dry, mild, good finish. *Last tasted Dec 2005* ★★★ *Drink soon.*

Riesling Grand Cru Schlossberg Cuvée Ste Catherine 'L'Inédit' Weinbach/Faller Medium-sweet (20g/l sugar), interesting flavour, fairly full-bodied, dry, slightly bitter end taste. *Nov 2005* ★★★? *Give it time.*

2004 ★★★ to ★★★★

For this vintage it was back to normal conditions after the excesses of 2003. The wines show good fruit and excellent acidity levels.

Gewurztraminer Hugel Palish, green-tinged; immature, undeveloped but typical Gewurz rose cachou aroma; medium-dry, soft, adequate flesh, crisp, clean, acidic finish. *Nov 2005* ★★★ *Drink soon.*

Gewurztraminer, Les Folostries Josmeyer Pale, bright; copybook Gewurz: sweet, rose-scented, lychees; medium-sweet, moderate weight, despite typical blunt, dry finish, refreshing. *May 2006* ★★★ *Drink soon.*

Gewurztraminer Grand Cru Hengst Zind-Humbrecht Medium-gold colour; low-keyed but scented rose cachou and youthful pineapple; bone dry, almost austere, high alcohol, distinctive flavour. *Nov 2005* ★(★★★) *2010–2015.*

Muscat Réserve Weinbach/Faller 70% Muscat d'Ottonel, 30% Muscatelle.

Muscat is the fourth 'noble' Alsace grape variety and, perhaps, the least often seen. Very pale; surprisingly low-keyed, I was expecting a florid, floral, very grapey aroma; medium-dryness and body, fragrant, spicy scented flavour. An attractive drink-alone wine. *Nov 2005* ★★★ *Drink soon.*

Muscat 'Tradition' Hugel No sooner than I had made the above note than, the following day, I tasted Hugel's, also a blend of Muscatelle and Ottonel. Pale; distinctly more Muscatelle grapiness – Ottonel tends to be more spicy, with melon and greengage; fairly but not very dry, a mild, attractive, grapey flavour. Worth trying. *Nov 2005* ★★★ *Drink soon.*

Riesling Grand Cru Brand Vendange Tardive Zind-Humbrecht Glorious golden colour; still immature but late-harvest honey; very sweet, modest alcohol (11.5%), lovely flavour, very good acidity. *Nov 2005* ★★★(★) *Now–2012.*

Riesling Cuvée Ste Catherine Weinbach/Faller Shimmery; very fragrant, delicious. Alsace Riesling at its most agreeable. *Jan 2006* ★★★★ *Now–2010.*

Riesling Rangen de Thann Clos St-Urbain Zind-Humbrecht Regarded as typical: excellent, not excessive ripeness benefiting from botrytis before the rain. A gush of refreshing gooseberry, green apple; medium-dry, 5.5g/l residual sugar, 13.7% alcohol (high for Riesling), lean, delicious flavour, youthful, grapefruit-like acidity. *Nov 2005* ★★(★★) *Now–2012.*

Riesling Grand Cru Schlossberg Weinbach/Faller Very pale; minerally, dry, delicious flavour, very good acidity. *Jan 2006* ★★(★★) *Now–2012.*

2005 ★★★★★

Almost perfect growing conditions. The harvest, which began at Domaine Weinbach on 27 September, was interrupted by rain from 1–5 October, but completed on the 21st. These are well balanced wines with good potential, especially Gewurztraminer and Pinot Gris. Alas, waiting to taste a wide range.

Germany

I happen to like German wines; by this I mean the quality wines mainly from well-established estates, with extraordinarily varied styles, ranging from bone dry to exquisitely sweet, and certainly not the cheap, sugar-and-water sort masquerading in traditional 'flute' bottles. Because German wines are considered a niche market, demand is specialised and there is little speculative or investment element, and so even the quality wines tend to be good value.

I regard Riesling, the grape that produces so many of Germany's top wines, as the most interesting and most versatile of all white wine grapes. Though Riesling is grown elsewhere in the world, only in Germany does it combine such charm and delicacy with deftness of touch.

Why do I list and describe so many old wines, ranging from Auslese to Trockenbeerenauslese (TBA) quality? Mainly to demonstrate their extraordinary quality and longevity. However, whereas notes on old and rare wines are my tribute to the great and the good, those of recent vintages should prove more practical.

Producers of quality German wine are ideally seeking a perfect balance of fruit and acidity. These low-alcohol *fruchtig* (fruity) wines are delightful drunk by themselves. The initial attempts to make *trocken* (dry) wines for food were not wholly successful. Removing the 'fruit' reduces the flavour. However, some extremely good *Erstes Gewächs* (first growth) dry wines are now being produced. They are for drinking not keeping.

Abbreviations used in the text for the German wine regions

(F) Franken or Franconia. Steely wines from Silvaner and the acidic Rieslaner.

(M) Mosel-Saar-Ruwer: the Mosel Valley along with two important tributaries, the Saar and the Ruwer. The most northerly of Europe's classic wine regions. Light, fruity, acidic wines, ranging from very dry to very rich.

(N) Nahe: geographically and by wine style between the Mosel and the Rheingau.

(P) Pfalz: between Rheinhessen and Alsace to the south, producing the best Gewürztraminers.

(Rg) Rheingau: the historic heart of German wine, on the right bank of the Rhine east and west of Wiesbaden, with the highest number of first growth vineyards. Firm, from dry, steely to the finest TBAs.

(Rh) Rheinhessen: on the left bank of the Rhine, with a handful of great estates overlooking the river. Inland, a lake of ordinary wine made from Müller-Thurgau and other easier, early-ripening grapes.

There are four other regions, all but the Ahr to the east of the Rhine:

(A) the Ahr Valley: north of the Mosel, specialising in red wine.

(B) Baden: the most southerly region. Very large production, both white and red wines.

(HB) Hessische Bergstrasse: little exported. None noted here.

(W) Württemberg: white and red.

Grape varieties

On the wine label the name of the grape always follows the village and vineyard name. Unless otherwise stated, all the wines noted in this chapter are Riesling.

Styles and qualities of German wine

German wine is classified according to the natural grape sugar content at harvest time, measured in degrees of Oechsle or must weight. The addition of sugar is not permitted in the category QmP ('quality' wine with distinction). This category has several levels. In ascending order of ripeness these are: **Kabinett**: dry to medium-dry; **Spätlese**: literally 'late-picked'. Ripe grapes, with moderate natural sugar content; **Auslese**: selected ripe bunches. Higher sugar content; **Beerenauslese** (or **BA**): selected fully ripe berries. Always sweet; **Eiswein**: sweet wines made from grapes frozen on the vine, with concentrated grape sugar. Since 1982 always at least BA level. **Trockenbeerenauslese** (or **TBA**): overripe berries affected by botrytis or 'noble rot' (Edelfäule in German). Rare, exceptionally sweet, concentrated wines. Only QmP wines are included in my notes, which are mainly confined to the higher levels, Auslese and above. Dry wines (Trocken and Erstes Gewächs) are not included.

Prior to 1971 growers could additionally qualify their better wines, usually from particularly successful casks, prefixing Auslese for example with feine, feinste, allerfeinste, edel. Now these superior wines are often identified by the capsule's colour and length – Goldkapsel, lange Goldkapsel – or by specific cask or Fuder numbers.

When to drink German wine

Most other great wine producers would envy the Germans and their delectable Rieslings – and other white grape varieties – grown in this relatively northern climate. The problem is this: with surprisingly few *exceptions they are lovely to drink the minute they are put on the market and most are drunk too soon. In connection with the notes about style on page 283, drink wines of **Kabinett** quality, and any others rated by me as ★★ or lower, soon; **Spätlesen** of ★★★ or above will develop further and will be at their best four to eight years after the vintage; drink **Auslesen** from seven to ten years, and those ★★★ or above up to 15 years. **Beerenauslesen** are lovely now but it would be a pity to drink them before they are 10–15 years old; **Trockenbeerenauslen**, mainly ★★★★★, have infinite life – as proven by the much older vintages in this chapter.*

18th and 19th centuries

It is perhaps worth reminding ourselves that the English have been importing Rhine, or 'Rhenish', wines for a thousand years. Not only were the wines palatable but transporting them was relatively safe and easy: down the Rhine and a short hop across the North Sea. From the Middle Ages to the 18th and early 19th centuries, 'Hock', the English term for Rhine wine, particularly 'old Hock', was fashionable and expensive; it bore no resemblance to the light, fruity wines of today. And in Victorian times good German wines, mainly from the Rheingau and Franken, achieved a high level of popularity.

VINTAGES AT A GLANCE

Outstanding ★★★★★ 1749, 1811, 1822, 1831, 1834, 1846, 1847, 1857, 1858, 1861, 1865, 1869, 1893

Very Good ★★★★ 1727, 1738, 1746, 1750, 1779, 1781, 1783, 1794, 1798, 1806, 1807, 1825, 1826, 1827, 1842, 1859, 1862, 1880, 1886

Good ★★★ 21 vintages in the 18th century, including 1748 in the text, and 20 vintages in the 19th century

1727 ★★★★

Rüdesheimer Apostelwein (Rg) From a large cask in the famous '12 Apostles' cellar beneath the Town Hall or *Ratskeller* in Bremen. Occasional half bottles appear at auction. The wine is drawn from the mother cask, which is then topped up with a young Rheingau of appropriate quality. In this way the large volume of the old wine is kept refreshed. Most recently, from a half bottle '*Réserve du Bremer Ratskeller*': Sercial madeira-like colour; bouquet also reminded me of an old madeira. After two hours in the glass, a smell of rich old stables and an hour after that, an amazing pungency left in the empty glass. On the palate medium-dry, lightish weight, a soft, gentler, slightly toasted, old straw flavour, tolerable acidity and clean finish. *Last noted Oct 1983* ★★ *for pleasure,* ★★★★★ *for interest.*

1748 ★★★
Schloss Johannisberger Cabinet Wein (Rg) Original 'flute' bottle with the oldest label in the castle cellars. Original cork. Warm old amber, with a rosy glow, almost like a faded old red wine; smell of wet hazelnuts; intolerably high acidity, alas undrinkable. *Oct 1985.*

1846 ★★★★★
Schloss Johannisberger Blaulack (Blue label) (Rg) Amber-gold; when first poured, faded fruit but fragrant, resembling charcoal and sultanas, cracking up after ten minutes; dry, positive flavour, like a refined old amontillado, with good length and remarkable for its age. *Nov 1984. As a drink ★★★, for its age ★★★★*

1862 ★★★★
A very big crop of fine wines.
Schloss Johannisberger Goldblaulack Auslese (Rg) Warm amber; slightly smoky, minty, raisiny bouquet, developing a rich, old straw nose. Medium-sweet, very assertive, high acidity, fragrant, exciting. *Nov 1984 ★★★★*

1893 ★★★★★
After 1811 and 1865, this was the best vintage of the 19th century. Very high levels of botrytis.
Erbacher Marcobrunn BA (Rg) **Schloss Reinhartshausen** Deep amber with touch of orange, and pure gold highlights; no faults; still sweet, a singed 'barley sugar' flavour with dry, raisiny finish. *Nov 1995 ★★★★*

1897 ★★
Steinberger Cabinet Wein (Rg) **Staatsweingut (Eltville)** Bright yellow-gold colour; fabulous, unusual and distinctive honeyed bouquet; rich yet dry, with very good flavour, depth and length. *Nov 1997 ★★★*

1900–1939

The reputation and demand in Britain for the finest Rhine wines reached its zenith in the period before the outbreak of World War One. Prices at the Kloster Eberbach auctions reached stratospheric levels but there was some concern about winemaking and authenticity, to the extent that in 1909 a wine law was enacted, introducing the concept of Naturwein or Naturrein ('naturally pure') for the unsugared wine, and stipulating that wine should come from the vineyard actually named on the label. After World War One, the devastatingly inflationary 1920s had a catastrophic effect, not so much on the actual quality of the wine made but on its traditional market. There was a timely boost in 1921, unquestionably the greatest German vintage of the 20th century and one which at last endorsed the high quality of the wines of the Mosel.

Although there were two good vintages in the 1930s, the market was greatly affected by the internment or flight of the Jewish merchants who had ably handled so much of the German wine trade up to this period.

VINTAGES AT A GLANCE

Outstanding ★★★★★ 1911, 1921, 1937
Very Good ★★★★ 1904, 1915, 1917, 1920, 1929, 1934
Good ★★★ 1900, 1901, 1905, 1907, 1926

1911 ★★★★★

Magnificent vintage, the best between 1900 and 1921.
Erbacher Marcobrunn TBA (Rg) Schloss Reinhartshausen Warm amber; blissful bouquet, raisiny, great depth; drying out a bit but good dry finish. *June 2004* ★★★

1915 ★★★★

Big harvest and very good quality.
Erbacher Marcobrunn Auslese Cabinet (Rg) Schloss Reinhartshausen 110° Oechsle. Rich amber, orange-gold highlights; touch of honey; medium-sweet, good flavour, dry, rather austere acidic finish but overall in good condition. *Nov 1995* ★★★

1920 ★★★★

Forster Ungeheuer Auslese (P) von Bühl Colour of dried apricots; bouquet of sultanas, honeyed botrytis; medium-sweet, fairly full-bodied, lovely old barley sugar flavour, good extract, length and aftertaste. *Oct 1988* ★★★★
Schloss Johannisberger Goldlack Auslese (Rg) Late-bottled. Unusual varietal blend, 55% Riesling and 45% Sylvaner. 115° Oechsle. Left in oak until it was bottled in 1930. Dashing and fragrant, some charm but a bit austere. *Nov 1984* ★★★★

1921 ★★★★★

The greatest vintage of the century. Small crop of extremely ripe, healthy grapes picked early after a scorching summer. Exceptionally rich wines.
Erbacher Honigberg Auslese (Rg) Schloss Reinhartshausen Very deep tawny; very sweet bouquet and flavour, old honey and toffee, considerable power and wonderful aftertaste. Of Beerenauslese quality. *Feb 2002* ★★★★★
Erbacher Rheinhell Auslese (Rg) Schloss Reinhartshausen Honeyed vanillin, whiff of caramel; distinctly dry, firm, good condition and length though, unsurprisingly, showing its age. *Last tasted June 2004* ★★
Schloss Johannisberger Cabinet (Rg) 105° Oechsle. Pure burnished gold; lightly grapey nose, remarkably fresh for its age. *Nov 1984* ★★★
Nackenheimer Rothenberg TBA Naturrein (Rh) Staatsweingut Amber; fabulous raisiny bouquet; very sweet, exquisite peachy flavour, wonderful acidity, great length. *March 2001* ★★★★★★ (6 stars)

Niersteiner Auflangen Auslese (Rh) **Franz Karl Schmitt** Marvellously rich colour, nose and taste. *Aug 1989* ★★★★★

Niersteiner Hermannshof TBA (Rh) **H F Schmitt** Orange-tinged amber; orange blossom bouquet; drying out a little but very rich, touch of caramel, good acidity. Pure old Riesling? Possibly Silvaner. *March 2002* ★★★

1927 ★★
Small production, below average quality.

Deidesheimer Hohenrain TBA (P) **von Bassermann-Jordan** Very deep brown with yellow-green rim; deliciously sweet, heavenly, butterscotch, crust of *crème brûlée*; still very sweet, Muscat and a touch of malt, with excellent life-preserving acidity. *May 2002* ★★★★

Kiedricher Robert Weil A simple village wine in contemporary green (not the customary brown) bottle; bouquet showing its age but became fragrant, creamy, vanilla; medium-dry, old, appley, dried peach skin flavour, good acidity. *Nov 2002.* ★★★★ *Remarkable for its class, vintage and age.*

1929 ★★★★
A lean decade in Germany, the 1929 vintage being the next best after 1921. These ripe and appealing wines were virtually all consumed in the 1930s.

Erbacher Marcobrunn Cabinet Auslese (Rg) **Schloss Reinhartshausen** Deep amber-gold; honey, apricots, tangerine bouquet; fairly sweet, rich old grapey flavour, great depth, good acidity, dry finish. *Last tasted June 2004* ★★★★

1934 ★★★★
Very satisfactory vintage.

Niersteiner Pettental und Auflangen TBA (Rh) **Franz Karl Schmitt** Prune-like amber; very powerful bouquet and flavour, bottle age and botrytis. Still sweet, immensely rich, flavour of peaches, apricots and caramel. Magnificent. *Sept 1996* ★★★★★

1937 ★★★★★
A great vintage in Germany. The best wines can still be excellent if well stored. My favourite classic German vintage. Many notes.

Brauneberger Juffer-Sonnenuhr Auslese (M) **Fritz Haag** Orange-gold; honeyed orange blossom; drying out, taste of peach skin, firm, marvellous acidity. *June 1992* ★★★★

Erbacher Marcobrunn TBA (Rg) **Schloss Reinhartshausen** Fairly deep amber; rich, pronounced bouquet; now medium-sweet but very rich, caramelised, excellent acidity, dry finish. *Last tasted June 2004* ★★★★

Schloss Johannisberger Rosalack Auslese (Rg) Two years in cask. Warm, rich, polished orange-gold; showing its age, like old apples in a hayloft but still rich and tangy; fairly sweet, still retaining good fruit and very good acidity. *Last tasted Nov 2005* ★★★★

1938 ★★
Average vintage; some good wines made but rarely seen.

Assmannshäuser Höllenberg Rot-Weiss Auslese (Rg)
Staatsweingut Colour of 10-year-old tawny port with ruddy glow; deliciously rich strawberry jam, then raisiny bouquet. Sweet, glorious, fabulous aftertaste. Remarkable for a 60-year-old German red. *Nov 1998* ★★★★

1940–1959

World War Two was as difficult for the German wine estates as for those of occupied France, with shortages of labour and materials. Only grim determination enabled the producers to take advantage of the great post-war vintages, notably the 1949.

By the mid-1950s, most leading British wine lists featured a wide range of German wines serviced by specialist importers. This period saw technological changes and viticultural experiments with new grape varieties; with the aim of producing easier to grow, earlier ripening and more prolific varieties in this difficult northerly region. However understandable, it led to an undermining of quality and image.

Vintages at a Glance

Outstanding ★★★★★ 1945, 1949, 1953, 1959
Very Good ★★★★ 1947
Good ★★★ 1942 (V), 1943, 1946, 1952

1940
Niersteiner Orbel Spätlese (Rh) **Heyl** Warm amber; bottle age, honeyed, touch of caramel and mushroom; fairly dry, showing its age. High acidity. *July 2005* ★

1941
Erbacher Hohenrain Kabinett (Rg) **Schloss Reinhartshausen** Pale old gold; floral, herbaceous, old honey; bone dry, clean, sound, lacking depth, very high acidity. *Feb 2002* ★★ *for its age and vintage.*

1942 ★★ to ★★★
Average to good wartime vintage. Only one wine tasted.
Erbacher Marcobrunn TBA (Rg) **Schloss Reinhartshausen** Peach blossom and apricots; still fairly sweet, lovely flavour. *Sept 1988* ★★★★

1943 ★★★
As in France, the best of the wartime vintages.
Assmannshäuser Höllenberg, Spätburgunder (Rg) **Staatsweingut** Medium, soft red; rich, high-toned scent of squashed strawberry and crushed cherry; very flavoury, fresh for its age. *Nov 1998* ★★★

Schloss Johannisberger BA Fass Nr 92 (Rg) Lively gold; bouquet exuding an almost Gewürztraminer spiciness; medium-sweet, good, but rather one-track and lacking fat. *Nov 1984* ★★★★

Wehlener Sonnenuhr feinste Auslese (M) **J J Prüm** Spicy, honeyed; fairly dry, good but unusual flavour, perfectly mature but blunt. *May 1983* ★★★★

1945 ★★★★★

A great but pitifully small vintage thanks to a hot, dry summer and understandable labour shortages.

Deidesheimer Kieselberg BA (P) **von Bühl** Deep amber; *crème brûlée* nose and taste; meaty, assertive, full, rich flavour. *Dec 1995* ★★★★

Deidesheimer Kieselberg Auslese Basserman-Jordan Several bottles: rich orange-gold with lime-green rim (some hazy); intensely rich, pure, raisiny, almost TBA bouquet; medium-sweet but rich, caramel and raisins, with dry, slightly bitter finish. Remarkably good. *Last tasted March 2003* ★★★★

Erbacher Marcobrunn Auslese (Rg) **Schloss Reinhartshausen** Rich orange colour, pale lime rim; very rich, soft, sweet orange peel and barley sugar bouquet; fairly sweet, powerful, tangy. Good dry finish. *Last tasted Feb 2002* ★★★

Marcobrunner feinste TBA (Rg) **Schloss Schönborn** Heavenly, still sweet with highish but inspired acidity. *Dec 1995* ★★★★★

1946 ★★★

A good vintage but not shipped and rarely seen.

1947 ★★★★

A very hot year. Very rich, soft wines of high quality.

Erbacher Brühl Beerenauslese (Rg) **Schloss Reinhartshausen** Fresh mushrooms nose; sweet, rich, high alcohol, very good acidity. *June 2004* ★★★★

Schloss Johannisberger Goldlack TBA (Rg) Medium-deep amber-gold highlights, lime rim; perfectly harmonious, scented, peaches, apricots; sweet, perfectly formed, lovely flesh, flavour, acidity. Great wine. *Nov 2001* ★★★★★

Schloss Vollrads TBA (Rg) Deep amber with apple-green rim; very powerful bouquet, singed raisins and honey; sweet, full-flavoured, high extract yet delicate. Glorious length and aftertaste. Great wine. *Sept 1988* ★★★★★

1948 ★★

Rated average to good. Two wines noted; both two stars.

1949 ★★★★★

A beautiful vintage. Perfectly balanced wines. By 1949 the vineyards had recovered, and so had the trade. A very popular vintage.

Erbacher Brühl Auslese (Rg) **Schloss Reinhartshausen** (Brühl is now called Schlossberg) Medium-deep orange-tawny; whiff of muscatelle raisins and citrus, honeyed depth; medium-sweet, rich, flavour and aftertaste of candied orange peel. Dry finish. *Feb 2002* ★★★★

Erbacher Marcobrunn TBA (Rg) **Schloss Reinhartshausen** Fairly deep amber with broad lime edge; glorious bouquet, raisiny, butterscotch; still sweet, rich with power and length, lovely flavour and perfect acidity. Good firm dry finish.

Great wine. *June 2004* ★★★★★
Schloss Johannisberger Auslese (Rg) **Schloss Johannisberg** 110°
Oechsle. Whiff of old apples; fairly sweet, rich, holding well. *Nov 1998* ★★★★
Steinberger Auslese (Rg) **Staatsweingut** Orange-gold; touch of fungi;
fairly sweet, rich, distinctive, creamy. *Feb 2000* ★★★★

1950 ★★
Few tasted. All dried out, austere, tart.

1951
Poor thin wines. Few exported. Only one fairly old note. Avoid.

1952 ★★★
A good vintage. Harvey's, in 1954, listed no fewer than 18 '52s, over half
bottled in Bristol. Only one relatively recent note.
Hattenheimer Stabel Spätlese (Rg) **Schloss Reinhartshausen** Pure
gold; musty at first, then honeycomb, lovely, creamy; rather stern '52 Rheingau
character, good body, clean dry finish. *March 1991* ★★★

1953 ★★★★★
Wines of enormous charm and appeal. The best can still be lovely now.
Eitelsbacher Karthäuserhofberg Kronenbourg Spätlese (M)
Tyrell Lovely colour; pure Riesling and vanilla; medium-sweet, glorious, sustained
by its crisp Ruwer acidity. *Nov 2005* ★★★★★
Erbacher Herrenberg Auslese Cabinet (Rg) **Schloss
Reinhartshausen** The Herrenberg vineyard is now called Schlossberg. An
astonishing warm, orange-gold; honey and raisins; fairly sweet, caramelised flavour,
touch of chocolate orange, dry finish. *Nov 1995* ★★★★
Erbacher Marcobrunn Edelbeerenauslese (Rg) **Schloss
Reinhartshausen** Deep gold; fragrant bouquet, orange peel, tangerine; fairly
sweet, touch of caramel but good acidity. Rather hard finish. *June 2004* ★★★★
Niersteiner Orbel Rehbach BA (Rh) **Heyl zu Herrnsheim** The best
site on the banks of the Rhine. Steep slope. Red slate. 122° Oechsle. 8.1g/l acidity.
Slight bottle variation. Fragrant, floral, delicate bouquet and flavour. Drying out a
little, fading gracefully. *Oct 1998. At best* ★★★★
Rauenthaler Baiken TBA (Rg) **Schloss Eltz** Orange blossom, – rather
Yquem-like; rich though drying out. Firm finish. *Nov 1997* ★★★★
Steinberger Edelbeerenauslese (Rg) **Kloster Eberbach** Several notes,
all superb. Warm, orange-gold; peach blossom fragrance; almost overpoweringly
rich, delicious, pure butterscotch flavour, great length, excellent acidity. The honey
of bottle age not *Edelfäule* (botrytis). *Last tasted March 2003* ★★★★★
Wehlener Sonnenuhr BA (M) **J J Prüm** Two similar notes: yellow;
fabulous bouquet, like ambrosial lemon curd; flavour to match. Fairly sweet, fleshy,
buttery texture. Lovely. *April 1999. At best* ★★★★★

1954
Disastrous weather.

1955 ★★

A moderately good vintage that was listed by British merchants in 1957, the high peak for German wine sales at Harvey's. Only tasted one since the late 1950s.

Durbacher Schlossberg Clevner Traminer (B) **Wolff-Metternich** Great rarity, only 300 bottles produced. Unusually a mix of red and white grapes, combining to produce an astonishing 200° Oechsle. Touch of tawny; floral; very sweet, glorious flavour but, to quibble, lacking a bit of length. *Dec 1995* ★★★★★

1956, 1957 and 1958

Poor quality and few wines tasted.

1959 ★★★★★

At last, to end a mixed and mainly disappointing decade, a magnificent vintage, though the excessively hot summer created unusual, indeed unprecedented, winemaking conditions. However, glorious wines were made from sun-enriched grape juice with an extraordinarily high sugar content; a record number of Beerenauslesen and TBA wines in the Mosel-Saar-Ruwer. The wines are now variable and mainly past their best, though the top wines can still be beautiful.

Erbacher Marcobrunn TBA (Rg) **Schloss Reinhartshausen** Warm amber; orange Muscat scent; lovely singed, Tokay-like flavour with wonderfully honeyed aftertaste. *Last tasted Nov 2000* ★★★★★

Hallgartener Schönhell TBA (Rg) **Fürst Löwenstein** Deep amber-gold; glorious, slightly singed, raisiny, smoky bouquet and taste. Still fat and fleshy though drying out. *Feb 2001* ★★★★

Hattenheimer Wisselbrunnen Beerenauslese (Rg) **Schloss Reinhartshausen** Superb wine. Several ecstatic notes. To sum up: amber-gold; fragrant, floral, honeyed; very sweet, lovely flavour, perfect balance, acidity and aftertaste. *Last noted July 2006* ★★★★★

Maximin Grünhäuser Herrenberg TBA (M) **von Schubert** Perfect combination of '59 ripeness and Ruwer acidity. Minerally lime blossom backed by soft, peachy scents and whiff of caramel; an amazing attack of flavour, mid-palate fragrance and teeth-gripping acidity. Finesse and zest. *March 2003* ★★★★★

Nackenheimer Rothenberg Auslese (Rh) **Gunderloch** Yquem-like yellow-gold; glorious fragrance, very rich, raisiny, very varietal Riesling, toasted butterscotch; fairly sweet, soft, rich, not as overwhelming as bouquet, flavour of black treacle. *March 2003* ★★★★

Rauenthaler Baiken TBA (Rg) **Staatsweingut** Intense concentration, magnificent, warranting six stars in 1983. Most recently: deep, glowing amber; intense fragrance, old honey, raisiny, apricot skins; great sweetness and richness, very good acidity. Fabulous wine. *Last tasted July 2005* ★★★★★

Rauenthaler Herrberg Spätlese (Rg) **von Simmern** Just to prove that a '59 Spätlese can keep well. Touch of orange; medium-dry, good structure, condition and length. *Feb 2000* ★★★

Scharzhofberger Auslese (M) **Egon Müller** Though the grapes were very ripe they lacked botrytis. Three fairly consistent notes: good varietal flavour and texture but lacking this extra zest. *Last tasted Sept 2004* ★★★ just.

Steinberger Edelbeerenauslese (Rg) **Staatsweingut** Rich orange-gold; creamy yet touch of hardness, rich but taut; extremely rich caramelly flavour, delicious but leaner than expected and, for a '59, high acidity. *Last tasted March 2003* ★★★★

Steinberger TBA (Rg) **Staatsweingut** 230° Oechsle, 148g/l residual sugar. Three notes, all memorable. Rich gold, orange highlights; *crème brûlée*; exceptionally rich, caramelly flavour though leaner than expected, great length. High acidity for a '59. Delicious. *Last tasted March 2003. At best* ★★★★★

Wehlener Sonnenuhr feinste Auslese (M) **J J Prüm** Remarkably pale, still retaining a youthful green tinge; lightly herbaceous, grapey; medium-sweet, fleshy, soft, perfect flavour, just enough acidity. *Last tasted April 1999. At best* ★★★★

1960–1979

The emphasis on new technology, techniques and experimental grape varieties continued apace in Germany. Too much attention was given to productivity and not enough to quality, the emphasis being on early-ripening varieties such as the prolific Müller-Thurgau. Other varieties were introduced more for their sugar content than any character, and when planted on alluvial soil on flat land – so much easier to manage than the steep slate slopes of the Mosel Valley – the production of easy, fairly sweet, less costly to make wines took off.

The 'rationalisation' of vineyards and names introduced by the 1971 German wine laws, ostensibly to simplify the marketing of the wines, had disastrous effects. Cheap, sugary and watery wines were marketed under familiar wine names. There emerged a flood of cheap Spätlese and Auslese wines from non-traditional varieties and less good districts. All this harmed the image of German wines and undermined the old-established quality-wine estates.

Vintages at a Glance

Outstanding ★★★★★ 1967 (v), 1971, 1973 (v)
Very Good ★★★★ 1964, 1975, 1976
Good ★★★ 1961 (v), 1962 (v), 1963 (v), 1966, 1969 (v), 1970, 1979

1960 ★
A return to poor weather. An abundance of mediocre wine.

1961 ★ to ★★★
Another poor summer in Germany. Wide variations in quality; no great sweet wines. None tasted recently.

1962 ★ to ★★★

A moderate vintage, best known for its Eiswein, the last grapes being picked in early December in below-freezing temperatures. Few notes.

Wehlener Sonnenuhr feine Auslese (M) **S A Prüm** Most recently: lime-gold; harmonious, grapey, lightly honeyed touch of kerosene; medium-sweet, lovely flavour, soft yet firm, perfect, understated acidity. *Last tasted Sept 1988* ★★★

Wöllsteiner Äffchen Sämling Auslese Eiswein (W) **Wirth** A prize-winner; straw-gold; ripe, rich nectarine fragrance; very sweet though light in style and a bit of a let-down on the palate, straw-flavoured. *Sept 1987* ★★★

1963 ★ to ★★★

Amazing how any decent drinkable wines could be made after such a growing season: the Rhine frozen, cold spring, late flowering, sunny July then rain through to an abrupt Indian summer at the end of October.

Casteller Schlossberg Rieslaner Spätlese (F) **Fürst Castell** Surprisingly good for an off vintage, dry but full and fragrant. *July 1997* ★★★

1964 ★★★★

A rich, ripe vintage following an almost too good summer, hours of sunshine even exceeding 1959. Similar problems: difficult winemaking in hot conditions, ripe grapes, high sugar content and low acidity.

Undoubtedly the vintage was most successful in the Mosel-Saar-Ruwer where the naturally high acidity of the Riesling grown on steep slate slopes counterbalanced the unusually ripe sweetness. Some wines are still lovely, others tired.

Bernkasteler Doctor Spätlese (M) **Thanisch** Delicious. *Dec 1997* ★★★★

Hattenheimer Wisselbrunn Cabinett TBA (Rg) **Schloss Reinhartshausen** Richly coloured; honey and raisins, bottle age and depth; sweet, rich, surprisingly acidic for a '64. *June 2004* ★★★

Rauenthaler Baiken Auslese (Rg) **Schloss Eltz** A perfect colour for its age, lovely flavour, 'drying out elegantly'. *June 1996* ★★★

Steinberger BA (Rg) **Staatsweingut** 'Calf's foot jelly', smooth, caramelly nose and aftertaste; sweet, flavour of quince, good acidity. *Nov 2000* ★★★★

Steinberger TBA (Rg) **Staatsweingut** Old gold; toffee, liquorice, pure old Riesling; still very sweet, fat, lovely flavour and aftertaste. *Nov 1997* ★★★★★

Wehlener Sonnenuhr feine Auslese Fuder 15 (M) **J J Prüm** Orange-gold; sweet, peachy, caramelly bottle age and botrytis nose and taste. For a '64 a bit lacking though drinking pleasantly. *April 1999* ★★ *Drink up.*

1965

Vying with 1956 as one of the worst vintages of the century.

1966 ★★★

Pale, firm, steely wines, with good sustaining acidity. A relatively small crop harvested late due to cold and rain. Due to cold, wet weather in early November few sweet wines were produced, save for some very late-picked grapes made into Eiswein. Few wines tasted recently, the following being a representative cross-section.

Erbacher Langenwingert Kabinett (Rg) **Schloss Reinhartshausen**
Palish, with lime-gold highlights; low-keyed, lime blossom; some sweetness,
melon-like flavour, fresh, refreshing acidity. *Feb 2002* ★★★
Zeltinger Schlossberg feine Auslese (M) **J J Prüm** Bright yellow-
gold; nose initially a waxy kerosene Riesling character that seemed to spread itself,
creamily; good, flavour and length, dry finish. *April 1999* ★★★

1967 ★ to ★★★★★

Fairly ordinary in the lower quality range but some excellent, late-picked,
underrated, botrytis-affected sweet wines. Those estates that held back for the
late autumn sunshine made superb TBAs.
Hattenheimer Hassel BA (Rg) **H Lang** 140° Oechsle, 9g/l acidity. Two
notes, a day apart. Almost identical descriptions including 'very Germanic', 'very
Wagnerian', 'almost unctuous'. A beautiful burnished gold; syrup of figs,
'butterscotch'. I liked it! *Last noted Oct 1998* ★★★★
Hattenheimer Schützenhaus Auslese (Rg) **Balthasar Ress** Powerful,
honeyed wine of *feine* Auslese quality. *Last noted Sept 1996* ★★★★
Schloss Johannisberger Goldlack TBA (Rg) Amber; rich, tangy; sweet,
crisp, lovely flavour, assertive, caramelly aftertaste. *Nov 2001* ★★★★
Wachenheimer Rechbächel TBA (P) **Bürklin-Wolf** 184° Oechsle,
9.3g/l acidity. Three experiences of this extraordinary wine. Tawny gold; the
sweetness and concentration of brown treacle! *Last noted Sept 1992* ★★★★★

1968

A poor year. Cold and wet. Thin, raw wines of low quality and short life.

1969 at best ★★★

Reasonably good, firm, acidic wines. After the '71s came along, the '69s were
largely forgotten. The best can still be very agreeable to drink.
Erdener Prälat hochfeine Auslese (M) **Dr Loosen** Natural sugar
content of grapes 100–105° Oechsle, close to Beerenauslese, hence the *hochfeine*
suffix. An attractive yellow colour; honeyed bottle-age and ripe grapes; medium-
sweet, fairly full-bodied for a Moselwein, even fat, but with very good acidity.
Touch of 'bracken' on the end taste. *Sept 1988* ★★★
Erdener Treppchen feinste Auslese (M) **Mönchhof** Yellow-gold; rich,
ripe, kerosene grapiness; medium-sweet, full, rich, creamy, honeyed. Dry finish.
June 1992 ★★★★★
Hallgartener Deutelsberg (Rg) **Engelmann** Pale for its age; low-keyed,
cress-like, opened up nicely; medium sweetness and body, curious flavour, lovely
acidity. *Feb 2000* ★★★
Kallstadter Saumagen BA (P) **Koehler-Ruprecht** Amber; rich, honeyed,
slightly caramelly; medium-sweet, assertive, 'oily' Riesling. *Feb 2000* ★★★
Oberemmeler Hütte feinste Auslese (M) **von Hövel** Yellow; peachy,
soft, sweet bouquet; sweet entry, firm dry finish. Honeyed. *June 1992* ★★★★
Wehlener Sonnenuhr hochfeine Auslese (M) **J J Prüm** Fragrant old
honey; less sweet than expected, fairly powerful, with good length. *April 1999* ★★★

1970 ★★★

Rather plodding wines due to late blossoming, dry summer and moderate autumn. Some growers took advantage of the late summer sunshine; one or two even picked as late as 6 January 1971!

Erbacher Rheinhell Beerenauslese (Rg) **Schloss Reinhartshausen**
Golden; very sweet, soft, delicious. *August 2003* ★★★★

Erbacher Rheinhell BA Strohwein (Rg) **Schloss Reinhartshausen** To make this, the individually picked, very ripe grapes were spread out on corrugated asbestos roof panels! Two notes. Most recently, a pure yellow-gold; very fragrant, Muscat-like; some sweetness though light style. The original acidity appears to have settled down. Perfect. *Last tasted Oct 1983. At best* ★★★★★

Graacher Himmelreich BA (M) **J J Prüm** Orange-gold; honeyed; rich but drying out, with a touch of leanness. Apricots and acidity. *April 1999* ★★★

Trierer Thiergarten Unterm Kreuz Auslese, Weihnachts-Eiswein-Edelwein (M) **von Nell** A remarkable wine made from grapes picked on 24 and 25 December. Eiswein honey; fairly sweet, good acidity. *July 1983* ★★★

Wehlener Sonnenuhr BA (M) **J J Prüm** Orange-gold; 'calf's foot jelly'; fairly sweet, honey and lime blossom. Excellent acidity. *April 1999* ★★★

1971 ★★★★★

A magnificent vintage. Early flowering, with sunshine and warmth from early July through to the autumn, the lack of rain concentrating the flesh. Healthy, fully mature grapes picked in ideal conditions. Arguably the most perfect in the Mosel and its tributaries: the best Saar and Ruwer wines for decades. Overall the quality was high, almost too high for the commercial houses.

Drink up the Spätlesen, but look out for Auslesen from the better estates. Most are woefully undervalued at auction. The scarcer and more expensive Beeren and Trockenbeerenauslesen are still magnificent. Many notes.

Casteller Trautberg Silvaner TBA (F) **Fürst Castell** Most recently: the colour of Verdelho or sweet sherry; apple-green rim; bouquet of toffee and cream, delicious, still lively; sweet, creamy, soft yet with tingling acidity. *Last tasted Oct 1997* ★★★★★

Erbacher Hohenrain Spätlese (Rg) **Schloss Reinhartshausen** Palish; rich, deep, classic kerosene Riesling; sweet, soft, lovely peachy flavour and good follow-through. Of *feinste* Spätlese quality. *Feb 2002* ★★★★★

Erbacher Schlossberg, Ruländer TBA (Rg) **Schloss Reinhartshausen** Richly coloured; rare grape, raisins, tangerines; unbelievably rich, amazing power, glorious. *June 2004* ★★★★★

Erdener Prälat Auslese (M) **Dr Loosen** 7.5% alcohol. Delicious, grapey. Many consistently good notes. *Last tasted Oct 2006* ★★★★

Graacher Himmelreich Eiswein BA (M) **J J Prüm** Ripe apricots; sweet, ripe, lovely peachy flavour. Dry finish. *Dec 1995* ★★★★★

Hattenheimer Engelmannsberg TBA (Rg) **Balthasar Ress** Deep amber; rich, caramelly; very sweet, rich, full, creamy, shapely. *May 1996* ★★★★★

Hattenheimer Nussbrunnen BA (Rg) **Schloss Schönborn** 130° Oechsle, 73.8g/l residual sugar, 7.7g/l total acidity, 12% alcohol and winner of several medals. Several notes. Yellow-gold; fragrant, minerally; not over-sweet, though fairly hefty, with lip-licking acidity. *Last tasted Oct 1998* ★★★★

Hattenheimer Wisselbrunnen TBA (Rg) **Schloss Reinhartshausen** 11% alcohol. An extraordinary orange-red colour, clearly due to extraction of pigment from the shrivelled, sun-baked grape skins during fermentation. Ambrosial bouquet, touch of muscatelle grapiness; sweet, lightish in style though with typical '71 fat and marvellous acidity. Still with years of life ahead. *Last noted Oct 1992* ★★★★(★)

Schloss Johannisberger Rosalack Auslese (Rg) Kerosene, honeyed botrytis and bottle age; fairly sweet, delicious flavour, good acidity. *March 1999* ★★★★

Kallstadter Saumagen, Huxelrebe TBA (P) **Gerhard Schulz** Very deep amber-gold; the Huxelrebe raisiny nose and taste. Very sweet still, good acidity. Should keep well. *Sept 1999* ★★★★

Kiedricher Gräfenberg Auslese (Rg) **Robert Weil** 125° Oechsle. Buttercup yellow; drying out a little, but good, ripe flesh. Lovely. *Nov 1999* ★★★★

Oestricher Lenchen BA (Rg) **Jos Spreitzer** A lovely, calm, harmonious, honeyed combination of botrytis and bottle age; fairly sweet, very good flavour and acidity, the latter a bit hard, with a lemon peel twist. *Last tasted Nov 2000* ★★★★

Rauenthaler Baiken Spätlese (Rg) **Staatsweingut** Yellow-gold; classic Riesling; rich, ripe, superb for Spätlese. *July 2005* ★★★★

Rauenthaler Rothenberg BA (Rg) **August Eser** Rich, very forthcoming, balanced. Perfect acidity. Long life ahead. *Nov 1996* ★★★★(★)

Scharzhofberger Auslese (M) **Egon Müller** Fabulous colour, warm gold; perfect in every way, sweetness, balance of fruit and acidity. There was no botrytis. The '71s were 'hard and inaccessible when young'. Not much change in four years: peachily perfect. *Last noted May 2000* ★★★★★

Wehlener Sonnenuhr Auslese Goldkapsel (M) **J J Prüm** Lovely golden colour; fragrant, creamy, harmonious bouquet; medium-sweet, lovely flavour, balance, length and fragrant finish. *Last tasted April 1999* ★★★★★

Wehlener Sonnenuhr BA (M) **J J Prüm** Medium-deep warm gold; honey, lime blossom, cream; very sweet, wonderful flavour and length. Perfect balance of fruit and acidity. *April 1999* ★★★★★ *Perfection now.*

Wehlener Sonnenuhr TBA (M) **J J Prüm** Golden; a fragrance and flavour that defy description. Sweet with dry finish. *April 1999* ★★★★★★ *(6 stars)*

Wehlener Sonnenuhr feinste TBA (M) **J J Prüm** Clearly one of J J's greatest-ever vintages. How could the 6-star TBA in my previous note be beaten? Only by the *feinste*, finest TBA of all: orange-gold highlights; 'ambrosial' raisins! Rich, so rich, almost toffee-like, peachy, marmalade; its great sweetness balanced by perfect acidity. *Nov 2005* ★★★★★★

Winkeler Hasensprung TBA (Rg) **von Hessen** Hefty, caramelised and very concentrated nose and taste. Very sweet still and with lovely aftertaste. *Nov 1997* ★★★★

1972 ★

Not notable though it did supply the trade with a quantity of lesser wines after the too-high quality, and costliness, of the '71s.

1973 ★★ to ★★★★★ (Eiswein only)

Abundant – in fact the biggest crop on record – and some charming light wines made for early consumption, diluted through overproduction. A few Eisweins of outstanding quality.

Erbacher Michelmark BA Eiswein (Rg) **zu Knyphausen** Picked at −16° C. 12g/l acidity. Gold medal winner 1974. Deep orange; caramel; intensely sweet, fat, muscatelle-like taste, wonderful acidity. *Last tasted Nov 2000* ★★★★★

Wallhäuser Mühlenberg, Ruländer Eiswein TBA (N) **Prinz zu Salm-Dalberg** Minty, fragrant bouquet; sweet, rich but not fat, with a pleasantly light delicate touch and delicious apricot flavour and lovely acidity. *Oct 1988* ★★★★★

1974

A dismal summer with one of the wettest autumns in memory.

1975 ★★★★

A good vintage but buyers seemed to lose interest in it as soon as the immediately attractive '76s appeared on the market. Even so the firmer, slightly more acidic '75s are holding up well. Some very good wines though there were variations of style and quality due to conflicting winemaking approaches. Good '75s are undervalued and those of genuine Auslese quality are holding well.

Assmannshäuser Höllenberg, Spätburgunder Weissherbst Auslese (Rg) **R König** Colour of warm straw with orange highlights; rich, slightly toffee-like nose and taste; medium sweetness and body, very rich, lovely aftertaste. *Sept 1996* ★★★

Erbacher Marcobrunn BA Staatsweingut Deep amber-gold; lovely bouquet and flavour, old honey and apricot stems, excellent acidity. *Nov 2005* ★★★★

Schloss Johannisberger Rosagoldlack BA (Rg) Most recently, a hefty classic; touch of spearmint and '75 acidity. *Last tasted Nov 2000* ★★★★(★)?

Scharzhofberger TBA (M) **Egon Müller** Amber with apple-green rim; rich, fragrant, raisiny; very sweet, fat, fleshy, simply glorious. *May 2000* ★★★★★

Ürziger Würzgarten Auslese (M) **Christoffel-Berres** Peaches and fruit salad; medium sweetness, despite mild mid-palate, quite powerful. Hard dry finish. *June 1992* ★★★

Wehlener Sonnenuhr Auslese lange Goldkapsel (M) **J J Prüm** The perfect time for a wine of this vintage quality. A beautiful, uplifting floral bouquet; perfect balance of sweetness and acidity. Lively and lovely. *April 1999* ★★★★★

1976 ★★★★

A gloriously ripe vintage. Soft, fleshy, extremely attractive wines, the only handicap being a certain lack of acidity. Though it was a year of great heat and drought, the weather was pleasantly warm from mid-September to early October, dampness returning to encourage the formation of *Edelfäule* (noble rot) later in the month.

The sort of year that brings out the best in the Mosel and, in particular, in the Saar and Ruwer, which normally produce fairly acidic wines. This

vintage had more than its fair share of lovely Auslesen and fabulous Beeren-
and Trockenbeerenauslesen wines. Many still lovely, some past their peak.

Berncasteler Doctor Auslese (M) Thanisch Vaseline gold; flowery fruit,
greengages, privet; a lovely rich 'oily' Riesling, but with a curiously hard finish.
Aug 1996 ★★★★

Bischoffinger Steinbuck, Ruländer TBA (B) W G Bischoffingen
Three notes. An astonishing wine, 235° Oechsle, 270g/l residual sugar, acidity
10.2g/l, 6.51% alcohol. The colour of Bual madeira; its hefty toffee and raisins
nose and flavour offset by its vital acidity. Immensely sweet. One of my notes said
'cod-liver oil and malt'!. Great length. Delicious. *Oct 1998* ★★★★★

Brauneberger Juffer-Sonnenuhr TBA (M) Fritz Haag Orange-
amber; singed raisins; sweet, incredibly rich and concentrated, superb aftertaste.
Great wine. *May 2000* ★★★★★

Erbacher Hohenrain Spätlese (Rg) Schloss Reinhartshausen Lovely
orange-tinged gold; ripe, honeyed botrytis bouquet; medium-sweet, lovely flavour,
sweet fruit and upturned acidic finish. Perfection. *Feb 2002* ★★★★★

Graacher Himmelreich Auslese lange Goldkapsel (M) J J Prüm
Fairly sweet, superripe, lovely, honeyed, peachy flavour. Assertive. *April 1999* ★★★★

Hattenheimer Engelmannsberg TBA (Rg) Balthasar Ress Amber;
spicy, verbena, spearmint, creamy; very sweet, raisiny, slightly caramelly flavour and
aftertaste. *May 1996* ★★★★

Hattenheimer Wisselbrunnen Auslese (Rg) Balthasar Ress Deep
orange; sweet, rich, raisiny, fat and fleshy, fragrant aftertaste. *Oct 2005* ★★★★

Schloss Johannisberger Goldlack (TBA) (Rg) Surprisingly deep,
lime-tinged and very rich 'legs'; rich, touch of malt; sweet of course, the most
alcoholic of the TBAs, toffee-like taste, good acidity. *Nov 2001* ★★★

Laubenheimer Karthäuser BA (N) Tesch A gold medal winner from
young (six-year-old) vines. Golden; honey and greengages; sweet, ripe, creamy, soft
Nahe character yet combining honeyed botrytis and lip-licking finish. *Nov 2000*
★★★★★

Lorcher Bodental-Steinberg Auslese (Rg) von Kanitz Wonderful
colour; crisp fruit; very distinctive flavour, peachy, high acidity for '76. *Nov 1998*
★★★★

Lorcher Bodental-Steinberg BA (Rg) von Kanitz Two similar notes:
by 1988 already a fairly deep, orange-gold resulting from the overripe botrytised
grapes: peaches, apricots and honey; fairly sweet, perfect *Edelfäule* flavour, but I
thought it was a bit lacking in acidity. More recently I considered the acidity
adequate, and predicted a long life ahead of it. It is probably perfect now. *Last
tasted Nov 1999* ★★★★

**Niersteiner Findling, Scheurebe Beerenauslese (Rh) Louis
Guntrum** Minty, distinctive; substantial (7.5% alcohol), slightly caramelly.
Guntrum's **Orbel Silvaner TBA** less distinctive but interesting. *Both tasted
July 2006, both* ★★★

Niersteiner Hölletraminer Gewürz, BA (Rh) Senfter Rose cachou
and lychees scent; fairly sweet, rich, distinctive Gewürztraminer exotic flavour.
April 1998 ★★★

Rauenthaler Baiken Auslese (Rg) Staatsweingut Glowing gold; honey
and apricot; rich, lovely flavour, perfection. *Aug 2005* ★★★★★

Scharzhofberger Auslese (M) **Egon Müller** Four notes. Most recently: a beautiful yellow-gold; its rich ripe Riesling fragrance developing a piquant whiff of spearmint. Lovely wine. *Last tasted May 2000* ★★★★

Scharzhofberger Auslese 'GK' AP 36 (M) **Egon Müller** Honeyed bottle age; rich, dry peachy finish. A modest Egon Müller masterpiece. *March 2006* ★★★★

Scharzhofberger Auslese Goldkapsel (M) **Egon Müller** Two notes. More recently: now deeper in colour, orange-tinged and with a bitty sediment said to be due to calcium affected by botrytis. A bit of a heavyweight. Full, rich. *Last tasted May 2000* ★★★★ *Drink up.*

Scharzhofberger TBA (M) **Egon Müller** Deep tawny, orange highlights, apple-green rim and rich 'legs'; an indescribably lovely bouquet, slightly raisiny, lime honey and acidity; tremendously rich, concentrated, dry finish, good length. *May 2000* ★★★★★★ *(6 stars) Perfect now.*

Schlossböckelheimer Kupfergrube Auslese (N) **Staatsweingut** Typical ripe Nahe fruit salad, with bottle age; rich, lovely flavour, adequate acidity. *Jan 1999* ★★★★

Schloss Vollrads TBA (Rg) Fairly deep, orange-tinged; very powerful nose, a bit hard and with the maltiness of Bavarian beer; sweet, full, very rich, meaty, toffee and chocolate, very assertive but also very fragrant with an extraordinary mint leaf aftertaste. *Sept 1990* ★★★★★

Traiser Bastei Beerenauslese (N) **Dr Crusius** Many notes. Several recently. Glowing amber-gold; deep, rich, caramelised botrytis; very rich, verging on unctuous. *Last tasted July 2006* ★★★★★

Wallufer Walkenberg BA (Rg) **Jost** A lovely wine: amber-gold; ripe botrytis and honeyed bottle age. Fairly substantial, sweet entry, dry finish. *Last tasted Nov 2000* ★★★★

Wehlener Sonnenuhr Auslese Goldkapsel (M) **J J Prüm** Two bottles, one cloudy with white sediment, a botrytis calcium fault. Tart. The second with lovely colour, nose and flavour. Delicious. *April 1999. At best* ★★★★

Wehlener Sonnenuhr Auslese lange Goldkapsel (M) **J J Prüm** Lovely gold; touch of orange; sweet, rich, gloriously honeyed flavour, good acidity and length. *April 1999* ★★★★★

Wehlener Sonnenuhr TBA (M) **J J Prüm** Two notes. Most recently: a tinge of orange appearing; raisiny, fragrant; fat, soft, barley sugar flavour and finish. One of Manfred Prüm's greatest wines. *Last tasted April 1999* ★★★★★

Winkeler Hasensprung TBA (Rg) **Deinhard** Three notes. Most recently, despite its lovely *crème brûlée* bouquet and lovely flavour, it was beginning to dry out a little. *Last tasted Jan 1998* ★★★★

1977 ★

Modest quality wines for early consumption. However, conditions were right to enable some Eiswein to be made.

Assmannshäuser Höllenberg, Spätburgunder Weissherbst Eiswein BA (Rg) **Staatsweingut** Warm amber; very good, sweet, raisiny, appley bouquet; very sweet, fat, great length and very high acidity. *Nov 1998* ★★★★

1978 ★★

A vintage of moderate quality. Late harvest. Small crop of useful, commercial wines.

Erbacher Hohenrain Eiswein (Rg) **Schloss Reinhartshausen** Fairly deep gold with orange highlights; bouquet like golden syrup and 'calf's foot jelly'; sweet, lip-licking honey and acidity, yet with a taste of late season rot. Long acidic finish. *Feb 2002* ★★★

Weinsberger Schemelsberg, Silvaner BA Eiswein Astonishing orange-tawny; honey and caramel; very sweet, very rich, gloriously long barley sugar/peachy flavour and good acidity. A rare jewel from Württemberg. *April 2003* ★★★★

1979 ★★★

On the whole, light and easy wines. There were Regional variations: the Rheingau and Pfalz had bigger and better harvests, the Rheinhessen was small but good and the Mosel small and quite good. The wines lacked the excitement, grandeur and finesse of a good classic vintage, but were pleasant to drink.

Braunerberger Juffer-Sonnenuhr Auslese Goldkapsel (M) **Fritz Haag** Consistent notes. Must weight 120° Oechsle, 89g/l residual sugar, 10g/l acidity, 7.5% alcohol. Pale, lime-tinged; delicate, floral, almost minty bouquet, edge of honeycomb sweetness; medium-sweet; delicious flavour, zestful. *Last tasted Oct 1998* ★★★★

Erbacher Steinmorgen Eiswein (Rg) **zu Knyphausen** Picked very late – 14 January 1980! Gold prize winner. 122° Oechsle, 11.8g/l acidity: beautiful, flawless bouquet; not as sweet as expected, good, firm flavour, dry finish. *Last noted Nov 1998* ★★★★

Niersteiner Auflangen, Silvaner BA Eiswein (Rh) **Louis Guntrum** The grapes were picked on 31 December, yet there was not much botrytis. 148° Oechsle. Deep gold; beautiful honey-sweet, pure raisin nose; fairly sweet, some plumpness yet still hard. Good acidity. *Sept 1988* ★★★★

Oestricher Lenchen Auslese Eiswein (Rg) **Wegeler** Yellow-gold; very good ripe kerosene Riesling nose and flavour. Mouthfilling. Not as sweet as expected. *Nov 1999* ★★★

Wöllsteiner Ziffchen, Optima-Ruländer BA (Rh) **P Müller** An exotic combination: the full-bodied juicy Ruländer (Pinot Gris) and the newer, grapey Optima. Fairly deep, waxy gold; intriguingly novel bouquet, spearmint; perhaps lacking length but with tingling acidity. *Last tasted Aug 1990* ★★★

1980–1989

An important decade. The taste in the UK for fine *fruchtig* wines had been corrupted by the flood of cheap 'sugar and water' wines. The attempt to produce drier wines resulted in some largely unsuccessful *trocken* and *halb-trocken* wines. The best were made from quality grapes whose sugar content was fully fermented out, the result being generally dry and with naturally higher alcoholic content. Happily, the great estates, some of which had, frankly, been under-performing, were revising their ideas.

VINTAGES AT A GLANCE
Outstanding ★★★★★ None
Very Good ★★★★ 1983, 1988, 1989 (v)
Good ★★★ 1985, 1986 (v), 1989 (v)

1980
A strange and difficult vintage for the grape grower. Avoid.

1981 ★★
Variable, mainly modest to moderate quality. Now of little or no interest.

1982 ★
Yet another mediocre vintage. This time a bumper harvest thanks to heavy rain. The biggest crop ever recorded in Germany, half as much again as 1973. Unpredictable wines. Best to avoid.
Wehlener Sonnenuhr lange Goldkapsel (M) **J J Prüm** Certainly an extra dimension here: sweeter, richer, botrytis, length. *April 1999* ★★★★

1983 ★★★★
The best vintage since 1976, thanks to better growing conditions. A judicious combination of rain and sun in September swelled and ripened the berries. However, there was little or no botrytis. Though highly rated at the time, the overall reputation of 1983 has eased back a little. It was, however, unreservedly successful in the Saar and Ruwer, as well as the Nahe. A most invigorating vintage, one of my favourites, still well worth looking out for and, of course, drinking.
Filzener Herrenberg Eiswein (M) **Reverchon** 149° Oechsle, 10% alcohol and amazingly high acidity, 18g/l. Bright yellow-gold; scent of lime blossom; sweet , of course, flavour of ripe peaches, with gooseberry-like, teeth-gripping acidity. Delicious. Exciting. *Last tasted Oct 1998* ★★★★
Forster Jesuitengarten Eiswein (P) **von Bühl** A delicious half bottle, sweet, delectable. *July 1998* ★★★★
Hochheimer Domdechaney Spätlese (Rg) **Werner** Most recently, still rich, good fruit, complete. *Nov 1999. For a Spätlese of this age,* ★★★★
Hochheimer Kirchenstück Auslese (Rg) **Künstler** Showing its class: deliciously fragrant; perfect fruit and acidity. *Sept 1996* ★★★★
Kreuznacher Krötenpfühl Eiswein (N) **Paul Anheuser** Orange-amber; bouquet of dried apricot skins and touch of caramel on the palate. Very rich. Marvellous acidity. *Aug 1999* ★★★★
Mülheimer Helenenkloster Eiswein (M) **Max Ferd. Richter** Rich yellow; lovely, stylish. *Aug 2000* ★★★★
Scharzhofberger Auslese (M) **Egon Müller** Glorious ripe peachy fragrance and flavour. Dry finish. *May 2000* ★★★★

Traiser Rotenfels Eiswein (N) **Dr Crusius** Surprisingly pale yellow; refined 'soft caramel', very fragrant Nahe 'fruit salad' nose; very strange, singed richness, lovely acidity. Will keep. *Nov 2000* ★★★(★)

Wallhäuser Mühlenberg Eiswein (N) **Prinz zu Salm-Dalberg** 154° Oechsle, 7.9g/l acidity. Pure topaz; barley sugar and honey; sweet overall though curiously dry mid-palate. Smooth, delicious. *Oct 1997* ★★★★

Wehlener Sonnenuhr Auslese lange Goldkapsel (M) **J J Prüm** For Manfred Prüm his 'long gold capsule' represents the highest expression of vintage and vineyard, certainly borne out by his '83: a lovely yellow-gold; fat, rich, creamy nose, fairly sweet, with extra botrytis dimensions, firm, fragrant aftertaste. *April 1999* ★★★★(★) *Years of life.*

Wehlener Sonnenuhr BA (M) **J J Prüm** Two notes. More recently, fragrant, minerally, aromatic, spicy, lovely flavour, shape, texture, balance and finish. *Last tasted April 1999* ★★★★★

Wehlener Sonnenuhr Eiswein (M) **J J Prüm** Orange amber; apricots and tangerines; very sweet, caramelly, superb. *Nov 2002* ★★★★★

1984

Poor, acidic wines; possibly the worst vintage of the decade in Germany. There was unseasonable weather throughout northern Europe.

1985 ★★★

In contrast to 1984, an attractive vintage. Wet summer was saved by fine autumn. At best, wines with charm rather than substance. A small selection of my more recent notes.

Brauneberger Juffer Auslese **Willi Haag** Pale; attractive; fairly sweet, light (7.8% alcohol), lovely flavour. Why waste it on quince tart and cream? *Jan 2004. By itself* ★★★★

Brüssele Kleinbottwarer Eiswein (W) **Adelmann** The grape sugar had reached 90° before icing, its final Oechsle over 200°. Fabulously sweet and creamy. *Dec 1995* ★★★★★

Casteller Bausch Mariensteiner Eiswein (F) **Fürst Castell** The first Eiswein made in Franconia. Very powerful honey and spice; very sweet with high tangy acidity, clean and crisp. *Last tasted in 1988* ★★★★

Erbacher Steinmorgen Auslese (Rg) **Freiherr zu Knyphausen** Picked 31 December at 115° Oechsle. Surprisingly pale; nutty nose; medium-sweet, touch of pineapple, marvellous acidity. *Nov 1995* ★★★

Ingelheimer Schloss Westerhaus Eiswein (Rh) **von Opel** Picked 31 December and 1 January 1986. 6.1% alcohol. Pure yellow-gold; glorious, zestful, grape, peach, mango and honey; very sweet, delicious crisp fruity flavour, perfect acidity. It was the best icewine I could recall. *Sept 1988* ★★★★★

Josephshöfer Auslese (M) **von Kesselstatt** The estate's exclusive vineyard in Graach. 8.5% alcohol. Rich, hefty, goaty nose; medium-dry, richness balanced by very good acidity. Vanilla aftertaste. *Nov 1990* ★★★(★) *Drink up.*

Scharzhofberger Auslese (M) **Egon Müller** Palish yellow; lovely, honeyed 'kerosene'; medium sweet, perfect balance, delicious flavour. Three recent bottles, one corked. *Last tasted May 2006. At best* ★★★★★

1986 ★ to ★★★

Very mixed results due, as always, to mixed weather conditions. Except in the south, September was cold and wet, delaying ripening, the Pfalz in particular benefiting from relatively fine, uninterrupted harvest conditions with excellent botrytis for the higher quality sweet wines. Elsewhere, violent storms in late October made the continuation of picking particularly difficult. Relatively few Auslesen produced, though the best are keeping well.

Mülheimer Helenenkloster Eiswein-Christwein (M) **Max Ferd. Richter** The necessary −10°C occurred on Christmas Day. 145° Oechsle. A lovely yellow-gold; glorious honey and cream nose and taste. Very sweet. Wonderful acidity. *Aug 1994* ★★★★★

1987

On the whole a poor vintage and relatively few wines tasted. The fairly large crop comprised mainly very acidic wines of lowly quality though in certain favoured sites some good, long-lasting Auslesen were made.

Hochheimer Hölle Eiswein (Rg) **Aschrott** Grapes picked 20 December: yellow-gold; creamy, vanilla, 'milk chocolate'; sweet, crisp, lovely flavour, good acidity. *June 1994* ★★★★

1988 ★★★★

An extremely good yet perhaps not fully appreciated vintage. Higher quality wines are still drinking well.

Eitelsbacher Karthäuserhofberg Abtsberg Auslese Palish apple-green; extraordinary, plump, peach-skin nose; dryish, fleshy and fresh, 8% alcohol. *July 2004* ★★★ *A good '88.*

Graacher Himmelreich Auslese (M) **J J Prüm** Medium-sweet, soft, nice fruit and flesh but with gum-gripping acidity. *April 1999* ★★★★ *Now–2012.*

Iphöfer Julius-Echter-Berg, Huxelrebe Auslese (F) **Juliusspital** Deserving its gold medal: gloriously grapey, raisiny nose; medium-sweet, combining ripe flesh with Franken steeliness, powerful (unusually high alcohol, 14.5%, for a German wine). *May 1999* ★★★

Scharzhofberg Auslese (M) **Egon Müller** A magnum: brilliant colour; lovely, refreshing bouquet; medium-sweet, delicate, lightly grapey flavour, excellent acidity. *June 1996* ★★★★

Wehlener Sonnenuhr Auslese lange Goldkapsel (M) **J J Prüm** Acidic, 'greengage' nose; an interesting conflict of flesh, fat and acidic bite. Rich yet dry finish. *April 1999* ★★★(★)

1989 ★★★ to ★★★★

On the whole a very good vintage and a large crop thanks to almost ideal growing conditions. The harvest began toward the beginning of September. Very ripe grapes and botrytis made it not the easiest of years for the lighter styles of wine, lack of acidity being a problem. Conditions for the richer *Prädikat* styles were very favourable, boosted by an Indian summer, which enabled superbly concentrated TBAs to be made. The higher quality wines are lovely now, and the best Auslesen, Beerenauslesen and TBAs have life in hand.

Bischoffinger Steinbuck, Ruländer TBA (B) **WG Bischoffingen** A top-quality co-operative wine: soft tawny; exotic, honey and muscatelle; very sweet, rich, fat, soft. *Sept 1995* ★★★★★

Brauneberger Juffer-Sonnenuhr Auslese (M) **Fritz Haag** Two consistent notes: very pale, lime-tinged, fabulous bouquet, a *mélange* of apricots, peaches, gooseberry-like acidity, vanilla; fairly sweet, tongue-teasing delicacy and acidity. *Last tasted Oct 1998* ★★★★★

Casteller Kugelspiel, Rieslaner BA (F) **Fürst Castell** Scent and flavour like honeyed strawberries and cream. Sweet, glorious, with Rieslaner's heavenly, almost scorching, acidity. *June 1997* ★★★★

Eltviller Sonnenberg Auslese (Rg) **Belz** Only 550 litres made. Sugar content too high (at 53°) to use SO_2 hence the surprisingly deep colour; very rich, very Riesling, floral, thick, honeyed botrytis; fairly sweet, delicious flavour, acidity and aftertaste. *Nov 2000* ★★★★

Erbacher Marcobrunn TBA (Rg) **Schloss Reinhartshausen** A heavily botrytised wine. Virtually two identical notes. Orange-gold; rich, raisiny; very sweet, rich yet not at all cloying, fabulous acidity. *Last noted April 1999* ★★★★★

Erdener Prälat Auslese (M) **Christoffel-Berres** 96° Oechsle, 11% alcohol: floral, honeycomb, kerosene Riesling; delicious fruit and acidity. *Noted Oct 1997* ★★★★

Erdener Treppchen Auslese (M) **Dr Loosen** Pale; flowery, greengages; fairly sweet, soft and rich (9% alcohol). *May 1998* ★★★

Forster Pechstein Eiswein (P) **Mossbacherhof** Gold; fragrant, lime; pineapple, grapefruit and honey flavour. Excellent acidity. *Sept 1997* ★★★★

Hattenheimer Nussbrunnen Auslese (Rg) **Balthasar Ress** Very exotic beeswax bouquet; a touch of hardness and a bit short. Stefan Ress said that it was his most difficult vintage for 20 years, and that the wine would probably soften with five to seven years more bottle-ageing. *Last noted April 1998* ★★★★ *Drink up.*

Hochheimer Reichestal Eiswein (Rg) **Künstler** Perfect gold; distinctive, harmonious, minerally, *fraises des bois*; sweet, refined, perfect length and acidity. *May 1996* ★★★★★

Kreuznacher Krötenpfuhl Auslese (N) **P Anheuser** An amazing colour; heavenly bouquet; full-flavoured, glorious fruit and acidity. More recently: 'honey and roses'; ripe. Lovely. *Last tasted June 1997* ★★★★

Maximin Grünhäuser Herrenberg Auslese (M) **von Schubert** Yellow-gold; classic Riesling aroma; soft, rich though drying out a little, touch of spearmint. *Last tasted July 2004* ★★★★

Münsterer Königsschloss, Scheurebe TBA (N) **M Schäfer** Deep rich amber; fabulous, creamy; very sweet, rich essence of grapes, very good acidity. *April 1996* ★★★★★

Oberhäuser Brücke BA (N) **Dönnhoff** Warm orange-gold; singed, toasted, raisiny nose, opening up fragrantly; intensely rich and sweet, full-bodied, creamy texture, lovely aftertaste. Great wine. *Nov 2000* ★★★★★

Rüdesheimer Berg Rottland TBA (Rg) **Breuer** Bright and beautiful; floral, glorious, honeyed 'face powder'; mammoth, tangy wine. *Feb 2000* ★★★★★

Rüdesheimer Berg Schlossberg BA (Rg) **Schloss Schönborn** Rich gold; glorious lychee scent; sweet, ripe wonderful consistency, texture, concentration. *May 1996* ★★★★

Saarburger Rausch Auslese lange Goldkapsel (M) **Geltz-Zilliken**
Sweet of course and simply delicious combination of fruit and acidity. Zilliken's
combined production of Eiswein and Beerenauslesen, 800 litres. *June 2002* ★★★★
Scharzhofberger BA (M) **von Kesselstatt** Pure lemon gold; classic, honey,
botrytis, not too sweet, lovely flavour. And excellent Saar acidity. *April 1996* ★★★★
Steinberger Auslese (Rg) **Staatsweingut** Two notes the same day: rich,
gold; fragrant; medium-sweet, lovely flavour and acidity. *Last noted Nov 1994* ★★★★
Wallufer Walkenberg TBA (Rg) **Jost** Pale gold; fragrant, sweet, powerful,
assertive, dried raisins. Toni Jost's first TBA. Superb. *Nov 2005* ★★★★★
Wehlener Sonnenuhr Auslese (M) **Dr Loosen** Pale for its age and style;
gentle yet rich, classic Riesling; medium-sweet, lovely ripe flavour, good acidity.
Ernst Loosen demonstrating his deft touch. *April 2004* ★★★★★
Wehlener Sonnenuhr Auslese (M) **J J Prüm** Ripe, peachy bouquet and
flavour. Lively acidity, lovely wine. *April 1999* ★★★★★
Wehlener Sonnenuhr BA (M) **S A Prüm** 135° Oechsle, 7.5g/l acidity, 9%
alcohol. Tutankhamen gold; creamy, slightly minty, honeyed; deliciously sweet,
creamy, fabulous flesh and length. *Oct 1997* ★★★★
Wehlener Sonnenuhr TBA (M) **J J Prüm** Surprisingly pale; floral, minty;
sweet yet not overpowering. Lovely. *Sept 1997* ★★★★★
Winkeler Hasensprung Auslese (Rg) **von Hessen** Three notes. 124°
Oechsle, 87.5g/l residual sugar, 12.25g/l acidity, 10% alcohol. Quite deep yellow-
gold; orange blossom, dried sultanas, peachy; not as sweet or hefty as expected.
Dry finish. *Last tasted Oct 1998* ★★★★

1990–1999

The first thing to say about this period is that growers in Germany
were fortunate; on the whole, weather conditions were favourable.
Even when the rains came, the growers coped remarkably well. The
market did not fully reflect the quality of wines being made and there
seemed to be no end to the demand for cheap wines which, in some
instances, I am told, were not really German at all but EU table wine
made from cheap Italian white wines spiced up with a sprinkling of
acidic German wine and marketed in traditional flute bottles with
fancy labels and German names. Nevertheless, strenuous efforts were
made to improve quality and standing by members of the VDP
representing the serious producers and major estates in each region.

Vintages at a Glance

Outstanding ★★★★★ 1990, 1993 (v)
Very Good ★★★★ 1992 (v), 1993 (v), 1994 (v), 1995 (v), 1996
(v), 1997, 1998, 1999
Good ★★★ 1991 (v), 1992 (v), 1994 (v), 1995 (v), 1996 (v)

1990 ★★★★★

The third good vintage in a row, but totally different to 1989 in several respects: much smaller crop, below the 10-year average, but firmer wines, many major estates having the highest sugar/acid levels but little botrytis. Another classic Riesling vintage, at best the finest wines since 1971.

Bernkasteler Johannisbrünnchen Eiswein (M) **J J Prüm** Rich lemon-gold; honey and mint, complete, needs time; sweet, lean, crisp yet lissom fleshiness. A fraction sticky and with youthful bite. *April 1999* ★★★(★)

Brauneberger Juffer Auslese (M) **Richter** Grapey nose, minty undertone; medium-sweet, 8% alcohol, good fruit and acidity. *April 1995* ★★★★

Brauneberger Juffer Sonnenuhr Auslese (M) **F Haag** Deep, harmonious, rich, complete. Sweet finish. *May 2000* ★★★ *Fully mature.*

Burg Ravensburger Dicker Franz, Schwarzriesling Spätlese trocken (B) **Burg-Ravensburg** 94° Oechsle, 13% alcohol. Colour of Morello cherry, browning; cherry again on nose; alcoholic; some residual sugar, attractive, clean, dry, acidic end. *Oct 1997* ★★★ *Ready now.*

Eitelsbacher Karthäuserhofberg Auslese Nr. 23 (M) **Tyrell** Nr 23 (no longer the *Fuder* number. Tank number!). Most recently: still very fresh, grapey acidity; fairly sweet, light (9% alcohol), glorious flavour. *Last tasted Oct 1994* ★★★★

Eitelsbacher Karthäuserhofberg Kronenbourg Auslese Tyrell Distinct varietal aroma; lovely flavour, touch of austerity. Very good. Long life. *Nov 2005* ★★★★

Erbacher Marcobrunn Spätlese Blaukapsel (Rg) **von Simmern** Old-fashioned, slightly spicy; medium-dry, positive, good finish. *Nov 1999* ★★ *Drink up.*

Erbacher Marcobrunn BA (Rg) **von Simmern** Deep, rich, minty, lime blossom; very sweet and fleshy, creamy texture. *Nov 2000* ★★★★★

Erbacher Marcobrunn TBA (Rg) **Schloss Schönborn** Fairly deep amber; very rich bouquet and flavour. Fragrant, great depth. Sweet, powerful, very good acidity and aftertaste. *Nov 2000* ★★★★★

Hattenheimer Wisselbrunn Beerenauslese Schloss Reinhartshausen Old gold; very syrupy, raisiny nose; sweet, rich, 9% alcohol, assertive, dry finish. Touch of austerity. Long life. *Oct 2000* ★★★★(★)

Hochheimer Domdechaney Auslese (Rg) **Aschrott** Unusual for me to have tasted so many Hochheimers of such a good vintage, from an area with a character all of its own, rich, perhaps more earthy. Domdechaney is the top vineyard site, Hölle 'half a point behind' and the Kirchenstück good, but more variable. Amber-gold; harmonious bouquet, rich, ripe, botrytis and bottle age; sweet, good flavour, 7.5% alcohol, excellent acidity, dry finish. *May 2007* ★★★★

Hochheimer Domdechaney Auslese (Rg) **Aschrott** Amber-gold; harmonious, rich, ripe botrytis and bottle age; sweet, good flavour 7.5% alcohol; excellent acidity, dry finish. *May 2007* ★★★★

Hochheimer Domdechaney Auslese (Rg) **Werner** Fairly distinctive style; botrytis, honey; fairly sweet, perfect weight (7.5% alcohol) and acidity. Honeyed aftertaste. *Nov 1996* ★★★★ *Should be perfect now.*

Hochheimer Hölle Auslese (Rg) **Aschrott** Five consistently good notes: very sweet, fat, lovely. The perfect mid-morning drink. *Last tasted March 1998* ★★★★ *Will continue.*

Hochheimer Hölle Auslese (Rg) **Künstler** Surprisingly deep yellow-gold; rich, honeyed bouquet and flavour, excellent length. *Nov 1999* ★★★★

Hochheimer Domdechaney Kirchenstück TBA (Rg) **Schloss Schönborn** 50-50 from the estate's Domdechaney and Kirchenstück sites, presumably because not enough was produced to sell separately. A highly successful, much be-medalled wine. 176°Oechsle, 240g/l residual sugar, 8.6g/l acidity, 7% alcohol. Three notes. Yellow-gold; peach-like, minty, honey and acidity; very sweet, plump around the waist, delicious. *Oct 1998* ★★★★★

Johannisberger Klaus TBA (Rg) **von Hessen** Extraordinary, singed *crème caramel* nose; very sweet, very rich, very high acidity. *Nov 1999* ★★★★★

Kiedricher Gräfenberg Auslese Goldkapsel (Rg) **Robert Weil** Pale; crisp, honeyed; fairly sweet, lovely flavour, elegant, good length. A typical Weil style. *Nov 1995* ★★★★★

Rauenthaler Baiken Auslese Kloster Eberbach Yellow with waxy sheen and gold highlights; lovely combination of honeyed botrytis and bottle age; fairly sweet, grapey, fleshy, excellent acidity and length. *Dec 2004* ★★★★

Rüdesheimer Bischofsberg BA (Rg) **Breuer** Golden colour; rich, peachy, refreshing bouquet; excellent acidity. *Nov 1998* ★★★★

Scharzhofberg Auslese (M) **von Schubert** Pale; classic kerosene Riesling aroma; a serious wine, rich, low alcohol (8.5%), good acidity. *Sept 2004* ★★★★

Scharzhofberger Auslese AP 30 (M) **Egon Müller** Extra dimension, soft, peachy, 8% alcohol, perfect balance and length. Delicious. *March 2006* ★★★★★ More to come.

Schlossgut Diel Auslese Goldkapsel (N) From two vineyards. Buttercup yellow; rich, fragrant, peachy; rich, honeyed, typical Nahe 'fruit salad' flavour, tingling acidity. *Nov 2005* ★★★★

Wehlener Sonnenuhr Spätlese (M) **J J Prüm** The best of an unimpressive 'flight' of Spätlesen ('90s to '95s). The most fragrant and sweetest, with rich, ripe fruit. *April 1999* ★★★ *Drink up*.

Wehlener Sonnenuhr Auslese Goldkapsel (M) **J J Prüm** Harmonious, honeyed botrytis; fairly sweet, rich, mouthfilling, complete. *April 1999* ★★★★ *Drink soon*.

Wehlener Sonnenuhr Auslese lange Goldkapsel (M) **J J Prüm** Several notes. *Last tasted Sept 1999* ★★★(★) *Now–2010*.

Wiltinger Braune Kupp Auslese (M) **Le Gallais** Egon Müller's 4-ha. 'monopole' vineyard. Magnificent, with typical Ruwer zestful acidity. *March 2006* ★★★★★

1991 ★★ to ★★★

Frankly, a far from great vintage. The lesser, drier wines were pleasant enough but, by and large, should have been consumed while young and fresh. One or two outstanding wines made by some estates. Pick and choose carefully.

Hattenheimer Hassel Eiswein (Rg) **H Lang** 165° Oechsle, 237g/l residual sugar, 12.5g/l total acidity, 8.3% alcohol. Two notes. Bright yellow; minerally, harmonious, peachy; an astonishing taste, refined honey and 'lip-licking' acidity. *Last noted Oct 1998* ★★★★★

Piesporter Goldtröpfchen Kabinett Haart A pity the 1971 Wine Laws debased this popular name. This is the real thing, produced by a top grower in a lesser vintage: very pale; pronounced Riesling aroma; fairly dry, light (8.5% alcohol), but with some flesh and a lovely pure varietal flavour, good balance. Complete. Not intended to age, but it held its own. *Oct 2005* ★★★

Schloss Johannisberger Blaulack Eiswein (Rg) Bright yellow; curious meaty, minty, then wet straw; very sweet, interesting but rustic. Creamy. Good acidity but tailed off. *Nov 2001* ★★★

Schloss Vollrads Eiswein Goldkapsel (Rg) Pale; honeyed orange blossom; lovely flavour, extremely high acidity. *Nov 1999* ★★★

1992 ★★ to ★★★★

Swings and roundabouts due, as always, to the constraints of the weather. Conditions started off favourably followed by a summer which, though hot, was plagued by rain and humidity. From early October the harvest proceeded satisfactorily but was interrupted by ten days of rain. Those producers who waited managed to produce some great wines in the Auslese to TBA range. It was also a very successful year for Eisweins.

Bischoffinger Rosenkranz, Ruländer TBA (B) **W Bischoffingen** To demonstrate what a major Baden co-operative can do. 205° Oechsle, 230g/l residual sugar, 11.6g/l total acidity. Astonishing colour, pure topaz with apple-green rim; raisiny, like a 6-putt Tokaji Aszú plus a touch of malt; treacle-sweet verging on unctuous, but creamy and with life-saving acidity. *Oct 1998* ★★★★★

Erbacher Marcobrunn BA (Rg) **Schloss R**einhartshausen 330g/l sugar, 7% alcohol. Two notes, first: relatively pale; crisp, fragrant, 'needs time'; very sweet, almost syrupy, glorious flesh. A similar subsequent note except colour deepening, fat and 'flesh' noted again. *Last tasted Oct 1999* ★★★(★)

Erbacher Siegelsberg TBA (Rg) **Schloss Reinhartshausen** Siegelsberg is not a great vineyard site but 'it works in all years'. 180° Oechsle; 8% alcohol. Tremendously high extract even without the residual sugar and only 90 litres produced. Amazing colour, orange-gold; harmonious, honeyed; enormously sweet and concentrated, swingeingly high acidity. *Nov 1997* ★★★★★ *Endless life.*

Forster Jesuitengarten BA (P) **von Bühl** Most recently, still a youthful yellow; lovely honey and lime bouquet and taste. Sweet, fleshy, good length. *Jan 2000* ★★★★★

Hattenheimer Wisselbrunnen Auslese (Rg) **zu Knyphausen** Fairly sweet, hefty style, rich, grapey, good acidity. *April 1998* ★★★

Hattenheimer Wisselbrunnen Beerenauslese (Rg) **Schloss Reinhartshausen** Apricot and gold coloured; rich, honeyed, raisiny; sweet, glorious flavour, 6% alcohol, very good acidity. Lovely. *Oct 2006* ★★★★★★

Hochheimer Stielweg, Spätburgunder Weissherbst Eiswein (Rg) **Aschrott** Picked 27 December. 135g/l residual sugar, 8% alcohol. Delicious, muscatelle-like grapiness. *Last tasted Oct 1995* ★★★★

Kiedricher Gräfenberg Auslese Goldkapsel (Rg) **Robert Weil** 143° Oechsle. Only 300 bottles produced. Gloriously rich amber-gold; youthful, peppery, spicy privet; sweet, marvellous flesh and texture, perfect acidity. '20 years of life'. *May 1996* ★★★★★

Kiedricher Gräfenberg BA Goldkapsel (Rg) **Robert Weil** Amber-gold; lime and orange blossom; very sweet, fat, power and beauty combined. Delicious. *Nov 1996* ★★★★★

Königsbacher Idig BA (Rh) **A Christmann** From the best vineyard in the Pfalz owned by Christmann: lime blossom fragrance; attractive; sweet enough, pleasant dry finish. Had higher expectations. *March 2003* ★★★

Oppenheimer Sackträger Gewürztraminer TBA (Rh) **Louis Guntrum** Nothing like a good ripe Gewürztraminer for instant appeal. Not subtle but striking: extraordinary colour, deep orange-amber; raisiny nose coated with caramel and chocolate; concentrated *crème brûlée*. Tokaji-like finish. *June 1999* ★★★★

Randersackerer Pfülben, Rieslaner TBA (F) **Juliusspital** Rieslaner is very much a Franken grape variety, as is Silvaner, very acidic but a perfect foil for this TBA: 254°Oechsle, 'the highest ever must weight in Germany'. Yellow-gold, orange tinge; fantastically sweet, rich, fat. A new experience. *July 1997* ★★★★★

Ruppertsberger Reiterpfad, Scheurebe BA (P) **von Bühl** The grapey Scheurebe at its exotic best, its surging scents a *mélange* of apricots, honey, mint, grapefruit; a 'sweet and sour' flavour. Lovely. *May 1998* ★★★★★

Wehlener Sonnenuhr Auslese Goldkapsel (M) **J J Prüm** Two notes. Still very pale but with lively and lovely nose and flavour. Medium-sweet. Light. Fragrant aftertaste. *Last noted May 2000* ★★★★ *Drink soon*.

Winkeler Hasensprung Eiswein (Rg) **von Hessen** Picked 30 December. Two notes. Still fairly pale; fragrant, caramelly nose; fairly sweet, rich, with a hard dry finish. *Last noted Nov 2000* ★★★★

1993 ★★★★ to ★★★★★

Overall this was a very good vintage with some outstanding wines produced despite variable weather during the summer and heavy rain at harvest time. The higher quality wines can be a revelation.

Assmannshäuser Frankenthal, Spätburgunder Weissherbst Eiswein (Rg) **Robert König** An astonishing wine: soft, ruddy colour; rich, raisiny, Tokaji-like and with indescribable fruits; sweet, rich but vibrant, 8% alcohol, delicious, fabulous finish. *Aug 2004* ★★★★★

Brauneberger Juffer-Sonnenuhr BA (M) **Fritz Haag** Pale; minty, with sharp, gooseberry-like nose, sweet, light style but elegant and with tingling acidity. *Sept 1997* ★★★

Eitelsbacher Karthäuserhofberg Auslese Tyrell Delicious flavour, medium-light (9.5% alcohol), excellent acidity. Perfect for a hot, humid summer day. *July 2004* ★★★★

Hattenheimer Nussbrunnen Auslese (Rg) **Balthasar Ress** Waxy yellow; lovely pineapple and greengage fragrance; not too sweet, fairly rich (10% alcohol), less acidic than its nose indicated. *Last noted May 2000* ★★★ *Pleasant drink*.

Kiedricher Gräfenberg Auslese (Rg) **Robert Weil** Glorious gold; still fresh and young; sweet, rich yet light (8.5% alcohol), ripe botrytis, excellent acidity. Beautiful. Will keep well. *June 1999* ★★★★ *Now–2010*.

Kiedricher Gräfenberg BA Goldkapsel (Rg) **Robert Weil** A superb wine: 186° Oechsle, 250g/l sugar, 12g/l acidity, 8.5% alcohol. Many notes. Most recently, sheer perfection. *Last noted April 1998* ★★★★★

Lieser Niederberg Helden Auslese (M) **Schloss Lieser** Very pale, green-tinged; crisp, fresh, slightly raw gooseberry nose; medium-sweet, light (7.5% alcohol), refreshing but short. *May 2000* ★★

Oberemmeler Hütte Auslese (M) **von Hövel** Delicious sweetness, weight, flavour and Saar acidity. Despite its youthfulness, lovely. *June 1996* ★★★★ *Will be lovely now.*

Scharzhofberger Auslese Goldkap 'GK' AP 24 **Egon Müller** Slight spritz; amazingly sweet, rich, fabulous flesh, tinge of acidity, superb length and aftertaste. No wonder Egon Müller wins all the prizes. *March 2006* ★★★★★

Scharzhofberger BA (M) **Egon Müller** Yellow; nose shy at first, then deep, peachy, with lovely botrytis; sweet, rich yet elegant, with glorious flavour and perfect acidity. *Sept 1997* ★★★★★

Schloss Schönborn TBA (Rg) **Schloss Schönborn** Lovely wine: pale gold; raisins, honey and lime blossom, very sweet of course (157° Oechsle, 194g/l residual sugar, 7.1g/l acidity, 8.5% alcohol). *July 1997* ★★★★★

Steinberger Auslese (Rg) **Staatsweingut** A quick taste of youthful perfection, scented, spicy, good future. *Nov 1994* ★★★★

Wehlener Sonnenuhr Auslese (M) **J J Prüm** Extremely pale; floral, almost Sauvignon Blanc-like gooseberry aroma; medium sweet, light style, good acidity. Very quaffable. *Jan 2005* ★★★

1994 ★★★ to ★★★★

Another top-class Riesling vintage, the second in a row. The crop was large and healthy, perhaps too large for some estates, who decided to green prune. Rain in all regions throughout September was heavy, but not disastrously so. Warm, misty weather proved ideal for botrytis. Some superb high-quality sweet ones are reaching full maturity and many still have more years in hand.

Assmannshäuser Höllenberg, Spätburgunder Weissherbst BA (Rg) **A Kesseler** Picking began on 12 September for Auslese and Beerenauslese, bunches being separated, even divided, dependant on the quality and ripeness of the grapes. Very pale; fragrant, like mature apples; very sweet (198° Oechsle) but crisp, glorious. *Nov 1995* ★★★★ *Probably at peak now.*

Assmannshäuser Höllenberg, Spätburg Weissherbst TBA (Rg) **A Kesseler** Grapes picked five days later than the Auslesen and Beerenauslesen. Pale; very fragrant, peachy; very sweet (200° Oechsle), rich but lissom, heavenly fragrance. *Nov 1995* ★★★★★ *Will develop fabulously.*

Brauneberger Juffer-Sonnenuhr BA (M) **Fritz Haag** 160° Oechsle, alcohol less than 7%. Glorious bouquet and flavour. Fleshy, with perfectly ripe fruit and acidity. *Last noted May 2000* ★★★★ *Now–2015.*

Eitelsbacher Karthäuserhofberg Auslese (M) **Tyrell** Christoph Tyrell showed his Spätlese and Auslese the June after the vintage. Both with very acidic Ruwer character, the Spätlese very steely, the Auslese somewhat richer. Far too raw and young. *June 1995* ★★★? *Auslese hopefully softened by now.*

Erdener Treppchen Auslese (M) **Dr Loosen** Ernst Loosen produced one of the best Spätlesen at the opening Grosser Ring tasting in 1995. His Auslese tasted nine months later was simply delicious, faultless. *Feb 1996* ★★★★

Forster Ungeheuer TBA (P) **von Bühl** An amazing colour, orange-amber; glorious, celestial raisins; incredibly sweet, concentrated, almost overpowering. *Jan 1996* ★★★★

Graacher Domprobst Auslese **Kerpen** Fairly pale; fragrant, characterful, kerosene Riesling aroma, rich, very good acidity. Unassuming. *May 2004* ★★★

Hallgartener Schönhell BA (Rg) **Hans Lang** 154° Oechsle, 170g/l residual sugar, 10.5g/l acidity, 8.5% alcohol. Pale gold colour; floral, forthcoming mint and cress aroma; sweet but lean and attenuated finish. *Nov 1998* ★★★(★) *Now–2010.*

Hattenheimer Pfaffenberg TBA (Rg) **von Schönborn** Rich, raisiny nose of great depth; very sweet, rich, lovely flavour, classic. *Nov 2005* ★★★★★

Hattenheimer Schützenhaus Eiswein (Rg) **Hans Lang** Colour of pale old brass; lovely apricot and honey bouquet; very sweet and fleshy, glorious flavour, excellent acidity. *Nov 2005* ★★★★★

Hochheimer Domdechaney Auslese (Rg) **Werner** Fragrant, lime, floral, privet; fairly sweet, ripe fleshy fruit, lovely flavour and length. Brilliant. *Nov 1996* ★★★★ *Drink now–2010.*

Hochheimer Hölle BA (Rg) **Künstler** A lovely, light-honey BA richness; glorious flavour, crisp acidity, earthy Hochheim aftertaste. *Nov 1997* ★★★★

Monzinger Halenberg BA (N) **Emrich-Schönleber** Considered a great vintage in the Nahe. Richly coloured with orange and gold highlights; Nahe 'fruit salad' fragrance, creamy, whiff of violets; very sweet, fleshy, 11% alcohol, glorious flavour – golden syrup with perfect counterbalancing acidity. A great producer. *Nov 2005* ★★★★★

Monzinger Frühlingsplätzchen Auslese Goldkapsel (N) **Emrich-Schönleber** Wonderful flesh and acidity. *Nov 2000* ★★★★ *Long life.*

Niederhäuser Hermannsberg TBA (N) **Staatsweingut** Astonishing richness and power. 267° Oechsle, 400g/l sugar, residual 108g/l. Amber-gold. Whereas the nose struggled to emerge, though refined, there was a positive assault on the palate. Amazingly sweet and rich. *Nov 2000* ★★★★★

Niederhäuser Hermannshöhle Auslese (N) **Dönnhoff** Another top Nahe 'fruit salad' maker. Delicious. *June 1999* ★★★

Randersackerer Marsberg, Rieslaner TBA (F) **Staatlicher Hofkeller** 222° Oechsle, a long, cool fermentation used for the first time. Grapes individually picked in late October and early November, and then sorted again: apple gold; fabulous bouquet, deeply honeyed, apricots and *crème brûlée* with flavour to match. Only 6% alcohol. *July 1997* ★★★★★

Ruppertsberger Reiterpfad, Scheurebe TBA (P) **von Bühl** Viscous orange-amber; strange, citrus-like high acidity; alcohol only 6% but the sweetest, fattest, most grapey wine I can recall, the Scheurebe giving it a peculiar sweaty, gooseberry-like flavour. Highly impressive but… *Jan 1996* ★★★★

Scharzhofberger BA (M) **Egon Müller** Beautiful golden colour; scent of privet and gooseberry; incredibly sweet, glorious flavour and flesh, high acidity. The Müllers informed us that this had been their highest must weight ever in BA and even TBA – so concentrated that no sulphur was needed. *May 2000* ★★★(★★★) *(6 stars). At least a 30-year life span.*

Würzburger Abstleite, Muskat Eiswein (F) **Juliusspital** Extraordinary smell of cats, mint and mandarin; sweet, rich, lovely flavour and style. *July 1997* ★★★★

1995 ★★ to ★★★★

Another successful vintage – but it was mainly limited to the later-picked Riesling wines, though there were some decent QbA and Kabinett wines for early drinking. Growers who waited to pick until October, the warmest for ten years, particularly in the Mosel-Saar-Ruwer, made superlative wines.

Eitelsbacher Karthäuserhofberg Eiswein (M) **Tyrell** Virtually colourless – rich, peachy; sweet, light style, zinging Ruwer acidity, delicious. *Sept 1997* ★★★★

Erdener Prälat Auslese Goldkapsel (M) **Dr Loosen** Two notes. Already gloriously developed, moving from 4 to 5 stars. Fairly sweet, peachy, perfection. *Last noted Aug 1997* ★★★★★ *Now–2015.*

Freinsheimer Musikantenbuchel, Scheurebe Auslese (P) **Lingenfelder** Colour of brass; orange blossom; sweet peachy/tangerine flavour, body (9% alcohol) and excellent acidity. *April 1999* ★★★

Graacher Domprobst BA (M) **Willi Schaefer** Schaefer is reputed to make the best wine in Graach, partly because of his two outstanding vineyards of which Domprobst is one. A superb '95: pale yellow; honeyed sweet, attractive flavour with 'hot' acidic end. Needs time. *Sept 1997* ★★★★

Schloss Johannisberger Rosagold (BA) (Rg) Pure amber; very fragrant clover honey; fairly sweet, very acidic, long. *Nov 2001* ★★★(★) *2005–2020.*

Johannisberger Vogelsang Auslese (Rg) **Johannishof-Eser** Pale; fresh, high-toned; delicate sweetness and crisp style. *Nov 2000* ★★★

Kiedricher Gräfenberg Auslese Nr 19 (Rg) **Robert Weil** Faultless, heavenly, fairly sweet but light, with lovely fruit and uplifting finish. *Feb 1998* ★★★★★ *Will go on.*

Maximin Grünhäuser Abtsberg Auslese (M) **von Schubert** Instantly fragrant, kerosene grapiness; medium-sweet, light (8.5% alcohol). Charming, with perfect Ruwer acidity. *Dec 2000* ★★★★ *Will keep.*

Oberemmeler Hütte Eiswein (M) **von Hövel** Two notes. Most recently, its nose had opened up; sweet of course and a nice touch of fat. *Last tasted Sept 1997* ★★★★

Oberhäuser Brücke BA (N) **Dönnhoff** Two notes. My favourite Nahe 'fruit salad'; sweet, fleshy but crisp. Delectable. *Last tasted May 1998* ★★★★ *Another 10–15 years in hand.*

Piesporter Goldtröpfchen BA (M) **Reinhold Haart** Certainly not any old Piesporter 'golden drops' (*Goldtröpfchen*), but a strange undertone. Sweet, rich of course. A wine to keep. *Sept 1997* ★★(★★)?

Rüdesheimer Berg Roseneck Auslese (Rg) **Allendorf** Scent like apples in a hayloft; medium-sweet, 10% alcohol, touch of peach kernels but fragrant. Teeth-gripping acidity. Needs more time. *Nov 1999* ★(★★)?

Rüdesheimer Berg Schlossberg BA (Rg) **Hess'isches Staatsweingut** Sweet, rich, assertive, very good flavour and acidity. *Nov 2000* ★★★(★)

Saarburger Rausch Eiswein (M) **Dr Wagner** Well known for his zestful dry Saar wines, Heinz Wagner also produces outstanding sweet wines and this was one of his best vintages. Not as sweet as expected. *Sept 1997* ★★★★

Scharzhofberger Auslese Goldkapsel (M) **Egon Müller** Surprisingly pale; peachy; firm and not as sweet as expected. Rich though and acidic. Needs time. *June 1996* ★★(★★)?

Schlossgut Diel Eiswein (N) Picked early (for an Eiswein), 5 November. Very sweet, fleshy, lovely. Next, herbaceous nose and strange flavour like squashed fruit salad. *Last noted Nov 1996* ★★★★

Serriger Schloss Saarsteiner Eiswein (M) **Schloss Saarstein** Also picked 5 November in the middle of the harvest, their earliest Eiswein ever. 140° Oechsle: crisp, glorious. Peachy; distinctive flavour, good fruit, some fat, high acidity. *Last tasted Sept 1997* ★★★★ *Will keep.*

Wehlener Sonnenuhr Auslese (M) **Dr Loosen** Touch of *spritz* which gave the wine a delicious uplift. Crisp young honey and grapefruit nose; most agreeable fruit and flesh, perfect acidity, length and finish. *Last enjoyed Jan 1997* ★★★★★

Wehlener Sonnenuhr lange Goldkapsel (M) **J J Prüm** Yellow-gold; hard, minty, complex; fairly sweet, peachy flavour, lovely acidity and finish. Years of life. *April 1999* ★★★(★)

Wiltinger Braune Kupp Auslese GK 95 **Le Gallais** 'GK' = Goldkapsel. Pure gold; deep, honeyed, hefty style; very sweet but counterbalanced with good Ruwer acidity. Superb wine. *March 2006* ★★★★

Wiltinger Schlagengraben Auslese fruchtsüss **Reinart** Very pale; rather grassy aroma; anticipated sweetness more than counterattacked by equally anticipated Saar acidity. (8.5% alcohol, acidity 9.4 g/l). A matter of taste. *May 2004* ★★★ *with Japanese cuisine.*

1996 ★ to ★★★★

An abnormally dry growing season. Cold led to uneven flowering in June, July was warm and August variable, with some hail. Cool but sunny in September. Picking started in early October, though the sugar was too low and acidity too high. Those estates that waited benefited from a late Indian summer which happily reversed the sugar/acid ratios. Many notes.

Blauer Spätburgunder 'SJ' Karl (B) **K H Johner** 'Selection Johner'. Probably Karl Heinz's best-ever wine, certainly a great '96. An attractive red; 'warm' chocolatey nose; sweet, delicious, slightly raspberry flavour with lovely oaky finish (also unusually, all Johner's wines are matured in *barriques*). *June 1999* ★★★(★)

Deidesheimer Hohenmorgen Auslese (P) **von Bassermann-Jordan** Picked 28 October. 112° Oechsle, 64g/l residual sugar, 9.6g/l total acidity, 10.81% alcohol. Pale melon yellow; a glorious, herbaceous, peachy and honey nose with greengage acidity, then rose petals; not as sweet as expected, lovely flavour, clean, dry finish. *Last tasted Oct 1998* ★★★(★) *Now–2010.*

Erbacher Michelmark Eiswein (Rg) **J Jung** Picked on Christmas Day at −15° C. 200° Oechsle, very high acidity, 19.5g/l. Lime, cress, rather metallic; very sweet, quite good flesh, attenuated, lip-licking acidity. *Nov 1998* ★★★

Erbacher Siegelsberg Auslese (Rg) **Schloss Reinhartshausen** 10% alcohol. Palish; peachy, minty; fairly sweet, lovely flavour, balance, acidity. *Last noted Sept 2000* ★★★

Erdener Prälat Auslese (M) **Dr Loosen** Very pale; low-keyed but peachy; medium-sweet, excellent acidity. *March 1999* ★★★(★) *Now–2010.*

Forster Ungeheuer Eiswein (P) **von Bassermann-Jordan** A most exotic nose; very sweet but perfectly balanced by high end acidity. 10.5% alcohol. *April 1998* ★★★★

Forst Ungeheuer 'GC' Spätlese trocken **Bürklin-Wolf** Impressive double magnum: palish; pure gold highlights; spicy; medium-dry, full-bodied (13%

alcohol), good extract, flavour and acidity. A highly successful 'food wine'. *March 2005* ★★★★

Haardter Bürgergarten, Rieslaner Auslese (P) **Müller-Cattoir**

Distinct peach and apricot fragrance; fairly sweet, light style (8.5% alcohol) but rich. A Pfalz renaissance under Müller-Catoir. Delicious flavour, Rieslaner acidity. *Feb 1999* ★★★★

Hochheimer Domdechaney Spätlese (Rg) **Aschrott/Künstler** the

first vintage made by Künstler following his acquisition of the Aschrott estate. Relatively young, he has put Hochheim back on the map. Very pale; cress-like; ripe, lovely flavour ★★★; **Hölle BA** almost colourless; glorious fruit, sweetness, length and aftertaste ★★★★(★); **Kirchenstück Spätlese** 'Künstler's best ever Spätlese'. Lovely fruit and acidity. *Then* ★★★(★) *Now–2010;* all tasted in September 1997, except the **Reichenstal Eiswein** yellow-gold; deep, rich, creamy, honeyed; very sweet, plump, touch of Hochheimer earthiness, delicious flavour, length and acidity. Künstler demonstrating his prowess. *March 2003* ★★★★★

Schloss Johannisberger Rosalack Auslese (Rg) A particularly

successful year at the Schloss. Palish yellow; leafy, herbaceous, spearmint; sweet, crisp acidity, good flavour, length and end taste. *Nov 2001* ★★★(★) *Now–2012.*

Kiedricher Gräfenberg Auslese **Robert Weil** Wilhelm Weil's wines are in

a class of their own: lovely yellow-gold; exquisite 'honey and flowers' scents and greengage-like acidity. Sweet, rich, lovely flesh and flavour. *Oct 2002* ★★★★

Kiedricher Gräfenberg Auslese Goldkapsel (Rg) **Robert Weil** One

of the loveliest of wines. Six notes. Now a deep amber-gold, perfection. *Last tasted Nov 2000* ★★★★★

Kiedricher Gräfenberg BA Goldkapsel (Rg) **Robert Weil** Pinkish

gold; sweet, heady lime blossom and honeyed botrytis; almost TBA richness. Lovely flavour. Rather harsh end-acidity. *Last noted Sept 1999* ★★★★(★) *Now–2020.*

Maximin Grünhäuser Abstberg Eiswein (M) **von Schubert** A

rainless season ending with successful Eiswein, von Schubert's perfect slopes and skill producing a more than interesting wine, exotic Riesling more like Muscatelle; sweet but with a lean touch of teeth-gripping acidity. Very fragrant aftertaste. *March 2003* ★★★★

Nackenheimer Rothenberg Auslese (Rh) **Gunderloch** Top producer.

Two notes. 100° Oechsle, 65g/l residual sugar, 9.2g/l acidity, 9.5% alcohol: greengage, gooseberry, steely nose; fairly sweet entry, dry finish, good fruit, excellent balance. *Oct 1998* ★★★★ *Now–2012.*

Niersteiner Oelberg Eiswein (Rh) **Balbach** No botrytis in 1996: 168°

Oechsle, 225g/l residual sugar, 13.5g/l vital acidity, modest 7% alcohol. Scent of orange blossom, lime, peaches, lean, not exactly shrill, more like a high note on a violin; sweet, fleshy fruit, good acidity, a joy to drink. *Oct 1998* ★★★★★

Rüdesheimer Berg Schlossberg, Spätburgunder Spätlese (Rg)

August Kesseler Very small yield, between 6 and 8hl/ha, high acidity, 12.5% alcohol. Fairly deep red, rich 'legs'; very good, crisp Pinot Noir aroma; dry, fragrant, lovely tannin and acidity, slightly smoky. Kesseler at his best. *Nov 1999* ★★★(★)

OF THE MANY '96S TASTED in 1997 the following were showing well: **Bernkasteler Doctor Auslese lange Goldkapsel** (M) **Thanisch** sweetness and flesh and quite attractive ★★★; **Brauneberger Juffer Auslese**

lange Goldkapsel (M) **Willi Haag** grapey; assertive, good flavour, length
and excellent acidity ★★★(★); **Brauneberger Sonnenuhr Auslese lange
Goldkapsel** (M) **Fritz Haag** excellent: sweet, with glorious acidity ★★★(★)
Possible 5 stars. Long life; **Erdener Prälat Auslese Goldkapsel** (M)
Christoffel-Berres grapey, lively acidity; fairly sweet, crisp, attractive ★★★(★);
Erdener Prälat Auslese Goldkapsel (M) **Dr Loosen** sweet, rich,
lovely flavour, acidity and length. Needs time ★★★(★★) *now–2016;* **Erdener
Prälat Auslese lange Goldkapsel** (M) **Dr Loosen** glorious, ripe,
creamy; sweet yet light at heart, nice flesh and acidity ★★★★(★) *long life;*
Hattenheimer Schützenhaus Goldkapsel (Rg) **zu Knyphausen**
pale; peachy fruit and flavour ★★★; **Mülheimer Helenenkloster Eiswein**
(M) **Max Ferd. Richter** picked on Boxing Day, 26 December. 167.3g/l residual
sugar, very high acidity (16.5g/l), 12% alcohol. Very sweet, delicious, touch of
pineapple, uplift of acidity and crisp finish ★★★★; **Oberhäuser Brücke
Auslese** (N) **Dönnhoff** 'fruit salad' and lime fragrance and flavour. Glorious,
spicy, excellent flavour and finish ★★★★(★); **Saarburger Rausch Auslese
Goldkapsel** (M) **Zilliken** virtually colourless; light, grassy; fairly sweet, touch
of youthful grapefruit. Needed time. *Probably ★★★ or more now;*
Scharzhofberger Auslese Goldkapsel (M) **Egon Müller** sweet, fleshy,
ripe, original (★★★★); **Trittenheimer Leiterchen Auslese Goldkapsel**
(M) **Milz-Laurentiushof** medium-dry – I expected it to be sweeter. Good,
ripe, yet crisp nose and flavour ★★★(★); **Ürziger Würzgarten Auslese
Goldkapsel** (M) **Dr Loosen** 'over 50% botrytis'. Delicious, but needing
more time. Excellent value. *At best ★★★★ Now–2016;* **Ürziger Würzgarten
Auslese lange Goldkapsel** (M) **Eymael** good wine. Sweet, fruity, fleshy
★★★★; **Wehlener Sonnenuhr Auslese** (M) **J J Prüm** fairly sweet, light
style, fragrant ★★★★; **Wehlener Sonnenuhr Auslese Goldkapsel** (M)
J J Prüm from J J's prime 19-ha vineyard. Palish, starbright; steely; medium-
sweet, lightish style (8.5% alcohol), crisp, flavoury with lip-tingling acidity ★★★★;
Wiltinger Braune Kupp Auslese Goldkapsel (M) **Le Gallais**
glorious peachy flavour with a deft touch and spritz prickle on the finish ★★★;
Winkeler Jesuitengarten Auslese (Rg) **Jacob Hamm** lovely, grapey
flavour and acidity ★★(★★); and **Zeltinger Sonnenuhr Auslese** (M)
Vereinigte Hospitien light, agreeable. Whatever sweetness there is, is upstaged
by the very dry acidic finish ★(★★)?

1997 ★★★★

This vintage was one of the best, with generous production, ripe grapes, high
sugar content, though little botrytis and good acidity. An Indian summer
with sun, warmth and clear blue skies enabled harvesting to begin early
October. Many growers had finished by the second week in November.
    Some superb ripe Rieslings of Auslese quality and above.
Bernkasteler Badstube TBA Molitor 300 g/l residual sugar; 210°
Oechsle, alcohol only 7%. Pure gold; rich, Sauternes-like nose; immensely sweet
and rich, creamy, glorious. *June 2005* ★★★★★
Brauneberger Juffer-Sonnenuhr Auslese Fritz Haag Consistently the
top producer in the middle Mosel: fragrant, pure Riesling kerosene aroma; fairly
sweet, soft, ripe, peachy flavour and tingling acidity. *March 2006* ★★★★

Dernauer Pfarrwingert, Spätburgunder Rotwein Auslese trocken (A) **Meyer-Näkel** Meyer-Näkel is now regarded as the top Ahr producer and his wine, from fully fermented-out Pinot Noir, is interesting: medium-deep red; strawberry aroma and flavour; touch of sweetness, bitter tannic finish. Certainly too young when tasted. Needs time and food. *June 1999* ★★(★★)

Erdener Treppchen BA (M) **Dr Loosen** Pale gold; very rich, lovely; low alcohol (6.5%), and perfect acidity. *June 1999* ★★★★

Graacher Himmelreich Auslese (M) **J J Prüm** An elderberry, minerally blossoming scent; mild, grapey flavour. *Last tasted May 2000* ★★★

Hattenheimer Wisselbrunnen BA (Rg) **Eser** Lime-tinged; light, fragrant, whiff of mint and peach kernels; sweet, curious style but with very fragrant flavour and aftertaste and good acidity. *Nov 2000* ★★★★ *Now–2010.*

Hochheimer Hölle Spätlese halbtrocken (Rg) **Künstler** Delicate, fragrant; medium-dry, lovely flavour, perfect finish. *June 1999* ★★★

Hochheimer Hölle Eiswein (Rg) **Joachim Flick** Palish, lime; lovely peachy fruit and acidity; sweet, very fragrant. *Nov 1998* ★★★★

Ihringer Winklerberg, Spätburgunder Rotwein '★★★' Auslese (B) **Dr Heger** Outstanding estate. Dr Heger probably made the best '97 in Baden. Very rich varietal aroma which opened up well, scented Pinot, caramel and tar; slightly sweet, very good oaky Pinot flavour, perhaps a bit jammy. *March 2000* ★★★

Iphofer Kalb Ehrenfelser Eiswein (F) **Wirsching** Lovely honeyed nose; sweet, delicious flavour, very dry acidic finish. *April 2000* ★★(★) *Now–2010.*

Kiedricher Gräfenberg Auslese Goldkapsel (Rg) **Robert Weil** Wilhelm Weil's trademark is fruity sweetness and charm. Three notes. Most recently: very pale; extraordinary forthcoming bouquet; very sweet, highly original. *Last noted Nov 1999* ★★★★(★) *Now–2015.*

Lieser Niederberg Helden Auslese '★★★' (M) **Schloss Lieser** For Wilhelm and Thomas Haag, one of their best vintages of the 1990s. 115° Oechsle, without botrytis, 7.5% alcohol. A sheer delight. Sweet, creamy, peachy. Lovely balance and finish. *May 2000* ★★★(★) *Now–2010.*

Nackenheimer Rothenberg Auslese Goldkapsel (Rh) **Gunderloch** No botrytis, dried grapes. Very pale; refreshing lime blossom fragrance; sweet, lean, crisp fruit with lip-licking acidity. A challenge well handled by a deservedly renowned producer. *March 2003* ★★★★

Wehlener Sonnenuhr Auslese (M) **J J Prüm** Two similar notes. Youthful, lime-tinged, minerally nose; medium-sweet, fragrant, alcohol 7.5%, dry finish. On both occasions slight spritz. *Last noted Sept 1999* ★★(★) *Now–2010.*

Wehlener Sonnenuhr Auslese Goldkapsel Cask 29 (M) **J J Prüm** Top of the range in this vintage. Low-keyed, minerally nose; sweet, soft peachy flavour. Lovely. 8% alcohol. Lovely now and with a great future. *April 1999* ★★★(★)

1998 ★★★★

A very good year in the south (i.e the Pfalz and Baden), less easy in the Mosel-Saar-Ruwer except for those top estates with well-drained sites planted with the late-ripening Riesling; there was plenty of rain which made life more difficult for early-ripening varieties on richer soils and flatter sites.

The growing season started with an early budbreak followed by a very wet April. A hot and sunny May produced excellent flowering conditions, two weeks earlier than normal in the Mosel, perfect in the Rheingau, and early – though cool – in June elsewhere. Low temperatures continued, with extensive rain. July was warm and dry though lacking sunshine, and the rest of the summer was extremely hot, with temperatures up to 40°C in the Rheingau and an all-time German record high of 41.2°C in the Middle Mosel. The good ripening weather continued into early September, thereafter there was almost continuous rain. The Mosel enjoyed one week of sun in October followed by storms and floods. Despite the wet, the grapes remained healthy. A large, miraculously good crop.

Dorsheimer Goldloch Auslese (N) Schlossgut Diel The Nahe valley enjoyed a 'sensational' harvest. Medium-sweet, very good flavour. Dry finish. A broader, more earthy style than the Mosels. *June 2000* ★(★★) *Now–2015.*

Geisenheimer Rothenberg Beerenauslese Goldkapsel Wegeler Very sweet, very rich, assertive, touch of caramel. *Oct 2005* ★★★★

Hattenheimer Wisselbrunn Eiswein Hans Lang Picked 27 Nov at –10°C. Very sweet but with high counterbalancing acidity (12 g/l). Exciting wine. *Nov 2005* ★★★★

Kiedricher Gräfenberg Auslese (Rg) Robert Weil Perfect mid-morning drink – a sensible half bottle. Grapeskin yellow-green; enticingly fragrant; not too sweet, light (8% alcohol), delicious flesh and flavour, excellent acidity. Ever dependable Weil. *July 2003* ★★★★★

Kiedricher Gräfenberg Spätlese Robert Weil Pale melon colour; attractive fruit, with almost Sauvignon acidity; sweeter than expected – but delicious flavour, melon and grapes. *Aug 2002* ★★★★

Königsbacher Idig Eiswein A Christmann Picked after a very wet vintage at -9° C, 162° Oechsle. Pale; spicy, steely, minerally; sweet but lean, with incredible bite. Will match the richest confection; though we enjoyed it with boiled potatoes. *March 2003* ★★★

Maximin Grünhäuser Abtsberg Spätlese (M) von Schubert Almost colourless; light, fragrant, flowery; medium-dry, light (8% alcohol), with delectable flavour, dry finish and lip-licking acidity. *Oct 2000* ★★★(★) *Now–2010.*

Münsterer Pittersberg Auslese (N) Krüger-Rumpf Two notes. Very pale; curious powdery nose; medium-sweet, light, fragrant Nahe style, with dancing acidity. *Last tasted Nov 2000* ★★(★★) *Now–2010.*

Nackenheimer Rothenberg Auslese (Rh) Gunderloch Two notes. Copybook balance of fruit and acidity, delectable, delicious. *Last noted Sept 2000* ★★★(★) *Verging on 5 stars. Now–2012.*

Niederhäuser Hermannshöhle Auslese (N) Dönnhoff Lovely: my ideal Nahe 'fruit salad' wine. *April 2000* ★★★(★) *Now–2012.*

Wehlener Sonnenuhr Auslese (M) J J Prüm Pale; lovely, fragrant, peachy; medium-sweet, fairly rich, grapey flavour, very good acidity ★★★(★) *Now–2012;* **Auslese Goldkapsel** though very good, the extra 'leg up' of quality designation not all that obvious. The same sort of sweetness and distinctive kerosene Riesling flavour ★★★(★) *Now–2015;* and **Auslese lange Goldkapsel** more colour, honeyed botrytis; sweet, lovely flesh, flavour, good length ★★★(★★) *Now–2020; all tasted in May 2000. All now–2015.*

1999 ★★★★

This was said to be one of the best vintages since 1976 thanks to a long, warm and exceptionally sunny summer despite, as in 1998, rain throughout the harvest. Well-ripened grapes on the best well-drained sites survived miraculously. All regions reported very ripe fruit and unusually low acidity. The Saar and Ruwer, where very high acidity is often a problem, were both particularly successful.

Berncasteler Doctor Auslese (M) **Thanisch** Minerally, grapey; medium-sweet, austere finish. Needs time. *June 2000* ★★(★★) *Now–2010.*

Brauneberger Juffer-Sonnenuhr Auslese Goldkapsel (M) **Fritz Haag** Crisp, classic; very good, fairly sweet, rich yet only 7% alcohol and light, grapey flavour. *May 2000* ★★★(★) *Now–2012.*

Eitelsbacher Karthäuserhofberg Auslese (M) **Tyrell** two notes. Beautifully mellow ★★★★ *Now–2010;* **Auslese Cask 22** a superior cask. Slightly more peachy. Firm. Slatey finish ★(★★★) *2009–2018;* and **Auslese Cask 23** more power, greater length, lovely aftertaste (★★★★) *2010–2020; all tasted in June 2000.*

Erbacher Marcobrunn Spätlese fruchtig (Rg) **Schloss Reinhartshausen** Pale, bright; distinctive, herbaceous; fairly sweet, crisp, grapey flavour, well balanced, delicious. *Feb 2002* ★★★ *Drink up.*

Erdener Prälat Auslese (M) **Dr Loosen** The Prälat vineyard has an exceptional microclimate capable of producing the richest wines of the Mosel. The nose, initially like pear drops, has great depth; firm on the palate, with lovely flavour and excellent acidity. *Last tasted June 2000* ★★(★★) *Now–2012.*

Erdener Prälat Auslese (M) **Mönchhof** the ideal wines to sip on a summer's day. Colourless; youthful grape and pineapple aroma; medium-sweet, light (8% alcohol), acidic (★★★) *Now–2010;* and **Auslese Goldkapsel** the often-repeated 'peachy/grapey' is not very exciting to read but this, for me, is the character of these Mosel-Saar-Ruwer wines. Even lower alcoholic content, 7.5%. Fairly sweet, delectable acidity ★(★★★) *Now–2012; both tasted June 2000.*

Iphöfer Kronsberg, Silvaner Spätlese (F) **Hans Wirsching** Silvaner, which can produce lacklustre and mawkish wines in some regions, comes into its own in Franken, and many growers compare their '99s to the excellent '75s, the highish acidity of both vintages adding to Silvaner's vivacity. Pale, with a good aroma and dry steely palate. *April 2000* ★★(★★) *Drink soon.*

Schloss Johannisberger Goldlack TBA (Rg) The youngest and last of the ten wines at their 900th anniversary tasting: medium-pale, waxy yellow; youthful; very sweet of course, fleshy, creamy, a touch metallic but needs bottle age. Great length and potential. *Nov 2001* (★★★★★) *2015–2040?*

Kanzemer Altenberg Auslese (M) **von Othegraven** Like almost all of the Saar and Ruwer wines, almost colourless; a light but delightful aroma like freshly peeled grapes; medium-sweet, much fuller-bodied than its appearance or nose indicated, and with grip. Will benefit from bottle age ★(★★) *at least. Now–2012;* and **Auslese Goldkapsel** a lovely, ripe, peachy nose, sweeter than the 'plain' Auslese and even more mouthfilling. This great estate is enjoying a renaissance. ★(★★★) *2009–2015. Both tasted June 2000.*

Kiedricher Gräfenberg Auslese Goldkapsel (Rg) **Weil** Pure pale Tutankhamen gold, touch of spritz; immediate uplift of honey, apricot, melon;

sweet, luscious, alcohol only 8%, soft ripe rich texture and gooseberry-like acidity. Superb. *July 2003* ★★★★(★) *Will keep.*

Lieser Niederberg Helden Auslese (M) **Schloss Lieser** Very pale; rich, febrile nose; sweeter, richer, more grapey flavour than their Spätlese, alcohol 8%, quite soft for its age. *May 2000* ★★(★★) *2008–2015?*

Maximin Grünhäuser Abtsberg Spätlese (Rg) **von Schubert** Almost colourless; extraordinary uplift of fragrance; medium-sweet, lovely acidity though a bit raw – needs time to round it off. *Jan 2001* ★(★★) *Now–2010.*

Niederhäuser Hermannshöhle Auslese (N) **Dönnhoff** Virtually colourless; another example of Helmut Dönnhoff's seamless winemaking. *June 2000* ★★(★★) *Now–2010.*

Oberemmeler Hütte Auslese and **Auslese '★'** (M) **von Hövel** Pale; fragrant; fairly sweet, mellow. *June 2002* ★★★★ *Now–2012.*

Piesporter Goldtröpfchen Auslese (M) **Reinhold Haart** Piesporter – the real thing. Colourless; a steely, slatey, very minerally young nose; medium-sweet, ripe, fairly assertive and that well-worn adjective 'peachy' occurring again. *June 2000* ★(★★★) *Now–2012.*

Schloss Proschwitz Eiswein (Sachsen) **Prinz zu Lipp** Formerly part of East Germany, Sachsen wine from this aristocratic estate is at last re-emerging. Palish, bright; very pleasing floral aroma; sweet, soft, fleshy, peachy. Delicious. *Tasted in Leipzig, March 2003* ★★★★ *No track record. Say, now–2012.*

Saarburger Rausch Auslese (M) **Zilliken** a classic Saar wine of an open, ripe style ★(★★) *Now–2010*; and **Auslese lange Goldkapsel** lovely, peachy, fairly assertive. Give it time ★★★★(★) *Now–2016. Both tasted June 2000.*

Scharzhofberg Auslese von Schubert An astonishing scent, leafy, varietal; medium-sweet, succulent, fragrant, glorious acidity. *Sept 2004* ★★★★

Scharzhofberger Spätlese (M) **Egon Müller** virtually colourless; fresh, youthful, whiff of lime; medium-sweet, a touch of 'baby fat', lightweight (8.5% alcohol), lovely flavour, glorious acidity. This is the equivalent of many other producers' Auslesen. *May 2000* ★(★★★) *Now–2012*; **Spätlese Fuder 36** very pale; fragrant, delicate; medium – neither sweet nor dry, light, gentle, lovely flavour, violets aftertaste. *Jan 2001* ★★★(★★) *Now–2012*; **Auslese Goldkapsel** most recently: sublime ensemble of *Edelfäule* richness and acidity. *Nov 2000* ★★(★★★); **BA** medium yellow-gold; scent of delectable peach skins; very sweet, of course, lovely plump fruit and perfect acidity. *June 2002* ★★★(★★★) *Lovely now but will develop fabulously.*

Trittenheimer Leiterchen Auslese (M) **Milz-Laurentiushof** They are sole owners of the Leiterchen and Felsenkopf vineyard sites and have an excellent reputation. The '99 Auslese had a curious, slightly appley nose, peachy though; medium-sweet, an attractive mouthfiller. *June 2000* ★★(★) *Now–2010.*

Wallhäuser Johannisberg Auslese (N) **Schloss Dalberg** An attractive, youthful, minty, grapey aroma and flavour; medium-sweet, touch of pineapple and raw apple. A pleasant summer wine. *June 2000* ★(★★) *Drink up.*

Winkeler Hasensprung Auslese (R) **Prinz von Hessen** Pale, lime-tinged; very distinctive and forthcoming, lime, greengage acidity; sweet, honeyed botrytis, fleshy, creamy. Lovely. *Oct 2005* ★★★★

2000–2005

This reputation of the Riesling has turned full circle. It is firmly back in the saddle as the king of Germany's quality wines, reaching its sublime heights particularly in the Mosel-Saar-Ruwer and the Rheingau regions. This is not to say that it does not thrive in other German wine regions, or that the other classic varieties, Gewürztraminer in the Pfalz for example and Silvaner and the racy Rieslaner in Franconia, do not count for anything. However, real quality is being driven by little more than a handful of great winemakers, some of whom are comparatively young.

In contrast to the richer styles there are some brilliant and uncompromising dry wines, excellent with food, which can also benefit from bottle age. A step in the right direction is the resurrection of *Erstes Gewächs* (first growths). Labels are being simplified, with a move to put vintage, estate or brand name, grape and quality on the front label, using the full village and vineyard name for only the estate's top wines.

VINTAGES AT A GLANCE

Outstanding ★★★★★ 2003 (v), 2005
Very Good ★★★★ 2001, 2002, 2003 (v)
Good ★★★ 2000 (v)

2000 ★★ to ★★★

'Average to good' is too sweeping; poor to really very good would cover this none-too-easy vintage. Overall a smaller crop than 1999, and 25% down in the Mosel-Saar-Ruwer.

As usual, the weather was to blame, torrential rain occurring in September, three times the average in some districts. The worst hit were the vineyards on flat land with rich soil and early-ripening grape varieties. The most successful wines were made from the later-ripening Riesling on sloping, well-drained vineyard sites. Those growers who could afford to green harvest in August, later to comb their vines, hand-picking the ripe, discarding the rotten grapes, handling and vinifying them effectively, were able to produce some most attractive wines.

Castell Schlossberg TBA (F) Fürst Castell An ancient aristocratic Franken estate, the village, the Schloss, even the medieval castle and best vineyard bear the Ducal name. Minty, herbaceous nose; sweet, powerful, impressive. *Sept 2003* ★★★

Erbacher Siegelsberg Kabinett fruchtig (Rg) Schloss Reinhartshausen Bright, pale, refreshing colour; light but fragrant, slightly minty bouquet; medium-sweet, light style, fresh, flavoury, rounded, charming. *Feb 2002*.

Erbacher Siegelsberg BA (Rg) **Schloss Reinhartshausen** An amazing amber-gold colour; sweet, peachy almost raisiny bouquet; less sweet than expected but rich, 'tangy', dry finish. *Feb 2002* ★★★★

Hattenheimer Nussbrunnen Auslese Schloss Reinhartshausen Fragrant, flowery aroma; sweet, good flesh, grapefruit-like acidity. *Aug 2003* ★★★★

Iphöfer Kronsberg, Scheurebe Spätlese trocken (F) **Hans Wirsching** Exotic Scheurebe aromas of 'tom-cats' and scent; dry, in some ways rather like Sauvignon Blanc but with very high alcohol (14%). *March 2001* ★(★★)

Maximin Grünhäuser Kabinett (M) **von Schubert** Floral aroma, glorious fruit; light (7.5% alcohol); very high acidity. Good length. *Jan 2002* ★★★

Ruppertsberger Reiterpfad TBA (P) **Bassermann-Jordan** Described as 'a difficult year', just 80 litres made of this extraordinary wine. 200° Oechsle, extremely high acidity: between 13–14°g/l. The colour of pale amber: calf's foot jelly and lanolin nose; very sweet, powerful yet alcohol only 11%. Good mid-palate and length. A Wagnerian Pfalz. *March 2003* ★★★★? *A matter of taste and time.*

Schloss Vollrads Auslese Picked Dec 21. Pale; very fragrant, minerally; fairly sweet yet still with an immature hard finish. *May 2005* ★★(★★) *Give it time.*

2001 possible ★★★★

In some ways this vintage is all that the 2000 had hoped to be; the same provisos apply: selective late-picking of Riesling on well-drained sites to obtain optimum results.

High hopes were dashed by a miserably wet September. Those who had the courage to wait were rewarded by a fabulous October with high temperatures for over a month. The harvest was late in the classic vineyards, from around the third week in October to mid-November. These are late-harvest wines of exceptional ripeness, with sweet qualities, notably Auslesen, Beerenauslesen and TBAs, which some producers compare with the '75s, even the '71s. A great Riesling year, particularly in the Mosel-Saar-Ruwer, the Nahe, Mittelrhein and the eastern Rheingau.

Bernkasteler Doctor Auslese (M) **Wegeler** The Wegeler estate is one of the three owners of this renowned vineyard. Broad, open, self-assured, flinty, grapefruit-like; medium-sweet, drier than expected, still a bit of a bite. Classic. Good future. *Nov 2005* ★★★(★★)

Eitelsbacher Karthäuserhofberg Spätlese (M) **Tyrell** Crisp, grapey aroma and flavour; youthful acidity. *June 2002* ★★(★)?

Erbacher Marcobrunn Beerenauslese (Rg) **Schloss Reinhartshausen** Lovely ripe, peachy nose and flavour. Sweet of course but counterbalanced with very good acidity. *March 2003* ★★★★

Erdener Prälat Auslese (M) **Loosen** Many notes. Enjoyed at our regular weekend 'elevenses'. Touch of honey; medium-sweet, rich, still youthful grapey flavour. Light (7.5% alcohol) but fleshy. *Last tasted Oct 2006* ★★★★

Kiedricher Gräfenberg Spätlese (Rg) **Weil** two youthful notes. Little colour – spotless grapes; lovely, grapey, touch of mint; usual Weil deft sweetness, smooth texture, 8% alcohol. A sheer delight; and **Auslese** glorious yellow-gold; exquisitely rich, 'honey and flowers'; enticing acidity. Sweet. Lovely flesh and flavour. *Both noted Oct 2002, both* ★★★★

Maximin Grünhauser Herrenberg Auslese (M) **von Schubert** A charmer; rich but not too sweet, glorious flavour, perfect acidity. Will soften with age. *Nov 2005* ★★★(★)

Oberemmeler Hütte Auslese (M) **von Hövel** Youthful nose. Pronounced *Edelfäule* and refreshing acidity yet soft and peachy on the palate. 7.5% alcohol. Nice balance. *June 2002* ★★★★ *Good future.*

Schloss Vollrads Spätlese (Rg) Mainly from vines over 10 years old. 10% botrytis, ca. 80 g/l sugar. Harmonious, complete, dry finish. *Nov 2005* ★★★

Wehlener Sonnenuhr Auslese (M) **Thanisch** Light, fragrant, crisp fruit; pleasing sweetness and weight, attractive and so easy to drink. *Nov 2003* ★★★

Zeltinger Sonnenuhr Auslese (M) **Molitor** Honeyed, sweet, excellent acidity. What more could one ask for? *June 2005* ★★★★ *just.*

2002 ★★★★

Excellent vintage overall, noted for its crisp, minerally, classic Rieslings, thanks to a cool growing season and Indian summer. Lesser growths drinking perfectly now. The best Spätlesen, all good Auslesen and above, temptingly attractive but will keep and develop.

Bernkasteler Doctor Auslese (M) **Wegeler** Rich sheen; very distinctive, honey and linden; medium sweetness and body, four-square, self-confident. *Nov 2005* ★★★ *possibly extra* (★)

Eitelsbacher Karthäuserhofberg Kabinett (M) **Tyrell** Pale; totally delicious, fragrant, lively dancing aroma; fruity, moderately light (9% alcohol), perfect Ruwer acidity. The ideal apéritif. Beats champagne! *Sept 2005* ★★★★

Erbacher Michelmark Eiswein (M) **Jacob Jung** Early harvested. Pale, mouthwatering lime-tinged colour, aroma and taste. Very sweet, precariously balanced by its very high acidity (13.4 g/l). Deliciously refreshing. Zestful. *Nov 2005* ★★★★

Geisenheimer Rothenberg Auslese (Rg) **Wegeler** Starbright; entrancing, privet-like, flowery; medium-sweet, flesh, 8% alcohol, very good acidity, dry finish. *Nov 2005* ★★★(★)

Kiedricher Gräfenberg Auslese Goldkapsel (Rg) **Weil** Several recent notes. Weil at its most inspired. Exemplary assemblage of surging lime blossom, honey, apricots and enticing acidity; very sweet, rich, fleshy, lightly touched botrytis, alcohol 8%, fresh lip-licking acidity. *Last tasted March 2006* ★★★★★

Münsterer Pittersberg Eiswein (Rh) **KrugerRumpf** Very pale; soft, sweet, grapey, honeyed, arboreal; sweet of course, deliciously crisp fruit salad and honey. Alcohol 9.5%. Lovely '02 acidity. *Aug 2005* ★★★★★

Oberemmeler Hütte Spätlese (M) **von Hövel** Almost colourless; delicate, grapey, acidic; medium-dry, light, 7.5% alcohol, refreshing, delicious. Who said German wines do not go well with food. Excellent with turbot. *Dec 2005* ★★★★

Schloss Vollrads Spätlese (Rg) Tasted in a line up, 2001–2004, the lowest alcohol (7.5%), the palest, medium-sweet, peachy, positive but not assertive, good acidity. *Nov 2005* ★★★★

Trittenheimer Altaerchen Eiswein (M) **F-J Riedel** From the upper Mosel, a grower new to me. Pale, 7% alcohol, sweet, delicious. *March 2005* ★★★★

Wiltinger Schlangengraben Eiswein (M) **Reinhart** Johann Peter Reinart, fifth generation, and his gold medal winning Eiswein with all the Saar characteristics, low alcohol (7.5%), high acidity (13g/l) balancing high residual sugar 176 g/l. Very sweet. Delicious. Needs more time. *May 2004* ★★★(★)

2003 up to ★★★★★

A hot sunny summer, even in the relatively northerly German vineyards, is not necessarily a blessing. The crucial balance can be disturbed. I have far too many notes and list here the most distinctive and, at least for me, interesting.

As always the lesser quality wines, particularly in a hot vintage like this, should be consumed early.

Bernkasteler Doctor Auslese Wegeler Pale yellow-gold; glorious, slightly raisiny bouquet; very sweet, delicious flavour, great length, persistence and aftertaste. Alcohol only 5.5%. *July 2006* ★★★★★

Bernkasteler Graben Auslese ★★ (Goldcap) (M) Molitor Extremely pale; steely yet spicy; medium-sweet yet 100 g/l sugar, lovely flavour, creamy. 11.5% alcohol. A medal winner. *June 2005* ★★★★

Brauneberger Juffer-Sonnenuhr Auslese (M) Fritz Haag Fuder 12 muted peach; certainly good but preferred their **Fuder 6** gentle, grapey, also medium-sweet with a prickle of acidity. *Both tasted Jan 2005* ★★★ to ★★★★

Erbacher Marcobrunn Auslese Edelsüs (Rg) Schloss Reinhartshausen Pure vanilla; good flavour 111g/l, residual sugar, delicious but not over-high acidity, 6.9g/l, light style, 9.5% alcohol. *June 2004* ★★★

Erbacher Marcobrunn TBA Goldkapsel (Rg) Schloss Reinhartshausen Rich gold; extremely sweet, rich but low alcohol (7%), creamy, fabulous. Just 100 litres made. Selected yeasts. Filtered. *June 2004* ★★★★★

Erdener Prälat Auslese Goldkapsel (M) Dr Loosen Top of Ernst Loosen's range at the opening presentation: lovely young fleshy aroma; delectably sweet. Delicious. Good future. *June 2004* ★★★★★

Escherndorfer Lump Beerenauslese (F) Horst Sauer Despite its clumsy name, a top Franconia vineyard and leading producer. Palish gold; aroma lurking but latent; delicious flavour, sexy acidity, slight spritz adding to its zest. *March 2005* ★★★★ *Delicious and great potential.*

Geisenheimer Rothenberg TBA (Rg) Wegeler A well-established estate with prime vineyard sites in the Rheingau, Mosel (notably part of the Doctor vineyard) and Pfalz and currently enjoying a renaissance. This was the top '03 tasted: butterscotch yellow; very sweet, 306° Oechsle, very fat, buttery, low alcohol (6%). *Nov 2005* ★★★★★

Graacher Himmelreich Auslese Goldcap (M) J J Prüm The reputation of 'J J', embodied by Manfred Prüm, has held a prime position in the Mosel hierarchy for many years; yet it seems to me to be occasionally out-of-step with its peers. When the many other fine estates show their most recent vintage, J J shows the previous vintage. This '03 tasted in 2005 had a very strange metallic nose; sweet, soft, 'goaty'. *June 2005* ★★★? (*see also J J's Wehleners*).

Hattenheimer Nussbrunnen (Rg) Schloss Reinhartshausen One of ten '05s presented to the Circle of Wine Writers to demonstrate the extraordinary range of styles made in one vintage in the four vineyards at this large, privately owned estate, and also to demonstrate the marked improvement in 0,ere three wines with startlingly high alcohol, ranging from 13.6 to 14.5% (the Erbacher Marcobrunn) destined to become **Erstes Gewächs**, first growths, rich, not dry as expected, with an impressive mid-term future. An interesting development ★★(★★); the TBA a tremendous contrast made from overripe grapes but no botrytis. Only 70 litres produced of this yellow-coloured, ripe, peachy, glorious wine with degree of acidity and percentage of alcohol both 7.5. *Both tasted June 2004* ★★★★★

Hattenheimer Wisselbrunnen Auslese Edelsüsse Goldkapsel and Beerenauslese (Rg) Schloss Reinhartshausen, the Edelsüsse as sweet as it sounds, balanced by delicious acidity. 9.5% alcohol, and the BA sweet, fleshy, glorious (11% alcohol). Both will evolve with age. *Both tasted June 2004* ★★★★

Maximin Grünhäuser Abtsberg Auslese Fuder 155 (M) von Schubert Sold for twice the price of the 'standard' (and lovely) Auslese wine, von Schubert's special cask, Number 155, really does have extra dimensions: sweet, soft, yet wonderful acidity, peachy, very intriguing aftertaste. Delicious. *Jan 2005* ★★★★(★)

Oberhäuser Brücke Auslese Goldcapsel (N) Dönnhof Exuding quintessential Nahe pineapple and fruit salad; sweet, low alcohol (8%), delicious flavour and style. Dönnhof, masterly but unassuming. *Jan 2005* ★★★★(★)

Saarburger Rausch (M) Geltz-Zilliken Tasted at the Grosser Ring auction in Trier at a year old, the Spätlese was mouth-drying though fragrant, the Auslese, picked with 20% botrytis, blended with Eiswein picked on 1 December was distinctly raw – needing time. The top wine, Auslese Lange Goldkapsel, which fetched three times the price, was a different ball game: ripe, peachy, fleshy, grapey with - of course - good acidity and future. *Sept 2004* ★★★(★)

Scharzhofberger (M) Egon Müller Without question, Egon Müller is the greatest producer in the Mosel-Saar-Ruwer and his wines almost invariably fetch the highest prices at auctions in Trier. His 2003 Kabinett, hard, young, with high Ruwer acidity; the Spätlese rich, peachy, medium-dry, delicious, the two Auslesen Goldkapsel '26' very pale; peaches and gooseberries on nose and palate, the '25' more closed but floral, lime blossom; glorious flavour, length and acidity. A snip at nearly 200 Euros a half bottle. *Sept 2004, up to* ★★★★★ *gold dust of the future.*

Schloss Vollrads Spätlese to TBA (Rg) One of the oldest (over 800 years) wine estates in Germany. In the Matuschka-Greiffenclau family until recently and currently being revived by brilliant new management. Spätlese very ripe grapes, no botrytis, fairly sweet, delicious, not fully knit. Needs time. Auslese 20% botrytis. Gold leaf highlights; sweet, rich, creamy (8% alcohol); Beerenauslese 160° Oechsle, very sweet, verging on unctuous but saved by its acidity. Raisiny, fleshy. A keeper; TBA 248° Oechsle, 6.5% alcohol. Worth noting that four TBAs were made: unbelievably the first grapes to be picked made a TBA, general picking continued for eight weeks, and the last picked was also a TBA. Rich, 'viral and calf's foot jelly'; incredibly sweet, concentrated, almost meaty. *At the Schloss. Nov 2005, up to* ★★★★★

Wehlener Sonnenuhr Auslese (M) J J Prüm J J owns a major part of this perfectly sited vineyard – conveniently viewed from the family house across the Mosel. Tasted on a couple of occasions: minerally, minty, steely aromas; an almost meaty, acidic character, 8% alcohol, needs time. *Last tasted June 2005* ★★(★★)?

2004 ★★★★

Aptly described as a 'benchmark' vintage. Pure, racy, classic Rieslings. The
minor growths, up to Kabinett level, are refreshing now. Spätlese and above
are firm yet delicious to drink now but it would be a mistake not to give
them time to spread their wings.

Berncasteler Doctor Auslese (M) Interesting to taste, albeit quickly,
Auslesen of the famous Doctor vineyard from two of the three owners.
Thanisch's with a lovely broad open aroma; medium-sweet, very good acidity,
dry, minerally finish ★★★; **Wegeler**'s almost colourless; curious, slightly rustic but
with some depth; lovely flavour, excellent acidity, hard finish. Needs bottle age.
★★★(★) *but close run. Both tasted June 2005.*

Brauneberger Juffer-Sonnenuhr Spätlese and **Auslese** (M) **Fritz
Haag** Confusingly there are two Haag estates in Brauneberg, the heart of the
middle Mosel, but it is Wilhelm of Fritz Haag who is one of the top producers of
Germany. His 2004 **Spätlese** very pale; fragrant, fruity, hint of lime; medium-
sweet, delicate flavour, a touch of bitterness on the finish, which will wear off.
Auslese a lovely grapey aroma and flavour, with grapefruit-like acidity. *Both
tasted June 2005* ★★★ *to* ★★★★

Dorsheimer Pittermännchen Auslese (N) **Diel** Armin Diel is a top
producer, a well-known critic of German wines, for which one requires courage.
His 2004 **Goldlack Kabinett** steely yet surprisingly sweet and earthy; the
Burgberg Spätlese green-tinged, very distinctive; medium-sweet fruit salad
and refreshing acidity. The **Auslese** characterful, still steely, lovely flavour. *All
tasted with pleasure June 2005* ★★★ *to* ★★★★

Eitelsberger Karthäuserhofberg Spätlese and **Auslese** (M) **Tyrell**
An exemplary estate and the prettiest label in Germany. The **Spätlese** virtually
colourless (the sign of flawless skins), very steely, greengage (probably grapefruit
nearer); medium-sweet, lovely flavour, crisp acidity, length and aftertaste; **Auslese**
minty, grapey, minerally nose, not as sweet as expected and touch of bitterness on
the finish. Needs time. *Both June 2005, both* ★★★★

A **Dr Loosen** trio: As previously mentioned Ernst Loosen is one of the (once)
young geniuses of not just the Mosel but of Germany. Of the '04s tasted, his
Ürziger Würzgarten Spätlese is minerally, stately and delicious, his
Wehlener Sonnenuhr Auslese ★★★★ also delicious, but the **Erdener
Prälat Auslese Goldkapsel** exceptional: crisp, minerally scents; very sweet,
rich, creamy, a lovely long flavoury finish ★★★★(★). *All tasted June 2005.*

Geisenheimer Rothenberg Auslese (Rg) **Wegeler** Honeyed botrytis,
grapefruit and pineapple scents; fairly sweet, 125g/l residual sugar. The strength yet
delicacy of a prima ballerina. *Nov 2005* ★★★(★)

Graacher Domprobst Auslese ★★ **Cask 88** (M) **Max Ferd. Richter**
An exceptional wine from a dependable producer whose wines are regularly
featured in Christie's Wine Courses. Virtually colourless; very sweet but leaner
than expected, classic, good length, needs time. *June 2005* ★★★(★)

Kiedricher Gräfenberg (Rg) **Weil** Wilhelm Weil's reputation – and
auction prices – rivals Egon Müller's at Scharzhofberg, his Gräfenberg vineyard
large and superbly sited. However, a great contrast of styles, Weil's invariably softer
and sweeter and, like Egon Müller's, his **Kabinett** is the quality of other
producers' Spätlesen, **Spätlese** of Auslese quality, and quite often **Auslese** equal

to other Beerenauslesen. I love these wines and will just comment on his 2004
Eiswein. A convenient half bottle: delectable, sweet, grapey nose; despite its
richness and thickness, light in heart, 6.5% alcohol. *April 2006* ★★★★(★)
Monzinger Halenberg (N) **Emrich-Schönleber** A producer way up the
Nahe valley who is making superb wines. His 2004 **Frühlingsplätzchen**
★★★★ lovely; the **Halenberg Auslese** youthful, minerally, needs bottle age;
the **Eiswein** his 'best ever': colourless; glorious fruit salad; very sweet, delicious.
How inadequate are words. ★★★★★ *All tasted June 2005.*
Scharzhofberger (M) **Egon Müller** What more can one say about this great
estate? His – not exactly 'everyday' – **Spätlese** and **Auslese** ★★★★★ but
the **Auslese Goldkapsel**, predictably, has extra dimensions. Its nose exudes a
glorious essence of peaches; very sweet of course, indescribably lovely flavour,
length and finish. Tempting now but will blossom with bottle age. ★★★★(★) *All
tasted June 2005.*
Schloss Vollrads (Rg) An unhurried tasting with the director Rowald Hepp.
Briefly **Kabinett** (a *fruchtig* style), slow fermentation in steel: pale, refreshing, 9%
alcohol; **Spätlese** 2½ weeks longer hang time. Sweeter, delicious flavour with
teeth-gripping acidity. 8.5% alcohol. Needs 2–3 more years; **Auslese** 50–60%
botrytis, 115° Oechsle, scent of privet, honey and Sauvignon Blanc-like acidity;
fairly sweet, 'singed' taste, delicious flavour, length and aftertaste. 8% alcohol. Not a
pudding wine. For pleasure and contemplation. *All tasted Nov 2005, up to* ★★★(★)
Wehlener Sonnenuhr Auslese (M) **J J Prüm** Extremely pale; minerally;
medium-sweet, fresh, good acidity. *June 2006* ★★★ *Drink soon.*

2005 ★★★★★

Germany's recent run of successful vintages culminated in the well-nigh
perfect 2005. From all reports, the major estates made the most of fully ripe,
healthy grapes and overall good growing conditions.

Two problems: the wines are so appealing that all Riesling lovers will be
tempted to drink them too soon; the other problem, for producer and trade,
is that production is roughly 20% below average. Having said this, overall, the
vintage is exceptional and at its zenith in the Mosel and its two tributaries,
the Saar and Ruwer. These remarkable Rieslings prove that a high level of
alcohol is not the be-all-and-end-all; and delicacy does not mean fragility.
Wines to enjoy, to remember, and for the self-disciplined to keep until their
peak has been reached.

To generalise, the wines of Kabinett quality are delicious now (in 2007),
so are most of the Spätlesen. However, I have concentrated on the superb
Auslesen wines. It can be assumed that other great and rare wines in 2005
will also be of the highest quality.
Berncasteler Doctor Auslese (M) **Thanisch** Earmarked for the annual
Grosser Ring auction. Sweet, creamy, apricots, 9.5% alcohol, very good acidity. *June
2006* ★★★★(★)
Bernkasteler Graben Auslese (M) **Wegeler** Sweet, minerally, delicious.
Good future. *June 2006* ★★★(★)
Eitelsbacher Karthäuserhofberg Auslese (M) **Tyrell** Virtually
colourless; peachy; fairly sweet, attractive component parts in the process of
'knitting'. Good acidity. Excellent potential. *June 2006* ★★(★★)

Geisenheimer Rothenberg TBA (Rg) Wegeler In at the birth of the crown jewel of the 2005 vintage, I first tasted this at the estate on 8 November 2005 while it was still 'working': not bright but very viscous; honeyed, gooseberry aroma; incredibly sweet, lovely even at this stage. By July 2006 it had recorded the highest must weight of the 2005 vintage in Germany. 400g/l residual sugar, 9g/l acidity, and a total of only 20 litres made. Less than two years later another sip of the greatest TBA of 2005. Slightly minty, floral, lime blossom scents; intensely sweet, immensely rich, creamy, great length, persistence of flavour, just 6% alcohol, perfect acidity. *Last tasted Feb 2007.*

Graacher Himmelreich Auslese (M) J J Prüm Having suggested that the venerable J J might be a little out of step I confess to the total enjoyment of this superb 2005: polish; a glorious scent of honey, lime blossom, peaches, so positive, so engaging, so long lasting that I was completely seduced. Quite sweet, lovely flesh, perfect balance of ripe fruit and acidity. If it is lovely now, think what it will be like in ten years time. *June 2007* ★★★★★

Kiedricher Gräfenberg Auslese (Rg) Weil Very pale; youthful, flowery; medium-sweet. Light style (8.5% alcohol), very agreeable flavour and acidity. *July 2006* ★★★(★) *Lovely now but will develop other nuances with bottle age.*

Lieser Niederberg Helden Auslese Goldkapsel Thomas Haag Thomas is the gifted son of the renowned Wilm Haag. Low-keyed as yet on the nose but very sweet, light (7.5% alcohol), good flesh and acidity. Already delicious but will develop. *June 2006* ★★(★★)

Monzinger Halenberg Auslese (N) Emrich-Schönleber Though enjoying the highest critical acclaim this family estate has a problem with an unfamiliar district and name. Beautiful wine. Nose very steely but fragrant, with a light grapiness; sweet, soft yet perfect acidity, good length. Will benefit from bottle age. *June 2006* ★★★(★)

Niederhauser Hermannshöhle Auslese (N) Dönnhof Colourless; minerally; sweet, glorious flesh, 7.5% alcohol, very good acidity. Helmut Dönnhof's aim is purity and finesse – of which he is a master. *June 2006* ★★★(★★)

Oberemmeler Hütte (M) von Kunow Auslese very pale, lime-tinged; steely, very minerally, needs time to 'knit'; medium-sweet, 9.5% alcohol, very appealing and excellent acidity ★★(★★); **Auslese Lange Goldkapsel** very sweet, very fleshy, extra dimensions, 9% alcohol, good length, a bit of an end bite. Needs bottle age. *June 2006* ★★(★★★)

Saarburger Rausch (M) Geltz–Zilliken Auslese minerally due to the slate soil, good flavour, low alcohol (7.5%) and fairly high acidity ★★★★; **Auslese Goldcapsel** again minerally but more lime; very sweet, fleshy, delectable. Great future. *June 2006* ★★(★★★)

Scharzhofberger Auslese Goldkapsel (M) Egon Müller Unquestionably the star performer, consistently producing great wines, most notably so in this vintage. Really indescribable, the scents flooding the nose; very sweet, low alcohol (7%), a lovely wine by any standards. *June 2006* ★★★★(★)

Scharzhofberger TBA (M) Egon Müller Almost incredible richness, viscous, sleekly – not sickly – sweet, fast, luscious. Beyond reach of mortal men – except a handful of the richest connoisseurs. *June 2006* ★★★(★★★) *(6 stars)*

California

Nowadays, 'New World' is an inappropriate way to describe California, a region of such towering importance. The endless striving for quality, the innovation, and the sheer panache have made the wines and wine people of California an enormous influence in the world of wine.

As will be very apparent, what follows is not a gazetteer. Moreover, there has been such an explosion of wineries that even a full-time resident of the 'golden state' would find it impossible to cover fully all producers and vintages. The notes that follow have been made on a variety of occasions within the past decade, including several major tastings. My intention is to give the reader an overview, particularly on the quality and state of maturity of vintages, and illustrated by a limited selection of major producers' wines.

Note: CS = Cabernet Sauvignon; M = Merlot

Classic older vintages: 1936–1969

These were exciting times and a crucial period of development following the end of prohibition in 1933. After a prolonged enforced rest, wine in California suddenly sprang to life. The immediate post-war vintages got off to a kick-start by a winemaker of genius, André Tchelistcheff at Beaulieu Vineyard (BV), with important contributions from Dr Maynard Amerine and fellow enologists at the University of California, Davis. Apart from 'BV', the oldest and most revered winery was Inglenook, producing excellent wines from 1940; and in the late 1940s Louis Martini and Charles Krug. The Napa Valley was the centre of excellence in California, and Cabernet Sauvignon the grape variety of choice. The winemaker reigned supreme. I was fortunate, particularly in the 1970s, to taste a wide range of classic wines and vintages of this period. 'The Beaulieu Vineyard Centenary Tasting' in 1999 was a notable event.

Outstanding vintages
1941, 1946, 1951, 1958, 1965, 1968, 1969 (v), 1974, 1985, 1991, 1994 (v), 1997, 1999, 2005

The half dozen or so major wineries in the Napa Valley in the 1950s were augmented by an influx of committed outsiders setting new standards. The decade of the 1960s saw further major developments throughout the 'golden state' including the establishment of the Robert Mondavi Winery in 1966.

VINTAGES AT A GLANCE

Outstanding ★★★★★ 1941, 1946, 1951, 1958, 1965,
1968, 1969 (v)
Very Good ★★★★ 1942, 1947, 1956, 1959, 1963, 1964, 1966
Good ★★★ 1944, 1949, 1955, 1960, 1961, 1967

THE BEAULIEU VINEYARD CENTENARY TASTING IN 1999:
Beaulieu Vineyard, Georges de Latour Cabernet Sauvignon, all
100% Cabernet Sauvignon and served in pairs. I have noted, very briefly, the
better bottles, preceded by the vintage and its rating at the time: 1936 ★★★ faded
and yeasty. Of academic interest only; 1939 ★★★ soft texture, mellow, sound;
1941 ★★★★★ great vintage. Sweet, soft yet assertive and very tannic; 1942
★★★★ very deep, almost opaque; medium-sweet, rich, soft, bricky Cabernet taste,
dried-out; 1943 ★★★ very deep. Rich, cheesy, meaty. Interesting, mouthfilling,
tarry; 1944 ★★★ very deep, too brown; singed mocha nose, considerable depth of
fruit, singed; sweet, soft, full, flavoury, surprising teeth-gripping tannin; 1946
★★★★★ excellent vintage. Very attractive colour, open, mature. Medium-sweet,
elegant, delicious, dry finish; 1947 ★★★★ (this was the first vintage that 'Georges
de Latour, Private Reserve' actually appeared on the label.) Medium-deep; good,
fragrant, autumnal bouquet; very interesting and very attractive, soft entry, dry
finish; 1949 ★★★★★ fine colour; very fragrant on the nose but palate cracking
up; 1950 ★★★★★ alas, hopelessly oxidised, like overripe banana skin; 1951
★★★★★ still very deep; old spice, sound; rich, fullish fruit, astringent finish. The
second bottle sweeter and softer. Still very good for its age; 1952 ★★ medium-
deep, attractive. Sweet and quite good on the palate, rich fruit and grip; 1953 ★★
rich, mature; curious scent and taste, tea-like, privet, sweet with tarry taste; 1954
★★ big bottle variation. The best: good appearance and nose, sweet, quite good
flavour. Some elegance; 1955 ★★★ palish; light, sweet, showing its age on nose
and palate. Decent length though; 1956 ★★★★ very disappointing: odd, cold,
singed mocha; sweet, soft, lacking; 1957 very unpleasant, astringent; 1958
★★★★★ medium-deep, still surprisingly youthful; showing its age, *gibier*, slightly
malty; losing fruit but an exciting gamey wine with liplicking tannin and marked
acidity. *Last tasted Oct 2000. In its prime* ★★★★★; 1959 ★★★★ the best, with vanilla
and raspberry scent, sweet and rich on the palate; 1960 ★★★★★ the best, almost
silky sweet on nose and palate, rich but showing its age; 1961 ★★★ low-keyed,
smelly, hollow, short; 1962 ★★ pale, open, rosy hue; sweet, fragrant Muscat and
walnuts bouquet. More like port. Alas, yeasty finish; 1963 ★★★★ very good
vintage, but at the BV tasting, drab and acidic; 1964 ★★★★ very high sugars. A
huge, austere wine in its youth, Médoc-like. Most recently: richly coloured;
bouquet to match, high-toned; sweet, malty fruit and not to my taste. Now
uneven and should be avoided; 1965 ★★★★★ great vintage. Perfection in its early
years. Rich with an attractive flavour and grip. *Once* ★★★★★, *now at best* ★★★;
1966 ★★★★ another good, ripe, early vintage. Showing quite well, still deeply
coloured; spicy, attractive, fragrant and forthcoming bouquet. Sweet, rich, good
fruit; 1967 ★★★ lovely colour, attractive fruit and weight; 1968 ★★★★★ great
vintage. 'Napa at its best' with all the virtues and components in abundance. Still

deep and still youthful; good nose; very sweet, assertive, packed with fruit; good length; and 1969 ★★ to ★★★★★ slight bottle variation but both very good: medium-deep, attractive; minty, tea-like aromas soared out of the glass; full, rich, good length, tannin and acidity. The second bottle more eucalyptus, astonishingly like Martha's Vineyard with elegant, teeth-gripping finish. *At best* ★★★★★

1970–1979

This was an extraordinary period of expansion; yet at the time of my first visit to California, in 1970, there were only a handful of major wineries in the Napa Valley, including the renowned BV. In this decade, a newcomer, Joe Heitz was carving a considerable reputation with his Martha's Vineyard, planted originally as Bella Oaks by a modest but hugely influential amateur, Dr Bernard (Barney) L. Rhodes. Since the 1950s Barney had contributed not only his knowledge and experience to wineries in the Napa and Sonoma valleys but had also financed several embryonic wineries.

VINTAGES AT A GLANCE

Outstanding ★★★★★ 1974
Very Good ★★★★ 1970, 1972 (v), 1973, 1978
Good ★★★ 1971, 1972 (v), 1975, 1976, 1979

1970 ★★★★
Small crop, one third of normal, the result of 28 nights of frost and an excessively hot summer.
Beaulieu Vineyard, Georges de Latour CS Coincidentally tasted on three occasions in 1999. Now medium-deep, crisp, fragrant, very sweet on the palate, rich but with very dry finish. *Last noted Sept 1999* ★★★★
Heitz, Martha's Vineyard CS Bottled August 1974. Most recently: still very deep; spicy, characteristic eucalyptus scent; very sweet, spicy, superb. *Last tasted May 2006* ★★★★★ *Now, will keep.*

1971 ★★★
Beaulieu Vineyard, Georges de Latour CS Medium, mature; fragrant, 'bricky'; sweet, full, rich, good fruit, touch of pungency. *July 1999* ★★★
Ridge, Monte Bello CS Bottled October 1973. Several notes. Very good colour; stewed, slightly 'medicinal' – very Médoc-like, better on palate, lean, a modest 12.2% alcohol, very tannic. An uncompromising Paul Draper classic. *Last tasted May 2006* ★★★ *Drink soon.*

1972 ★★★ to ★★★★
Beaulieu Vineyard, Georges de Latour CS Fairly deep; rich, fragrant, gingery, herbaceous; very sweet, full-bodied, still tannic. *July 1999* ★★★

Clos du Val CS Curiously attractive, vegetal; very sweet, good flavour, modest alcohol (12%), good length, tannic. *May 2006* ★★★★ *Drink soon.*

1973 ★★★★
A very good vintage.
Beaulieu Vineyard, Georges de Latour CS Two very disappointing bottles: cheesy, slightly sour nose and flavour. *July 1999.*
Stag's Leap Wine Cellars, CS 'SLV' (Stag's Leap Vineyards) Mature, attractive; not very distinctive, whiff of Pinot; Bordeaux-like weight and style. A reasonable 13% alcohol. *May 2006* ★★★ *Drink up.*

1974 ★★★★★
A great vintage. A long, cool growing season and very hot harvest weather.
Beaulieu Vineyard, Georges de Latour CS Two bottles brought to the BV Centenary tasting earned high marks, particularly on the palate: very sweet, full of fruit, perfect flavour and weight. *Last tasted July 1999* ★★★★, *on the fringe of 5-star. But I suggest drinking it soon.*
Heitz, Martha's Vineyard CS Many notes, none less than magnificent. Most recently, in magnum: a lovely mature appearance; pure eucalyptus; lavender; sweet, assertive, quite a bite, moderate alcohol (13%). Almost a Mouton-Rothschild caricature. Glorious. *Last tasted Nov 2005* ★★★★★ *Still perfection.*
Joseph Phelps, Napa Red Fully mature; strange, arboreal, American oak nose and flavour. A survivor. *May 2003* ★★ *Drink up.*

1975 ★★★
Cold season and the vines retarded. Variable quality.

1976 ★★★
Drought year. Stressed vines and a small crop. Drink up.
Beaulieu Vineyard, Georges de Latour CS It was a pity that so many of the BV wines at the centenary tasting in 1999 were in such poor condition. The two '76s were not good enough, one too sweet, malty. The other better on the nose but with an edge of acidity. *Last tasted July 1999. Should be better than this.*

1977 ★★
Drought year.
Beaulieu Vineyard, Georges de Latour CS Rich, pleasant but rather static nose; very sweet, good fruit, attractive, a lot to it, tannic. *July 1999* ★★★

1978 ★★★★
A very good, substantial and late vintage.
Beaulieu Vineyard, Georges de Latour CS Medium-deep, rich 'legs'; sweet, attractive and a certain delicacy; delicious flavour, crisp fruit, body, extract and charm. *One of the best of the entire range of BV vintages tasted July 1999* ★★★★★
Chateau Montelena, CS Superripe grapes, 10 days on skins, two years in barrel. The first estate-bottled vintage. Still fairly deep, good colour, mature; wonderful fruit, evolving interestingly, stably, vinous, then, after 25 minutes, spearmint; sweet, lovely flavour, balance, length and finish. *Oct 2000* ★★★★★

Stag's Leap Wine Cellars, Cask 23 A magnum: opaque core; low-keyed nose; distinctive, curious earthy, meaty, oyster shell taste. Very impressive. Holding well. *Last tasted March 1998* ★★★★★ *Still developing.*

1979 ★★★

Cool vintage. Useful wines.

Beaulieu Vineyard, Georges de Latour CS Very good notes in the early and mid-1990s. Most recently, below-standard bottles at the extensive BV vertical: sour cheese, peppery; better on the palate, rich and full, but edgy. *Last tasted July 1999. Should be* ★★★ *at least.*

Chateau Montelena, CS The second vintage, and a great success at the Paris tasting in 1976. Recently: rich, mature; low-keyed, 'bricky' nose that evolved and held well in the glass; overall dry, high-toned somewhat volatile finish, still tannic, a touch of astringency. *Oct 2000* ★★★

Stag's Leap Wine Cellars, Cask 23 A jeroboam: deep, opaque core, nose uneven, slightly raw and peppery; dry, full-bodied, tannic like the '79 Médocs. *Last tasted Oct 2000* ★★?

1980–1999

This was a period of considerable growth in California. In a matter of ten years the Napa had grown from just half a dozen well-established wineries to dozens and then hundreds, the valley floor and sides becoming almost literally carpeted with vines and architect-designed wineries. Although there was also expansion in Sonoma and from south of San Francisco Bay along the Central Coast to Santa Barbara, Napa was – frankly still is – the focal point. The profusion of vines, the enthusiasm and increasing skills of California winemakers and, most recently, the emphasis on the quality of the grapes – for this is where all good wine starts – is inestimable. The 1990s saw some very impressive wines and an unprecedented range of new 'cult' wines.

VINTAGES AT A GLANCE

Outstanding ★★★★★ 1985, 1991, 1994 (v), 1997, 1999
Very Good ★★★★ 1980, 1982, 1986 (v), 1989 (v), 1990, 1992, 1993 (v), 1994 (v), 1995 (v)
Good ★★★ 1981 (v), 1984, 1986 (v), 1988, 1989 (v), 1993 (v), 1994 (v), 1995 (v), 1996, 1998 (v)

1980 ★★★★

A good vintage following a long cool summer with almost daily fog rolling in across the hills from the Pacific Ocean; a warm September ended with a heatwave which sent the sugar levels soaring. These are wines of power rather than elegance. I have tasted many wines but few within the past decade.

1981 at best ★★★

Hot growing season with the earliest harvest – mid-August – in living memory. Fleshy reds, moderate quality. Few recent notes.

Beaulieu Vineyard, Georges de Latour CS Three bottles, one corked, at the Beaulieu Vineyard Centenary tasting, the other two raw, edgy, horrid. *Tasted at Vinopolis, London, July 1999.*

Chalone Pinot Noir Mature; lovely nose and very good varietal flavour, but very tannic. *In New York, March 1997* ★★★(★)

Diamond Creek, Volcanic Hill CS Diamond Creek's three adjacent vineyards are all 100% Cabernet Sauvignon. The oldest vintage poured at a delightful picnic lunch under the trees: excellent, dry finish. *June 2001* ★★★★

1982 ★★★★

Long cool summer, temperatures picking up in August and September, though interrupted by heavy localised rains and a tropical storm in late September. Moderately large crop of good grapes producing some very ripe wines. Few recent notes.

Beaulieu Vineyard, Georges de Latour CS Deeply impressive; nose at the very edge of decrepitude though miraculously fruity, forthcoming, with a touch of raisins and, in its perverse way, undeniably attractive; very sweet on the palate, its high alcohol and extract masking the tannin. I liked neither the weight nor the style. *Last noted July 1999* ★★★

Carneros Creek, Fay Vineyard CS Good sweet fruit, soft, attractive. *March 1998* ★★

Grace Family Vineyards, CS Most recently: level right into the neck, medium, mature, light sediment; some sweetness, curious flavour, crisp fruit, quite a bite. Not as impressive as it should have been. *June 1999* ★★★

Dunn, Howell Mountain CS Still deep, rich and velvety; sweet, 'thick', brambly bouquet which held well; a touch of ripe sweetness, good fruit, perfect weight (13% alcohol) but a very hot, dry, tannic finish. *Last tasted Nov 1997* ★★★★ *Will doubtless continue.*

OF THE MANY OTHER VERY GOOD '82S tasted between 1986 and 1991 the best were: **Beringer, Knights Valley CS** mouthfilling and tannic, 'smelling like the armpit of a healthy, clean-living youth after exercise' ★★★★; **Caymus Vineyards, Special Selection CS** a bit over the top, speciously spicy. Like strawberry jam in the mouth ★★★; **Chateau Montelena, CS** ripe, good length ★(★★★); **Diamond Creek, Red Rock Terrace CS** fragrant, great impact, lean, tannic ★★(★★); **Douglas Vineyards, CS** bottled by Zaca Mesa. Delicious ★★★(★); **Groth, CS** good wine ★★★(★); **Heitz, Martha's Vineyard CS** spicy, packed with fruit ★★★(★★); **William Hill, CS** Pomerol-like, good texture, elegant ★★★; **Inglenook, CS Reserve Cask** extraordinary bouquet and flavour ★★★★; **Jordan, CS** (Merlot 15.5%) ripe, lovely ★★★; **Robert Mondavi, Reserve CS** fragrant, ready ★★★; and **Opus One** cherry red, good fruit and length ★★★

1983 ★★

The wettest winter on record. The summer was more like spring and there was heavy rain in mid-August. I mainly tasted wines of this vintage between 1985 and 1987. Few recent notes.

Beaulieu Vineyard, Georges de Latour CS Medium-deep, very rich 'legs'; initially indistinct but quite fragrant; sweet, soft, good fruit and flavour. Drying tannin. *July 1999* ★★★ *(just)*.

Stag's Leap Wine Cellars, Cask 23 A magnum: very deep; good fruit, complete; sweet, excellent body and balance. *March 1998* ★★★★

1984 ★★★

A moderately good vintage. A long dry period from early spring to the end of the harvest with record high temperatures in May. Few recent notes.

Beaulieu Vineyard, Georges de Latour CS Mature, rich 'legs'; low-keyed but fragrant nose; agreeable flavour, texture and balance – if anything a bit four-square. Also an attenuated sharp finish. *July 1999* ★★★ *(just)*.

Caymus Vineyards, Special Selection CS Aged four years in 60-gallon Limousin and Nevers oak barrels. Soft ruby; high-toned; dry, firm, crisp fruit, dry finish. *Nov 1998* ★★★

Groth, CS Sweet, appealing; soft fruit, rich (12.5% alcohol), easy drinking. *Dec 2000* ★★★

1985 ★★★★★

An extremely good vintage, and one of my favourites. There was a fine, dry, fairly cool summer, apart from a heatwave in June. Heavy rain in September stopped the harvest, continuing afterwards in short, cool spells. However, the sun returned at the end of the month to complete the ripening.

I tasted blind 55 of the best Cabernet Sauvignon wines in January 1991. It was an eye-opener. There is no space here to list them all, so I am starting with those wines for which I have a more recent note.

Beaulieu Vineyard, Georges de Latour CS Deep, richly coloured, maturing; attractive fruit; very flavoury but with a rather piquant, acidic finish. Most recently, at the Beaulieu Vineyard centenary tasting in London: now medium-deep, still with good, rich 'legs'; low-keyed; good fruit, complete. Very good though not sensational. *July 1999* ★★★★

Chateau Montelena, CS Richly coloured; full-bodied (13.5% alcohol); velvety yet tannic. *Last tasted Sept 1997* ★★★★

Dominus Most recently: still ruby; very strange nose, rich, hefty, toasted; dry, tannic, still raw. *Sept 1997* ★★(★)

Heitz, Martha's Vineyard CS In 1991, its eucalyptus nose a giveaway; full, sweet, meaty. Most recently, corked. *Last tasted April 2000. At best* ★★★★ *Should be perfect, even 5-star now.*

Ridge, York Creek CS (including 10% Merlot and 2% Cabernet Franc). Bottled May 1987. Fairly deep, mature; very strange nose and fishy, 'seaweed', metallic, iron taste (12.1% alcohol). Not sure what to make of this. *Dec 2000.*

Stag's Leap Wine Cellars, Cask 23 Still very deep, opaque core but showing some maturity; a lovely, ripe, harmonious bouquet; sweet, beautiful flavour, perfect balance. *Last tasted Oct 2000* ★★★★★ *At its sublime peak.*

Stag's Leap Wine Cellars, 'SLV' CS Deeply coloured, still youthful; crisp, berry-like aroma and taste. Perfect tannin and acidity. *March 1998* ★★★★
OF THE OTHER '85 REDS TASTED BLIND IN 1991, I rated the following as 5-star: **Mayacamas** soft yet penetrating nose; lissom, lean, fruity, tannic; **Joseph Phelps, Insignia** (CS 60%, Merlot 25%, Cabernet Franc 15%) an extraordinary scent, bell peppers, whiff of spearmint then lime blossom; very distinctive flavour, tannic; **Rutherford Hill, 'XVS' Napa CS** impressively deep; very fragrant; wonderful fruit and other components to match.
OF THE OTHER '85 REDS tasted blind in 1991, the following were close to the leaders, say 4-star plus: **Beringer, Knights Valley Proprietor's Growth CS; Buena Vista, Private Reserve Carneros CS; Diamond Creek, Red Rock Terrace** and **Volcanic Hill; Grgich Hills, Napa CS; Hess Collection, CS; Robert Mondavi, Reserve CS; Joseph Phelps, Insignia, Auction Reserve; Shafer, Hillside Select CS; Silver Oak, Alexander Valley CS; Simi, Alexander Valley Reserve CS;** and **Sterling, Reserve.**

1986 ★★★ to ★★★★ variable

'One long spring'. A protracted harvest, the final crop of Cabernets being picked in early October.
Beaulieu Vineyard, Georges de Latour CS Fine, deep colour; nose opened up with attractive fig-like fruit; some sweetness, good fruit, crisp but dry, very tannic and touch of edgy acidity. *Last tasted July 1999* ★★★
Mayacamas CS Fairly deep, velvety; vegetal, arboreal; medium dryness and weight, distinctive. *May 2003* ★★★ *Drink now.*
Chateau Montelena, CS Very deep, rich, maturing; fragrant, berry-like, rich development; powerful, alcoholic, masculine, loaded with tannin. *Oct 2000* ★★★(★) *For those who like to chew and spit out, or to keep.*
Opus One (CS 86.5%, Cabernet Franc 9.6%, Merlot 3.9%) Dark cherry; very Bordeaux-like fruit, smooth, leather and honey, an hour or so later, fragrant, tea leaves; sweet entry, nice weight (12.5% alcohol), ripe, 'very pleasant to drink now'. *Dec 1997* ★★★★
Stag's Leap Wine Cellars, 'SLV' CS Magnum: distinct whiff of coffee-mocha – like walking past a coffee shop. Sweet, flavour to match. Black cherry fruit. *Celebrating the winery's 25th anniversary, March 1998* ★★★
A FEW '86 CABERNET SAUVIGNONS tasted between 1989 and 1992:
Forman, CS (including Merlot 15%, Cabernet Franc 10% and a fraction of Petit Verdot – one of the earliest vintages I can recall where this late-ripening Bordeaux varietal was used). Lovely scent, spicy; crisp, very fragrant ★★(★★); **Hess Collection, CS** good but very tannic (★★★); **Mount Veeder, CS** nose like fresh peas; sweet, full-bodied (13.8% alcohol), rich, masked tannin. Plausibly attractive ★★★; and **Sequoia Grove, CS** soft, fleshy, attractive ★★(★).
A FAIRLY WIDE RANGE OF '86 PINOT NOIRS TASTED IN THEIR YOUTH. The following were showing well: **Acacia, St Clair Vineyard** ★★★★; **Bouchaine, Carneros Napa** ★★★; **Calera, Jensen** ★★★; **Carneros Creek, Loath's** ★★★; **Saintsbury, Carneros** ★★★; **Sanford, Sanford & Benedict** a La Tâche lookalike! ★★★★; **Sterling, Winery Lake** ★★★; and **Zaca Mesa, Reserve** ★★★★

1987 ★★

Modest. The potential crop was affected by a series of heatwaves in May. A dry summer, a cool September, then rain and excessive heat leading to an early harvest, the smallest in California for five years.

Chateau Montelena, CS Deep, rich, a tight, mature rim; very good, crisp, berry-like nose; sweet, full, rich, lovely. *Oct 2000* ★★★★

Opus One (CS 95%, Cabernet Franc 3%, Merlot 2%) 'Very Bordeaux-like'! Good flavour and flesh. *Last noted dining at Ch Mouton-Rothschild, Sept 1998* ★★★★

1988 ★★★

A difficult year and another small yield. Even from my few notes, it was clearly a good vintage.

Beaulieu Vineyard, Georges de Latour CS Fragrant; remarkably soft, sweet, velvety entry, delicious flavour, slightly bitter, tannic finish. *July 1999* ★★★★

1989 ★★ to ★★★★

Third year of drought was eased by spring rains. Summer was cool but pleasant. Early harvest interrupted by heavy rains, cold, and fog, rot affecting remaining grapes. Then an earthquake! On the whole, attractive wines. Most are perfect for drinking now.

Beaulieu Vineyard, Georges de Latour CS Using a new generation of American oak for ageing: deep, plummy; slightly mint leaf scent, then opening up with attractive, ripe fruit on nose and palate. Sweet, fairly hefty, very tannic. *July 1999* ★★★★(★)

Stag's Leap Wine Cellars, Fay Vineyard CS More mature; slightly vegetal nose; easy, stylish, elegant. Dry finish. *March 1998* ★★★

1990 ★★★★

Smaller crop than 1989 but harvested in near-perfect conditions, particularly in the Napa. A splendid vintage.

Beaulieu Vineyard, Georges de Latour CS Soft fruit, opening up fragrantly; lovely crisp fruit, sweet mid-palate, dry, refreshing finish. *Last tasted July 1999* ★★★★

Caymus Vineyards, Special Selection CS (100%) The oldest of the five-vintage vertical at an 'Extraordinary California Wines' tasting: substantial, but very fragrant and stylish. *Last tasted Dec 2000* ★★★(★)

Robert Mondavi, Reserve CS A 'veritable farmyard and hen droppings' nose', as I have also noted in the red wines of certain well-known châteaux in the Médoc. *Last noted June 2001* ★★★ *in its way.*

Ridge, Monte Bello CS Very deep; nose harmonious, elegant, berry-like; fairly sweet, fullish, good fruit, flavour and balance. *Last tasted Dec 2000* ★★★★

Ridge, York Creek Bordeaux blend, CS 85%. Deep, velvety; lovely scent, soft, fleshy, 13.5% alcohol, good fruit, good acidity, delicious. Paul Draper showing his genius. *Last tasted March 2005* ★★★★ *Now–2012.*

Stag's Leap Wine Cellars, Cask 23 Deep, but maturing; well-developed nose, rich, touch of mocha; sweet, complete, richness masking tannins. *Dec 2000* ★★★★★

1991 ★★★★★

Excellent vintage. Successful flowering promising an abundant harvest, but the summer was also cool by Californian standards. An unbroken Indian summer brought the grapes to full maturity. The net result was intensity of colour; good natural degrees of acidity thanks to the extended cool summer, and levels of alcohol conducive to finesse rather than massive structure. One cloud on the horizon was the spread of phylloxera, particularly in the Napa, where it was devastating whole blocks of vines on the valley floor.

Araujo, Eisele Vineyard CS Medium-deep, still with youthful rim; very Bordeaux-like 'cheese' and berries, spicy, minty, opening up well; medium dryness and body, lean, good flavour and an interesting opening shot. *Dec 2000* ★★★(★)

Beaulieu Vineyard, Georges de Latour CS Deep; low-keyed, spicy, opening up with whiff of mulberry, then more fig-like; sweet from start to finish, masking substantial tannins. *July 1999* ★★★(★)

Beringer, Napa CS Crisp varietal aroma; good rich flavour and finish. *Sept 2004* ★★★ *Drink now.*

Caymus Vineyards, Special Selection CS (100%) Medium-deep ruby; well-developed, crisp fruit, opening up spicily; dryish, stylish, marked tannin and acidity. *Dec 2000* ★★(★★)

Chateau Montelena, Montelena Estate Heavy sediment noted. Still fairly youthful; a bit of bottle stink soon cleared, soft, harmonious; very attractive, spicy, lean, elegant, Bordeaux-like, dry finish. *Oct 2000* ★★★(★)

Dalla Valle, 'Maya' (CS 55%, Cabernet Franc 45%) Opaque; minty, the Cabernet Franc crisp aroma distinguishable, holding harmoniously; medium-sweet, good texture, mature fruit, marked, rather harsh tannin. *Dec 2000* ★★★(★★)

Diamond Creek, Red Rock Terrace CS Medium-deep; fragrant; crisp, dry, more acidity than tannin. *June 2001* ★★★

Dominus, Napanook Vineyard (CS 90%) Opaque, intense; very sweet, ripe, full-bodied (13.5% alcohol), good fruit. *Feb 1997* ★★★(★)

Harlan Estate Very deep, intense; spicy but swingeingly tannic and, frankly, undrinkable. *Last tasted June 2001.*

Robert Mondavi, Reserve CS Opaque core though showing some maturity; sweet, full (13.5% alcohol), a touch of iron. *June 2001* ★★★(★)

Opus One (CS 88%, Cabernet Franc 6%, Merlot 5%, Malbec 1%) Deep, velvety, 'legs' like Romanesque arches; crisp, fruity, mouthwatering, very sweet, fairly full-bodied (13.5%), tolerable tannin, good acidity. *Dec 1997* ★★★(★)

Ridge, Monte Bello Very deep, rich; elegant, harmonious, crisp berries; more meaty than the '90; medium sweetness and body, rich, lovely flavour. A class act. *Dec 2000* ★★★★★

1992 ★★★★

For the first time in six years there was adequate winter rainfall to ease drought conditions. Flowering early and successful. Early summer was unsettled but by mid-July the warmth had returned, with a hot August. Warm days and cool nights resulted in an early, almost perfect harvest.

Araujo, Eisele Vineyard CS Fairly deep; sweet, harmonious with a rich, tarry uplift; fullish, vaguely Ch Latour-like, good fruit and discreet oak. *Dec 2000* ★★★★(★)

Beaulieu Vineyard, Georges de Latour CS Rich 'legs', nose and taste. Scents of vanilla, raspberry; very sweet, full, chewy, good fruit and balance. *July 1999* ★★★(★)

Caymus Vineyards, Special Selection CS Very deep though hint of maturity; nose restrained but with good fruit and whiff of eucalyptus, opening up crisply; medium-sweet, lovely flavour, fragrant, oaky. *Dec 2000* ★★★★(★)

Colgin, Herb Lamb Vineyard CS A cult wine made by the cult producer Helen Turley. Rich 'legs'; fairly high volatile acidity; concentrated, spicy. Impressive, but scarcely a food wine. *Dec 1998* (★★★★★) *if you like this sort of wine.*

Dalla Valle, 'Maya' (CS 55%, Cabernet Franc 45%) Low-keyed; dry, lean, somewhat raw tannin and acidity. Not for me. *At Waddesdon Manor, Dec 2000* ★★(★)?

Dominus, Napanook Vineyard (Cabernet Sauvignon 64%, Cabernet Franc 15%, Merlot 19%, Petit Verdot 2%) Fairly deep, velvety, mature rim, rich, initially vegetal, sweetened in the glass, harmonious, soft toffee, finally lovely fruit; sweet, soft. Good fruit yet slightly raw finish. *March 2002* ★★★

Harlan Estate Good fruit, rich, touch of tar; very dry, like a supercharged Médoc. I found it tiring to the palate. *At Waddesdon Manor* ★★★

Opus One (Cabernet Sauvignon 90%, Cabernet Franc 8%, Merlot 2%) Very fragrant, crisp with dancing fruitiness; intriguing flavour, cherry-like fruit, though full-bodied (13.9% alcohol), not heavy. Marvellous acidity. *Dec 1997* ★★★★(★)

Ridge, Monte Bello Impressively deep but by no means hefty. Medium-sweet, agreeable weight and flavour. *Dec 2000* ★★★★(★)

Screaming Eagle, CS 'The cult of cults'! Made from a small parcel of wines in a bigger vineyard owned by Jean Phillips and production is limited to 175–200 cases per vintage. In 1992, just 170 cases were made and sold for a phenomenal price on allocation. Fairly deep, mature; decent nose; medium sweetness and weight, crisp fruit. Unquestionably good. A very agreeable wine – for rich collectors only. *Dec 2000* ★★★★★

Shafer, Hillside Select CS Opaque core; very meaty-malty character; sweet, hefty, crisp, spicy with 'interesting tannins!' Unsurprisingly heady. *June 2001* ★★(★★) *Top of the class.*

Stag's Leap Wine Cellars, Cask 23 Most recently, medium-deep, bright garnet; nose very rich but not sweet, touch of mocha and smell of the barrel cellar; sweet, fullish, very attractive. *Last tasted Dec 2000* ★★★(★) *Possibly 5 stars when fully developed.*

Stag's Leap Wine Cellars, Fay Vineyard CS Very fragrant, herbaceous, lively. *March 1998* ★★★(★)

Stag's Leap Wine Cellars, 'SLV' CS A wet dog, slightly sweaty (tannic) nose; sweet, more powerful than the Fay. Good grip. *March 1998* ★★(★★)

1993 ★★ to ★★★★

Extremely variable quality and an overall loss of about 10% of the crop due to bizarre, erratic, and totally unpredictable weather conditions from spring to harvest time. Unusually cold and rainy in the early summer followed by heatwaves alternating with cold spells into October.

Anderson's 'Éloge', Conn Valley Soft, mature; curious meaty, sweaty (tannic) nose; better on palate; very sweet, full of fruit, 13.5% alcohol, hot, dry finish. Certainly interesting. *Dec 2003* ★★★ *Drink soon.*

Araujo, Eisele Vineyard CS Very deep, intense, rich 'legs'; minty and meaty developing fruit and spice; medium-sweet, full-bodied, amply supplied with fruit and spice. Very tannic. Needs food. *Dec 2000* ★★(★★★)

Beaulieu Vineyard, Georges de Latour CS 100%, 50-50 American and French oak. A great whoosh of high-toned, minty fragrance, then green olives; very sweet, full-bodied, chewy, brambly fruit, rather raw texture. *Last noted July 1999* ★★(★★) *Now–2010.*

Colgin, Herb Lamb Vineyard CS Made by Helen Turley. Still deep, with opaque core; very fleshy, crystallised violets scent; sweet, very rich and spicy. A bit of a show-off. *Last tasted Dec 1998* ★★★ *Impressive, but this is not my style of wine.*

Dalla Valle, 'Maya' Only 300 cases made. Fairly deep; very good, rich, meaty nose which sweetened in the glass; good body, fruit, extract. For me the best of their '90–'94 range. *Dec 2000* ★★★(★★)

Harlan Estate Deep; good fruit and oak, opened up richly, both 'thick' and spirity – hard to explain; good fruit and spice, full-bodied. Not wholly convinced. *Dec 2000* ★(★★)?

Opus One (Cabernet Sauvignon 89%, Cabernet Franc 7%, Merlot 4%) Good colour, still a rim of purple; beautiful, good depth, complete – a most attractive wine, spicy with a powerful finish. Needs time. *Dec 1997* ★★(★★★) *Now–2012?*

Ridge, Monte Bello Deep, full-flavoured and tannic. Both classic and idiosyncratic at the same time. *Dec 2000* ★★(★★)

Screaming Eagle, CS Production 135 cases. The oldest vintage in a fascinating vertical: deep, rich core, maturing nicely; certainly impressive, forthcoming – almost a gusher, very fragrant, great depth; sweet, well balanced, delicious, masked tannin. *Jan 2003* ★★★★ *Lovely now.*

Shafer, Hillside Select CS Dry, lean, crisp, good acidity. *June 2001* ★(★★★)

Silver Oak, Alexander Valley, CS Warm, mature; sweet, rich style; taut, 13% alcohol, showing its age. *Sept 2005* ★★ *Declining. Drink up.*

Stag's Leap Wine Cellars, Cask 23 Slight bottle variation. Fairly deep, intense; complete, good fruit, attenuated and acidic. *March 1998* ★★(★) *Now–2010.*

1994 variable, up to ★★★★★

Too much rain; cool conditions. Generally uneven and mediocre though Napa and Sonoma reds better than most. Excellent Cabernet Sauvignon.

Araujo, Eisele Vineyard CS (including Cabernet Franc 4% and Petit Verdot 3%). Still very deep; very good, spicy nose and flavour. Tannic. New oak finish. *Last tasted Dec 2000* ★★(★★★)

Beaulieu Vineyard, Georges de Latour CS Plummy, figgy fruit; like a young Bordeaux; very sweet, rich fruit. All front end and middle. (New clones) *July 1999* (★★★)? *Hard to assess.*

Beringer, CS Very good fruit. Delicious. *Last tasted Jan 1999* ★★★(★)

Caymus Vineyards, Napa Valley CS ('Regular' not Special Selection: 80% of the grapes bought from local growers). Very deep, velvety; low-keyed, tarry; lovely flavour, great length, stylish but very tannic, with bitter finish. Very fragrant, totally different to the preceding '92. Delicious to drink by itself. *Last noted Dec 2000* ★★★★★

Chateau Montelena, Montelena Estate Starting to mature; deliciously sweet nose and taste, rich, with edgy tannin and acid finish. *Oct 2000* ★★(★★)

Colgin, Herb Lamb Vineyard CS Deep, rich; gushing scent, crystallised violets and taste. Unquestionably dashing and flavoury. Very tannic. *Dec 1998* ★★★★ *I cannot resist seduction.*

Dalla Valle, 'Maya' Opaque, immature; low-keyed nose, oak, meaty then minty; full of fruit, good length but a swingeingly tannic finish. *Dec 2000* ★★(★★★) *Hugely impressive but simply not the wine for me.*

Diamond Creek, Volcanic Hill CS (100% Cabernet Sauvignon) Immature mauve, rich 'legs'; dry, very crisp. *June 2001* (★★★)

Dominus, Napanook Vineyard CS 72%, the lowest since the first vintage (2000), M 12%, Cabernet Franc 11%, Petit Verdot 5%. Fairly deep, still a touch of ruby; figgy, herbaceous; dry, touch of rusticity, very dry finish. Disappointing. *Last tasted July 2003* ★★ *Drink up.*

Harlan Estate Very deep; initially fruity, meaty, oak, but I liked it less and less. Better on the palate: good texture; power, flesh and fruit. Dry finish. *Dec 2000* ★★★(★★) *for those who like this sort of wine.*

Robert Mondavi, 'Ode to Napa', Pinot Noir Magnum. Soft red, mature; vegetal, figgy; sweet, good flavour, decent enough. I was tempted to add 'Ode dear'. *Sept 2003* ★★★ *Drink up.*

Niebaum–Coppola, Rubicon (Cabernet Sauvignon and Merlot) Deep, youthful; brambly, spicy, lovely; fullish (14.1% alcohol), long, dry finish. *Dec 1998* ★★★★

Opus One (Cabernet Sauvignon 93%, Cabernet Franc 4%, Merlot 2%, Malbec 1%) Heaven knows – or perhaps the winemaker does – what the Malbec adds. Good, deep, impressive appearance; Bordeaux-like cedar nose, sweet, very scented; a powerhouse, far too immature even to taste. Overall dry, crisp, fruit dominant, long trajectory. *Dec 1997* ★(★★★)? *I presume a long life.*

Joseph Phelps, Insignia (Cabernet Sauvignon 88%, Merlot 10%, Cabernet Franc 2%) Mainly from vineyards on the Rutherford Bench and Stags Leap area of the Napa. Opaque core, intense, very rich 'legs'; 'classic', touch of smokiness; sweet, tarry fruit – not unlike Ch Pontet-Canet in certain vintages – well made, rich, tannic. *Nov 1998* ★★★(★★)

Ridge, Monte Bello CS and Merlot. Highly polished dark cherry; crisp, classic Cabernet-dominated nose; full-flavoured yet a moderate 12% alcohol, spicy blackcurrant and oak, good length and aftertaste. *Last tasted Oct 2005* ★★★(★★) *Now–2015.*

Screaming Eagle, CS 175 cases. Mature, open rim; lighter style than the '93, more herbaceous, fragrant citrus whiff; fairly dry, vegetal, astringent tannin and acidity. *Last tasted Jan 2003* ★★(★) *Drink up.*

Shafer, Hillside Select CS Sweet, delicious to taste but not my idea of an ideal food wine. *June 2001* ★★★★

Stag's Leap Wine Cellars, Cask 23 Fairly deep, brown-rimmed; vegetal; some sweetness, full-bodied, drinking pretty well. *Dec 2000* ★★★(★) *Ready now but will keep.*

1995 ★★ to ★★★★

Another difficult year with varying results. Flooded vineyards were a problem and cold weather prolonged flowering, which had the knock-on effect of delaying the eventual harvest for two to four weeks. Some delicious wines.

Araujo, Eisele Vineyard CS Deep, fairly intense; low-keyed at first but opening up fragrantly; medium sweetness and body, delicious flavour, crisp fruit, good tannin and acidity. The fifth consecutive vintage which led me to the conclusion that Araujo deserved its cult following. *Dec 2000* ★★(★★★)

Caymus Vineyards, Special Selection CS Very deep; meaty, well developed nose, deliciously emerging Cabernet aroma; well constituted. Rather oaky. *Dec 2000* ★★★(★)

Colgin, Herb Lamb Vineyard CS Opaque; nose not as exaggerated as the '93 and '94; complete, impressive, even enjoyable. *Last tasted Dec 1998* ★★★(★)

Diamond Creek, Volcanic Hill CS (Cabernet Sauvignon 100%). One of the most consistently fine Napa Cabernets; the sweet and spicy '95 no exception. *June 2001* ★★★★

Dominus, Napanook Vineyard (Cabernet Sauvignon 80%, Cabernet Franc 10%, Merlot 6%, Petit Verdot 4%). Dark cherry, still youthful; extraordinarily scented, rich, spicy, mocha; very sweet, full-bodied (14.1% alcohol) soft entry and mid-palate, good length, rich, soft tannins, touch of iron. *March 2002* ★★★(★★)

Harlan Estate Spicy, oaky nose which opened up fairly spectacularly; good fruit and all the component parts were correct, but noticeably tannic. Frankly, I found Harlan uneven. *Dec 2000* ★★★(★)

Opus One (Cabernet Sauvignon 86%, Cabernet Franc 7%, Merlot 5%, Malbec 2%. Skin contact 39 days, 18 months in new French oak). Medium depth and intensity; bright, fragrant, crisp fruit and oak, its bouquet developing sweetly; rich fruit, good flavour, fair length, touch of tar and tannin. *March 2002* ★★★(★★)

PlumpJack, Reserve CS Impressively deep, youthful; very fragrant, Bordeaux-like nose; excellent flavour and balance. Classic. *Dec 2000* ★★★★

Qupé, Syrah Dark cherry; harmonious, fig-like varietal aroma, lovely fruit, spicy – like herbs from Provence; full of character, complete. A lovely wine. *Jan 1997* ★★★★

Ridge, Monte Bello Dry, firm, very good. *Dec 2000* ★★★(★)

Screaming Eagle, CS 225 cases. Rich, soft, maturing nicely; soft fruit, harmonious; sweet, easy, good length, silky tannins, delightful. *Jan 2003* ★★★★★ Now–2012.

Stag's Leap Wine Cellars, CS Fay Vineyard Delicious, crisp, tannic. *Nov 1998* ★★★(★)

Shafer, Hillside Select CS Opaque, velvety; impossible to smell in a cellar which combined young wine and wet concrete; fairly dry and full-bodied, crisp fruit. *June 2001* ★★(★★)

1996 ★★★

A variable year. Cool spring, but one of the earliest budbreaks; rain in May caused vines to 'shatter' during flowering. Heatwaves in July and August, then abruptly cooling in the Napa and delaying ripening. The increased 'hang time' is supposed to add complexity. Cabernet Sauvignon and Merlot were the least affected.

Chateau Montelena, Montelena Estate Very deep; nicely evolved, soft, rich, 'hot vintage' scent; sweet, full, masked tannins. *Oct 2000* ★★★(★)

Diamond Creek, Red Rock Terrace CS Fine, deep, velvety; very good fruit and flesh. Complete. Tannic. *Tasted Nov 1999* ★★★★

Dominus, Napanook Vineyard (CS 82%, Cabernet Franc 10%, Merlot 4%, Petit Verdot 4%). Deep, rich, maturing; fragrant, citrus-like, opening up into soft brown sugar, then, after an hour, extraordinarily full and harmonious; sweet, soft, delicious fruit, crystallised violets. Outstanding. *March 2002* ★★★★★

Froman Vineyards, 'La Strada', Pinot Noir Opaque, intense; no discernable varietal character, hefty style, hardly drinkable. If this is the new 'global taste', well … *April 2004. Not classable.*

Opus One (CS 86%, Cabernet Franc 8%, Merlot 3%, Malbec 3%.) Deep, floral, vegetal nose, fruit and oak; attractive spicy flavour, fullish body (13.5% alcohol) a touch lean and very tannic. *March 2002* ★★(★★)

Peter Michael, Les Pavots Virtually opaque; complete; sweet, rich, full of fruit, reasonably masked tannins. *Oct 2000* ★★★(★)

Robert Mondavi, Special Reserve CS (including Cabernet Franc 3%, Merlot 2%). Very good nose, forthcoming, slightly scented; good fruit, body and length. *Last noted Oct 2000* ★★(★★)

Robert Mondavi, Barrel-Aged Reserve CS Lovely colour; crisp; good fruit, very dry finish. *March 2000* ★★(★)

Robert Mondavi, Oakville District CS A perfectly decent, not very expressive wine served with rack of lamb. *March 2000* ★★★

Pahlmeyer, Napa, Bordeaux blend Curious, unknit; better on palate, sweet, rich, chunky fruit, substantial 14.3% alcohol. *Sept 2005* ★★ *possible* ★★★

Screaming Eagle Production now up to 500 cases. Still youthful; sweaty tannic nose; medium dryness and body. Swingeingly tannic. *Jan 2003* ★★(★★)?

Shafer, Hillside Select CS Deep purple, violet edge; sweet, chewy, lovely fruit, extract masking tannin. *June 2001* (★★★★)

Shafer, Merlot Deep, plummy; hefty, meaty fruit; sweet, fleshy, hefty, delicious in its way. *June 2001* ★★★★

1997 ★★★★★

After a run of small vintages, a bumper crop with yields up by 24% compared to 1996, though there was some unevenness due to tropical storms in Sonoma and Napa in August and September. The high proportion of premium wines helped to relieve price inflation.

Arietta Kongsgaard and Hatton – Cabernet Franc 81%, Merlot 19%, from the Hudson vineyards planted in 1980. Deep, rich, velvety; crisp fruit, floral, developing an extremely sweet pineapple scent; sweet, rich, lovely texture and flavour. Spicy. Tannic. *Last tasted March 2002* ★★★★(★)

Beringer Collection, Napa CS Most recently: very deep but maturing; very distinctive, good Bordeaux lookalike; good fruit, fragrant, smattering of mocha, 14% alcohol, well balanced, delicious. *Last tasted Jan 2003* ★★★★

Cain, Cain Five CS 87%, Cabernet Franc 11%, Petit Verdot 1%, Malbec 1%. Fairly deep, plummy; crisp, berry-like fruit; medium sweetness and weight, full of fruit, dry finish. *Dec 2001* ★★★

Chateau Montelena, Montelena Estate Dark cherry; good, young fruit, developing well, sweet, rich, a good mouthful. *Oct 2000* ★★(★★)

Dominus, Napanook Vineyard CS 86.5%, Cabernet Franc 9%, Merlot 4.5%. Very deep, rich, velvety and less mature looking than the '96 Opus One tasted alongside; a rich, two-part, as yet unknit nose, muffled fruit; sweet on the palate too with a soft entry, good mid-palate fruit but very tannic, astringent finish. *March 2002* (★★★★)

Heller Estate, Signature Release, Carmel Valley, CS I visited this lovely winery when it was called Durney Vineyards. Now revitalised. Opaque core, velvety, rim the colour of plum skin; thick ripe fruit; sweet, delicious, good length but very high alcohol (14.5%) and tannin giving it a bit of a kick. *May 2002* ★★★ *Will have mellowed by now.*

Robert Mondavi, Reserve CS Very good flavour and length, but a touch of leanness and refreshing acidity. Needs time. *Last noted June 2001* ★★(★★)

Niebaum-Coppola, Napa Valley, Zinfandel, Edizione Pennino Unsurprisingly deep and velvety; sweet fruit; a big (14.1% alcohol), well-made wine with a nice uplift on the finish. *Oct 2003* ★★★ *Drink soon.*

Opus One CS 84%, Cabernet Franc 10%, Malbec 4%, Petit Verdot 2%. Early harvest. Largest crop of the decade thinned to the lowest per-acre yield. An exuberant fountain of full, rich Cabernet aroma, a touch of coffee, mocha and malt. Simmered down after an hour in the glass. Sweet, very attractive citrus and spice flavour. Very tannic. *March 2002* ★★(★★)

PlumpJack, Reserve CS Spicy, attractive. Still very tannic. *Dec 2000* ★★(★★)

Screaming Eagle 500 cases produced. Medium-deep, advanced; rich, chocolatey, whiff of tar; sweet, very good fruit, teeth-gripping tannin. *Jan 2003.* Then ★★(★★) *Now approaching maturity.*

Shafer, Hillside Select CS Deep, plummy; dry, crisp, well stacked, certainly interesting, with spicy aftertaste. Too alcoholic: 14%. *June 2001* ★(★★★)

Stag's Leap Wine Cellars, Cask 23 Dark cherry, rich, velvety; crisp varietal aroma, sweaty tannin; fairly sweet, very good fruit, touch of tannic bitterness. *Nov 2002* ★★(★★) *Needs time.*

1998 ★★★?

Unquestionably a difficult year: February the worst on record, a cool and wet spring, unsuitable weather during flowering. Short, erratic bouts of intense heat in the summer and by mid-September hardly a single grape picked. The latest harvest in living memory, ending mid-November.

Arietta, Merlot Good but as yet unknit nose, arboreal, touch of citrus fruit, opening up and settling down nicely; sweet, fleshy, delicious. *March 2002* ★★★★

Arietta, Napa Valley Cabernet Franc 60%, Merlot 40%. Deep, crisp fruit, floral scents, opening up richly, mocha and oak; the sweetest of the 'flight' ('96 to '99) with a lovely flavour, spicy, dry, slightly astringent finish. *March 2002* ★★(★★)

Clos du Val, Stags Leap District CS Maturing nicely; distinct Bordeaux varietal aroma, well made as always. Crisp, flavoury. *Sept 2004* ★★★ *Now–2012.*

Diamond Creek, Volcanic Hill CS Opaque core, purple rim; lovely, intense fruit on nose and palate. Alas, no opportunity to taste the wines of Al's two other vineyards (Gravelly Meadow and Red Rock Terrace) but judging from this, they will be good. *Picnicking at the winery, June 2001* ★★(★★★)?

Dominus Sweet, very good. *April 2002* ★★★★

Kongsgaard, Napa Valley Syrah (100%, planted 1980. Only 80 cases produced). Extremely good nose: sweet, leafy, oaky, touch of tangerine, developed well; some flavour, overall dry, somewhat astringent. Needs further bottle age. *March 2002.*

Screaming Eagle 60 to 65% aged in new French oak barriques for 18–20 months, bottled unfiltered. Deep, velvety sheen, rich 'legs'; very appealing varietal aromas, a whiff of tar, both breadth and depth; sweetish ripe entry, rich fruit, very dry tannic finish. Undoubtedly good. *Jan 2003. Then* ★★(★★) *Doubtless mature now.*

1999 ★★★★★

One of the longest, coolest ripening periods, supercharged by an almost week-long burst of heat at the end of September leading into November, one of the latest-ever harvests. Small crop and the major red varieties were very successful.

Arietta, Merlot Kongsgaard and Hatton Very deep, intense, immature; sweet, floral, curiously toffee-like; medium-sweet, good fruit but harsh, oaky, teeth-gripping tannins. *March 2002* (★★★)?

Arietta, Napa Valley Kongsgaard and Hatton (Cabernet Franc 60%, Merlot 40%). Opaque, velvety; good crisp fruit, rich, singed nose and flavour. Sweet, spicy, dry, tannic, oaky aftertaste. Lovely wine. *March 2002* ★★(★★★)

Au Bon Climat, Bien Nacido Pinot Noir Soft, cherry-tinted; sweet, harmonious, very well made. *Last tasted Sept 2001* ★(★★★)

Dominus, Napanook Vineyard (Cabernet Sauvignon 75%, Cabernet Franc 13%, Merlot 9%, Petit Verdot 3% – not using new oak). Dark cherry; very attractive nose, developed sweetly, rather jammy; sweet, soft and firm, delicious, richness masking tannin. *March 2002* ★★★(★★)

Duckhorn, Merlot Something of a speciality and always a true expression – in Californian terms – of Merlot. Crisp fruit, sweet, fleshy, minty, delicious. *Oct 2002* ★★★ *Drink now.*

Heitz, Martha's Vineyard Opaque, velvety; characteristic eucalyptus (Joe Heitz always hated my repeating this, despite my reassurance that it was unmistakable – and reminded me of Mouton-Rothschild); sweet, delicious and expensive. *Sept 2004* ★★★(★) *Now–2012.*

Kongsgaard, Napa Valley Syrah (100%, in 50% new burgundian oak. Impressively deep; very sweet, oaky/spicy nose of great depth, brambly fruit; sweet, fleshy fruit, very spicy, tannic. I thought too oaky. *March 2002* ★(★★★)

Marimar Torres, Don Miguel Vineyard Pinot Noir Good, scented, varietal aroma; delicious flavour, very oaky/spicy finish. *Oct 2001* ★★★(★)

Spring Mountain, Syrah 100% clones from Chapoutier (Hermitage) and Beaucastel (Châteauneuf). 22 months in French oak, 1100 cases produced. Very deep, plummy; a positively explosive combination, sweet, flesh, mammoth (14.8% alcohol). What I describe as an Osso buco wine. Undoubtedly impressive. *Last tasted April 2003* ★★(★★★) *if this is your type of wine.*

2000–2005

There are now around 3000 wineries in California but the 'Golden State' is not without its problems – weather conditions during the growing and harvesting seasons vary enormously. Prices are often exorbitant, and not just for the 'cult' wines. But if the trade and consumer are prepared to pay, so be it. This period has also seen what is, to me, an unhealthy concentration on high-strength wines; 14.5% is now the norm and many wines exceed 15%. At this level of alcohol one certainly notes deep, often opaque, colour, mountains of ripe fruit and sweetness – all immensely impressive but too heady to drink by itself and, frankly, too heavy with food. Wineries blame the demand on wine magazine reviews, while – 'moving with the times' – they are demanding later picked and increasingly riper wines, which for the growers is expensive (if they are paid by weight). These remarks apply equally to white wines, notably Chardonnays, not covered in this chapter; also to other New World producers and, it must be admitted, even to Bordeaux. Surely, there must be a return to eminently drinkable wines, rather than heady blockbusters: wines of elegance and finesse, to sip, worthy of contemplation. I live in hope.

VINTAGES AT A GLANCE
Outstanding ★★★★★ 2001, 2002
Very Good ★★★★ 2000, 2003, 2005
Good ★★★ 2004

2000 ★★★★
An outstanding growing season. Budbreak, flowering and *véraison* all ahead of schedule. Then a long cool ripening period resulted in a prolonged harvest ending in early November. Apart from competition, premium wine prices too high and the US dollar too strong, discouraging exports.
Au Bon Climat, Santa Maria Valley, Pinot Noir Sweet, remarkably good, vanillin, perfectly constructed. 13.5% alcohol. *June 2003* ★★★★★ *Then youthful but first rate. Now–2015.*
Bonny Doon Vineyards, Santa Cruz, Syrah Rich purple, almost opaque; very attractive nose, whiff of asparagus; sweet, yet with teeth-gripping tannin, hefty style though reasonable strength (13.5% alcohol). Delicious. *Jan 2003* ★★★★ *Drink soon*
Clos du Val, Napa, CS Maturing, rich 'legs'; very distinctive, discreet new oak. Sweet, delicious flavour, 13.5% alcohol, spicy, good tannin and acidity. *Last tasted May 2006* ★★★(★) *2008–2015.*
Robert Mondavi, Napa, CS 100% CS. Opaque, intense; very good, classic blackcurrant CS and tannin; very sweet entry, good flavour, 14% alcohol, very dry finish. *Last tasted Oct 2005* ★★★(★) *Soon–2012.*

Niebaum-Coppola, Napa, Zinfandel Opaque, intense, peppery; crisp, impressive, very oaky on the palate. *Oct 2003* ★(★★★) *Very good with rack of lamb, but needs more time.*

Ridge, Monte Bello CS A class act, as always. Moderate, sensible weight (13.4%), very tannic. Needs time. *May 2006* ★(★★★) *2010–2020.*

Saintsbury, Reserve Pinot Noir Medium-pale, correct; ripe; sweet, integrated 14.5% alcohol, very attractive. Copybook. *Sept 2004* ★★★★ *Now–2012.*

Spring Mountain Vineyard CS 66%, M 34%. Fairly deep, velvety; rich, tarry; very soft entry and fruit masking tannin. Good in its way. A 'Napa Valley Red Wine' released Jan 2003 at a modest $50. *Jan 2004* ★★(★) *Say Now–2012.*

Stag's Leap Wine Cellars, Fay Vineyard CS (10% M) Lovely colour, good fruit, alcohol substantial 14.2%, touch of iron, hot finish. Good wine. *Sept 2004* ★★★(★) *2010–2020.*

Marimar Torres Estate, Don Miguel Vineyard, Russian River, Pinot Noir Complicated, but it works. Six clones; aged in 35% new French oak; unfiltered. Plummy, ruby, maturing; very pronounced varietal aroma; sweet, soft fruit, 14% alcohol, perhaps a bit too easy for its age, but attractive. *Feb 2003* ★★★ *Will keep but drink soon.*

Turley Zinfandel Not a huge admirer of this renowned winemaker and, for me, a rare enough Zin. Unquestionably impressive; very sweet, rich but outrageous 15% alcohol. Knockout drops. *Nov 2003. Admittedly youthful. A matter of taste.*

Williams Selyem, Pinot Noir Delicious fragrance, arboreal, whiff of privet, vanilla; very sweet, spicy, 14.2% alcohol, oaky finish. *Sept 2005* ★★★★ *Now–2012.*

2001 (★★★★★)

An outstanding vintage, certainly in Napa and Sonoma. Despite an uneasy start, with a too-easy budbreak being hit by frost, there was the worst spring frost in 20 years. The summer, however, was well-nigh perfect, leading to an early harvest, with Cabernet Sauvignon grapes in particular being smaller, with thick skins and concentrated flesh.

Au Bon Climat, Knox Alexander, Pinot Noir Correct, palish, lovely colour; classic California, slightly vegetal, touch of vanilla; fairly sweet, lovely flavour, ideal weight (13.5% alcohol), dry finish. *July 2005* ★★★★ *Drink soon.*

Au Bon Climat, 'La Bauge', Santa Maria Valley, Pinot Noir Good colour and nose, very good flavour and weight (13.5% alcohol). *May 2006* ★★★ *Drink soon.*

Brogan Cellars, Benn Tierra Vineyard, Pinot Noir Sweet, very scented, vanilla; chewy, berry-like fruit, modest – for Russian River Pinots, 13% alcohol. *Oct 2006* ★★★ *Drink soon.*

Cakebread Cellars, CS Luminous; very distinctive; sweet, floral fruit, very tannic, oaky finish. *Sept 2004* ★★★ *Good but too oaky. Now–2012.*

Cyrus, Alexander Valley CS 57%, M 32 %, Cabernet Franc 11%, one year in old oak, then in new oak. Deep, velvety; crisp, herbaceous, mocha and 'stone fruit'; very forthcoming, rich fruit, 13.9% alcohol, very tannic. *April 2005* ★★(★★) *Now–2015.*

Diamond Creek, Volcanic Hill, CS Very rich core; still hard; ripe, good texture, very dry finish ★(★★); **Red Rock Terrace** fairly deep ruby; very good CS aroma; sweet, delicious, chewy ★★(★); **Gravelly Meadow** hard, undeveloped; good flavour and underlying fruit. The best of the trio ★(★★★). *All tasted Nov 2004. Now–2016.*

Joseph Phelps, Insignia, CS (11% M) Velvety; muffled varietal aroma; sweet, delicious flavour, 13.9% alcohol, hot finish, drying tannins. *Sept 2004* ★★(★★) *Now–2016.*

Marimar Estate, Don Miguel Vineyard, Pinot Noir 39% new oak. Bottled Aug 2002. Good but low-keyed, varietal, dry. *June 2005* ★★(★) *Drink soon.*

Screaming Eagle, CS Fairly deep, velvety; vibrant; full-bodied (14.5% alcohol) yet with refreshing citrus touch. Very dry, powerful finish. Impressive. *April 2005* ★★(★★★) *2010–2020.*

Robert Mondavi, CS 100% CS. Many notes. Deep, intense, good 'legs'; attractive, harmonious varietal nose; sweet, fleshy, hefty (14.5% alcohol), soft yet with a dry tannic finish. *Last tasted Nov 2006* ★★(★★) *Now–2012.*

Shafer, Hillside Select, CS Much as I like and admire the Shafer family, I find their minimum 14% alcohol somehow misguided. Even so, impressive: opaque, velvety; good fruit, albeit a touch 'green'; too sweet, very rich, though packed with fruit, a touch of iron, an absurd 14.9% alcohol, silky leathery tannins. *May 2006* ★★★ *or more if you like the style.*

Stag's Leap Wine Cellars, Cask 23 CS Rich, maturing; nose low-keyed but opened up; better on palate, more Bordeaux-like, 14.2% alcohol, good flavour, tannin and acidity. Outstanding. *May 2006* ★★(★★) *2010–2020.*

Staglin, CS Impressively deep; strange 'fishy' nose, good in its way; sweet, good flavour, too alcoholic (14.8%), oaky/smoky, good aftertaste. *May 2006* ★★★(★) *Drink soon–2012?*

Trefethen Estate, CS Opaque core; unknit, sweaty tannin; sweet, classic berry-like flavour, high but well supported, 14.5% alcohol. *Sept 2004* ★★(★★) *Now–2015?*

2002 ★★★★★

Good growing conditions throughout the State, certainly favourable for the Cabernet Sauvignons. Benevolent spring, cool and beneficial summer weather, the overall quality of the fruit excellent, and said by some winemakers to be the best for over ten years.

Acacia, St Clair Vineyard, Pinot Noir Attractive, open, purple rim; low-keyed yet fragrant; ripe, delicious flavour, 14.4% alcohol, slightly spicy, noticeable tannin and acidity. *July 2005* ★★★(★) *Now–2013.*

Cuvaison, Carneros, Pinot Noir Estate Selection Plummy purple; very strange burgundian *merde* nose and taste. Too sweet. *July 2005* ★★ *Drink up.*

Delicato Family Vineyards, Shiraz Deep, velvety, youthful purple rim; crisp fruit; sweet, brambly, reasonable body (13.5% alcohol) but too oaky. Needs bottle age. *Aug 2003* ★★(★) *Hard to predict.*

Gloria Ferrer, Carneros, Pinot Noir Thick, hefty, brambly fruit; very sweet, very oaky, moderate weight (13.5% alcohol). *April 2005* ★★★ *just. 2008–2012.*

Franciscan, Oakville Estate, Napa, CS Deep, youthful; very Cabernet Franc-like raspberry nose; very good 'food wine'. *May 2005* ★★(★) *Now–2012.*

The Hess Collection, Mountain Cuvée, CS (Merlot with Malbec and

Syrah). Intriguing fruit, touch of tar, then caramelly; soft fleshy, entry, a crescendo of flavour, 14.5% alcohol, soft sweet tannins. *April 2005* ★★★? *Now–2015.*

La Crema, 'Nine Barrels' Russian River, Pinot Noir Youthful black cherry; good varietal aroma; very dry, good finish. *April 2005* ★★★ *Now–2012.*

Joseph Phelps. Insignia, Napa, CS Impressively deep, lovely, long 'legs'; slightly vegetal, whiff of eucalyptus; assertive, impressive, 14.4% alcohol, very good in its way but too sweet. *May 2006* ★★★ *or* ★★★★ *depending on one's personal taste. Now–2012?*

Saintsbury Carneros, Pinot Noir Several notes. Delicious forthcoming fruit; distinctly sweet entry, lovely flavour, 13.5% alcohol, dry finish. *Last tasted July 2005* ★★★★ *Now–2012.*

2003 ★★★★

The 'sunshine state' did not live up to its sunny reputation with a tricky unsettled growing season: warm February brought on the budding but was succeeded by unseasonably cold and wet spring which hampered growth. Normality resumed in May but the summer was hot, with major heatwaves in July. Average temperatures in August; early September rainy then hot, accelerating ripeness. Napa sets the standards and the best producers' Cabernets are ripe, concentrated, with firm tannins.

Au Bon Climat, Santa Maria Valley, Pinot Noir Medium-pale, soft, classic Pinot colour; 'beetroot' and mint nose; sweet, very good flavour to match. Quite a bite. *Jan 2006* ★★★(★) *Now–2012.*

Terlato Vineyard, Dry Creek, Syrah Fairly deep ruby; 'hot', dusty nose; medium-sweet, weight of bottle matches 14.5% alcohol, brambly fruit, scented flavour, dry tannin and oak finish. Not very varietal but fairly impressive. *Feb 2006* ★★??

Titus Vineyard, CS Opaque core yet trying to mature; very refreshing, black fruit, whiff of eucalyptus – very Napa; sweet entry, crisp, hefty (14.5% alcohol), with raw harsh bitter finish. Impressive but not for me. *May 2006* ★★(★) *Maybe 5 years bottle age?*

Marimar Torres, Pinot Noir 'Christmas Selection' 80% new oak. Unfiltered. Fairly deep; sweet, varietal; medium-sweet, full-bodied (14% in very small print – in case anyone like me is put off), delicious flavour; good, dry but very oaky finish. *April 2007* ★★★★ *Now–2012.*

2004 ★★★

A somewhat precocious growing season, advanced budding, unusually hot spring, cooler May and June, end August to early September hot resulting in one of the earliest harvests for decades. High-quality Cabernet Sauvignon.

2005 ★★★★

Almost a complete contrast to 2004. Cold spring delayed flowering, followed by an unusually cool summer, culminating in a late harvest, the second largest on record. Higher than usual levels of acidity gave hopes of high quality.

Vintage Champagne

I cannot think of any other wine which automatically, unconsciously, conjures up such a variety of (mainly) happy associations. It is, par excellence, the wine of celebration. Unlike many white wines, the best champagne not only keeps but develops in bottle. It is commonly assumed that the grape varieties (Pinot Noir, Pinot Meunier and Chardonnay), the chalky soil and northerly climate are what make champagne champagne. Well, yes, but the plus factor is blending. At the top of the pile is vintage champagne made from vineyards classified 100% in the finest districts of Champagne.

The French think the English are mad to drink and, seemingly, to enjoy old champagne. But there is a moment when a venerable champagne, its carbon dioxide bubbles congregated in the neck of the bottle, can, rather like a well-hung pheasant, be richly sublime. The purpose in this chapter is to summarise the quality and condition of champagne vintages, with mainly recent tasting notes focussing on the best and/or most typical wines.

18th century to 1919

Champagne has always been well regarded, fashionable and expensive. It first appeared in James Christie's catalogues in 1768, two years after the start of his auction house, and customarily commanded prices twice that of the finest claret. In those days it was dry and still, not sparkling, and Sillery was the most esteemed. Despite the Napoleonic wars either side of 1800, which fairly understandably caused shortages and even higher prices, champagne continued to be imported into Britain. The real explosion of demand started in the second half of the 19th century, the trade press reporting an unhealthy pressure on prices culminating with the 1874 vintage, the most renowned of the period, which reached record prices at Christie's. The *fin de siècle* is associated with extravagant lifestyles in both France and Britain; but, in fact, Chile was then the biggest importer of champagne – a period which was completely knocked off course following the outbreak of World War One.

Outstanding vintages
1857, 1874, 1892, 1899, 1904, 1911, 1920, 1921, 1928, 1937, 1945, 1952, 1959, 1964, 1971, 1982, 1985, 1988, 1990, 1996, 2005

VINTAGES AT A GLANCE

Outstanding ★★★★★ 1857, 1874, 1892, 1899, 1904, 1911
Very Good ★★★★ 1870, 1914
Good ★★★ 1915, 1919

1892 ★★★★★

Along with the 1874 and 1899 this was one of the finest champagne vintages of the period.
Perrier-Jouët, Extra Original corks. Slight bottle variation. The first the colour of warm gold with pinpricks of carbon dioxide; low-keyed but lovely old straw bouquet; medium-dry, fair body; excellent flavour, length and finish. Now more like an old white burgundy but with a prickle at its edge. The other bottle was a slightly paler yellow gold, totally flat; sweet, sound, good flavour but lacking bite. *Feb 1994. At best* ★★★★

1899 ★★★★★

Great vintage. Alas never tasted.

1907 ★

Not a great vintage but a remarkable survivor.
Heidsieck Monopole. Disgorged in 1916 shortly before the ship it was on sank in the Baltic on its way to Russia, remaining submerged in silt until recently salvaged. Most recently, yellow-gold; nutty 'sea breeze' nose; distinct sweetness, strange flavour, excellent acidity, unbelievably good for its age and submerged provenance. *Last tasted Sept 2000. At its best* ★★★★

1911 ★★★★★

A great vintage, the best between 1874 and 1921. There was a small crop of excellent wines.
Pol Roger Probably disgorged in the mid-1950s. Most recently, the wine had an excellent colour, very slight prickle, a touch of cloudiness towards the bottom of the bottle; lovely smoky nose; perfect flavour, weight, texture, balance and finish. Perfection. *Last tasted July 1993* ★★★★★

1914 ★★★★

World War One broke out in August; the German army had reached the champagne vineyards even before the harvest began. It made life difficult for the pickers but good wine was made.
Pol Roger Two notes, both bottles disgorged in the middle of World War Two. Most recently, pure amber gold, quite still, no bubbles; soft, old straw nose, slight whiff of *cacao*; full-flavoured, a very slight prickle, remarkably sweet and enjoyable. *Last tasted June 1997* ★★★

1915 ★★★

Early harvest. Fine, well-balanced wines. Only one old note.
Moët & Chandon, Dry Impérial. Sound, still signs of life, nice old wine. *1968* ★★★

1920–1944

The 1920s and '30s were two totally contrasting decades followed by the problems of World War Two and the German occupation of France. The 1920s were well served by six good to outstanding vintages, two, the '21 and '28, vying to qualify as the greatest vintage of the century, although when the latter appeared on the market, the exuberant period of its year of birth had been overtaken by the Great Depression. Despite prohibition, champagne continued to find its way into the USA, and there were sufficient people of wealth in Britain to support a de luxe product. The trade, however, was overstocked and the early to mid-1930s period was nothing short of disastrous for the champagne producer, a situation exacerbated by the abundant vintage in 1934. German troops occupied Champagne from May 1940 until liberation in August 1944.

Although I am an advocate of old champagne with original corks, wines of this age are safer newly disgorged.

VINTAGES AT A GLANCE

Outstanding ★★★★★ 1920, 1921, 1928, 1937
Very Good ★★★★ 1923, 1929, 1934, 1943
Good ★★★ 1926, 1942

1920 ★★★★★
Very good quality. Cold August but followed by a gloriously sunny September. These wines were doubtless consumed rapidly in the middle of the frothy 1920s as none seem to have survived.

1921 ★★★★★
A long, exceedingly hot summer produced outstanding white wines, as elsewhere in Europe, and champagne was no exception. A small crop harvested from 19 September. This was the vintage debut of Dom Pérignon, Moët & Chandon's de luxe cuvée.
Pol Roger Variable. Most recently, a bottle disgorged in April 1966: surprisingly pale for its age and vintage, pale gold, no mousse; a sweet, creamy, harmonious bouquet with a whiff of coffee; touch of sweetness on the palate, glorious flavour and excellent acidity. 'The best-ever '21'. *March 1997. At best* ★★★★★

1923 ★★★★
A very good vintage but small crop.
Veuve Clicquot, Brut Several notes. Most recently, two bottles, one drab, sweeter and better on nose and palate, the other a lovely gold colour; sweet nose; touch of fungi; dry, firm, remarkably firm and fresh though with swingeing acidity. *Both April 1997. At best* ★★★★

1928 ★★★★★

An excellent vintage. Firm, crisp, well-constituted, long-lasting wines. But now risky.

Heidsieck, Dry Monopole Firm cork, good level. Lovely colour, pure amber; sweet, rich, meaty but maderised; flavour like old sherry or *vin jaune* but very attractive in its way, its acidity giving it much needed support and a dry finish. Second bottle with slightly more vivacity, creamy old nose, acidic. *Both July 1995* ★★ *or* ★★★, *a matter of taste.*

Perrier-Jouët, Finest Extra Quality, Reserve for Great Britain Excellent level: bright old gold colour but lacking life; toasted, slightly maderised; by no means 'extra dry', quite a bit of sweetness. Lovely old flavour and pleasant dry prickle on the finish. More recently, a very similar bottle from my own cellar, a better, more honeyed nose and lovely flavour. *Both 1994 and 1998* ★★★★

Veuve Clicquot Several notes. First tasted 50 years after the vintage. 'A beauty' ★★★★★. Most recently, its level just below the foil: golden, lifeless, not star bright; sweet old straw nose; delicious old flavour, clean, excellent acidity. *March 1998. At best* ★★★★

1929 ★★★★

A lovely vintage, abundant, with great charm. Not as firm or acidic as the '28.

Veuve Clicquot, Brut Several notes. Most recently, probably re-disgorged in the late 1960s, it had a certain haziness and a curious minty 'ivy-leaf' scent. By no means Brut, with a very distinctive, notably sweet taste, considerable charm, a prickle of carbon dioxide and fabulous acidity. *April 1997* ★★★★

1934 ★★★★

A very good abundant vintage. Timely, for it came on to the market to invigorate those recovering from the Depression.

Pol Roger Three notes, the only bottle tasted in the 1990s being from a small stock of old champagne bought at Christie's. It had a heavy wax seal over the original cap but the level was just below the bottom of the foil. The cork seemed firm but it had not kept out the air. Although the wine had a lovely, palish amber colour it had no life; the nose, though powerful, was slightly mushroomy and maderised. Yet sweet, rich, and, once one had got used to its creaking character, quite pleasant. The *coup de grâce* was a slightly grubby finish. *Jan 1996. Solo* ★, *but when mixed in the glass with a younger vintage* ★★★

1937 ★★★★★

Great vintage. Firm, crisp, long-lasting wines taking advantage of the acidity common to all '37s. If you like old champagne, this is a good vintage to experiment with, but the wine must have come from a good cellar. Few recent notes.

Veuve Clicquot Bright yellow; old straw, slightly malty; dry, surprisingly sound. *Dec 1992* ★★★ *for its age.*

1942 ★★★

Good wines.

Veuve Clicquot, Dry Most recently, slight variation but on the whole, despite showing their age, remarkably good. At best, now more sweet than dry, creamy, lovely flavour, vanillin aftertaste. *Last tasted April 1997* ★★★

1943 ★★★★
A very good year, more successful than in any other classic French wine region and the first major vintage to be shipped after the war. Also, freshly disgorged in 1953 it was sold in Britain as the Coronation Cuvée to celebrate the accession of Queen Elizabeth II. These newly disgorged wines rarely retain their freshness.

Delbeck, Extra Sec One note of a well-preserved, 50-year-old half bottle in excellent condition: palish; rich bouquet; medium-dry, good flavour. *Dec 1992* ★★★★

Moët & Chandon, Dry Impérial Another interesting comparison. The first, original bottling: pale; smoky bouquet; dry, fabulous flavour; the second, Moët's Coronation Cuvée disgorged in 1953 had an odd straw nose and taste. *Dec 1992. At best* ★★★★★

1945–1979

Despite the superb quality of the immediate post-war champagne vintages, particularly the trio, '45, '47 and '49, there was still a back-log of pre-war stock in the UK. The decades of the 1950s and 1960s each produced a quartet of really good vintages which, if well kept, will still appeal to the British who prefer their champagne calm and characterful like a mature Montrachet.

Although Moët's Dom Pérignon, the precursor of the modern spate of de luxe champagnes, was launched pre-war, it was in the post-war period that these champagnes started to take off, with Roederer Cristal in 1945, Taittinger's Comtes de Champagne in 1952, and Laurent-Perrier's Grand Siècle, a novel blend of three vintages ('52, '53 and '55), launched in 1960.

VINTAGES AT A GLANCE
Outstanding ★★★★★ 1945, 1952, 1959, 1964, 1971
Very Good ★★★★ 1947, 1949, 1953, 1955, 1961, 1962, 1966, 1970, 1976, 1979
Good ★★★ 1969, 1973, 1975

1945 ★★★★★
Small crop of excellent wines. The firmness and acidity gave the '45s vigour and a long life. The best, and best kept wines, will still be delicious if you prefer your champagne like a lovely old white burgundy.

Pol Roger Several notes. Most recently, medium-pale, yellow gold, a faint prickle; scent and flavour of freshly peeled mushrooms. Delicious, wonderful fruit (a high proportion of Pinot Noir) and length. *March 1997* ★★★★★

Ruinart Good colour; crisp, excellent flavour and condition. *Dec 1992* ★★★★★

OTHER GOOD '45S **Pommery & Greno** in perfect condition. *Dec 1992* ★★★★; **Roederer** perfect at 30 years of age – I would love to taste it again; and, older still, good bottles of **Heidsieck, Monopole**.

1947 ★★★★

Very good, thanks to a bakingly hot summer and an unusually early harvest. Production well below average.

Krug, Private Cuvée, Brut Two notes. Most recently, still in its immediate post-war blue bottle, the wine had been disgorged in the mid-1950s: medium straw gold; wonderfully rich, complete, harmonious bouquet and flavour. Medium-sweet, rich, good length, a touch of *crème brûlée* on the finish. *May 1997* ★★★★★

Pol Roger Several notes, all excellent. Most recently what appeared to be an original bottling, labelled '*Reserve for Great Britain*'. Lovely bright gold with faint and fine mousse; gloriously full, rich, old straw bouquet; fairly dry, nutty, delicious old flavour. Very good for its age. *April 1997* ★★★★★

Veuve Clicquot, Dry Many notes. Most recently, a magnum (Brut) from Clicquot's cellars, disgorged three months prior: beautiful colour, a sluggish flow of very fine bubbles; nose like freshly peeled mushrooms; uncompromisingly dry, even austere, but complete and drinking well, with a walnut-dry finish. *April 1997* ★★★★

1949 ★★★★

A very good vintage following a long, hot, dry summer.

1952 ★★★★★

Excellent: firm, long-lasting wines. Worth looking out for.

Bollinger First tasted in 1957 and several notes since. Most recently, sheer perfection. *Jan 1991* ★★★★★ *Should still be good – if well cellared.*

Gosset, Brut Disgorged 1974. 1% dosage. Two notes. Most recently, the second oldest – after the Monopole 1907 – at a Christie's pre-sale tasting: pale, pinprick bubbles; harmonious old bouquet; dry, clean, considerable delicacy and very fragrant. *Last tasted Oct 1998* ★★★★

Veuve Clicquot, Brut A magnum: yellow gold, very fine bubbles; nutty, bottle age straw nose developing creamily; medium-dry, full-bodied, firm, assertive, delicious flavour, lively acidity on finish. *April 1997* ★★★★★

1953 ★★★★

Supple, elegant wines benefiting from a good growing season and early harvest.

Krug The late Paul Krug, the father of Rémi and Henri, considered this his best vintage between 1945 and 1955. It had achieved perfection by the end of the 1960s but continued to develop, gaining colour and bottle age. Alas, not tasted recently but it was perfection in 1983. *Then* ★★★★★